16.50

825

D0982739

INFLUENCES OF

GEOGRAPHIC ENVIRONMENT

INFLUENCES OF

GEOGRAPHIC ENVIRONMENT

ON THE BASIS OF RATZEL'S SYSTEM
OF
ANTHROPO-GEOGRAPHY

BY

ELLEN CHURCHILL SEMPLE

AUTHOR OF "AMERICAN HISTORY AND ITS GEOGRAPHIC
CONDITIONS"

NEW YORK / RUSSELL & RUSSELL

TO THE MEMORY

OF

FRIEDRICH RATZEL

Hither, as to their fountain, other stars
Repairing in their golden urns draw light.
MILTON.

GF
31
S5
1968

PREFACE

THE present book, as originally planned over seven years ago, was to be a simplified paraphrase or restatement of the principles embodied in Friedrich Ratzel's *Anthropo-Geographie*. The German work is difficult reading even for Germans. To most English and American students of geographic environment it is a closed book, a treasure-house bolted and barred. Ratzel himself realized "that any English form could not be a literal translation, but must be adapted to the Anglo-Celtic and especially to the Anglo-American mind." The writer undertook, with Ratzel's approval, to make such an adapted restatement of the principles, with a view to making them pass current where they are now unknown. But the initial stages of the work revealed the necessity of a radical modification of the original plan.

Ratzel performed the great service of placing anthropogeography on a secure scientific basis. He had his forerunners in Montesquieu, Alexander von Humboldt, Buckle, Ritter, Kohl, Peschel and others; but he first investigated the subject from the modern scientific point of view, constructed his system according to the principles of evolution, and based his conclusions on world-wide inductions, for which his predecessors did not command the data. To this task he brought thorough training as a naturalist, broad reading and travel, a profound and original intellect, and amazing fertility of thought. Yet the field which he had chosen was so vast, and its material so complex, that even his big mental grasp could not wholly compass it. His conclusions, therefore, are not always exhaustive or final.

Moreover, the very fecundity of his ideas often left him no time to test the validity of his principles. He enunciates one brilliant generalization after another. Sometimes he reveals the mind of a seer or poet, throwing out conclusions which are highly suggestive, on the face of them convincing,

but which on examination prove untenable, or at best must be set down as unproven or needing qualification. But these were just the slag from the great furnace of his mind, slag not always worthless. Brilliant and far-reaching as were his conclusions, he did not execute a well-ordered plan. Rather he grew with his work, and his work and its problems grew with him. He took a mountain-top view of things, kept his eyes always on the far horizon, and in the splendid sweep of his scientific conceptions sometimes overlooked the details near at hand. Herein lay his greatness and his limitation.

These facts brought the writer face to face with a serious problem. Ratzel's work needed to be tested, verified. The only solution was to go over the whole field from the beginning, making research for the data as from the foundation, and checking off the principles against the facts. This was especially necessary, because it was not always obvious that Ratzel had based his inductions on sufficiently broad data; and his published work had been open to the just criticism of inadequate citation of authorities. It was imperative, moreover, that any investigation of geographic environment for the English-speaking world should meet its public well supported both by facts and authorities, because that public had not previously known a Ritter or a Peschel.

The writer's own investigation revealed the fact that Ratzel's principles of anthropo-geography did not constitute a complete, well-proportioned system. Some aspects of the subject had been developed exhaustively, these of course the most important; but others had been treated inadequately, others were merely a hint or an inference, and yet others were represented by an hiatus. It became necessary, therefor, to work up certain important themes with a thoroughness commensurate with their significance, to reduce the scale of others, and to fill up certain gaps with original contributions to the science. Always it was necessary to clarify the original statement, where that was adhered to, and to throw it into the concrete form of expression demanded by the Anglo-Saxon mind.

One point more. The organic theory of society and state permeates the *Anthropo-geographie*, because Ratzel formulated his principles at a time when Herbert Spencer exercised a wide influence upon European thought. This theory, now generally abandoned by sociologists, had to be eliminated from any restatement of Ratzel's system. Though it was applied in the original often in great detail, it stood there nevertheless rather as a scaffolding around the finished edifice; and the stability of the structure after this scaffolding is removed shows how extraneous to the whole it was. The theory performed, however, a great service in impressing Ratzel's mind with the life-giving connection between land and people.

The writer's own method of research has been to compare typical peoples of all races and all stages of cultural development, living under similar geographic conditions. If these peoples of different ethnic stocks but similar environments manifested similar or related social, economic or historical development, it was reasonable to infer that such similarities were due to environment and not to race. Thus, by extensive comparison, the race factor in these problems of two unknown quantities was eliminated for certain large classes of social and historical phenomena.

The writer, moreover, has purposely avoided definitions, formulas, and the enunciation of hard-and-fast rules; and has refrained from any effort to delimit the field or define the relation of this new science of anthropo-geography to the older sciences. It is unwise to put tight clothes on a growing child. The eventual form and scope of the science, the definition and organization of its material must evolve gradually, after long years and many efforts of many workers in the field. The eternal flux of Nature runs through anthropo-geography, and warns against precipitate or rigid conclusions. But its laws are none the less well founded because they do not lend themselves to mathematical finality of statement. For this reason the writer speaks of geographic factors and influences, shuns the word geographic determinant, and speaks with extreme caution of geographic control.

The present volume is offered to the public with a deep sense of its inadequacy; with the realization that some of its principles may have to be modified or their emphasis altered after wider research; but also with the hope that this effort may make the way easier for the scholar who shall some day write the ideal treatise on anthropo-geography.

In my work on this book I have only one person to thank, the great master who was my teacher and friend during his life, and after his death my inspiration.

ELLEN CHURCHILL SEMPLE.

LOUISVILLE, KENTUCKY.

January, 1911.

CONTENTS

CHAPTER IV.

MOVEMENTS OF PEOPLES IN THEIR GEOGRAPHICAL
SIGNIFICANCE

CHAPTER V.

GEOGRAPHICAL LOCATION

CHAPTER VI.

GEOGRAPHICAL AREA

CHAPTER VII.
GEOGRAPHICAL BOUNDARIES

CHAPTER VIII.
COAST PEOPLES

CHAPTER IX.
OCEANS AND ENCLOSED SEAS

CHAPTER X.
MAN'S RELATION TO THE WATER

CHAPTER XI.
THE ANTHROPO-GEOGRAPHY OF RIVERS

CHAPTER XII.

CONTINENTS AND THEIR PENINSULAS

CHAPTER XIII.

ISLAND PEOPLES

CHAPTER XIV.
PLAINS, STEPPES AND DESERTS

CHAPTER XV.
MOUNTAIN BARRIERS AND THEIR PASSES

Man as part of the mobile envelope of the earth—Inaccessibility

CHAPTER XVI.

INFLUENCES OF A MOUNTAIN ENVIRONMENT

CHAPTER XVII.

THE INFLUENCES OF CLIMATE UPON MAN

xvi CONTENTS

LIST OF MAPS.

THE INFLUENCES OF
GEOGRAPHIC ENVIRONMENT

CHAPTER I

THE OPERATION OF GEOGRAPHIC FACTORS IN
HISTORY

MAN is a product of the earth's surface. This means not **Man a** merely that he is a child of the earth, dust of her dust; but **product of** that the earth has mothered him, fed him, set him tasks, **surface.** directed his thoughts, confronted him with difficulties that have strengthened his body and sharpened his wits, given him his problems of navigation or irrigation, and at the same time whispered hints for their solution. She has entered into his bone and tissue, into his mind and soul. On the mountains she has given him leg muscles of iron to climb the slope; along the coast she has left these weak and flabby, but given him instead vigorous development of chest and arm to handle his paddle or oar. In the river valley she attaches him to the fertile soil, circumscribes his ideas and ambitions by a dull round of calm, exacting duties, narrows his outlook to the cramped horizon of his farm. Up on the wind-swept plateaus, in the boundless stretch of the grasslands and the waterless tracts of the desert, where he roams with his flocks from pasture to pasture and oasis to oasis, where life knows much hardship but escapes the grind of drudgery, where the watching of grazing herd gives him leisure for contemplation, and the wide-ranging life a big horizon, his ideas take on a certain gigantic simplicity; religion becomes monotheism, God becomes one, unrivalled like the sand of the desert and the grass of the steppe, stretching on and on without break or change. Chewing over and over the cud of his simple belief as the one food of his unfed mind, his faith becomes fanaticism; his big spacial ideas, born of that ceaseless regular wandering, outgrow the land that bred them and bear their legitimate fruit in wide imperial conquests.

Man can no more be scientifically studied apart from the ground which he tills, or the lands over which he travels, or the seas over which he trades, than polar bear or desert cactus can be understood apart from its habitat. Man's relations to his environment are infinitely more numerous and complex than those of the most highly organized plant or animal. So complex are they that they constitute a legitimate and necessary object of special study. The investigation which they receive in anthropology, ethnology, sociology and history is piecemeal and partial, limited as to the race, cultural development, epoch, country or variety of geographic conditions taken into account. Hence all these sciences, together with history so far as history undertakes to explain the causes of events, fail to reach a satisfactory solution of their problems largely because the *geographic factor* which enters into them all has not been thoroughly analyzed. Man has been so noisy about the way he has "conquered Nature," and Nature has been so silent in her persistent influence over man, that the geographic factor in the equation of human development has been overlooked.

Stability of geographic factors in history.

In every problem of history there are two main factors, variously stated as heredity and environment, man and his geographic conditions, the internal forces of race and the external forces of habitat. Now the geographic element in the long history of human development has been operating strongly and operating persistently. Herein lies its importance. It is a stable force. It never sleeps. This natural environment, this physical basis of history, is for all intents and purposes immutable in comparison with the other factor in the problem —shifting, plastic, progressive, retrogressive man.

Persistent effect of remoteness.

History tends to repeat itself largely owing to this steady, unchanging geographic element. If the ancient Roman consul in far-away Britain often assumed an independence of action and initiative unknown in the provincial governors of Gaul, and if, centuries later, Roman Catholicism in England maintained a similar independence towards the Holy See, both facts have their cause in the remoteness of Britain from the center of political or ecclesiastical power in Rome. If the independence of the Roman consul in Britain was duplicated later by the attitude of the Thirteen Colonies toward England, and again within the young Republic by the headstrong self-reliance, impatient of government authority, which characterized the early Trans-Allegheny commonwealths in their aggressive Indian policy, and led them to make war and conclude treaties for the cession of land like sovereign states; and if this attitude of independence in the over-mountain men reappeared in a spirit of political defection looking toward secession from the Union and a new combination with their British neighbor on the Great Lakes or the Spanish beyond the Mississippi, these are all the identical effects of geographical remoteness made yet more remote by barriers of mountain and sea. This is the long reach which weakens the arm of authority, no matter what the race or country or epoch.

As with geographical remoteness, so it is with geographical proximity. The history of the Greek peninsula and the Greek people, because of their location at the threshold of the Orient, has contained a constantly recurring Asiatic element. This comes out most often as a note of warning; like the *motif* of Ortrud in the opera of "Lohengrin," it mingles ominously in every chorus of Hellenic enterprise or pæan of Hellenic victory, and finally swells into a national dirge at the Turkish conquest of the peninsula. It comes out in the legendary history of the Argonautic Expedition and the Trojan War; in the arrival of Phœnician Cadmus and Phrygian Pelops in Grecian lands; in the appearance of Tyrian ships on the coast of the Peloponnesus, where they gather the purple-yielding murex and kidnap Greek women. It appears more conspicuously in the Asiatic sources of Greek culture; more dramatically in the Persian Wars, in the retreat of Xenophon's Ten Thousand, in Alexander's conquest of Asia, and Hellenic domination of Asiatic trade through Syria to the Mediterranean. Again in the thirteenth century the lure of the Levantine trade led Venice and Genoa to appropriate certain islands and promontories of Greece as commercial bases nearer to Asia. In 1396 begins the absorption of Greece into the Asiatic em-

Effect of proximity.

pire of the Turks, the long dark eclipse of sunny Hellas, till it issues from the shadow in 1832 with the achievement of Greek independence.

Persistent effect of natural barriers.
If the factor is not one of geographical location, but a natural barrier, such as a mountain system or a desert, its effect is just as persistent. The upheaved mass of the Carpathians served to divide the westward moving tide of the Slavs into two streams, diverting one into the maritime plain of northern Germany and Poland, the other into the channel of the Danube Valley which guided them to the Adriatic and the foot of the Alps. This same range checked the westward advance of the mounted Tartar hordes. The Alps long retarded Roman expansion into central Europe, just as they delayed and obstructed the southward advance of the northern barbarians. Only through the partial breaches in the wall known as passes did the Alps admit small, divided bodies of the invaders, like the Cimbri and Teutons, who arrived, therefore, with weakened power and at intervals, so that the Roman forces had time to gather their strength between successive attacks, and thus prolonged the life of the declining empire. So in the Middle Ages, the Alpine barrier facilitated the resistance of Italy to the German emperors, trying to enforce their claim upon this ancient seat of the Holy Roman Empire.

It was by river-worn valleys leading to passes in the ridge that Etruscan trader, Roman legion, barbarian horde, and German army crossed the Alpine ranges. To-day well-made highways and railroads converge upon these valley paths and summit portals, and going is easier; but the Alps still collect their toll, now in added tons of coal consumed by engines and in higher freight rates, instead of the ancient imposts of physical exhaustion paid by pack animal and heavily accoutred soldier. Formerly these mountains barred the weak and timid; to-day they bar the poor, and forbid transit to all merchandise of large bulk and small value which can not pay the heavy transportation charges. Similarly, the wide barrier of the Rockies, prior to the opening of the first overland railroad, excluded all but strong-limbed and strong-hearted pioneers from the fertile valleys of California and Oregon, just as it excludes coal and iron even from the Colorado mines, and checks the free movement of laborers to the fields and factories of California, thereby tightening the grip of the labor unions upon Pacific coast industries.

As the surface of the earth presents obstacles, so it offers channels for the easy movement of humanity, grooves whose direction determines the destination of aimless, unplanned migrations, and whose termini become, therefore, regions of historical importance. Along these nature-made highways history repeats itself. The maritime plain of Palestine has been an established route of commerce and war from the time of Sennacherib to Napoleon.[1] The Danube Valley has admitted to central Europe a long list of barbarian invaders, covering the period from Attila the Hun to the Turkish besiegers of Vienna in 1683. The history of the Danube Valley has been one of warring throngs, of shifting political frontiers, and unassimilated races; but as the river is a great natural highway, every neighboring state wants to front upon it and strives to secure it as a boundary.

Persistent effect of nature-made highways.

The movements of peoples constantly recur to these old grooves. The unmarked path of the voyageur's canoe, bringing out pelts from Lake Superior to the fur market at Montreal, is followed to-day by whaleback steamers with their cargoes of Manitoba wheat. To-day the Mohawk depression through the northern Appalachians diverts some of Canada's trade from the Great Lakes to the Hudson, just as in the seventeenth century it enabled the Dutch at New Amsterdam and later the English at Albany to tap the fur trade of Canada's frozen forests. Formerly a line of stream and portage, it carries now the Erie Canal and New York Central Railroad.[2] Similarly the narrow level belt of land extending from the mouth of the Hudson to the eastern elbow of the lower Delaware, defining the outer margin of the rough hill country of northern New Jersey and the inner margin of the smooth coastal plain, has been from savage days such a natural thoroughfare. Here ran the trail of the Lenni-Lenapi Indians; a little later, the old Dutch road between New Amsterdam and the Delaware trading-posts; yet later the King's Highway from New York to Philadelphia. In 1838 it became the route of the Delaware and Raritan Canal, and more recently of the Pennsylvania Railroad between New York and Philadelphia.[3]

The early Aryans, in their gradual dispersion over northwestern India, reached the Arabian Sea chiefly by a route running southward from the Indus-Ganges divide, between the eastern border of the Rajputana Desert and the western foot of the Aravalli Hills. The streams flowing down from this range across the thirsty plains unite to form the Luni River, which draws a dead-line to the advance of the desert. Here a smooth and well-watered path brought the early Aryans of India to a fertile coast along the Gulf of Cambay.[4] In the palmy days of the Mongol Empire during the seventeenth century, and doubtless much earlier, it became an established trade route between the sea and the rich cities of the upper Ganges.[5] Recently it determined the line of the Rajputana Railroad from the Gulf of Cambay to Delhi.[6] Barygaza, the ancient seaboard terminus of this route, appears in Pliny's time as the most famous emporium of western India, the resort of Greek and Arab merchants.[7] It reappears later in history with its name metamorphosed to Baroche or Broach, where in 1616 the British established a factory for trade,[8] but is finally superseded, under Portuguese and English rule, by nearby Surat. Thus natural conditions fix the channels in which the stream of humanity most easily moves, determine within certain limits the direction of its flow, the velocity and volume of its current. Every new flood tends to fit itself approximately into the old banks, seeks first these lines of least resistance, and only when it finds them blocked or pre-empted does it turn to more difficult paths.

Regions of historical similarity. Geographical environment, through the persistence of its influence, acquires peculiar significance. Its effect is not restricted to a given historical event or epoch, but, except when temporarily met by some strong counteracting force, tends to make itself felt under varying guise in all succeeding history. It is the permanent element in the shifting fate of races. Islands show certain fundamental points of agreement which can be distinguished in the economic, ethnic and historical development of England, Japan, Melanesian Fiji, Polynesian New Zealand, and pre-historic Crete. The great belt of deserts and steppes extending across the Old World gives us a vast territory of rare historical uniformity. From time immemorial they have borne and bred tribes of wandering herdsmen; they have sent out the invading hordes who, in successive waves of conquest, have overwhelmed the neighboring river lowlands of Eurasia and Africa. They have given birth in turn to Scythians, Indo-Aryans, Avars, Huns, Saracens, Tartars and Turks, as to the Tuareg tribes of the Sahara, the Sudanese and Bantu folk of the African grasslands. But whether these various peoples have been Negroes, Hamites, Semites, Indo-Europeans or Mongolians, they have always been pastoral nomads. The description given by Herodotus of the ancient Scythians is applicable in its main features to the Kirghis and Kalmuck who inhabit the Caspian plains to-day. The environment of this dry grassland operates now to produce the same mode of life and social organization as it did 2,400 years ago; stamps the cavalry tribes of Cossacks as it did the mounted Huns, energizes its sons by its dry bracing air, toughens them by its harsh conditions of life, organizes them into a mobilized army, always moving with its pastoral commissariat. Then when population presses too hard upon the meager sources of subsistence, when a summer drought burns the pastures and dries up the water-holes, it sends them forth on a mission of conquest, to seek abundance in the better watered lands of their agricultural neighbors. Again and again the productive valleys of the Hoangho, Indus, Ganges, Tigris and Euphrates, Nile, Volga, Dnieper and Danube have been brought into subjection by the imperious nomads of arid Asia, just as the "hoe-people" of the Niger and upper Nile have so often been conquered by the herdsmen of the African grasslands. Thus, regardless of race or epoch —Hyksos or Kaffir—history tends to repeat itself in these rainless tracts, and involves the better watered districts along their borders when the vast tribal movements extend into these peripheral lands.

Climatic influences are persistent, often obdurate in their **Climatic** control. Arid regions permit agriculture and sedentary life **influences.** only through irrigation. The economic prosperity of Egypt to-day depends as completely upon the distribution of the Nile

DENSITY OF POPULATION IN EASTERN HEMISPHERE

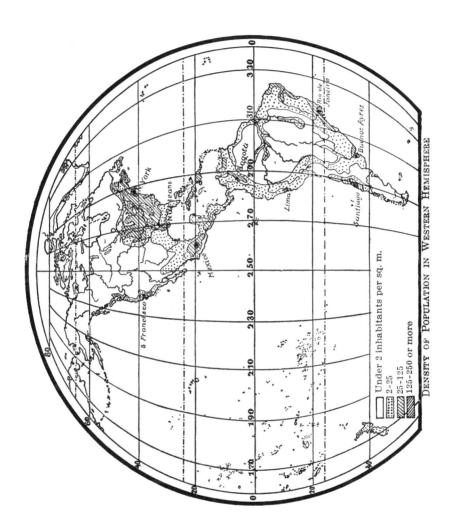

DENSITY OF POPULATION IN WESTERN HEMISPHERE

Under 2 inhabitants per sq. m.
2-25
25-125
125-250 or more

waters as in the days of the Pharaohs. The mantle of the ancient Egyptian priest has fallen upon the modern British engineer. Arctic explorers have succeeded only by imitating the life of the Eskimos, adopting their clothes, food, fuel, dwellings, and mode of travel. Intense cold has checked both native and Russian development over that major portion of Siberia lying north of the mean annual isothern of 0 degree C. (32 degrees F.); and it has had a like effect in the corresponding part of Canada. (Compare maps pages 8 and 9.) It allows these sub-arctic lands scant resources and a population of less than two to the square mile. Even with the intrusion of white colonial peoples, it perpetuates the savage economy of the native hunting tribes, and makes the fur trader their modern exploiter, whether he be the Cossack tribute-gatherer of the lower Lena River, or the factor of the Hudson Bay Company. The assimilation tends to be ethnic as well as economic, because the severity of the climate excludes the white woman. In the same way the Tropics are a vast melting-pot. The debilitating effects of heat and humidity, aided by tropical diseases, soon reduce intruding peoples to the dead level of economic inefficiency characteristic of the native races. These, as the fittest, survive and tend to absorb the new-comers, pointing to hybridization as the simplest solution of the problem of tropical colonization.

The relation of geography to history. The more the comparative method is applied to the study of history—and this includes a comparison not only of different countries, but also of successive epochs in the same country— the more apparent becomes the influence of the soil in which humanity is rooted, the more permanent and necessary is that influence seen to be. Geography's claim to make scientific investigation of the physical conditions of historical events is then vindicated. "Which was there first, geography or history?" asks Kant. And then comes his answer: "Geography lies at the basis of history." The two are inseparable. History takes for its field of investigation human events in various periods of time; anthropo-geography studies existence in various regions of terrestrial space. But all historical development takes place on the earth's surface, and therefore is more or less molded by its geographic setting. Geography, to reach accurate conclusions, must compare the operation of its factors in different historical periods and at different stages of cultural development. It therefore regards history in no small part as a succession of geographical factors embodied in events. Back of Massachusetts' passionate abolition movement, it sees the granite soil and boulder-strewn fields of New England; back of the South's long fight for the maintenance of slavery, it sees the rich plantations of tidewater Virginia and the teeming fertility of the Mississippi bottom lands. This is the significance of Herder's saying that "history is geography set into motion." What is to-day a fact of geography becomes to-morrow a factor of history. The two sciences cannot be held apart without doing violence to both, without dismembering what is a natural, vital whole. All historical problems ought to be studied geographically and all geographic problems must be studied historically. Every map has its date. Those in the Statistical Atlas of the United States showing the distribution of population from 1790 to 1890 embody a mass of history as well as of geography. A map of France or the Russian Empire has a long historical perspective; and on the other hand, without that map no change of ethnic or political boundary, no modification in routes of communication, no system of frontier defences or of colonization, no scheme of territorial aggrandizement can be understood.

The study of physical environment as a factor in history was unfortunately brought into disrepute by extravagant and ill-founded generalization, before it because the object of investigation according to modern scientific methods. And even to-day principles advanced in the name of anthropo-geography are often superficial, inaccurate, based upon a body of data too limited as to space and time, or couched in terms of unqualified statement which exposes them to criticism or refutation. Investigators in this field, moreover, are prone to get a squint in their eye that makes them see one geographic factor to the exclusion of the rest; whereas it belongs to the very nature of physical environment to combine a whole group of influences, working all at the same time under the law of the resolution of forces. In this plexus of influences, some

Multiplicity of geographic factors.

operate in one direction and some in another; now one loses
its beneficent effect like a medicine long used or a garment
outgrown; another waxes in power, reinforced by a new geographic factor which has been released from dormancy by the
expansion of the known world, or the progress of invention
and of human development.

Evolution of geographic relations. These complex geographic influences cannot be analyzed
and their strength estimated except from the standpoint of
evolution. That is one reason these half-baked geographic
principles rest heavy on our mental digestion. They have
been formulated without reference to the all-important fact
that the geographical relations of man, like his social and
political organization, are subject to the law of development.
Just as the embryo state found in the primitive Saxon tribe
has passed through many phases in attaining the political
character of the present British Empire, so every stage in this
maturing growth has been accompanied or even preceded by
a steady evolution of the geographic relations of the English
people.

Owing to the evolution of geographic relations, the physical environment favorable to one stage of development may
be adverse to another, and *vice versa*. For instance, a small,
isolated and protected habitat, like that of Egypt, Phœnicia,
Crete and Greece, encourages the birth and precocious growth
of civilization; but later it may cramp progress, and lend
the stamp of arrested development to a people who were once
the model for all their little world. Open and wind-swept
Russia, lacking these small, warm nurseries where Nature could
cuddle her children, has bred upon its boundless plains a massive, untutored, homogeneous folk, fed upon the crumbs of
culture that have fallen from the richer tables of Europe.
But that item of area is a variable quantity in the equation.
It changes its character at a higher stage of cultural development. Consequently, when the Muscovite people, instructed
by the example of western Europe, shall have grown up intel-
lectually, economically and politically to their big territory,
its area will become a great national asset. Russia will come
into its own, heir to a long-withheld inheritance. Many of
its previous geographic disadvantages will vanish, like the

diseases of childhood, while its massive size will dwarf many previous advantages of its European neighbors.

This evolution of geographic relations applies not only to the local environment, but also to the wider world relations of a people. Greeks and Syrians, English and Japanese, take a different rank among the nations of the earth to-day from that held by their ancestors 2,000 years ago, simply because the world relations of civilized peoples have been steadily expanding since those far-back days of Tyrian and Athenian supremacy. The period of maritime discoveries in the fifteenth and sixteenth centuries shifted the foci of the world relations of European states from enclosed seas to the rim of the Atlantic. Venice and Genoa gave way to Cadiz and Lagos, just as sixteen centuries before Corinth and Athens had yielded their ascendency to Rome and Ostia. The keen but circumscribed trade of the Baltic, which gave wealth and historical preeminence to Lübeck and the other Hanse Towns of northern Germany from the twelfth to the seventeenth century, lost its relative importance when the Atlantic became the maritime field of history. Maritime leadership passed westward from Lübeck and Stralsund to Amsterdam and Bristol, as the historical horizon widened. England, prior to this sudden dislocation, lay on the outskirts of civilized Europe, a terminal land, not a focus. The peripheral location which retarded her early development became a source of power when she accumulated sufficient density of population for colonizing enterprises, and when maritime discovery opened a way to trans-oceanic lands.[9]

Meanwhile, local geographic advantages in the old basins remain the same, although they are dwarfed by the development of relatively greater advantages elsewhere. The broken coastline, limited area and favorable position of Greece make its people to-day a nation of seamen, and enable them to absorb by their considerable merchant fleet a great part of the trade of the eastern Mediterranean,[10] just as they did in the days of Pericles; but that youthful Aegean world which once constituted so large a part of the *oikoumene*, has shrunken to a modest province, and its highways to local paths. The coast cities of northern Germany still maintain a large commerce in the Baltic, but no longer hold the pre-eminence of the old Hanse Towns. The glory of the Venetian Adriatic is gone; but that the sea has still a local significance is proven by the vast sums spent by Austria and Hungary on their hand-made harbors of Trieste and Fiume.[11]   The analytical geographer, therefore, while studying a given combination of geographic forces, must be prepared for a momentous readjustment and a new interplay after any marked turning point in the economic, cultural, or world relations of a people.

Interplay of geographic factors.   Skepticism as to the effect of geographic conditions upon human development is apparently justifiable, owing to the multiplicity of the underlying causes and the difficulty of distinguishing between stronger and weaker factors on the one hand, as between permanent and temporary effects on the other.   We see the result, but find it difficult to state the equation producing this result.   But the important thing is to avoid seizing upon one or two conspicuous geographic elements in the problem and ignoring the rest.   The physical environment of a people consists of all the natural conditions to which they have been subjected, not merely a part.   Geography admits no single blanket theory.   The slow historical development of the Russian folk has been due to many geographic causes—to excess of cold and deficiency of rain, an outskirt location on the Asiatic border of Europe exposed to the attacks of nomadic hordes, a meager and, for the most part, ice-bound coast which was slowly acquired, an undiversified surface, a lack of segregated regions where an infant civilization might be cradled, and a vast area of unfenced plains wherein the national energies spread out thin and dissipated themselves.   The better Baltic and Black Sea coasts, the fertility of its Ukraine soil, and location next to wide-awake Germany along the western frontier have helped to accelerate progress, but the slow-moving body carried too heavy a drag.

The law of the resolutions of forces applies in geography as in the movement of planets.   Failure to recognize this fact often enables superficial critics of anthropo-geography to make a brave show of argument.   The analysis of these interacting forces and of their various combinations requires careful investigation.   Let us consider the interplay of the forces of land and sea apparent in every country with a maritime location. In some cases a small, infertile, niggardly country conspires with a beckoning sea to drive its sons out upon the deep; in others a wide territory with a generous soil keeps its well-fed children at home and silences the call of the sea. In ancient Phœnicia and Greece, in Norway, Finland, New England, in savage Chile and Tierra del Fuego, and the Indian coast district of British Columbia and southern Alaska, a long, broken shoreline, numerous harbors, outlying islands, abundant timber for the construction of ships, difficult communication by land, all tempted the inhabitants to a seafaring life. While the sea drew, the land drove in the same direction. There a hilly or mountainous interior putting obstacles in the way of landward expansion, sterile slopes, a paucity of level, arable land, an excessive or deficient rainfall withholding from agriculture the reward of tillage—some or all of these factors combined to compel the inhabitants to seek on the sea the livelihood denied by the land. Here both forces worked in the same direction.

In England conditions were much the same, and from the sixteenth century produced there a predominant maritime development which was due not solely to a long indented coastline and an exceptional location for participating in European and American trade. Its limited island area, its large extent of rugged hills and chalky soil fit only for pasturage, and the lack of a really generous natural endowment,[12] made it slow to answer the demands of a growing population, till the industrial development of the nineteenth century exploited its mineral wealth. So the English turned to the sea—to fish, to trade, to colonize. Holland's conditions made for the same development. She united advantages of coastline and position with a small infertile territory, consisting chiefly of water-soaked grazing lands. When at the zenith of her maritime development, a native authority estimated that the soil of Holland could not support more than one-eighth of her inhabitants. The meager products of the land had to be eked out by the harvest of the sea. Fish assumed an important place in the diet of the Dutch, and when a process of curing it was discovered, laid the foundation of Holland's export

Land and sea in co-operation.

trade. A geographical location central to the Baltic and North Sea countries, and accessible to France and Portugal, combined with a position at the mouth of the great German rivers made it absorb the carrying trade of northern Europe.[13] Land and sea coöperated in its maritime development.

Land and sea opposed.   Often the forces of land and sea are directly opposed. If a country's geographic conditions are favorable to agriculture and offer room for growth of population, the land forces prevail, because man is primarily a terrestrial animal. Such a country illustrates what Chisholm, with Attic nicety of speech, calls "the influence of bread-power on history,"[14] as opposed to Mahan's sea-power. France, like England, had a long coastline, abundant harbors, and an excellent location for maritime supremacy and colonial expansion; but her larger area and greater amount of fertile soil put off the hour of a redundant population such as England suffered from even in Henry VIII's time. Moreover, in consequence of steady continental expansion from the twelfth to the eighteenth century and a political unification which made its area more effective for the support of the people, the French of Richelieu's time, except those from certain districts, took to the sea, not by national impulse as did the English and Dutch, but rather under the spur of government initiative. They therefore achieved far less in maritime trade and colonization.[15] In ancient Palestine, a long stretch of coast, poorly equipped with harbors but accessible to the rich Mediterranean trade, failed to offset the attraction of the gardens and orchards of the Jezreel Valley and the pastures of the Judean hills, or to overcome the land-born predilections and aptitudes of the desert-bred Jews. Similarly, the river-fringed peninsulas of Virginia and Maryland, opening wide their doors to the incoming sea, were powerless, nevertheless, to draw the settlers away from the riotous productiveness of the wide tidewater plains. Here again the geographic force of the land outweighed that of the sea and became the dominant factor in directing the activities of the inhabitants.

The two antagonistic geographic forces may be both of the land, one born of a country's topography, the other of its location. Switzerland's history has for centuries shown the conflict of two political policies, one a policy of cantonal and communal independence, which has sprung from the division of that mountainous country into segregated districts, and the other one of political centralization, dictated by the necessity for coöperation to meet the dangers of Switzerland's central location mid a circle of larger and stronger neighbors. Local geographic conditions within the Swiss territory fixed the national ideal as a league of "sovereign cantons," to use the term of their constitution, enjoying a maximum of individual rights and privileges, and tolerating a minimum of interference from the central authority. Here was physical dismemberment coupled with mutual political repulsion. But a location at the meeting place of French, German, Austrian and Italian frontiers laid upon them the distasteful necessity of union within to withstand aggressions crowding upon them from without. Hence the growth of the Swiss constitution since 1798 has meant a fight of the Confederation against the canton in behalf of general rights, expanding the functions of the central government, contracting those of canton and commune.[16]

Every country forms an independent whole, and as such finds its national history influenced by its local climate, soil, relief, its location whether inland or maritime, its river highways, and its boundaries of mountain, sea, or desert. But it is also a link in a great chain of lands, and therefore may feel a shock or vibration imparted at the remotest end. The gradual desiccation of western Asia which took a fresh start about 2,000 years ago caused that great exodus and displacement of peoples known as the *Völkerwanderung*, and thus contributed to the downfall of Rome; it was one factor in the Saxon conquest of Britain and the final peopling of central Europe. The impact of the Turkish hordes hurling themselves against the defenses of Constantinople in 1453 was felt only forty years afterward by the far-off shores of savage America. Earlier still it reached England as the revival of learning, and it gave Portugal a shock which started its navigators towards the Cape of Good Hope in their search for a sea route to India. The history of South Africa is intimately connected with the Isthmus of Suez. It owes its Portuguese,

Local and remote geographic factors.

Dutch, and English populations to that barrier on the Mediterranean pathway to the Orient; its importance as a way station on the outside route to India fluctuates with every crisis in the history of Suez.

Direct and indirect effects of environment.   The geographic factors in history appear now as conspicuous direct effects of environment, such as the forest warfare of the American Indian or the irrigation works of the Pueblo tribes, now as a group of indirect effects, operating through the economic, social and political activities of a people. These remoter secondary results are often of supreme importance; they are the ones which give the final stamp to the national temperament and character, and yet in them the causal connection between environment and development is far from obvious. They have, therefore, presented pitfalls to the precipitate theorizer. He has either interpreted them as the direct effect of some geographic cause from which they were wholly divorced and thus arrived at conclusions which further investigation failed to sustain; or seeing no direct and obvious connection, he has denied the possibility of a generalization.

Montesquieu ascribes the immutability of religion, manners, custom and laws in India and other Oriental countries to their warm climate.[17]   Buckle attributes a highly wrought imagination and gross superstition to all people, like those of India, living in the presence of great mountains and vast plains, knowing Nature only in its overpowering aspects, which excite the fancy and paralyze reason. He finds, on the other hand, an early predominance of reason in the inhabitants of a country like ancient Greece, where natural features are on a small scale, more comprehensible, nearer the measure of man himself.[18]   The scientific geographer, grown suspicious of the omnipotence of climate and cautious of predicating immediate psychological effects which are easy to assert but difficult to prove, approaches the problem more indirectly and reaches a different solution. He finds that geographic conditions have condemned India to isolation. On the land side, a great sweep of high mountains has restricted intercourse with the interior; on the sea side, the deltaic swamps of the Indus and Ganges Rivers and an unbroken shoreline, backed by mountains on the west of the peninsula and by coastal marshes and lagoons on the east, have combined to reduce its accessibility from the ocean. The effect of such isolation is ignorance, superstition, and the early crystallization of thought and custom. Ignorance involves the lack of material for comparison, hence a restriction of the higher reasoning processes, and an unscientific attitude of mind which gives imagination free play. In contrast, the accessibilty of Greece and its focal location in the ancient world made it an intellectual clearing-house for the eastern Mediterranean. The general information gathered there afforded material for wide comparison. It fed the brilliant reason of the Athenian philosopher and the trained imagination which produced the masterpieces of Greek art and literature.

Heinrich von Treitschke, in his recent "Politik," imitates the direct inference of Buckle when he ascribes the absence of artistic and poetic development in Switzerland and the Alpine lands to the overwhelming aspect of nature there, its majestic sublimity which paralyzes the mind.[19] He reinforces his position by the fact that, by contrast, the lower mountains and hill country of Swabia, Franconia and Thuringia, where nature is gentler, stimulating, appealing, and not overpowering, have produced many poets and artists. The facts are incontestable. They reappear in France in the geographical distribution of the awards made by the Paris *Salon* of 1896. Judged by these awards, the rough highlands of Savoy, Alpine Provence, the massive eastern Pyrenees, and the Auvergne Plateau, together with the barren peninsula of Brittany, are singularly lacking in artistic instinct, while art flourishes in all the river lowlands of France. Moreover, French men of letters, by the distribution of their birthplaces, are essentially products of fluvial valleys and plains, rarely of upland and mountain.[20]

This contrast has been ascribed to a fundamental ethnic distinction between the Teutonic population of the lowlands and the Alpine or Celtic stock which survives in the isolation of highland and peninsula, thus making talent an attribute of race. But the Po Valley of northern Italy, whose population contains a strong infusion of this supposedly stultifying Alpine blood, and the neighboring lowlands and hill country

Indirect mental effects.

of Tuscany show an enormous preponderance of intellectual and artistic power over the highlands of the peninsula.[21] Hence the same contrast appears among different races under like geographic conditions. Moreover, in France other social phenomena, such as suicide, divorce, decreasing birth-rate, and radicalism in politics, show this same startling parallelism of geographic distribution,[22] and these cannot be attributed to the stimulating or depressing effect of natural scenery upon the human mind.

Mountain regions discourage the budding of genius because they are areas of isolation, confinement, remote from the great currents of men and ideas that move along the river valleys. They are regions of much labor and little leisure, of poverty to-day and anxiety for the morrow, of toil-cramped hands and toil-dulled brains. In the fertile alluvial plains are wealth, leisure, contact with many minds, large urban centers where commodities and ideas are exchanged. The two contrasted environments produce directly certain economic and social results, which, in turn, become the causes of secondary intellectual and artistic effects. The low mountains of central Germany which von Treitschke cites as homes of poets and artists, owing to abundant and varied mineral wealth, are the seats of active industries and dense populations,[23] while their low reliefs present no serious obstacle to the numerous highways across them.' They, therefore, afford all conditions for culture.

Indirect effects in differentiation of colonial peoples.

Let us take a different example. The rapid modification in physical and mental constitution of the English transplanted to North America, South Africa, Australia and New Zealand has been the result of several geographic causes working through the economic and social media; but it has been ascribed by Darwin and others to the effect of climate. The prevailing energy and initiative of colonists have been explained by the stimulating atmosphere of their new homes. Even Natal has not escaped this soft impeachment. But the enterprise of colonials has cropped out under almost every condition of heat and cold, aridity and humidity, of a habitat at sea-level and on high plateau. This blanket theory of climate cannot, therefore, cover the case. Careful analysis supersedes it by a whole group of geographic factors working directly and indirectly. The first of these was the dividing ocean which, prior to the introduction of cheap ocean transportation and bustling steerage agents, made a basis of artificial selection. Then it was the man of abundant energy who, cramped by the narrow environment of a Norwegian farm or Irish bog, came over to America to take up a quarter-section of prairie land or rise to the eminence of Boston police sergeant. The Scotch immigrants in America who fought in the Civil War were nearly two inches taller than the average in the home country.[24] But the ocean barrier culled superior qualities of mind and character also—independence of political and religious conviction, and the courage of those convictions, whether found in royalist or Puritan, Huguenot or English Catholic.

Such colonists in a remote country were necessarily few and could not be readily reinforced from home. Their new and isolated geographical environment favored variation. Heredity passed on the characteristics of a small, highly selected group. The race was kept pure from intermixture with the aborigines of the country, owing to the social and cultural abyss which separated them, and to the steady withdrawal of the natives before the advance of the whites. The homogeneity of island peoples seems to indicate that individual variations are in time communicated by heredity to a whole population under conditions of isolation; and in this way modifications due to artificial selection and a changed environment become widely spread. *Indirect effect through isolation.*

Nor is this all. The modified type soon becomes established, because the abundance of land at the disposal of the colonists and the consequent better conditions of living encourage a rapid increase of population. A second geographic factor of mere area here begins to operate. Ease in gaining subsistence, the greater independence of the individual and the family, emancipation from carking care, the hopeful attitude of mind engendered by the consciousness of an almost unlimited opportunity and capacity for expansion, the expectation of large returns upon labor, and, finally, the profound influence of this hopefulness upon the national character, all combined, produce a social rejuvenation of the race. New conditions present new problems which call for prompt and original solution, make a demand upon the ingenuity and resourcefulness of the individual, and therefore work to the same end as his previous removal from the paralyzing effect of custom in the old home country. Activity is youth and sluggishness or paralysis is age. Hence the energy, initiative, adaptability, and receptivity to new ideas—all youthful qualities—which characterize the Anglo-Saxon American as well as the English Africander, can be traced back to the stimulating influences, not of a bracing or variable climate, but of the abundant opportunities offered by a great, rich, unexploited country. Variation under new natural conditions, when safe-guarded by isolation, tends to produce modification of the colonial type; this is the direct effect of a changed environment. But the new economic and social activities of a transplanted people become the vehicle of a mass of indirect geographic influences which contribute to the differentiation of the national character.

General importance of indirect effects.

The tendency to overlook such links between conspicuous effects and their remote, less evident geographic causes has been common in geographic investigation. This direct rather than indirect approach to the heart of the problem has led to false inferences or to the assumption that reliable conclusions were impossible. Environment influences the higher, mental life of a people chiefly through the medium of their economic and social life; hence its ultimate effects should be traced through the latter back to the underlying cause. But rarely has this been done. Even so astute a geographer as Strabo, though he recognizes the influence of geographic isolation in differentiating dialects and customs in Greece,[25] ascribes some national characteristics to the nature of the country, especially to its climate, and the others to education and institutions. He thinks that the nature of their respective lands had nothing to do with making the Athenians cultured, the Spartans and Thebans ignorant; that the predilection for natural science in Babylonia and Egypt was not a result of environment but of the institutions and education of those countries.[26] But here arise the questions, how far custom and education in their turn depend upon environment; to what degree natural conditions, molding economic and political development, may through them fundamentally affect social customs, education, culture, and the dominant intellectual aptitudes of a people. It is not difficult to see, back of the astronomy and mathematics and hydraulics of Egypt, the far off sweep of the rain-laden monsoons against the mountains of Abyssinia and the creeping of the tawny Nile flood over that river-born oasis.

Plutarch states in his "Solon" that after the rebellion of Kylon in 612 B.C. the Athenian people were divided into as many political factions as there were physical types of country in Attica. The mountaineers, who were the poorest party, wanted something like a democracy; the people of the plains, comprising the greatest number of rich families, were clamorous for an oligarchy; the coast population of the south, intermediate both in social position and wealth, wanted something between the two. The same three-fold division appeared again in 564 B.C. on the usurpation of Peisistratus.[27] Here the connection between geographic condition and political opinion is clear enough, though the links are agriculture and commerce. New England's opposition to the War of 1812, culminating in the threat of secession of the Hartford Convention, can be traced back through the active maritime trade to the broken coastline and unproductive soil of that glaciated country. *Indirect political and moral effects.*

In all democratic or representative forms of government permitting free expression of popular opinion, history shows that division into political parties tends to follow geographical lines of cleavage. In our own Civil War the dividing line between North and South did not always run east and west. The mountain area of the Southern Appalachians supported the Union and drove a wedge of disaffection into the heart of the South. Mountainous West Virginia was politically opposed to the tidewater plains of old Virginia, because slave labor did not pay on the barren "upright" farms of the Cumberland Plateau; whereas, it was remunerative on the wide fertile plantations of the coastal lowland. The ethics of the question were obscured where conditions of soil and topography made the institution profitable. In the mountains, as also in New England, a law of diminishing financial returns had for its corollary a law of increasing moral insight. In this case, geographic conditions worked through the medium of direct economic effects to more important political and ethical results.

The roots of geographic influence often run far underground before coming to the surface, to sprout into some flowering growth; and to trace this back to its parent stem is the necessary but not easy task of the geographer.

Time element. The complexity of this problem does not end here. The modification of human development by environment is a natural process; like all other natural processes, it involves the cumulative effects of causes operating imperceptibly but persistently through vast periods of time. Slowly and deliberately does geography engrave the sub-titles to a people's history. Neglect of this time element in the consideration of geographic influences accounts equally for many an exaggerated assertion and denial of their power. A critic undertakes to disprove modification through physical environment by showing that it has not produced tangible results in the last fifty or five hundred years. This attitude recalls the early geologists, whose imaginations could not conceive the vast ages necessary in a scientific explanation of geologic phenomena.

The theory of evolution has taught us in science to think in larger terms of time, so that we no longer raise the question whether European colonists in Africa can turn into negroes, though we do find the recent amazing statement that the Yankee, in his tall, gaunt figure, "the colour of his skin, and the formation of his hair, has begun to differentiate himself from his European kinsman and approach the type of the aboriginal Indians."[28] Evolution tells the story of modification by a succession of infinitesimal changes, and emphasizes the permanence of a modification once produced long after the causes for it cease to act. The mesas of Arizona, the earth sculpture of the Grand Canyon remain as monuments to the erosive forces which produced them. So a habitat leaves upon man no ephemeral impress; it affects him in one way at a low stage of his development, and differently at a later or higher stage, because the man himself and his relation to his environment have been modified in the earlier period; but traces of that earlier adaptation survive in his maturer life. Hence man's relation to his environment must be looked at through the perspective of historical development. It would be impossible to explain the history and national character of the contemporary English solely by their twentieth century response to their environment, because with insular conservatism they carry and cherish vestiges of times when their islands represented different geographic relations from those of to-day. Witness the wool-sack of the lord chancellor. We cannot understand the location of modern Athens, Rome or Berlin from the present day relations of urban populations to their environment, because the original choice of these sites was dictated by far different considerations from those ruling to-day. In the history of these cities a whole succession of geographic factors have in turn been active, each leaving its impress of which the cities become, as it were, repositories.

The importance of this time element for a solution of anthropo-geographic problems becomes plainer, where a certain locality has received an entirely new population, or where a given people by migration change their habitat. The result in either case is the same, a new combination, new modifications superimposed on old modifications. And it is with this sort of case that anthropo-geography most often has to deal. So restless has mankind been, that the testimony of history and ethnology is all against the assumption that a social group has ever been subjected to but one type of environment during its long period of development from a primitive to a civilized society. Therefore, if we assert that a people is the product of the country which it inhabits at a given time, we forget that many different countries which its forbears occupied have left their mark on the present race in the form of inherited aptitudes and traditional customs acquired in those remote ancestral habitats. The Moors of Granada had passed through a wide range of ancestral experiences; they bore the impress of Asia, Africa and Europe, and on their expulsion from Spain carried back with them to Morocco traces of their peninsula life.

A race or tribe develops certain characteristics in a certain region, then moves on, leaving the old abode but not all the

Effect of a previous habitat.

accretions of custom, social organization and economic method there acquired. These travel on with the migrant people; some are dropped, others are preserved because of utility, sentiment or mere habit. For centuries after the settlement of the Jews in Palestine, traces of their pastoral life in the grasslands of Mesopotamia could be discerned in their social and political organization, in their ritual and literature. Survivals of their nomadic life in Asiatic steppes still persist among the Turks of Europe, after six centuries of sedentary life in the best agricultural land of the Balkan Peninsula. One of these appears in their choice of meat. They eat chiefly sheep and goats, beef very rarely, and swine not at all.[29] The first two thrive on poor pastures and travel well, so that they are admirably adapted to nomadic life in arid lands; the last two, far less so, but on the other hand are the regular concomitant of agricultural life. The Turk's taste to-day, therefore, is determined by the flocks and herds which he once pastured on the Trans-Caspian plains. The finished terrace agriculture and methods of irrigation, which the Saracens had learned on the mountain sides of Yemen through a schooling of a thousand years or more, facilitated their economic conquest of Spain. Their intelligent exploitation of the country's resources for the support of their growing numbers in the favorable climatic conditions which Spain offered was a light-hearted task, because of the severe training which they had had in their Arabian home.

The origin of Roman political institutions is intimately connected with conditions of the naturally small territory where arose the greatness of Rome. But now, after two thousand years we see the political impress of this narrow origin spreading to the governments of an area of Europe immeasurably larger than the region that gave it birth. In the United States, little New England has been the source of the strongest influences modifying the political, religious and cultural life of half a continent; and as far as Texas and California these influences bear the stamp of that narrow, unproductive environment which gave to its sons energy of character and ideals.

Trans-planted religions.

Ideas especially are light baggage, and travel with migrant

peoples over many a long and rough road. They are wafted like winged seed by the wind, and strike root in regions where they could never have originated. Few classes of ideas bear so plainly the geographic stamp of their origin as religious ones, yet none have spread more widely. The abstract monotheism sprung from the bare grasslands of western Asia made slow but final headway against the exuberant forest gods of the early Germans. Religious ideas travel far from their seed-beds along established lines of communication. We have the almost amusing episode of the brawny Burgundians of the fifth century, who received the Arian form of Christianity by way of the Danube highway from the schools of Athens and Alexandria, valiantly supporting the niceties of Greek religious thought against the Roman version of the faith which came up the Rhone Valley.

If the sacred literature of Judaism and Christianity take weak hold upon the western mind, this is largely because it is written in the symbolism of the pastoral nomad. Its figures of speech reflect life in deserts and grasslands. For these figures the western mind has few or vague corresponding ideas. It loses, therefore, half the import, for instance, of the Twenty-third Psalm, that picture of the nomad shepherd guiding his flock across parched and trackless plains, to bring them at evening, weary, hungry, thirsty, to the fresh pastures and waving palms of some oasis, whose green tints stand out in vivid contrast to the tawny wastes of the encompassing sands. "He leadeth me beside the still waters," not the noisy rushing stream of the rainy lands, but the quiet desert pool that reflects the stars. What real significance has the tropical radiance of the lotus flower, the sacred symbol of Buddhism, for the Mongolian lama in the cold and arid borders of Gobi or the wind-swept highlands of sterile Tibet? And yet these exotic ideas live on, even if they no longer bloom in the uncongenial soil. But to explain them in terms of their present environment would be indeed impossible.

A people may present at any given time only a partial response to their environment also for other reasons. This may be either because their arrival has been too recent for the new habitat to make its influence felt; or because, even after long

Partial response to environment.

residence, one overpowering geographic factor has operated to the temporary exclusion of all others. Under these circumstances, suddenly acquired geographic advantages of a high order or such advantages, long possessed but tardily made available by the release of national powers from more pressing tasks, may institute a new trend of historical development, resulting more from stimulating geographic conditions than from the natural capacities or aptitudes of the people themselves. Such developments, though often brilliant, are likely to be short-lived and to end suddenly or disastrously, because not sustained by a deep-seated national impulse animating the whole mass of the people. They cease when the first enthusiasm spends itself, or when outside competition is intensified, or the material rewards decrease.

The case of Spain   An illustration is found in the mediæval history of Spain. The intercontinental location of the Iberian Peninsula exposed it to the Saracen conquest and to the constant reinforcements to Islam power furnished by the Mohammedanized Berbers of North Africa. For seven centuries this location was the dominant geographic factor in Spain's history. It made the expulsion of the Moors the sole object of all the Iberian states, converted the country into an armed camp, made the gentleman adventurer and Christian knight the national ideal. It placed the center of political control high up on the barren plateau of Castile, far from the centers of population and culture in the river lowlands or along the coast. It excluded the industrial and commercial development which was giving bone and sinew to the other European states. The release of the national energies by the fall of Granada in 1492 and the now ingrained spirit of adventure enabled Spain and Portugal to utilize the unparalleled advantage of their geographical position at the junction of the Mediterranean and Atlantic highways, and by their great maritime explorations in the fifteenth and sixteenth centuries, to become foremost among European colonial powers. But the development was sporadic, not supported by any widespread national movement. In a few decades the maritime preëminence of the Iberian Peninsula began to yield to the competition of the Dutch and English, who were, so to speak, saturated with their own maritime environment. Then followed the rapid decay of the sea power of Spain, followed by that of Portugal, till by 1648 even her coasting trade was in the hands of the Dutch, and Dutch vessels were employed to maintain communication with the West Indies.[30]

We have a later instance of sporadic development under the stimulus of new and favorable geographic conditions, with a similar anti-climax. The expansion of the Russians across the lowlands of Siberia was quite in harmony with the genius of that land-bred people; but when they reached Bering Sea, the enclosed basin, the proximity of the American continent, the island stepping-stones between, and the lure of rich seal-skins to the fur-hunting Cossacks determined a sudden maritime expansion, for which the Russian people were unfitted. Beginning in 1747, it swept the coast of Alaska, located its American administrative center first on Kadiak, then on Baranof Island, and by 1812 placed its southern outposts on the California coast near San Francisco Bay and on the Farralone Islands.[31] Russian convicts were employed to man the crazy boats built of green lumber on the shores of Bering Sea, and Aleutian hunters with their *bidarkas* were impressed to catch the seal.[32] The movement was productive only of countless shipwrecks, many seal skins, and an opportunity to satisfy an old grudge against England. The territory gained was sold to the United States in 1867. This is the one instance in Russian history of any attempt at maritime expansion, and also of any withdrawal from territory to which the Muscovite power had once established its claim. This fact alone would indicate that only excessively tempting geographic conditions led the Russians into an economic and political venture which neither the previously developed aptitudes of the people nor the conditions of population and historical development on the Siberian seaboard were able to sustain. *Sporadic response to a new environment.*

The history and culture of a people embody the effects of previous habitats and of their final environment; but this environment means something more than local geographic conditions. It involves influences emanating from far beyond the borders. No country, no continent, no sea, mountain or river is restricted to itself in the influence which it either exer- *The larger conception of environment.*

cises or receives. The history of Austria cannot be understood merely from Austrian ground. Austrian territory is part of the Mediterranean hinterland, and therefore has been linked historically with Rome, Italy, and the Adriatic. It is a part of the upper Danube Valley and therefore shares much of its history with Bavaria and Germany, while the lower Danube has linked it with the Black Sea, Greece, the Russian steppes, and Asia. The Asiatic Hungarians have pushed forward their ethnic boundary nearly to Vienna. The Austrian capital has seen the warring Turks beneath its walls, and shapes its foreign policy with a view to the relative strength of the Sultan and the Czar.

Unity of the earth. The earth is an inseparable whole. Each country or sea is physically and historically intelligible only as a portion of that whole. Currents and wind-systems of the oceans modify the climate of the nearby continents, and direct the first daring navigations of their peoples. The alternating monsoons of the Indian Ocean guided Arab merchantmen from ancient times back and forth between the Red Sea and the Malabar coast of India.[33] The Equatorial Current and the northeast trade-wind carried the timid ships of Columbus across the Atlantic to America. The Gulf Stream and the prevailing westerlies later gave English vessels the advantage on the return voyage. Europe is a part of the Atlantic coast. This is a fact so significant that the North Atlantic has become a European sea. The United States also is a part of the Atlantic coast: this is the dominant fact of American history. China forms a section of the Pacific rim. This is the fact back of the geographic distribution of Chinese emigration to Annam, Tonkin, Siam, Malacca, the Philippines, East Indies, Borneo, Australia, Hawaiian Islands, the Pacific Coast States, British Columbia, the Alaskan coast southward from Bristol Bay in Bering Sea, Ecuador and Peru.

As the earth is one, so is humanity. Its unity of species points to some degree of communication through a long prehistoric past. Universal history is not entitled to the name unless it embraces all parts of the earth and all peoples, whether savage or civilized. To fill the gaps in the written record it must turn to ethnology and geography, which by tracing the distribution and movements of primitive peoples can often reconstruct the most important features of their history.

Anthropo-geographic problems are never simple. They must all be viewed in the long perspective of evolution and the historical past. They require allowance for the dominance of different geographic factors at different periods, and for a possible range of geographic influences wide as the earth itself. In the investigator they call for pains-taking analysis and, above all, an open mind.

NOTES TO CHAPTER I

1. George Adam Smith, Historical Geography of the Holy Land, pp. 149-157. New York, 1897.

2. A. P. Brigham, Geographic Influences in American History, Chap. I. Boston, 1903.

3. R. H. Whitbeck, Geographic Influences in the Development of New Jersey, *Journal of Geography*, Vol. V, No. 6. January, 1908.

4. Hans Helmolt, History of the World, Vol. II, p. 372. London and New York, 1902-1906.

5. Jean Baptiste Tavernier, Travels in India, 1641-1667. Vol. I, chap. V and map. London, 1889.

6. Sir Thomas Holdich, India, p. 305. London, 1905.

7. Bunbury, History of Ancient Geography, Vol. II, pp. 464-465, 469. London, 1883.

8. *Imperial Gazetteer for India*, Vol. III, p. 109. London, 1885.

9. G. G. Chisholm, The Relativity of Geographic Advantages, *Scottish Geog. Mag.*, Vol. XIII, No. 9, Sept. 1897.

10. Hugh Robert Mill, International Geography, p. 347. New York, 1902.

11. Joseph Partsch, Central Europe, pp. 228-230. London, 1903.

12. H. J. Mackinder, Britain and the British Seas, pp. 317-323. London, 1904.

13. Captain A. T. Mahan, Influence of Sea Power upon History, pp. 36-38. Boston, 1902.

14. G. G. Chisholm, Economic Geography, *Scottish Geog. Mag.*, March, 1908.

15. Captain A. T. Mahan, Influence of Sea Power upon History, pp. 37-38. Boston, 1902.

16. Boyd Winchester, The Swiss Republic, pp. 123, 124, 145-147. Philadelphia, 1891.

17. Montesquieu, Spirit of the Laws, Book XIV, chap. IV.

18. Henry Buckle, History of Civilization in England, Vol. I, pp. 86-106.

19. Heinrich von Treitschke, *Politik*, Vol. I, p. 225. Leipzig, 1897. This whole chapter on *Land und Leute* is suggestive.

20. W. Z. Ripley, Races of Europe, pp. 524-525. New York, 1899.

21. *Ibid.*, 526.

22. *Ibid.*, 517-520, 533-536.

23. Joseph Partsch, Central Europe, pp. 256-257, 268-271. London, 1903.

24. W. Z. Ripley, Races of Europe, p. 89. New York, 1899.

25. Strabo, Book VII, chap. I, 2.

26. Strabo, Book II, chap. III, 7.

27. Plutarch, Solon, pp. 13, 29, 154.

28. Hans Helmolt, History of the World, Vol. II, pp. 244-245. New York, 1902-1906.

29. Roscher, *National-oekonomik des Ackerbaues*, p. 33, note 3. Stuttgart, 1888.

30. Captain A. T. Mahan, Influence of Sea Power upon History, pp. 41-42, 50-53. Boston, 1902.

31. H. Bancroft, History of California, Vol. I, pp. 298, 628-635. San Francisco.

32. Agnes Laut, Vikings of the Pacific, pp. 64-82. New York, 1905.

33. Bunbury, History of Ancient Geography, Vol. II, pp. 351, 470-471. London, 1883.

CHAPTER II

CLASSES OF GEOGRAPHIC INFLUENCES

INTO almost every anthropo-geographical problem the element of environment enters in different phases, with different
modes of operation and varying degrees of importance. Since
the causal conception of geography demands a detailed analysis of all the relations between environment and human development, it is advisable to distinguish the various classes of
geographic influences.

Four fundamental classes of effects can be distinguished. Physical
1. The first class includes direct physical effects of environ- effects.
ment, similar to those exerted on plants and animals by their
habitat. Certain geographic conditions, more conspicuously
those of climate, apply certain stimuli to which man, like
the lower animals, responds by an adaption of his organism to his environment. Many physiological peculiarities of
man are due to physical effects of environment, which doubtless operated very strongly in the earliest stages of human
development, and in those shadowy ages contributed to the
differentiation of races. The unity of the human species is as
clearly established as the diversity of races and peoples, whose
divergences must be interpreted chiefly as modifications in
response to various habitats in long periods of time.

Such modifications have probably been numerous in the Variation
persistent and unending movements, shiftings, and migrations and natural
which have made up the long prehistoric history of man. If the conditions.
origin of species is found in variability and inheritance, variation is undoubtedly influenced by a change of natural conditions. To quote Darwin, "In one sense the conditions of life
may be said, not only to cause variability, either directly or
indirectly, but likewise to include natural selection, for the
conditions determine whether this or that variety shall survive."[1] The variability of man does not mean that every ex-

ternal influence leaves its mark upon him, but that man as an organism, by the preservation of beneficent variations and the elimination of deleterious ones, is gradually adapted to his environment, so that he can utilize most completely that which it contributes to his needs. This self-maintenance under outward influences is an essential part of the conception of life which Herbert Spencer defines as the correspondence between internal conditions and external circumstances, or August Comte as the harmony between the living being and the surrounding medium or *milieu*.

According to Virchow, the distinction of races rests upon hereditary variations, but heredity itself cannot become active till the characteristic or *Zustand* is produced which is to be handed down.[2] But environment determines what variation shall become stable enough to be passed on by heredity. For instance, we can hardly err in attributing the great lung capacity, massive chests, and abnormally large torsos of the Quichua and Aymara Indians inhabiting the high Andean plateaus to the rarified air found at an altitude of 10,000 or 15,000 feet above sea level. Whether these have been acquired by centuries of extreme lung expansion, or represent the survival of a chance variation of undoubted advantage, they are a product of the environment. They are a serious handicap when the Aymara Indian descends to the plains, where he either dies off or leaves descendants with diminishing chests.[3] [See map page 101.]

Stature and environment.

Darwin holds that many slight changes in animals and plants, such as size, color, thickness of skin and hair, have been produced through food supply and climate from the external conditions under which the forms lived.[4] Paul Ehrenreich, while regarding the chief race distinctions as permanent forms, not to be explained by external conditions, nevertheless concedes the slight and slow variation of the sub-race under changing conditions of food and climate as beyond doubt.[5] Stature is partly a matter of feeding and hence of geographic condition. In mountain regions, where the food resources are scant, the varieties of wild animals are characterized by smaller size in general than are corresponding species in the lowlands. It is a noticeable fact that dwarfed horses or ponies have originated in islands, in Iceland, the Shetlands, Corsica and Sardinia. This is due either to scanty and unvaried food or to excessive inbreeding, or probably to both. The horses introduced into the Falkland Islands in 1764 have deteriorated so in size and strength in a few generations that they are in a fair way to develop a Falkland variety of pony.[6]   On the other hand, Mr. Homer Davenport states that the pure-bred Arabian horses raised on his New Jersey stock farm are in the third generation a hand higher than their grandsires imported from Arabia, and of more angular build. The result is due to more abundant and nutritious food and the elimination of long desert journeys.

The low stature of the natives prevailing in certain "misery spots" of Europe, as in the Auvergne Plateau of southern France, is due in part to race, in part to a disastrous artificial selection by the emigration of the taller and more robust individuals, but in considerable part to the harsh climate and starvation food-yield of that sterile soil; for the children of the region, if removed to the more fertile valleys of the Loire and Garonne, grow to average stature.[7]   The effect of a scant and uncertain food supply is especially clear in savages, who have erected fewer buffers between themselves and the pressure of environment. The Bushmen of the Kalahari Desert are shorter than their Hottentot kindred who pasture their flocks and herds in the neighboring grasslands.[8] Samoyedes, Lapps, and other hyperborean races of Eurasia are shorter than their more southern neighbors, the physical record of an immemorial struggle against cold and hunger. The stunted forms and wretched aspect of the Snake Indians inhabiting the Rocky Mountain deserts distinguished these clans from the tall buffalo-hunting tribes of the plains.[9] Any feature of geographic environment tending to affect directly the physical vigor and strength of a people cannot fail to prove a potent factor in their history.

Oftentimes environment modifies the physique of a people indirectly by imposing upon them certain predominant activities, which may develop one part of the body almost to the point of deformity. This is the effect of increased use or disuse which Darwin discusses. He attributes the thin legs and

Physical effects of dominant activities.

thick arms of the Payaguas Indians living along the Paraguay River to generations of lives spent in canoes, with the lower extremities motionless and the arm and chest muscles in constant exercise.[10] Livingstone found these same characteristics of broad chests and shoulders with ill-developed legs among the Barotse of the upper Zambesi;[11] and they have been observed in pronounced form, coupled with distinctly impaired powers of locomotion, among the Tlingit, Tsimshean, and Haida Indians of the southern Alaskan and British Columbia coast, where the geographic conditions of a mountainous and almost strandless shore interdicted agriculture and necessitated sea-faring activities.[12] An identical environment has produced a like physical effect upon the canoemen of Tierra del Fuego[13] and the Aleutian Islanders, who often sit in their boats twenty hours at a time.[14] These special adaptations are temporary in their nature and tend to disappear with change of occupation, as, for instance, among the Tlingit Indians, who develop improved leg muscles when employed as laborers in the salmon canneries of British Columbia.

Effects of climate. Both the direct and indirect physical effects of environment thus far instanced are obvious in themselves and easily explained. Far different is it with the majority of physical effects, especially those of climate, whose mode of operation is much more obscure than was once supposed. The modern geographer does not indulge in the naive hypothesis of the last century, which assumed a prompt and direct effect of environment upon the form and features of man. Carl Ritter regarded the small, slit eyes and swollen lids of the Turkoman as "an obvious effect of the desert upon the organism." Stanhope Smith ascribed the high shoulders and short neck of the Tartars of Mongolia to their habit of raising their shoulders to protect the neck against the cold; their small, squinting eyes, overhanging brows, broad faces and high cheek bones, to the effect of the bitter, driving winds and the glare of the snow, till, he says, "every feature by the action of the cold is harsh and distorted."[15] These profound influences of a severe climate upon physiognomy he finds also among the Lapps, northern Mongolians, Samoyedes and Eskimo.

Most of these problems are only secondarily grist for the

geographer's mill. For instance, when the Aryans descended
to the enervating lowlands of tropical India, and in that debilitating climate lost the qualities which first gave them supremacy, the change which they underwent was primarily a
physiological one. It can be scientifically described and explained therefore only by physiologists and physico-chemists;
and upon their investigations the geographer must wait before
he approaches the problem from the standpoint of geographical distribution. Into this sub-class of physical effects come Acclimat-
all questions of acclimatization.[16] These are important to the ization.
anthropo-geographer, just as they are to colonial governments
like England or France, because they affect the power of national or racial expansion, and fix the historical fate of tropical
lands. The present populations of the earth represent physical adaptation to their environments. The intense heat and
humidity of most tropical lands prevent any permanent occupation by a native-born population of pure whites. The ca-
tarrhal zone north of the fortieth parallel in America soon
exterminates the negroes.[17]

The Indians of South America, though all fundamentally
of the same ethnic stock, are variously acclimated to the warm,
damp, forested plains of the Amazon; to the hot, dry, treeless
coasts of Peru; and to the cold, arid heights of the Andes.
The habitat that bred them tends to hold them, by restricting
the range of climate which they can endure. In the zone of
the Andean slope lying between 4,000 and 6,000 feet of altitude, which produces the best flavored coffee and which must
be cultivated, the imported Indians from the high plateaus
and from the low Amazon plains alike sicken and die after a
short time; so that they take employment on these coffee plantations for only three or five months, and then return to their
own homes. Labor becomes nomadic on these slopes, and in
the intervals these farm lands of intensive agriculture show the
anomaly of a sparse population only of resident managers.[18]
Similarly in the high, dry Himalayan valley of the upper
Indus, over 10,000 feet above sea level, the natives of Ladak
are restricted to a habitat that yields them little margin
of food for natural growth of population but forbids them to
emigrate in search of more,—applies at the same time the

lash to drive and the leash to hold, for these highlanders soon die when they reach the plains.[19]   Here are two antagonistic geographic influences at work from the same environment, one physical and the other social-economic.   The Ladaki have reached an interesting resolution of these two forces by the institution of polyandry, which keeps population practically stationary.

Pigmen-tation and cli-mate.   The relation of pigmentation to climate has long interested geographers as a question of environment; but their specula-tions on the subject have been barren, because the preliminary investigations of the physiologist, physicist and chemist are still incomplete.   The general fact of increasing nigrescence from temperate towards equatorial regions is conspicuous enough, despite some irregularity of the shading.[20]   This fact points strongly to some direct relation between climate and pigmentation, but gives no hint how the pigmental processes are affected.   The physiologist finds that in the case of the negro, the dark skin is associated with a dense cuticle, diminished perspiration, smaller chests and less respiratory power, a lower temperature and more rapid pulse,[21] all which variations may enter into the problem of the negro's coloring. The question is therefore by no means simple.

Yet it is generally conceded by scientists that pigment is a protective device of nature.   The negro's skin is comparatively insensitive to a sun heat that blisters a white man.   Living-stone found the bodies of albino negroes in Bechuana Land always blistered on exposure to the sun,[22] and a like effect has been observed among albino Polynesians, and Melanesians of Fiji.[23]   Paul Ehrenreich finds that the degree of coloration de-pends less upon annual temperature than upon the direct effect of the sun's rays; and that therefore a people dwelling in a cool, dry climate, but exposed to the sun may be darker than another in a hot, moist climate but living in a dense forest. The forest-dwelling Botokudos of the upper San Francisco River in Brazil are fairer than the kindred Kayapo tribe, who inhabit the open campos; and the Arawak of the Purus River forests are lighter than their fellows in the central Matto Grosso.[24]   Sea-faring coast folk, who are constantly exposed to the sun, especially in the Tropics, show a deeper pigmentation than their kindred of the wooded interior.[25]   The coast Moros of western Mindanao are darker than the Subanos, their Malay brethren of the back country, the lightness of whose color can be explained by their forest life.[26]   So the Duallas of the Kamerun coast of Africa are darker than the Bakwiri inhabiting the forested mountains just behind them, though both tribes belong to the Bantu group of people.[27]   Here light, in contradistinction to heat, appears the dominant factor in pigmentation.   A recent theory, advanced by von Schmae-del in 1895, rests upon the chemical power of light.   It holds that the black pigment renders the negro skin insensitive to the luminous or actinic effects of solar radiation, which are far more destructive to living protoplasm than the merely calorific effects.[28]

Coloration responds to other more obscure influences of en-vironment.   A close connection between pigmentation and ele-vation above sea level has been established: a high altitude operates like a high latitude.   Blondness increases appreciably on the higher slopes of the Black Forest, Vosges Mountains, and Swiss Alps, though these isolated highlands are the stronghold of the brunette Alpine race.[29]   Livi, in his treatise on military anthropometry, deduced a special action of moun-tains upon pigmentation on observing a prevailing increase of blondness in Italy above the four-hundred meter line, a phenomenon which came out as strongly in Basilicata and Calabria provinces of the south as in Piedmont and Lombardy in the north.[30]   The dark Hamitic Berbers of northern Africa have developed an unmistakable blond variant in high valleys of the Atlas range, which in a sub-tropical region ris 3 to the height of 12,000 feet.   Here among the Kabyles the popula-tion is fair; grey, blue or green eyes are frequent, as is also reddish blond or chestnut hair.[31]   Waitz long ago affirmed this tendency of mountaineers to lighter coloring from his study of primitive peoples.[32]   The modification can not be attributed wholly to climatic contrast between mountain and plain.   Some other factor, like the economic poverty of the environment and the poor food-supply, as Livi suggests, has had a hand in the result; but just what it is or how it has operated cannot yet be defined.[33]

Pigmenta-tion and altitude.

Difficulty of generalization.

Enough has been said to show that the geographer can formulate no broad generalization as to the relation of pigmentation and climate from the occurrence of the darkest skins in the Tropics; because this fact is weakened by the appearance also of lighter tints in the hottest districts, and of darker ones in arctic and temperate regions. The geographer must investigate the questions when and where deeper shades develop in the skins of fair races; what is the significance of dark skins in the cold zones and of fair ones in hot zones. His answer must be based largely on the conclusions of physiologists and physicists, and only when these have reached a satisfactory solution of each detail of the problem can the geographer summarize the influence of environment upon pigmentation. The rule can therefore safely be laid down that in all investigation of geographic influences upon the permanent physical characteristics of races, the geographic distribution of these should be left out of consideration till the last, since it so easily misleads.[34] Moreover, owing to the ceaseless movements of mankind, these effects do not remain confined to the region that produced them, but pass on with the wandering throng in whom they have once developed, and in whom they endure or vanish according as they prove beneficial or deleterious in the new habitat.

Psychical effects.

II. More varied and important are the psychical effects of geographic environment. As direct effects they are doubtless bound up in many physiological modifications; and as influences of climate, they help differentiate peoples and races in point of temperament. They are reflected in man's religion and his literature, in his modes of thought and figures of speech. Blackstone states that "in the Isle of Man, to take away a horse or ox was no felony, but a trespass, because of the difficulty in that little territory to conceal them or to carry them off; but to steal a pig or a fowl, which is easily done, was a capital misdemeanour, and the offender punished with death." The judges or deemsters in this island of fishermen swore to execute the laws as impartially "as the herring's backbone doth lie in the middle of the fish."[35] The whole mythology of the Polynesians is an echo of the encompassing ocean. The cosmography of every primitive people, their first crude effort in the science of the universe, bears the impress of their habitat. The Eskimo's hell is a place of darkness, storm and intense cold;[36] the Jew's is a place of eternal fire. Buddha, born in the steaming Himalayan piedmont, fighting the lassitude induced by heat and humidity, pictured his heaven as Nirvana, the cessation of all activity and individual life.

Intellectual effects of environment may appear in the enrichment of a language in one direction to a rare nicety of expression; but this may be combined with a meager vocabulary in all other directions. The greatest cattle-breeders among the native Africans, such as the Hereros of western Damaraland and the Dinkas of the upper White Nile, have an amazing choice of words for all colors describing their animals—brown, dun, red, white, dapple, and so on in every gradation of shade and hue. The Samoyedes of northern Russia have eleven or twelve terms to designate the various grays and browns of their reindeer, despite their otherwise low cultural development.[37] The speech of nomads has an abundance of expressions for cattle in every relation of life. It includes different words for breeding, pregnancy, death, and slaughtering in relation to every different kind of domestic animal. The Magyars, among whom pastoral life still survives on the low plains of the Danube and Theiss, have a generic word for herd, *csorda*, and special terms for herds of cattle, horses, sheep, and swine.[38] While the vocabulary of Malays and Polynesians is especially rich in nautical terms, the Kirghis shepherd tribes who wander over the highlands of western Asia from the Tian Shan to the Hindu Kush have four different terms for four kinds of mountain passes. A *daban* is a difficult, rocky defile; an *art* is very high and dangerous; a *bel* is a low, easy pass, and a *kutal* is a broad opening between low hills.[39]

To such influences man is a passive subject, especially in the earlier stages of his development; but there are more important influences emanating from his environment which affect him as an active agent, challenge his will by furnishing the motives for its exercise, give purpose to his activities, and determine the direction which they shall take.[40] These mold his mind and character through the media of his

Indirect effect upon language.

economic and social life, and produce effects none the less important because they are secondary. About these anthropo-geography can reach surer conclusions than regarding direct psychical effects, because it can trace their mode of operation as well as define the result. Direct psychical effects are more matters of conjecture, whose causation is asserted rather than proved. They seem to float in the air, detached from the solid ground under foot, and are therefore subject matter for the psychologist rather than the geographer.

The great man in history. What of the great man in this geographical interpretation of history? It seems to take no account of him, or to put him into the melting-pot with the masses. Both are to some extent true. As a science, anthropo-geography can deal only with large averages, and these exclude or minimize the exceptional individual. Moreover, geographic conditions which give this or that bent to a nation's purposes and determine its aggre-gate activities have a similar effect upon the individual; but he may institute a far-seeing policy, to whose wisdom only gradually is the people awakened. The acts of the great man are rarely arbitrary or artificial; he accelerates or retards the normal course of development, but cannot turn it counter to the channels of natural conditions. As a rule he is a product of the same forces that made his people. He moves with them and is followed by them under a common impulse. Daniel Boone, that picturesque figure leading the van of the westward movement over the Allegheny Mountains, was born of his frontier environment and found a multitude of his kind in that region of backwoods farms to follow him into the wil-derness. Thomas Jefferson of Virginia, in the Louisiana Pur-chase, carried out the policy of expansion adumbrated in Gov-ernor Spottswood's expedition with the Knights of the Golden Horseshoe over the Blue Ridge in 1712. Jefferson's daring consummation of the purchase without government authority showed his community of purpose with the majority of the people. Peter the Great's location of his capital at St. Peters-burg, usually stigmatized as the act of a despot, was made in response to natural conditions offering access to the Baltic nations, just as certainly as ten centuries before similar con-ditions and identical advantages led the early Russian merchants to build up a town at nearby Novgorod, in easy water connection with the Baltic commerce.[41]

III. Geographic conditions influence the economic and social development of a people by the abundance, paucity, or general character of the natural resources, by the local ease or difficulty of securing the necessaries of life, and by the possibility of industry and commerce afforded by the environment. From the standpoint of production and exchange, these influences are primarily the subject matter of economic and commercial geography; but since they also permeate national life, determine or modify its social structure, condemn it to the dwarfing effects of national poverty, or open to it the cultural and political possibilities resident in national wealth, they are legitimate material also for anthropo-geography. *Economic and social effects.*

They are especially significant because they determine the size of the social group. This must be forever small in areas of limited resources or of limited extent, as in the little islands of the world and the yet smaller oases. The desert of Chinese Turkestan supports, in certain detached spots of river-born fertility, populations like the 60,000 of Kashgar, and from this size groups all the way down to the single families which Younghusband found living by a mere trickle of a stream flowing down the southern slope of the Tian Shan. Small islands, according to their size, fertility, and command of trade, may harbor a sparse and scant population, like the five hundred souls struggling for an ill-fed existence on the barren Westman Isles of Iceland; or a compact, teeming, yet absolutely small social group, like that crowding Malta or the Bermudas. Whether sparsely or compactly distributed, such groups suffer the limitations inherent in their small size. They are forever excluded from the historical significance attaching to the large, continuously distributed populations of fertile continental lands. *Size of the social group.*

IV. The next class belongs exclusively to the domain of geography, because it embraces the influence of the features of the earth's surface in directing the movements and ultimate distribution of mankind. It includes the effect of natural barriers, like mountains, deserts, swamps, and seas, in ob- *Effect upon movements of peoples.*

structing or deflecting the course of migrating people and in giving direction to national expansión; it considers the tendency of river valleys and treeless plains to facilitate such movements, the power of rivers, lakes, bays and oceans either to block the path or open a highway, according as navigation is in a primitive or advanced stage; and finally the influence of all these natural features in determining the territory which a people is likely to occupy, and the boundaries which shall separate from their neighbors.

River routes. The lines of expansion followed by the French and English in the settlement of America and also the extent of territory covered by each were powerfully influenced by geographic conditions. The early French explorers entered the great east-west waterway of the St. Lawrence River and the Great Lakes, which carried them around the northern end of the Appalachian barrier into the heart of the continent, planted them on the low, swampy, often navigable watershed of the Mississippi, and started them on another river voyage of nearly two thousand miles to the Gulf of Mexico. Here were the conditions and temptation for almost unlimited expansion; hence French Canada reached to the head of Lake Superior, and French Louisiana to the sources of the Missouri. To the lot of the English fell a series of short rivers with fertile valleys, nearly barred at their not distant sources by a wall of forested mountains, but separated from one another by low watersheds which facilitated lateral expansion over a narrow belt between mountains and sea. Here a region of mild climate and fertile soil suited to agriculture, enclosed by strong natural boundaries, made for compact settlement, in contrast to the wide diffusion of the French. Later, when a growing population pressed against the western barrier, mountain gates opened at Cumberland Gap and the Mohawk Valley; the Ohio River and the Great Lakes became interior thoroughfares, and the northwestern prairies lines of least resistance to the western settler. Rivers played the same part in directing and expediting this forward movement, as did the Lena and the Amoor in the Russian advance into Siberia, the Humber and the Trent in the progress of the Angles into the heart of Britain, the Rhone and

Danube in the march of the Romans into central Europe. The geographical environment of a people may be such as to segregate them from others, and thereby to preserve or even intensify their natural characteristics; or it may expose them to extraneous influences, to an infusion of new blood and new ideas, till their peculiarities are toned down, their distinctive features of dialect or national dress or provincial customs eliminated, and the people as a whole approach to the composite type of civilized humanity. A land shut off by mountains or sea from the rest of the world tends to develop a homogeneous people, since it limits or prevents the intrusion of foreign elements; or when once these are introduced, it encourages their rapid assimilation by the strongly interactive life of a confined locality. Therefore large or remote islands are, as a rule, distinguished by the unity of their inhabitants in point of civilization and race characteristics. Witness Great Britain, Ireland, Japan, Iceland, as also Australia and New Zealand at the time of their discovery. The highlands of the Southern Appalachians, which form the "mountain backyards" of Kentucky, Tennessee and North Carolina, are peopled by the purest English stock in the United States, descendants of the backwoodsmen of the late eighteenth century. Difficulty of access and lack of arable land have combined to discourage immigration. In consequence, foreign elements, including the elsewhere ubiquitous negro, are wanting, except along the few railroads which in recent years have penetrated this country. Here survive an eighteenth century English, Christmas celebrated on Twelfth Night, the spinning wheel, and a belief in Joshua's power to arrest the course of the sun.[42]

An easily accessible land is geographically hospitable to all new-comers, facilitates the mingling of peoples, the exchange of commodities and ideas. The amalgamation of races in such regions depends upon the similarity or diversity of the ethnic elements and the duration of the common occupation. The broad, open valley of the Danube from the Black Sea to Vienna contains a bizarre mixture of several stocks—Turks, Bulgarians, various families of pure Slavs, Roumanians, Hungarians, and Germans. These elements are too diverse and

(margin note: Segregation and accessibility.)

their occupation of the valley too recent for amalgamation to have advanced very far as yet. The maritime plain and open river valleys of northern France show a complete fusion of the native Celts with the Saxons, Franks, and Normans who have successively drifted into the region, just as the Teutonic and scanter Slav elements have blended in the Baltic plains from the Elbe to the Vistula.

Change of habitat. Here are four different classes of geographic influences, all which may become active in modifying a people when it changes its habitat. Many of the characteristics acquired in the old home still live on, or at best yield slowly to the new environment. This is especially true of the direct physical and psychical effects. But a country may work a prompt and radical change in the social organization of an immigrant people by the totally new conditions of economic life which it presents. These may be either greater wealth or poverty of natural resources than the race has previously known, new stimulants or deterrents to commerce and intercourse, and new conditions of climate which affect the efficiency of the workman and the general character of production. From these a whole complex mass of secondary effects may follow.

The Aryans and Mongols, leaving their homes in the cool barren highlands of Central Asia where nature dispensed her gifts with a miserly hand, and coming down to the hot, low, fertile plains of the Indian rivers, underwent several fundamental changes in the process of adaptation to their new environment. An enervating climate did its work in slaking their energies; but more radical still was the change wrought by the contrast of poverty and abundance, enforced asceticism and luxury, presented by the old and new home. The restless, tireless shepherds became a sedentary, agricultural people; the abstemious nomads,—spare, sinewy, strangers to indulgence—became a race of rulers, revelling in luxury, lording it over countless subjects; finally, their numbers increased rapidly, no longer kept down by the scant subsistence of arid grasslands and scattered oases.

In a similar way, the Arab of the desert became transformed into the sedentary lord of Spain. In the luxuriance of field and orchard which his skilful methods of irrigation and til-

lage produced, in the growing predominance of the intellectual
over the nomadic military life, of the complex affairs of city
and mart over the simple tasks of herdsman or cultivator, he
lost the benefit of the early harsh training and therewith
his hold upon his Iberian empire. Biblical history gives us the
picture of the Sheik Abraham, accompanied by his nephew
Lot, moving up from the rainless plains of Mesopotamia with
his flocks and herds into the better watered Palestine. There
his descendants in the garden land of Canaan became an agricultural people; and the problem of Moses and the Judges was
to prevent their assimilation in religion and custom to the
settled Semitic tribes about them, and to make them preserve
the ideals born in the starry solitudes of the desert.

The change from the nomadic to the sedentary life repre- **Retro-**
sents an economic advance. Sometimes removal to strongly **gression**
in new
contrasted geographic conditions necessitates a reversion to a **habitat.**
lower economic type of existence. The French colonists who
came to Lower Canada in the seventeenth and eighteenth centuries found themselves located in a region of intense cold,
where arable soil was inferior in quality and limited in amount,
producing no staple like the tobacco of Virginia or the wheat of
Maryland or the cotton of South Carolina or the sugar of
the West Indies, by which a young colony might secure a
place in European trade. But the snow-wrapped forests of
Canada yielded an abundance of fur-bearing animals, the
fineness and thickness of whose pelts were born of this frozen
north. Into their remotest haunts at the head of Lake Superior or of Hudson Bay, long lines of rivers and lakes opened
level water roads a thousand miles or more from the crude
little colonial capital at Quebec. And over in Europe beaver
hats and fur-trimmed garments were all the style! So the
plodding farmer from Normandy and the fisherman from
Poitou, transferred to Canadian soil, were irresistibly drawn
into the adventurous life of the trapper and fur-trader. The
fur trade became the accepted basis of colonial life; the
voyageur and *courier de bois,* clad in skins, paddling up ice-
rimmed streams in their birch-bark canoes, fraternizing with
Indians who were their only companions in that bleak interior,
and married often to dusky squaws, became assimilated to the

savage life about them and reverted to the lower hunter stage of civilization.[43]

The Boers of South Africa.

Another pronounced instance of rapid retrogression under new unfavorable geographic conditions is afforded by the South African Boer. The transfer from the busy commercial cities of the Rhine mouths to the far-away periphery of the world's trade, from the intensive agriculture of small deltaic gardens and the scientific dairy farming of the moist Netherlands to the semi-arid pastures of the high, treeless *veldt*, where they were barred from contact with the vivifying sea and its ship-borne commerce, has changed the enterprising seventeenth century Hollander into the conservative pastoral Boer. Dutch cleanliness has necessarily become a tradition to a people who can scarcely find water for their cattle. The comfort and solid bourgeois elegance of the Dutch home lost its material equipment in the Great Trek, when the long wagon journey reduced household furniture to its lowest terms. House-wifely habits and order vanished in the semi-nomadic life which followed.[44] The gregarious instinct, bred by the closely-packed population of little Holland, was transformed to a love of solitude, which in all lands characterizes the people of a remote and sparsely inhabited frontier. It is a common saying that the Boer cannot bear to see another man's smoke from his *stoep*, just as the early Trans-Allegheny pioneer was always on the move westward, because he could not bear to hear his neighbor's watch-dog bark. Even the Boer language has deteriorated under the effects of isolation and a lower status of civilization. The native *Taal* differs widely from the polished speech of Holland; it preserves some features of the High Dutch of two centuries ago, but has lost inflexions and borrowed words for new phenomena from the English, Kaffirs and Hottentots; can express no abstract ideas, only the concrete ideas of a dull, work-a-day world.[45]

The new habitat may eliminate many previously acquired characteristics and hence transform a people, as in the case of the Boers; or it may intensify tribal or national traits, as in the seafaring propensities of the Angles and Saxons when transferred to Britain, and of the seventeenth century English when transplanted to the indented coasts of New England; or it may tolerate mere survival or the slow dissuetude of qualities which escape any particular pressure in the new environment, and which neither benefit nor handicap in the modified struggle for existence.

NOTES TO CHAPTER II

1. Darwin, Origin of Species, Chap. V, p. 166. New York, 1895.
2. R. Virchow, *Rassenbildung und Erblichkeit*, Bastian Festschrift, pp. 14, 43, 44. Berlin, 1896.
3. Darwin, Descent of Man, pp. 34-35. New York, 1899.
4. Darwin, Origin of Species, Chap. I, pp. 8-9. New York, 1895.
5. P. Ehrenreich, *Die Urbewohner Brasiliens*, p. 30. Braunschweig, 1897.
6. Ratzel, *Die Erde und das Leben*, Vol. I, pp. 364, 365. Leipzig and Vienna, 1901.
7. W. Z. Ripley, Races of Europe, pp. 79-86, 96, 100. New York, 1899.
8. T. Waitz, Anthropology, pp. 57-58. Edited by J. F. Collingwood. London, 1863.
9. Schoolcraft, Indian Tribes of the United States, Vol. I, pp. 198-200, 219. Philadelphia, 1853.
10. Darwin, Descent of Man, p. 33. New York, 1899.
11. D. Livingstone, Missionary Travels, p. 266. New York, 1858.
12. Alaska, *Eleventh Census Report*, pp. 54, 56. Washington, 1893, and Albert P. Niblack, The Coast Indians of Southern Alaska and Northern British Columbia, p. 237. Washington, 1888.
13. Fitz-Roy, Voyage of the Beagle, Vol. II, pp. 130-132, 137, 138. London, 1839.
14. H. Bancroft, Native Races, Vol. I, pp. 88-89. San Francisco, 1886.
15. S. Stanhope Smith, Essay on the Causes of the Variety of Complexion and Figure in the Human Species, pp. 103-110. New Brunswick and New York, 1810.
16. For full discussion see A. R. Wallace's article on acclimatization in Encyclopedia Britanica, and W. Z. Ripley, Races of Europe. Chap. XXI. New York, 1899.
17. D. G. Brinton, Races and Peoples, pp. 39-41. Philadelphia, 1901.
18. Darwin, Descent of Man, pp. 34-35. New York, 1899.
19. E. F. Knight, Where Three Empires Meet, pp. 137-138. London, 1897.
20. W. Z. Ripley, Races of Europe, pp. 58-71, Map. New York, 1899.
21. *Ibid.*, p. 566. D. G. Brinton, Races and Peoples, pp. 29-30. Philadelphia, 1901.
22. D. Livingstone, Missionary Travels, p. 607. New York, 1858.
23. Williams and Calvert, Fiji and the Fijians, p. 83. New York, 1859.

24. P. Ehrenreich, *Die Urbewohner Brasiliens*, p. 32. Braunschweig, 1897.

25. T. Waitz, Anthropology, pp. 46-49. Edited by Collingwood, London, 1863.

26. *Philippine Census*, Vol. I, p. 552. Washington, 1903.

27. F. Ratzel, History of Mankind, Vol. III, p. 106. London, 1908.

28. Major Charles E. Woodruff, The Effect of Tropical Light on the White Man, New York, 1905, is a suggestive but not convincing discussion of the theory.

29. W. Z. Ripley, Races of Europe, pp. 74-77. New York, 1899.

30. Quoted in G. Sergi, The Mediterranean Race, p. 73. London and New York, 1901.

31. *Ibid.*, pp. 63-69, 74-75.

32. T. Waitz, Anthropology, pp. 44-45. Edited by J. F. Collingwood, London, 1863.

33. W. Z. Ripley, Races of Europe, p. 76. New York, 1899.

34. For able discussion, see Topinard, Anthropology, pp. 385-392. Tr. from French, London, 1894.

35. J. Johnson, Jurisprudence of the Isle of Man, pp. 44, 71. Edinburgh, 1811.

36. Charles F. Hall, Arctic Researches and Life among the Eskimo, p. 571. New York, 1866. Franz Boas, The Central Eskimo, *Sixth Annual Report of the Bureau of Ethnology*, pp. 588-590. Washington, 1888.

37. Ratzel, History of Mankind, Vol. I, p. 35. London, 1896-1898.

38. Roscher, *National-Oekonomik des Ackerbaues*, p. 34, note 8. Stuttgart, 1888.

39. Elisee Reclus, The Earth and Its Inhabitants, *Asia*, Vol. I, p. 171. New York, 1895.

40. Alfred Hettner, *Die Geographie des Menschen*, pp. 409-410 in *Geographische Zeitschrift*, Vol. XIII, No. 8. Leipzig, 1907.

41. S. B. Boulton, The Russian Empire, pp. 60-64. London, 1882.

42. E. C. Semple, The Anglo-Saxons of the Kentucky Mountains, *The Geographical Journal*, Vol. XVII, No. 6, pp. 588-623. London, 1901.

43. E. C. Semple, American History and its Geographic Conditions, pp. 25-31. Boston, 1903. The Influence of Geographic Environment on the Lower St. Lawrence, Bull. *Amer. Geog. Society*, Vol. XXXVI, p. 449-466. New York, 1904.

44. A. R. Colquhoun, Africander Land, pp. 200-201. New York, 1906.

45. *Ibid.*, pp. 140-145. James Bryce, Impressions of South Africa, p. 398. New York, 1897.

CHAPTER III

SOCIETY AND STATE IN RELATION TO THE LAND

EVERY clan, tribe, state or nation includes two ideas, a People people and its land, the first unthinkable without the other. and land. History, sociology, ethnology touch only the inhabited areas of the earth. These areas gain their final significance because of the people who occupy them; their local conditions of climate, soil, natural resources, physical features and geographic situation are important primarily as factors in the development of actual or possible inhabitants. A land is fully comprehended only when studied in the light of its influence upon its people, and a people cannot be understood apart from the field of its activities. More than this, human activities are fully intelligible only in relation to the various geographic conditions which have stimulated them in different parts of the world. The principles of the evolution of navigation, of agriculture, of trade, as also the theory of population, can never reach their correct and final statement, unless the data for the conclusions are drawn from every part of the world, and each fact interpreted in the light of the local conditions whence it sprang. Therefore anthropology, sociology and history should be permeated by geography.

In history, the question of territory,—by which is meant Political mere area in contrast to specific geographic conditions— geography has constantly come to the front, because a state obviously and history. involved land and boundaries, and assumed as its chief function the defence and extension of these. Therefore political geography developed early as an offshoot of history. Political science has often formulated its principles without regard to the geographic conditions of states, but as a matter of fact, the most fruitful political policies of nations have almost invariably had a geographic core. Witness the colonial policy of Holland, England, France and Portugal, the free-trade policy of England, the militantism of Germany, the whole complex question of European balance of power and the Bosporus, and the Monroe Doctrine of the United States. Dividing lines between political parties tend to follow approximately geographic lines of cleavage; and these make themselves apparent at recurring intervals of national upheaval, perhaps with centuries between, like a submarine volcanic rift. In England the southeastern plain and the northwestern uplands have been repeatedly arrayed against each other, from the Roman conquest which embraced the lowlands up to about the 500-foot contour line,[1] through the War of the Roses and the Civil War,[2] to the struggle for the repeal of the Corn Laws and the great Reform Bill of 1832.[3] Though the boundary lines have been only roughly the same and each district has contained opponents of the dominant local party, nevertheless the geographic core has been plain enough.

Political versus social geography.

The land is a more conspicuous factor in the history of states than in the history of society, but not more necessary and potent. Wars, which constitute so large a part of political history, have usually aimed more or less directly at acquisition or retention of territory; they have made every petty quarrel the pretext for mulcting the weaker nation of part of its land. Political maps are therefore subject to sudden and radical alterations, as when France's name was wiped off the North American continent in 1763, or when recently Spain's sovereignty in the Western Hemisphere was obliterated. But the race stocks, languages, customs, and institutions of both France and Spain remained after the flags had departed. The reason is that society is far more deeply rooted in the land than is a state, does not expand or contract its area so readily. Society is always, in a sense, *adscripta glebae;* an expanding state which incorporates a new piece of territory inevitably incorporates its inhabitants, unless it exterminates or expels them. Yet because racial and social geography changes slowly, quietly and imperceptibly, like all those fundamental processes which we call growth, it is not so easy and obvious a task to formulate a natural law for the territorial relations of the various hunter, pastoral nomadic, agricultural, and industrial types of society as for those of the growing state.

Most systems of sociology treat man as if he were in some way detached from the earth's surface; they ignore the land basis of society. The anthropo-geographer recognizes the various social forces, economic and psychologic, which sociologists regard as the cement of societies; but he has something to add. He sees in the land occupied by a primitive tribe or a highly organized state the underlying material bond holding society together, the ultimate basis of their fundamental social activities, which are therefore derivatives from the land. He sees the common territory exercising an integrating force,—weak in primitive communities where the group has established only a few slight and temporary relations with its soil, so that this low social complex breaks up readily like its organic counterpart, the low animal organism found in an amoeba; he sees it growing stronger with every advance in civilization involving more complex relations to the land,—with settled habitations, with increased density of population, with a discriminating and highly differentiated use of the soil, with the exploitation of mineral resources, and finally with that far-reaching exchange of commodities and ideas which means the establishment of varied extra-territorial relations. Finally, the modern society or state has grown into every foot of its own soil, exploited its every geographic advantage, utilized its geographic location to enrich itself by international trade, and when possible, to absorb outlying territories by means of colonies. The broader this geographic base, the richer, more varied its resources, and the more favorable its climate to their exploitation, the more numerous and complex are the connections which the members of a social group can establish with it, and through it with each other; or in other words, the greater may be its ultimate historical significance. The polar regions and the subtropical deserts, on the other hand, permit man to form only few and intermittent relations with any one spot, restrict economic methods to the lower stages of development, produce only the small, weak, loosely organized horde, which never evolves into a state so long as it remains in that retarding environment.

Land basis of society.

Morgan's Societas.

Man in his larger activities, as opposed to his mere physiological or psychological processes, cannot be studied apart from the land which he inhabits. Whether we consider him singly or in a group—family, clan, tribe or state—we must always consider him or his group in relation to a piece of land. The ancient Irish sept, Highland clan, Russian mir, Cherokee hill-town, Bedouin tribe, and the ancient Helvetian canton, like the political state of history, have meant always a group of people and a bit of land. The first presupposes the second. In all cases the form and size of the social group, the nature of its activities, the trend and limit of its development will be strongly influenced by the size and nature of its habitat. The land basis is always present, in spite of Morgan's artificial distinction between a theoretically landless *societas*, held together only by the bond of common blood, and the political *civitas* based upon land.[4] Though primitive society found its conscious bond in common blood, nevertheless the land bond was always there, and it gradually asserted its fundamental character with the evolution of society.

The savage and barbarous groups which in Morgan's classification would fall under the head of *societas* have nevertheless a clear conception of their ownership of the tribal lands which they use in common. This idea is probably of very primitive origin, arising from the association of a group with its habitat, whose food supply they regard as a monopoly.[5] This is true even of migratory hunting tribes. They claim a certain area whose boundaries, however, are often ill-defined and subject to fluctuations, because the lands are not held by permanent occupancy and cultivation. An exceptional case is that of the Shoshone Indians, inhabiting the barren Utah basin and the upper valleys of the Snake and Salmon Rivers, who are accredited with no sense of ownership of the soil. In their natural state they roved about in small, totally unorganized bands or single families, and changed their locations so widely, that they seemed to lay no claim to any particular portion. The hopeless sterility of the region and its poverty of game kept its destitute inhabitants constantly on the move to gather in the meager food supply, and often restricted the social group to the family.[6] Here the bond between land

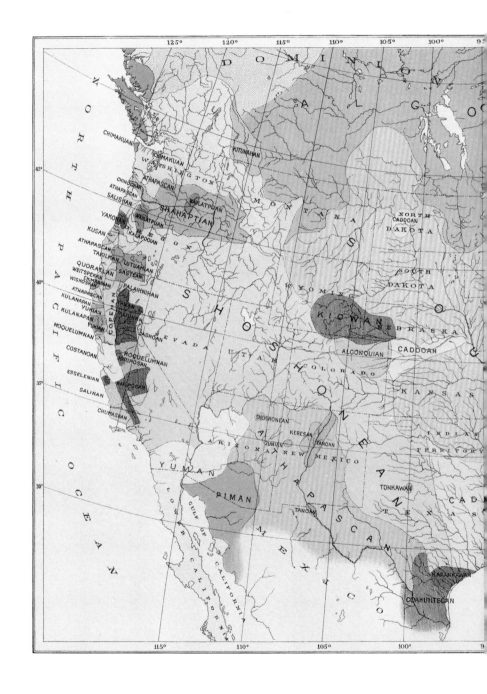

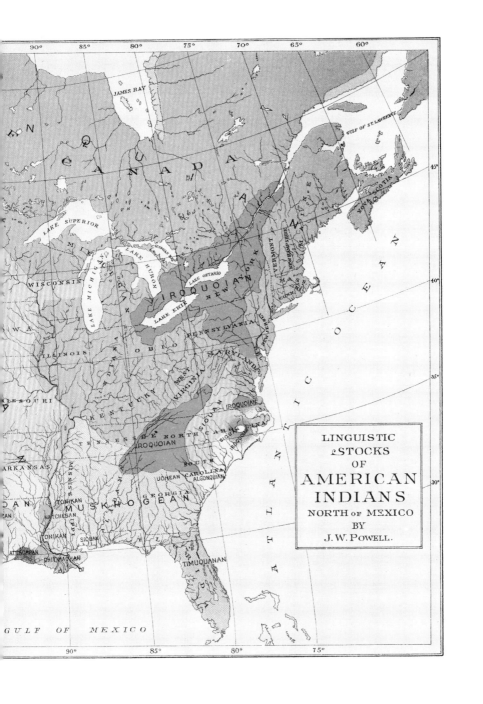

LINGUISTIC
ℓSTOCKS
OF
AMERICAN
INDIANS
NORTH OF MEXICO
BY
J. W. POWELL.

and tribe, and hence between the members of the tribe, was the weakest possible.

The usual type of tribal ownership was presented by the Comanches, nomadic horse Indians who occupied the grassy plains of northern Texas. They held their territory and the game upon it as the common property of the tribe, and jealously guarded the integrity of their domain.[7] The chief Algonquin tribes, who occupied the territory between the Ohio River and the Great Lakes, had each its separate domain, within which it shifted its villages every few years; but its size depended upon the power of the tribe to repel encroachment upon its hunting grounds. Relying mainly on the chase and fishing, little on agriculture, for their subsistence, their relations to their soil were superficial and transitory, their tribal organization in a high degree unstable.[8] Students of American ethnology generally agree that most of the Indian tribes east of the Mississippi were occupying definite areas at the time of the discovery, and were to a considerable extent sedentary and agricultural. Though nomadic within the tribal territory, as they moved with the season in pursuit of game, they returned to their villages, which were shifted only at relatively long intervals.[9]

The political organization of the native Australians, low as they were in the social scale, seems to have been based chiefly on the claim of each wretched wandering tribe to a definite territory.[10] In north central Australia, where even a very sparse population has sufficed to saturate the sterile soil, tribal boundaries have become fixed and inviolable, so that even war brings no transfer of territory. Land and people are identified. The bond is cemented by their primitive religion, for the tribe's spirit ancestors occupied this special territory.[11] In a like manner a very definite conception of tribal ownership of land prevails among the Bushmen and Bechuanas of South Africa; and to the pastoral Hereros the alienation of their land is inconceivable.[12] [See map page 105.]

A tribe of hunters can never be more than a small horde, because the simple, monotonous savage economy permits no concentration of population, no division of labor except that between the sexes, and hence no evolution of classes. The

Land bond in hunter tribes.

common economic level of all is reflected in the simple social organization,[13] which necessarily has little cohesion, because the group must be prepared to break up and scatter in smaller divisions, when its members increase or its savage supplies decrease even a little. Such primitive groups cannot grow into larger units, because these would demand more roots sent down into the sustaining soil; but they multiply by fission, like the infusorial monads, and thereafter lead independent existences remote from each other. This is the explanation of multiplication of dialects among savage tribes.

Land bond in fisher tribes.

Fishing tribes have their chief occupation determined by their habitats, which are found along well stocked rivers, lakes, or coastal fishing grounds. Conditions here encourage an early adoption of sedentary life, discourage wandering except for short periods, and facilitate the introduction of agriculture wherever conditions of climate and soil permit. Hence these fisher folk develop relatively large and permanent social groups, as testified by the ancient lake-villages of Switzerland, based upon a concentrated food-supply resulting from a systematic and often varied exploitation of the local resources. The coöperation and submission to a leader necessary in pelagic fishing often gives the preliminary training for higher political organization.[14] All the primitive stocks of the Brazilian Indians, except the mountain Ges, are fishermen and agriculturists; hence their annual migrations are kept within narrow limits. Each linguistic group occupies a fixed and relatively well defined district.[15] Stanley found along the Congo large permanent villages of the natives, who were engaged in fishing and tilling the fruitful soil, but knew little about the country ten miles back from the river. These two generous means of subsistence are everywhere combined in Polynesia, Micronesia and Melanesia; there they are associated with dense populations and often with advanced political organization, as we find it in the feudal monarchy of Tonga and the savage Fiji Islands.[16] Fisher tribes, therefore, get an early impulse forward in civilization;[17] and even where conditions do not permit the upward step to agriculture, these tribes have permanent relations with their land, form stable social groups, and often utilize their location on a natural highway to develop systematic trade. For instance, on the northwest coast of British Columbia and Southern Alaska, the Haida, Tlingit and Tsimshean Indians have portioned out all the land about their seaboard villages among the separate families or households as hunting, fishing, and berrying grounds. These are regarded as private property and are handed down from generation to generation. If they are used by anyone other than the owner, the privilege must be paid for. Every salmon stream has its proprietor, whose summer camp can be seen set up at the point where the run of the fish is greatest. Combined with this private property in land there is a brisk trade up and down the coast, and a tendency toward feudalism in the village communities, owing to the association of power and social distinction with wealth and property in land.[18]

Among pastoral nomads, among whom a systematic use of their territory begins to appear, and therefore a more definite relation between land and people, we find a more distinct notion than among wandering hunters of territorial ownership, the right of communal use, and the distinct obligation of common defense. Hence the social bond is drawn closer. The nomad identifies himself with a certain district, which belongs to his tribe by tradition or conquest, and has its clearly defined boundaries. Here he roams between its summer and winter pastures, possibly one hundred and fifty miles apart, visits its small arable patches in the spring for his limited agricultural ventures, and returns to them in the fall to reap their meager harvest. Its springs, streams, or wells assume enhanced value, are things to be fought for, owing to the prevailing aridity of summer; while ownership of a certain tract of desert or grassland carries with it a certain right in the bordering settled district as an area of plunder.[19] *Land bond in pastoral societies.*

The Kara-Kirghis stock, who have been located since the sixteenth century on Lake Issik-Kul, long ago portioned out the land among the separate families, and determined their limits by natural features of the landscape.[20] Sven Hedin found on the Tarim River poles set up to mark the boundary between the Shah-yar and Kuchar tribal pastures.[21] John de Plano Carpini, traveling over southern Russia in 1246, immediately after the Tartar conquest, found that the Dnieper, Don, Volga and Ural rivers were all boundaries between domains of the various millionaries or thousands, into which the Tartar horde was organized.[22] The population of this vast country was distributed according to the different degrees of fertility and the size of the pastoral groups.[23] Volney observed the same distinction in the distribution of the Bedouins of Syria. He found the barren cantons held by small, widely scattered tribes, as in the Desert of Suez; but the cultivable cantons, like the Hauran and the Pachalic of Aleppo, closely dotted by the encampments of the pastoral owners.[24]

The large range of territory held by a nomadic tribe is all successively occupied in the course of a year, but each part only for a short period of time. A pastoral use of even a good district necessitates a move of five or ten miles every few weeks. The whole, large as it may be, is absolutely necessary for the annual support of the tribe. Hence any outside encroachment upon their territory calls for the united resistance of the tribe. This joint or social action is dictated by their common interest in pastures and herds. The social administration embodied in the apportionment of pastures among the families or clans grows out of the systematic use of their territory, which represents a closer relation between land and people than is found among purely hunting tribes. Overcrowding by men or livestock, on the other hand, puts a strain upon the social bond. When Abraham and Lot, typical nomads, returned from Egypt to Canaan with their large flocks and herds, rivalry for the pastures occasioned conflicts among their shepherds, so the two sheiks decided to separate. Abraham took the hill pastures of Judea, and Lot the plains of Jordan near the settled district of Sodom.[25]

Geographical mark of low-type societies.

The larger the amount of territory necessary for the support of a given number of people, whether the proportion be due to permanent poverty of natural resources as in the Eskimo country, or to retarded economic development as among the Indians of primitive America or the present Sudanese, the looser is the connection between land and people, and the lower the type of social organization. For such groups the organic theory of society finds an apt description.

To quote Spencer, "The original clusters, animal and social, are not only small, but they lack density. Creatures of low type occupy large spaces considering the small quantity of animal substance they contain; and low-type societies spread over areas that are wide relatively to the number of their component individuals."[26] In common language this means small tribes or even detached families sparsely scattered over wide areas, living in temporary huts or encampments of tepees and tents shifted from place to place, making no effort to modify the surface of the land beyond scratching the soil to raise a niggardly crop of grain or tubers, and no investment of labor that might attach to one spot the sparse and migrant population. [See density maps pages 8 and 9.]

The superiority over this social type of the civilized state Land and lies in the highly organized utilization of its whole geographic state. basis by the mature community, and in the development of government that has followed the increasing density of population and multiplication of activities growing out of this manifold use of the land. Sedentary agriculture, which forms its initial economic basis, is followed by industrialism and commerce. The migratory life presents only limited accumulation of capital, and restricts narrowly its forms. Permanent settlement encourages accumulation in every form, and under growing pressure of population slowly reveals the possibilities of every foot of ground, of every geographic advantage. These are the fibers of the land which become woven into the whole fabric of the nation's life. These are the geographic elements constituting the soil in which empires are rooted; they rise in the sap of the nation.

The geographic basis of a state embodies a whole complex Strength of physical conditions which may influence its historical de- of the velopment. The most potent of these are its size and zonal land bond location; its situation, whether continental or insular, inland in the or maritime, on the open ocean or an enclosed sea; its bounda- state. ries, whether drawn by sea, mountain, desert or the faint demarking line of a river; its forested mountains, grassy plains, and arable lowlands; its climate and drainage system; finally its equipment with plant and animal life, whether indigenous or imported, and its mineral resources. When a state has taken advantage of all its natural conditions, the land becomes a constituent part of the state,[27] modifying the people which inhabit it, modified by them in turn, till the connection between the two becomes so strong by reciprocal interaction, that the people cannot be understood apart from their land. Any attempt to divide them theoretically reduces the social or political body to a cadaver, valuable for the study of structural anatomy after the method of Herbert Spencer, but throwing little light upon the vital processes.

Weak land tenure of hunting and pastoral tribes. A people who makes only a transitory or superficial use of its land has upon it no permanent or secure hold. The power to hold is measured by the power to use; hence the weak tenure of hunting and pastoral tribes. Between their scattered encampments at any given time are wide interstices, inviting occupation by any settlers who know how to make better use of the soil. This explains the easy intrusion of the English colonists into the sparsely tenanted territory of the Indians, of the agricultural Chinese into the pasture lands of the Mongols beyond the Great Wall, of the American pioneers into the hunting grounds of the Hudson Bay Company in the disputed Oregon country.[28] The frail bonds which unite these lower societies to their soil are easily ruptured and the people themselves dislodged, while their land is appropriated by the intruder. But who could ever conceive of dislodging the Chinese or the close-packed millions of India? A modern state with a given population on a wide area is more vulnerable than another of like population more closely distributed; but the former has the advantage of a reserve territory for future growth.[29] This was the case of Kursachsen and Brandenburg in the sixteenth century, and of the United States throughout its history. But beside the danger of inherent weakness before attack, a condition of relative underpopulation always threatens a retardation of development. Easy-going man needs the prod of a pressing population. [Compare maps pages 8 and 103 for examples.]

Land and food supply. Food is the urgent and recurrent need of individuals and of society. It dictates their activities in relation to their land at every stage of economic development, fixes the locality of the encampment or village, and determines the size of the territory from which sustenance is drawn. The length of residence in one place depends upon whether the springs of its food supply are perennial or intermittent, while the abundance of their flow determines how large a population a given piece of land can support.

Hunter and fisher folk, relying almost exclusively upon what their land produces of itself, need a large area and derive from it only an irregular food supply, which in winter diminishes to the verge of famine. The transition to the pastoral stage has meant the substitution of an artificial for a natural basis of subsistence, and therewith a change which more than any other one thing has inaugurated the advance from savagery to civilization.[30] From the standpoint of economics, the forward stride has consisted in the application of capital in the form of flocks and herds to the task of feeding the wandering horde;[31] from the standpoint of alimentation, in the guarantee of a more reliable and generally more nutritious food supply, which enables population to grow more steadily and rapidly; from the standpoint of geography, in the marked reduction in the per capita amount of land necessary to yield an adequate and stable food supply. Pastoral nomadism can support in a given district of average quality from ten to twenty times as many souls as can the chase; but in this respect is surpassed from twenty to thirtyfold by the more productive agriculture. While the subsistence of a nomad requires 100 to 200 acres of land, for that of a skillful farmer from 1 to 2 acres suffice.[32] In contrast, the land of the Indians living in the Hudson Bay Territory in 1857 averaged 10 square miles per capita; that of the Indians in the United States in 1825, subsidized moreover by the government, $1\frac{1}{4}$ square miles.[33]

With transition to the sedentary life of agriculture, society makes a further gain over nomadism in the closer integration of its social units, due to permanent residence in larger and more complex groups; in the continuous release of labor from the task of mere food-getting for higher activities, resulting especially in the rapid evolution of the home; and finally in the more elaborate organization in the use of the land, leading to economic differentiation of different locali-

Advance from natural to artificial basis of subsistence.

Land in relation to agriculture.

ties and to a rapid increase in the population supported by a given area, so that the land becomes the dominant cohesive force in society. [See maps pages 8 and 9.]

Migratory agriculture. Agriculture is adopted at first on a small scale as an adjunct to the chase or herding. It tends therefore to partake of the same extensive and nomadic character[34] as these other methods of gaining subsistence, and only gradually becomes sedentary and intensive. Such was the superficial, migratory tillage of most American Indians, shifting with the village in the wake of the retreating game or in search of fresh unexhausted soil. Such is the agriculture of the primitive Korkus in the Mahadeo Hills in Central India. They clear a forested slope by burning, rake over the ashes in which they sow their grain, and reap a fairly good crop in the fertilized soil. The second year the clearing yields a reduced product and the third year is abandoned. When the hamlet of five or six families has exhausted all the land about it, it moves to a new spot to repeat the process.[35]

The same superficial, extensive tillage, with abandonment of fields every few years, prevails in the Tartar districts of the Russian steppes, as it did among the cattle-raising Germans at the beginning of their history. Tacitus says of them, *Arva per annos mutant et superest ager*,[36] commenting at the same time upon their abundance of land and their reluctance to till. Where nomadism is made imperative by aridity, the agriculture which accompanies it tends to become fixed, owing to the few localities blessed with an irrigating stream to moisten the soil. These spots, generally selected for the winter residence, have their soil enriched, moreover, by the long stay of the herd and thus avoid exhaustion.[37] Often, however, in enclosed basins the salinity of the irrigating streams in their lower course ruins the fields after one or two crops, and necessitates a constant shifting of the cultivated patches; hence agriculture remains subsidiary to the yield of the pastures. This condition and effect is conspicuous along the termini of the streams draining the northern slope of the Kuen Lun into the Tarim basin.[38]

Geographic checks to progress. The desultory, intermittent, extensive use of the land practised by hunters and nomads tends, under the growing pressure of population, to pass into the systematic, continuous, intensive use practised by the farmer, except where nature presents positive checks to the transition. The most obvious check consists in adverse conditions of climate and soil. Where agriculture meets insurmountable obstacles, like the intense cold of Arctic Siberia and Lapland, or the alkaline soils of Nevada and the Caspian Depression, or the inadequate rainfall of Mongolia and Central Arabia, the land can produce no higher economic and social groups than pastoral hordes. Hence shepherd folk are found in their purest types in deserts and steppes, where conditions early crystallized the social form and checked development. [Rainfall map chap. XIV.]

Adverse conditions of climate and soil are not the only Native factors in this retardation. The very unequal native equip- animal and ment of the several continents with plant and animal forms plant life likely to accelerate the advance to nomadism and agriculture as factors. also enters into the equation. In Australia, the lack of a single indigenous mammal fit for domestication and of all cereals blocked from the start the pastoral and agricultural development of the natives. Hence at the arrival of the Europeans, Australia presented the unique spectacle of a whole continent with its population still held in the vise of nature. The Americas had a limited variety of animals susceptible of domestication, but were more meagerly equipped than the Old World. Yet the Eskimo failed to tame and herd the reindeer, though their precarious food-supply furnished a motive for the transition. Moreover, an abundance of grass and reindeer moss (*Cladonia rangiferina*), and congenial climatic conditions favored it especially for the Alaskan Eskimo, who had, besides, the nearby example of the Siberian Chukches as reindeer herders.[39] The buffalo, whose domesticability has been proved, was never utilized in this way by the Indians, though the Spaniard Gomara writes of one tribe, living in the sixteenth century in the southwestern part of what is now United States territory, whose chief wealth consisted in herds of tame buffalo.[40] North America, at the time of the discovery, saw only the dog hanging about the lodges of the Indians; but in South America the llama and alpaca, confined to the higher levels of the Andes (10,000 to

15,000 feet elevation) were used in domestic herds only in the mountain-rimmed valleys of ancient Peru, where, owing to the restricted areas of these intermontane basins, stock-raising early became stationary,[41] as we find it in the Alps. Moreover, the high ridges of the Andes supported a species of grass called *ichu*, growing up to the snowline from the equator to the southern extremity of Patagonia. Its geographical distribution coincided with that of the llama and alpaca, whose chief pasturage it furnished.[42] In contrast, the absence of any wild fodder plants in Japan, and the exclusion of all foreign forms by the successful competition of the native bamboo grass have together eliminated pastoral life from the economic history of the island.

The Old World, on the other hand, furnished an abundant supply of indigenous animals susceptible of domestication, and especially those fitted for nomadic life, such as the camel, horse, ass, sheep and goat. Hence it produced in the widespread grasslands and deserts of Europe, Asia, and Africa the most perfect types of pastoral development in its natural or nomadic form. Moreover, the early history of the civilized agricultural peoples of these three continents reveals their previous pastoral mode of life.

North and South America offered over most of their area conditions of climate and soil highly favorable to agriculture, and a fair list of indigenous cereals, tubers, and pulses yielding goodly crops even to superficial tillage. Maize especially was admirably suited for a race of semi-migratory hunters. It could be sown without plowing, ripened in a warm season even in ninety days, could be harvested without a sickle and at the pleasure of the cultivator, and needed no preparation beyond roasting before it was ready for food.[43] The beans and pumpkins which the Indians raised also needed only a short season. Hence many Indian tribes, while showing no trace of pastoral development, combined with the chase a semi-nomadic agriculture; and in a few districts where geographic conditions had applied peculiar pressure, they had accomplished the transition to sedentary agriculture.

Every advance to a higher state of civilization has meant a progressive decrease in the amount of land necessary for the

Land per capita under various cultural and geographic conditions.

support of the individual, and a progressive increase in the relations between man and his habitat. The stage of social development remaining the same, the per capita amount of land decreases also from poorer to better endowed geographical districts, and with every invention which brings into use some natural resource. The following classification[44] illustrates the relation of density of population to various geographic and socio-economic conditions.

Hunter tribes on the outskirts of the habitable area, as in Arctic America and Siberia, require from 70 to 200 square miles per capita; in arid lands, like the Kalahari Desert and Patagonia, 40 to 200 square miles per capita; in choice districts and combining with the chase some primitive agriculture, as did the Cherokee, Shawnee and Iroquois Indians, the Dyaks of Borneo and the Papuans of New Guinea, ½ to 2 square miles per capita.

Pastoral nomads show a density of from 2 to 5 to the square mile; practicing some agriculture, as in Kordofan and Sennar districts of eastern Sudan, 10 to 15 to the square mile. Agriculture, undeveloped but combined with some trade and industry as in Equatorial Africa, Borneo and most of the Central American states, supports 5 to 15 to the square mile; practised with European methods in young or colonial lands, as in Arkansas, Texas, Minnesota, Hawaii, Canada and Argentine, or in European lands with unfavorable climate, up to 25 to the square mile.

Pure agricultural lands of central Europe support 100 to the square mile, and those of southern Europe, 200; when combining some industry, from 250 to 300. But these figures rise to 500 or more in lowland India and China. Industrial districts of modern Europe, such as England, Belgium, Saxony, Departments Nord and Rhone in France, show a density of 500 to 800 to the square mile. [See maps pages 8 and 9.]

With every increase of the population inhabiting a given area, and with the consequent multiplication and constriction of the bonds uniting society with its land, comes a growing necessity for a more highly organized government, both to reduce friction within and to secure to the people the land on Density of population and government.

which and by which they live. Therefore protection becomes a prime function of the state. It wards off outside attack which may aim at acquisition of its territory, or an invasion of its rights, or curtailment of its geographic sphere of activity. The modern industrial state, furthermore, with the purpose of strengthening the nation, assists or itself undertakes the construction of highways, canals, and railroads, and the maintenance of steamship lines. These encourage the development of natural resources and of commerce, and hence lay the foundation for an increased population, by multiplying the relations between land and people.

Territorial expansion of the state.

A like object is attained by territorial expansion, which often follows in the wake of commercial expansion. This strengthens the nation positively by enlarging its geographic base, and negatively by forcing back the boundaries of its neighbors. The expansion of the Thirteen Colonies from the Atlantic slope to the Mississippi River and the Great Lakes by the treaty concluding the Revolution was a strong guarantee of the survival of the young Republic against future aggressions either of England or Spain, though it exchanged the scientific or protecting boundary of the Appalachian Mountains for the unscientific and exposed boundary of a river. The expansion to the Rocky Mountains by the Louisiana purchase not only gave wider play to national energies, stimulated natural increase of population, and attracted immigration, but it eliminated a dangerous neighbor in the French, and placed a wide buffer of untenanted land between the United States and the petty aggressions of the Spanish in Mexico. Rome's expansion into the valley of the Po, as later into Trans-Alpine Gaul and Germany, had for its purpose the protection of the peninsula against barbarian inroads. Japan's recent aggression against the Russians in the Far East was actuated by the realization that she had to expand into Korea at the cost of Muscovite ascendency, or contract later at the cost of her own independence.

Checks to population.

If a state lacks the energy and national purpose, like Italy, or the possibility, like Switzerland, for territorial

expansion, and accepts its boundaries as final, the natural increase of population upon a fixed area produces an increased
density, unless certain social forces counteract it. Without
these forces, the relation of men to the land would have tended
to modify everywhere in the same way. Increase in numbers
would have been attended by a corresponding decrease in the
amount of land at the disposal of each individual. Those
states which, like Norway and Switzerland, cannot expand and
which have exploited their natural resources to the utmost,
must resign themselves to the emigration of their redundant
population. But those which have remained within their own
boundaries and have adopted a policy of isolation, like China,
feudal Japan during its two and a half centuries of seclusion,
and numerous Polynesian islands, have been forced to war
with nature itself by checking the operation of the law of
natural increase. All the repulsive devices contributing to
this end, whether infanticide, abortion, cannibalism, the sanctioned murder of the aged and infirm, honorable suicide, polyandry or persistent war, are the social deformities consequent
upon suppressed growth. Such artificial checks upon population are more conspicuous in natural regions with sharply defined boundaries, like islands and oases, as Malthus observed;[45]
but they are visible also among savage tribes whose boundaries
are fixed not by natural features but by the mutual repulsion
and rivalry characterizing the stage of development, and
whose limit of population is reduced by their low economic
status.

There is a great difference between those states whose inhabi- Extra-terri-
tants subsist exclusively from the products of their own coun- torial
try and those which rely more or less upon other lands. Great relations.
industrial states, like England and Germany, which derive
only a portion of their food and raw material from their
own territory, supply their dense populations through international trade. Interruption of such foreign commerce is
disastrous to the population at home; hence the state by a
navy protects the lines of communication with those far-
away lands of wheat fields and cattle ranch. This is no purely
modern development. Athens in the time of Pericles used her
navy not only to secure her political domination in the

Aegean, but also her connections with the colonial wheat lands about the Euxine. The modern state strives to render this circle of trade both large and permanent by means of commercial treaties, customs-unions, trading-posts and colonies. Thus while society at home is multiplying its relations with its own land, the state is enabling it to multiply also its relations with the whole producing world. While at home the nation is becoming more closely knit together through the common bond of the fatherland, in the world at large humanity is evolving a brotherhood of man by the union of each with all through the common growing bond of the earth. Hence we cannot avoid the question: Are we in process of evolving a social idea vaster than that underlying nationality? Do the Socialists hint to us the geographic basis of this new development, when they describe themselves as an international political party?

Geography in the philosophy of history. It is natural that the old philosophy of history should have fixed its attention upon the geographic basis of historical events. Searching for the permanent and common in the outwardly mutable, it found always at the bottom of changing events the same solid earth. Biology has had the same experience. The history of the life forms of the world leads always back to the land on which that life arose, spread, and struggled for existence. The philosophy of history was superior to early sociology, in that its method was one of historical comparison, which inevitably guided it back to the land as the material for the first generalization. Thus it happens that the importance of the land factor in history was approached first from the philosophical side. Montesquieu and Herder had no intention of solving sociological and geographical problems, when they considered the relation of peoples and states to their soil; they wished to understand the purpose and destiny of man as an inhabitant of the earth.

Theory of progress from the standpoint of geography. The study of history is always, from one standpoint, a study of progress. Yet after all the century-long investigation of the history of every people working out its destiny in its given environment, struggling against the difficulties of its habitat, progressing when it overcame them and retrograding

when it failed, advancing when it made the most of its opportunities and declining when it made less or succumbed to
an invader armed with better economic or political methods
to exploit the land, it is amazing how little the land, in which
all activities finally root, has been taken into account in the
discussion of progress. Nevertheless, for a theory of progress
it offers a solid basis. From the standpoint of the land
social and political organizations, in successive stages of
development, embrace ever increasing areas, and make them
support ever denser populations; and in this concentration
of population and intensification of economic development
they assume ever higher forms. It does not suffice that a people, in order to progress, should extend and multiply only its
local relations to its land. This would eventuate in arrested development, such as Japan showed at the time of Perry's visit.
The ideal basis of progress is the expansion of the world relations of a people, the extension of its field of activity and
sphere of influence far beyond the limits of its own territory,
by which it exchanges commodities and ideas with various
countries of the world. Universal history shows us that, as
the geographical horizon of the known world has widened from
gray antiquity to the present, societies and states have expanded their territorial and economic scope; that they have
grown not only in the number of their square miles and in
the geographical range of their international intercourse, but
in national efficiency, power, and permanence, and especially
in that intellectual force which feeds upon the nutritious food
of wide comparisons. Every great movement which has widened
the geographical outlook of a people, such as the Crusades in
the Middle Ages, or the colonization of the Americas, has
applied an intellectual and economic stimulus. The expanding field of advancing history has therefore been an essential concomitant and at the same time a driving force in the
progress of every people and of the world.

Since progress in civilization involves an increasing ex- Man's
ploitation of natural advantages and the development of closer increasing
relations between a land and its people, it is an erroneous dependence
idea that man tends to emancipate himself more and more upon nature.
from the control of the natural conditions forming at once

the foundation and environment of his activities. On the contrary, he multiplies his dependencies upon nature;[46] but while increasing their sum total, he diminishes the force of each. There lies the gist of the matter. As his bonds become more numerous, they become also more elastic. Civilization has lengthened his leash and padded his collar, so that it does not gall; but the leash is never slipped. The Delaware Indians depended upon the forests alone for fuel. A citizen of Pennsylvania, occupying the former Delaware tract, has the choice of wood, hard or soft coal, coke, petroleum, natural gas, or manufactured gas. Does this mean emancipation? By no means. For while fuel was a necessity to the Indian only for warmth and cooking, and incidentally for the pleasureable excitement of burning an enemy at the stake, it enters into the manufacture of almost every article that the Pennsylvanian uses in his daily life. His dependence upon nature has become more far-reaching, though less conspicuous and especially less arbitrary.

Increase in kind and amount. These dependencies increase enormously both in variety and amount. Great Britain, with its twenty thousand merchant ships aggregating over ten million tons, and its immense import and export trade, finds its harbors vastly more important to-day for the national welfare than in Cromwell's time, when they were used by a scanty mercantile fleet. Since the generation of electricity by water-power and its application to industry, the plunging falls of the Scandinavian Mountains, of the Alps of Switzerland, France, and Italy, of the Southern Appalachians and the Cascade Range, are geographical features representing new and unsuspected forms of national capital, and therefore new bonds between land and people in these localities. Russia since 1844 has built 35,572 miles (57,374 kilometers) of railroad in her European territory, and thereby derived a new benefit from her level plains, which so facilitate the construction and cheap operation of railroads, that they have become in this aspect alone a new feature in her national economy. On the other hand, the galling restrictions of Russia's meager and strategically confined coasts, which tie her hand in any wide maritime policy, work a greater hardship to-day than they did a hundred years ago, since her growing population creates a more insistent demand for international trade. In contrast to Russia, Norway, with its paucity of arable soil and of other natural resources, finds its long indented coastline and the coast-bred seamanship of its people a progressively important national asset. Hence as ocean-carriers the Norwegians have developed a merchant marine nearly half as large again as that of Russia and Finland combined—1,569,646 tons[47] as against 1,084,165 tons.

This growing dependence of a civilized people upon its land is characterized by intelligence and self-help. Man forms a partnership with nature, contributing brains and labor, while she provides the capital or raw material in ever more abundant and varied forms. As a result of this coöperation, held by the terms of the contract, he secures a better living than the savage who, like a mendicant, accepts what nature is pleased to dole out, and lives under the tyranny of her caprices.

NOTES TO CHAPTER III

1. H. J. Mackinder, Britain and the British Seas, p. 196. London, 1904.
2. Gardner, Atlas of English History, Map 29. New York, 1905.
3. Hereford George, Historical Geography of Great Britain, pp. 58-60. London, 1904.
4. Lewis Morgan, Ancient Society, p. 62. New York, 1878.
5. Franklin H. Giddings, Elements of Sociology, p. 247. New York, 1902.
6. Schoolcraft, The Indian Tribes of the United States, Vol. I, pp. 198-200, 224. Philadelphia, 1853.
7. Ibid., Vol. I, pp. 231-232, 241.
8. Roosevelt, The Winning of the West, Vol. I, pp. 70-73, 88. New York, 1895.
9. McGee and Thomas, Prehistoric North America, pp. 392-393, 408, Vol. XIX, of History of North America, edited by Francis W. Thorpe, Philadelphia, 1905. Eleventh Census Report on the Indians, p. 51. Washington, 1894.
10. Hans Helmolt, History of the World, Vol. II, pp. 249-250. New York, 1902-1906.
11. Spencer and Gillen, Northern Tribes of Central Australia, pp. 13-15. London, 1904.
12. Ratzel, History of Mankind, Vol. I, p. 126. London, 1896-1898.
13. Roscher, National-Oekonomik des Ackerbaues, p. 24. Stuttgart, 1888.

72 SOCIETY AND STATE IN RELATION TO LAND

14. Ratzel, History of Mankind, Vol. I, p. 131. London, 1896-1898.
15. Paul Ehrenreich, *Die Einteilung und Verbreitung der Völkerstämme Brasiliens*, Peterman's *Geographische Mittheilungen*, Vol. XXXVII, p. 85. Gotha, 1891.
16. Roscher, *National-Oekonomik des Ackerbaues*, p. 26, Note 5. Stuttgart, 1888.
17. *Ibid.*, p. 27.
18. Albert Niblack, The Coast Indians of Southern Alaska and Northern British Columbia, pp. 298-299, 304, 337-339. Washington, 1888.
19. Ratzel, History of Mankind, Vol. III, p. 173. London, 1896-1898.
20. *Ibid.*, Vol. III, pp. 173-174.
21. Sven Hedin, Central Asia and Tibet, Vol. I, p. 184. New York and London, 1903.
22. John de Plano Carpini, Journey in 1246, p. 130. *Hakluyt Society*, London, 1904.
23. Journey of William de Rubruquis in 1253, p. 188. *Hakluyt Society*, London, 1903.
24. Volney, quoted in Malthus, Principles of Population, Chap. VII, p. 60. London, 1878.
25. Genesis, Chap. XIII, 1-12.
26. Herbert Spencer, Principles of Sociology, Vol. I, p. 457. New York.
27. Heinrich von Treitschke, *Politik*, Vol. I, pp. 202-204. Leipzig, 1897.
28. E. C. Semple, American History and Its Geographic Conditions, pp. 206-207. Boston, 1903.
29. Roscher, *Grundlagen des National-Oekonomie*, Book VI. *Bevolkerung*, p. 694, Note 5. Stuttgart, 1886.
30. Edward John Payne, History of the New World Called America, Vol. I, p. 303-313. Oxford and New York, 1892.
31. Roscher, *National-Oekonomik des Ackerbaues*, pp. 31, 52. Stuttgart, 1888.
32. *Ibid.*, p. 56, Note 5.
33. For these and other averages, Sir John Lubbock, Prehistoric Times, pp. 593-595. New York, 1872.
34. Roscher, *National-Oekonomik des Ackerbaues*, pp. 79-80, p. 81, Note 7. Stuttgart, 1888. William I. Thomas, Source Book for Social Origins, pp. 96-112. Chicago, 1909.
35. Capt. J. Forsyth, The Highlands of Central India, pp. 101-107, 168. London, 1889.
36. Tacitus, *Germania*, III.
37. Roscher, *National-Oekonomik des Ackerbaues*, p. 32, Note 15 on p. 36. Stuttgart, 1888.
38. E. Huntington, The Pulse of Asia, pp. 202, 203, 212, 213, 236-237. Boston, 1907.
39. Sheldon Jackson, Introduction of Domesticated Reindeer into Alaska, pp. 20, 25-29, 127-129. Washington, 1894.
40. Quoted in Alexander von Humboldt, Aspects of Nature in Different Lands, pp. 62, 139. Philadelphia, 1849.
41. Edward John Payne, History of the New World Called America, Vol. I, pp. 311-321, 333-354, 364-366. New York, 1892.
42. Prescott, Conquest of Peru, Vol. I, p. 47. New York, 1848.

43. McGee and Thomas, Prehistoric North America, Vol. XIX, pp. 151-161, of *The History of North America*, edited by Francis W. Thorpe, Philadelphia, 1905.
44. Ratzel, *Anthropo-geographie*, Vol. II, pp. 264-265.
45. Malthus, Principles of Population, Chapters V and VII. London, 1878.
46. Nathaniel Shaler, Nature and Man in America, pp. 147-151. W. Z. Ripley, Races of Europe, Chap. I, New York, 1899.
47. Justus Perthes, *Taschen-Atlas*, pp. 44, 47. Gotha, 1910.

CHAPTER IV

THE MOVEMENTS OF PEOPLES IN THEIR GEO-
GRAPHICAL SIGNIFICANCE

Universal-
ity of
these move-
ments.
THE ethnic and political boundaries of Europe to-day are the residuum of countless racial, national, tribal and individual movements reaching back into an unrecorded past. The very names of Turkey, Bulgaria, England, Scotland and France are borrowed from intruding peoples. New England, New France, New Scotland or Nova Scotia and many more on the American continents register the Trans-Atlantic nativity of their first white settlers. The provinces of Galicia in Spain, Lombardy in Italy, Brittany in France, Essex and Sussex in England record in their names streams of humanity diverted from the great currents of the *Völkerwanderung*. The Romance group of languages, from Portugal to Roumania, testify to the sweep of expanding Rome, just as the wide distribution of the Aryan linguistic family points to many roads and long migrations from some unplaced birthplace. Names like Cis-Alpine and Trans-Alpine Gaul in the Roman Empire, Trans-Caucasia, Trans-Caspia and Trans-Baikalia in the Russian Empire, the Transvaal and Transkei in South Africa, indicate the direction whence the advancing people have come.

Stratifi-
cation of
races.
Ethnology reveals an east and west stratification of linguistic groups in Europe, a north and south stratification of races, and another stratification by altitude, which reappears in all parts of the world, and shows certain invading dominant races occupying the lowlands and other displaced ones the highlands. This definite arrangement points to successive arrivals, a crowding forward, an intrusion of the strong into fertile, accessible valleys and plains, and a dislodgment of the weak into the rough but safe keeping of mountain range or barren peninsula, where they are brought to bay. Ethnic fragments, linguistic survivals, or merely place names, dropped

like discarded baggage along the march of a retreating army, bear witness everywhere to tragic recessionals.

Every country whose history we examine proves the recipient of successive streams of humanity. Even sea-girt England has received various intruding peoples from the Roman occupation to the recent influx of Russian Jews. In prehistoric times it combined several elements in its population, as the discovery of the "long barrow" men and "round barrow" men by archæologists, and the identification of a surviving Iberian or Mediterranean strain by ethnologists go to prove.[1] Egypt, Mesopotamia, and India tell the same story, whether in their recorded or unrecorded history. Tropical Africa lacks a history; but all that has been pieced together by ethnologists and anthropologists, in an effort to reconstruct its past, shows incessant movement,—growth, expansion and short-lived conquest, followed by shrinkage, expulsion or absorption by another invader.[2] To this constant shifting of races and peoples the name of historical movement has been given, because it underlies most of written history, and constitutes the major part of unwritten history, especially that of savage and nomadic tribes. Two things are vital in the history of every people, its ethnic composition and the wars it wages in defense or extension of its boundaries. Both rest upon historical movements,—intrusions, whether peaceful or hostile, into its own land, and encroachments upon neighboring territory necessitated by growth. Back of all such movements is natural increase of population beyond local means of subsistence, and the development of the war spirit in the effort to secure more abundant subsistence either by raid or conquest of territory.

Among primitive peoples this movement is simple and monotonous. It involves all members of the tribe, either in pursuit of game, or following the herd over the tribal territory, or in migrations seeking more and better land. Among civilized peoples it assumes various forms, and especially is differentiated for different members of the social group. The civilized state develops specialized frontiersmen, armies, explorers, maritime traders, colonists, and missionaries, who keep a part of the people constantly moving and directing

The name Historical Movement.

Evolution of the Historical Movement.

external expansion, while the mass of the population converts the force once expended in the migrant food-quest into internal activity. Here we come upon a paradox. The nation as a whole, with the development of sedentary life, increases its population and therewith its need for external movements; it widens its national area and its circle of contact with other lands, enlarges its geographical horizon, and improves its internal communication over a growing territory; it evolves a greater mobility within and without, which attaches, however, to certain classes of society, not to the entire social group. This mobility becomes the outward expression of a whole complex of economic wants, intellectual needs, and political ambitions. It is embodied in the conquests which build up empires, in the colonization which develops new lands, in the world-wide exchange of commodities and ideas which lifts the level of civilization, till this movement of peoples becomes a fundamental fact of history.

Nature of primitive movements.

This movement is and has been universal and varied. When most unobtrusive in its operation, it has produced its greatest effects. To seize upon a few conspicuous migrations, like the *Völkerwanderung* and the irruption of the Turks into Europe, made dramatic by their relation to the declining empires of Rome and Constantinople, and to ignore the vast sum of lesser but more normal movements which by slow increments produce greater and more lasting results, leads to wrong conclusions both in ethnology and history. Here, as in geology, great effects do not necessarily presuppose vast forces, but rather the steady operation of small ones. It is often assumed that the world was peopled by a series of migrations; whereas everything indicates that humanity spread over the earth little by little, much as the imported gypsy moth is gradually occupying New England or the water hyacinth the rivers of Florida. Louis Agassiz observed in 1853 that "the boundaries within which the different natural combinations of animals are known to be circumscribed upon the surface of the earth, coincide with the natural range of distinct types of man."[3] The close parallelism between Australian race and flora, Eskimo race and Arctic fauna, points to a similar manner of dispersion. Wallace, in describing how the Russian frontier

of settlement slowly creeps forward along the Volga, encroaching upon the Finnish and Tartar areas, and permeating them
with Slav blood and civilization, adds that this is probably the
normal method of expansion.[4] Thucydides describes the same
process of encroachment, displacement, and migration in
ancient Hellas.[5] Strabo quotes Posidonius as saying that the
emigration of the Cimbrians and other kindred tribes from
their native seats was gradual and by no means sudden.[6]
The traditions of the Delaware Indians show their advance
from their early home in central Canada southward to the
Delaware River and Chesapeake Bay to have been a slow zigzag movement, interrupted by frequent long halts, leaving
behind one laggard group here and sending out an offshoot
there, who formed new tribes and thereby diversified the
stock.[7] It was an aimless wandering, without destination and
purpose other than to find a pleasanter habitat. The Vandals
appear first as "a loose aggregation of restless tribes who must
not be too definitely assigned to any precise district on the
map," somewhere in central or eastern Prussia.[8] Far-reaching
migrations aiming at a distant goal, like the Gothic and
Hunnish conquests of Italy, demand both a geographical
knowledge and an organization too high for primitive peoples,
and therefore belong to a later period of development.[9]

The long list of recorded migrations has been supplemented by the researches of ethnologists, which have revealed
a multitude of prehistoric movements. These are disclosed in
greater number and range with successive investigation.
The prehistoric wanderings of the Polynesians assume far
more significance to-day than a hundred years ago, when
their scope was supposed to have its western limit at Fiji and
the Ellice group. They have now been traced to almost every
island of Melanesia; vestiges of their influence have been
detected in the languages of Australia, and the culture of the
distant coasts of Alaska and British Columbia. The western pioneers of America knew the Shoshone Indians as small
bands of savages, constantly moving about in search of food
in the barren region west of the Rocky Mountains, and occasionally venturing eastward to hunt buffalo on the plains. Recent investigation has identified as offshoots of this retarded

Number and range.

Shoshonean stock the sedentary agriculturalists of the Moqui Pueblo, and the advanced populations of ancient Mexico and Central America.[10]   Here was a great human current which through the centuries slowly drifted from the present frontier of Canada to the shores of Lake Nicaragua. Powell's map of the distribution of the linguistic stocks of American Indians is intelligible only in the light of constant mobility. Haebler's map of the South American stocks reveals the same restless past. This cartographical presentation of the facts, giving only the final results, suggests tribal excursions of the nature of migrations; but ethnologists see them as the sum total of countless small movements which are more or less part of the normal activity of an unrooted savage people. [Map page 101.]

Otis Mason finds that the life of a social group involves a variety of movements characterized by different ranges or scopes.   I. The daily round from bed to bed.   II. The annual round from year to year, like that of the Tunguse Orochon of Siberia who in pursuit of various fish and game change their residence within their territory from month to month, or the pastoral nomads who move with the seasons from pasture to pasture. III. Less systematic outside movements covering the tribal sphere of influence, such as journeys or voyages to remote hunting or fishing grounds, forays or piratical descents upon neighboring lands eventuating usually in conquest, expansion into border regions for occasional occupation or colonization.   IV. Participation in streams of barter or commerce.   V. And at a higher stage in the great currents of human intercourse, experience, and ideas, which finally compass the world.[11]   In all this series the narrower movement prepares for the broader, of which it constitutes at once an impulse and a part.

Importance of such movements in history.
The real character and importance of these movements have been appreciated by broad-minded historians.   Thucydides elucidates the conditions leading up to the Peloponnesian War by a description of the semi-migratory population of Hellas, the exposure of the more fertile districts to incursions, and the influence of these movements in differentiating Dorian from Ionian Greece.[12]   Johannes von Muller, in the introduction to his history of Switzerland, assigns to federations and migra-

tions a conspicuous rôle in historical development. Edward
A. Ross sees in such movements a thorough-going selective
process which weeds out the unfit, or rather spares only the
highly fit. He lays down the principle that repeated migrations tend to the creation of energetic races of men. He adds,
"This principle may account for the fact that those branches
of a race achieve the most brilliant success which have wan-
dered the farthest from their ancestral home. . . . The Arabs
and Moors that skirted Africa and won a home in far-away
Spain, developed the most brilliant of the Saracen civilizations.
Hebrews, Dorians, Quirites, Rajputs, Hovas were far invaders
No communities in classic times flourished like the cities of
Asia created by the overflow from Greece. Nowhere under the
Czar are there such vigorous, progressive communities as in
Siberia.[13] Brinton distinguishes the associative and disper-
sive elements in ethnography. The latter is favored by the
physical adaptability of the human race to all climates and
external conditions; it is stimulated by the food-quest, the
pressure of foes, and the resultant restlessness of an unstable
primitive society.[14]

The earth's surface is at once factor and basis in these
movements. In an active way it directs them; but they in turn
clothe the passive earth with a mantle of humanity. This
mantle is of varied weave and thickness, showing here the
simple pattern of a primitive society, there the intricate design
of advanced civilization; here a closely woven or a gauzy
texture, there disclosing a great rent where a rocky peak or the
ice-wrapped poles protrude through the warm human covering.
This is the magic web whereof man is at once woof and weaver,
and the flying shuttle that never rests. Given a region, what
is its living envelope, asks anthropo-geography. Whence and
how did it get there? What is the material of warp and woof?
Will new threads enter to vary the color and design? If
so, from what source? Or will the local pattern repeat itself
over and over with dull uniformity?

It was the great intellectual service of Copernicus that he
conceived of a world in motion instead of a world at rest. So
anthropo-geography must see its world in motion, whether it
is considering English colonization, or the westward expansion

Geographi-
cal inter-
pretation
of histori-
cal move-
ment.

of the Southern slave power in search of unexhausted land, or the counter expansion of the free-soil movement, or the early advance of the trappers westward to the Rockies after the retreating game, or the withdrawal thither of the declining Indian tribes before the protruding line of white settlement, and their ultimate confinement to ever shrinking reservations. In studying increase of population, it sees in Switzerland chalet and farm creeping higher up the Alp, as the lapping of a rising tide of humanity below; it sees movement in the projection of a new dike in Holland to reclaim from the sea the land for another thousand inhabitants, movement in Japan's doubling of its territory by conquest, in order to house and feed its redundant millions.

The whole complex relation of unresting man to the earth is the subject matter of anthropo-geography. The science traces his movements on the earth's surface, measures their velocity, range, and recurrence, determines their nature by the way they utilize the land, notes their transformation at different stages of economic development and under different environments. Just as an understanding of animal and plant geography requires a previous knowledge of the various means of dispersal, active and passive, possessed by these lower forms of life, so anthropo-geography must start with a study of the movements of mankind.

Mobility of primitive peoples. First of all is to be noted an evolution in the mobility of peoples. In the lower stages of culture mobility is great. It is favored by the persistent food-quest over wide areas incident to retarded economic methods, and by the loose attachment of society to the soil. The small social groups peculiar to these stages and their innate tendency to fission help the movements to ramify. The consequent scattered distribution of the population offers wide interstices between encampments or villages, and into these vacant spaces other wandering tribes easily penetrate. The rapid decline of the Indian race in America before the advancing whites was due chiefly to the division of the savages into small groups, scattered sparsely over a wide territory. Hunter and pastoral peoples need far more land than they can occupy at any one time. Hence the temporarily vacant spots invite incursion. Moreover, the

slight impedimenta carried by primitive folk minimize the
natural physical obstacles which they meet when on the march.
The lightly equipped war parties of the Shawnee Indians used
gorges and gaps for the passage of the Allegheny Mountains
which were prohibitive to all white pioneers except the lonely
trapper. Finally, this mobility gets into the primitive mind.
The *Wanderlust* is strong. Long residence in one territory is
irksome, attachment is weak. Therefore a small cause suffices
to start the whole or part of the social body moving. A temporary failure of the food supply, cruelty or excessive exac-
tion of tribute on the part of the chief, occasions an exodus.
The history of every negro tribe in Africa gives instances of
such secessions, which often leave whole districts empty and
exposed to the next wandering occupant. Methods of preventing such withdrawals, and therewith the diminution of his
treasury receipts and his fighting force, belong to the policy
of every negro chieftain.

The checks to this native mobility of primitive peoples are Natural
two: physical and mental. In addition to the usual barriers barriers to
of mountains, deserts, and seas before the invention of boats, movement.
primeval forests have always offered serious obstacles to man
armed only with stone or bronze axe, and they rebuffed even
man of the iron age. War and hunting parties had to move
along the natural clearings of the rivers, the tracks of animals,
or the few trails beaten out in time by the natives themselves.
Primitive agriculture has never battled successfully against
the phalanx of the trees. Forests balked the expansion of the
Inca civilization on the rainy slope of the Andes, and in Central Africa the negro invaded only their edges for his yam
fields and plantain groves. The earliest settlements in ancient
Britain were confined to the natural clearings of the chalk
downs and oolitic uplands; and here population was chiefly
concentrated even at the close of the Roman occupation. Only
gradually, as the valley woodlands were cleared, did the richer
soil of the alluvial basins attract men from the high, poor
ground where tillage required no preliminary work. But after
four centuries of Roman rule and Roman roads, the clearings
along the river valleys were still mere strips of culture mid an
encompassing wilderness of woods. When the Germanic in-

vaders came, they too appropriated the treeless downs and were blocked by the forests.[15] On the other hand, grasslands and savannahs have developed the most mobile people whom we know, steppe hunters like the Sioux Indians and Patagonians. Thus while the forest dweller, confined to the highway of the stream, devised only canoe and dugout boat in various forms for purposes of transportation, steppe peoples of the Old World introduced the use of draft and pack animals, and invented the sledge and cart.

Effect of geographical horizon.   Primitive peoples carry a drag upon their migrations in their restricted geographical outlook; ignorance robs them of definite goals. The evolution of the historical movement is accelerated by every expansion of the geographical horizon. It progresses most rapidly where the knowledge of outlying or remote lands travels fastest, as along rivers and thalassic coasts. Rome's location as toll-gate keeper of the Tiber gave her knowledge of the upstream country and directed her conquest of its valley; and the movement thus started gathered momentum as it advanced. Cæsar's occupation of Gaul meant to his generation simply the command of the roads leading from the Mediterranean to the northern sources of tin and amber, and the establishment of frontier outposts to protect the land boundaries of Italy; this represented a bold policy of inland expansion for that day. The modern historian sees in that step the momentous advance of history beyond the narrow limits of the Mediterranean basin, and its gradual inclusion of all the Atlantic countries of Europe, through whose maritime enterprise the historical horizon was stretched to include America. In the same way, mediæval trade with the Orient, which had familiarized Europe with distant India and Cathay, developed its full historico-geographical importance when it started the maritime discoveries of the fifteenth century. The expansion of the geographical horizon in 1512 to embrace the earth inaugurated a widespread historical movement, which has resulted in the Europeanization of the world.

Civilization and mobility.   Civilized man is at once more and less mobile than his primitive brother. Every advance in civilization multiplies and tightens the bonds uniting him with his soil; makes him a sedentary instead of a migratory being. On the other hand every advance in civilization is attended by the rapid clearing of the forests, by the construction of bridges and interlacing roads, the invention of more effective vehicles for transportation whereby intercourse increases, and the improvement of navigation to the same end. Civilized man progressively modifies the land which he occupies, removes or reduces obstacles to intercourse, and thereby approximates it to the open plain. Thus far he facilitates movements. But while doing this he also places upon the land a dense population, closely attached to the soil, strong to resist incursion, and for economic reasons inhospitable to any marked accession of population from without. Herein lies the great difference between migration in empty or sparsely inhabited regions, such as predominated when the world was young, and in the densely populated countries of our era. As the earth grew old and humanity multiplied, peoples themselves became the greatest barriers to any massive migrations, till in certain countries of Europe and Asia the historical movement has been reduced to a continual pressure, resulting in compression of population here, repression there. Hence, though political boundaries may shift, ethnic boundaries scarcely budge. The greatest wars of modern Europe have hardly left a trace upon the distribution of its peoples. Only in the Balkan Peninsula, as the frontiers of the Turkish Empire have been forced back from the Danube, the alien Turks have withdrawn to the shrinking territory of the Sultan and especially to Asia Minor.

Where a population too great to be dislodged occupies the land, conquest results in the eventual absorption of the victors and their civilization by the native folk, as happened to the Lombards in Italy, the Vandals in Africa and the Normans in England. Where the invaders are markedly superior in culture though numerically weak, conquest results in the gradual permeation of the conquered with the religion, economic methods, language, and customs of the new-comers.[16] The latter process, too, is always attended by some intermixture of blood, where no race repulsion exists, but this is small in comparison to the diffusion of civilization. This was the method by which

[margin: Diffusion of culture.]

Greek traders and colonists Hellenized the countries about the eastern Mediterranean, and spread their culture far back from the shores which their settlements had appropriated. In this way Saracen armies soon after the death of Mohammed Arabized the whole eastern and southern sides of the Mediterranean from Syria to Spain, and Arab merchants set the stamp of their language and religion on the coasts of East Africa as far as Moçambique. The handful of Spanish adventurers who came upon the relatively dense populations of Mexico and Peru left among them a civilization essentially European, but only a thin strain of Castilian blood. Thus the immigration of small bands of people sufficed to influence the culture of that big territory known as Latin America.

Ethnic intermixture.

That vast sum of migrations, great and small, which we group under the general term of historical movement has involved an endless mingling of races and cultures. As Professor Petrie has remarked, the prevalent notion that in prehistoric times races were pure and unmixed is without foundation. An examination of the various forms of the historical movement reveals the extent and complexity of this mingling process.

In the first place, no migration is ever simple; it involves a number of secondary movements, each of which in turn occasions a new combination of tribal or racial elements. The transference of a whole people from its native or adopted seat to a new habitat, as in the *Völkerwanderungen*, empties the original district, which then becomes a catchment basin for various streams of people about its rim; and in the new territory it dislodges a few or all of the occupants, and thereby starts up a fresh movement as the original one comes to rest.

Nor is this all. A torrent that issues from its source in the mountains is not the river which reaches the sea. On its long journey from highland to lowland it receives now the milky waters of a glacier-fed stream, now a muddy tributary from agricultural lands, now the clear waters from a limestone plateau, while all the time its racing current bears a burden of soil torn from its own banks. Now it rests in a lake, where it lays down its weight of silt, then goes on, perhaps across an arid stretch where its water is sucked up by the thirsty air

or diverted to irrigate fields of grain. So with those rivers of
men which we call migrations. The ethnic stream may start
comparatively pure, but it becomes mixed on the way. From
time to time it leaves behind laggard elements which in turn
make a new racial blend where they stop. Such were the six
thousand Aduatici whom Cæsar found in Belgian Gaul. These
were a detachment of the migrating Cimbri, left there in
charge of surplus cattle and baggage while the main body went
on to Italy.[17]

A migration rarely involves a single people even at the Complex
start. It becomes contagious either by example or by the currents
subjection of several neighboring tribes to the same impelling of migration.
force, by reason of which all start at or near the same time.
We find the Cimbri and Teutons combined with Celts from the
island of Batavia[18] in the first Germanic invasion of the Roman
Empire. Jutes, Saxons and Angles started in close succession
for Britain, and the Saxon group included Frisians.[19] An
unavoidable concomitant of great migrations, especially
those of nomads, is their tendency to sweep into the vortex
of their movement any people whom they brush on the way.
Both individuals and tribes are thus caught up by the current.
The general convergence of the central German tribes towards
the Danube frontier of the Roman Empire during the Marcomannic War drew in its train the Lombards from the lower
Elbe down to the middle Danube and Theiss.[20] The force of
the Lombards invading Italy in 568 included twenty thousand
Saxons from Swabia, Gepidae from the middle Danube, Bulgarians, Slavs from the Russian Ukraine, together with various tribes from the Alpine district of Noricum and the fluvial
plains of Pannonia. Two centuries later the names of these
non-Lombard tribes still survived in certain villages of Italy
which had formed their centers.[21] The army which Attila
the Hun brought into Gaul was a motley crowd, comprising
peoples of probable Slav origin from the Russian steppes,
Teutonic Ostrogoths and Gepidae, and numerous German
tribes, besides the Huns themselves. When this horde withdrew after the death of Attila, Gepidae and Ostrogoths settled
along the middle Danube, and the Slavonic contingent along
the Alpine courses of the Drave and Save Rivers.[22] The

Vandal migration which in 409 invaded Spain included the Turanian Alans and the German Suevi. The Alans found a temporary home in Portugal, which they later abandoned to join the Vandal invasion of North Africa, while the Suevi settled permanently in the northwestern mountains of Spain. The Vandals occupied in Spain two widely separated districts, one in the mountain region of Galicia next to the Suevi, and the other in the fertile valley of Andalusia in the south, while the northeastern part of the peninsula was occupied by intruding Visigoths.[23]   Add to these the original Iberian and Celtic stocks of the peninsula and the Roman strain previously introduced, and the various elements which have entered into the Spanish people become apparent.[24]

Cultural modification during migration.   The absorption of foreign elements is not confined to large groups whose names come down in history, nor is the ensuing modification one of blood alone. Every land migration or expansion of a people passes by or through the territories of other peoples; by these it is inevitably influenced in point of civilization, and from them individuals are absorbed into the wandering throng by marriage or adoption, or a score of ways. This assimilation of blood and local culture is facilitated by the fact that the vast majority of historical movements are slow, a leisurely drift. Even the great *Völkerwanderung*, which history has shown us generally in the moment of swift, final descent upon the imperial city, in reality consisted of a succession of advances with long halts between. The Vandals, whose original seats were probably in central or eastern Prussia, drifted southward with the general movement of the German barbarians toward the borders of the Empire late in the second century, and, after the Marcomannic War (175 A. D.), settled in Dacia north of the lower Danube under the Roman sway. In 271 they were located on the middle Danube, and sixty years afterwards in Moravia. Later they settled for seventy years in Pannonia within the Empire, where they assimilated Roman civilization and adopted the Arian form of Christianity from their Gothic neighbors.[25]   In Spain, as we have seen, they occupied Galicia and Andalusia for a time before passing over into Africa in 429. Here was a migration lasting two centuries and a half, reaching from the Baltic to the southern shores of the Mediterranean, starting on the bleak sterile plains of the north amid barbarous neighbors, ending in the sunny grain fields and rich cities of Roman Africa. The picture which we get of the victorious Vandals parceling out the estates of Roman nobles, and, from the standpoint of their more liberal faith, profiting by the dissensions of the two Catholic sects of Africa, shows us a people greatly modified by their long sweep through the civilized outskirts of the Empire. So it was with the Lombards and Goths who invaded Italy.

Among primitive tribes, who move in smaller groups and must conform closely to the dictates of their environment, the modifying effects of people and land through which they pass are conspicuous. Ratzel describes the gradual withdrawal of a Hottentot people from western Cape Colony far into the arid interior before the advance of Kaffirs and Europeans by saying: "The stock and name of the Namaquas wandered northward, acquiring new elements, and in course of time filling the old mold with new contents."[26] This is the typical result of such primitive movements. The migration of the Delaware Indians from an early home somewhere northwest of the Great Lakes to their historical habitat between the Hudson and Potomac Rivers was a slow progress, which somewhere brought them into contact with maize-growing tribes, and gave them their start in agriculture.[27] The transit lands through which these great race journeys pass exercise a modifying effect chiefly through their culture and their peoples, less through their physical features and climate. For that the stay of the visitants is generally too brief.

Even early maritime migrants did not keep their strains pure. The untried navigator sailing from island to headland, hugging the coast and putting ashore for water, came into contact with the natives. Cross currents of migration can be traced in Polynesian waters, where certain islands are nodal points which have given and received of races and culture through centuries of movement. The original white population of Uruguay differed widely from that of the other Spanish republics of South America. Its nucleus was a large

Effect of early maritime migration.

immigration of Canary Islanders. These were descendants of Spaniards and the native Guanches of the Canaries, mingled also with Norman, Flemish and Moorish blood.[28] The Norse on their way to Iceland may have picked up a Celtic element in the islands north of Scotland; but from the Faroe group onward they found only empty Iceland and Greenland. This was an exceptional experience. Early navigation, owing to its limitations, purposely restricted itself to the known. Men voyaged where men had voyaged before and were to be found. Journeys into the untenanted parts of the world were rare. However, the probable eastward expansion of the Eskimo along the Arctic rim of North America belongs in this class, so that this northern folk has suffered no modification from contact with others, except where Alaska approaches Asia.

The transit land.

The land traversed by a migrating horde is not to be pictured as a dead road beneath their feet, but rather as a wide region of transit and transition, potent to influence them by its geography and people, and to modify them in the course of their passage. The route which they follow is a succession of habitats, in which they linger and domicile themselves for a while, though not long enough to lose wholly the habits of life and thought acquired in their previous dwelling place. Although nature in many places, by means of valleys, low plains, mountain passes or oasis lines, points out the way of these race movements, it is safer to think and speak of this way as a transit land, not as a path or road. Even where the district of migration has been the sea, as among the Caribs of the Antilles Islands, the Moros of the Philippines, and the Polynesians of the Pacific, man sends his roots like a water plant down into the restless element beneath, and reflects its influence in all his thought and activities.

War as a form of the historical movement.

Every aggressive historical movement, whether bold migration or forcible extension of the home territory, involves displacement or passive movement of other peoples (except in those rare occupations of vacant lands), who in turn are forced to encroach upon the lands of others. These conditions involve war, which is an important form of the historical movement, contributing to new social contacts and fusion of racial stocks.

Raids and piratical descents are often the preliminary of great historical movements. They first expand the geographical horizon, and end in permanent settlements, which involve finally considerable transfers of population, summoned to strengthen the position of the interloper. Such was the history of the Germanic invasions of Britain, the Scandinavian settlements on the shores of Iceland, Britain, and France, and the incursions of Saharan tribes into the Sudanese states. Among pastoral nomads war is the rule; the tribe, a mobilized nation, is always on a war footing with its neighbors. The scant supply of wells and pasturage, inadequate in the dry season, involves rivalry and conflict for their possession as agricultural lands do not. Failure of water or grass is followed by the decline of the herds, and then by marauding expeditions into the river valleys to supply the temporary want of food. When population increases beyond the limits of subsistence in the needy steppes, such raids become the rule and end in the conquest of the more favored lands, with resulting amalgamation of race and culture.[29]

The wars of savage and pastoral peoples affect the whole **Primitive** tribe. All the able-bodied men are combatants, and all the **war.** women and children constitute the spoils of war in case of defeat. This fact is important, since the purpose of primitive conflicts is to enslave and pillage, rather than to acquire land. The result is that a whole district may be laid waste, but when the devastators withdraw, it is gradually repopulated by bordering tribes, who make new ethnic combinations. After the destruction of the Eries by the Iroquois in 1655, Ohio was left practically uninhabited for a hundred and fifty years. Then the Iroquoian Wyandots extended their settlements into northwestern Ohio from their base in southern Michigan, while the Miami Confederacy along the southern shore of Lake Michigan pushed their borders into the western part. The Muskingum Valley in the eastern portion was occupied about 1750 by Delawares from eastern Pennsylvania, the Scioto by Shawnees, and the northeast corner of the territory by detachments of Iroquois, chiefly Senecas.[30] The long wars between the Algonquin Indians of the north and the Appalachian tribes of the south kept the district of Kentucky a No Man's Land, in convenient vacancy for occupation by the white settlers, when they began the westward movement.[31] [Map page 156.]

Slavery as form of historical movement.

This desolation is produced partly by killing, but chiefly by enslavement of prisoners and the flight of the conquered. Both constitute compulsory migrations of far-reaching effect in the fusion of races and the blending of civilizations. The thousands of Greek slaves who were brought to ancient Rome contributed to its refinement and polish. All the nations of the known world, from Briton to Syrian and Jew, were represented in the slave markets of the imperial capital, and contributed their elements to the final composition of the Roman people. When we read of ninety-seven thousand Hebrews whom Titus sold into bondage after the fall of Jerusalem, of forty thousand Greeks sold by Lucullus after one victory, and the auction *sub corona* of whole tribes in Gaul by Cæsar, the scale of this forcible transfer becomes apparent, and its power as an agent of race amalgamation. Senator Sam Houston of Texas, speaking of the Comanche Indians, in the United States Senate, December 31, 1854, said: "There are not less than two thousand prisoners (whites) in the hands of the Comanches, four hundred in one band in my own state . . . They take no prisoners but women and boys."[32] It was customary among the Indians to use captured women as concubines and to adopt into the tribe such boys as survived the cruel treatment to which they were subjected. Since the Comanches in 1847 were variously estimated to number from nine to twelve thousand,[33] so large a proportion of captives would modify the native stock.

In Africa slavery has been intimately associated with agriculture as a source of wealth, and therefore has lent motive to intertribal wars. Captives were enslaved and then gradually absorbed into the tribe of their masters. Thus war and slavery contributed greatly to that widespread blending of races which characterizes negro Africa. Slaves became a medium of exchange and an article of commerce with other continents. The negro slave trade had its chief importance in the eyes of ethnologists and historians because, in distributing the black races in white continents, it has given a "negro question" to the United States, superseded the native

Indian stock of the Antilles by negroes, and left a broad negro strain in the blood of Colombia, Venezuela, and Brazil. This particular historical movement, which during the two centuries of its greatest activity involved larger numbers than the Tartar invasion of Russia or the Turkish invasion of Europe, for a long period gave to black Africa the only historical importance which it possessed for the rest of the world.[34]

In higher stages of political development, war aiming at the subjugation of large territories finds another means to fuse the subject peoples and assimilate them to a common standard of civilization. The purpose is unification and the obliteration of local differences. These are also the unconscious ends of evolution by historical movement. With this object, conquerors the world over have used a system of tribal and racial exchanges. It was the policy of the Incas of ancient Peru to remove conquered tribes to distant parts of the realm, and supply their places with colonists from other districts who had long been subjected and were more or less assimilated.[35] In 722 B. C. the Assyrian king, Sargon, overran Samaria, carried away the Ten Tribes of Israel beyond the Tigris and scattered them among the cities of Media, where they probably merged with the local population. To the country left vacant by their wholesale deportation he transplanted people from Babylon and other Mesopotamian cities.[36] The descendants of these, mingled with the poorer class of Jews still left there, formed the despised Samaritans of the time of Christ. The Kingdom of Judah later was despoiled by Nebuchadnezzar of much of its population, which was carried off to Babylon.

Fusion by deported and military colonies.

This plan of partial deportation and colonization characterized the Roman method of Romanization. Removal of the conquered from their native environment facilitated the process, while it weakened the spirit and power of revolt. The Romans met bitter opposition from the mountain tribes when trying to open up the northern passes of the Apennines. Consequently they removed the Ligurian tribe of the Apuanians, forty-seven thousand in number, far south to Samnium. When in 15 B. C. the region of the Rhaetian Alps was joined

to the Empire, forty thousand of the inhabitants were transplanted from the mountains to the plain. The same method
was used with the Scordisci and Dacians of the Danube. More
often the mortality of war so thinned the population, that the
settlement of Roman military colonies among them sufficed to
keep down revolt and to Romanize the surviving fragment.
The large area of Romance speech found in Roumania and
eastern Hungary, despite the controversy about its origin,[37]
seems to have had its chief source in the extensive Roman
colonies planted by the Emperor Trajan in conquered Dacia.[38]
In Iberian Spain, which bitterly resisted Romanization, the
process was facilitated by the presence of large garrisons of
soldiers. Between 196 and 169 B. C. the troops amounted to
one hundred and fifty thousand, and many of them remained
in the country as colonists.[39]   Compare the settlement of
Scotch troops in French Canada by land grants after 1763,
resulting in the survival to-day of sandy hair, blue eyes, and
highland names among the French-speaking *habitants* of Murray Bay and other districts. The Turks in the fifteenth century brought large bodies of Moslem converts from Asia Minor
to garrison Macedonia and Thessaly, thereby robbing the
Anatolian Plateau of half its original population.   Into the
vacuum thus formed a current of nomads from inner Asia has
poured ever since.[40]

**Withdrawal
and flight.**   Every active historical movement which enters an already
populated country gives rise there to passive movements,
either compression of the native folk followed by amalgamation, or displacement and withdrawal. The latter in some
degree attends every territorial encroachment. Only where
there is an abundance of free land can a people retire as a whole
before the onslaught, and maintain their national or racial
solidarity. Thus the Slavs seem largely to have withdrawn before the Germans in the Baltic plains of Europe. The Indians
of North and South America retired westward before the advance of the whites from the Atlantic coast. The Cherokee
nation, who once had a broad belt of country extending from
the Tennessee Valley through South Carolina to the ocean,[41]
first retracted their frontier to the Appalachian Mountains;
in 1816 they were confined to an ever shrinking territory on

the middle Tennessee and the southern end of the highlands; in 1818 they began to retire beyond the Mississippi, and in 1828 beyond the western boundary of Arkansas.[42] The story of the Shawnees and Delawares is a replica of this.[43] In the same way Hottentots and Kaffirs in South Africa are withdrawing northward and westward into the desert before the protruding frontier of white settlement, as the Boers before the English treked farther into the veldt. [See map page 105.]

Where the people attacked or displaced is small or a broken remnant, it often takes refuge among a neighboring or kindred tribe. The small Siouan tribes of the Carolinas, reduced to fragments by repeated Iroquois raids, combined with their Siouan kinsmen the Catawbas, who consequently in 1743 included twenty dialects among their little band.[44] The Iroquoian Tuscaroras of North Carolina, defeated and weakened by the whites in 1711, fled north to the Iroquois of New York, where they formed the Sixth Nation of the Confederation. The Yamese Indians, who shifted back and forth between the borders of Florida and South Carolina, defeated first by the whites and then by the Creeks, found a refuge for the remnant of their tribe among the Seminoles, in whom they merged and disappeared as a distinct tribe[45]—the fate of most of these fragmentary peoples. [See map page 54.]

When the fugitive body is large, it is forced to split up in order to escape. Hence every fugitive movement tends to assume the character of a dispersal, all the more as organization and leadership vanish in the catastrophe. The fissile character of primitive societies especially contributes to this end, so that almost every story of Indian and native African warfare tells of shattered remnants fleeing in several directions. Among civilized peoples, the dispersal is that of individuals and has far-reaching historical effects. After the destruction of Jerusalem, the Jews were scattered over the earth, the debris of a nation. The religious wars of France during the sixteenth and seventeenth centuries caused Huguenots to flee to Switzerland, Germany, Holland, England, and South Carolina; they even tried to establish a colony on the coast of Brazil. Everywhere they contributed a valuable element to the economic and social life of the community

Dispersal in flight.

which they joined. The great schism in the Russian Church became an agent of emigration and colonization. It helped to spread the Russian nationality over remote frontier regions of the empire which previously had been almost exclusively Asiatic; and distributed groups of dissenters in the neighboring provinces of Turkey, Roumania, Austria, Poland and Prussia.[46]

Natural regions of retreat.
The hope of safety from pursuit drives fugitive peoples into isolated and barren places that are scarcely accessible or habitable, and thereby extends the inhabited area of the earth long before mere pressure of population would have stretched it to such limits. We find these refugee folk living in pile villages built over the water, in deserts, in swamps, mangrove thickets, very high mountains, marshy deltas, and remote or barren islands, all which can be classified as regions of retreat. Fugitives try to place between themselves and their pursuers a barrier of sea or desert or mountains, and in doing this have themselves surmounted some of the greatest obstacles to the spread of the human race.

Districts of refuge located centrally to several natural regions of migration receive immigrants from many sides, and are therefore often characterized by a bizarre grouping of populations. The cluster of marshy islands at the head of the Adriatic received fugitives from a long semi-circle of north Italian cities during the barbarian invasions. Each refugee colony occupied a separate island, and finally all coalesced to form the city of Venice. Central mountain districts like the Alps and Caucasus contain "the sweepings of the plains." The Caucasus particularly, on the border between Europe and Asia, contains every physical type and representative of every linguistic family of Eurasia, except pure Aryan. Nowhere else in the world probably is there such a heterogeneous lot of peoples, languages and religions. Ripley calls the Caucasus "a grave of peoples, of languages, of customs and physical types."[47] Its base, north and south, and the longitudinal groove through its center from east to west have been swept by various racial currents, which have cast up their flotsam into its valleys. The pueblos of our arid Southwest, essentially an area of asylum, are inhabited by Indians of four distinct stocks, and only one of them, the Moquis, show clearly kinship to another tribe outside this territory,[48] so that they are survivals. The twenty-eight different Indian stocks huddled together in small and diverse linguistic groups between the Pacific Ocean and the eastern slope of the Sierra Nevada and Cascade Range[49] leave the impression that these protected valleys, similar to the Caucasus in their ethnic diversity, were an asylum for remnants of depleted stocks who had fled to the western highlands before the great Indian migrations of the interior.[50] Making their way painfully and at great cost of life through a region of mountain and desert, they came out in diminished bands to survive in the protection of the great barrier. Of the twenty-one Indian linguistic stocks which have become extinct since the arrival of the white man, fifteen belong to this transmontane strip of the Pacific slope[51]—evidence of the fragmentary character of these stocks and their consequently small power of resistance. [See map page 54.]

Advance to a completely sedentary life, as we see it among modern civilized nations, prohibits the migration of whole peoples, or even of large groups when maintaining their political organization. On the other hand, however, sedentary life and advanced civilization bring rapid increase of population, improved methods of communication, and an enlarged geographical horizon. These conditions encourage and facilitate emigration and colonization, forms of historical movement which have characterized the great commercial peoples of antiquity and the overcrowded nations of modern times. These forms do not involve a whole people, but only individuals and small groups, though in time the total result may represent a considerable proportion of the original population. The United States in 1890 contained 980,938 immigrants from Canada and Newfoundland,[52] or just one-fifth the total population of the Dominion in that same year. Germany since 1820 has contributed at least five million citizens to non-European lands. Ireland since 1841 has seen nearly four millions of its inhabitants drawn off to other countries,[53] an amount only little less than its present population. It is estimated that since 1851 emigration has carried off from

Emigration and colonization.

County Clare and Kerry seventy-two per cent. of the average population; and yet those counties are still crowded.[54] Among those who abandon their homes in search of easier conditions of living, certain ages and certain social and industrial classes predominate. A typical emigrant group to America represents largely the lower walks of life, includes an abnormal proportion of men and adults, and about three-fourths of it are unskilled laborers and agriculturists.[55]

Colonization, the most potent instrument of organized expansion, has in recent centuries changed the relative significance of the great colonial nations of Europe. It raised England from a small insular country to the center of a world power. It gave sudden though temporary preëminence to Spain and Portugal, a new lease of life to little Holland, and ominous importance to Russia. Germany, who entered the colonial field only in 1880, found little desirable land left; and yet it was especially Germany who needed an outlet for her redundant population. With all these states, as with ancient Phoenicia, Greece and Yemen, the initial purpose was commerce or in some form the exploitation of the new territory. Colonies were originally trading stations established as safe termini for trade routes.[56] Colonial government, as administered by the mother country, originally had an eye single for the profits of trade: witness the experience of the Thirteen Colonies with Great Britain. Colonial wars have largely meant the rivalry of competing nations seeking the same markets, as the history of the Portuguese and Dutch in the East Indies, and the English and French in America prove. The first Punic War had a like commercial origin—rivalry for the trade of *Magna Græcia* between Rome and Carthage, the dominant colonial powers of the western Mediterranean. Such wars result in expansion for the victor.

Commerce.   Commerce, which so largely underlies colonization, is itself a form of historical movement. It both causes and stimulates great movements of peoples, yet it differs from these fundamentally in its relation to the land. Commerce traverses the land to reach its destination, but takes account of natural features only as these affect transportation and travel. It has to do with systems of routes and goals, which it aims to reach as quickly as possible. It reduces its cortege to essentials; eliminates women and children. Therefore it surmounts natural barriers which block the advance of other forms of the historical movement. Merchant caravans are constantly crossing the desert, but not so peoples. Traders with loaded yaks or ponies push across the Karakorum Mountains by passes where a migrating horde would starve and freeze. The northern limit of the Mediterranean race in Spain lies sharply defined along the crest of the Pyrenees, whose long unbroken wall forms one of the most pronounced boundaries in Europe;[57] yet traders and smugglers have pushed their way through from time immemorial. Long after Etruscan merchants had crossed northward over the Alps, Roman expansion and colonization made a detour around the mountains westward into Gaul, with the result that the Germans received Roman civilization not straight from the south, but secondhand through their Gallic neighbors west of the Rhine.

Commerce, though differing from other historical movements, may give to these direction and destination. The trader is frequently the herald of soldier and settler. He becomes their guide, takes them along the trail which he has blazed, and gives them his own definiteness of aim. The earliest Roman conquest of the Alpine tribes was made for the purpose of opening the passes for traders and abolishing the heavy transit duties imposed by the mountaineers.[58] Furtraders inaugurated French expansion to the far west of Canada, and the Russian advance into Siberia. The ancient amber route across Russia from the Baltic to the Euxine probably guided the Goths in their migration from their northern seats to the fertile lands in southern Russia, where they first appear in history as the Ostrogoths.[59] The caravan trade across the Sahara from the Niger to the Mediterranean coast has itself embodied an historical movement, by bringing out enough negro slaves appreciably to modify the ethnic composition of the population in many parts of North Africa.[60] It was this trade which also suggested to Prince Henry of Portugal in 1415, when campaigning in Morocco, the plan of reaching the Guinea Coast by sea and diverting its gold dust and slaves to the port of Lisbon, a movement

Commerce a guide to various movements.

which resulted in the Portuguese circumnavigation of Africa.[61]

Every staple place and trading station is a center of geographical information; it therefore gives an impulse to expansion by widening the geographical horizon. The Lewis and Clark Expedition found the Mandan villages at the northern bend of the Missouri River the center of a trade which extended west to the Pacific, through the agency of the Crow and Paunch Indians of the upper Yellowstone, and far north to the Assiniboine and Saskatchewan Rivers. Here in conversation with British and French fur-traders of the Northwest Company's posts, they secured information about the western country they were to explore.[62] Similarly the trade of the early Jesuit missions at La Pointe near the west end of Lake Superior annually drew the Indians from a wide circle sweeping from Green Bay and the Fox River in the south, across the Mississippi around to the Lake of the Woods and far north of Lake Superior.[63] Here Marquette first heard of the great river destined to carry French dominion to the Gulf of Mexico.

Movements due to religion. Trade often finds in religion an associate and coadjutor in directing and stimulating the historical movement. China regards modern Christian missions as effective European agencies for the spread of commercial and political power. Jesuit and fur-trader plunged together into the wilds of colonial Canada; Spanish priest and gold-seeker, into Mexico and Peru. American missionary pressed close upon the heels of fur-trader into the Oregon country. Jason Lee, having established a Methodist mission on the Willamette in 1834, himself experienced sudden conversion from religionist to colonizer. He undertook a temporary mission back to the settled States, where he preached a stirring propaganda for the settlement and appropriation of the disputed Oregon country, before the British should fasten their grip upon it. The United States owes Hawaii to the expansionist spirit of American missionaries. Thirty years after their arrival in the islands, they held all the important offices under the native government, and had secured valuable tracts of lands, laying the foundation of the landed aristocracy of planters established there to-day. Their sons and grandsons took the lead in the Revolution of 1893, and in the movement for annexation to the United States. Thus sometimes do the meek inherit the earth.

The famous pilgrimages of the world, in which the commercial element has been more or less conspicuous,[64] have contributed greatly to the circulation of peoples and ideas, especially as they involve multitudes and draw from a large circle of lands. Their economic, intellectual and political effects rank them as one phase of the historical movement. Herodotus tells of seven hundred thousand Egyptians flocking to the city of Bubastis from all parts of Egypt for the festival of Diana.[65] The worship of Ashtoreth in Bambyce in Syria drew votaries from all the Semitic peoples except the Jews. As early as 386 A. D. Christian pilgrims flocked to Jerusalem from Armenia, Persia, India, Ethiopia, and even from Gaul and Britain. Jerusalem gave rise to those armed pilgrimages, the Crusades, with all their far-reaching results. The pilgrimages to Rome, which in the Jubilee of 1300 brought two hundred thousand worshipers to the sacred city, did much to consolidate papal supremacy over Latin Christendom.[66] As the roads to Rome took the pious wayfarers through Milan, Venice, Genoa, Florence, Bologna, and other great cities of Italy, they were so many channels for the distribution of Italian art and culture over the more untutored lands of western Europe.

Though Mecca is visited annually by only seventy or eighty thousand pilgrims, it puts into motion a far greater number over the whole Mohammedan world, from westernmost Africa to Chinese Turkestan.[67] Yearly a great pilgrimage, numbering in 1905 eighty thousand souls, moves across Africa eastward through the Sudan on its way to the Red Sea and Mecca. Many traders join the caravans of the devout both for protection and profit, and the devout themselves travel with herds of cattle to trade in on the way. The merchants are prone to drop out and settle in any attractive country, and few get beyond the populous markets of Wadai. The British and French governments in the Sudan aid and protect these pilgrimages; they recognize them as a political force, because

Religious pilgrimages.

they spread the story of the security and order of European rule.[68] The markets of western Tibet, recently opened to Indian merchants by the British expedition to Lhassa, promote intercourse between the two countries especially because of the sacred lakes and mountains in their vicinity, which are goals of pilgrimage alike to Hindu and Tibetan Buddhist. They offer an opportunity to acquire merit and profit at the same time, an irresistible combination to the needy, pious Hindu. Therefore across the rugged passes of the Himalayas he drives his yaks laden with English merchandise, an unconscious instrument for the spread of English influence, English civilization and the extension of the English market, as the Colonial Office well understands.[69]

Historical movement and race distribution.   The forms which have been assumed by the historical movement are varied, but all have contributed to the spread of man over the habitable globe. The yellow, white and red races have become adapted to every zone; the black race, whether in Africa, Australia or Melanesia, is confined chiefly to the Tropics. A like conservatism as to habitat tends to characterize all sub-races, peoples, and tribes of the human family. The fact which strikes one in studying the migrations of these smaller groups is their adherence each to a certain zone or heat belt defined by certain isothermal lines (see map chap. XVII.), their reluctance to protrude beyond its limits, and the restricted range and small numerical strength of such protrusions as occur. This seems to be the conservatism of the mature race type, which has lost some of its plasticity and shuns or succumbs to the ordeal of adaptation to contrasted climatic conditions, except when civilization enables it partially to neutralize their effects.

Migrations in relation to zones and heat belts.   In South America, Caribs and Arawaks showed a strictly tropical distribution from Hayti to the southern watershed of the Amazon. The Tupis, moving down the Parana-La Plata system, made a short excursion beyond the Tropic of Capricorn, though not beyond the hot belt, then turned equator-ward again along the coast.[70] In North America we find some exceptions to the rule. For instance, though the main area of the Athapascan stock is found in the frigid belt of Canada and Alaska, north of the annual isotherm of $0°$ C.

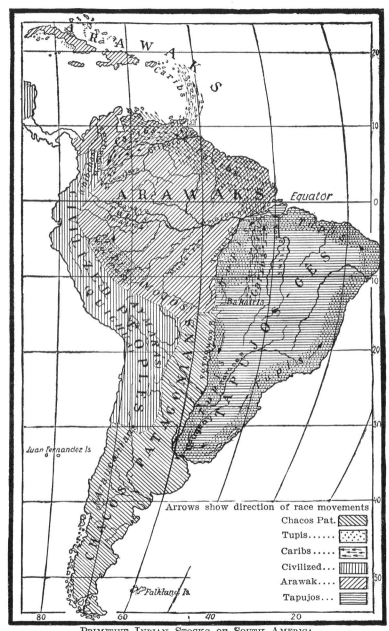

PRIMITIVE INDIAN STOCKS OF SOUTH AMERICA
(From Helmolt's *History of the World*. By permission of Dodd,
Mead & Co.)

(32° F.) small residual fragments of these people are scattered also along the Pacific coast of Oregon and California, marking the old line of march of a large group which drifted southward into Arizona, New Mexico, Texas and the northern part of Mexico. The Shoshone stock, which originally occupied the Great Basin and western intermontane plateau up to the borders of Canada, sent out offshoots which developed into the ancient civilized tribes of tropical Mexico and Central America. Both these emigrations to more southern zones were part of the great southward trend characterizing all movements on the Pacific side of the continent, probably from an original ethnic port of entry near Bering Strait; and part also of the general southward drift in search of more genial climate, which landed the van of northern Siouan, Algonquin and Iroquoian stocks in the present area of South Carolina, Georgia, Alabama, Mississippi and Louisiana, while the base of their territory stretched out to its greatest width in southern Canada and contiguous parts of the United States. [See map page 54.][71]

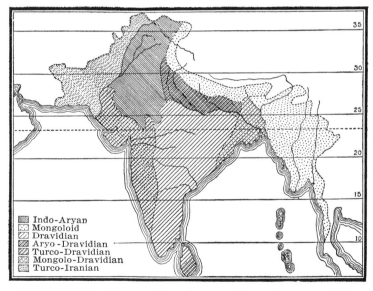

ETHNOGRAPHICAL MAP OF INDIA FROM THE INDIAN CENSUS OF 1901.

If we turn to the eastern hemisphere, we find the Malays Range of
and Malayo-Polynesians, differentiated offshoots of the Mon- movements
golian stock, restricted to the Tropics, except where Poly- in Asia.

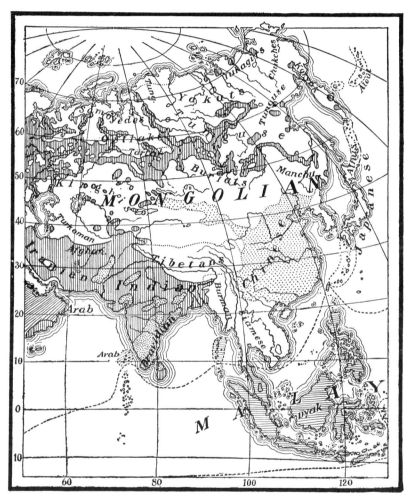

ETHNOGRAPHICAL MAP OF ASIA.
Vertical Shading in the North is Slav.

nesians have spread to outlying New Zealand. The Chinese
draw their political boundary nearly along the Tropic of Can-

cer, but they have freely lapped over this frontier into Indo-China as far as Singapore.[72] Combined with this expansion was the early infiltration of the Chinese into the Philippines, Borneo, and the western Sunda Isles, all distinctly tropical. The fact that the Chinese show a physical capacity for acclimatization found in no other race explains in part their presence into the Tropics. In contrast, the Aryan folk of India, whether in their pure type as found in the Punjab and Rajputana Desert, or mingled with the earlier Dravidian race, belong to the hot belt but scarcely reach the Tropic of Cancer,[73] though their language has far overshot this line both in the Deccan and the Ganges Delta. One spore of Aryan stock, in about 450 B. C., moved by sea from the Bay of Cambay to Ceylon; mingling there with the Tamil natives, they became the progenitors of the Singhalese, forming a hybrid tropical offshoot.

Europe, except for its small sub-arctic area, has received immigrants, according to the testimony of history and ethnology, only from the temperate parts of Asia and Africa, with the one exception of the Saracens of Arabia, whose original home lay wholly within the hot climate belt of 20° C. (68° F.). Saracen expansion, in covering Persia, Syria, and Egypt, still kept to this hot belt; only in the Barbary Coast of Africa and in Spain did it protrude into the temperate belt. Though this last territory was extra-tropical, it was essentially semi-arid and sub-tropical in temperature, like the dry trade-wind belt whence the Saracens had sprung.

Range of movements in Africa.   The Semitic folk of Arabia and the desert Hamites of northern Africa, bred by their hot, dry environment to a nomadic life, have been drawn southward over the Sahara across the Tropic into the grasslands of the Sudan, permeating a wide zone of negro folk with the political control, religion, civilization and blood of the Mediterranean north. Here similar though better conditions of life, a climate hotter though less arid, attracted Hamitic invasion, while the relatively dense native population in a lower stage of economic development presented to the commercial Semites the attraction of lucrative trade. South of the equator the native Bantu Kaffirs, essentially a tropical people, spread beyond their zonal border

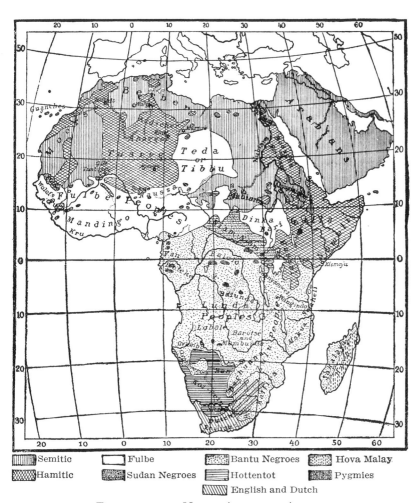

Semitic   Fulbe   Bantu Negroes   Hova Malay
Hamitic   Sudan Negroes   Hottentot   Pygmies
English and Dutch

ETHNOGRAPHICAL MAP OF AFRICA AND ARABIA.

to the south coast of Africa at 33° S. L., and displaced the yellow Hottentots[74] before the arrival of the Dutch in 1602; while in the early nineteenth century we hear of the Makololo, a division of this same Kaffir stock, leaving their native seats near the southern sources of the Vaal River at 28° S. L. and moving some nine hundred miles northward to the Barotse territory on the upper Zambesi at 15° S. L.[75] This again was a movement of a pastoral people across a tropic to other grasslands, to climatic conditions scarcely different from those which they had left.

Coloniza-
tion and
latitude.
The modern colonial movements which have been genuine race expansions have shown a tendency not only to adhere to their zone, but to follow parallels of latitude or isotherms. The stratification of European peoples in the Americas, excepting Spanish and Portuguese, coincides with heat zones. Internal colonization in the United States reveals the same principle.[76] Russian settlements in Asia stretch across Siberia chiefly between the fiftieth and fifty-fifth parallels; these same lines include the ancient Slav territory in Germany between the Vistula and Weser. The great efflux of home-seekers, as opposed to the smaller contingent of mere conquerors and exploiters, which has poured forth from Europe since the fifteenth century, has found its destinations largely in the temperate parts of the Americas, Australia, New Zealand, and South Africa. Even the Spanish overlords in Mexico and Peru domiciled themselves chiefly in the highlands, where altitude in part counteracts tropical latitude. European immigration into South America to-day greatly predominates in the temperate portions,—in Argentine, Uruguay, Paraguay, southern Brazil and southern Chile. While Argentine's population includes over one million white foreigners, who comprise twenty per cent. of the total,[77] Venezuela has no genuine white immigration. Its population, which comprises only one per cent. of pure whites, consists chiefly of negroes, mulattoes, and Sambos, hybrids of negro and Indian race. In British Guiana, negroes and East Indian coolies, both importations from other tropical lands, comprise eighty-one per cent. of the population.[78]

The movement of Europeans into the tropical regions of

Asia, Australasia, Africa and America, like the American advance into the Philippines, represents commercial and political, not genuine ethnic expansion. Except where it resorts to hybridization, it seeks not new homesteads, but the profits of tropical trade and the markets for European manufactures found in retarded populations. These it secures either by a small but permanently domiciled ruling class, as formerly in Spanish and Portuguese America, or by a body of European officials, clerks, agents and soldiers, sent out for a term of years. Such are the seventy-six thousand Britishers who manage the affairs of commerce and state in British India, and the smaller number of Dutch who perform the same functions in the Dutch East India islands. The basis of this system is exploitation. It represents neither a high economic, ethical, nor social ideal, and therefore lacks the stamp of geographic finality.

A migrating or expanding people, when free to choose, is Movement prone to seek a new home with like geographic conditions to to like the old. Hence the stamp once given by an environment tends geographic to perpetuate itself. All people, especially those in the lower conditions. stages of culture, are conservative in their fundamental activities. Agriculture is intolerable to pastoral nomads, hunting has little attraction for a genuine fisher folk. Therefore such peoples in expansion seek an environment in which the national aptitudes, slowly evolved in their native seats, find a ready field. Thus arise natural provinces of distribution, whose location, climate, physical features, and size reflect the social and economic adaptation of the inhabitants to a certain type of environment. A shepherd folk, when breaking off from its parent stock like Abraham's family from their Mesopotamian kinsmen, seeks a land rich in open pastures and large enough to support its wasteful nomadic economy. A seafaring people absorb an ever longer strip of seaboard, like the Eskimo of Arctic America, or throw out their settlements from inlet to inlet or island to island, as did Malays and Polynesians in the Pacific, ancient Greeks and Phoenicians in the subtropical Mediterranean, and the Norse in the northern seas. The Dutch, bred to the national profession of diking and draining, appear in their element in the water-logged coast of Sumatra and Guiana,[79] where they cultivate lands reclaimed from the sea; or as colonists in the Vistula lowlands, whither Prussia imported them to do their ancestral task, just as the English employed their Dutch prisoners after the wars with Holland in the seventeenth century to dike and drain the fens of Cambridgeshire and Lincolnshire. Moreover, the commercial talent of the Dutch, trained by their advantageous situation on the North Sea about the Rhine mouths, guided their early traders to similar locations elsewhere, like the Hudson and Delaware Rivers, or planted them on islands either furnishing or commanding extensive trade, such as Ceylon, Mauritius, the East Indies, or the Dutch holdings in the Antilles.

Much farther down in the cultural scale we find the fisher tribes of Central Africa extending their villages from point to point along the equatorial streams, and the river Indians of South America gradually spreading from headwaters to estuary, and thence to the related environment of the coast. The Tupis, essentially a water race, have left traces of their occupation only where river or coast enabled them to live by their inherited aptitudes.[80]   The distribution of the ancient mounds in North America shows their builders to have sought with few exceptions protected sites near alluvial lowlands, commanding rich soil for cultivation and the fish supply from the nearby river.   Mountaineer folk often move from one upland district to another, as did the Lombards of Alpine Pannonia in their conquest of Lombardy and Apennine Italy, where all their four duchies were restricted to the highlands of the peninsula.[81]   The conquests of the ancient Incas and the spread of their race covered one Andean valley after another for a stretch of one thousand five hundred miles, wherever climatic and physical conditions were favorable to their irrigated tillage and highland herds of llamas. They found it easier to climb pass after pass and mount to ever higher altitudes, rather than descend to the suffocating coasts where neither man nor beast could long survive, though they pushed the political boundary finally to the seaboard. [Map page 101.]

Movement to better geographic conditions.

The search for better land, milder climate, and easier conditions of living starts many a movement of peoples which, in view of their purpose, necessarily leads them into an environment sharply contrasted to their original habitat. Such has been the radial outflow of the Mongoloid tribes down from the rugged highlands of central Asia to the fertile river lowlands of the peripheral lands; the descent of the Iran pastors upon the agricultural folk of the Indus, Ganges and Mesopotamian valleys, and the swoop of desert-born conquerors upon the unresisting tillers of well-watered fields in all times, from the ancient Hyksos of the Nile to the modern Fulbe of the Niger Valley.

The attraction of a milder climate has caused in the north- Southward ern hemisphere a constantly recurring migration from north and west-ward drifts to south. In primitive North America, along the whole broad in the Atlantic slope, the predominant direction of Indian migra- northern tions was from north to south, accompanied by a drift hemi-from west to east.[82] On the Pacific side of the continent also sphere. the trend was southward. This is generally conceded regardless of theory as to whether the Indians first found entrance to the continent at its northeast or northwest corner. It was a movement toward milder climates.[83] Study of the *Völkerwanderungen* in Europe reveals two currents or drifts in varied combination, one from north to south and the other from east to west, but both of them aimed at regions of better climate; for the milder temperature and more abundant rainfall of western Europe made a country as alluring to the Goths, Huns, Alans, Slavs, Bulgars and Tartars of Asiatic deserts and Russian steppes, as were the sunny Mediterranean peninsulas to the dwellers of the bleak Baltic coasts. This is one geographic fact back of the conspicuous westward movement formulated into an historical principle: "Westward the star of empire takes its course." The establishment of European colonies on the western side of the Atlantic, their extension thence to the Pacific and ever westward, till European culture was transplanted to the Philippines by Spain and more recently by the United States, constitute the most remarkable sustained movement made by any one race.

But westward movements are not the only ones. On the Eastward Pacific slope of Asia the star has moved eastward. From movements. highland Mongolia issued the throng which originally popu-

lated the lowlands of China; and ever since, one nomad conqueror after the other has descended thence to rule the fruitful plains of Chili and the teeming populations of the Yangtze
Valley.[84] Russia, blocked in its hoped for expansion to the west
by the strong powers of central Europe, stretched its dominion
eastward to the Pacific and for a short time over to Alaska.
The chief expansion of the German people and the German
Empire in historical times has also been from west to east; but
this eastward advance is probably only retracing the steps
taken by many primitive Teutonic tribes as they drifted
Rhineward from an earlier habitat along the Vistula.

Return movements.

Since the world is small, it frequently happens that a people after an interval of generations, armed with a higher
civilization, will reënter a region which it once left when too
crude and untutored to develop the possibilities of the land,
but which its better equipment later enables it to exploit.
Thus we find a backward expansion of the Chinese westward to
the foot of the Pamir, and an internal colonization of the
empire to the Ili feeder of Lake Balkash. The expansion of
the Japanese into Korea and Saghalin is undoubtedly such a
return current, after an interval long enough to work a complete transformation in the primitive Mongolians who found
their way to that island home. Sometimes the return represents the ebbing of the tide, rather than the back water of a
stream in flood. Such was the retreat of the Moors from
Spain to the Berber districts of North Africa, whither they
carried echoes of the brilliant Saracen civilization in the
Iberian Peninsula. Such has been the gradual withdrawal of
the Turks from Europe back to their native Asia, and slow
expulsion of the Tartar tribes from Russia to the barren
Asiatic limits of their former territory. [See map page 225.]

Regions of at-traction and repulsion.

Voluntary historical movements, seeking congenial or choice
regions of the earth, have left its less favored spots undisturbed. Paucity of resources and isolation have generally
insured to a region a peaceful history; natural wealth has
always brought the conqueror. In ancient Greece the fruitful plains of Thessaly, Boeotia, Elis and Laconia had a
fatal attraction for every migrating horde; Attica's rugged
surface, poor soil, and side-tracked location off the main line

of travel between Hellas and the Peloponnesus saved it from many a rough visitant,[85] and hence left the Athenians, according to Thucydides, an indigenous race. The fertility of the Rhine Valley has always attracted invasion, the barren Black Forest range has repelled and obstructed it.

The security of such unproductive highlands lies more in their failure to attract than in their power to resist conquest. When to abundant natural resources, a single spot adds a reputation for wealth, magnificence, an exceptional position for the control of territory or commerce, it becomes a geographical magnet. Such was Delphi for the Gauls of the Balkan Peninsula in the third century, Rome for the Germanic and Hunnish tribes of the *Völkerwanderung*, Constantinople for the Normans, Turks and Russians, Venice for land-locked Austria, the Mississippi highway and the outlet at New Orleans for our Trans-Allegheny pioneers.

Sometimes the goal is fabulous or mythical, but potent to lure, like the land of El Dorado, abounding in gold and jewels, which for two centuries spurred on Spanish exploration in America. Other than purely material motives may initiate or maintain such a movement, an ideal or a dream of good, like the fountain of eternal youth which brought Ponce de Leon to Florida, the search for the Islands of the Blessed, or the spirit of religious propaganda which stimulated the spread of the Spanish in Mexico and the French in Canada, or the hope of religious toleration which has drawn Quaker, Puritan, Huguenot, and Jew to America. It was an idea of purely spiritual import which directed the century-long movement of the Crusades toward Jerusalem, half Latinized the Levant, and widened the intellectual horizon of Europe. A national or racial sentiment which enhaloes a certain spot may be pregnant with historical results, because at any moment it may start some band of enthusiasts on a path of migration or conquest. The Zionist agitation for the return of oppressed Jews to Palestine, and the establishment of the Liberian Republic for the negroes in Africa rest upon such a sentiment. The reverence of the Christian world for Rome as a goal of pilgrimages materially enhanced the influence of Italy as a school of culture during the Middle Ages. The spiritual and ethnic

Psychical influences in certain movements.

association of the Mohammedan world with Mecca is always fraught with possible political results. The dominant tribes of the Sudan, followers of Islam, who proudly trace back a fictitious line of ancestry to the Arabs of Yemen, are readily incited to support a new prophet sprung from the race of Mecca.[86] The pilgrimages which the Buddhists of the Asiatic highlands make to the sacred city of Lhassa ensure China's control over the restless nomads through the instrumentality of the Grand Lama of Tibet.

Results of historical movement.   Historical movements are varied as to motive, direction, numerical strength, and character, but their final results are two, differentiation and assimilation. Both are important phases of the process of evolution, but the latter gains force with the progress of history and the increase of the world's population.

Differentiation and area.   A people or race which, in its process of numerical growth, spreads over a large territory subjects itself to a widening range of geographic conditions, and therefore of differentiation. The broad expansion of the Teutonic race in Europe, America, Australia and South Africa has brought it into every variety of habitat. If the territory has a monotonous relief like Russia, nevertheless, its mere extent involves diversity of climate and location. The diversity of climate incident to large area involves in turn different animal and plant life, different crops, different economic activities. Even in lowlands the relief, geologic structure, and soil are prone to vary over wide districts. The monotonous surface of Holland shows such contrasts. So do the North German lowlands; here the sandy barren flats of the "geest" alternate with stretches of fertile silt deposited by the rivers or the sea,[87] and support different types of communities, which have been admirably described by Gustav Frenssen in his great novel of Jön Uhl. The flat surface of southern Illinois shows in small compass the teeming fertility of the famous "American bottom," the poor clay soil of "Egypt" with its backward population, and the rich prairie land just to the north with its prosperous and progressive farmer class.

When the relief includes mountains, the character not only of the land but of the climate changes, and therewith the type of community. Hence neighboring districts may produce strongly contrasted types of society. Madison County of Kentucky, lying on the eastern margin of the Bluegrass region, contains the rich landed estates, negro laboring class and aristocratic society characteristic of the "planter" communities of the old South; and only twenty miles southeast of Richmond, the center of this wealth and refinement, it includes also the rough barren hill country of the Cumberland Plateau, where are found one-room cabins, moonshine stills, feuds, and a backward population sprung from the same pure English stock as the Bluegrass people.

Here is differentiation due to the immediate influences of environment. The phenomenon reappears in every part of the world, in every race and every age. The contrast between the ancient Greeks of the mountains, coasts and alluvial valleys shows the power of environment to direct economic activities and to modify culture and social organization. So does the differences between the coast, steppe, and forest Indians of Guiana,[88] the Kirghis of the Pamir pastures and the Irtysh River valley, the agricultural Berbers of the Atlas Mountains and the Berber nomads of the Sahara, the Swiss of the high, lonely Engadine and those of the crowded Aar valley.

Contrasted environ- ments.

Contrasted environments effect a natural selection in another way and thereby greatly stimulate differentiation, whenever an intruding people contest the ownership of the territory with the inhabitants. The struggle for land means a struggle also for the best land, which therefore falls to the share of the strongest peoples. Weaklings must content themselves with poor soils, inaccessible regions of mountain, swamp or desert. There they deteriorate, or at best strike a slower pace of increase or progress. The difference between the people of the highlands and plains of Great Britain or of France is therefore in part a distinction of race due to this geographical selection,[89] in part a distinction of economic development and culture due to geographic influences. Therefore the piedmont belts of the world, except in arid lands, are cultural, ethnic and often political lines of cleavage, showing marked differentiation on either side. Isotherms are other such cleavage lines, marking the limits beyond which an aggressive people did not desire to expand because of an uncongenial climate. The distinction between Anglo-Saxon and Latin America is one of zone as well as race. Everywhere in North America the English stock has dominated or displaced French and Spanish competitors down to the Mexican frontier.

As the great process of European colonization has permeated the earth and multiplied its population, not only the best land but the amount of this has commenced to differentiate the history of various European nations, and that in a way whose end cannot yet be definitely predicted. The best lands have fallen to the first-comers strong enough to hold them. People who early develop powers of expansion, like the English, or who, like the French and Russians, formulate and execute vast territorial policies, secure for their future growth a wide base which will for all time distinguish them from late-comers into the colonial field, like Germany and Italy. These countries see the fecundity of their people redounding to the benefit of alien colonial lands, which have been acquired by enterprising rivals in the choice sections of the temperate zone. German and Italian colonies in torrid, unhealthy, or barren tropical lands, fail to attract emigrants from the mother country, and therefore to enhance national growth.

Two-type populations. When colonizers or conquerors appropriate the land of a lower race, we find a territory occupied at least for a time by two types of population, constituting an ethnic, social and often economic differentiation. The separation may be made geographical also. The Indians in the United States have been confined to reservations, like the Hottentots to the twenty or more "locations" in Cape Colony. This is the simplest arrangement. Whether the second or lower type survives depends upon their economic and social utility, into which again geographic conditions enter. The Indians of Canada are a distinct economic factor in that country as trappers for the Hudson Bay Company, and they will so remain till the hunting grounds of the far north are exhausted. The native agriculturists in the Tropics are indispensable to the unacclimated whites. The negroes of the South, introduced for an economic purpose, find their natural habitat in the Black Belt.

Here we have an ethnic division of labor for geographical reasons. Castes or social classes, often distinguished by shades of color as in Brahman India, survive as differentiations indicating old lines of race cleavage. There is abundant evidence that the upper classes in Germany, France, Austria, and the British Isles are distinctly lighter of hair and eyes than the peasantry.[90] The high-class Japanese are taller and fairer than the masses. Nearly all the African tribes of the Sudan and bordering Sahara include two distinct classes, one of lighter and one of darker shade. Many Fulbe tribes distinguish these classes by the names of "Blacks" and "Whites."[91] The two-type people are the result of historical movements.

Differentiation results not only from contrasted geographic conditions, but also from segregation. A moving or expanding throng in search of more and better lands drops off one group to occupy a fertile valley or plain, while the main body goes on its way, till it reaches a satisfactory destination or destinations. The tendency to split and divide, characteristic of primitive peoples, is thus stimulated by migration and expansion. Each offshoot, detached from the main body, tends to diverge from the stock type. If it reaches a naturally isolated region, where its contact without is practically cut off, it grows from its own loins, emphasizes its group characteristic by close in-breeding, and tends to show a development related to biological divergence under conditions of isolation. Since man is essentially a gregarious animal, the size of every such migrating band will always prevent the evolution of any sharply defined variety, according to the standard of biology. Nevertheless, the divergent types of men and societies developed in segregated regions are an echo of the formation of new species under conditions of isolation which is now generally acknowledged by biological science. Isolation was recognized by Darwin as an occasional factor in the origin of species and especially of divergence; in combination with migration it was made the basis of a theory of evolution by Moritz Wagner in 1873;[92] and in recent years has come to be regarded as an essential in the explanation of divergence of types, as opposed to differentiation.[93]

Differentiation and isolation.

The traditions of the Delaware Indians and Sioux in the north of the United States territory, and of the Creeks in the south, commence with each stock group as a united body, which, as it migrates, splits into tribes and sends out offshoots developing different dialects. Here was tribal differentiation after entry into the general stock area, the process going on during migration as well as after the tribes had become established in their respective habitats. Culture, however, made little progress till after they became sedentary and took up agriculture to supplement the chase.[94] Tribes sometimes wander far beyond the limits of their stock, like the Iroquoian Cherokees of East Tennessee and North Carolina or the Athapascan Navajos and Apaches of arid New Mexico and Arizona, who had placed twenty or thirty degrees of latitude between themselves and their brethren in the basins of the Yukon and Mackenzie rivers. Such inevitably come into contrasted climatic conditions, which further modify the immigrants. [See map page 54.]

Wide digressions differentiate them still further from the parent stock by landing them amid different ethnic and social groups, by contact with whom they are inevitably modified. The Namaqua Hottentots, living on the southern margin of the Hottentot country near the frontier of the European settlements in Cape Colony, acquired some elements of civilization, together with a strain of Boer and English blood, and in some cases even the Dutch vernacular. They were therefore differentiated from their nomadic and warlike kinsmen in the grasslands north of the Orange River, which formed the center of the Hottentot area.[95] A view of the ancient Germans during the first five or six centuries after Christ reveals differentiation by various contacts in process along all the ragged borders of the Germanic area. The offshoots who pushed westward across the Rhine into Belgian Gaul were rapidly Celticized, abandoning their semi-nomadic life for sedentary agriculture, assimilating the superior civilization which they found there, and steadily merging with the native population. They became *Belgae*, though still conscious of their Teutonic origin.[96] The Batavians, an offshoot of the ancient Chatti living near the Thuringian Forest, appropriated the river island between the Rhine and the Waal. There in the seclusion of their swamps, they became a distinct national unit, retaining their backward German culture and primitive type of German speech, which the Chatti themselves lost by contact with the High Germans.[97] Far away on the southeastern margin of the Teutonic area the same process of assimilation to a foreign civilization went on a little later when the Visigoths, after a century of residence on the lower Danube in contact with the Eastern Empire, adopted the Arian form of Christianity which had arisen in the Greek peninsula.[98] The border regions of the world show the typical results of the historical movement—differentiation from the core or central group through assimilation to a new group which meets and blends with it along the frontier.

Entrance into a naturally isolated district, from which subsequent incursions are debarred, gives conditions for divergence and the creation of a new type. On the other hand, where few physical barriers are present to form these natural pockets, the process of assimilation goes on over a wide field. Europe is peculiar among the family of continents for its "much divided" geography, commented upon by Strabo. Hence its islands, peninsulas and mountain-rimmed basins have produced a variegated assemblage of peoples, languages and culture. Only where it runs off into the monotonous immensity of Russia do we find a people who in their physical traits, language, and civilization reflect the uniformity of their environment.[99]

Africa's smooth outline, its plateau surface rimmed with mountains which enclose but fail to divide, and its monotonous configuration have produced a racial and cultural uniformity as striking as Europe's heterogeneity. Constant movements and commixture, migration and conquest, have been the history of the black races, varied by victorious incursions of the Hamitic and Semitic whites from the north, which, however, have resulted in the amalgamation of the two races after conquest.[100] Constant fusion has leveled also the social and political relations of the people to one type; it has eliminated primordial groups, except where the dwarf hunters have taken refuge in the equatorial forests and the

Geographic conditions of heterogeneity and homogeneity.

Bushmen in the southwestern deserts, just as it has thwarted the development of higher social groups by failure to segregate and protect. It has sown the Bantu speech broadcast over the immense area of Central Africa, and is disseminating the Hausa language through the agency of a highly mixed commercial folk over a wide tract of the western Sudan. The long east-and-west stretch of the Sudan grasslands presents an unobstructed zone between the thousand-mile belt of desert to the north and the dense equatorial forests to the south, between hunger and thirst on one side, heat and fever and impenetrable forests on the other. Hence the Sudan in all history has been the crowded Broadway of Africa. Here pass commercial caravans, hybrid merchant tribes like the Hausa, throngs of pilgrims, streams of peoples, herds of cattle moving to busy markets, rude incursive shoppers or looters from the desert, coming to buy or rob or rule in this highway belt. [See map page 105.]

Differentiation versus assimilation. Historical development advances by means of differentiation and assimilation. A change of environment stimulates variation. Primitive culture is loath to change; its inertia is deep-seated. Only a sharp prod will start it moving or accelerate its speed; such a prod is found in new geographic conditions or new social contacts. Divergence in a segregated spot may be overdone. Progress crawls among a people too long isolated, though incipient civilization thrives for a time in seclusion. But in general, accessibility, exposure to some measure of ethnic amalgamation and social contact is essential to sustained progress. [101] As the world has become more closely populated and means of communication have improved, geographical segregation is increasingly rare. The earth has lost its "corners." All parts are being drawn into the circle of intercourse. Therefore differentiation, the first effect of the historical movement, abates; the second effect, assimilation, takes the lead.

Elimination by historical movement. The ceaseless human movements making for new combinations have stimulated development. They have lifted the level of culture, and worked towards homogeneity of race and civilization on a higher plane. Since the period of the great discoveries inaugurated by Columbus enabled the historical movement to compass the world, whole continents, like North America and Australia, have been reclaimed to civilization by colonization. The process of assimilation is often ruthless in its method. Hence it has been attended by a marked reduction in the number of different ethnic stocks, tribes, languages, dialects, social and cultural types through wide-spread elimination of the weak, backward or unfit. [102] These have been wiped out, either by extermination or the slower process of absorption. The Indian linguistic stocks in the United States have been reduced from fifty-three to thirty-two; and of those thirty-two, many survive as a single tribe or the shrinking remnant of one. [103] In Africa the slave trade has caused the annihilation of many small tribes.[104] The history of the Hottentots, who have been passive before the active advance of the English, Dutch and Kaffirs about them, shows a race undergoing a widespread process of hybridization[105] and extermination.[106]

Strong peoples, like the English, French, Russians and Chinese, occupy ever larger areas. Where an adverse climate precludes genuine colonization, as it did for the Spanish in Central and South America, and for the English and Dutch in the Indies, they make their civilization, if not their race, permeate the acquired territory, and gradually impose on it their language and economic methods. The Poles, who once boasted a large and distinguished nationality, are being Germanized and Russified to their final national extinction. The Finns, whose Scandinavian offshoot has been almost absorbed in Sweden,[107] are being forcibly dissolved in the Muscovite dominion by powerful reägents, by Russian schoolmasters, a Russian priesthood, Russian military service.

No new types of races have been developed either by amalgamation or by transfer to new climatic and economic conditions in historic times. Contrasted geographic conditions long ago lost their power to work radical physical changes in the race type, because man even with the beginnings of civilization learned to protect himself against extremes of climate. He therefore preserved his race type, which consequently in the course of ages lost much of its plasticity and therewith its capacity to evolve new varieties. [108]

No new ethnic type.

Where ethnic amalgamations on a large scale have occurred as a result of the historical movement, as in Mexico, the Sudan and Central Africa, the local race, being numerically stronger than the intruders and better adapted to the environment, has succeeded in maintaining its type, though slightly modified, side by side with the intruders. The great historical movements of modern times, however, have been the expansion of European peoples over the retarded regions of the world. These peoples, coming into contact with inferior races, and armed generally with a race pride which was antagonistic to hybrid marriages, preserved their blood from extensive intermixture. Hybridism, where it existed, was an ephemeral feature restricted to pioneer days, when white women were scarce, or to regions of extreme heat or cold, where white women and children could with difficulty survive. Even in Spanish America, where ethnic blendings were most extensive, something of the old Spanish pride of race has reasserted itself.

Checks to differentiation. Improved communication maintains or increases the ranks of the intruders from the home supply. The negroes in North America, imported as they were *en masse*, then steadily recruited by two centuries of the slave trade, while their race integrity was somewhat protected by social ostracism, have not been seriously modified physically by several generations of residence in a temperate land. Their changes have been chiefly cultural. The Englishman has altered only superficially in the various British colonial lands. Constant intercourse and the progress of inventions have enabled him to maintain in diverse regions approximate uniformity of physical well-being, similar social and political ideals. The changed environment modifies him in details of thought, manner, and speech, but not in fundamentals.

Moreover, civilized man spreading everywhere and turning all parts of the earth's surface to his uses, has succeeded to some extent in reducing its physical differences. The earth as modified by human action is a conspicuous fact of historical development. [109] Irrigation, drainage, fertilization of soils, terrace agriculture, denudation of forests and forestration of prairies have all combined to diminish the contrasts between diverse environments, while the acclimatization of plants, animals and men works even more plainly to the same end of uniformity. The unity of the human race, varied only by superficial differences, reflects the unity of the spherical earth, whose diversities of geographical feature nowhere depart greatly from the mean except in point of climate. Differentiation due to geography, therefore, early reached its limits. For assimilation no limit can be forseen.

In view of this constant differentiation on the one hand, Geographical and assimilation on the other, the historical movement has origins. made it difficult to trace race types to their origin; and yet this is a task in which geography must have a hand. Borrowed civilizations and purloined languages are often so many disguises which conceal the truth of ethnic relationships. A long migration to a radically different habitat, into an outskirt or detached location protected from the swamping effects of cross-breeding, results eventually in a divergence great enough to obliterate almost every cue to the ancient kinship. The long-headed Teutonic race of northern Europe is regarded now by ethnologists as an offshoot of the long-headed brunette Mediterranean race of African origin, which became bleached out under the pale suns of Scandinavian skies. The present distribution of the various Teutonic stocks is a geographical fact; their supposed cradle in the Mediterranean basin is a geographical hypothesis. The connecting links must also be geographical. They must prove the former presence of the migrating folk in the intervening territory. A dolichocephalic substratum of population, with a negroid type of skull, has in fact been traced by archaeologists all over Europe through the early and late Stone Ages. The remains of these aboriginal inhabitants are marked in France, even in sparsely tenanted districts like the Auvergne Plateau, which is now occupied by the broad-headed Alpine race; and they are found to underlie, in point of time, other brachycephalic areas, like the Po Valley, Bavaria and Russia. [110]

The origin of a people can be investigated and stated only in terms of geography. The problem of origin can be solved only by tracing a people from its present habitat, through the country over which it has migrated, back to its original seat. Here are three geographical entities which can be laid down upon a map, though seldom with sharply defined boundaries. They represent three successive geographic locations, all embodying geographic conditions potent to influence the people and their movement. Hence the geographical element emerges in every investigation as to origins, whether in ethnology, history, philology, mythology or religion. The transit land, the course between start and finish, is of supreme importance. Especially is this true for religion, which is transformed by travel. Christianity did not conquer the world in the form in which it issued from the cramped and isolated environment of Palestine, but only after it had been remodelled in Asia Minor, Egypt, Greece and Rome, and cosmopolized in the wide contact of the Mediterranean basin. The Roman speech and civilization, which spread through the Romance speaking peoples of Europe, were variously diluted and alloyed before being transplanted by French, Spaniard and Portuguese to American shores, there to be further transformed.

Large centers of dispersion.   In view of the countless springs and tributaries that combine to swell the current of every historical movement, anthropo-geography looks for the origin of a people not in a narrowly defined area, but in a broad, ill-defined center of dispersion, from which many streams simultaneously and successively flow out as from a low-rimmed basin, and which has been filled from many remoter sources. Autochthones, aborigines are therefore merely scientific tropes, indicating the limit beyond which the movement of people cannot be traced in the gray light of an uncertain dawn. The vaguer and more complex these movements on account of their historical remoteness, the wider their probable range. The question as to the geographical origin of the Aryan linguistic family of peoples brings us to speculative sources, more or less scientifically based, reaching from Scandinavia and Lithuania to the Hindu Kush Mountains and northern Africa. [111] The sum total of all these conjectural cradles, amounting to a large geographical area, would more nearly approximate the truth as to Aryan origins. For the study of the historical movement makes it clear that a large, highly differentiated ethnic or linguistic family presupposes a big center and a long period of dispersion, protracted wanderings, and a diversified area both for their migrations and successive settlements.

The slighter the inner differences in an ethnic stock, whether in culture, language or physical traits, the smaller was their center of distribution and the more rapid their dispersal. The small initial habitat restricts the chances of variation through isolation and contrasted geographic conditions, as does also the short duration of their subsequent separation. The amazing uniformity of the Eskimo type from Bering Strait to eastern Greenland can only thus be explained, even after making allowance for the monotony of their geographic conditions and remoteness from outside influences. The distribution of the Bantu dialects over so wide a region in Central Africa and with such slight divergences presupposes narrow limits both of space and time for their origin, and a short period since their dispersal.[112]

Small centers.

Small centers of dispersion are generally natural districts with fixed boundaries, favored by their geographical location or natural resources or by both for the development of a relatively dense population. When this increases beyond the local limits of subsistence, there follows an emigration in point of number and duration out of all proportion to the small area whence it issues. Ancient Phoenicia, Crete, Samos, mediaeval Norway, Venice, Yemen, modern Malta, Gilbert Islands, England and Japan furnish examples. Such small favored areas, when they embody also strong political power, may get the start in the occupation of colonial lands. This gives them a permanent advantage, if their colonies are chosen with a view to settlement in congenial climates, as were those of the English, rather than the more ephemeral advantage of trade, as were those of the Dutch and Portuguese in the Tropics. It seems also essential to these centers of dispersion, that, to be effective, they must command the wide choice of outlet and destination afforded by the mighty common of the sea. Only the Inca Empire in South America gives us an example of the extensive political expansion of a small mountain state.

Tests of origin.

The question arises whether any single rule can as yet be formulated for identifying the original seats of existing peoples. By some ethnologists and historians such homes have been sought where the people are distributed in the largest area, as the Athapascan and Algonquin Indians are assigned to a northern source, because their territories attained their greatest continuous extent in Canada, but were intermittent or attenuated farther south. The fact that colonial peoples often multiply inordinately in new lands, and there occupy a territory vastly greater than that of the mother country, points to the danger in such a generalization. Of the ten millions of Jews in the world, only a handful remain in the ancient center of dispersion in Palestine, while about eight millions are found in Poland and the contiguous territories of western Russia, Roumania, Austria-Hungary and eastern Germany. Moreover, history and the German element in the "Yiddish" speech of the Russian Jews point to a secondary center of dispersion in the Rhine cities and Franconia, whither the Jews were drawn by the trade route up the Rhone Valley in the third century. [113]

A more scientific procedure is to look for the early home of a race in the locality around which its people or family of peoples centers in modern times. Therefore we place the cradle of the negro race in Africa, rather than Melanesia. Density often supplies a test, because colonial lands are generally more sparsely inhabited than the mother country. But even this conclusion fails always to apply, as in the case of Samos, which has a population vastly more dense than any section of the Grecian mainland. The largest compact area including at once the greatest density of population and the greatest purity of race would more nearly indicate the center of dispersion; because purity of race is incompatible with long migrations, as we have seen, though in the native seat it may be affected by intrusive elements. When this purity of race is combined with archaic forms of language and culture, as among the Lithuanians of Aryan speech among the Baltic swamps, it may indicate that the locality formed a segregated corner of the early center of dispersion. It seems essential to such an original seat that, whether large or small, it should be marked by some degree of isolation, as the condition for the development of specific racial characteristics. The complexity of this question of ethnic origins is typical of anthropo-geographic problems, typical also in the warning which it gives against any rigidly systematic method of solution. The whole science of anthropo-geography is as yet too young for hard-and-fast rules, and its subject matter too complex for formulas.

NOTES TO CHAPTER IV

1. H. J. Mackinder, Britain and the British Seas, pp. 179-187. London, 1904. W. Z. Ripley, The Races of Europe, pp. 306-310, 319-326. New York, 1899.
2. Compare observations of Georg Schweinfurth, The Heart of Africa, Vol. I, pp. 312-313. London, 1873.
3. Nott and Gliddon, Types of Mankind, p. lvii. Philadelphia, 1868.
4. D. M. Wallace, Russia, pp. 151-155. New York, 1904.
5. Thucydides, Book I, chap. II.
6. Strabo, Book II, chap. III, 7.
7. McGee and Thomas, Prehistoric North America, pp. 408-414, Vol. XIX of History of North America, edited by T. N. Thorpe. Philadelphia, 1905.
8. Hodgkin, Italy and Her Invaders, Vol. II, p. 214. Oxford, 1892.
9. Sir John Lubbock, Prehistoric Times, p. 587. New York, 1872.
10. D. G. Brinton, The American Race, pp. 116-119. Philadelphia, 1901.
11. O. T. Mason, Primitive Travel and Transportation, pp. 249-250. Smithsonian Report, Washington, 1896.
12. Thucydides, Book I, chap. II.
13. Edward A. Ross, Foundations of Sociology, pp. 359-363, 386-389. New York, 1905.
14. D. G. Brinton, Races and Peoples, pp. 73-75. Philadelphia, 1901.
15. John Richard Green, The Making of England, Vol. I, pp. 9-11, 45-46, 52-54, 57, 62. London, 1904.
16. James Bryce, The Migration of the Races of Men Considered Historically, Scottish Geographical Magazine, Vol. VIII, pp. 400-421, and Smithsonian Report for 1893, pp. 567-588.
17. Cæsar, De Bello Gallico, Book II, chap. 29.
18. Motley, Rise of the Dutch Republic, Vol. I, p. 5. New York, 1883.
19. John Richard Green, The Making of England, Vol. I, p. 46. London, 1904.

20. Hodgkin, Italy and Her Invaders, Vol. V, pp. 99-101. Oxford, 1895.

21. *Ibid.*, Vol. V, pp. 156-157.

22. Hodgkin, Italy and Her Invaders, Vol. II, pp. 107, 195. Oxford, 1892.

23. *Ibid.*, Vol. II, pp. 219-223, 230.

24. W. Z. Ripley, Races of Europe, pp. 276-277. New York, 1899.

25. Hodgkin, Italy and Her Invaders, Vol. II, pp. 214-219. Oxford, 1892.

26. Ratzel, History of Mankind, Vol. II, p. 296. London, 1896-1898.

27. McGee and Thomas, Prehistoric North America, pp. 408-412, Vol. XIX of *History of North America*. Philadelphia, 1905.

28. Hugh R. Mill, International Geography, p. 858. New York, 1902.

29. Roscher, *National-Oekonomik des Ackerbaues*, pp. 44-48. Stuttgart, 1888.

30. Cyrus Thomas, The Indians of North America in Historical Times, p. 261. Vol. II of *History of North America*, Philadelphia, 1903.

31. Roosevelt, Winning of the West, Vol. I, pp. 134-135, 250. New York, 1895. Justin Winsor, The Westward Movement, p. 16. Boston, 1899.

32. Eleventh Census, *Report on the Indians*, p. 54. Washington, 1894.

33. *Ibid.*, p. 531.

34. Hans Helmolt, History of the World, Vol. III, p. 411. New York, 1902-1906.

35. Edward John Payne, History of the New World Called America, Vol. II, pp. 57-58. Oxford, 1899.

36. *II Kings*, Chap. XVII, 6-24.

37. W. Z. Ripley, Races of Europe, pp. 432-434. New York, 1899.

38. Hans Helmolt, History of the World, Vol. V, pp. 353-354. New York, 1902-1906.

39. *Ibid.*, Vol. VI, p. 15.

40. D. G. Hogarth, The Nearer East, p. 247. London, 1902.

41. Roosevelt, Winning of the West, Vol. I, p. 248. New York, 1895.

42. C. C. Royce, The Cherokee Nation of Indians, pp. 130-131. Maps VIII and IX. *Fifth Annual Report of Bureau of Ethnology*, Washington, 1887.

43. Albert Gallatin, Report on the Indians in 1836, reprinted in Eleventh Census, *Report on the Indians*, p. 33. Washington, 1894.

44. Cyrus Thomas, Indians of North America in Historical Times, pp. 94, 96. Vol. II of *History of North America*, Philadelphia, 1903.

45. *Ibid.*, Vol. II, pp. 100-101.

46. Anatole Leroy-Beaulieu, The Empire of the Tsars, Vol. III, pp. 333-334. New York, 1902.

47. W. Z. Ripley, Races of Europe, pp. 437-438. New York, 1899.

48. D. G. Brinton, The American Race, pp. 115-116. Philadelphia, 1901.

49. H. Bancroft, The Native Races, Vol. III, pp. 559, 635-638. San Francisco, 1886.

50. Cyrus Thomas, Indians of North America in Historical Times, pp. 381-382, Vol. II of *History of North America*. Philadelphia, 1903.

51. Eleventh Census, *Report on the Indians*, p. 35. Washington, 1894.

52. Eleventh Census, *Report on Population*, Vol. I, p. cxxxviii. Washington, 1894.

53. Justus Perthes, *Taschen Atlas*, p. 38. Gotha, 1905.

54. Richmond Mayo-Smith, Emigration and Immigration, p. 24. New York.

55. *Ibid.*, pp. 79-80, 113-115.

56. Capt. A. T. Mahan, Influence of Sea Power upon History, pp. 27-28. Boston, 1902.

57. W. Z. Ripley, Races of Europe, pp. 247, 272-274. New York, 1899.

58. Cæsar, *Bello Gallico*, Book III, chap. I.

59. Hodgkin, Italy and Her Invaders, Vol. I, Part I, pp. 34-43. Oxford, 1892.

60. Ratzel, History of Mankind, Vol. III, pp. 242, 245, 250, 257. London, 1896-1898.

61. John Fiske, Discovery of America, Vol. I, pp. 316-317. Boston, 1893.

62. Elliott Coues, History of the Lewis and Clark Expedition, Vol. I. pp. 193-198, 203-212, 240. New York, 1893.

63. Francis Parkman, La Salle and the Discovery of the Great West, pp. 39-40, Note 2. Boston, 1904.

64. George G. Chisholm, Commercial Geography, pp. 56-57. London, 1904.

65. Herodotus, Book II, 60.

66. Encyclopædia Britanica, Article Pilgrimages.

67. E. Huntington, The Pulse of Asia, p. 88. Boston, 1907.

68. Boyd Alexander, From the Niger to the Nile, Vol. II, pp. 3-7. London, 1907.

69. C. A. Sherring, Western Tibet and the British Borderland, pp. 3-4, 144-145, 280-284. London, 1906.

70. Hans Helmolt, History of the World, Vol. I, pp. 189-191. Map p. 190. New York and London, 1902-1906.

71. J. W. Powell, Map of Linguistic Stocks of American Indians, Annual Report of Bureau of Ethnology, Vol. VII.

72. Archibald Little, The Far East, Ethnological Map, p. 8. Oxford, 1905.

73. Census of India, 1901, General Report by H. H. Risley and E. A. Gait, Vol. I, Part I, pp. 500-504; and Ethnographic Appendices by H. H. Risley, Vol. I, map, p. 60. Calcutta, 1903. P. Vidal de la Blache, *Le Peuple de l'Inde, d'après la série des recensements*, pp. 431-434, *Annales de Géographie*, Vol. XV. Paris, 1906.

74. Hans Helmolt, History of the World, Vol. III, pp. 422, 424, 434-436. New York, 1902-1906.

75. D. Livingstone, Missionary Travels, pp. 97-102. New York, 1858.

76. James Bryce, Migrations of the Races of Men Considered Historically, *Scottish Geographical Magazine*, Vol. VIII, pp. 400-421, May, 1892.

77. Justus Perthes, *Taschen Atlas*, p. 78. Gotha, 1905.

78. *Ibid.*, p. 80.

79. Hugh R. Mill, International Geography, p. 878. New York, 1902.

80. Hans Helmolt, History of the World, Vol. I, pp. 189-191. New York, 1902-1906.

81. Hodgkin, Italy and Her Invaders, Vol. VI, pp. 23-27, 38-42, 63-68, 83-87. Oxford, 1896.

82. McGee and Thomas, Prehistoric North America, Chap. XXI, Vol. XIX of *History of North America*, Philadelphia, 1905.

83. *Ibid.*, pp. 83, 87, Map of Migrations, p. 3.

84. Archibald Little, The Far East, pp. 34-38. Oxford, 1905.

85. Strabo, Book VIII, chap. I, 2.

86. Heinrich Barth, Travels in North and Central Africa, Vol. II, p. 548. New York, 1857.

87. Joseph Partsch, Central Europe, pp. 104-105. London, 1903.

88. E. F. im Thurn, Among the Indians of Guiana, pp. 167-171, 202-207. London, 1883.

89. W. Z. Ripley, Races of Europe, p. 237. New York, 1899.

90. Ibid., p. 469.

91. H. Barth, Human Society in Northern Central Africa, Journal of the Royal Geog. Society, Vol. XXX, p. 116. London, 1860.

92. Moritz Wagner, Die Entstehung der Arten durch räumliche Sonderung. Basel, 1889.

93. H. W. Conn, The Method of Evolution, pp. 282-295. New York, 1900.

94. McGee and Thomas, Prehistoric North America, pp. 418, 424, Vol. XIX of History of North America. Philadelphia, 1905.

95. Ratzel, History of Mankind, Vol. II, pp. 280-283. London, 1896-1898.

96. Cæsar, Bello Gallico, Book II, chap. IV.

97. H. Helmolt, History of the World, Vol. VI, pp. 32-33. New York, 1902-1906.

98. Hodgkin, Italy and Her Invaders, Vol. I, Part I, pp. 75, 81, 82. Oxford, 1895.

99. W. Z. Ripley, Races of Europe, pp. 34, 341-342. New York, 1899.

100. H. Helmolt, History of the World, Vol. III, pp. 400, 417. New York, 1902-1906.

101. A. C. Haddon, The Study of Man, p. xix. New York and London, 1898.

102. James Bryce, Migrations of the Races of Men Considered Historically, Scottish Geographical Magazine, Vol. VIII, pp. 400-421. May, 1892.

103. Eleventh Census, Report on the Indians, pp. 34-35. Washington, 1894.

104. H. Helmolt, History of the World, Vol. III, p. 42. New York, 1902-1906.

105. Ratzel, History of Mankind, Vol. II, pp. 279-283. London, 1896-98.

106. Jerome Dowd, The Negro Races, Vol. I, pp. 47-48, 61-62. New York, 1907.

107. Sweden, Its People and Its Industries, p. 93. Edited by G. Sundbärg, Stockholm, 1904.

108. Sir John Lubbock, Prehistoric Times, pp. 589-593. New York, 1872.

109. G. P. Marsh, The Earth as Modified by Human Action. New York, 1877.

110. W. Z. Ripley, Races of Europe, pp. 261-267. New York, 1899.

111. Ibid., pp. 475-485.

112. Ratzel, History of Mankind, Vol. II, pp. 402-405. London, 1896-1898.

113. W. Z. Ripley, Races of Europe, pp. 371-372. Map, p. 374. New York, 1899.

CHAPTER V

GEOGRAPHICAL LOCATION

THE location of a country or people is always the supreme Importance
geographical fact in its history. It outweighs every other of geograph-
single geographic force. All that has been said of Russia's ical lo-
vast area, of her steppes and tundra wastes, of her impotent cation.
seaboard on land-locked basins or ice-bound coasts, of her
poverty of mountains and wealth of rivers, fades into the
background before her location on the border of Asia. From
her defeat by the Tartar hordes in 1224 to her attack upon
the Mongolian rulers of the Bosporus in 1877, and her recent
struggle with Japan, most of her wars have been waged
against Asiatics. Location made her the bulwark of Central Europe against Asiatic invasion and the apostle of Western civilization to the heart of Asia. If this position on the
outskirts of Europe, remote from its great centers of development, has made Russia only partially accessible to European
culture and, furthermore, has subjected her to the retarding
ethnic and social influences emanating from her Asiatic neighbors,[1] and if the rough tasks imposed by her frontier situation have hampered her progress, these are all the limitations
of her geographical location, limitations which not even the
advantage of her vast area has been able to outweigh.

Area itself, important as it is, must yield to location. Location may mean only a single spot, and yet from this spot
powerful influences may radiate. No one thinks of size when
mention is made of Rome or Athens, of Jerusalem or Mecca,
of Gibraltar or Port Arthur. Iceland and Greenland guided
early Norse ships to the continent of America, as the Canaries and Antilles did those of Spain; but the location of the
smaller islands in sub-tropical latitudes and in the course of
the northeast trade-winds made them determine the first
permanent path across the western seas.

The historical significance of many small peoples, and the

historical insignificance of many big ones even to the *nil*
point, is merely the expression of the preponderant importance of location over area. The Phœnicians, from their narrow strip of coast at the foot of Mount Lebanon, were disseminators of culture over the whole Mediterranean. Holland owed her commercial and maritime supremacy, from the
thirteenth to the middle of the seventeenth century, to her
exceptional position at the mouth of the great Rhine highway
and at the southern angle of the North Sea near the entrance
to the unexploited regions of the Baltic. The Iroquois tribes,
located where the Mohawk Valley opened a way through the
Appalachian barrier between the Hudson River and Lake
Ontario, occupied both in the French wars and in the Revolution a strategic position which gave them a power and importance out of all proportion to their numbers.

Location often assumes a fictitious political value, due to
a combination of political interests. The Turkish power owes
its survival on the soil of Europe to-day wholly to its position
on the Bosporus. Holland owes the integrity of her kingdom, and Roumania that of hers, to their respective locations
at the mouths of the Rhine and the Danube, because the interest of western Europe demands that these two important
arteries of commerce should be held by powers too weak ever
to tie them up. The same principle has guaranteed the neutrality of Switzerland, whose position puts it in control of
the passes of the Central Alps from Savoy to the Tyrol;
and, more recently, that of the young state of Panama,
through which the Isthmian Canal is to pass.

Content of the term location. Geographical location necessarily includes the idea of the
size and form of a country. Even the most general state-
ment of the zonal and interoceanic situation of Canada, the
United States, Mexico, and the Russian Empire, indicates the
area and contour of their territories. This is still more
conspicuously the case with naturally defined regions, such as
island and peninsula countries. But location includes a complex of yet larger and more potent relations which go with
mere attachment to this or that continent, or to one or
another side of a continent. Every part of the world gives
to its lands and its people some of its own qualities; and so

again every part of this part. Arabia, India and Farther India, spurs of the Asiatic land-mass, have had and will always have a radically different ethnic and political history from Greece, Italy and Spain, the corresponding peninsulas of Europe, because the histories of these two groups are bound up in their respective continents. The idea of a European state has a different content from that of an Asiatic, or North American or African state; it includes a different race or combination of races, different social and economic development, different political ideals. Location, therefore, means climate and plant life at one end of the scale, civilization and political status at the other.

This larger conception of location brings a correspondingly larger conception of environment, which affords the solution of many otherwise hopeless problems of anthropogeography. It is embodied in the law that the influences of a land upon its people spring not only from the physical features of the land itself, but also from a wide circle of lands into which it has been grouped by virtue of its location. Almost every geographical interpretation of the ancient and modern history of Greece has been inadequate, because it has failed sufficiently to emphasize the most essential factor in this history, namely, Greece's location at the threshold of the Orient. This location has given to Greek history a strong Asiatic color. It comes out in the accessibility of Greece to ancient Oriental civilization and commerce, and is conspicuous in every period from the Argonautic Expedition to the achievement of independence in 1832 and the recent efforts for the liberation of Crete. This outpost location before the Mediterranean portals of the vast and arid plains of southwestern Asia, exposed to every tide of migration or conquest sent out by those hungry lands, had in it always an element of weakness. In comparison with the shadow of Asia, which constantly overhung the Greek people and from 1401 to 1832 enveloped them, only secondary importance can be attributed to advantageous local conditions as factors in Greek history.

It is a similar intercontinental location in the isthmian region between the Mediterranean on the west and the ancient

(margin note: Intercontinental location.)

maritime routes of the Red Sea and Persian Gulf on the east, which gave to Phœnicia the office of middleman between the Orient and Occident,[2] and predestined its conquest, now by the various Asiatic powers of Mesopotamia, now by the Pharaohs of Egypt, now by European Greeks and Romans, now by a succession of Asiatic peoples, till to-day we find it incorporated in the Asiatic-European Empire of Turkey. Proximity to Africa has closely allied Spain to the southern continent in flora, fauna, and ethnic stock. The long-headed, brunette Mediterranean race occupies the Iberian Peninsula and the Berber territory of northwest Africa.[3] This community of race is also reflected in the political union of the two districts for long periods, first under the Carthaginians, then the Romans, who secured Hispania by a victory on African soil, and finally by the Saracens. This same African note in Spanish history recurs to-day in Spain's interest in Morocco and the influence in Moroccan affairs yielded her by France and Germany at the Algeciras convention in 1905, and in her ownership of Ceuta and five smaller *presidios* on the Moroccan coast. Compare Portugal's former ownership of Tangier.

In contradistinction to continental and intercontinental location, anthropo-geography recognizes two other narrower meanings of the term. The innate mobility of the human race, due primarily to the eternal food-quest and increase of numbers, leads a people to spread out over a territory till they reach the barriers which nature has set up, or meet the frontiers of other tribes and nations. Their habitat or their specific geographic location is thus defined by natural features of mountain, desert and sea, or by the neighbors whom they are unable to displace, or more often by both.

Natural versus vicinal location. A people has, therefore, a twofold location, an immediate one, based upon their actual territory, and a mediate or vicinal one, growing out of its relations to the countries nearest them. The first is a question of the land under their feet; the other, of the neighbors about them. The first or natural location embodies the complex of local geographic conditions which furnish the basis for their tribal or national existence. This basis may be a peninsula, island, archipelago, an oasis, an arid steppe, a mountain system, or a fertile lowland. The stronger the vicinal location, the more dependent is the people upon the neighboring states, but the more potent the influence which it can, under certain circumstances, exert upon them. Witness Germany in relation to Holland, France, Austria and Poland. The stronger the natural location, on the other hand, the more independent is the people and the more strongly marked is the national character. This is exemplified in the people of mountain lands like Switzerland, Abyssinia and Nepal; of peninsulas like Korea, Spain and Scandinavia; and of islands like England and Japan. To-day we stand amazed at that strong primordial brand of the Japanese character which nothing can blur or erase.

Clearly defined natural locations, in which barriers of mountains and sea draw the boundaries and guarantee some degree of isolation, tend to hold their people in a calm embrace, to guard them against outside interference and infusion of foreign blood, and thus to make them develop the national genius in such direction as the local geographic conditions permit. In the unceasing movements which have made up most of the historic and prehistoric life of the human race, in their migrations and counter-migrations, their incursions, retreats, and expansions over the face of the earth, vast unfenced areas, like the open lowlands of Russia and the grasslands of Africa, present the picture of a great thoroughfare swept by pressing throngs. Other regions, more secluded, appear as quiet nooks, made for a temporary halt or a permanent rest. Here some part of the passing human flow is caught as in a vessel and held till it crystallizes into a nation. These are the conspicuous areas of race characterization. The development of the various ethnic and political offspring of the Roman Empire in the naturally defined areas of Italy, the Iberian Peninsula, and France illustrates the process of national differentiation which goes on in such secluded locations.

A marked influence upon this development is generally ascribed to the protection afforded by such segregated districts. But protection alone is only a negative force in the life of a people; it leaves them free to develop in their own

Naturally defined location.

way, but does not say what that way shall be. On the other hand, the fact that such a district embraces a certain number of geographic features, and encompasses them by obstructive boundaries, is of immense historical importance; because this restriction leads to the concentration of the national powers, to the more thorough utilization of natural advantages, both racial and geographical, and thereby to the growth of an historical individuality. Nothing robs the historical process of so much of its greatness or weakens so much its effects as its dispersion over a wide, boundless area. This was the disintegrating force which sapped the strength of the French colonies in America. The endless valleys of the St. Lawrence and the Mississippi and the alluring fur trade tempted them to an expansion that was their political and economic undoing. Russia's history illustrates the curse of a distant horizon. On the other hand, out of a restricted geographical base, with its power to concentrate and intensify the national forces, grew Rome and Greece, England and Japan, ancient Peru and the Thirteen Colonies of America.

Vicinal location.   If even the most detached and isolated of these natural locations be examined, its people will, nevertheless, reveal a transitional character, intermediate between those of its neighbors, because from these it has borrowed both ethnic stock and culture. Great Britain is an island, but its vicinal location groups it with the North Sea family of people. Even in historic times it has derived ancient Belgian stock, Roman, Anglo-Saxon, Danish and Scandinavian from the long semicircle of nearby continental lands, which have likewise contributed so much to the civilization of the island. Similarly, Japan traces the sources of its population to the north of Asia by way of the island of Sakhalin, to the west through Korea, and to the Malay district of the south, whence the Kuro Siwa has swept stragglers to the shores of Kiu-siu. Like England, Japan also has drawn its civilization from its neighbors, and then, under the isolating influence of its local environment, has individualized both race and culture. Here we have the interplay of the forces of natural and vicinal location.

A people situated between two other peoples form an

ethnic and cultural link between the two. The transitional type is as familiar in anthropo-geography as in biology. The only exception is found in the young intrusion of a migrating or conquering people, like that of the Hungarians and Turks in southeastern Europe, and of the Berger Tuaregs and Fulbes among the negroes of western Sudan; or of a colonizing people, like that of the Russians in Mongolian Siberia and of Europeans among the aborigines of South Africa. Even in these instances race amalgamation tends to take place along the frontiers, as was the case in Latin America and as occurs to-day in Alaska and northern Canada, where the "squaw man" is no rarity. The assimilation of culture, at least in a superficial sense, may be yet more rapid, especially where hard climatic conditions force the interloper to imitate the life of the native. The industrial and commercial Hollander, when transplanted to the dry grasslands of South Africa, became pastoral like the native Kaffirs. The French voyageur of Canada could scarcely be distinguished from the Indian trapper; occupation, food, dress, and spouse were the same. Only a lighter tint of skin distinguished the half-breed children of the Frenchman. The settlers of the early Trans-Allegheny commonwealths, at least for a generation or two, showed little outward difference in mode of life from that of the savage community among which they dwelt. [4]

The more alike the components of such a vicinal group of people, the easier, freer and more effective will be the mediating function of the central one. Germany has demonstrated this in her long history as intermediary between the nations of southeastern and western Europe. The people of Poland, occupying a portion of the Baltic slope of northern Europe, fended by no natural barriers from their eastern and western neighbors, long constituted a transition form between the two. Though affiliated with Russia in point of language, the Poles are Occidental in their religion; and their head-form resembles that of northern Germany rather than that of Russia. [5] The country belongs to western Europe in the density of its population (74 to the square kilometer or 190 to the square mile), which is quadruple that of re-

Vicinal groups of similar or diverse race and culture.

maining European Russia, and also in its industrial and social development. The partition of Poland among the three neighboring powers was the final expression of its intermediate location and character. [6] One part was joined politically to the Slav-German western border of Russia, and another to the German-Slav border of Germany, while the portion that fell to the Austrian Empire simply extended the northern Slav area of that country found in Bōhemia, Moravia, and the Slovak border of Hungary. [Map page 223.]

If the intermediate people greatly differs in race or civilization from both neighbors, it exercises and receives slight influence. The Mongols of Central Asia, between China on one side and Persia and India on the other, have been poor vehicles for the exchange of culture between these two great districts. The Hungarians, located between the Roumanians and Germans on the east and west, Slovaks and Croatians on the north and south, have helped little to reconcile race differences in the great empire of the Danube.

Thalassic vicinal location.

The unifying effect of vicinal location is greatly enhanced if the neighboring people are grouped about an enclosed sea which affords an easy highway for communication. The integrating force of such a basin will often overcome the disintegrating force of race antagonisms. The Roman Empire in the Mediterranean was able to evolve an effective centralized government and to spread one culture over the neighboring shores, despite great variety of nationality and language and every degree of cultural development. A certain similarity of natural conditions, climatic and otherwise, from the Iberian Peninsula to the borders of the Syrian desert, also aided in the process of amalgamation.

Where similarity of race already forms a basis for congeniality, such circumthalassic groups display the highest degree of interactive influence. These contribute to a further blending of population and unification of culture, by which the whole circle of the enclosing lands tends to approach one standard of civilization. This was the history of the Baltic coast from the thirteenth to the sixteenth centuries, when the German Hansa distributed the material products of Europe's highest civilization from Russian Novgorod to Norway. The

North Sea group, first under the leadership of Holland, later under England's guidance, became a single community of advancing culture, which was a later reflection of the early community of race stretching from the Faroe and Shetland Islands to the Rhine and the Elbe. This same process has been going on for ages about the marginal basins of eastern Asia, the Yellow and Japan Seas. Community of race and culture stamps China, Korea and Japan. A general advance in civilization under the leadership of Japan, the England of the East, now inaugurates the elevation of the whole group.

An even closer connection exists between adjoining peoples who are united by ties of blood and are further made economically dependent upon one another, because of a contrast in the physical conditions and, therefore, in the products of their respective territories. Numerous coast and inland tribes, pastoral and agricultural tribes are united because they are mutually necessary. In British Columbia and Alaska the fishing Indians of the seaboard long held a definite commercial relation to the hunting tribes of the interior, selling them the products and wares of the coast, while monopolizing their market for the inland furs. Such was the position of the Ugalentz tribe of Tlingits near the mouth of the Copper River in relation to the up-stream Athapascans ; of the Kinik tribe at the head of Cook's Inlet in relation to the inland Atnas, [7] of the Chilcats of Chilkoot Inlet to the mountain Tinnehs. Similarly, the hunting folk of the Kalahari Desert in South Africa attach themselves to influential tribesmen of the adjacent Bechuana grasslands, in order to exchange the skins of the desert animals for spears, knives, and tobacco. [8] Fertile agricultural lands adjoining pastoral regions of deserts and steppes have in all times drawn to their border markets the mounted plainsmen, bringing the products of their herds to exchange for grain ; and in all times the abundance of their green fields has tempted their ill-fed neighbors to conquest, so that the economic bond becomes a preliminary to a political bond and an ethnic amalgamation growing out of this strong vicinal location. The forest lands of Great Russia supplement the grain-bearing Black Lands

Complementary locations.

of Little Russia; the two are united through geographico-economic conditions, which would not permit an independent existence to the smaller, weaker section of the south, ever open to hostile invasion from Asia. [9]

Types of location.

Leaving now the ethnic and economic ties which may strengthen the cohesive power of such vicinal grouping, and considering only its purely geographic aspects, we distinguish the following types:

I. Central location. Examples: The Magyars in the Danube Valley; the Iroquois Indians on the Mohawk River and the Finger Lakes; Russia from the 10th to the 18th century; Poland from 1000 to its final partition in 1795; Bolivia, Switzerland, and Afghanistan.

II. Peripheral location: Ancient Phœnicia; Greek colonies in Asia Minor and southern Italy; the Roman Empire at the accession of Augustus; the Thirteen Colonies in 1750; island and peninsula lands.

III. Scattered location: English and French settlements in America prior to 1700; Indians in the United States and the Kaffirs in South Africa; Portuguese holdings in the Orient, and French in India.

IV. Location in a related series: Oasis states grouped along desert routes; islands along great marine routes.

Continuous and scattered location.

All peoples in their geographical distribution tend to follow a social and political law of gravitation, in accordance with which members of the same tribe or race gather around a common center or occupy a continuous stretch of territory, as compactly as their own economic status, and the physical conditions of climate and soil will permit. This is characteristic of all mature and historically significant peoples who have risen to sedentary life, maintained their hold on a given territory, and, with increase of population, have widened their boundaries. The nucleus of such a people may be situated somewhere in the interior of a continent, and with growing strength it may expand in every direction; or it may originate on some advantageous inlet of the sea and spread thence up and down the coast, till the people have possessed themselves of a long-drawn hem of land and used this peripheral location to intercept the trade between their back country and the sea.

These are the two types of continuous location. In contrast to them, a discontinuous or scattered location characterizes the sparse distribution of primitive hunting and pastoral tribes; or the shattered fragments of a conquered people, whose territory has been honeycombed by the land appropriation of the victors; or a declining, moribund people, who, owing to bad government, poor economic methods, and excessive competition in the struggle for existence, have shrunk to mere patches. As a favorable symptom, scattered location regularly marks the healthy growth of an expanding people, who throw out here and there detached centers of settlement far beyond the compact frontier, and fix these as the goal for the advance of their boundary. It is also a familiar feature of maritime commercial expansion, which is guided by no territorial ambition but merely aims to secure widely distributed trading stations at favorable coast points, in order to make the circle of commerce as ample and resourceful as possible. But this latter form of scattered location is not permanently sound. Back of it lies the short-sighted policy of the middleman nation, which makes wholly inadequate estimate of the value of land, and is content with an ephemeral prosperity.

A broad territorial base and security of possession are the **Central** guarantees of national survival. The geographic conditions **versus peri-** which favor one often operate against the other. Peripheral **pheral lo-** location means a narrow base but a protected frontier along **cation.** the sea; central location means opportunity for widening the territory, but it also means danger. A state embedded in the heart of a continent has, if strong, every prospect of radial expansion and the exercise of wide-spread influence; but if weak, its very existence is imperilled, because it is exposed to encroachments on every side. A central location minus the bulwark of natural boundaries enabled the kingdom of Poland to be devoured piecemeal by its voracious neighbors. The kingdom of Burgundy, always a state of fluctuating boundaries and shifting allegiances, fell at last a victim to its central location, and saw its name obliterated from the map. Hungary, which, in the year 1000, occupied a restricted inland location on the middle Danube, by the

14th century broke through the barriers of its close-hugging neighbors, and stretched its boundaries from the Adriatic to the Euxine; two hundred years later its territory contracted to a fragment before the encroachments of the Turks, but afterwards recovered in part its old dimensions. Germany has, in common with the little Sudanese state of Wadai, an influential and dangerous position. A central location in the Sudan has made Wadai accessible to the rich caravan trade from Tripoli and Barca on the north, from the great market town of Kano in Sokoto on the west, and from the Nile Valley and Red Sea on the east. But the little state has had to fight for its life against the aggressions of its western rival Bornu and its eastern neighbor Darfur. And now more formidable enemies menace it in the French, who have occupied the territory between it and Bornu, and the English, who have already caught Darfur in the dragnet of the Egyptian Sudan. [10]

Danger of central location. Germany, crowded in among three powerful neighbors like France, Russia, and Austria, has had no choice about maintaining a strong standing army and impregnable frontier defenses. The location of the Central European states between the Baltic and the Balkans has exposed them to all the limitations and dangers arising from a narrow circle of land neighbors. Moreover, the diversified character of the area, its complex mountain systems, and diverging river courses have acted as disintegrating forces which have prevented the political concentration necessary to repel interference from without. The Muscovite power, which had its beginning in a modest central location about the sources of the Dwina, Dnieper and Volga, was aided by the physical unity of its unobstructed plains, which facilitated political combination. Hence, on every side it burst through its encompassing neighbors and stretched its boundaries to the untenanted frontier of the sea. Central location was the undoing of the Transvaal Republic. Its efforts to expand to the Indian Ocean were blocked by its powerful British rival at every point—at Delagoa Bay in 1875 by treaty with Portugal, at Santa Lucia Bay in 1884, and through Swaziland in 1894. The Orange Free State was maimed in the same way when, in 1868, she tried to stretch out an arm through Basutoland to the sea.[11] Here even weak neighbors were effective to curtail the seaward growth of these inland states, because they were made the tools of one strong, rapacious neighbor. A central position teaches always the lesson of vigilance and preparedness for hostilities, as the Boer equipment in 1899, the military organization of Germany, and the bristling fortresses on the Swiss Alpine passes prove.

How intimate and necessary are the relations between central and peripheral location is shown by the fact that all states strive to combine the two. In countries like Norway, France, Spain, Japan, Korea and Chile, peripheral location predominates, and therefore confers upon them at once the security and commercial accessibility which result from contact with the sea. Other countries, like Russia, Germany and Austro-Hungary, chiefly central in location, have the strategic and even the commercial value of their coasts reduced by the long, tortuous course which connects them with the open ocean. Therefore, we find Russia planning to make a great port at Ekaterina Harbor on the northernmost point of her Lapland coast, where an out-runner from the Gulf Stream ensures an ice-free port on the open sea. [12] An admirable combination of central and peripheral location is seen in the United States. Here the value of periphery is greatly enhanced by the interoceanic location of the country; and the danger of entanglements arising from a marked central location is reduced by the simplicity of the political neighborhood. But our country has paid for this security by an historical aloofness and poverty of influence. Civilized countries which are wholly central in their location are very few, only nine in all. Six of these are mountain or plateau states, like Switzerland and Abyssinia, which have used the fortress character of their land to resist conquest, and have preferred independence to the commercial advantages to be gained only by affiliation with their peripheral neighbors.

Mutual relations between center and periphery.

Central and peripheral location presuppose and supplement one another. One people inhabits the interior of an island or continent whose rim is occupied by another. The first suffers from exclusion from the sea and therefore strives

Inland and coastward expansion.

to get a strip of coast. The coast people feel the drawback of their narrow foothold upon the land, want a broader base in order to exploit fully the advantages of their maritime location, fear the pressure of their hinterland when the great forces there imprisoned shall begin to move; so they tend to expand inland to strengthen themselves and weaken the neighbor in their rear. The English colonies of America, prior to 1763, held a long cordon of coast, hemmed in between the Appalachian Mountains and the sea. Despite threats of French encroachments from the interior, they expanded from this narrow peripheral base into the heart of the continent, and after the Revolution reached the Mississippi River and the northern boundary of the Spanish Floridas. They now held a central location in relation to the long Spanish periphery of the Gulf of Mexico. True to the instincts of that location, they began to throw the weight of their vast hinterland against the weak coastal barrier. This gave way, either to forcible appropriation of territory or diplomacy or war, till the United States had incorporated in her own territory the peripheral lands of the Gulf from Florida Strait to the Rio Grande. [See map page 156.]

Russian expansion in Asia.   In Asia this same process has been perennial and on a far greater scale. The big arid core of that continent, containing many million square miles, has been charged with an expansive force. From the appearance of the Aryans in the Indus Valley and the Scythians on the borders of Macedonia, it has sent out hordes to overwhelm the peripheral lands from the Yellow Sea to the Black, and from the Indian Ocean to the White Sea.[13] To-day Russia is making history there on the pattern set by geographic conditions. From her most southerly province in Trans-Caspia, conquered a short twenty-five years ago, she is heading towards the Indian Ocean. The Anglo-Russian convention of August 31st, 1907, yielding to Russia all northern Persia as her sphere of influence, enables her to advance half way to the Persian Gulf, though British statesmen regard it as a check upon her ambition, because England has secured right to the littoral. But Russia by this great stride toward her goal is working with causes, satisfied to let the effects follow at their leisure.

She has gained the best portion of Persia, comprising the six largest cities and the most important lines of communication radiating from the capital. [14] This country will make a solid base for her further advance to the Persian Gulf; and, when developed by Russian enterprise in railroad building and commerce, it will make a heavy weight bearing down upon the coast. The Muscovite area which is pressing upon England's Persian littoral reaches from Ispahan and Yezd to the far-away shores of the Arctic Ocean.

In the essentially complementary character of interior and periphery are rooted all these coastward and landward movements of expansion. Where an equilibrium seems to have been reached, the peoples who have accepted either the one or the other one-sided location have generally for the time being ceased to grow. Such a location has therefore a passive character. But the surprising elasticity of many nations may start up an unexpected activity which will upset this equilibrium. Where the central location is that of small mountain states, which are handicapped by limited resources and population, like Nepal and Afghanistan, or overshadowed by far more powerful neighbors, like Switzerland, the passive character is plain enough. In the case of larger states, like Servia, Abyssinia, and Bolivia, which offer the material and geographical base for larger populations than they now support, it is often difficult to say whether progression or retrogression is to be their fate. As a rule, however, the expulsion of a people from a peripheral point of advantage and their confinement in the interior gives the sign of national decay, as did Poland's loss of her Baltic seaboard. Russia's loss of her Manchurian port and the resignation of her ambition on the Chinese coasts is at least a serious check. On the other hand, if an inland country enclosed by neighbors succeeds in somewhere getting a maritime outlet, the sign is hopeful. The century-old political slogan of Hungary, "To the sea, Magyars!" has borne fruit in the Adriatic harbor of Fiume, which is to-day the pride of the nation and in no small degree a basis for its hope of autonomy. The history of Montenegro took on a new phase when from its mountain seclusion it recently secured the short strip of seaboard which

Periphery as goal of expansion.

it had won and lost so often. Such peripheral holdings are the lungs through which states breathe.

Reaction between center and periphery.

History and the study of race distribution reveal a mass of facts which represent the contrast and reaction between interior and periphery. The marginal lands of Asia, from northern Japan, where climatic conditions first make historical development possible, around the whole fringe of islands, peninsulas and border lowlands to the Aegean coast of Asia Minor, present a picture of culture and progress as compared with the high, mountain-rimmed core of the continent, condemned by its remoteness and inaccessibility to eternal retardation. Europe shows the same contrast, though in less pronounced form. Its ragged periphery, all the way from the Balkan Gibraltar at Constantinople to the far northern projections of Scandinavia and Finland, shows the value of a seaward outlook both in culture and climate. Germany beyond the Elbe and Austria beyond the Danube begin to feel the shadow of the continental mass behind them; and from their eastern borders on through Russia the benumbing influence of a central location grows, till beyond the Volga the climatic, economic, social and political conditions of Asia prevail. Africa is all core: contour and relief have combined to reduce its periphery to a narrow coastal hem, offering at best a few vantage points for exploitation to the great maritime merchant peoples of the world. Egypt, embedded in an endless stretch of desert like a jewel in its matrix, was powerless to shake off the influence of its continental environment. Its location was predominantly central; its culture bore the stamp of isolation and finally of arrested development. Australia, the classic ground of retardation, where only shades of savagery can be distinguished, offered the natives of its northern coast some faint stimuli in the visits of Malay seamen from the nearby Sunda Islands; but its central tribes, shielded by geographic segregation from external influences, have retained the most primitive customs and beliefs.[15]

Expanding Europe has long been wrestling with Africa, but it can not get a grip, owing to the form of its antagonist; it finds no limb by which the giant can be tripped and thrown.

Asia presents a wide border of marginal lands, some of them like Arabia and India being almost continental in their proportions. Since Europe began her career of maritime and colonial expansion in the sixteenth and seventeenth centuries, she has seized upon these peripheral projections as if they were the handles on a pilot wheel, and by them she has steered the course of Asia ever since. These semi-detached outlyers of the continent have enabled her to stretch a girdle of European influences around the central core. Such influences, through the avenues of commerce, railway concessions, missionary propaganda, or political dominion, have permeated the accessible periphery and are slowly spreading thence into the interior. China and Persia have felt these influences not less than India and Tongking; Japan, which has most effectually preserved its political autonomy, has profited by them most.

This historical contrast between center and periphery of continents reappears in smaller land masses, such as peninsulas and islands. The principle holds good regardless of size. The whole fringe of Arabia, from Antioch to Aden and from Mocha to Mascat, has been the scene of incoming and outgoing activities, has developed live bases of trade, maritime growth, and culture, while the inert, somnolent interior has drowsed away its long eventless existence. The rugged, inaccessible heart of little Sardinia repeats the story of central Arabia in its aloofness, its impregnability, backwardness, and in the purity of its race. Its accessible coast, forming a convenient way-station on the maritime crossroads of the western Mediterranean, has received a succession of conquerors and an intermittent influx of every ethnic strain known in the great basin.

The story of discovery and colonization, from the days of Periphery in ancient Greek enterprise in the Mediterranean to the recent colonization. German expansion along the Gulf of Guinea, shows the appropriation first of the rims of islands and continents, and later that of the interior. A difference of race and culture between inland and peripheral inhabitants meets us almost everywhere in retarded colonial lands. In the Philippines, the wild people of Luzon, Mindoro and the Visa-

yas are confined almost entirely to the interior, while civilized or Christianized Malays occupy the whole seaboard,
except where the rugged Sierra Madre Mountains, fronting
the Pacific in Luzon, harbor a sparse population of primitive Negritos.[16]   For centuries Arabs held the coast of East
Africa, where their narrow zone of settlement bordered on
that of native blacks, with whom they traded.   Even ancient
Greece showed a wide difference in type of character and culture between the inland and maritime states.   The Greek
landsman was courageous and steadfast, but crude, illiterate,
unenterprising, showing sterility of imagination and intellect;
while his brother of the seaboard was active, daring, mercurial, imaginative, open to all the influences of a refining
civilization.[17]   To-day the distribution of the Greeks along
the rim of the Balkan peninsula and Asia Minor, in contrast
to the Turks and Slavs of the interior, is distinctly a peripheral phenomenon.[18]

The rapid inland advance from the coast of oversea
colonists is part of that restless activity which is fostered by
contact with the sea and supported by the command of
abundant resources conferred by maritime superiority.   The
Anglo-Saxon invasion of England, as later the English
colonization of America, seized the rim of the land, and
promptly pushed up the rivers in sea-going boats far into
the interior.   But periphery may give to central region something more than conquerors and colonists.   From its active
markets and cosmopolitan exchanges there steadily filter
into the interior culture and commodities, carried by peaceful
merchant and missionary, who, however, are often only the
harbingers of the conqueror.   The accessibility of the periphery tends to raise it in culture, wealth, density of population, and often in political importance, far in advance of
the center.

Dominant
historical
side.

The maritime periphery of a country receives a variety of
oversea influences, blends and assimilates these to its own
culture, Hellenizes, Americanizes or Japanizes them, as the
case may be, and then passes them on into the interior.   Here
no one foreign influence prevails.   On the land boundaries
the case is different.   Each inland frontier has to reckon with

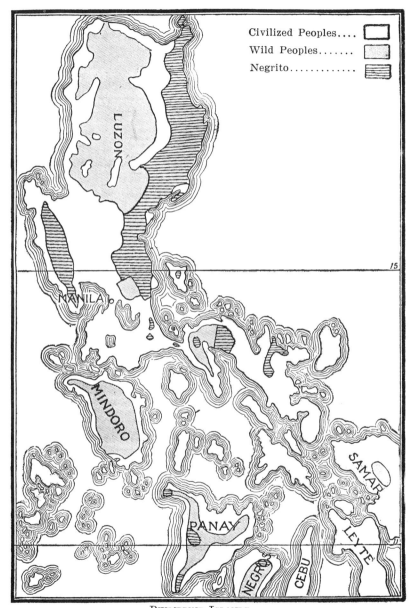

PHILIPPINE ISLANDS.
Distribution of Civilized and Wild Peoples

a different neighbor and its undiluted influence. A predominant central location means a succession of such neighbors, on all sides friction which may polish or rub sore. The distinction between a many-sided and a one-sided historical development depends upon the contact of a people with its neighbors. Consider the multiplicity of influences which have flowed in upon Austria from all sides. But not all such influences are similar in kind or in degree. The most powerful neighbor will chiefly determine on which boundary of a country its dominant historical processes are to work themselves out in a given epoch. Therefore, it is of supreme importance to the character of a people's history on which side this most powerful neighbor is located Russia had for several centuries such a neighbor in the Tartar hordes along its southeastern frontier, and therefore its history received an Asiatic stamp; so, too, did that of Austria and Hungary in the long resistance to Turkish invasion. All three states suffered in consequence a retardation of development on their western sides. After the turmoil on the Asiatic frontier had subsided, the great centers of European culture and commerce in Italy, Germany and the Baltic lands began to assert their powers of attraction. The young Roman Republic drew up its forces to face the threatening power of Carthage in the south, and thereby was forced into rapid maritime development; the Roman Empire faced north to meet the inroads of the barbarians, and thereby was drawn into inland expansion. All these instances show that a vital historical turning-point is reached in the development of every country, when the scene of its great historical happenings shifts from one side to another.

The Mediterranean side of Europe.   In addition to the aggressive neighbor, there is often a more sustained force that may draw the activities of a people toward one or another boundary of their territory. This may be the abundance of land and unexploited resources lying on a colonial frontier and attracting the unemployed energies of the people, such as existed till recently in the United States, [19] and such as is now transferring the most active scenes of Russian history to far-away Siberia. But a stronger attraction is that of a higher civilization and domin-

ant economic interests. So long as the known world was confined to the temperate regions of Europe, Asia and Africa,
together with the tropical districts of the Indian Ocean, the
necessities of trade between Orient and Occident and the
historical prestige of the lands bordering on the Mediterranean placed in this basin the center of gravity of the cultural, commercial and political life of Europe. The continent
was dominated by its Asiatic corner; its every country took on
an historical significance proportionate to its proximity and
accessibility to this center. The Papacy was a Mediterranean
power. The Crusades were Mediterranean wars. Athens,
Rome, Constantinople, Venice, and Genoa held in turn the
focal positions in this Asiatic-European sea; they were on the
sunny side of the continent, while Portugal and England lay
in shadow. Only that portion of Britain facing France felt
the cultural influences of the southern lands. The estuaries
of the Mersey and Clyde were marshy solitudes, echoing to
the cry of the bittern and the ripple of Celtic fishing-boat.

After the year 1492 inaugurated the Atlantic period of Change of
history, the western front of Europe superseded the Medi- historical
terranean side in the historical leadership of the continent. front.
The Breton coast of France waked up, the southern seaboard
dozed. The old centers in the Aegean and Adriatic became
drowsy corners. The busy traffic of the Mediterranean was
transferred to the open ocean, where, from Trafalger to Norway, the western states of Europe held the choice location on
the world's new highway. Liverpool, Plymouth, Glasgow,
Hamburg, Rotterdam, Antwerp, Cherbourg, Lisbon and
Cadiz were shifted from shadowy margin to illuminated center, and became the foci of the new activity. Theirs was a
new continental location, maintaining relations of trade and
colonization with two hemispheres. Their neighbors were
now found on the Atlantic shores of the Americas and the
peripheral lands of Asia. These cities became the exponents
of the intensity with which their respective states exploited
the natural advantages of this location.

The experience of Germany was typical of the change of
front. From the tenth to the middle of the sixteenth century, this heir of the old Roman Empire was drawn toward

Italy by every tie of culture, commerce, and political ideal. This concentration of interest in its southern neighbor made it ignore a fact so important as the maritime development of the Hanse Towns, wherein lay the real promise of its future, the hope of its commercial and colonial expansion. The shifting of its historical center of gravity to the Atlantic seaboard therefore came late, further retarded by lack of national unity and national purposes. But the present wide circle of Germany's transoceanic commerce incident upon its recent industrial development, the phenomenal increase of its merchant marine, the growth of Hamburg and Bremen, the construction of ship canals to that short North Sea coast, and the enormous utilization of Dutch ports for German commerce, all point to the attraction of distant economic interests, even when meagerly supported by colonial possessions.

Location, therefore, while it is the most important single geographic factor, is at the same time the one most subject to the vicissitudes attending the anthropo-geographical evolution of the earth. Its value changes with the transfer of the seats of the higher civilizations from sub-tropical to temperate lands; from the margin of enclosed sea to the hem of the open ocean; from small, naturally defined territories to large, elastic areas; from mere periphery to a combination of periphery and interior, commanding at once the freedom of the sea and the resources of a wide hinterland.

Contrasted historical sides.   Even in Europe, however, where the Atlantic leaning of all the states is so marked as to suggest a certain dependence, the strength of this one-sided attraction is weakened by the complexity and closeness of the vicinal grouping of the several nations. Germany's reliance upon the neighboring grain fields of Russia and Hungary and the leather of the southern steppes counteracts somewhat the far-off magnet of America's wheat and cattle. England experienced a radical change of geographic front with the sailing of the Cabots; but the enormous tonnage entering and passing from the North Sea and Channel ports for her European trade[20] show the attraction of the nearby Continent. Oftentimes we find two sides of a country each playing simultaneously a different, yet an equally important historical part, and thus distributing the historical activities, while diversifying the historical development of the people. The young United States were profoundly influenced as to national ideals and their eventual territorial career by the free, eager life and the untrammeled enterprise of its wilderness frontier beyond the Alleghenies, while through the Atlantic seaboard it was kept in steadying contact with England and the inherited ideals of the race. Russia is subjected to different influences on its various fronts; it is progressive, industrial, socialistic on its European side in Poland; expansive and radical in a different way in colonial Siberia; aggressive in the south, bending its energies toward political expansion along the Mediterranean and Persian Gulf seaboards. In all such countries there is a constant shifting and readjustment of extra-territorial influences.

It is otherwise in states of very simple vicinal grouping, coupled with only a single country or at best two. Spain, from the time Hamilcar Barca made it a colony of ancient Carthage, down to the decline of its Saracen conquerors, was historically linked with Africa. Freeman calls attention to "the general law by which, in almost all periods of history, either the masters of Spain have borne rule in Africa or the masters of Africa have borne rule in Spain." The history of such simply located countries tends to have a correspondingly one-sided character. Portugal's development has been under the exclusive influence of Spain, except for the oversea stimuli brought to it by the Atlantic. England's long southern face close to the French coast had for centuries the effect of interweaving its history with that of its southern neighbor. The conspicuous fact in the foreign history of Japan has been its intimate connection with Korea above all the other states.[21] Egypt, which projects as an alluvial peninsula into an ocean of desert from southwestern Asia, has seen its history, from the time of the Shepherd Kings to that of Napoleon, repeatedly linked with Palestine and Syria. Every Asiatic or European conquest of these two countries has eventually been extended to the valley of the Nile; and Egypt's one great period of ex-

One-sided historical relations.

pansion saw this eastern coast of the Mediterranean as far as the Euphrates united to the dominion of the Pharaohs. Here is a one-sided geographical location in an exaggerated form, emphasized by the physical and political barrenness of the adjacent regions of Africa and the strategic importance of the isthmian district between the Mediterranean and Indian Ocean.

Scattered location due to geographic conditions.

The forms of vicinal location thus far considered presuppose a compact or continuous distribution, such as characterizes the more fertile and populous areas of the earth. Desert regions, whether due to Arctic cold or extreme aridity, distribute their sparse population in small groups at a few favored points, and thus from physical causes give rise to the anthropo-geographical phenomenon of scattered location. Districts of intense cold, which sustain life only in contact with marine supplies of food, necessitate an intermittent distribution along the seaboard, with long, unoccupied stretches between. This is the location we are familiar with among the Eskimo of Greenland and Alaska, among the Norse and Lapps in the rugged Norwegian province of Finmarken, where over two-thirds of the population live by fishing. In the interior districts of this province about Karasjok and Kantokeino, the reindeer Lapps show a corresponding scattered grouping here and there on the inhospitable slopes of the mountains.[22] In that one-half of Switzerland lying above the altitude where agriculture is possible, population is sprinkled at wide intervals over the sterile surface of the highlands.

A somewhat similar scattered location is found in arid deserts, where population is restricted to the oases dropped here and there at wide intervals amid the waste of sand. But unlike those fragments of human life on the frozen outskirts of the habitable world, the oasis states usually constitute links in a chain of connection across the desert between the fertile lands on either side, and therefore form part of a series, in which the members maintain firm and necessary economic relations. Every caravan route across the Sahara is dotted by a series of larger or smaller tribal settlements. Tripoli, Sokna, Murzuk, Bilma and Bornu form one such chain; Algiers, El Golea, Twat, the salt mines of Taudeni,

DISTRIBUTION OF SETTLEMENT IN THE NORWEGIAN
PROVINCE OF FINMARKEN.

Arawan and Timbuctoo, another. Bagdad, Hayil, Boreyda
and Mecca trace the road of pilgrim and merchant starting
from the Moslem land of the Euphrates to the shrine of Mohammed.[23]

Not unlike this serial grouping of oasis states along cara- Island way
van routes through the desert are the island way stations station on
that rise out of the waste of the sea and are connected by the routes.
great maritime routes of trade. Such are the Portuguese
Madeiras, Bissagos, and San Thomé on the line between Lisbon and Portuguese Loanda in West Africa; and their other
series of the Madeiras, Cape Verde, and Fernando, which
facilitated communication with Pernambuco when Brazil was

a Portuguese colony. The classic example of this serial grouping is found in the line of islands, physical or political, which trace England's artery of communication with India— Gibraltar, Malta, Cyprus, Perim, Aden, Sokotra, and Ceylon, besides her dominant position at Suez.

Scattered location of primitive tribes. Quite different from this scattered distribution, due to physical conditions, in an otherwise uninhabited waste is that wide dispersal of a people in small detached groups which is the rule in lower stages of culture, and which bespeaks the necessity of relatively large territorial reserves for the uneconomic method of land utilization characteristic of hunting, fishing, pastoral nomadism, and primitive agriculture. A distribution which claims large areas, without, however, maintaining exclusive possession or complete occupation, indicates among advanced peoples an unfinished process, [24] especially unfinished expansion, such as marked the early French and English colonies in America and the recent Russian occupation of Siberia. Among primitive peoples it is the normal condition, belongs to the stage of civilization, not to any one land or any one race, though it has been called the American form of distribution.

Not only are villages and encampments widely dispersed, but also the tribal territories. The Tupis were found by the Portuguese explorers along the coast of eastern Brazil and in the interior from the mouth of the La Plata to the lower Amazon, while two distant tribes of the Tupis were dropped down amid a prevailing Arawak population far away among the foothills of the Andes in two separate localities on the western Amazon.[25] [See map page 101.] The Athapascans, from their great compact northern area between Hudson Bay, the Saskatchewan River, and the Eskimo shores of the Arctic Ocean sent southward a detached offshoot comprising the Navajos, Apaches and Lipans, who were found along the Rio Grande from its source almost to its mouth; and several smaller fragments westward who were scattered along the Pacific seaboard from Puget Sound to northern California.[26] The Cherokees of the southern Appalachians and the Tuscaroras of eastern North Carolina were detached groups of the Iroquois, who had their chief seat about the lower Great

Lakes and the St. Lawrence. Virginia and North Carolina harbored also several tribes of Sioux,[27] who were also represented in southern Mississippi by the small Biloxi nation, though the chief Sioux area lay between the Arkansas and Saskatchewan rivers. Similarly the Caddoes of Louisiana and eastern Texas had one remote offshoot on the Platte River and another, the Arikaras, on the upper Missouri near its great bend. [See map page 54.] But the territory of the Caddoes, in turn, was sprinkled with Choctaws, who belonged properly east of the Mississippi, but who in 1803 were found scattered in fixed villages or wandering groups near the Bayou Teche, on the Red River, the Washita, and the Arkansas.[28] Their villages were frequently interspersed with others of the Biloxi Sioux.

This fragmentary distribution appears in Africa among people in parallel stages of civilization. Dr. Junker found it as a universal phenomenon in Central Africa along the watershed between the White Nile and the Welle-Congo. Here the territory of the dominant Zandeh harbored a motley collection of shattered tribes, remnants of peoples, and intruding or refugee colonies from neighboring districts.[29] The few weak bonds between people and soil characterizing retarded races are insufficient to secure permanent residence in the face of a diminished game supply, as in the case of the Choctaws above cited, or of political disturbance or oppression, or merely the desire for greater independence, as in that of so many African tribes.

A scattered location results in all stages of civilization when an expanding or intruding people begins to appropriate the territory of a different race. Any long continued infiltration, whether peaceful or aggressive, results in race islands or archipelagoes distributed through a sea of aborigines. Semitic immigration from southern Arabia has in this way striped and polka-dotted the surface of Hamitic Abyssinia.[30] Groups of pure German stock are to-day scattered through the Baltic and Polish provinces of Russia.[31] [See map page 223.] In ancient times the advance guard of Teutonic migration crossed the Rhenish border of Gaul, selected choice sites here and there, after the manner of

Ethnic islands of expansion.

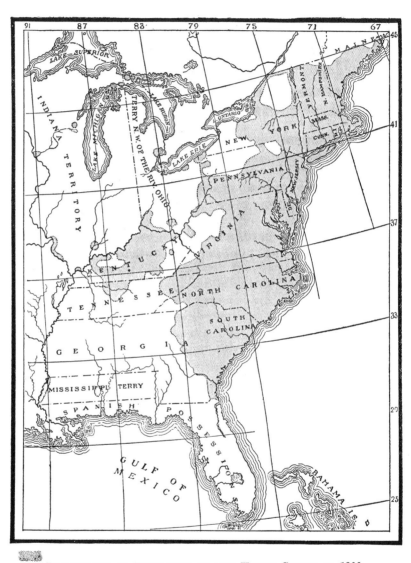

DISTRIBUTION OF POPULATION IN THE UNITED STATES IN 1800.

Ariovistus, and appeared as enclaves in the encompassing Gallic population. While the Anahuac plateau of Mexico formed the center of the Aztec or Nahuatl group of Indians, outlying colonies of this stock occurred among the Maya people of the Tehuantepec region, and in Guatemala and Nicaragua.[32]

Such detached fragments or rather spores of settlement characterize all young geographical boundaries, where ethnic and political frontiers are still in the making. The early French, English, Dutch, and Swedish settlements in America took the form of archipelagoes in a surrounding sea of Indian-owned forest land; and in 1800, beyond the frontier of continuous settlement in the United States long slender peninsulas and remote outlying islands of white occupation indicated American advance at the cost of the native. Similarly the Portuguese, at the end of the sixteenth century, seized and fortified detached points along the coast of East Africa at Sofala, Malindi, Mombassa, Kilwa, Lamu, Zanzibar and Barava, which served as way stations for Portuguese ships bound for India, and were outposts of expansion from their Moçambique territory.[33] The snow-muffled forests of northern Siberia have their solitudes broken at wide intervals by Russian villages, located only along the streams for fishing, gold-washing and trading with the native. These lonely clearings are outposts of the broad band of Muscovite settlement which stretches across southern Siberia from the Ural Mountains to the Angara River.[34] [See map page 103.]

The most exaggerated example of scattered political location existing to-day is found in the bizarre arrangement of European holdings on the west coast of Africa between the Senegal and Congo rivers. Here in each case a handful of governing whites is dropped down in the midst of a dark-skinned population in several districts along the coast. The six detached seaboard colonies of the French run back in the interior into a common French-owned hinterland formed by the Sahara and western Sudan, which since 1894 link the Guinea Coast colonies with French Algeria and Tunis; but the various British holdings have no territorial cohesion at

Political islands of expansion

any point, nor have the Spanish or Portuguese or German. The scattered location of these different European possessions is for the most part the expression of a young colonizing activity, developed in the past fifty years, and signalized by the vigorous intrusion of the French and Germans into the field. To the anthropo-geographer the map of western Africa presents the picture of a political situation wholly immature, even embryonic. The history of similar scattered outposts of political expansion in America, India and South Africa teaches us to look for extensive consolidation.

Ethnic islands of survival.   Race islands occur also when a land is so inundated by a tide of invasion or continuous colonization that the original inhabitants survive only as detached remnants, where protecting natural conditions, such as forests, jungles, mountains or swamps, provide an asylum, or where a sterile soil or rugged plateau has failed to attract the cupidity of the conqueror. The dismembered race, especially one in a lower status of civilization, can be recognized as such islands of survival by their divided distribution in less favored localities, into which they have fled, and in which seldom can they increase and recombine to recover their lost heritage. In Central Africa, between the watersheds of the Nile, Congo and Zambesi, there is scarcely a large native state that does not shelter in its forests scattered groups of dwarf hunter folk variously known as Watwa, Batwa, and Akka.[35]   They serve the agricultural tribes as auxiliaries in war, and trade with them in meat and ivory, but also rob their banana groves and manioc patches. The local dispersion of these pygmies in small isolated groups among stronger peoples points to them as survivals of a once wide-spread aboriginal race, another branch of which, as Schweinfurth suggested, is probably found in the dwarfed Bushmen and Hottentots of South Africa.[36] [See map page 105.]

Similar in distribution and in mode of life are the aborigines of the Philippines, the dwarf Negritos, who are still found inhabiting the forests in various localities. They are dispersed through eight provinces of Luzon and in several other islands, generally in the interior, whither they have been driven by the invading Malays.[37] [See map page 147.] But

the Negritos crop out again in the mountain interior of Formosa and Borneo, in the eastern peninsula of Celebes, and in
various islands of the Malay Archipelago as far east as Ceram
and Flores, amid a prevailing Malay stock. Toward the west
they come to the surface in the central highland of Malacca,
in the Nicobar and Andaman Islands, and in several mountain and jungle districts of India. Here again is the typical
geographic distribution of a moribund aboriginal race, whose
shrivelled patches merely dot the surface of their once wide
territory.[38] The aboriginal Kolarian tribes of India are
found under the names of Bhils, Kols and Santals scattered
about in the fastnesses of the Central Indian jungles, the Vindhyan Range, and in the Rajputana Desert, within the area
covered by Indo-Aryan occupation.[39] [See map page 103.]

Such broad, intermittent dispersal is the anthropological Discontinu-
prototype of the "discontinuous distribution" of biol- ous dis-
ogists. By this they mean that certain types of plants and tribution.
animals occur in widely separated regions, without the presence of any living representatives in the intermediate area.
But they point to the rock records to show that the type once
occupied the whole territory, till extensive elimination occurred, owing to changes in climatic or geologic conditions or
to sharpened competition in the struggle for existence,
with the result that the type survived only in detached localities offering a favorable environment.[40] In animal and
plant life, the ice invasion of the Glacial Age explains most of
these islands of survival; in human life, the invasion of
stronger peoples. The Finnish race, which in the ninth century covered nearly a third of European Russia, has been
shattered by the blows of Slav expansion into numerous fragments which lie scattered about within the old ethnic boundary from the Arctic Ocean to the Don-Volga watershed.[41]
The encroachments of the whites upon the red men of
America early resulted in their geographical dispersion.
The map showing the distribution of population in 1830
reveals large detached areas of Indian occupancy embedded
in the prevailing white territory.[42] The rapid compression of
the tribal lands and the introduction of the reservation system resulted in the present arrangement of yet smaller and

more widely scattered groups. Such islands of survival tend constantly to contract and diminish in number with the growing progress, density, and land hunger of the surrounding race. The Kaffir islands and the Hottentot "locations" in South Africa, large as they now are, will repeat the history of the American Indian lands, a history of gradual shrinkage and disappearance as territorial entities.

Contrasted location.

Every land contains in close juxtaposition areas of sharply contrasted cultural, economic and political development, due to the influence of diverse natural locations emphasizing lines of ethnic cleavage made perhaps by some great historical struggle. In mountainous countries the conquered people withdraw to the less accessible heights and leave the fertile valleys to the victorious intruders. The two races are thus held apart, and the difference in their respective modes of life forced upon them by contrasted geographic conditions tends still farther for a time to accentuate their diversity. The contrasted location of the dislodged Alpine race, surviving in all the mountains and highlands of western Europe over against the Teutonic victors settled in the plains,[43] has its parallel in many parts of Asia and Africa; it is almost always coupled with a corresponding contrast in mode of life, which is at least in part geographically determined. In Algeria, the Arab conquerors, who form the larger part of the population, are found in the plains where they live the life of nomads in their tents; the Berbers, who were the original inhabitants, driven back into the fastnesses of the Atlas ranges, form now an industrious, sedentary farmer class, living in stone houses, raising stock, and tilling their fields as if they were market gardeners.[44] In the Andean states of South America, the eastern slopes of the Cordilleras, which are densely forested owing to their position in the course of the trade-winds, harbor wild, nomadic tribes of hunting and fishing Indians who differ in stock and culture from the Inca Indians settled in the drier Andean basins.[45] [See map page 101.]

Geographical polarity.

Every geographical region of strongly marked character possesses a certain polarity, by reason of which it attracts certain racial or economic elements of population, and

repels others.   The predatory tribes of the desert are constantly reinforced by refugee outlaws from the settled agricultural communities along its borders.[46]   The mountains which
offer a welcome asylum for the persecuted Waldenses have
no lure for the money-making Jew, who is therefore rarely
found there.   The negroes of the United States are more and
more congregating in the Gulf States, making the "Black
Belt" blacker.   The fertile tidewater plains of ante-bellum Virginia and Maryland had a rich, aristocratic white population
of slave-holding planters; the mountain backwoods of the Appalachian ranges, whose conditions of soil and relief were ill
adapted for slave cultivation, had attracted a poorer democratic farmer class, who tilled their small holdings by their
own labor and consequently entertained little sympathy for
the social and economic system of the tidewater country.   This
is the contrast between mountain and plain which is as old
as humanity.   It presented problems to the legislation of
Solon, and caused West Virginia to split off from the mother
State during the Civil War.[47]

Each contrasted district has its own polarity; but with
this it attracts not one but many of the disruptive forces
which are pent up in every people or state.   Certain conditions of climate, soil, and tillable area in the Southern States
of the Union made slave labor remunerative, while opposite
conditions in the North combined eventually to exclude it
thence.   Slave labor in the South brought with it in turn a
whole train of social and economic consequences, notably the
repulsion of foreign white immigration and the development
of shiftless or wasteful industrial methods, which further
sharpened the contrast between the two sections.   The same
contrast occurs in Italian territory between Sicily and Lombardy.   Here location at the two extremities of the peninsula
has involved a striking difference in ethnic infusions in the two
districts, different historical careers owing to different vicinal
grouping, and dissimilar geographic conditions.   These effects
operating together and attracting other minor elements of
divergence, have conspired to emphasize the already strong
contrast between northern and southern Italy.

In geographical location can be read the signs of growth

Geograph-
ical
marks of
growth.

or decay. There are racial and national areas whose form is indicative of development, expansion, while others show the symptoms of decline. The growing people seize all the geographic advantages within their reach, whether lying inside their boundaries or beyond. In the latter case, they promptly extend their frontiers to include the object of their desire, as the young United States did in the case of the Mississippi River and the Gulf coast. European peoples, like the Russians in Asia, all strive to reach the sea; and when they have got there, they proceed to embrace as big a strip of coast as possible. Therefore the whole colonization movement of western and central Europe was in the earlier periods restricted to coasts, although not to such an excessive degree as that of the Phœnicians and Greeks. Their own maritime location had instructed them as to the value of seaboards, and at the same time made this form of expansion the simplest and easiest.

Marks of inland expansion. On the other hand, that growing people which finds its coastward advance blocked, and is therefore restricted to landward expansion, seizes upon every natural feature that will aid its purpose. It utilizes every valley highway and navigable river, as the Russians did in the case of the Dnieper, Don, Volga, Kama and Northern Dwina in their radial expansion from the Muscovite center at Moscow, and as later they used the icy streams of Siberia in their progress toward the Pacific; or as the Americans in their trans-continental advance used the Ohio, Tennessee, the Great Lakes, and the Missouri. They reach out toward every mountain pass leading to some choice ultramontane highway. Bulges or projecting angles of their frontier indicate the path they plan to follow, and always include or aim at some natural feature which will facilitate their territorial growth. The acquisition of the province of Ticino in 1512 gave the Swiss Confederation a foothold upon Lake Maggiore, perhaps the most important waterway of northern Italy, and the possession of the Val Leventina, which now carries the St. Gotthard Railroad down to the plains of the Po. Every bulge of Russia's Asiatic frontier, whether in the Trans-Caucasus toward the Mesopotamian basin and the Persian Gulf, or up the Murghab and Tedjend rivers toward the gates of Herat, is directed at some mountain pass and an outlet seaward beyond.

If this process of growth bring a people to the borders of a desert, there they halt perhaps for a time, but only, as it were, to take breath for a stride across the sand to the nearest oasis. The ancient Egyptians advanced by a chain of oases —Siwa, Angila, Sella and Sokna, across the Libyan Desert to the Syrtis Minor. The Russians in the last twenty-five years have spread across the arid wastes of Turkestan by way of the fertile spots of Khiva, Bukhara and Merv to the irrigated slopes of the Hindu Kush and Tian Shan Mountains. The French extended the boundaries of Algiers southward into the desert to include the caravan routes focusing at the great oases of Twat and Tidekelt, years before their recent appropriation of the western Sahara.

As territorial expansion is the mark of growth, so the sign Marks of of decline is the relinquishment of land that is valuable or decline. necessary to a people's well-being. The gradual retreat of the Tartars and in part also of the Kirghis tribes from their best pasture lands along the Volga into the desert or steppes indicates their decrease of power, just as the withdrawal of the Indians from their hunting grounds in forest and prairie was the beginning of their decay. Bolivia maimed herself for all time when in 1884 she relinquished to Chile her one hundred and eighty miles of coast between the Rio Lao and the twenty-fourth parallel. Her repeated efforts later to recover at least one seaport on the Pacific indicate her own estimate of the loss by which she was limited to an inland location, and deprived of her maritime periphery.[48]

The habits of a people and the consequent demands which Interpretation of they make upon their environment must be taken into account scattered in judging whether or not a restricted geographical location and maris indicative of a retrograde process. The narrow marginal ginal location distribution of the Haida, Tlingit, and Tsimshean Indians on tion. the islands and coastal strips of northwestern America means simply the selection of sites most congenial to those inveterate fisher tribes. The fact that the English in the vicinity of the Newfoundland Banks settled on a narrow rim of coast in order to exploit the fisheries, while the French peasants penetrated into the interior forests and farmlands of Canada, was no sign of territorial decline. English and French were both on the forward march, each in their own way. The scattered peripheral location of the Phœnician trading stations and later of the Greek colonies on the shores of the Mediterranean was the expression of the trading and maritime activity of those two peoples. Centuries later a similar distribution of Arab posts along the coast of East Africa, Madagascar and the western islands of the Sunda Archipelago indicated the great commercial expansion of the Mohammedan traders of Oman and Yemen. The lack came when this distribution, normal as a preliminary form, bore no fruit in the occupation of wide territorial bases. [See map page 251.]

Prevalence of ethnic islands of decline.   In general, however, any piecemeal or marginal location of a people justifies the question as to whether it results from encroachment, dismemberment, and consequently national or racial decline. This inference as a rule strikes the truth. The abundance of such ethnic islands and reefs— some scarcely distinguishable above the flood of the surrounding population—is due to the fact that when the area of distribution of any life form, whether racial or merely animal, is for any cause reduced, it does not merely contract but breaks up into detached fragments. These isolated groups often give the impression of being emigrants from the original home who, in some earlier period of expansion, had occupied this outlying territory. At the dawn of western European history, Gaul was the largest and most compact area of Celtic speech. For this reason it has been regarded as the land whence sprang the Celts of Britain, the Iberian Peninsula, the Alps and northern Italy. Freeman thinks that the Gauls of the Danube and Po valleys were detachments which had been left behind in the great Celtic migration toward the west;[49] but does not consider the possibility of a once far more extensive Celtic area, which, as a matter of fact, once reached eastward to the Weser River and the Sudetes Mountains and was later dismembered.[50] The islands of Celtic speech which now mark the western flank of Great Britain and Ireland are shrunken fragments of a Celtic linguistic area which, as place-names indicate, once comprised the whole country.[51] Similarly, all over Russia Finnic place-names testify to the former occupation of the country by a people now submerged by the immigrant Slavs, except where they emerge in ethnic islands in the far north and about the elbow of the Volga.[52] [See map page 225.] Beyond the compact area of the Melanesian race occupying New Guinea and the islands eastward to the Fiji and Loyalty groups, are found scattered patches of negroid folk far to the westward, relegated to the interiors of islands and peninsulas. The dispersed and fragmentary distribution of this negroid stock has suggested that it formed the older and primitive race of a wide region extending from India to Fiji and possibly even beyond.[53]

Ethnic or political islands of decline can be distinguished from islands of expansion by various marks. When survivals of an inferior people, they are generally characterized by inaccessible or unfavorable geographic location. When remnants of former large colonial possessions of modern civilized nations, they are characterized by good or even excellent location, but lack a big compact territory nearby to which they stand in the relation of outpost. Such are the Portuguese fragments on the west coast of India at Goa, Damaon, and Diu Island, and the Portuguese half of the island of Timor with the islet of Kambing in the East Indies. Such also are the remnants of the French empire in India, founded by the genius of François Dupleix, which are located on the seaboard at Chandarnagar, Carical, Pondicherry, Yanaon and Mahe. They tell the geographer a far different story from that of the small detached French holding of Kwang-chan Bay and Nao-chan Island on the southern coast of China, which are outposts of the vigorous French colony of Tongking.

Contrast between ethnic islands of growth and decline.

The scattered islands of an intrusive people, bent upon conquest or colonization, are distinguished by a choice of sites favorable to growth and consolidation, and by the rapid extension of their boundaries until that consolidation is achieved; while the people themselves give signs of the rapid differentiation incident to adaptation to a new environment.

166   GEOGRAPHICAL LOCATION

NOTES TO CHAPTER V

1. Anatole Leroy-Beaulieu, The Empire of the Tsars, Vol. I, pp. 98-101. New York, 1893.
2. George Adam Smith, Historical Geography of the Holy Land, pp. 5-8, 12, 13, 19-28, 37. New York, 1897.
3. W. Z. Ripley, Races of Europe, pp. 272-273. New York, 1899.
4. Monette, History of the Valley of the Mississippi, Vol. II, chap. I. 1846.
5. W. Z. Ripley, Races of Europe, pp. 336, 334. Map. p. 53. New York, 1899.
6. J. Partsch, Central Europe, p. 137. London, 1903.
7. Eleventh Census, Report for Alaska, pp. 66, 67, 70. Washington, 1893.
8. Livingstone, Travels in South Africa, p. 56. New York, 1858.
9. Anatole Leroy-Beaulieu, The Empire of the Tsars, Vol I, pp. 36, 108. New York, 1893.
10. Boyd Alexander, From the Niger to the Nile, Vol. II, pp. 127-130, 170. London, 1907.
11. James Bryce, Impressions of South Africa, pp. 147, 150, 170-173. New York, 1897.
12. Alexander P. Engelhardt, A Russian Province of the North, pp. 135, 140-147, 165, 170. Translated from the Russian. London, 1899.
13. For full and able discussion, see H. J. Mackinder, The Geographical Pivot of History, in the *Geographical Journal*, April, 1904. London.
14. The Anglo-Russian Agreement, with map, in *The Independent*, October, 10, 1907.
15. Spencer and Gillen, The Northern Tribes of Central Australia, p. xii. London, 1904.
16. Census of the Philippine Islands, Vol. I, p. 526; Vol. II, pp. 34-35, 50-52 and map. Washington, 1903.
17. Grote, History of Greece, Vol. II, pp. 225-226. New York, 1859.
18. W. Z. Ripley, The Races of Europe, pp. 402-410, map. New York, 1899.
19. Frederick J. Turner, The Significance of the Frontier in American History, in the *Annual Report of the American Historical Association* for 1893, pp. 199-227. Washington, 1894.
20. Hugh R. Mill, International Geography, pp. 150-152. New York, 1902.
21. W. E. Griffis, The Mikado's Empire, Vol. I, pp. 75, 83. New York, 1903. Henry Dyer, Dai Nippon, pp. 59, 69. New York, 1904.
22. Norway, Official Publication, pp. 4, 83, 99, and map. Christiania, 1900.
23. D. G. Hogarth, The Nearer East, pp. 221-224, map. London, 1902.
24. Heinrich von Treitschke, *Politik*, Vol. I, p. 224. Leipzig, 1897.
25. Helmolt, History of the World, Vol. I, pp. 189-191. New York, 1902-1906.
26. Eleventh Census, *Report on the Indians*, pp. 36-37. Washington, 1894.
27. John Fiske, Old Virginia and her Neighbors, Vol. II, p. 299. Boston, 1897.

28. Eleventh Census, *Report on the Indians*, pp. 30-31. Washington, 1894.

29. Dr. William Junker, Travels in Africa, 1882-1886, pp. 30, 31, 34, 37, 44, 50-54, 64, 94-95, 140, 145-148. London, 1892.

30. Ratzel, History of Mankind, Vol. III, pp. 193-195. London, 1896-1898.

31. Anatole Leroy-Beaulieu, Empire of the Tsars, Vol. I, pp. 124-129. New York, 1893.

32. D. G. Brinton, The American Race, p. 266. Philadelphia, 1901.

33. Helmolt, History of the World, Vol. III, pp. 484, 485. New York, 1902-06.

34. Nordenskiold, The Voyage of the Vega, p. 291. New York, 1882.

35. H. M. Stanley, Through the Dark Continent, Vol. II, pp. 100-103, 218. In Darkest Africa, Vol. I, pp. 208, 261, 374-375; Vol. II, pp. 40-44.

36. Georg Schweinfurth, The Heart of Africa, Vol. II, chap. XI, 3rd edition, London.

37. Census of the Philippine Islands, Vol. I, pp. 411, 436, 532, 533. Washington, 1903.

38. Quatrefages, The Pygmies, pp. 24-51. New York, 1895.

39. Sir T. H. Holdich, India, pp. 202-203, map. London, 1905.

40. Darwin, Origin of Species, Vol. II, chap. XII. New York, 1895.

41. Anatole Leroy-Beaulieu, The Empire of the Tsars, Vol. I, pp. 66-70, maps facing pp. 64 and 80. New York, 1893.

42. Eleventh Census of the United States, *Report on Population*, Part I, map p. 23. Washington, 1894.

43. W. Z. Ripley, Races of Europe, Chapters 7, 8, 11. New York, 1899.

44. H. R. Mill, International Geography, p. 910. New York, 1902.

45. *Ibid.*, pp. 832, 836.

46. Ratzel, History of Mankind, Vol. III, pp. 175, 257. London, 1896-1898.

47. E. C. Semple, American History and its Geographic Conditions, pp. 280-287. Boston, 1903.

48. C. E. Akers, History of South America, 1854-1894, pp. 501-502, 556-562. New York, 1904.

49. E. A. Freeman, Historical Geography of Europe, p. 14. London, 1882.

50. Helmolt, History of the World, Vol. VI, pp. 125-132, map. New York, 1902-1906. Ripley, Races of Europe, pp. 274, 297, 308, 472-473. New York, 1899.

51. H. J. Mackinder, Britain and the British Seas, pp. 183-191. London, 1904.

52. W. Z. Ripley, Races of Europe, pp. 26, 353, 361-365. Map. New York, 1899.

53. Ratzel, History of Mankind, Vol. I, 214-218. London, 1896-1898.

CHAPTER VI

GEOGRAPHICAL AREA

The size of the earth.

EVERY consideration of geographical area must take as its starting point the 199,000,000 square miles (510,000,000 square kilometers) of the earth's surface. Though some 8,000,000 square miles (21,000,000 square kilometers) about the poles remain unexplored, and only the twenty-eight per cent. of the total constituting the land area is the actual habitat of man, still the earth as a whole is his planet. Its surface fixes the limits of his* possible dwelling place, the range of his voyages and migrations, the distribution of animals and plants on which he must depend. These conditions he has shared with all forms of life from the amoeba to the civilized nation. The earth's superficial area is the primal and immutable condition of earth-born, earth-bound man; it is the common soil whence is sprung our common humanity. Nations belong to countries and races to continents, but humanity belongs to the whole world. Naught but the united forces of the whole earth could have produced this single species of a single genus which we call Man.

Relation of area to life.

The relation of life to the earth's area is a fundamental question of bio-geography. The amount of that area available for terrestrial life, the proportion of land and water, the reduction or enlargement of the available surface by the operation of great cosmic forces, all enter into this problem, which changes from one geologic period to another. The present limited plant life of the Arctic regions is the impoverished successor of a vegetation abundant enough at the eighty-third parallel to produce coal. That was in the Genial Period, when the northern hemisphere with its broad land-masses presented a far larger area for the support of life than to-day. Then the Glacial Period spread an ice-sheet from the North Pole to approximately the fiftieth parallel, forced back life to the lower latitudes, and confined the bio-sphere to the smaller land-masses of the southern hemisphere and a girdle north of the equator. The sum total of life on the globe was greatly reduced at the height of glaciation, and since the retreat of the ice has probably never regained the abundance of the Middle Tertiary; so that our period is probably one of relative impoverishment and faulty adjustment both of life to life and of life to physical environment.[1] The continent of North America contained a small vital area during the Later Cretaceous Period, when a notable encroachment of the sea submerged the Atlantic coastal plain, large sections of the Pacific coast, the Great Plains, Texas and the adjacent Gulf plain up the Mississippi Valley to the mouth of the Ohio.[2]

The task of estimating the area supporting terrestrial life which the earth presented at any given time is an important one, not only because the amount of life depends upon this area, but because every increase of available area tends to multiply conditions favorable to variation. Darwin shows that largeness of area, more than anything else, affords the best conditions for rapid and improved variation through natural selection; because a large area supports a larger number of individuals in whom chance variations, advantageous in the struggle for existence, appear oftener than in a small group. This position is maintained also by the most recent evolutionists.[3] *Area and differentiation.*

On purely geographical grounds, also, a large area stimulates differentiation by presenting a greater diversity of natural conditions, each of which tends to produce its appropriate species or variety.[4] Consider the different environments found in a vast and varied continent like Eurasia, which extends from the equator far beyond the Arctic Circle, as compared with a small land-mass like Australia, relatively monotonous in its geographic conditions; and observe how much farther evolution has progressed in the one than in the other, in point of animal forms, races and civilization. If we hold with Moritz Wagner and others that isolation in naturally defined regions, alternating with periods of migration, offers the necessary condition for the rapid evolution of type forms, and thus go farther than Darwin, who regards isolation merely as a fortunate contributory circumstance, we find that for the evolution of mankind it is large areas like Eurasia which afford the greatest number and variety of these naturally segregated habitats, and at the same time the best opportunity for vast historical movements.

The struggle for space.
Evolution needs room but finds the earth's surface limited. Everywhere old and new forms of life live side by side in deadly competition; but the later improved variety multiplies and spreads at the cost of less favored types. The struggle for existence means a struggle for space.[5] This is true of man and the lower animals. A superior people, invading the territory of its weaker savage neighbors, robs them of their land, forces them back into corners too small for their support, and continues to encroach even upon this meager possession, till the weaker finally loses the last remnant of its domain, is literally crowded off the earth, becomes extinct as the Tasmanians and so many Indian tribes have done.[6] The superiority of such expansionists consists primarily in their greater ability to appropriate, thoroughly utilize and populate a territory. Hence this is the faculty by which they hasten the extinction of the weaker; and since this superiority is peculiar to the higher stages of civilization, the higher stages inevitably supplant the lower.

Area an index of social and political development.
The successive stages of social development—savage, pastoral nomadic, agricultural, and industrial—represent increasing density of population, increasing numerical strength of the social group, and finally increasing geographical area, resulting in a vastly enlarged social group or state. Increase in the population of a given land is accompanied by a decrease in the share which each individual can claim as his own. This progressive readjustment to a smaller proportion of land brings in its train the evolution of all economic and social processes, reacting again favorably on density of population and resulting eventually in the greatly increased social group and enlarged territory of the modern civilized state. Hence we may lay down the rule that change in areal relations, both of the individual to his decreasing quota of land, and of the state to its increasing quota of the earth's

surface is an important index of social and political evolution. Therefore the rise and decline not only of peoples but of whole civilizations have depended upon their relations to area. Therefore problems of area, such as the expansion of a small territory, the economic and political mastery of a large one, dominate all history.

Humanity's area of distribution and historical movement **The Oikou-** we call the Oikoumene. It forms a girdle around the earth **mene.** between the two polar regions, and embraces the Tropics, the Temperate Zones, and a part of the North Frigid, in all, five-sixths of the earth's surface. This area of distribution is unusually large. Few other living species so nearly permeate the whole vital area, and many of these have reached their wide expansion only in the company of man. Only about 49,000,000 square miles (125,000,000 square kilometers) of the Oikoumene is land and therefore constitutes properly the habitat of man. But just as we cannot understand a nation from the study of its own country alone, but must take into consideration the wider area of its spreading activities, so we cannot understand mankind without including in his world not only his habitat but also the vastly larger sphere of his activities, which is almost identical with the earth itself. The most progressive peoples to-day find their scientific, economic, religious and political interests embracing the earth.

Mankind has in common with all other forms of life the **Unity** tendency toward expansion. The more adaptable and mobile **of the** an organism is, the wider the distribution which it attains **human** and the greater the rapidity with which it displaces its weaker **species in** kin. In the most favored cases it embraces the whole vital **relation to** area of the earth, leaving no space free for the development **the earth.** of diversity of forms, and itself showing everywhere only superficial distinctions. Mankind has achieved such wide distribution. Before his persistent intrusions and his mobility, the earth has no longer any really segregated districts where a strongly divergent type of the man animal might develop. Hence mankind shows only superficial distinctions of hair, color, head-form and stature between its different groups. It has got beyond the point of forming species, and is restricted to the slighter variations of races. Even these are few in comparison with the area of the earth's surface, and their list tends to decrease. The Guanches and Tasmanians have vanished, the Australians are on the road to extinction; and when they shall have disappeared, there will be one variety the less in humanity. So the process of assimilation advances, here by the simple elimination of weaker divergent types of men, there by amalgamation and absorption into the stock of the stronger.

This unity of the human species has been achieved in spite of the fact that, owing to the three-fold predominance of the water surface of the globe, the land surface appears as detached fragments which rise as islands from the surrounding ocean. Among these fragments we have every gradation in size, from the continuous continental mass of Eurasia-Africa with its 31,000,000 square miles, the Americas with 15,000,000, Australia with nearly 3,000,000, Madagascar with 230,000, and New Zealand with 104,000, down to Guam with its 199 square miles, Ascension with 58, Tristan da Cunha with 45, and the rocky islet of Helgoland with its scant 150 acres. All these down to the smallest constitute separate vital districts.

Isolation and differentiation.

Small, naturally defined areas, whether their boundaries are drawn by mountains, sea, or by both, always harbor small but markedly individual peoples, as also peculiar or endemic animal forms, whose differentiation varies with the degree of isolation. Such peoples can be found over and over again in islands, peninsulas, confined mountain valleys, or desert-rimmed oases. The cause lies in the barriers to expansion and to accessions of population from without which confront such peoples on every side. Broad, uniform continental areas, on the other hand, where nature has erected no such obstacles are the habitats of wide-spread peoples, monotonous in type. The long stretch of coastal lowlands encircling the Arctic Ocean and running back into the wide plains of North America and Eurasia show a remarkable uniformity of animal and plant forms[7] and a striking similarity of race through the Lapps, the Samoyedes of northern Russia, the various Mongolian tribes of Arctic Siberia to Bering Strait, and the Eskimo, that curiously transitional race, formerly classified as Mongolian and more recently as a divergent Indian stock; for the Eskimos are similar to the Siberians in stature, features, coloring, mode of life, in everything but head-form, though even the cephalic indices approach on the opposite shores of Bering Sea.[8] Where geography draws no dividing line, ethnology finds it difficult to do so. Where the continental land-masses converge is found similarity or even identity of race, easy gradations from one type to another; where they diverge most widely in the peninsular extremities of South America, South Africa and Australia, they show the greatest dissimilarity in their native races, and a corresponding diversity in their animal life.[9] Geographical proximity combined with accessibility results in similarity of human and animal occupants, while a corresponding dissimilarity is the attendant of remoteness or of segregation. Therefore, despite the distribution of mankind over the total habitable area of the earth, his penetration into its detached regions and hidden corners has maintained such variations as still exist in the human family.

If the distribution of the several races be examined in the light of this conclusion, it becomes apparent that the races who have succeeded in appropriating only limited portions of the earth's surface, though each may be a marked variant of the human family, are characterized by few inner diversities, either of physical features or culture. Their subdivisions feel only in a slight degree the differentiating effects of geographic remoteness, which in a small area operates with weakened force; and they enjoy few of those diversities of environment which stimulate variation. They form close and distinct ethnic unities also because their scant numbers restrict the appearance of variations. The habitat of the negro race in Africa south of the Sahara, relatively small, limited in its zonal location almost wholly to the Tropics, poorly diversified both in relief and contour, has produced only a retarded and monotonous social development based upon tropical agriculture or a low type of pastoral life. The still smaller, still less varied habitat of the Australian race, again tropical or sub-tropical in location, has

Monotonous race type of small area.

produced over its whole extent only one grade of civilization and that the lowest, one physical, mental and moral type.[10]

Wide race distribution and inner diversities. The Mongoloid area of distribution, on the other hand, is so large that it necessarily includes a great range of climates and variety of geographic conditions. [Maps pages 103 and 225.] Representatives of this race, reflecting their diversified habitats, show many ethnic differentiations. They reveal also every stage and phase of cultural development from the industrialism of Japan, with its artistic and literary concomitants, to the savage economy and retarded intellectual life of the Chukches fisher tribes or the Giljak hunters of Sakhalin. The white race, identified primarily with Europe, that choice and diversified continent, comprised also a large area of southwestern Asia and the northern third of Africa. It thus extended from the Arctic Circle well within the Tropics. Its area included every variety of geographic condition and originally every degree of cultural development; but the rapid expansion in recent centuries of the most advanced peoples of this race has made them the apostles of civilization to the whole world. It has also given them, through the occupation of Australia and the Americas, the widest distribution and the most varied habitats. As agents of the modern historical movement, however, they are subjected to all its assimilating effects, which tend to counteract the diversities born of geographic segregation, and to raise all branches of the white race to one superior cosmopolitan type. On the other hand, the vast international division of labor and specialization of production, geographically based and entailed by advancing economic development, besides the differences of traditions and ideals reaching far back into an historic past and rooted in the land, will serve to maintain many subtle inner differences between even the most progressive nations.

Area and language. Hence the wide area which Darwin found to be most favorable to improved variation and rapid evolution in animals, operates to the same end in human development, and its influence becomes a law of anthropo-geography. It permeates the higher aspects of life. The wide, varied area occupied by the Germanic tribes of Europe permitted the evolution of the many dialects which finally made the richness of modern German speech. English has gained in vocabulary and idiom with every expansion of its area. New territories mean to a people new pursuits, new relations, new wants; and all these become reflected in their speech. Languages, like peoples, cease to grow with national stagnation.[11] To such stagnation movement or expansion is the surest antidote. America will in time make its contribution to the English tongue. The rich crop of slang that springs up on the frontier is not wholly to be deplored. The crudeness and vigor of cowboy speech are marks of youth: they are also promises of growth. Language can not live by dictionary alone. It tends to form new variants with every change of habitat. The French of the Canadian *habitant* has absorbed Indian and English words, and adapted old terms to new uses;[12] but it is otherwise a survival of seventeenth century French. Boer speech in South Africa shows the same thing—absorption of new Kaffir and English words, coupled with marks of retardation due to isolation. Religion in the same way gains by wide dispersal. Christianity is one thing in St. Petersburg, another among the Copts of Cairo, another in Rome, another in London, and yet another in Boston. Buddhism takes on a different color in Ceylon, Tibet, China and Japan. In religion as in other phases of human development, differentiation must mean eventual enrichment, a larger content of the religious idea, to which each faith makes its contribution.

The larger the area occupied by a race or people, other geographic conditions being equal, the surer the guarantee of their permanence, and the less the chance of their repression or annihilation. A broad geographic base means generally abundant command of the resources of life and growth. Though for a growing people of wide possessions, like the Russians, the significance of the land may not be obvious, it becomes apparent enough in national decline and decay; for these even in their incipiency betray themselves in a loss of territory. A people which, voluntarily or otherwise, renounces its hold upon its land is on the downward path. Nothing else could show so plainly the national

Large area a guarantee of racial or national permanence.

vitality of Japan as her tenacious purpose to get back Port Arthur taken from her by the Shimonoseki treaty in 1895. A people may decrease in numbers without serious consequences if it still retains its land; for herein lies its resources by which it may again hope to grow. The recurring loss of millions of lives in China from the wide-sweeping floods of the Hoangho is a passing episode, forgotten as soon as the mighty stream is re-embanked and the flooded plains reclaimed. The Civil War in the United States involved a temporary diminution of population and check to progress, but no lasting national weakness because no loss of territory. But the expulsion of the American Indians from their well-stocked hunting grounds in the Mississippi Valley and Atlantic plain to more restricted and barren lands in the far West, and the withdrawal of the Australian natives from the fertile coasts to the desert interior have meant racial renunciation of the sources of life.

Hence a people who are conquered and dislodged from their territory, as were the ancient Britons by the Saxons, the Slavs from the land between the Elbe and the Niemen by the mediæval Germans, and the Kaffirs in South Africa by the Dutch and English, the Ainos from Hondo by the Japanese, and the whole original Alpine race by the later coming Teutons from the fertile valleys and plains into the more barren highlands of western Europe, have little or no chance of regaining their own. When conquest results not in dislodgement, but only in the subjection of an undisturbed native population to a new ruling class, the vanquished retain their hold, only slightly impaired, perhaps, upon their strength-giving fields, recover themselves, and sooner or later conquer their conquerors either by absorption or revolution. This was the history of ancient Egypt with its Shepherd Kings, of England with its Norman lords, of Mexico and Peru with their Spanish victors.

Weakness of small states.

A large area throws around all the life forms which it supports the protection of its mere distances, which facilitate defense in competition with other forms, render attack difficult, and afford room for retreat under pursuit. On the other hand, the small area is easily compassed by the invaders, and its inhabitants soon brought to bay. Since there is a general correspondence between size of area and number of inhabitants, where physical conditions and economic development are similar, a small area involves a further handicap of numerical weakness of population. Greece has always suffered from the small size of the peninsula and the further political dismemberment entailed by its geographic subdivisions. Despite superior civilization and national heroism, it has fallen a victim to almost every invader. Belgium, Holland, Switzerland exist as distinct nations only on sufferance. Finland's history since 1900 shows that the day for the national existence of small peoples is passing.[13] The fragmentary political geography of the Danube basin gives the geographer the impression of an artist's crayon studies of details, destined later to be incorporated in a finished picture. Their small areas promise short-lived autonomy. The recent absorption of Bosnia and Herzegovina by Austria indicates the destiny of these Danubian states as fixed by the law of increasing territorial aggregates.

What is true of states is true also of peoples. The extinction of the retarded "provisional peoples" of the earth progresses more rapidly in small groups than in large, and in small islands more quickly than in continental areas. Of the twenty-one Indian stocks or families which have died out in the United States, fifteen belonged to the small bands once found in the Pacific coast states, and four more were similar fragments found on the lower Mississippi and its bayous.[14] [See map page 54.] The native Gaunches of Teneriffe Island disappeared long ago. The last Tasmanian died in 1876. New Zealand, whose area is four times that of Tasmania, and therefore gives some respite before the encroachments of the whites, still harbors 47,835 Maoris, or little over one-third the native population of the island in 1840.[15] But these compete for the land with nearly one million English colonists, and in the limited area of the islands they will eventually find no place of retreat before the relentless white advance.

To the Australians, on the other hand, much inferior to the Maoris, the larger area of their continent affords exten-

Protection of large area to primitive peoples.

sive deserts and steppes into which the natives have withdrawn and whither the whites do not care to follow. Hence mere area, robbed of every other favorable geographical circumstance, has contributed to the survival of the 230,000 natives in Australia. Similarly the Arawaks were early wiped out on the island of Cuba and the Caribs on San Domingo and the smaller Antilles by the truculent methods of the Spanish conquerors, while both stocks survive on the continent of South America. Even the truculent methods of the Spanish conquerors could make little impression upon the relatively massive populations of Mexico and Peru, whose survival and latter-day recovery of independence can be ascribed largely though not solely to their ample territorial base. So the vast area of the United States and Canada has afforded a hinterland of asylum to the retreating Indians, whose moribund condition, especially in the United States, is betrayed by their scattered distribution in small, unfavorable localities. On the other hand, the vast extent of Arctic and sub-Arctic Canada, combined with the adverse climatic conditions of the region, will guarantee the northern Indians a longer survival. In Tierra del Fuego, the encroachments of sheep-farmers and gold-miners from Patagonia twenty years ago, by fencing off the land and killing off the wild guanaco, threatened the existence of this animal and of the Onas natives of the island. These, soon brought to bay in that natural enclosure, attacked the farmers, whose reprisals between 1890 and 1900 reduced the number of the Onas from 2,000 to 800 souls.[16]

Contrast of large and small areas in bio-geography. The same law holds good in bio-geography; here, too, area gives strength and a small territorial foothold means weakness. The native flora and fauna of New Zealand seem involved in the same process of extinction as the native race. The Maoris themselves have observed this fact and applied the principle to their own obvious fate. They have seen hardy imported English grasses offering deadly competition to the indigenous vegetation; the Norway rat, entering by European ships, extirpating the native variety; the European house fly, purposely imported and distributed to destroy the noxious indigenous species.[17] The same unequal combat between imported plants and animals, equipped by the fierce Iliads of continental areas, and the local flora and fauna has taken place on the little island of St. Helena, to the threatened destruction of the native forms.[18]

The preponderant migration of animals from the northern to the southern hemisphere is attributed by Darwin to the greater extent of land in the north, whereby the northern types have existed in greater numbers and have been so perfected through natural selection and competition, that they have surpassed the southern forms in dominating power and therefore have encroached successfully.[19] Also the races and nations of the northern continents have seriously invaded the southern land-masses and are still expanding. It is the largest continent, Eurasia, which has been the chief center of dispersal.

The Temperate Zone of North America will always harbor a more powerful people than the corresponding zone of South America, because the latter continent begins to contract and tapers off to a point where the other at the northern Tropic begins to spread out. Therefore North America possesses more abundantly all the advantages accruing to a continent from a location in the Temperate Zone. The wide basis of the North Slavs in Russia and Siberia has given them a natural leadership in the whole Slav family, just as the broad unbroken area of ever expanding Prussia gave that state the ascendency in the German Empire over the geographically partitioned and politically dismembered surface of southern Germany. English domination of the United Kingdom is based not only upon race, location, geographical features and resources, but also on the larger size of England. So in the United States, abolitionist statesmen adopted the most effective means of fighting slavery when they limited its area by law, while permitting free states to go on multiplying in the new territory of the vast Northwest.

Political domination of large areas.

In a peninsula political ascendency often falls to the broad base connecting it with the continent, because this part alone has the area to support a large population, and moreover commands a large hinterland, whence it continually draws new and invigorating blood. The geographical basis of the Aryan and later the Mongol supremacy in India was the wide zone of lowlands between the Indus and the Brahmaputra. [See map page 103.] The only ancient Greek state ever able to dominate the Balkan Peninsula was non-Hellenic Macedonia, after it had extended its boundaries to the Euxine and the Adriatic. To-day a much larger area in this same peninsular base harbors the widespread southern Slavs, who numerically and economically far outweigh Albanians and Greeks, and who could with ease achieve political domination over the small Turkish minority, were it not for the European fear of a Slavic Bosporus, and its union with Russia. The Cisalpine Gauls of the wide Po basin repeatedly threatened the existence of the smaller but more civilized Etruscan and Latin tribes. The latter, maturing their civilization under the concentrating influences of a limited area, at last dominated the larger Celtic district to the north. But in the nineteenth century this district took the lead in the movement for a United Italy, and now exercises the strong influence in Italian affairs which belongs to it by reason of its superior area, location, and more vigorous race. [See map of Italy's population, Chap. XVI.]

The broad territorial base of the Anglo-Saxon race, Slavs, Germans and Chinese promises a long ethnic life, whereas the narrow foothold of the Danes, Dutch, Greeks, and the Turks in Europe carries with it the persistent risk of conquest and absorption by a larger neighbor. Such a fate repeatedly threatens these people, but has thus far been warded off, now by the protection of an isolating environment, now by the diplomatic intervention of some not disinterested power. The scattered fragments of Osman stock in European Turkey, which constitute only about ten per cent. of the total population, and are almost lost in the surrounding mass of Slavs and Greeks, provide a poor guarantee for the duration of the race and their empire on European soil. On the other hand, the Osmani who are compactly spread over the whole interior of Asia Minor have a better prospect of national survival.

Area and literature. An important factor in the preservation of national consciousness and the spread of national influence is always a national language and literature. This principle is recognized by the government of the Czar in its Russification of Finland,[20] Poland, and the German centers in the Baltic provinces, when it substitutes Russian for the local language in education, law courts and all public offices, and restricts the publication of local literature. The survival of a language and its literature is intimately connected with area and the population which that area can support. The extinction of small, weak peoples has its counterpart in the gradual elimination of dialects and languages having restricted territorial sway, whose fate is foreshadowed by the unequal competition of their literatures with those of numerically stronger peoples. An author writing in a language like the Danish, intelligible to only a small public, can expect only small returns for his labor in either influence, fame, or fortune. The return may be so small that it is prohibitive. Hence we find the Danish Hans Christian Andersen and the Norwegian Ibsen writing in German, as do also many Scandinavian scientists. Georg Brandes abandons his native Danish and seeks a larger public by making English the language of his books. The incentive to follow a literary career, especially if it includes making a living, is relatively weak among a people of only two or three millions, but gains enormously among large and cultivated peoples, like the seventy million German-speaking folk of Europe, or the one hundred and thirty millions of English speech scattered over the world. The common literature which represents the response to this incentive forms a bond of union among the various branches of these peoples, and may be eventually productive of political results.

Growth has been the law of human societies since the birth of man's gregarious instinct. It has manifested itself in the formation of ever larger social groups, appropriating ever larger areas. It has registered itself geographically in the protrusion of ethnic boundaries, economically in more intensive utilization of the land, socially in increasing density of population, and politically in the formation of ever larger national territorial aggregates. The lowest stages of culture reveal small tribes, growing very slowly or at times not at all, disseminated over areas small in themselves but large for

Small geographic base of primitive societies.

the number of their inhabitants, hence sparsely populated. The size of these primitive holdings depends upon the natural food supply yielded by the region. They assume wide dimensions but support groups of only a few families on the chill rocky coasts of Tierra del Fuego or the sterile plains of central Australia; and they contract to smaller areas dotted with fairly populous villages in the fertile districts of the middle Congo or bordering the rich coast fishing grounds of southern Alaska and British Columbia. But always land is abundant, and is drawn upon in widening circles when the food supply becomes inadequate or precarious.

Influence of small confined areas. Where nature presents barriers to far-ranging food-quests, man is forced to advance from the natural to the artificial basis of subsistence; he leaves the chase for the sedentary life of agriculture. Extensive activities are replaced by intensive ones, wide dispersal of tribal energies by concentration. The extensive forests and grassy plains of the Americas supported abundant animal life and therefore afforded conditions for the long survival of the hunting tribes; nature put no pressure upon man to coerce him to progress, except in the small mountain-walled valleys of Peru and Mexico, and in the restricted districts of isthmian Central America. Here game was soon exhausted. Agriculture became an increasing source of subsistence and was forced by limited area out of its migratory or *essartage* stage of development into the sedentary. As fields become fixed in such enclosed areas, so do the cultivators. Here first population becomes relatively dense, and thereby necessitates more elaborate social and political organization in order to prevent inner friction.

The geographically enclosed district has the further advantage that its inhabitants soon come to know it out to its boundaries, understand its possibilities, exploit to the utmost its resources, and because of the closeness of their relationship to it and to each other come to develop a conscious national spirit. The population, since it cannot easily spread beyond the nature-set limits, increases in density. The members of the compact society react constantly upon one another and exchange the elements of civilization. Thus the small territory is characterized by the early maturity of a highly individualized civilization, which then, with inherent power of expansion, proceeds to overleap its narrow borders and conquer for itself a wide sphere of influence. Hand in hand with this process goes political concentration, which aids the subsequent expansion. Therefore islands, oases, slender coastal strips and mountain valleys repeatedly show us small peoples who, in their seclusion, have developed a tribal or national consciousness akin in its intensity to clan feeling. This national feeling is conspicuous in the English, Japanese, Swiss and Dutch, as it was in the ancient city-states of Greece. The accompanying civilization, once brought to maturity in its narrow breeding place, spreads under favorable geographic conditions over a much larger space, which the accumulated race energy takes for its field of activity. The flower which thus early blooms may soon fade and decay; nevertheless the geographically evolved national consciousness persists and retains a certain power of renewal. This has been demonstrated in the Italians and modern Greeks, in the Danes and the Icelanders. In the Jews it has resisted exile from their native land, complete political dissolution, and dispersal over the habitable world. Long and often as Italy had to submit to foreign dominion, the idea of the national unity of the peninsula was never lost.

In vast unobstructed territories, on the other hand, the evil of wide, sparse dispersal is checked only by natural increase of population and the impinging of one growing people upon another, which restricts the territory of either. When the boundary waste between the small scattered tribal groups has been occupied, encroachment from the side of the stronger follows; then comes war, incorporation of territory, amalgamation of race and coalescence, or the extinction of the weaker. The larger people, commanding its larger area, expands numerically and territorially, and continues to throw out wider frontiers, till it meets insurmountable natural obstacles or the confines of a people strong as itself. After a pause, during which the existing area is outgrown and population begins to press harder upon the limits of subsistence, the weight of a nation is thrown against the barrier, be it physical or political. In consequence, the old boundaries are

The process of territorial growth.

enlarged, either by successful encroachment upon a neighbor, or, in case of defeat, by incorporation in the antagonist's territory. But even defeat brings participation in a larger geographic base, wider coöperation, a greater sum total of common national interests, and especially the protection of the larger social group. The Transvaal and the Orange Free State find compensation for the loss of independence by their incorporation in the British Empire, even if gradual absorption be the destiny of the Boer stock.

Area and growth. Of adjacent areas equally advanced in civilization and in density of population but of unequal size, the larger must dominate because its people have the resistance and aggressive force inherent in the larger mass. This is the explanation of the absorption of so many colonies and conquerors by the native races, when no great cultural abyss or race antagonism separates the two. The long rule of the Scandinavians in the Hebrides ended in their absorption by the local Gaelic stock, simply because their settlements were too small and the number of their women too few. The lowlands on the eastern coasts of Scotland accommodated larger bands of Norse, who even to-day can be distinguished from the neighboring Scotch of the Highlands; but on the rugged western coast, where only small and widely separated deltas at the heads of the fiords offered a narrow foothold to the invaders, their scattered ethnic islands were soon inundated by the contiguous population.[21] The Teutonic elements, both English and Norwegian, which for centuries filtered into Ireland, have been swallowed up in the native Celtic stock, except where religious antagonisms served to keep the two apart. So the dominant Anglo-Saxon population of England was a solvent for the Norman French, and the densely packed humanity of China for their Manchu conquerors.

On the other hand, extensive areas, like early North America and Australia, sparsely inhabited by small scattered groups who have only an attenuated connection with their soil and therefore only a feeble hold upon their land, cannot compete with small areas, if these have the dense and evenly distributed population which ensures a firm tenure of the

land. Small, geographically confined areas foster this compact and systematic occupation on the part of their inhabitants, since they put barriers in the way of precipitate and
disintegrating expansion; and this characteristic compensates
in some degree and for a period at least for the weakness
otherwise inherent in the narrow territorial base.

Every race, people, and state has had the history of *Historical advance from small to large areas.*
progress from a small to a large area. All have been small
in their youth. The bit of land covered by Roma Quadrata
has given language, customs, laws, culture, and a faint strain
of Latin blood to nations now occupying half a million square
miles of Europe. The Arab inundation, which flooded the
vast domain of the Caliphs, traced back to that spring of
ethnic and religious energy which welled up in the arid
plain of Mecca and the Arabian oases. The world-wide
maritime expansion of the English-speaking people had its
starting point in the lowlands of the Elbe. The makers of
empire in northern China were cradled in the small highland
valley of the Wei River. The little principality of Moscow
was the nucleus of the Russian Empire.

Penetration into a people's remote past comes always upon
some limited spot which has nurtured the young nation, and
reveals the fact that territorial expansion is the incontestible
feature of their history. This advance from small to large
characterizes their political area, the scope of their trade
relations, their spheres of activity, the size of their known
world, and finally the sway of their religions. Every religion
in its early stages of development bears the stamp of a narrow
origin, traceable to the circumscribed habitat of the primitive
social group, or back of that to the small circle of lands constituting the known world whence it sprang. First it is tribal,
and makes a distinction between my God and thy God; but
even when it has expanded to embody a universal system, it still
retains vestigial forms of its narrow past. Jerusalem, Mecca
and Rome remain the sacred goal of pilgrimages, while the
vaster import of a monotheistic faith and the higher ethical
teaching of the brotherhood of man have encircled the world.

When religion, language and race have spread, in their
wake comes the growing state. Everywhere the political area

tends gradually to embrace the whole linguistic area of which it forms a part, and finally the yet larger race area.   Only the diplomacy of united Europe has availed to prevent France from absorbing French-speaking Belgium, or Russia from incorporating into her domain that vast Slav region extending from the Drave and Danube almost to the Gulf of Corinth, now parcelled out among seven different states, but bound to the Muscovite empire by ties of related speech, by race and religion.   The detachment of the various Danubian principalities from the uncongenial dominion of the Turks, though a dismemberment of a large political territory and a seeming backward step, can be regarded only as a leisurely preliminary for a new territorial alignment.   History's movements are unhurried; the backward step may prepare for the longer leap forward.   It is impossible to resist the conclusion that the vigorous, reorganized German Empire will one day try to incorporate the Germanic areas found in Austria, Switzerland and Holland.

Gradations in area and in development.   Throughout the life of any people, from its fœtal period in some small locality to its well rounded adult era marked by the occupation and organization of a wide national territory, gradations in area mark gradations of development.   And this is true whether we consider the compass of their commercial exchanges, the scope of their maritime ventures, the extent of their linguistic area, the measure of their territorial ambitions, or the range of their intellectual interests and human sympathies.   From land to ethics, the rule holds good.   Peoples in the lower stages of civilization have contracted spacial ideas, desire and need at a given time only a limited territory, though they may change that territory often; they think in small linear terms, have a small horizon, a small circle of contact with others, a small range of influence, only tribal sympathies; they have an exaggerated conception of their own size and importance, because their basis of comparison is fatally limited.   With a mature, widespread people like the English or French, all this is different; they have made the earth their own, so far as possible.

Just because of this universal tendency towards the occupation of ever larger areas and the formation of vaster political aggregates, in making a sociological or political estimate of different peoples, we should never lose sight of the fact that all racial and national characteristics which operate towards the absorption of more land and impel to political expansion are of fundamental value. A ship of state manned by such a crew has its sails set to catch the winds of the world.

Territorial expansion is always preceded by an extension of the circle of influence which a people exerts through its traders, its deep-sea fishermen, its picturesque marauders and more respectable missionaries, and earlier still by a widening of its mere geographical horizon through fortuitous or systematic exploration. The Northmen visited the coasts of Britain and France first as pirates, then as settlers. Norman and Breton fishermen were drawing in their nets on the Grand Bank of Newfoundland thirty years before Cartier sailed up the St. Lawrence. Japanese fishing boats preceded Japanese colonists to the coasts of Yezo. Trading fleets were the forerunners of the Greek colonies along the Black Sea and Mediterranean, and of Phœnician settlements in North Africa, Sicily and Spain. It was in the wake of trapper and fur trader that English and American pioneer advanced across our continent to the Pacific; just as in French Canada Jesuit priest and voyageur opened the way for the settler. Religious propaganda was yoked with greed of conquest in the campaigns of Cortez and Pizarro. Modern statesmen pushing a policy of expansion are alive to the diplomatic possibilities of missionaries endangered or their property destroyed. They find a still better asset to be realized on territorially in enterprising capitalists settled among a weaker people, by whom their property is threatened or overtaxed, or their trade interfered with. The British acquisition of Hongkong in 1842 followed a war with China to prevent the exclusion of the English opium trade from the Celestial Empire. The annexation of the Transvaal resulted from the expansion of English capitalists to the Rand mines, much as the advance of the United States flag to the Hawaiian Islands followed American sugar planters thither. American capital in the Caribbean states of South America has repeatedly

Prelimi-
naries to
ethnic and
political
expansion.

tried to embroil those countries with the United States government; and its increasing presence in Cuba is undoubtedly ominous for the independence of the island, because with capital go men and influence.

When the foreign investor is not a corporation but a government, the expanding commercial influence looks still more surely to tangible political results; because such national enterprises have at bottom a political motive, however much overlaid by an economic exterior. When the British government secured a working majority of the Suez Canal stock, it sealed the fate of Egypt to become ultimately a province of the British Empire. Russian railroads in Manchuria were the well-selected tool for the Russification and final annexation of the province. The weight of American national enterprise in the Panama Canal Zone sufficed to split off from the Colombian federation a peripheral state, whose detachment is obviously a preliminary for eventual incorporation into United States domain. The efforts of the German government to secure from the Sultan of Turkey railroad concessions through Asia Minor for German capitalists has aroused jealousy in financial and political circles in St. Petersburg, and prompted a demand from the Russian Foreign Office upon Turkey for the privilege of constructing railroads through eastern Asia Minor.[22]

Signifi-
cance of
sphere of
activity or
influence.

Beyond the home of a people lies its sphere of influence or activities, which in the last analysis may be taken as a protest against the narrowness of the domestic habitat. It represents the larger area which the people wants and which in course of time it might advantageously occupy or annex. It embodies the effort to embrace more varied and generous natural conditions, whereby the struggle for subsistence may be made less hard. Finally, it is an expression of the law that for peoples and races the struggle for existence is at bottom a struggle for space. Geography sees various forms of the historical movement as the struggle for space in which humanity has forever been engaged. In this struggle the stronger peoples have absorbed ever larger portions of the earth's surface. Hence, through continual subjection to new conditions here or there and to a greater sum total of various conditions, they gain in power by improved variation, as well as numerically by the enlargement of their geographic base. The Anglo-Saxon branch of the Teutonic stock has, by its phenomenal increase, overspread sections of whole continents, drawn from their varied soils nourishment for its finest efflorescence, and thereby has far out-grown the Germanic branch by which, at the start, it was overshadowed. The fact that the British Empire comprises 28,615,000 square kilometers or exactly one-fifth of the total land area of the earth, and that the Russian Empire contains over one-seventh, are full of encouragement for Anglo-Saxon and Slav, but contain a warning to the other peoples of the world.

The large area which misleads a primitive folk into exces- Nature of sive dispersion and the dissipation of their tribal powers, expansion offers to an advanced people, who in some circumscribed and old habitat have learned the value of land, the freest conditions countries. for their development. A wide, unobstructed territory, occupied by a sparse population of wandering tribes capable of little resistance to conquest or encroachment, affords the most favorable conditions to an intruding superior race. Such conditions the Chinese found in Mongolia and Manchuria, the Russians in Siberia, and European colonists in the Americas, Australia and Africa. Almost unlimited space and undeveloped resources met their land hunger and their commercial ambition. Their numerical growth was rapid, both by the natural increase reflecting an abundant food supply, and by accessions from the home countries. Expansion advanced by strides. In contrast to this care-free, easy development in a new land, growth in old countries like Europe and the more civilized parts of Asia means a slow protrusion of the frontier, made at the cost of blood; it means either the absorption of the native people, because there are no unoccupied corners into which they can be driven, or the imposition upon them of an unwelcome rule exercised by alien officials. Witness the advance of the Russians into Poland and Finland, of the Germans into Poland and Alsace-Lorraine, of the Japanese into Korea, and of the English into crowded India.

The rapid unfolding of the geographical horizon

in a young land communicates to an expanding people new springs of mobility, new motives for movement out and beyond the old confines, new goals holding out new and undreamt of benefits. Life becomes fresh, young, hopeful. Old checks to natural increase of population are removed. Emigrant bands beat out new trails radiating from the old home. They go on individual initiative or state-directed enterprises; but no matter which, the manifold life in the far-away periphery reacts upon the center to vivify and rejuvenate it.

Relation of ethnic to political expansion. The laws of the territorial growth of peoples and of states are in general the same. The main differences between the two lies in the fact that ethnic expansion, since it depends upon natural increase, is slow, steady, and among civilized peoples is subject to slight fluctuations; while the frontiers of a state, after a long period of permanence, can suddenly be advanced by conquest far beyond the ethnic boundaries, often, however, only to be as quickly lost again. Therefore the important law may be laid down, that the more closely the territorial growth of a state keeps pace with that of its people, and the more nearly the political area coincides with the ethnic, the greater is the strength and stability of the state. This is the explanation of the vigor and permanence of the early English colonies in America. The slow westward protrusion of their frontier of continuous settlement within the boundaries of the Allegheny Mountains formed a marked contrast to the wide sweep of French voyageur camp and lonely trading-station in the Canadian forests, and even more to the handful of priests and soldiers who for three centuries kept an unsteady hold upon the Spanish empire in the Western Hemisphere. The political advance of the United States across the continent from the Alleghenies to the Mississippi, thence to the Rocky Mountains, and thence to the Pacific was always preceded by bands of enterprising settlers, who planted themselves beyond the frontier and beckoned to the flag to follow. The great empires of antiquity were enlarged mechanically by conquest and annexation. They were mosaics, not growths. The cohesive power of a common ethnic bond was lacking; so was the

modern substitute for this to be found in close economic interdependence maintained by improved methods of communication. Hence these empires soon broke up again along lines
of old geographic and ethnic cleavage. For Rome, the
cementing power of the Mediterranean and the fairly unified
civilization which this enclosed sea had been evolving since
the dawn of Cretan and Phœnician trade, compensated in
part for the lack of common speech and national ideals
throughout the political domain. But the Empire proved
in the end to be merely a mosaic, easily broken.

The second point of difference between the expansion of Relation
peoples and of states lies in their respective relation to the of people
political frontier. This confines the state like a stockade, and state
fixing the territorial limits of its administrative functions; to political
but for the subjects of the state it is an imaginary line, boundary.
powerless to check the range of their activities, except when
a military or tariff war is going on. The state boundary, if
it coincides with a strong natural barrier, may for decades
or even centuries succeed in confining a growing people, if
these, by intelligent economy, increase the productivity of
the soil whose area they are unable to extend. Yet the time
comes even for these when they must break through the barriers and secure more land, either by foreign conquest or
colonization. The classic example of the confinement of a
people within its political boundaries is the long isolation
of Japan from 1624 to 1854. The pent-up forces there
accumulated, in a population which had doubled itself in
the interval and which by hard schooling was made receptive
to every improved economic method, manifest themselves in
the insistent demand for more land which has permeated
all the recent policy of Japan. But the history of Japan is
exceptional. The rule is that the growing people slowly but
continually overflow their political boundary, which then
advances to cover the successive flood plains of the national
inundation, or yet farther to anticipate the next rise. This
has been the history of Germany in its progress eastward
across the Elbe, the Oder, the Vistula and the Niemen. The
dream of a greater empire embraces all the German-speaking
people from Switzerland, Tyrol and Steiermark to those out-

lying groups in the Baltic provinces of Russia and the related offshoot in Holland.[23] [See map page 223.]

Though political boundaries, especially where they coincide with natural barriers, may restrict the territorial growth of a people, on the other hand, political expansion is always a stimulus to racial expansion, because it opens up more land and makes the conditions of life easier for an increasing people, by relieving congestion in the older areas. More than this, it materially aids while guiding and focusing the out-going streams of population. Thus it keeps them concentrated for the reinforcement of the nation in the form of colonies, and tends to reduce the political evil of indiscriminate emigration, by which the streams are dissipated and diverted to strengthen other nations. Witness the active internal colonization practiced by Germany in her Polish territory,[24] by Russia in Siberia, in an effort to make the ethnic boundary hurry after and overtake the political frontier.

Expansion of civilization.

Just as the development of a people and state is marked by advance from small to ever larger areas, so is that of a civilization. It may originate in a small district; but more mobile than humanity itself, it does not remain confined to one spot, but passes on from individual to individual and from people to people. Greece served only as a garden in which the flowers of Oriental and Egyptian civilization were temporarily transplanted. As soon as they were modified and adapted to their new conditions, their seed spread over all Europe. The narrow area of ancient Greece, which caused the early dissemination of its people over the Mediterranean basin, and thereby weakened the political force of the country at home, was an important factor in the wide distribution of its culture. Commerce, colonization and war are vehicles of civilization, where favorable geographic conditions open the way for trade in the wake of the victorious army. The imposition of Roman dominion meant everywhere the gift of Roman civilization. The Crusaders brought back from Syria more than their scars and their trophies. Every European factory in China, every Hudson Bay Company post in the wilds of northern Canada, every Arab settlement in savage Africa is surrounded by a sphere of trade; and this in turn is enclosed in a wider sphere of influence through which its civilization, though much diluted, has filtered. The higher the civilization, the wider the area which it masters. The manifold activities of a civilized people demand a large sphere of influence, and include, furthermore, improved means of communication which enable it to control such a sphere.

Even a relatively low civilization may spread over a vast area if carried by a highly mobile people. Mohammedanism, which embodies a cultural system as well as a religion, found its vehicles of dispersal in the pastoral nomads occupying the arid land of northern Africa and western Asia, and thus spread from the Senegal River to Chinese Turkestan. It was carried by the maritime Arabs of Oman and Yemen to Malacca and Sumatra, where it was communicated to the seafaring Malays. These island folk, who approximate the most highly civilized peoples in their nautical efficiency, distributed the meager elements of Mohammedan civilization over the Malay Archipelago. [See map of the Religions of the Eastern Hemisphere, in chapter XIV.]

The larger the area which a civilized nation occupies, the more numerous are its points of contact with other peoples, and the less likely is there to be a premature crystallization of its civilization from isolation. Extension of area on a large scale means eventually extension of the seaboard and access to those multiform international relations which the ocean highway confers. The world wide expansion of the British Empire has given it at every outward step wider oceanic contact and eventually a cosmopolitan civilization. The same thing is true of the other great colonial empires of history, whether Portuguese, Spanish, Dutch or French; and even of the great continental empires, like Russia and the United States. The Russian advance across Siberia, like the American advance across the Rockies, meant access to the Pacific, and a modification of its civilization on those remote shores. *Cultural advantages of large political area.*

A large area means varied vicinal locations and hence differentiation of civilization, at least along the frontier. How rapidly the vivifying influences of this contact will penetrate into the bulk of the interior depends upon size, location as scattered or compact, and general geographic conditions like navigable rivers or mountains, which facilitate or bar intercourse with that interior. The Russian Empire has eleven different nations, speaking even more different languages, on its western and southern frontiers. Its long line of Asiatic contact will inevitably give to the European civilization transplanted hither in Russian colonies a new and perhaps not unfruitful development. The Siberian citizen of future centuries may compare favorably with his brother in Moscow. Japan, even while impressing its civilization upon the reluctant Koreans, will see itself modified by the contact and its culture differentiated by the transplanting; but the content of Japanese civilization will be increased by every new variant thus formed.

Politico-economic advantages.
The larger the area brought under one political control, the less the handicap of internal friction and the greater its economic independence. Vast territory has enabled the United States to maintain with advantage a protective tariff, chiefly because the free trade within its own borders was extensive. The natural law of the territorial growth of states and peoples means an extension of the areas in which peace and coöperation are preserved, a relative reduction of frontiers and of the military forces necessary to defend them,[25] diminution in the sum total of conflicts, and a wider removal of the border battle fields. In place of the continual warfare between petty tribes which prevailed in North America four hundred years ago, we have to-day the peaceful competition of the three great nations which have divided the continent among them. The political unification of the Mediterranean basin under the Roman Empire restricted wars to the remote land frontiers. The foreign wars of Russia, China, and the United States in the past century have been almost wholly confined to the outskirts of their big domains, merely scratching the rim and leaving the great interior sound and undisturbed. Russia's immense area is the military ally on which she can most surely count. The long road to Moscow converted Napoleon's victory into a defeat;

and the resistless advance of the Japanese from Port Arthur to the Sungari River led only to a peace robbed of the chief fruits of victory. The numerous wars of the British Empire have been limited to this or that corner, and have scarcely affected the prosperity of the great remainder, so that their costs have been readily borne and their wounds rapidly healed.

The territorial expansion of peoples and states is attended by an evolution of their spacial conceptions and ideals. Primitive peoples, accustomed to dismemberment in small tribal groups, bear all the marks of territorial contraction. Their geographical horizon is usually fixed by the radius of a few days' march. Inter-tribal trade and intercourse reach only rudimentary development, under the prevailing conditions of mutual antagonism and isolation, and hence contribute little to the expansion of the horizon. Knowing only their little world, such primitive groups overestimate the size and importance of their own territory, and are incapable of controlling an extensive area. This is the testimony of all travellers who have observed native African states. Though the race or stock distribution may be wide, like that of the Athapascan and Algonquin Indians, and their war paths long, like the campaigns of the Iroquois against the Cherokees of the Tennessee River, yet the unit of tribal territory permanently occupied is never large. *Political area and the national horizon.*

Small naturally defined regions, which take the lead in historical development because they counteract the primitive tendency towards excessive dispersal, are in danger of teaching too well their lesson of concentration. In course of time geographic enclosure begins to betray its limitations. The extent of a people's territory influences their estimate of area *per se*, determines how far land shall be made the basis of their national purposes, fixes the territorial scale of their conquests and their political expansion. This is a conspicuous psychological effect of a narrow local environment. A people embedded for centuries in a small district measure area with a short yardstick. The ancient Greeks devised a philosophic basis for the advantages of the small state, which is extolled in the writings of Plato and Aristotle.[26] Aristotle *National estimates of area.*

wanted it small enough "to be comprehended at one glance of the statesman's eye." Plato's ideal democracy, by rigid laws limiting the procreative period of women and men and providing for the death of children born out of this period or out of wedlock, restricted its free citizens to 5,040 heads of families, [27] all living within reach of the agora, and all able to judge from personal knowledge of a candidate's fitness for office. This condition was possible only in dwarf commonwealths like the city-states of the Hellenic world. The failure of the Greeks to build up a political structure on a territorial scale commensurate with their cultural achievements and with the wide sphere of their cultural influence can be ascribed chiefly to their inability to discard the contracted territorial ideas engendered by geographic and political dismemberment. The little Judean plateau, which gave birth to a universal religion, clung with provincial bigotry to the narrow tribal creed and repudiated the larger faith of Christ, which found its appropriate field in Mediterranean Europe.

Estimates of area in small maritime states. Maritime peoples of small geographic base have a characteristic method of expansion which reflects their low valuation of area. Their limited amount of arable soil necessitates reliance upon foreign sources of supply, which are secured by commerce. Hence they found trading stations or towns among alien peoples on distant coasts, selecting points like capes or inshore islets which can be easily defended and which at the same time command inland or maritime routes of trade. The prime geographic consideration is location, natural and vicinal. The area of the trading settlement is kept as small as possible to answer its immediate purpose, because it can be more easily defended. [28] Such were the colonies of the ancient Phœnicians and Greeks in the Mediterranean, of the Medieval Arabs and the Portuguese on the east coast of Africa and in India. This method reached its ultimate expression in point of small area, seclusion, and local autonomy, perhaps, in the Hanse factories in Norway and Russia.[29] But all these widespread nuclei of expansion remained barren of permanent national result, because they were designed for a commercial end, and ignored the larger national mission and surer economic base found in acquisition of territory. Hence they were short-lived, succumbing to attack or abandoned on the failure of local resources, which were ruthlessly exploited.

That precocious development characteristic of small nat- urally defined areas shows its inherent weakness in the tend- ency to accept the enclosed area as a nature-made standard of national territory. The earlier a state fixes its frontier without allowance for growth, the earlier comes the cessation of its development. Therefore the geographical nurseries of civilization were infected with germs of decay. Such was the history of Egypt, of Yemen, of Greece, Crete, and Phœnicia. These are the regions which, as Carl Ritter says, have given the whole fruit of their existence to the world for its future use, have conferred upon the world the trust which they once held, afterward to recede, as it were, from view.[30] They were great in the past, and now they belong to those immortal dead whose greatness has been incor- porated in the world's life—"the choir invisible" of the nations.

Limitations of small territorial conceptions.

The advance from a small, self-dependent community to interdependent relations with other peoples, then to ethnic expansion or union of groups to form a state or empire is a great turning point in any history. Thereby the clan or tribe discards the old paralyzing seclusion of the primitive society and the narrow habitat, and joins that march of ethnic, political and cultural progress which has covered larger and larger areas, and by increase of com- mon purpose has cemented together ever greater aggre- gates.

Evolution of terri- torial policies.

Nothing is more significant in the history of the English in America than the rapid evolution of their spacial ideals, their abandonment of the small territorial conception brought with them from the mother country and embodied, for example, in that munificent land grant, fifty by a hun- dred miles in extent, of the first Virginia charter in 1606, and their progress to schemes of continental expansion. Every accession of territory to the Thirteen Colonies and to the Republic gave an impulse to growth. Expansion kept pace with opportunity. Only in small and isolated New England did the contracted provincial point of view persist. It manifested itself in a narrow policy of concentration and curtailment, which acquiesced in the occlusion of the Mississippi River to the Trans-Allegheny settlements by Spain in 1787, and which later opposed the purchase of the Louisiana territory[31] and the acquisition of the Philippines.

All peoples who have achieved wide expansion have developed in the process vast territorial policies. This is true of the pastoral nomads who in different epochs have inundated Europe, northern Africa and the peripheral lands of Asia, and of the great colonial nations who in a few decades have brought continents under their dominion. In nomadic hordes it is based upon habitual mobility and the possession of herds, which are at once incentive and means for extending the geographical horizon; but it suffers from the evanescent character of nomadic political organization, and the tendency toward dismemberment bred in all pastoral life by dispersal over scattered grazing grounds. Hence the empires set up by nomad conquerors like the Saracens and Tartars soon fall apart.

Colonial expansion.

Among highly civilized agricultural and industrial peoples, on the other hand, a vast territorial policy is at once cause and effect of national growth; it is at once an innate tendency and a conscious purpose tenaciously followed. It makes use of trade and diplomacy, of scientific invention and technical improvement, to achieve its aims. It becomes an accepted mark of political vigor and an ideal even among peoples who have failed to enlarge their narrow base. The model of Russian expansion on the Pacific was quickly followed by awakened Japan, stirred out of her insular complacence by the threat of Muscovite encroachment. Germany and Italy, each strengthened and enlarged as to national outlook by recent political unification, have elbowed their way into the crowded colonial field. The French, though not expansionists as individuals, have an excellent capacity for collective action when directed by government. The officials whom Louis XIV sent to Canada in the seventeenth century executed large schemes of empire reflecting the dilation of French frontiers in Europe. These ideals of expansion seem to have been communicated by the power of example, or the threat of danger in them, to the English colonists in Virginia and Pennsylvania, and later to Washington and Jefferson.

The best type of colonial expansion is found among the English-speaking people of America, Australia and South Africa. Their spacial ideas are built on a big scale. Distances do not daunt them. The man who could conceive a Cape-to-Cairo railroad, with all the schemes of territorial aggrandizement therein implied, had a mind that took continents for its units of measure; and he found a fitting monument in a province of imperial proportions whereon was inscribed his name. Bryce tells us that in South Africa the social circle of "the best people" includes Pretoria, Johannesburg, Kimberley, Bloemfontein and Cape Town—a social circle with a diameter of a thousand miles! [32]

The mind of colonials.

The spirit of our western frontier, so long as there was a frontier, was the spirit of movement, of the conquest of space. It found its expression in the history of the Wilderness Road and the Oregon Trail. When the center of population in the United States still lingered on the shore of Chesapeake Bay, and the frontier of continuous settlement had not advanced beyond the present western boundary of Virginia and Pennsylvania, the spacious mind of Thomas Jefferson foresaw the Mississippi Valley as the inevitable and necessary possession of the American people, and looked upon the trade of the far-off Columbia River as a natural feeder of the Mississippi commerce. [33]

Emerson's statement that the vast size of the United States is reflected in the big views of its people applies not only to political policy, which in the Monroe Doctrine for the first time in history has embraced a hemisphere; nor is it confined to the big scale of their economic processes. Emerson had in mind rather their whole conception of national mission and national life, especially their legislation, [34] for which he anticipated larger and more Catholic aims than obtain in Europe, hampered as it is by countless political and linguistic boundaries, and barred thereby from any far-reaching unity of purpose and action.

Canada, British South Africa, Australia and the United States, though widely separated, have in common a certain wide outlook upon life, a continental element in the national mind, bred in their people by their generous territories. The American recognizes his kinship of mind with these colonial Englishmen as something over and above mere kinship of race. It consists in their deep-seated common democracy, the democracy born in men who till fields and clear forests, not as plowmen and wood-cutters, but as makers of nations. It consists in identical interests and points of view in regard to identical problems growing out of the occupation and development of new and almost boundless territories. Race questions, paucity of labor, highways and railroads, immigration, combinations of capital, excessive land holdings, and illegal appropriation of land on a large scale, are problems that meet them all. The monopolistic policy of the United States in regard to American soil as embodied in the Monroe Doctrine, and the expectation lurking in the mental background of every American that his country may eventually embrace the northern continent, find their echo in Australia's plans for wider empire in the Pacific. The Commonwealth of Australia has succeeded in getting into its own hands the administration of British New Guinea (90,500 square miles.) It has also secured from the imperial government the unusual privilege of settling the relations between itself and the islands of the Pacific, because it regards the Pacific question as the one question of foreign policy in which its interests are profoundly involved. In the same way the British in South Africa, sparsely scattered though they are, feel an imperative need of further expansion, if their far-reaching schemes of commerce and empire are to be realized.

Colonials as road builders.

The effort to annihilate space by improved means of communication has absorbed the best intellects and energies of expanding peoples. The ancient Roman, like the Incas of Peru, built highways over every part of the empire, undaunted by natural obstacles like the Alps and Andes. Modern expansionists are railroad builders. Witness the long list of strategic lines, constructed or subsidized by various governments during the past half century—the Union Pacific, Central Pacific, Canadian Pacific, Trans-Siberian, Cairo-Khartoum, Cape Town-Zambesi, and now the proposed Trans-Saharan road, designed to unite the Mediterranean and Guinea colonies of French Africa. The equipment of the American roads, with their heavy rails, giant locomotives, and enormous freight cars, reveals adaptation to a commerce that covers long distances between strongly differentiated areas of production, and that reflects the vast enterprises of this continental country. The same story comes out in the ocean vessels which serve the trade of the Great Lakes, and in the acres of coal barges in a single fleet which are towed down the Ohio and Mississippi by one mammoth steel tug.

The abundant natural resources awaiting development in **Practical** such big new countries give to the mind of the people an **bent of** essentially practical bent. The rewards of labor are so great **colonials.** that the stimulus to effort is irresistible. Economic questions take precedence of all others, divide political parties, and consume a large portion of national legislation; while purely political questions sink into the background. Civilization takes on a material stamp, becomes that "dollar civilization" which is the scorn of the placid, paralyzed Oriental or the old world European. The genius of colonials is essentially practical. Impatience of obstacles, short cuts aiming at quick returns, wastefulness of land, of forests, of fuel, of everything but labor, have long characterized American activities. The problem of an inadequate labor supply attended the sudden accession of territory opened for European occupation by the discovery of America, and caused a sudden recrudescence of slavery, which as an industrial system had long been outgrown by Europe. It has also given immense stimulus to invention, and to the formation of labor unions, which in the newest colonial fields, like Australia and New Zealand, have dominated the government and given a Utopian stamp to legislation.

Yet underlying and permeating this materialism is a youthful idealism. Transplanted to conditions of greater opportunity, the race becomes rejuvenated, abandons outgrown customs and outworn standards, experiences an enlargement of vision and of hope, gathers courage and energy equal to its task, manages somehow to hitch its wagon to a star.

NOTES TO CHAPTER VI

1. Chamberlain and Salisbury, Geology, Vol. III, pp. 483-485. New York, 1906.
2. *Ibid.*, p. 137 and map p. 138.
3. Darwin, Origin of Species, Vol. I, chap. IV, pp. 124-132; Vol. II, chap. XII, p. 134. New York, 1895. H. W. Conn, The Method of Evolution, p. 54. London and New York, 1900.
4. *Ibid.*, pp. 194-197, 226-227, 239-242, 342-350.
5. Ratzel, *Der Lebensraum, eine bio-geographische Studie*, p. 51. Tubingen, 1901.
6. D. G. Brinton, Races and Peoples, pp. 271, 293-295. Philadelphia, 1901.
7. A. Heilprin, Geographical Distribution of Animals, pp. 57-61. London, 1894.
8. W. Z. Ripley, Races of Europe, p. 39, maps pp. 43, 78. New York, 1899.
9. Darwin, Origin of Species, Vol. II, chap. XII, pp. 130-131. New York, 1895.
10. Richard Semon, In the Australian Bush, p. 211. London, 1899.
11. J. H. W. Stuckenburg, Sociology, Vol. I, p. 324. New York and London, 1903.
12. E. C. Semple, The Influences of Geographic Environment on the Lower St. Lawrence. Bulletin American Geographical Society, Vol. XXXVI, pp. 464-465. 1904.
13. E. Limedorfer, Finland's Plight, *Forum*, Vol. XXXII, pp. 85-93.
14. Eleventh Census, Report on the Indians, p. 35. Washington, 1894.
15. A. R. Wallace, Australasia, Vol. I, p. 454. London, 1893.
16. W. S. Barclay, Life in Terra del Fuego, *The Nineteenth Century*, Vol. 55, p. 97. January, 1904.
17. A. R. Wallace, Australasia, Vol. I, pp. 454-455. London, 1893.
18. Darwin, Origin of Species, Vol. II, chap. XIII, p. 178. New York, 1895.
19. *Ibid.*, Vol. II, chap. XII, p. 167-168.
20. Nesbit Bain, Finland and the Tsar, *Fortnightly Review*, Vol. 71, p. 735. E. Limedorfer, Finland's Plight, *Forum*, Vol. 32, pp. 85-93.
21. Archibald Geikie, The Scenery of Scotland, pp. 398-399. London, 1887.
22. Railways in Asia Minor, *Littell's Living Age*, Vol. 225, p. 196.
23. J. Ellis Barker, Modern Germany, pp. 38-66. London, 1907.
24. The Polish Danger in Prussia, *Westminster Review*, Vol. 155, p. 375.
25. Heinrich von Treitschke, *Politik*, Vol. I, pp. 223-224. Leipzig, 1897.

26. Plato, Critias, 112. Aristotle, Politics, Book II, chap. VII; Book IV, chap. IV; Book VII, chap. IV.

27. Plato, *De Legibus*, Book V, chaps. 8, 9, 10, 11.

28. Roscher, *National-Oekonomik des Handels und Gewerbefleisses*, pp. 180-187. Stuttgart, 1899.

29. Blanqui, History of Political Economy, pp. 150-152. New York, 1880.

30. Carl Ritter, Comparative Geography, p. 63. New York, 1865.

31. E. C. Semple, American History and its Geographic Conditions, pp. 42-43, 109, 110. Boston, 1903.

32. James Bryce, Impressions of South Africa, pp. 405-6. New York, 1897.

33. P. L. Ford, Writings of Thomas Jefferson, Vol. VIII. Letter to John Bacon, April 30, 1803; and Confidential Message to Congress on the Expedition to the Pacific, January 18, 1803.

34. Emerson, The Young American, in Nature Addresses and Lectures, pp. 369-371. Centenary Edition, Boston.

CHAPTER VII

GEOGRAPHICAL BOUNDARIES

The
boundary
zone in
nature.

NATURE abhors fixed boundary lines and sudden transitions; all her forces combine against them. Everywhere she keeps her borders melting, wavering, advancing, retreating. If by some cataclysm sharp lines of demarcation are drawn, she straightway begins to blur them by creating intermediate forms, and thus establishes the boundary zone which characterizes the inanimate and animate world. A stratum of limestone or sandstone, when brought into contact with a glowing mass of igneous rock, undergoes various changes due to the penetrating heat of the volcanic outflow, so that its surface is metamorphosed as far as that heat reaches. The granite cliff slowly deposits at its base a rock-waste slope to soften the sudden transition from its perpendicular surface to the level plain at its feet. The line where a land-born river meets the sea tends to become a sandbar or a delta, created by the river-borne silt and the wash of the waves, a form intermediate between land and sea, bearing the stamp of each, fluid in its outlines, ever growing by the persistent accumulation of mud, though ever subject to inundation and destruction by the waters which made it. The alluvial coastal hems that edge all shallow seas are such border zones, reflecting in their flat, low surfaces the dead level of the ocean, in their composition the solid substance of the land; but in the miniature waves imprinted on the sands and the billows of heaped-up boulders, the master workman of the deep leaves his mark. [See map page 243.]

Under examination, even our familiar term coastline proves to be only an abstraction with no corresponding reality in nature. Everywhere, whether on margin of lake or gulf, the actual phenomenon is a coast zone, alternately covered and abandoned by the waters, varying in width from a few inches to a few miles, according to the slope of the land, the range of the tide and the direction of the wind. It has one breadth at the minimum or neap tide, but increases often two or three fold at spring tide, when the distance between ebb and flood is at its maximum. At the mouth of Cook's Inlet on the southern Alaskan coast, where the range of tides is only eight feet, the zone is comparatively narrow, but widens rapidly towards the head of the inlet, where the tide rises twenty-three feet above the ebb line, and even to sixty-five feet under the influence of a heavy southwest storm. On flat coasts we are familiar with the wide frontier of salt marshes, that witness the border warfare of land and sea, alternate invasion and retreat. In low-shored estuaries like those of northern Brittany and northwestern Alaska, this amphibian girdle of the land expands to a width of four miles, while on precipitous coasts of tideless sea basins it contracts to a few inches. Hence this boundary zone changes with every impulse of the mobile sea and with every varying configuration of the shore. Movement and external conditions are the factors in its creation. They make something that is only partially akin to the two contiguous forms. Here on their outer margins land and ocean compromise their physical differences, and this by a law which runs through animate and inanimate nature. Wherever one body moves in constant contact with another, it is subjected to modifying influences which differentiate its periphery from its interior, lend it a transitional character, make of it a penumbra between light and shadow. The modifying process goes on persistently with varying force, and creates a shifting, changing border zone which, from its nature, cannot be delimited. For convenience' sake, we adopt the abstraction of a boundary line; but the reality behind this abstraction is the important thing in anthropo-geography.

All so-called boundary lines with which geography has to do have this same character,—coastlines, river margins, ice or snow lines, limits of vegetation, boundaries of races or religions or civilizations, frontiers of states. They are all the same, stamped by the eternal flux of nature. Beyond the solid ice-pack which surrounds the North Pole is a wide

Gradations in the boundary zone.

girdle of almost unbroken drift ice, and beyond this is an irregular concentric zone of scattered icebergs which varies in breadth with season, wind and local current; a persistent decrease in continuity from solid pack to open sea. The line of perpetual snow on high mountains advances or retreats from season to season, from year to year; it drops low on chilly northern slopes and recedes to higher altitudes on a southern exposure; sends down long icy tongues in dark gorges, and leaves outlying patches of old snow in shaded spots or beneath a covering of rock waste far below the margin of the snow fields.

In the struggle for existence in the vegetable world, the tree line pushes as far up the mountain as conditions of climate and soil will permit. Then comes a season of fiercer storms, intenser cold and invading ice upon the peaks. Havoc is wrought, and the forest drops back across a zone of border warfare—for war belongs to borders—leaving behind it here and there a dwarfed pine or gnarled and twisted juniper which has survived the onslaught of the enemy. Now these are stragglers in the retreat, but are destined later in milder years to serve as outposts in the advance of the forest to recover its lost ground. Here we have a border scene which is typical in nature—the belt of unbroken forest, growing thinner and more stunted toward its upper edge, succeeded by a zone of scattered trees, which may form a cluster perhaps in some sheltered gulch where soil has collected and north winds are excluded, and higher still the whitened skeleton of a tree to show how far the forest once invaded the domain of the waste.

Oscillating boundaries of the habitable area. The habitable area of the earth everywhere shows its boundaries to be peripheral zones of varying width, now occupied and now deserted, protruding or receding according to external conditions of climate and soil, and subject to seasonal change. The distribution of human life becomes sparser from the temperate regions toward the Arctic Circle, foreshadowing the unpeopled wastes of the ice-fields beyond. The outward movement from the Tropics poleward halts where life conditions disappear, and there finds its boundary; but as life conditions advance or retreat with the seasons, so does that

boundary. On the west coast of Greenland the Eskimo village of Etah, at about the seventy-eighth parallel, marks the
northern limit of permanent or winter settlement; but in summer the Eskimo, in his kayak, follows the musk-ox and seal
much farther north and there leaves his igloo to testify to
the wide range of his poleward migration. Numerous relics
of the Eskimo and their summer encampments have been
found along Lady Franklin Bay in northern Grinnell Land
(81° 50′ N. L.), but in the interior, on the outlet streams
of Lake Hazen, explorers have discovered remains of habitations which had evidently, in previous ages, been permanently occupied.[1] The Murman Coast of the Kola Peninsula
has in summer a large population of Russian fishermen and
forty or more fishing stations; but when the catch is over at
the end of August, and the Arctic winter approaches, the
stations are closed, and the three thousand fishermen return
to their permanent homes on the shores of the White Sea.[2]
Farther east along this polar fringe of Russia, the little village of Charbarova, located on the Jugor Strait, is inhabited in summer by a number of Samoyedes, who pasture
their reindeer over on Vaygats Island, and by some Russians and Finns, who come from the White Sea towns to trade
with the Samoyedes and incidentally to hunt and fish. But in
the fall, when a new ice bridge across the Strait releases the
reindeer from their enclosed pasture on the island, the Samoyedes withdraw southward, and the merchants with their
wares to Archangel and other points. This has gone on for
centuries.[3] On the Briochov Islands at the head of the
Yenisei estuary Nordenskiold found a small group of houses
which formed a summer fishing post in 1875, but which was
deserted by the end of August.[4]

An altitude of about five thousand feet marks the limit of Altitude
village life in the Alps; but during the three warm months boundary
of the year, the summer pastures at eight thousand feet or zones.
more are alive with herds and their keepers. The boundary
line of human life moves up the mountains in the wake of
spring and later hurries down again before the advance of
winter. The Himalayan and Karakorum ranges show whole
villages of temporary occupation, like the summer trading

town of Gartok at 15,000 feet on the caravan route from Leh to Lhassa, or Shahidula (3,285 meters or 10,925 feet) on the road between Leh and Yarkand;[5] but the boundary of permanent habitation lies several thousand feet below. Comparable to these are the big hotels that serve summer stage-coach travel over the Alps and Rockies, but which are deserted when the first snow closes the passes. Here a zone of altitude, as in the polar regions a zone of latitude, marks the limits of the habitable area.

"Wallace's Line" a typical boundary zone.

The distribution of animals and races shows the limit of their movements or expansion. Any boundary defining the limits of such movements can not from its nature be fixed, and hence can not be a line. It is always a zone. Yet "Wallace's Line," dividing the Oriental from the Australian zoological realm, and running through Macassar Strait southward between Bali and Lombok, is a generally accepted dictum. The details of Wallace's investigation, however, reveal the fact that this boundary is not a line, but a zone of considerable and variable width, enclosing the line on either side with a marginal belt of mixed character. Though Celebes, lying to the east of Macassar Strait, is included in the Australian realm, it has lost so large a proportion of Australian types of animals, and contains so many Oriental types from the west, that Wallace finds it almost impossible to decide on which side of the line it belongs.[6] The Oriental admixture extends yet farther east over the Moluccas and Timor. Birds of Javan or Oriental origin, to the extent of thirty genera, have spread eastward well across Wallace's Line; some of these stop short at Flores, and some reach even to Timor,[7] while Australian cockatoos, in turn, have been seen on the west coast of Bali but not in Java. Heilprin avoids the unscientific term line, because he finds his zoological realms divided by "transition regions," which are intermediate in animal types as they are in geographical location.[8] Wallace notes a similar "debatable land" in the Rajputana Desert east of the Indus, which is the border district between the Oriental and Ethiopian realms.[9]

Boundaries as limits of movements or expansion.

Such boundaries mark the limits of that movement which is common to all animate things. Every living form spreads until it meets natural conditions in which it can no longer survive, or until it is checked by the opposing expansion of some competing form. If there is a change either in the life conditions or in the strength of the competing forms, the boundary shifts. In the propitious climate of the Genial Period, plants and animals lived nearer to the North Pole than at present; then they fell back before the advance of the ice sheet. The restless surface of the ocean denies to man a dwelling place; every century, however, the Dutch are pushing forward their northern boundary by reclamation of land from the sea; but repeatedly they have had to drop back for a time when the water has again overwhelmed their hand-made territory.

The boundaries of race and state which are subjected to greatest fluctuations are those determined by the resistance of other peoples. The westward sweep of the Slavs prior to the eighth century carried them beyond the Elbe into contact with the Germans; but as these increased in numbers, outgrew their narrow territories and inaugurated a counter-movement eastward, the Slavs began falling back to the Oder, to the Vistula, and finally to the Niemen. Though the Mohawk Valley opened an easy avenue of expansion westward for the early colonists of New York, the advance of settlements up this valley for several decades went on at only a snail's pace, because of the compact body of Iroquois tribes holding this territory. In the unoccupied land farther south between the Cumberland and Ohio rivers the frontier went forward with leaps and bounds, pushed on by the expanding power of the young Republic. [See map page 156.]

Peoples as barriers.

Anything which increases the expanding force of a people —the establishment of a more satisfactory government by which the national consciousness is developed, as in the American and French revolutions, the prosecution of a successful war by which popular energies are released from an old restraint, mere increase of population, or an impulse communicated by some hostile and irresistible force behind—all are registered in an advance of the boundary of the people in question and a corresponding retrusion of their neighbor's frontier.

Boundary zone as index of growth or decline.

The border district is the periphery of the growing or declining race or state. It runs the more irregularly, the greater are the variations in the external conditions as represented by climate, soil, barriers, and natural openings, according as these facilitate or obstruct advance. When it is contiguous with the border of another state or race, the two form a zone in which ascendency from one side or the other is being established. The boundary fluctuates, for equilibrium of the contending forces is established rarely and for only short periods. The more aggressive people throws out across this debatable zone, along the lines of least resistance or greatest attraction, long streamers of occupation; so that the frontier takes on the form of a fringe of settlement, whose interstices are occupied by a corresponding fringe of the displaced people. Such was its aspect in early colonial America, where population spread up every fertile river valley across a zone of Indian land; and such it is in northern Russia to-day, where long narrow Slav bands run out from the area of continuous Slav settlement across a wide belt of Mongoloid territory to the shores of the White Sea and Arctic Ocean.[10] [See maps pages 103 and 225.]

The border zone is further broadened by the formation of ethnic islands beyond the base line of continuous settlement, which then advances more or less rapidly, if expansion is unchecked, till it coalesces with these outposts, just as the forest line on the mountains may reach, under advantageous conditions, its farthest outlying tree. Such ethnic peninsulas and islands we see in the early western frontiers of the United States from 1790 to 1840, when that frontier was daily moving westward.[11] [See map page 156.]

Breadth of the boundary zone.

The breadth of the frontier zone is indicative of the activity of growth on the one side and the corresponding decline on the other, because extensive encroachment in the same degree disintegrates the territory of the neighbor at whose cost such encroachment is made. A straight, narrow race boundary, especially if it is nearly coincident with a political boundary, points to an equilibrium of forces which means, for the time being at least, a cessation of growth. Such boundaries are found in old, thickly populated countries, while the wide, ragged border zone belongs to new, and especially to colonial peoples. In the oldest and most densely populated seats of the Germans, where they are found in the Rhine Valley, the boundaries of race and empire are straight and simple; but the younger, eastern border, which for centuries has been steadily advancing at the cost of the unequally matched Slavs, has the ragged outline and sparse population of a true colonial frontier. Between two peoples who have had a long period of growth behind them, the oscillations of the boundary decrease in amplitude, as it were, and finally approach a state of rest. Each people tends to fill out its area evenly; every advance in civilization, every increase of population, increases the stability of their tenure, and hence the equilibrium of the pressure upon the boundary. Therefore, in such countries, racial, linguistic and cultural boundaries tend to become simpler and straighter.

The growth is more apparent, or, in other words, the border zone is widest and most irregular, where a superior people intrudes upon the territory of an inferior race. Such was the broad zone of thinly scattered farms and villages amid a prevailing wilderness and hostile Indian tribes which, in 1810 and 1820, surrounded our Trans-Allegheny area of continuous settlement in a one to two hundred mile wide girdle. Such has been the wide, mobile frontier of the Russian advance in Siberia and until recently in Manchuria, which aimed to include within a dotted line of widely separated railway-guard stations, Cossack barracks, and penal colonies, the vast territory which later generations were fully to occupy. Similar, too, is the frontier of the Dutch and English settlements in South Africa, which has been pushed forward into the Kaffir country—a broad belt of scattered cattle ranches and isolated mining hives, dropped down amid Kaffir hunting and grazing lands. Broader still was that shadowy belt of. American occupation which for four decades immediately succeeding the purchase of Louisiana stretched in the form of isolated fur-stations, lonely trappers' camps, and shifting traders' *rendezvous* from the Mississippi to the western slope of the Rockies and the northern watershed of the Missouri, where it met the corre-

The broad frontier zone of active expansion.

sponding nebulous outskirts of the far-away Canadian state on the St. Lawrence River.

The same process with the same geographical character has been going on in the Sahara, as the French since 1890 have been expanding southward from the foot of the Atlas Mountains in Algeria toward Timbuctoo at the cost of the nomad Tuaregs. Territory is first subdued and administered by the military till it is fully pacified. Then it is handed over to the civil government. Hence the advancing frontier consists of a military zone of administration, with a civil zone behind it, and a weaker wavering zone of exploration and scout work before it.[12] Lord Curzon in his Romanes lecture describes the northwest frontier of India as just such a three-ply border.

Economic factors in expanding frontiers. The untouched resources of such new countries tempt to the widespread superficial exploitation, which finds its geographical expression in a broad, dilating frontier. Here the man-dust which is to form the future political planet is thinly disseminated, swept outward by a centrifugal force. Furthermore, the absence of natural barriers which might block this movement, the presence of open plains and river highways to facilitate it, and the predominance of harsh conditions of climate or soil rendering necessary a savage, extensive exploitation of the slender resources, often combine still further to widen the frontier zone. This was the case in French Canada and till recent decades in Siberia, where intense cold and abundant river highways stimulated the fur trade to the practical exclusion of all other activities, and substituted for the closely grouped, sedentary farmers with their growing families the wide-ranging trader with his Indian or Tunguse wife and his half-breed offspring. Under harsh climatic conditions, the fur trade alone afforded those large profits which every infant colony must command in order to survive; and the fur trade meant a wide frontier zone of scattered posts amid a prevailing wilderness. The French in particular, by the possession of the St. Lawrence and Mississippi rivers, the greatest systems in America, were lured into the danger of excessive expansion, attenuated their ethnic element, and failed to raise the economic status of their wide border district, which could therefore offer only

slight resistance to the spread of solid English settlement.[13]
Yet more recently, the chief weakness of the Russians in
Siberia and Manchuria—apart from the corruption of the
national government—was the weakness of a too remote and
too sparsely populated frontier, and of a people whose inner
development had not kept pace with their rate of expansion.

Wasteful exploitation of a big territory is easier than the
economical development of a small district. This is one line
of least resistance which civilized man as well as savage
instinctively follows, and which explains the tendency toward excessive expansion characteristic of all primitive and
nascent peoples. For such peoples natural barriers which
set bounds to this expansion are of vastly greater importance than they are for mature or fully developed peoples.
The reason is this: the boundary is only the expression of
the outward movement or growth, which is nourished from
the same stock of race energy as is the inner development.
Either carried to an excess weakens or retards the other.
If population begins to press upon the limits of subsistence,
the acquisition of a new bit of territory obviates the necessity
of applying more work and more intelligence to the old area,
to make it yield subsistence for the growing number of
mouths; the stimulus to adopt better economic methods is
lost. Therefore, natural boundaries drawn by mountain,
·sea and desert, serving as barriers to the easy appropriation of new territory, have for such peoples a far deeper
significance than the mere determination of their political
frontiers by physical features, or the benefit of protection.

The land with the most effective geographical boundaries
is a naturally defined region like Korea, Japan, China,
Egypt, Italy, Spain, France or Great Britain—a land characterized not only by exclusion from without through its
encircling barriers, but also by the inclusion within itself of
a certain compact group of geographic conditions, to whose
combined influences the inhabitants are subjected and from
which they cannot readily escape. This aspect is far more
important than the mere protection which such boundaries
afford. They are not absolutely necessary for the development of a people, but they give it an early start, accelerate

Value of barrier boundaries.

the process, and bring the people to an early maturity; they stimulate the exploitation of all the local geographic advantages and resources, the formation of a vivid tribal or national consciousness and purpose, and concentrate the national energies when the people is ready to overleap the old barriers. The early development of island and peninsula peoples and their attainment of a finished ethnic and political character are commonplaces of history. The stories of Egypt, Crete and Greece, of Great Britain and Japan, illustrate the stimulus to maturity which emanates from such confining boundaries. The wall of the Appalachians narrowed the westward horizon of the early English colonies in America, guarded them against the excessive expansion which was undermining the French dominion in the interior of the continent, set a most wholesome limit to their aims, and thereby intensified their utilization of the narrow land between mountains and sea. France, with its limits of growth indicated by the Mediterranean, Pyrenees, Atlantic, Channel, Vosges, Jura and Western Alps, found its period of adolescence shortened and, like Great Britain, early reached its maturity. Nature itself set the goal of its territorial expansion, and by crystallizing the political ideal of the people, made that goal easier to reach, just as the dream of "United Italy" realized in 1870 had been prefigured in contours drawn by Alpine range and Mediterranean shore-line.

The sea as the absolute boundary   The area which a race or people occupies is the resultant of the expansive force within and the obstacles without, either physical or human. Insurmountable physical obstacles are met where all life conditions disappear, as on the borders of the habitable world, where man is barred from the unpeopled wastes of polar ice-fields and unsustaining oceans. The frozen rim of arctic lands, the coastline of the continents, the outermost arable strip on the confines of the desert, the barren or ice-capped ridge of high mountain range, are all such natural boundaries which set more or less effective limits to the movement of peoples and the territorial growth of states. The sea is the only absolute boundary, because it alone blocks the continuous, unbroken expansion of a people. When the Saxons of the lower Elbe spread to the island of

Britain, a zone of unpeopled sea separated their new settlements from their native villages on the mainland. Even the most pronounced land barriers, like the Himalayas and Hindu Kush, have their passways and favored spots for short summer habitation, where the people from the opposite slopes meet and mingle for a season. Sandy wastes are hospitable at times. When the spring rains on the mountains of Abyssinia start a wave of moisture lapping over the edges of the Nubian desert, it is immediately followed by a tide of Arabs with their camels and herds, who make a wide zone of temporary occupation spread over the newly created grassland, but who retire in a few weeks before the desiccating heat of summer.[14]

Nevertheless, all natural features of the earth's surface which serve to check, retard or weaken the expansion of peoples, and therefore hold them apart, tend to become racial or political boundaries; and all present a zone-like character. The wide ice-field of the Scandinavian Alps was an unpeopled waste long before the political boundary was drawn along it. "It has not in reality been a definite natural *line* that has divided Norway from her neighbour on the east; it has been a *band* of desert land, up to hundreds of miles in width. So utterly desolate and apart from the area of continuous habitation has this been, that the greater part of it, the district north of Trondhjem, was looked upon even as recently as the last century as a common district. Only nomadic Lapps wandered about in it, sometimes taxed by all three countries. A parcelling out of this desert common district was not made toward Russia until 1826. Toward Sweden it was made in 1751."[15] In former centuries the Bourtanger Moor west of the River Ems used to be a natural desert borderland separating East and West Friesland, despite the similarity of race, speech and country on either side of it. It undoubtedly contributed to the division of Germany and the Netherlands along the present frontier line, which has been drawn the length of this moor for a hundred kilometers.[16]

[margin note: Natural boundaries as bases of ethnic and political boundaries*]*

Any geographical feature which, like this, presents a practically uninhabitable area, forms a scientific boundary, not

[margin note: Primitive waste boundaries.*]*

only because it holds apart the two neighboring peoples and thereby reduces the contact and friction which might be provocative of hostilities, but also because it lends protection against attack. This motive, as also the zone character of all boundaries, comes out conspicuously in the artificial border wastes surrounding primitive tribes and states in the lower status of civilization. The early German tribes depopulated their borders in a wide girdle, and in this wilderness permitted no neighbors to reside. The width of this zone indicated the valor and glory of the state, but was also valued as a means of protection against unexpected attack.[17] Cæsar learned that between the Suevi and Cherusci tribes dwelling near the Rhine *"silvam esse ibi, infinita magnitudine quae appelletur Bacenis; hanc longe introrsus pertinere et pro nativo muro objectam Cheruscos ab Suevis Suevosque ab Cheruscis injuriis incursionibusque prohibere."*[18] The same device appears among the Huns. When Attila was pressing upon the frontier of the Eastern Empire in 448 A. D., his envoys sent to Constantinople demanded that the Romans should not cultivate a belt of territory, a hundred miles wide and three hundred miles long, south of the Danube, but maintain this as a March.[19] When King Alfonso I. (751-764 A. D.) of mountain Asturias began the reconquest of Spain from the Saracens, he adopted the same method of holding the foe at arm's length. He seized Old Castile as far as the River Duoro, but the rest of the province south of that stream he converted into a waste boundary by transporting the Christians thence to the north side, and driving the Mohammedans yet farther southward.[20] Similarly Xenophon found that the Armenian side of the River Kentrites, which formed the boundary between the Armenian plains and the highlands of Karduchia, was unpeopled and destitute of villages for a breadth of fifteen miles, from fear of the marauding Kurds.[21] In the eastern Sudan, especially in that wide territory along the Nile-Congo watershed occupied by the Zandeh, Junker found the frontier wilderness a regular institution owing to the exposure of the border districts in the perennial intertribal feuds.[22] The same testimony comes from Barth,[23] Boyd Alexander,[24] Speke,[25] and other explorers in the Sudan and the neighboring parts of equatorial Africa.

The vast and fertile region defined by the Ohio and Ten- Border
nessee rivers, lay as a debatable border between the Algonquin wastes of
Indians of the north and the Appalachians of the south. Indian lands.
Both claimed it, both used it for hunting, but neither dared
dwell therein.[26] Similarly the Cherokees had no definite
understanding with their savage neighbors as to the limits
of their respective territories The effectiveness of their claim
to any particular tract of country usually diminished with
every increase of its distance from their villages. The consequence was that a considerable strip of territory between
the settlements of two tribes, Cherokees and Creeks for instance, though claimed by both, was practically considered
neutral ground and the common hunting ground of both.[27]
The Creeks, whose most western villages from 1771 to 1798
were located along the Coosa and upper Alabama rivers,[28]
were separated by 300 miles of wilderness from the Chickasaws to the northwest, and by a 150-mile zone from the
Choctaws. The most northern Choctaw towns, in turn, lay
160 miles to the south of the Chickasaw nation, whose compact settlements were located on the watershed between the
western sources of the Tombigby and the head stream of the
Yazoo.[29] The wide intervening zone of forest and canebrake
was hunted upon by both nations.[30]

Sometimes the border is preserved as a wilderness by formal agreement. A classic example of this case is found
in the belt of untenanted land, fifty to ninety kilometers wide,
which China and Korea once maintained as their boundary.
No settler from either side was allowed to enter, and all
travel across the border had to use a single passway, where
three times annually a market was held.[31] On the Russo-
Mongolian border south of Lake Baikal, the town of Kiakhta,
which was established in 1688 as an entrepôt of trade between
the two countries, is occupied in its northern half by Russian
factories and in its southern by the Mongolian-Chinese quarters, while between the two is a neutral space devoted to com- Alien in-
merce.[32] trusions

These border wastes do not always remain empty, however, into border
even when their integrity is respected by the two neighbors wastes.

whom they serve to divide; alien races often intrude into their unoccupied reaches. The boundary wilderness between the Sudanese states of Wadai and Dar Fur harbors several semi-independent states whose insignificance is a guarantee of their safety from conquest.[33] Similarly in the wide border district between the Creeks on the east and the Choctaws on the west were found typical small, detached tribes—the Chatots and Thomez of forty huts each on the Mobile River, the Tensas tribe with a hundred huts on the Tensas River, and the Mobilians near the confluence of the Tombigby and Alabama.[34] Along the desolate highland separating Norway and Sweden the nomadic Lapps, with their reindeer herds, have penetrated southward to 62° North Latitude, reinforcing the natural barrier by another barrier of alien race. From this point southward, the coniferous forests begin and continue the border waste in the form of a zone some sixty miles wide; this was unoccupied till about 1600, when into it slowly filtered an immigration of Finns, whose descendants to-day constitute an important part of the still thin population along the frontier to the heights back of Christiania. Only thirty miles from the coast does the border zone between Norway and Sweden, peopled chiefly by intruding foreign stocks, Lapps and Finns, contract and finally merge into the denser Scandinavian settlements.[35]

Where the border waste offers favorable conditions of life and the intruding race has reached a higher status of civilization, it multiplies in this unpeopled tract and soon spreads at the cost of its less advanced neighbors. The old No Man's Land between the Ohio and Tennessee was a line of least resistance for the expanding Colonies, who here poured in a tide of settlement between the northern and southern Indians, just as later other pioneers filtered into the vague border territory of weak tenure between the Choctaws and Creeks, and there on the Tombigby, Mobile and Tensas rivers, formed the nucleus of the State of Alabama.[36]

Politico-economic significance of the waste boundary.

This untenanted hem of territory surrounding so many savage and barbarous peoples reflects their superficial and unsystematic utilization of their soil, by reason of which the importance of the land itself and the proportion of population to area are greatly reduced. It is a part of that un-economic and extravagant use of the land, that appropriation of wide territories by small tribal groups, which characterizes the lower stages of civilization, as opposed to the exploitation of every square foot for the support of a teeming humanity, which marks the most advanced states. Each stage puts its own valuation upon the land according to the return from it which each expects to get. The low valuation is expressed in the border wilderness, by which a third or even a half of the whole area is wasted; and also in the readiness with which savages often sell their best territory for a song.

For the same reason they leave their boundaries undefined; a mile nearer or farther, what does it matter? Moreover, their fitful or nomadic occupation of the land leads to oscillations of the frontiers with every attack from without and every variation of the tribal strength within. Their unstable states rarely last long enough in a given form or size to develop fixed boundaries; hence, the vagueness as to the extent of tribal domains among all savage peoples, and the conflicting land claims which are the abiding source of war. Owing to these overlapping boundaries—border districts claimed but not occupied—the American colonists met with difficulties in their purchase of land from the Indians, often paying twice for the same strip.

Even civilized peoples may adopt a waste boundary where Common the motive for protection is peculiarly strong, as in the half- boundary mile neutral zone of lowland which ties the rock of Gibraltar districts. to Spain. On a sparsely populated frontier, where the abundance of land reduces its value, they may throw the boundary into the form of a common district, as in the vast, disputed Oregon country, accepted provisionally as a district of joint occupancy between the United States and Canada from 1818 to 1846, or that wide highland border which Norway so long shared with Russia and Sweden. In South America, where land is abundant and population sparse, this common boundary belt is not rare. It suggests a device giving that leeway for expansion desired by all growing states. By the treaty of 1866, the frontier between Chile and Bolivia crossed the Atacama desert at 24°

South Latitude; but the zone between 23° and 25° was left under the common jurisdiction of the two states, for exploitation of the guano deposits and mineral wealth.[37] A common border district on a much larger scale is found between Brazil and the eastern frontier of French Guiana. It includes a belt 185 miles (300 kilometers) wide between the Oyapok and Arawary rivers, and is left as a neutral district till its fate is decided by arbitration.[38] All these instances are only temporary phases in the evolution of a political frontier from wide, neutral border to the mathematically determined boundary line required by modern civilized states.

Tariff free zones.

Even when the boundary line has been surveyed and the boundary pillars set up, the frontier is prone to assert its old zonal nature, simply because it marks the limits of human movements. Rarely, for instance, does a customs boundary coincide with a political frontier, even in the most advanced states of Europe, except on the coasts. The student of Baedecker finds a gap of several miles on the same railroad between the customs frontier of Germany and France, or France and Italy. Where the border district is formed by a high and rugged mountain range, the custom houses recede farther and farther from the common political line upon the ridge, and drop down the slope to convenient points, leaving between them a wide neutral tariff zone, like that in Haute Savoie along the massive Mont Blanc Range between France and Italy.

Allied to this phase, yet differing from it, is the "Zona Libre" or Free Zone, 12 miles broad and 1,833 miles long, which forms the northern hem of Mexico from the Gulf to the Pacific. Here foreign goods pay only 18 1-2 per cent., formerly only 2 1-2 per cent., of the usual federal duties. Goods going on into the interior pay the rest of the tariff at the inner margin of the Zone. This arrangement was adopted in 1858 to establish some sort of commercial equilibrium between the Mexican towns of the Rio Grande Valley, which were burdened by excessive taxation on internal trade, and the Texas towns across the river, which at this time enjoyed a specially low tariff. Consequently prices of food and manufactured goods were twice or four times as high on the Mexican as on the American side. The result was persistent smuggling, extensive emigration from the southern to the northern bank, and the commercial decline of the frontier states of Mexico, till the Zona Libre adjusted the commercial discrepancy.[39] Since 1816 a tariff free zone a league wide has formed the border of French Savoy along the Canton and Lake of Geneva, thus uniting this canton by a free passway with the Swiss territory at the upper end of the lake.[40]

When the political boundary has evolved by a system of contraction out of the wide waste zone to the nicely determined line, that line, nevertheless, is always encased, as it were, in a zone of contact wherein are mingled the elements of either side. The zone includes the peripheries of the two contiguous racial or national bodies, and in it each is modified and assimilated to the other. On its edges it is strongly marked by the characteristics of the adjacent sides, but its medial band shows a mingling of the two in ever-varying proportions; it changes from day to day and shifts backward and forward, according as one side or the other exercises in it more potent economic, religious, racial, or political influences. *Boundary zones of mingled race elements.*

Its peripheral character comes out strongly in the mingling of contiguous ethnic elements found in every frontier district. Here is that zone of transitional form which we have seen prevails so widely in nature. The northern borderland of the United States is in no small degree Canadian, and the southern is strongly Mexican. In the Rio Grande counties of Texas, Mexicans constituted in 1890 from 27 to 55 per cent. of the total population, and they were distributed in considerable numbers also in the second tier of counties. A broad band of French and English Canadians overlaps the northern hem of United States territory from Maine to North Dakota.[41] In the New York and New England counties bordering on the old French province of Quebec, they constitute from 11 to 22 per cent. of the total population, except in two or three western counties of Maine which have evidently been mere passways for a tide of *habitants* moving on to more attractive conditions of life in the counties just to the south.[42] But even these large figures do not adequately represent the British-American element within our boundaries, because they leave out of account the native-born of Canadian parents who have been crossing our borders for over a generation.

Ethnic border zones in the Alps.   If we turn to northern Italy, where a mountain barrier might have been expected to segregate the long-headed Mediterranean stock from the broad-headed Alpine stock, we find as a matter of fact that the ethnic type throughout the Po basin is markedly brachycephalic and becomes more pronounced along the northern boundary in the Alps, till it culminates in Piedmont along the frontier of France, where it becomes identical with the broad-headed Savoyards.[43] More than this, Provençal French is spoken in the Dora Baltea Valley of Piedmont; and along the upper Dora Riparia and in the neighboring valleys of the Chisone and Pellice are the villages of the refugee Waldenses, who speak an idiom allied to the Provençal. More than this, the whole Piedmontese Italian is characterized by its approach to the French, and the idiom of Turin sounds very much like Provençal.[44] To the north there is a similar exchange between Italy and Switzerland with the adjacent Austrian province of the Tyrol. In the rugged highlands of the Swiss Grisons bordering upon Italy, we find a pure Alpine stock, known to the ancients as the Rhaetians, speaking a degenerate Latin tongue called Romansch, which still persists also under the names of Ladino and Frioulian in the Alpine regions of the Tyrol and Italy. In fact, the map of linguistic boundaries in the Grisons shows the dovetailing of German, Italian, and Romansch in a broad zone.[45] The traveller in the southern Tyrol becomes accustomed in the natives to the combination of Italian coloring, German speech, and Alpine head form; whereas, if on reaching Italy he visits the hills back of Vicenza, he finds the German settlements of Tredici and Sette Communi, where German customs, folklore, language, and German types of faces still persist, survivals from the days of German infiltration across the Brenner Pass.[46]

The Slav-German boundary.   Where Slavs and Teutons come together in Central Europe, their race border is a zone lying approximately between 14 and 24 degrees East Longitude; it is crossed by alternate

SLAV-GERMAN BOUNDARY IN EUROPE.

peninsulas of predominant Germans and Austrians from the one side, Czechs and Poles from the other, the whole spattered over by a sprinkling of the two elements. Rarely, and then only for short stretches, do political and ethnic boundaries coincide. The northern frontier hem of East Prussia lying between the River Niemen and the political line of demarcation is quite as much Lithuanian as German, while German stock dots the whole surface of the Baltic provinces of Russia as far as St. Petersburg. The eastern rim of the Kaiser's empire as far south as the Carpathians presents a broad band of the Polish race, averaging about fifty kilometers (30 miles) in width, sparsely sprinkled with German settlements; these are found farther east also as an ethnic archipelago dotting the wide Slav area of Poland. The enclosed basin of Bohemia, protected on three sides by mountain walls and readily accessible to the Slav stock at the sources of the Vistula, enabled the Czechs to penetrate far westward and there maintain themselves; but in spite of encompassing mountains, the inner or Bohemian slopes of the Boehmer Wald, Erz, and Sudetes ranges constitute a broad girdle of almost solid German population.[47] In the Austrian provinces of Moravia and Silesia, which form the southeastward continuation of this Slav-German boundary zone, 60 per cent. of the population are Czechs, 33 per cent. are German, and 7 per cent., found in the eastern part of Silesia, are Poles.[48]

An ethnic map of the western Muscovite Empire in Europe shows a marked infiltration into White and Little Russia of West Slavs from Poland, and in the province of Bessarabia alternate areas of Russians and Roumanians. The latter in places form an unbroken ethnic expansion from the home kingdom west of the Pruth, extending in solid bands as far as the Dniester, and throwing out ethnic islands between this stream and the Bug.

Assimilation of culture in boundary zones. In the northern provinces of Russia, in the broad zone shared by the aboriginal Finns and the later-coming Slavs, Wallace found villages in every stage of Russification. "In one everything seemed thoroughly Finnish; the inhabitants had a reddish-olive skin, very high cheek bones, obliquely set eyes, and a peculiar costume; none of the women and very few of the men could understand Russian and any Russian

Poles
Swedes
Magyars
Russian
German

ETHNOGRAPHICAL MAP OF RUSSIA.

MONGOLOID: Kalmucks, Kirghis, Nogai, Tartars, Bashkirs, Voguls, Ostiaks, Samoyedes.
ZIRIAN: Mingled Mongoloid and Finnish.

who visited the place was regarded as a foreigner. In the second, there were already some Russian inhabitants; the others had lost something of their purely Finnish type, many of the men had discarded the old costume and spoke Russian fluently, and a Russian visitor was no longer shunned. In a third, the Finnish type was still further weakened; all the men spoke Russian, and nearly all the women understood it; the old male costume had entirely disappeared and the old female was rapidly following it; and intermarriage with the Russian population was no longer rare. In a fourth, intermarriage had almost completely done its work, and the old Finnish element could be detected merely in certain peculiarities of physiognomy and accent." This amalgamation extends to their religions—prayers wholly pagan devoutly uttered under the shadow of a strange cross, next the Finnish god Yumak sharing honors equally with the Virgin, finally a Christianity pure in doctrine and outward forms except for the survival of old pagan ceremonies in connection with the dead.[49]

At the confluence of the Volga and Kama rivers, this boundary zone of Russians and Finns meets the borderland of the Asiatic Mongols; and here is found an intermingling of races, languages, religions, and customs scarcely to be equalled elsewhere. Finns are infused with Tartar as well as Russian blood, and Russians show Tartar as well as Finnish traits. The Bashkirs, who constitute an ethnic peninsula running from the solid Mongolian mass of Asia, show every type of the mongrel.[50] [See map page 225.]

Boundary zones of assimilation in Asia   If we turn to Asia and examine the western race boundary of the expanding Chinese, we find that a wide belt of mingled ethnic elements, hybrid languages, and antagonistic civilizations marks the transition from Chinese to Mongolian and Tibetan areas. The eastern and southern frontiers of Mongolia, formerly marked by the Great Wall, are now difficult to define, owing to the steady encroachment of the agricultural Chinese on the fertile edges of the plateau, where they have converted the best-watered pastures of the Mongols into millet fields and vegetable gardens, leaving for the nomad's herds the more sterile patches between.[51] Every line of least resistance—climatic, industrial, commercial—sees the Chinese widening this transitional zone. He sprinkles his crops over the "Land of Grass," invades the trade of the caravan towns, sets up his fishing station on the great northern bend of the Hoangho in the Ordos country, three hundred miles beyond the Wall, to exploit the fishing neglected by the Mongols.[52] The well-watered regions of the Nan-Shan ranges has enabled him to drive a long, narrow ethnic wedge, represented by the westward projection of Kansu Province between Mongolia and Tibet, into the heart of the Central Plateau. [See map page 103.] Here the nomad Si Fan tribes dwell side by side with Chinese farmers,[53] who themselves show a strong infusion of the Mongolian and Tibetan blood to the north and south, and whose language is a medley of all three tongues.[54]

In easternmost Tibet, in the elevated province of Minjak (2,600 meters or 8,500 feet), M. Huc found in 1846 a great number of Chinese from the neighboring Sze-Chuan and Yun-nan districts keeping shops and following the primary trades and agriculture. The language of the Tibetan natives showed the effect of foreign intercourse; it was not the pure speech of Lhassa, but was closely assimilated to the idiom of the neighboring Si Fan speech of Sze-Chuan and contained many Chinese expressions. He found also a modification of manners, customs, and costumes in this peripheral Tibet; the natives showed more of the polish, cunning, and covetousness of the Chinese, less of the rudeness, frankness, and strong religious feeling characteristic of the western plateau man.[55] Just across the political boundary in Chinese territory, the border zone of assimilation shows predominance of the Chinese element with a strong Tibetan admixture both in race and civilization.[56] Here Tibetan traders with their yak caravans are met on the roads or encamped in their tents by the hundred about the frontier towns, whither they have brought the wool, sheep, horses, hides and medicinal roots of the rough highland across that "wild borderland which is neither Chinese nor Tibetan." The Chinese population consists of hardy mountaineers, who eat millet and maize instead of rice. The prevailing architecture is Tibetan and

Boundary zones of mountain Tibet.

the priests on the highways are the red and yellow lamas from the Buddhist monasteries of the plateau. "The Country is a cross between China and Tibet." [57]

Even the high wall of the Himalayas does not suffice to prevent similar exchanges of ethnic elements and culture between southern Tibet and northern India. Lhassa and Giamda harbor many emigrants from the neighboring Himalayan state of Bhutan, allow them to monopolize the metal industry, in which they excel, and to practise undisturbed their Indian form of Buddhism.[58] The southern side of this zone of transition is occupied by a Tibetan stock of people inhabiting the Himalayan frontiers of India and practising the Hindu religion.[59] In the hill country of northern Bengal natives are to be seen with the Chinese queue hanging below a Hindu turban, or wearing the Hindu caste mark on their broad Mongolian faces. With these are mingled genuine Tibetans who have come across the border to work in the tea plantations of this region.[60] [See map page 102.]

Relation of ethnic and cultural assimilation. The assimilation of culture within a boundary zone is in some respects the result of race amalgamation, as, for instance, in costume, religion, manners and language; but in economic points it is often the result of identical geographic influences to which both races are alike subjected. For example, scarcity of food on the arid plateau of Central Asia makes the Chinese of western Kansu eat butter and curds as freely as do the pastoral Mongols, though such a diet is obnoxious to the purely agricultural Chinese of the lowlands.[61] The English pioneer in the Trans-Allegheny wilderness shared with the Indians an environment of trackless forests and savage neighbors; he was forced to discard for a time many essentials of civilization, both material and moral. Despite a minimum of race intermixture, the men of the Cumberland and Kentucky settlements became assimilated to the life of the red man; they borrowed his scalping knife and tomahawk, adopted his method of ambush and extermination in war; like him they lived in great part by the chase, dressed in furs and buckskin, and wore the noiseless moccasin. Here the mere fact of geographical location on a remote frontier, and of almost complete isolation from the centers of English life

on the Atlantic slope, and the further fact of persistent contact with a lower status of civilization, resulted in a temporary
return to primitive methods of existence, till the settlements
secured an increase of population adequate for higher industrial development and for defence.

A race boundary involves almost inevitably a cultural
boundary, often, too, a linguistic and religionary, occasionally a political boundary. The last three are subject to wide
fluctuation, frequently overstepping all barriers of race and
contrasted civilizations. Though one often accompanies
another, it is necessary to distinguish the different kinds of
boundaries and to estimate their relative importance in the
history of a people or state. We may lay down the rule
that the greater, more permanent, and deep-seated the contrasts on the two sides of a border, the greater is its significance ; and that, on this basis, boundaries rank in importance,
with few exceptions, in the following order: racial, cultural,
linguistic, and political. The less marked the contrasts, in
general, the more rapid and complete the process of assimilation in the belt of borderland.

The significance of the border zone of assimilation for The
political expansion lies in the fact that it prepares the way boundary
for the advance of the state boundary from either side; in it zone in
the sharp edge of racial and cultural antagonism is removed, expansion.
or for this antagonism a new affinity may be substituted.
The zone of American settlement, industry, and commerce
which in 1836 projected beyond the political boundary of
the Sabine River over the eastern part of Mexican Texas
facilitated the later incorporation of the State into the Union,
just as a few years earlier the Baton Rouge District of
Spanish West Florida had gravitated to the United States
by reason of the predominant American element there, and
thus extended the boundary of Louisiana to the Pearl River.
When the political boundary of Siberia was fixed at the
Amur River, the Muscovite government began extending
the border zone of assimilation far to the south of that stream
by the systematic Russification of Manchuria, with a view to
its ultimate annexation. Schleswig-Holstein and Alsace-
Lorraine, by reason of their large German population, have

been readily incorporated into the German Empire. Only in Lorraine has a considerable French element retarded the process. The considerable sprinkling of Germans over the Baltic provinces of Russia and Poland west of the Vistula, and a certain Teutonic stamp of civilization which these districts have received, would greatly facilitate the eastward extension of the German Empire; while their common religions, both Protestant and Roman Catholic, would help obliterate the old political fissure. Thus the borderland of a country, so markedly differentiated from its interior, performs a certain historical function, and becomes, as it were, an organ of the living, growing race or state.

Tendency toward defection along political frontiers. Location on a frontier involves remoteness from the center of national, cultural, and political activities; these reach their greatest intensity in the core of the nation and exercise only an attenuated influence on the far-away borders, unless excellent means of communication keep up a circulation of men, commodities, and ideas between center and periphery. For the frontier, therefore, the centripetal force is weakened; the centrifugal is strengthened often by the attraction of some neighboring state or tribe, which has established bonds of marriage, trade, and friendly intercourse with the outlying community. Moreover, the mere infusion of foreign blood, customs, and ideas, especially a foreign religion, which is characteristic of a border zone, invades the national solidarity. Hence we find that a tendency to political defection constantly manifests itself along the periphery. A long reach weakens the arm of authority, especially where serious geographical barriers intervene; hence border uprisings are usually successful, at least for a time. When accomplished, they involve that shrinkage of the frontiers which we have found to be the unmistakable symptom of national decline.

This defection shows itself most promptly in conquered border tribes of different blood, who lack the bond of ethnic affinity, and whose remoteness emboldens them to throw off the political yoke. The decay of the Roman Empire, after its last display of energy under Trajan, was registered in the revolt of its peripheral districts beyond the Euphrates, Danube, and Rhine, as also in the rapid Teutonization of eastern

Gaul, which here prepared the way for the assertion of independence. The border satraps of the ancient Persian Empire were constantly revolting, as the history of Asia Minor shows. Aragon, Old Castile, and Portugal were the first kingdoms in the Iberian Peninsula to throw off Saracen dominion. Mountain ranges and weary stretches of desert roads enabled the rebellions in Chinese Turkestan and the border districts of Sungaria in 1863 to be maintained for several years.[62]

A feeble grasp upon remote peripheral possessions is often further weakened by the resistance of an immigrant population from beyond the boundary, which brings with it new ideas of government. This was the geographical history of the Texan revolt. A location on the far northern outskirts of Mexican territory, some twelve hundred miles from the capital, rendered impossible intelligent government control, the enforcement of the laws, and prompt defence against the Indians. Remoteness weakened the political cohesion. More than this, the American ethnic boundary lapped far over eastern Texas, forming that border zone of two-fold race which we have come to know. This alien stock, antagonistic to the national ideals emanating from the City of Mexico, dominant over the native population by reason of its intelligence, energy, and wealth, ruptured the feeble political bond and asserted the independence of Texas. Quite similar was the history of the "Independent State of Acre," which in 1899 grew up just within the Bolivian frontier under the leadership of Brazilian caoutchouc gatherers, resisted the collection of taxes by the Bolivian government, and four years later secured annexation to Brazil.[63]

Centrifugal forces on the frontier.

Even when no alien elements are present to weaken the race bond, if natural barriers intervene to obstruct and retard communications between center and periphery, the frontier community is likely to develop the spirit of defection, especially if its local geographic, and hence social, conditions are markedly different from those of the governing center. This is the explanation of that demand for independent statehood which was rife in our Trans-Allegheny settlements from 1785 to 1795, and of that separatist movement which advocated political alliance with either the British colonies to the north or the Spanish to the west, because these were nearer and offered easier access to the sea. A frontier location and an intervening mountain barrier were important factors in the Whisky Rebellion in western Pennsylvania, just as similar conditions later suggested the secession of the Pacific States from the Union. Disaffection from the government was manifested by the Trek Boers of early South Africa, "especially by those who dwelt in the outlying districts where the Government had exerted and could exert little control." In 1795 the people of Graaf-Reinet, a frontier settlement of that time, revolted against the Dutch South African Company and set up a miniature republic.[64]

The spirit of colonial frontiers.

The spirit of the colonial frontier is the spirit of freedom, the spirit of men who have traveled far, who are surcharged with energy, enterprise and self-reliance, often with impatience of restraint. A severe process of elimination culls out for the frontier a population strikingly differentiated from the citizens of the old inhabited centers. Then remoteness of location and abundance of opportunity proceed to emphasize the qualities which have squeezed through the sieve of natural and social selection. This is the type bred upon our own frontier, which, West beyond West, has crossed the continent from the backwoods of the Allegheny Mountains to the Pacific. The Siberian frontier develops much the same type on the eastern edge of the Russian Empire. Here army officers find a compensation for their rough surrounding in the escape from the excessive bureaucracy of the capitals. Here is to be noted the independence, self-reliance and self-respect characteristic of other colonial frontiers. The Russian of the Asiatic border is proud to call himself a Siberian: he is already differentiated in his own consciousness. The force of Moscow tradition and discipline is faint when it reaches him, it has traveled so far. Even the elaborate observances of the orthodox Greek Church tend to become simplified on the frontier. The question naturally arises whether in the Russian Empire, as in the United States, the political periphery will in time, react upon the center, infuse it with the spirit of progress and youth.[65]

When to a border situation is added a geographic location affording conditions of long-established isolation, this tendency to maintain political autonomy becomes very pronounced. This is the explanation of so many frontier mountain states that have retained complete or partial independence, such as Nepal, Bhutan, the Asturias, which successfully withstood Saracen attack, and Montenegro, which has repelled alike Venetian, Servian, and Turkish dominion. Europe especially has numerous examples of these unabsorbed border states, whose independence represents the equilibrium of the conflicting political attractions about them. But all these smallest fragments of political territory have either some commercial or semi-political union with one or another of their neighbors. The little independent principality of Liechtenstein, wedged in between Switzerland and the Tyrol, is included in the customs union of Austro-Hungary. The small, independent duchy of Luxemburg, which has been attached in turn to all the great states which have grown up along its borders, is included in the *Zollverein* of Germany. The republic of Andorra, far up in a lofty valley of the Pyrenees, which has maintained its freedom for a thousand years, acknowledges certain rights of suzerainty exercised by France and the Spanish bishopric of Urgel.[66]

Oftentimes a state gains by recognizing this freedom-loving spirit of the frontier, and by turning it to account for national defence along an exposed boundary. In consequence of the long wars between Scotland and England, to the Scotch barons having estates near the Border were given the Wardenships of the Marches, offices of great power and dignity; and their clans, accustomed only to the imperfect military organization demanded by the irregular but persistent hostilities of the time and place, developed a lawless spirit. Prohibited from agriculture by their exposed location, they left their fields waste, and lived by pillage and cattle-lifting from their English and even their Scotch neighbors. The valor of these southern clans, these "reivers of the Border," was the bulwark of Scotland against the English, but their mutinous spirit resisted the authority of the king and led them often to erect semi-independent principalities.[67]

Border nomads as frontier police.

China has fringed her western boundaries with quasi-independent tribes whose autonomy is assured and whose love of freedom is a guarantee of guerilla warfare against any invader from Central Asia. The Mantze tribes in the mountain borders of Sze-Chuan province have their own rulers and customs, and only pay tribute to China.[68] The highlands of Kansu are sprinkled with such independent tribes. Sometimes a definite bargain is entered into—a self-governing military organization and a yearly sum of money in return for defence of the frontier. The Mongol tribes of the Charkar country or "Borderland" just outside the Great Wall northwest of Pekin constitute a paid army of the Emperor to guard the frontier against the Khalkhas of northern Mongolia, the tribe of Genghis Khan.[69] Similarly, semi-independent military communities for centuries made a continuous line of barriers against the raids of the steppe nomads along the southern and southeastern frontiers of Russia, from the Dnieper to the Ural rivers. There were the "Free Cossacks," located on the debatable ground between the fortified frontier of the agricultural steppe and marauding Crimean Tartars. Nominally subjects of the Czar, they obeyed him when it suited them, and on provocation rose in open revolt. The Cossacks of the Dnieper, who to the middle of the seventeenth century formed Poland's border defence against Tartar invasion, were jealous of any interference with their freedom. They lent their services on occasions to the Sultan of Turkey, and even to the Crimean Khan; and finally, in 1681, attached themselves and their territory to Russia.[70] Here speaks that spirit of defection which is the natural product of the remoteness and independence of frontier life. The Russians also attached to themselves the Kalmucks located between the lower Volga and Don, and used them as a frontier defence against their Tartar and Kirghis neighbors.[71] In this case, as in that of the Cossacks and the Charkars of eastern Mongolia, we have a large body of men living in the same arid grassland, leading the same pastoral life, and carrying on the same kind of warfare as the nomadic marauders whose pillaging, cattle-lifting raids they aim to suppress. The imperial orders to the

Charkars limit them strictly to the life of herdmen, with the purpose of maintaining their mobility and military efficiency. So in olden times, for the Don Cossacks agriculture was prohibited on pain of death, lest they should lose their taste for the live-stock booty of a punitive raid. A still earlier instance of this utilization of border nomads is found in the first century after Christ, when the Romans made the Arabian tribe of Beni Jafre, dwelling on the frontier of Syria, the warders of the eastern marches of the Empire.[72]

The advancing frontier of an expanding people often carries them into a sparsely settled country where the unruly members of society can with advantage be utilized as colonists. After centralized and civilized Russia began to encroach with the plow upon the pastures of the steppe Cossacks, and finally suppressed these military republics, the more turbulent and obstinate remnants of them she colonized along the Kuban and Terek rivers, to serve as bulwarks against the incursions of the Caucasus tribes and as the vanguard of the advance southward.[73]

This is one principle underlying the transportation of criminals to the frontier. They serve to hold the new country. There these waste elements of civilization are converted into a useful by-product. They may be only political radicals or religious dissenters: if so, so much the better colonial material. The Russian government formerly transported the rebellious sect of the Molokans or Unitarians to the outskirts of the Empire, where the danger of contagion was reduced. Hence they are to be found to-day scattered in the Volga province of Samara, on the border of the Kirghis steppe, in the Crimea, the Caucasus, and Siberia, still faithful and still persecuted.[74] Since 1709 the Russian advance into Siberia has planted its milestones in settlements formed of prisoners of war, political exiles, and worse offenders.[75] Penal colonists located on the shores of Kamchatka helped build and man the crazy boats which set out for Alaska at the end of the eighteenth century. China settles its thieves and cheats among the villages of its own border provinces of Shensi[76] and Kansu; but its worst criminals it transports far away to the Ili country on the western frontier of the

Lawless citizens deported to frontiers.

Empire, where they have doubtless contributed to the spirit of revolt that has there manifested itself.[77]

Drift of lawless elements to the frontiers.
The abundance of opportunity and lack of competition in a new frontier community, its remoteness from the center of authority, and its imperfect civil government serve to attract thither the vicious, as well as the sturdy and enterprising. The society of the early Trans-Allegheny frontier included both elements. The lawless who drifted to the border formed gangs of horse thieves, highwaymen, and murderers, who called forth from the others the summary methods of lynch law.[78] North Carolina, which in its early history formed the southern frontier of Virginia, swarmed with ruffians who had fled thither to escape imprisonment or hanging, and whose general attitude was to resist all regular authority and especially to pay no taxes.[79] Similarly, that wide belt of mountain forest which forms the waste boundary between Korea and Manchuria is the resort of bandits, who have harried both sides of the border ever since this neutral district was established in the thirteenth century.[80] The frontier communities of the Russian Cossacks in the seventeenth and eighteenth centuries were regular asylums for runaway serfs and peasants who were fleeing from taxation; their hetmans were repeatedly fugitive criminals. The eastern border of Russia formed by the Volga basin in 1775 was described as "an asylum for malcontents and vagabonds of all kinds, ruined nobles, disfrocked monks, military deserters, fugitive serfs, highwaymen, and Volga pirates"—disorderly elements which contributed greatly to the insurrection led by the Ural Cossacks in that year.[81] "The Debatable Land," a tract between the Esk and Sark rivers, formerly claimed by both England and Scotland, was long the haunt of thieves, outlaws and vagabonds, as indeed was the whole Border, subject as it was to the regular jurisdiction of neither side.[82]

Asylums beyond the border.
Just beyond the political boundary, where police authority comes to an end and where pursuit is cut short or retarded, the fleeing criminal finds his natural asylum. Hence all border districts tend to harbor undesirable refugees from the other side. Deserters and outlaws from China proper sprinkle the eastern districts of Mongolia.[83] Marauding

bands of Apaches and Sioux, after successful depredations on American ranches, for years fled across the line into Mexico and Canada before the hammering hoof-beats of Texas Ranger and United States cavalry, until a treaty with Mexico in 1882, authorizing such armed pursuit to cross the boundary, cut off at least one asylum.[84]   Our country exchanges other undesirable citizens with its northern and southern neighbors in cases where no extradition treaty provides for their return; and the borders of the individual states are crossed and recrossed by shifty gentlemen seeking to dodge the arm of the law.   The fact that so many State boundaries fall in the Southern Appalachians, where illicit distilling and feud murders provide most of the cases on the docket, has materially retarded the suppression of these crimes by increasing the difficulty both of apprehending the offender and of subpœnaing the reluctant witness.

Dissatisfied, oppressed, or persecuted members of a political community are prone to seek an asylum across the nearest border, where happier or freer conditions of life are promised.   There they contribute to that mixture of race which characterizes every boundary zone, though as an embittered people they may also help to emphasize any existing political or religious antagonism.   The Revocation of the Edict of Nantes in 1685 was followed by an exodus of Huguenots from France to the Protestant states of Switzerland, the Palatinate of the Rhine, and Holland, as also across the Channel into southern England; just as in recent years the Slav borderland of eastern Germany has received a large immigration of Polish Jews from Russia.   When the Polish king in 1571 executed the leader of the Dnieper Cossacks, thousands of these bold borderers left their country and joined the community of the Don; and in 1722 after the Dnieper community had been crushed by Peter the Great, a similar exodus took place across the southern boundary into the Crimea, whereby the Tartar horde was strengthened, just as a few years before, during an unsuccessful revolt of the Don Cossacks, some two thousand of the malcontents crossed the southern frontier to the Kuban River in Circassia.[85]   The establishment of American independence in 1783 saw an ex-

Border refugees and ethnic mingling.

odus of loyalists from the United States into the contiguous districts of Ontario, New Brunswick, and Spanish Florida. Five years later discontent with the Federal Government for its dilatory opposition to the occlusion of the Mississippi and the lure of commercial betterment sent many citizens of the early Trans-Allegheny commonwealths to the Spanish side of the Mississippi,[86] while the Natchez District on the east bank of the river contained a sprinkling of French who had become dissatisfied with Spanish rule in Louisiana and changed their domicile.

These are some of the movements of individuals and groups which contribute to the blending of races along every frontier, and make of the boundary a variable zone, as opposed to the rigid artificial line in terms of which we speak.

NOTES TO CHAPTER VII

1. A. W. Greely, Report of the Lady Franklin Bay Expedition, Vol. I, ₚp. 28-33, 236. Misc. Doc. No. 393. Washington, 1888.

2. A. P. Engelhardt, A Russian Province of the North, pp. 123-130. Translated from the Russian. London, 1899.

3. Nordenskiold, Voyage of the Vega, pp. 60-62. New York, 1882.

4. Ibid., pp. 146, 161.

5. Col. F. E. Younghusband, The Heart of a Continent, pp. 194-199. London, 1904.

6. A. R. Wallace, Geographical Distribution of Animals, Vol. I, pp. 387-389, 426-431, 436-438. London, 1876.

7. Ibid., 409, 424.

8. A. Heilprin, Geographical Distribution of Animals, pp. 105-108. London, 1894.

9. A. R. Wallace, Geographical Distribution of Animals, Vol. I, pp. 313, 321-322. London, 1876.

10. Anatole Leroy-Beaulieu, The Empire of the Tsars, Vol. I, ethnographical map. New York, 1893.

11. Eleventh Census of the United States, Population, Part I., maps on pp. xviii-xxiii.

12. L. March Phillipps, In the Desert, pp. 64-68, 77. London, 1905.

13. Fully treated in E. C. Semple, American History and Its Geographic Conditions, pp. 22-31. Boston, 1903.

14. Sir S. W. Baker, The Nile Tributaries of Abyssinia, pp. 88, 128-129, 135. Hartford, 1868.

15. Norway, Official Publication for the Paris Exhibition, pp. 3-4 and map. Christiania, 1900.

16. J. Partsch, Central Europe, p. 297. London, 1903.

17. Cæsar, *Bello Gallico*, Book IV, chap. 3 and Book VI, chap. 23.

18. *Ibid.*, Book VI, chap. 10.

19. T. Hodgkin, Italy and Her Invaders, Vol. II, p. 56, note I. Oxford, 1892.

20. Helmolt, History of the World, Vol. IV, p. 510. New York, 1902-1906.

21. Grote, History of Greece, Vol. IX, chap. 70, pp. 99, 115. New York, 1859.

22. Dr. Wilhelm Junker, Travels in Africa, pp. 18, 45, 79, 87, 115, 117, 138, 191, 192, 200, 308, 312, 325, 332. Translated from the German. London, 1892.

23. H. Barth, Human Society in North Central Africa, *Journal Royal Geographical Society*, Vol. XXX, pp. 123-124. London, 1860.

24. Boyd Alexander, From the Niger to the Nile, Vol. II, pp. 163 164. London, 1907.

25. John H. Speke, Discovery of the Sources of the Nile, pp. 74, 89, 91, 94, 95, 173, 176-177, 197. New York, 1868.

26. Theodore Roosevelt, The Winning of the West, Vol. I, pp. 50, 70, 135. New York, 1895.

27. C. C. Royce, The Cherokee Nations of Indians, p. 140. *Fifth Annual Report of the Bureau of Ethnology.* Washington, 1884.

28. Albert J. Pickett, History of Alabama, pp. 79-89, 113-115, 1851. Reprint, Birmingham, 1900. James Adair, History of the American Indians, p. 257. London, 1775.

29. *Ibid.*, pp. 252-3, 282.

30. Albert J. Pickett, History of Alabama, pp. 133-135. 1851. Reprint, Birmingham, 1900.

31. Archibald Little, The Far East, p. 249. Oxford. 1905.

32. M. Huc, Travels in Tartary, Thibet and China, 1844-1846, Vol. I, p. 74. Translated from the French. Reprint, Chicago, 1898.

33. Nachtigal, *Sahara und Sudan*, Vol. I, pp. 102, 448; Vol. III, pp. 203-205, 314. Leipzig, 1889. Boyd Alexander, From the Niger to the Nile, Vol. II, p. 170. London, 1907.

34. Albert J. Pickett, History of Alabama, pp. 118-119. 1851. Reprint, Birmingham, 1900.

35. Norway, Official Publication for the Paris Exhibition, pp. 5, 83-84. Christiania, 1900.

36. Albert J. Pickett, History of Alabama, pp. 416, 417, 461, 467. 1857. Reprint, Birmingham, 1900.

37. C. E. Akers, History of South America, 1854-1904, p. 435. New York, 1904.

38. H. R. Mill, International Geography, p. 883. New York, 1902.

39. Matias Romero, Mexico and the United States, pp. 433-441. New York, 1898.

40. E. Hertslet, The Map of Europe by Treaty, 1814-1875, Vol. I, pp. 422, 425, 426; Vol. II, p. 1430.

41. Eleventh Census of the United States, *Population*, Part I., map No. 10 and p. cxliii.

42. *Ibid.* Based on comparison of Tables 15 and 33 for the States mentioned.

43. W. Z. Ripley, Races of Europe, pp. 250-253. New York, 1899.

44. W. Deecke, Italy, pp. 325, 347, 349. Translated from the German. London, 1904.

45. Sydow-Wagner, *Methodischer Schul-Atlas, Völker und Sprachen-karten*, No. 13. Gotha, 1905. W. Z. Ripley, Races of Europe, pp. 282-284. New York, 1899.

46. *Ibid.*, pp. 255-257. W. Deecke, Italy, p. 357. London, 1904.

47. Sydow-Wagner, *Methodischer Schul-Atlas, Völker und Sprachen-karten* No. 13. Gotha, 1905.

48. Hugh R. Mill, International Geography, p. 309. New York, 1902.

49. D. M. Wallace, Russia, pp. 151-155. New York, 1904.

50. W. Z. Ripley, Races of Europe, p. 362. New York, 1899.

51. Archibald Little, The Far East. Map p. 8 and pp. 171-172. Oxford, 1905. M. Huc, Travels in Tartary, Thibet and China, 1844-1846. Vol. I, pp. 2-4, 21, 197-201, 284. Reprint, Chicago, 1898.

52. *Ibid.*, Vol. I, pp. 166-170.

53. *Ibid.*, Vol II, p. 23.

54. *Ibid.*, Vol. I, 312-313.

55. *Ibid.*, Vol. II, pp. 319-322, 327.

56. M. Huc, Journey through the Chinese Empire, Vol. I, p. 36. New York, 1871.

57. Isabella Bird Bishop, The Yangtze Valley and Beyond, Vol. II, pp. 70-71, 88, 91, 92, 104-109, 113, 117, 133, 134, 155, 194, 195. London, 1900.

58. M. Huc, Travels in Tartary, Thibet and China, 1844-1846, Vol. II, pp. 155-156, 264. Reprint, Chicago, 1898.

59. C. A. Sherring, Western Tibet and the British Borderland, pp. 60, 65-73, 205, 347-358. London, 1906. Statistical Atlas of India, pp. 61-62, maps. Calcutta, 1895. *Imperial Gazetteer of India*, Vol. I, p. 295-296. Oxford, 1907.

60. Eliza R. Scidmore, Winter India, pp. 106-108. New York, 1903.

61. M. Huc, Travels in Tartary, Thibet, and China, 1844-1846, Vol. I, pp. 312-313. Reprint, Chicago, 1898.

62. Alexis Krausse, Russia in Asia, pp. 174-175. New York, 1899.

63. Charles E. Akers, History of South America, 1854-1904, p. 562. New York, 1904.

64. James Bryce, Impressions of South Africa, pp. 108-109. New York, 1897.

65. O. P. Crosby, Tibet and Turkestan, pp. 15-20.

66. H. R. Mill, International Geography, p. 378. New York, 1902. H. Spencer, A Visit to Andorra, *Fortnightly Review*, Vol. 67, pp. 44-60. 1897.

67. Wm. Robertson, History of Scotland, pp. 19-20. New York, 1831. The Scotch Borderers, *Littell's Living Age*, Vol 40, p. 180.

68. Isabella Bird Bishop, The Yangtze Valley and Beyond, Vol. II, pp. 209-210. London, 1900.

69. M. Huc, Travels in Tartary, Thibet and China, 1844-1846, Vol. I, pp. 41, 42, 97. Reprint, Chicago, 1898.

70. D. M. Wallace, Russia, pp. 352-356. New York, 1904. Article on Cossacks in Encyclopedia Britannica.

71. Pallas, Travels in Southern Russia, Vol. I, pp. 126-129; 442; Vol. II, pp. 330-331. London, 1812.

72. G. Adam Smith, Historical Geography of the Holy Land, p. 9. New York, 1897.

73. D. M. Wallace, Russia, p. 358. New York, 1904. Walter K. Kelly, History of Russia, Vol. II, pp. 394-395. London, 1881.

74. D. M. Wallace, Russia, p. 298. New York, 1904.

75. Alexis Krausse, Russia in Asia, pp. 43, 53. New York, 1899.

76. Francis H. Nichol, Through Hidden Shensi, pp. 139-140. New York, 1902.

77. M. Huc, Travels in Tartary, Thibet and China, 1844-1846, Vol. I, p. 23. Reprint, Chicago, 1898.

78. Theodore Roosevelt, The Winning of the West, Vol. I, pp. 130-132. New York, 1895.

79. John Fiske, Old Virginia and Her Neighbors, Vol. II, pp. 311, 315-321. Boston, 1897.

80. Archibald Little, The Far East, p. 249. Oxford, 1905.

81. Alfred Rambaud, History of Russia, Vol. II, pp. 45, 199-200. Boston, 1886.

82. Malcolm Lang, History of Scotland, Vol. I, pp. 42-43. London, 1800. The Scotch Borderland, Gentleman's Magazine, Vol. CCLX, p. 191. 1886.

83. Friedrich Ratel, History of Mankind, Vol. III, p. 175. London, 1896.

84. A. B. Hart, Foundations of American Foreign Policy, pp. 81-82. New York, 1901.

85. Alfred Rambaud, History of Russia, Vol. II, pp. 45, 50. Boston, 1886.

86. Justin Winsor, The Westward Movement, p. 366. Boston, 1899.

CHAPTER VIII

COAST PEOPLES

The coast a zone of transition.

Of all geographical boundaries, the most important is that between land and sea. The coast, in its physical nature, is a zone of transition between these two dominant forms of the earth's surface; it bears the mark of their contending forces, varying in its width with every stronger onslaught of the unresting sea, and with every degree of passive resistance made by granite or sandy shore. So too in an anthropogeographical sense, it is a zone of transition. Now the life-supporting forces of the land are weak in it, and it becomes merely the rim of the sea; for its inhabitants the sea means food, clothes, shelter, fuel, commerce, highway, and opportunity. Now the coast is dominated by the exuberant forces of a productive soil, so that the ocean beyond is only a turbulent waste and a long-drawn barrier: the coast is the hem of the land. Neither influence can wholly exclude the other in this amphibian belt, for the coast remains the intermediary between the habitable expanse of the land and the international highway of the sea. The break of the waves and the dash of the spray draw the line beyond which human dwellings cannot spread; for these the shore is the outermost limit, as for ages also in the long infancy of the races, before the invention of boat and sail, it drew the absolute boundary to human expansion. In historical order, its first effect has been that of a barrier, and for the majority of peoples this it has remained; but with the development of navigation and the spread of human activities from the land over sea to other countries, it became the gateway both of land and sea—at once the outlet for exploration, colonization, and trade, and the open door through which a continent or island receives contributions of men or races or ideas from transoceanic shores. Barrier and threshold: these are the *rôles* which

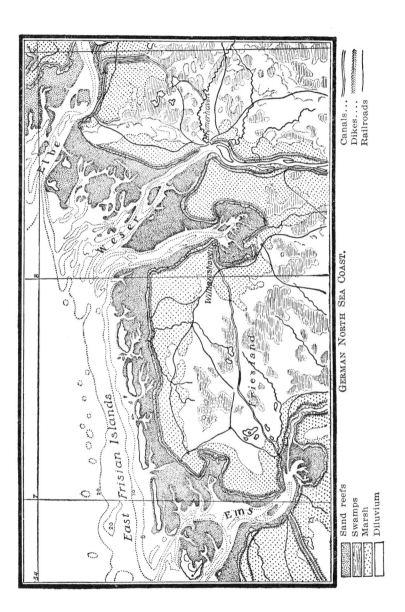

GERMAN NORTH SEA COAST.

Canals....
Dikes....
Railroads

Sand reefs
Swamps
Marsh
Diluvium

coasts have always played in history. To-day we see them side by side. But in spite of the immense proportions assumed by transmarine intercourse, the fact remains that the greater part of the coasts of the earth are for their inhabitants only a barrier and not an outlet, or at best only a base for timorous ventures seaward that rarely lose sight of the shore.

Width of coastal zones.
As intermediary belt between land and sea, the coast becomes a peculiar habitat which leaves its mark upon its people. We speak of coast strips, coastal plains, "tidewater country," coast cities; of coast tribes, coast peoples, maritime colonies; and each word brings up a picture of a land or race or settlement permeated by the influences of the sea. The old term of "coastline" has no application to such an intermediary belt, for it is a zone of measurable width; and this width varies with the relief of the land, the articulation of the coast according as it is uniform or complex, with the successive stages of civilization and the development of navigation among the people who inhabit it.

Along highly articulated coasts, showing the interpenetration of sea and land in a broad band of capes and islands separated by tidal channels and inlets, or on shores deeply incised by river estuaries, or on low shelving beaches which screen brackish lagoons and salt marshes behind sand reefs and dune ramparts, and which thus form an indeterminate boundary of alternate land and water, the zone character of the coast in a physical sense becomes conspicuous. In an anthropological sense the zone character is clearly indicated by the different uses of its inner and outer edge made by man in different localities and in different periods of history.

The inner edge.
The old German maritime cities of the North Sea and the Baltic were located on rivers from 6 to 60 miles from the open sea, always on the inner edge of the coastal belt. Though primarily trading towns, linked together once in the sovereign confederacy of the Hanseatic League, they fixed their sites on the last spurs of firm ground running out into the soft, yielding alluvium, which was constantly exposed to inundation. Land high enough to be above the ever threatening flood of river and storm-driven tide on this flat coast, and

solid enough to be built upon, could not be found immediately on the sea. The slight elevations of sandy "geest" or detrital spurs were limited in area and in time outgrown. Hence the older part of all these river towns, from Bremen to Königsberg, rests upon hills, while in every case the newer and lower part is built on piles or artificially raised ground on the alluvium.[1] So Utrecht, the Ultrajectum of the Romans, selected for its site a long raised spur running out from the solid ground of older and higher land into the water-soaked alluvium of the Netherlands. It was the most important town of all this region before the arts of civilization began the conquest by dike and ditch of the amphibian coastal belt which now comprises one-fourth of the area and holds one-half the population of the Netherlands.[2] So ancient London marked the solid ground at the inner edge of the tidal flats and desolate marshes which lined the Thames estuary, as the Roman Camulodunum and its successor Colchester on its steep rise or *dun* overlooked the marshes of the Stour inlet.[3] Farther north about the Wash, which in Roman days extended far inland over an area of fens and tidal channels, Cambridge on the River Cam, Huntingdon and Stamford on the Nen, and Lincoln on the Witham—all river seaports—defined the firm inner edge of this wide low coast. In the same way the landward rim of the tidal waters and salt marshes of the Humber inlet was described by a semicircle of British and Roman towns—Doncaster, Castleford, Todcaster, and York.[4] On the flat or rolling West African coastland, which lines the long shores of the Gulf of Guinea with a band 30 to 100 miles wide, the sandy, swampy tracts immediately on the sea are often left uninhabited; native population is distributed most frequently at the limit of deep water, and here at head of ship-navigation the trading towns are found.[5]

While, on low coasts at any rate, the inner edge tends to mark the limit of settlement advancing from the interior, as the head of sea navigation on river and inlet it has also been the goal of immigrant settlers from oversea lands. The history of modern maritime colonization, especially in America, shows that the aim of regular colonists, as opposed to

Inner edge as head of sea navigation.

mere traders, has been to penetrate as far as possible into the land while retaining communication with the sea, and thereby with the mother country. The small boats in use till the introduction of steam navigation fixed this line far inland and gave the coastal zone a greater breadth than it has at present, and a more regular contour. In colonial America this inner edge coincided with the "fall-line" of the Atlantic rivers, which was indicated by a series of seaport towns; or with the inland limit of the tides, which on the St. Lawrence fell above Quebec, and on the Hudson just below Albany.

Shifting of the inner edge.

With the recent increase in the size of vessels, two contrary effects are noticed. In the vast majority of cases, the inner edge, as marked by ports, moves seaward into deeper water, and the zone narrows. The days when almost every tobacco plantation in tidewater Virginia had its own wharf are long since past, and the leaf is now exported by way of Norfolk and Baltimore. Seville has lost practically all its sea trade to Cadiz, Rouen to Havre, and Dordrecht to Rotterdam. In other cases the zone preserves its original width by the creation of secondary ports on or near the outer edge, reserved only for the largest vessels, while the inner harbor, by dredging its channel, improves its communication with the sea. Thus arises the phenomenon of twin ports like Bremen and Bremerhaven, Dantzig and Neufahrwasser, Stettin and Swinemünde, Bordeaux and Pauillac, London and Tilbury. Or the original harbor seeks to preserve its advantage by canalizing the shallow approach by river, lagoon, or bay, as St. Petersburg by the Pantiloff canal through the shallow reaches of Kronstadt Bay; or Königsberg by its ship canal, carried for 25 miles across the Frisches Haff to the Baltic;[6] or Nantes by the Loire ship canal, which in 1892 was built to regain for the old town the West Indian trade recently intercepted by the rising outer port of St. Nazaire, at the mouth of the Loire estuary.[7] In northern latitudes, however, the outer ports on enclosed sea basins like the Baltic become dominant in the winter, when the inner ports are ice-bound. Otherwise the outer port sinks with every improvement in the channel between the inner port and the sea. Hamburg has so constantly deepened the Elbe passage that its outport of Cuxhaven has had little chance to rise, and serves only as an emergency harbor; while on the Weser, maritime leadership has oscillated between Bremen and Bremerhaven.[8] So the whole German coast and the Russian Baltic have seen a more or less irregular shifting backward and forward of maritime importance between the inner and the outer edges.

The width of the coast zone is not only prevented from contracting by dredging and canaling, but it is even increased. By deepening the channel, the chief port of the St. Lawrence River has been removed from Quebec 180 miles upstream to Montreal, and that of the Clyde from Port Glasgow 16 miles to Glasgow itself, so that now the largest ocean steamers come to dock where fifty years ago children waded across the stream at ebb tide. Such artificial modifications, however, are rare, for they are made only where peculiarly rich resources or superior lines of communication with the hinterland justify the expenditures; but they find their logical conclusion in still farther extensions of sea navigation into the interior by means of ship canals, where previously no waterway existed. Instances are found in the Manchester ship canal and the Welland, which, by means of the St. Lawrence and the Great Lakes, makes Chicago accessible to ocean vessels. Though man distinguishes between sea and inland navigation in his definitions, in his practice he is bound by no formula and recognizes no fundamental difference where rivers, lakes, and canals are deep enough to admit his sea-going craft.

Artificial extension of inner edge.

Such deep landward protrusions of the head of marine navigation at certain favored points, as opposed to its recent coastward trend in most inlets and rivers, increase the irregularity of the inner edge of the coast zone by the marked discrepancy between its maximum and minimum width. They are limited, however, to a few highly civilized countries, and to a few points in those countries. But their presence testifies to the fact that the evolution of the coast zone with the development of civilization shows the persistent importance of this inner edge.

Outer edge in original settlement.

The outer edge finds its greatest significance, which is for the most part ephemeral, in the earlier stages of navigation, maritime colonization, and in some cases of original settlement. But this importance persists only on steep coasts furnishing little or no level ground for cultivation and barred from interior hunting or grazing land; on many coral and volcanic islands of the Pacific Ocean whose outer rim has the most fertile soil and furnishes the most abundant growth of coco palms, and whose limited area only half suffices to support the population; and in polar and sub-polar districts, where harsh climatic conditions set a low limit to economic

Outer edge and food supply. development. In all these regions the sea must provide most of the food of the inhabitants, who can therefore never lose contact with its waters. In mountainous Tierra del Fuego, whose impenetrably forested slopes rise directly from the sea, with only here and there a scanty stretch of stony beach, the natives of the southern and western coasts keep close to the shore. The straits and channels yield them all their food, and are the highways for all their restless, hungry wanderings.[9] The steep slopes and dense forests preclude travel by land, and force the wretched inhabitants to live as much in their canoes as in their huts. The Tlingit and Haida Indians of the mountainous coast of southern Alaska locate their villages on some smooth sheltered beach, with their houses in a single row facing the water, and the ever-ready canoe drawn up on shore in front. They select their sites with a view to food supply, and to protection in case of attack. On the treeless shores of Kadiak Island and of the long narrow Alaska Peninsula near by, the Eskimo choose their village location for an accumulation of driftwood, for proximity to their food supply, and a landing-place for their kayaks and bidarkas. Hence they prefer a point of land or gravel spit extending out into the sea, or a sand reef separating a salt-water lagoon from the open sea. The Aleutian Islanders regard only accessibility to the shell-fish on the beach and their pelagic hunting and fishing; and this consideration has influenced the Eskimo tribes of the wide Kuskokwin estuary to such an extent, that they place their huts only a few feet above ordinary high tide, where they are constantly exposed to overflow from the sea.[10] Only among the great tidal channels of the Yukon delta are they distributed over the whole wide coastal zone, even to its inner edge.

The coast Chukches of northeastern Siberia locate their tent villages on the sand ramparts between the Arctic Ocean and the freshwater lagoons which line this low tundra shore. Here they are conveniently situated for fishing and hunting marine animals, while protected against the summer inundations of the Arctic rivers.[11] The whole western side of Greenland, from far northern Upernivik south to Cape Farewell, shows both Eskimo and Danish settlements almost without exception on projecting points of peninsulas or islands, where the stronger effect of the warm ocean current, as well as proximity to the food supply, serve to fix their habitations; although the remains of the old Norse settlements in general are found in sheltered valleys with summer vegetation, striking off from the fiords some 20 miles back from the outer coast.[12] Cæsar found that the ancient Veneti, an immigrant people of the southern coast of Brittany, built their towns on the points of capes and promontories, sites which gave them ready contact with the sea and protection against attack from the land side, because every rise of the tide submerged the intervening lowlands.[13] Here a sterile plateau hinterland drove them for part of their subsistence to the water, and the continuous intertribal warfare of small primitive states to the sea-girt asylums of the capes.

In the early history of navigation and exploration, striking features of this outer coast edge, like headlands and capes, became important sea marks. The promontory of Mount Athos, rising 6,400 feet above the sea between the Hellespont and the Thessalian coast, and casting its shadow as far as the market-place of Lemnos, was a guiding point for mariners in the whole northern Aegean.[14] For the ancient Greeks Cape Malia was long the boundary stone to the unknown wastes of the western Mediterranean, just as later the Pillars of Hercules marked the portals to the *mare tenebrosum* of the stormy Atlantic. So the Sacred Promontory (Cape St. Vincent) of the Iberian Peninsula defined for Greeks and Romans the southwestern limit of the habitable

Outer edge in early navigation.

world.[15]   Centuries later the Portuguese marked their advance
down the west coast of Africa, first by Cape Non, which so
long said "No!" to the struggling mariner, then by Cape
Bojador, and finally by Cape Verde.

In coastwise navigation, minor headlands and inshore
islands were points to steer by; and in that early maritime
colonization, which had chiefly a commercial aim, they
formed the favorite spots for trading stations.   The Phœnicians in their home country fixed their settlements by preference on small capes, like Sidon and Berytus, or on inshore
islets, like Tyre and Aradus,[16] and for their colonies and trading stations they chose similar sites, whether on the coast of
Sicily,[17] Spain, or Morocco.[18]   Carthage was located on a
small hill-crowned cape projecting out into the Bay of Carthage.   The two promontories embracing this inlet were
edged with settlements, especially the northern arm, which
held Utica and Hippo,[19] the latter on the site of the modern
French naval station of Bizerta.

Outer edge
and
piracy.

In this early Hellenic world, when Greek sea-power was in
its infancy, owing to the fear of piracy, cities were placed
a few miles back from the coast; but with the partial cessation of this evil, sites on shore and peninsula were preferred
as being more accessible to commerce,[20] and such of the older
towns as were in comparatively easy reach of the seaboard
established there each its own port.   Thus we find the ancient
urban pairs of Argos and Nauplia, Troezene and Pogon,
Mycenæ and Eiones, Corinth commanding its Aegean port
of Cenchreæ 8 miles away on the Saronic Gulf to catch the
Asiatic trade, and connected by a walled thoroughfare a mile
and a half long with Lechæum, a second harbor on the Cor-
inthian Gulf which served the Italian commerce.[21]   In the same
group belonged Athens and its Piræus, Megara and Pegæ,
Pergamus and Elaæ in western Asia Minor.[22]   These ancient
twin cities may be taken to mark the two borders of the coast
zone.   Like the modern ones which we have considered above,
their historical development has shown an advance from the
inner toward the outer edge, though owing to different
causes.   However, the retired location of the Baltic and North
Sea towns of Germany served as a partial protection against

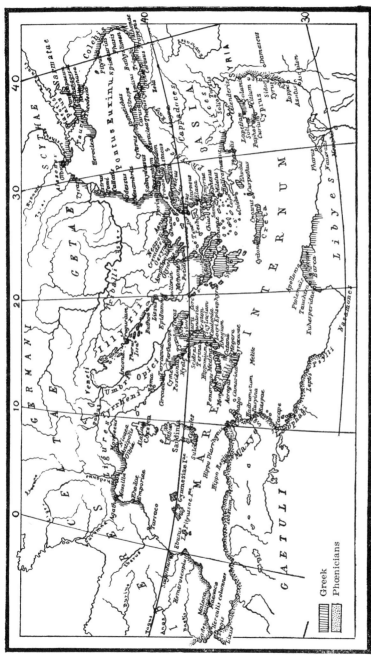

MAP OF ANCIENT PHOENICIAN AND GREEK COLONIES.

the pirates who, in the Middle Ages, scoured these coasts.[23] Lubeck, originally located nearer the sea than at present, and frequently demolished by them, was finally rebuilt farther inland up the Trave River.[24] Later the port of Travemünde grew up at the mouth of the little estuary.

Outer edge in colonization. The early history of maritime colonization shows in general two geographic phases: first, the appropriation of the islet and headland outskirts of the seaboard, and later—it may be much later—an advance toward the inner edge of the coast, or yet farther into the interior. Progress from the earlier to the maturer phase depends upon the social and economic development of the colonizers, as reflected in their valuation of territorial area. The first phase, the outcome of a low estimate of the value of land, is best represented by the Phœnician and earliest Greek colonies, whose purposes were chiefly commercial, and who sought merely such readily accessible coastal points as furnished the best trading stations on the highway of the Mediterranean and the adjacent seas. The earlier Greek colonies, like those of the Triopium promontory forming the south-western angle of Asia Minor, Chalcidice, the Thracian Chersonesus, Calchedon, Byzantium, the Pontic Heraclea, and Sinope, were situated on peninsulas or headlands, that would afford a convenient anchor ground; or, like Syracuse and Mitylene, on small inshore islets, which were soon outgrown, and from which the towns then spread to the mainland near by. The advantages of such sites lay in their accessibility to commerce, and in their natural protection against the attack of strange or hostile mainland tribes. For a nation of merchants, satisfied with the large returns but also with the ephemeral power of middlemen, these considerations sufficed. While the Phœnician trading posts in Africa dotted the outer rim of the coast, the inner edge of the zone was indicated by Libyan or Ethiopian towns, where the inhabitants of the interior bartered their ivory and skins for the products of Tyre.[25] So that commercial expansion of the Arabs down the east coast of Africa in the first and again in the tenth century seized upon the offshore islands of Zanzibar, Pemba, and Mafia, the small inshore islets like Mombasa and Lamu,

and the whole outer rim of the coast from the equator southward to the Rovuma River.[26] The Sultan of Zanzibar, heir
to this coastal strip, had not expanded it a decade ago, when
he had to relinquish the long thread of his continental possessions.

But when a people has advanced to a higher conception **Inland ad-**
of colonization as an outlet for national as well as commer- **vance of**
cial expansion, and when it sees that the permanent prosper- **colonies.**
ity of both race and trade in the new locality depends upon
the occupation of larger tracts of territory and the development of local resources as a basis for exchanges, their settlements spread from the outer rim of the coasts to its inner
edge and yet beyond, if alluvial plains and river highways
are present to tempt inland expansion. Such was the history
of many later colonies of the Greeks[27] and Carthaginians,
and especially of most modern colonial movements, for these
have been dominated by a higher estimate of the value of
land.

After the long Atlantic journey, the outposts of the American coast were welcome resting-places to the early European
voyagers, but, owing to their restricted area and therefore
limited productivity, they were soon abandoned, or became
mere bases for inland expansion. The little island of Cutty-
hunk, off southern Massachusetts, was the site of Gosnold's
abortive attempt at colonization in 1602, like Raleigh's
attempt on Roanoke Island in 1585, and the later one of Pop-
ham on the eastern headland of Casco Bay. The Pilgrims
paused at the extremity of Cape Cod, and again on Clark's
Island, before fixing their settlement on Plymouth Bay. Mon-
hegan Island, off the Maine coast, was the site of an early
English trading post, which, however, lasted only from 1623
to 1626;[28] and the same dates fix the beginning and end of a
fishing and trading station established on Cape Ann, and removed later to Salem harbor. The Swedes made their first
settlement in America on Cape Henlopen, at the entrance of
Delaware Bay; but their next, only seven years later, they
located well up the estuary of the Delaware River. Thus for
the modern colonist the outer edge of the coast is merely
the gateway of the land. From it he passes rapidly to the

settlement of the interior, wherever fertile soil and abundant resources promise a due return upon his labor.

Interpenetration of land and sea. Since it is from the land, as the inhabited portion of the earth's surface, that all maritime movements emanate, and to the land that all oversea migrations are directed, the reciprocal relations between land and sea are largely determined by the degree of accessibility existing between the two. This depends primarily upon the articulation of a land-mass, whether it presents an unbroken contour like Africa and India, or whether, like Europe and Norway, it drops a fringe of peninsulas and a shower of islands into the bordering ocean. Mere distance from the sea bars a country from its vivifying contact; every protrusion of an ocean artery into the heart of a continent makes that heart feel the pulse of life on far-off, unseen shores. The Baltic inlet which makes a seaport of St. Petersburg 800 miles (1,300 kilometers) back from the western rim of Europe, brings Atlantic civilization to this half-Asiatic side of the continent. The solid front presented by the Iberian Peninsula and Africa to the Atlantic has a narrow crack at Gibraltar, whence the Mediterranean penetrates inland 2,300 miles (3,700 kilometers), and converts the western foot of the Caucasus and the roots of the Lebanon Mountains into a seaboard. By means of the Arabian Sea, the Indian Ocean runs northward 1,300 miles (2,200 kilometers) from Cape Comorin to meet the Indus delta; and then turns westward 700 miles farther through the Oman and Persian gulfs to receive the boats from the Tigris and Euphrates. Such marine inlets create islands and peninsulas, which are characterized by proximity to the sea on all or many sides; and in the interior of the continents they produce every degree of nearness, shading off into inaccessible remoteness from the watery highway of the deep.

The success with which such indentations open up the interior of the continents depends upon the length of the inlets and the size of the land-mass in question. Africa's huge area and unbroken contour combine to hold the sea at arm's length, Europe's deep-running inlets open that small continent so effectively that Kazan, Russia's most eastern city of considerable size, is only 750 miles (1,200 kilometers) distant from the nearest White Sea, Baltic, and Azof ports. Asia, the largest of all the continents, despite a succession of big indentations that invade its periphery from Sinai peninsula to East Cape, has a vast inland area hopelessly far from the surrounding oceans.

In order to determine the coast articulation of any coun- try or continent, Carl Ritter and his followers divided area by shoreline, the latter a purely mathematical line represent- ing the total contour length. By this method Europe's ratio is one linear mile of coast to 174 square miles of area, Aus- tralia's 1 : 224, Asia's 1 : 490, and Africa's 1 : 700. This means that Europe's proportion of coast is three times that of Asia and four times that of Africa; that a country like Norway, with a shoreline of 12,000 miles traced in and out along the fiords and around the larger islands,[29] has only 10 square miles of area for every mile of seaboard, while Germany, with every detail of its littoral included in the measurement, has only 1,515 miles of shoreline and a ratio of one mile of coast to every 159 square miles of area.

Ratio of shoreline to area.

The criticism has been made against this method that it compares two unlike measures, square and linear, which more- over increase or decrease in markedly different degrees, ac- cording as larger or smaller units are used. But for the pur- poses of anthropo-geography the method is valid, inasmuch as it shows the amount of area dependent for its marine out- line upon each mile of littoral. A coast, like every other boundary, performs the important function of intermediary in the intercourse of a land with its neighbors; hence the length of this sea boundary materially affects this function. Area and coastline are not dead mathematical quantities, but like organs of one body stand in close reciprocal activ- ity, and can be understood only in the light of their persistent mutual relations. The division of the area of a land by the length of its coastline yields a quotient which to the anthropo-geographer is not a dry figure, but an index to the possible relations between seaboard and interior. A comparison of some of these ratios will illustrate this fact.

Germany's shoreline, traced in contour without including details, measures 787 miles; this is just one-fifth that of

Italy and two-fifths that of France, so that it is short. But since Germany's area is nearly twice Italy's and a little larger than that of France, it has 267 square miles of territory for every mile of coast, while Italy has only 28 square miles, and France 106. Germany has towns that are 434 miles from the nearest seaboard, but in Italy the most inland point is only 148 miles from the Mediterranean.[30] If we turn now to the United States and adopt Mendenhall's estimate of its general or contour coastline as 5,705 miles, we find that our country has 530 square miles of area dependent for its outlet upon each mile of seaboard. This means that our coast has a heavy task imposed upon it, and that its commercial and political importance is correspondingly enhanced; that the extension of our Gulf of Mexico littoral by the purchase of Florida and the annexation of Texas were measures of self-preservation, and that the unbroken contour and mountain-walled face of our Pacific littoral is a serious national handicap.

Criticism of this ormula.

But this method is open to the legitimate and fundamental criticism that, starting from the conception of a coast as a mere line instead of a zone, it ignores all those features which belong to every littoral as a strip of the earth's surface—location, geologic structure, relief, area, accessibility to the sea in front and to the land behind, all which vary from one part of the world's seaboard to another, and serve to differentiate the human history of every littoral. Moreover, of all parts of the earth's surface, the coast as the hem of the sea and land, combining the characters of each, is most complex. It is the coast as a human habitat that primarily concerns anthropo-geography. A careful analysis of the multifarious influences modifying one another in this mingled environment of land and water reveals an intricate interplay of geographic forces, varying from inland basin to marginal sea, from marginal sea to open ocean, and changing from one historical period to another—an interplay so mercurial that it could find only a most inadequate expression in the rigid mathematical formula of Carl Ritter.

Accessibility of coasts from hinterland.

As the coast, then, is the border zone between the solid, inhabited land and the mobile, untenanted deep, two important factors in its history are the accessibility of its back country on the one hand, and the accessibility of the sea on the other. A littoral population barred from its hinterland by mountain range or steep plateau escarpment or desert tract feels little influence from the land; level or fertile soil is too limited in amount to draw inland the growing people, intercourse is too difficult and infrequent, transportation too slow and costly. Hence the inhabitants of such a coast are forced to look seaward for their racial and commercial expansion, even if a paucity of good harbors limits the accessibility of the sea; they must lead a somewhat detached and independent existence, so far as the territory behind them is concerned. Here the coast, as a peripheral organ of the interior, as the outlet for its products, the market for its foreign exchanges, and the medium for intercourse with its maritime neighbors, sees its special function impaired. But it takes advantage of its isolation and the protection of a long sea boundary to detach itself politically from its hinterland, as the histories of Phœnicia, the Aegean coast of Asia Minor, Dalmatia, the republics of Amalfi, Venice, and Genoa, the county of Barcelona, and Portugal abundantly prove. At the same time it profits by its seaboard location to utilize the more varied fields of maritime enterprise before it, in lieu of the more or less forbidden territory behind it. The height and width of the landward barrier, the number and practicability of the passways across it, and especially the value of the hinterland's products in relation to their bulk, determine the amount of intercourse between that hinterland and its mountain or desert barred littoral.

The interior is most effectively cut off from the periphery, where a mountain range or a plateau escarpment traces the inner line of the coastland, as in the province of Liguria in northern Italy, Dalmatia, the western or Malabar coast of India, most parts of Africa, and long stretches of the Pacific littoral of the Americas. The highland that backs the Norwegian coast is crossed by only one railroad, that passing through the Trondhjem depression; and this barrier has served to keep Norway's historical connection with Sweden far less intimate than with Denmark. The long inlet of

Mountain-barred hinterlands.

the Adriatic, bringing the sea well into the heart of Southern Europe, has seen nevertheless a relatively small maritime development, owing to the wall of mountains that everywhere shuts out the hinterland of its coasts. The greatness of Venice was intimately connected with the Brenner Pass over the Alps on the one hand, and the trade of the eastern Mediterranean on the other. Despite Austro-Hungary's crucial interest in the northeast corner of the Adriatic as a maritime outlet for this vast inland empire, and its herculean efforts at Trieste and Fiume to create harbors and to connect them by transmontane railroads with the valley of the Danube, the maritime development of this coast is still restricted, and much of Austria's trade goes out northward by German ports.[31] Farther south along the Dalmatian and Albanian coasts, the deep and sheltered bays between the half-submerged roots of the Dinaric Alps have developed only local importance, because they lack practicable connection with the interior. This was their history too in early Greek and Roman days, for they found only scant support in the few caravans that crossed by the Roman road to Dyrrachium to exchange the merchandise of the Aegean for the products of the Ionian Isles. Spain has always suffered from the fact that her bare, arid, and unproductive tableland almost everywhere rises steeply from her fertile and densely populated coasts; and therefore that the two have been unable to coöperate either for the production of a large maritime commerce or for national political unity. Here the diverse conditions of the littoral and the wall of the great central terrace of the country have emphasized that tendency to defection that belongs to every periphery, and therefore necessitated a strong centralized government to consolidate the restive maritime provinces with their diverse Galician, Basque, Catalonian, and Andalusian folk into one nation with the Castilians of the plateau.[32]

Accessible hinterlands. Where mountain systems run out endwise into the sea, the longitudinal valleys with their drainage streams open natural highways from the interior to the coast. This structure has made the Atlantic side of the Iberian Peninsula far more open than its Mediterranean front, and therefore contributed to its leadership in maritime affairs since 1450. So from the shores of Thrace to the southern point of the Peloponnesus, all the valleys of Greece open out on the eastern or Asiatic side. Here every mountain-flanked bay has had its own small hinterland to draw upon, and every such interior has been accessible to the civilization of the Aegean; here was concentrated the maritime and cultural life of Hellas.[33] The northern half of Andean Colombia, by way of the parallel Atrato, Rio Cauco, and Magdalena valleys, has supported the activities of its Caribbean littoral, and through these avenues has received such foreign influences as might penetrate to inland Bogota. In like manner, the mountain-ridged peninsula of Farther India keeps its interior in touch with its leading ports through its intermontane valleys of the Irawadi, Salwin, Menam, and Mekong rivers.

Low coasts rising by easy gradients to wide plains, like those of northern France, Germany, southern Russia, and the Gulf seaboard of the United States, profit by an accessible and extensive hinterland. Occasionally, however, this advantage is curtailed by a political boundary reinforced by a high protective tariff, as Holland, Belgium, and East Prussia[34] know to their sorrow.

These low hems of the land, however, often meet physical obstructions to ready communications with the interior in the silted inlets, shallow lagoons, marshes, or mangrove swamps of the littoral itself. Here the larger drainage streams give access across this amphibian belt to the solid land behind. Where they flow into a tide-swept bay like the North Sea or the English Channel, they scour out their beds and preserve the connection between sea and land;[35] but debouchment into a tideless basin like the Caspian or the Gulf of Mexico, even for such mighty streams as the Volga and the Mississippi, sees the slow silting up of their mouths and the restriction of their agency in opening up the hinterland. Thus the character of the bordering sea may help to determine the accessibility of the coast from the land side. **Accessibility of coasts from the sea.** Its accessibility from the sea depends primarily upon its degree of articulation; and this articulation depends upon whether the littoral belt has suffered elevation or subsidence.

When the inshore sea rests upon an uplifted bottom, the contour of the coast is smooth and unbroken, because most of the irregularities of surface have been overlaid by a deposit of waste from the land; so it offers no harbor except here and there a silted river mouth, while it shelves off through a broad amphibian belt of tidal marsh, lagoon, and sand reef to a shallow sea. Such is the coast of New Jersey, most of the Gulf seaboard of the United States and Mexico, the Coromandel coast of India, and the long, low littoral of Upper Guinea. Such coasts harbor a population of fishermen living along the strands of their placid lagoons,[36] and stimulate a timid inshore navigation which sometimes develops to extensive coastwise intercourse, where a network of lagoons and deltaic channels forms a long inshore passage, as in Upper Guinea, but which fears the break of the surf outside.[37]

The rivers draining these low uplifted lands are deflected from their straight path to the sea by coastwise deposits, and idly trail along for miles just inside the outer beach; or they are split up into numerous offshoots among the silt beds of a delta, to find their way by shallow, tortuous channels to the ocean, so that they abate their value as highways between sea and land. The silted mouths of the Nile excluded the larger vessels even of Augustus Cæsar's time and admitted only their lighters,[38] just as to-day the lower Rufigi River loses much of its value to German East Africa because of its scant hospitality to vessels coming from the sea.

Embayed coasts.   The effect of subsidence, even on a low coastal plain, is to increase accessibility from the sea by flooding the previous river valleys and transforming them into a succession of long shallow inlets, alternating with low or hilly tongues of land. Such embayed coasts form our Atlantic seaboard from Delaware Bay, through Chesapeake Bay to Pamlico Sound, the North Sea face of England, the funnel-shaped "förden" or firths on the eastern side of Jutland and Schleswig-Holstein, and the ragged sounds or "Bodden" that indent the Baltic shore of Germany from the Bay of Lubeck to the mouth of the Oder River.[39] Although the shallowness of the bordering sea and the sand-bars and sand reefs which characterize all flat coasts here also exclude the largest vessels, such coasts

have nevertheless ample contact with both land and sea.
They tend to develop, therefore, the activities appropriate
to both. A fertile soil and abundant local resources, as in
tidewater Maryland and Virginia, make the land more attractive than the sea; the inhabitants become farmers rather
than sailors. On the other hand, an embayed coastland
promising little return to the labor of tillage, but with abundant fisheries and a superior location for maritime trade, is
sure to profit by the accessible sea, and achieve the predominant maritime activity which characterized the mediæval
Hanse Towns of northern Germany and colonial New
England.

Subsidence that brings the beat of the surf against the *Maritime*
bolder reliefs of the land produces a ragged, indented coast, *activity*
deep-water inlets penetrating far into the country, hilly or *on steep*
mountainous tongues of land running far out into the sea *coasts.*
and breaking up into a swarm of islands and rocks, whose
outer limits indicate approximately the old prediluvial line
of shore.[40] Such are the fiord regions of Norway, southern
Alaska, British Columbia, Greenland, and southern Chile;
the Rias or submerged river valley coast of northwestern
Spain; and the deeply sunken mountain flank of Dalmatia,
whose every lateral valley has become a bay or a strait between mainland and island. All these coasts are characterized by a close succession of inlets, a limited amount of level
country for settlement or cultivation, and in their rear a
steep slope impeding communication with their hinterland.
Inaccessibility from the land, a high degree of accessibility
from the sea, and a paucity of local resources unite to
thrust the inhabitants of such coasts out upon the deep, to
make of them fishermen, seamen, and ocean carriers. The
same result follows where no barrier on the land side exists,
but where a granitic or glaciated soil in the interior discourages agriculture and landward expansion, as in Brittany,
Maine, and Newfoundland. In all these the land repels and
the sea attracts. Brittany furnishes one-fifth of all the sailors in France's merchant marine,[41] and its pelagic fishermen
sweep the seas from Newfoundland to Iceland. Three-fifths
of the maritime activity of the whole Austrian Empire is

confined to the ragged coast of Dalmatia, which furnishes
to-day most of the sailors for the imperial marine, just as in
Roman days it manned the Adriatic fleet of the Cæsars.[42]
The Haida, Tsimshean, and Tlingit Indians of the ragged
western coast of British Columbia and southern Alaska
spread their villages on the narrow tide-swept hem of the
land, and subsist chiefly by the generosity of the deep. They
are poor landsmen, but excellent boat-makers and seamen,
venturing sometimes twenty-five miles out to sea to gather
birds' eggs from the outermost fringe of rocks.

Contrasted coastal belts.   As areas of elevation or subsidence are, as a rule, extensive, it follows that coasts usually present long stretches of
smooth simple shoreline, or a long succession of alternating
inlet and headland. Therefore different littoral belts show
marked contrasts in their degree of accessibility to the sea,
and their harbors appear in extensive groups of one type—
fiords, river estuaries, sand or coral reef lagoons, and embayed mountain roots. A sudden change in relief or in geologic history sees one of these types immediately succeeded
by a long-drawn group of a different type. Such a contrast
is found between the Baltic and North Sea ports of Denmark
and Germany, the eastern and southern seaboards of England, the eastern and western sides of Scotland, and the
Pacific littoral of North America north and south of Juan
de Fuca Strait, attended by a contrasted history.

A common morphological history, marked by mountain
uplift, glaciation, and subsidence, has given an historical
development similar in not a few respects to the fiord coasts
of New England, Norway, Iceland, Greenland, the Alaskan
"panhandle," and southern Chile. Large subsidence areas
on the Mediterranean coasts from the Strait of Gibraltar to
the Bosporus have in essential features duplicated each
other's histories, just as the low infertile shores of the Baltic
from Finland to the Skager Rack have had much in common
in their past development.

Where, however, a purely local subsidence, as in Kamerun
Bay and Old Calabar on the elsewhere low monotonous stretch
of the Upper Guinea coast,[43] or a single great river estuary,
as in the La Plata and the Columbia, affords a protected

anchorage on an otherwise portless shore, such inlets assume increased importance. In the long unbroken reach of our Pacific seaboard, San Francisco Bay and the Columbia estuary are of inestimable value; while, by the treaty of 1848 with Mexico, the international boundary line was made to bend slightly south of west from the mouth of the Gila River to the coast, in order to include in the United States territory the excellent harbor of San Diego. The mere nicks in the rim of Southwest Africa constituting Walfish Bay and Angra Pequena assume considerable value as trading sta tions and places of refuge along that 1,200-mile reach of inhospitable coast extending from Cape Town north to Great Fish Bay.[44] It is worthy of notice in passing that, though both of these small inlets lie within the territory of German Southwest Africa, Walfish Bay with 20 miles of coast on either side is a British possession, and that two tiny islets which commands the entrance to the harbor of Angra Pequena, also belong to Great Britain. On the uniform coast of East Africa, the single considerable indentation formed by Delagoa Bay assumes immense importance, which, however, is due in part to the mineral wealth of its Transvaal hinterland. From this point northward for 35 degrees of latitude, a river mouth, like that fixing the site of Beira, or an inshore islet affording protected harborage, like that of Mombasa, serves as the single ocean gateway of a vast territory, and forms the terminus of a railroad—proof of its importance.

The maritime evolution of all amply embayed coasts, except in Arctic and sub-Arctic regions inimical to all historical development, shows in its highest stage the gradual elimination of minor ports, and the concentration of maritime activity in a few favored ones, which have the deepest and most capacious harbors and the best river, canal, or railroad connection with the interior. The earlier stages are marked by a multiplicity of ports, showing in general activity nearly similar in amount and in kind. England's merchant marine in the fourteenth century was distributed in a large group of small but important ports on the southern coast, all which, owing to their favorable location, were engaged in the French and Flemish trade; and in another group on the east coast, *Evolution of ports.*

reaching from Hull to Colchester, which participated in the Flemish, Norwegian, and Baltic trade.[45] Most of these have now declined before the overpowering competition of a few such seaboard marts as London, Hull, and Southampton. The introduction of steam trawlers into the fishing fleets has in like manner led to the concentration of the fishermen in a few large ports with good railroad facilities, such as Aberdeen and Grimsby, while the fishing villages that fringed the whole eastern and southern coasts have been gradually depopulated.[46] So in colonial days, when New England was little more than a cordon of settlements along that rockbound littoral, almost every inlet had its port actively engaged in coastwise and foreign commerce in the West Indies and the Guinea Coast, in cod and mackerel fisheries, in whaling and shipbuilding, and this with only slight local variations. This widespread homogeneity of maritime activity has been succeeded by strict localization and differentiation, and reduction from many to few ports. So, for the whole Atlantic seaboard of the United States, evolution of seaports has been marked by increase of size attended by decrease of numbers.

Offshore islands. A well dissected coast, giving ample contact with the sea, often fails nevertheless to achieve historical importance, unless outlying islands are present to ease the transition from inshore to pelagic navigation, and to tempt to wider maritime enterprise. The long sweep of the European coast from northern Norway to Brittany has played out a significant part of its history in that procession of islands formed by Iceland, the Faroes, Shetland, Orkneys, Great Britain, Ireland and the Channel Isles, whether it was the navigator of ancient Armorica steering his leather-sailed boat to the shores of Cæsar's Britain, or the modern Breton fisherman pulling in his nets off the coasts of distant Iceland. The dim outline of mountainous Cyprus, seen against a far-away horizon from the slopes of Lebanon, beckoned the Phœnician ship-master thither to trade and to colonize, just as the early Etruscan merchants passed from their busy ironworks on the island of Elba over the narrow strait to visible Corsica.[47] It was on the eastern side of Greece, with its deep embayments, its valleys opening out to the Aegean, with its 483 islands scattered thickly as stars in the sky, and its Milky Way of the Cyclades leading to the deep, rich soils of the Asia Minor coast, with its sea-made contact with all the stimulating influences and dangers emanating from the Asiatic littoral, that Hellenic history played its impressive drama. Here was developed the spirit of enterprise that carried colonies to far western Sicily and Italy, while the western or rear side had a confined succession of local events, scarce worthy the name of history. Neither mountain-walled Epirus nor Corcyra had an Hellenic settlement in 735 B. C., at a date when the eastern Greeks had reached the Ionian coast of the Aegean and had set up a lonely group of colonies even on the Bay of Naples. Turning to America, we find that the Antilles received their population from the only two tribes, first the Arawaks and later the Caribs, who ever reached the indented northern coast of South America between the Isthmus of Panama and the mouth of the Orinoco. Here the small islands of the Venezuelan coast, often in sight, lured these peoples of river and shore to open-sea navigation, and drew them first to the Windward Isles, then northward step by step or island by island, to Hayti and Cuba.[48]

In all these instances, offshore islands tempt to expansion and thereby add to the historical importance of the near-by coast. Frequently, however, they achieve the same result by offering advantageous footholds to enterprising voyagers from remote lands, and become the medium for infusing life into hitherto dead coasts. The long monotonous littoral of East Africa from Cape Guadafui to the Cape of Good Hope, before the planting here of Portuguese way-stations on the road to India in the sixteenth century, was destitute of historical significance, except that stretch opposite the islands of Zanzibar and Pemba, which Arab merchants in the tenth century appropriated as the basis for their slave and ivory trade. The East Indies and Ceylon have been so many offshore stations whence, first through the Portuguese, and later through the Dutch and English, European influences percolated into southeastern Asia. Asia, with its island-strewn shores, has diffused its influences over a broad

Offshore islands as vestibules of the mainland.

zone of the western Pacific, and through the agency of its active restless Malays, even halfway across that ocean. In contrast, the western coast of the Americas, a stretch nearly 10,000 miles from Tierra del Fuego to the Aleutian chain, has seen its aboriginal inhabitants barred from seaward expansion by the lack of offshore islands, and its entrance upon the historical stage delayed till recent times.

In general it can be said that islandless seas attain a later historical development than those whose expanse is rendered less forbidding by hospitable fragments of land. This factor, as well as its location remote from the old and stimulating civilization of Syria and Asia Minor, operated to retard the development of the western Mediterranean long after the eastern basin had reached its zenith.

Previous habitat of coast-dwellers. Coast-dwelling peoples exhibit every degree of intimacy with the water, from the amphibian life of many Malay tribes who love the wash of the waves beneath their pile-built villages, to the Nama Bushmen who inhabit the dune-walled coast of Southwest Africa, and know nothing of the sea. In the resulting nautical development the natural talents and habits of the people are of immense influence; but these in turn have been largely determined by the geographical environment of their previous habitat, whether inland or coastal, and by the duration in time, as well as the degree and necessity, of their contact with the sea. The Phœnicians, who, according to their traditions as variously interpreted, came to the coast of Lebanon either from the Persian Gulf or the Red Sea,[49] brought to their favorable maritime location a different endowment from that of the land-trading Philistines, who moved up from the south to occupy the sand-choked shores of Palestine,[50] or from that of the Jews, bred to the grasslands of Mesopotamia and the gardens of Judea, who only at rare periods in their history forced their way to the sea.[51] The unindented coast stretching from Cape Carmel south to the Nile delta never produced a maritime people and never achieved maritime importance, till a race of experienced mariners like the Greeks planted their colonies and built their harbor moles on the shores of Sharon and Philistia.[52] So on the west face of Africa, from the Senegal southward along the whole Guinea Coast to Benguela, all evidences of kinship and tradition among the local tribes point to an origin on the interior plains and a recent migration seaward,[53] so that no previous schooling enabled them to exploit the numerous harbors along this littoral, as did later the sea-bred Portuguese and English.

Not only the accessibility of the coast from the sea, but also its habitability enters as a factor into its historical importance. A sandy desert coast, like that of Southwest Africa and much of the Peruvian littoral, or a sterile mountain face, like that of Lower California, excludes the people of the country from the sea. Saldanha Bay, the one good natural harbor on the west coast of Cape Colony, is worthless even to the enterprising English, because it has no supply of fresh water.[54] The slowness of the ancient Egyptians to take the short step forward from river to marine navigation can undoubtedly be traced to the fact that the sour swamps, barren sand-dunes, and pestilential marshes on the seaward side of the Nile delta must have always been sparsely populated as they are to-day,[55] and that a broad stretch of sandy waste formed their Red Sea littoral.

Habitability of coasts as factor in maritime development.

On the other hand, where the hem of the continents is fertile enough to support a dense population, a large number of people are brought into contact with the sea, even where no elaborate articulation lengthens the shoreline. When this teeming humanity of a garden littoral is barred from landward expansion by desert or mountain, or by the already overcrowded population of its own hinterland, it wells over the brim of its home country, no matter how large, and overflows to other lands across the seas. The congested population of the fertile and indented coast of southern China, though not strictly speaking a sea-faring people, found an outlet for their redundant humanity and their commerce in the tropical Sunda Islands. By the sixth century their trading junks were doing an active business in the harbors of Java, Sumatra, and Malacca; they had even reached Ceylon and the Persian Gulf, and a little later were visiting the great focal market of Aden at the entrance of the Red Sea.[56] A strong infusion of Chinese blood improved the Malay stock in the Sunda Islands, and later in North Borneo and certain of the Philippines, whither their traders and emigrants turned in the fourteenth century, when they found their opportunities curtailed in the archipelago to the south by the spread of Islam.[57] Now the "yellow peril" threatens the whole circle of these islands from Luzon to Sumatra.

Similarly India, first from its eastern, later from its western coast, sent a stream of traders, Buddhist priests, and colonists to the Sunda Islands, and especially to Java, as early as the fifth century of our era, whence Indian civilization, religion, and elements of the Sanskrit tongue spread to Borneo, Sumatra, Bali, Lombok, and even to some smaller islands among the Molucca group.[58] The Hindus became the dominant commercial nation of the Indian Ocean long before the great development of Arabian sea power, and later shared the trade of the East African coast with the merchants of Oman and Yemen.[59] To-day they form a considerable mercantile class in the ports of Mascat, Aden, Zanzibar, Pemba, and Natal.

Geographic conditions for brilliant maritime development. On the coasts of large fertile areas like China and India, however, maritime activity comes not as an early, but as an eventual development, assumes not a dominant, but an incidental historical importance. The coastlands appearing early on the maritime stage of history, and playing a brilliant part in the drama of the sea, have been habitable, but their tillable fields have been limited either in fertility, as in New England, or in amount, as in Greece, or in both respects, as in Norway. But if blessed with advantageous location for international trade and many or even a few fairly good harbors, such coasts tend to develop wide maritime dominion and colonial expansion.[60]

Great fertility in a narrow coastal belt barred from the interior serves to concentrate and energize the maritime activities of the nation. The 20-mile wide plain stretching along the foot of the Lebanon range from Antioch to Cape Carmel is even now the garden of Syria.[61] In ancient Phœnician days its abundant crops and vines supported luxuriant cities and a teeming population, which sailed and traded and colonized to the Atlantic outskirts of Europe and Africa.

Moreover, their maritime ventures had a wide sweep as early as 1100 B. C. Quite similar to the Phœnician littoral and almost duplicating its history, is the Oman seaboard of eastern Arabia. Here again a fertile coastal plain sprinkled with its "hundred villages," edged with a few tolerable harbors, and backed by a high mountain wall with an expanse of desert beyond, produced a race of bold and skilful navigators,[62] who in the Middle Ages used their location between the Persian Gulf and the Arabian Sea to make themselves the dominant maritime power of the Indian ocean. With them maritime expansion was typically wide in its sweep and rapid in its development. Even before Mohammed's time they had reached India; but under the energizing influences of Islam, by 758 they had established a flourishing trade with China, for which they set up way stations or staple-points in Canton and the Sunda Islands.[63] First as voyagers and merchants, then as colonists, they came, bringing their wares and their religion to these distant shores. Marco Polo, visiting Sumatra in 1260, tells us the coast population was "Saracen," but this was probably more in religion than in blood.[64] Oman ventures, seconded by those of Yemen, reached as far south as east. The trading stations of Madisha and Barawa were established on the Somali coast of East Africa in 908, and Kilwa 750 miles further south in 925. In the seventeenth century the Oman Arabs dislodged the intruding Portuguese from all this coast belt down to the present northern boundary of Portuguese East Africa. Even so late as 1850 their capital, Mascat, sent out fine merchantmen that did an extensive carrying trade, and might be seen loading in the ports of British India, in Singapore, Java, and Mauritius.

Brittany's active part in the maritime history of France is due not only to its ragged contour, its inshore and off-shore islands, its forward location on the Atlantic which brought it near to the fisheries of Newfoundland and the trade of the West Indies, but also to the fact that the "Golden Belt," which, with but few interruptions, forms a band of fertility along the coast, has supported a denser population than the sterile granitic soils of the interior,[65]

Soil of coastlands as factor.

while the sea near by varied and enriched the diet of the inhabitants by its abundance of fish, and in its limy seaweed yielded a valuable fertilizer for their gardens.[66] The small but countless alluvial deposits at the fiord heads in Norway, aided by the products of the sea, are able to support a considerable number of people. Hence the narrow coastal rim of that country shows always a density of population double or quadruple that of the next density belt toward the mountainous interior, and contains seventeen out of Norway's nineteen towns having more than 5,000 inhabitants.[67] It is this relative fertility of the coastal regions, as opposed to the sterile interior, that has brought so large a part of Norway's people in contact with the Atlantic and helped give them a prominent place in maritime history.

Barren coast of fertile hinterland. Occasionally an infertile and sparsely inhabited littoral bordering a limited zone of singular productivity, especially if favorably located for international trade, will develop marked maritime activity, both in trade and commercial colonization. Such was Arabian Yemen, the home of the ancient Sabæans on the Red Sea, stretching from the Straits of Bab-el-Mandeb north-westward for 500 miles. Here a mountain range, rising to 10,000 feet and bordering the plateau desert of central Arabia, condenses the vapors of the summer monsoon and creates a long-drawn oasis, where terraced coffee gardens and orchards blossom in the irrigated soil; but the arid coastal strip at its feet, harboring a sparse population only along its tricking streams, developed a series of considerable ports as outlets for the abundant products and crowded population of the highlands.[68] A location on the busy sea lane leading from the Indian Ocean to the Mediterranean, near the meeting place of three continents, made the merchants of the Yemen coast, like the Oman Arabs to the north, middlemen in the trade of Europe with eastern Africa and India.[69] Therefore, even in the second century these Sabæans had their trading stations scattered along the east coast of Africa as far south as Zanzibar.[70] In 1502 Vasco da Gama found Arabs, either of Oman or Yemen, yet farther south in Sofala, the port for the ivory and gold trade. Some of them he employed as pilots to steer his course to India.[71]

History makes one fact very plain: a people who dwell by Scope and
the sea, and to whom nature applies some lash to drive them importance
out upon the deep, command opportunity for practically un- of seaward
limited expansion. In this way small and apparently ill- expansion.
favored strips of the earth's surface have become the seats
of wide maritime supremacy and colonial empire. The scattered but extensive seaboard possession of little Venice and
Genoa in the latter centuries of the Middle Ages are paralleled in modern times by the large oversea dominions of the
English and Dutch.

Seaward expansions of peoples are always of great moment and generally of vast extent, whether they are the coastward movements of inland peoples to get a foothold upon the
great oceanic highway of trade and civilization, as has been
the case with the Russians notably since the early eighteenth
century, and with numerous interior tribes of West Africa
since the opening of the slave trade; or whether they represent the more rapid and extensive coastwise and oversea
expansions of maritime nations like the English, Dutch, and
Portuguese. In either event they give rise to widespread dis-
placements of peoples and a bizarre arrangement of race elements along the coast. When these two contrary movements
meet, the shock of battle follows, as the recent history of the
Russians and Japanese in Manchuria and Korea illustrates,
the wars of Swedes and Russians for the possession of the
eastern Baltic littoral, and the numerous minor conflicts that
have occurred in Upper Guinea between European commercial
powers and the would-be trading tribes of the bordering
hinterland.

A coast region is a peculiar habitat, inasmuch as it is more Ethnic
or less dominated by the sea. It is exposed to inundation by contrast
tidal wave and to occupation by immigrant fleets. It may between
be the base for out-going maritime enterprise or the goal of coast and interior
some oversea movement, the dispenser or the recipient of col- peoples.
onists. The contrast between coast-dwellers and the near-by
inland people which exists so widely can be traced not only to
a difference of environment, but often to a fundamental difference of race or tribe caused by immigration to accessible
shores. The Greeks, crowded in their narrow peninsula of

limited fertility, wove an Hellenic border on the skirts of the Black Sea and eastern Mediterranean lands, just as the Carthaginians added a fringe of aliens to North Africa, where the Punic people of the coast presented a marked contrast to the Berbers of the interior. [See map page 251.]

An ethnographical map of Russia to-day shows a narrow but almost continuous rim of Germans stretching from the River Niemen north through the Baltic coast of Courland, Livland, and Esthland, as far as Revel; and again, a similar band of Swedes along the seaboard of Finland, from a point east of Helsingfors on the south around to Uleaborg on the north,[72] dating from the time when Finland was a political dependency of Sweden, and influenced by the fact that the frozen Gulf of Bothnia every winter makes a bridge of ice between the two shores. [See map page 225.]

Ethnic contrasts in the Pacific islands.

Everywhere in the Melanesian archipelago, where Papuans and Malays dwell side by side, the latter as the new-comers are always found in possession of the coast, while the darker aborigines have withdrawn into the interior. So in the Philippines, the aboriginal Negritos, pure or more often mixed with Malayan blood, as in the Mangyan tribe of central Mindoro, are found crowded back into the interior by the successive invasions of Malays who have encircled the coasts. [See map page 147.] The Zamboanga peninsula of Mindanao has an inland pagan population of primitive Malayan race called Subanon, who have been displaced from the littoral by the seafaring Samal Moros, Mohammedanized Malays from the east shores of Sumatra and the adjacent islands, who spread northward about 1300 under the energizing impulse of their new religion.[73] Even at so late a date as the arrival of Magellan, the Subanon seem to have still occupied some points of the coast,[74] just as the savage Ainos of the island of Yezo touched the sea about Sapporo only forty years ago, though they are now surrounded by a seaboard rim of Japanese.[75]

Ethnic contrasts in the Americas.

If we turn to South America, we find that warlike Tupi, at the time of the discovery, occupied the whole Brazilian coast from the southern tropic north to eastern Guiana, while the highlands of eastern Brazil immediately in their rear were populated by tribes of Ges, who had been displaced by the coastwise expansion of the Tupi canoemen.[76] [See map page 101.] And to-day this same belt of coastland has been appropriated by a foreign population of Europeans and Negroes, while the vast interior of Brazil shows a predominance of native Indian stocks, only broken here and there by a lonely *enclave* of Portuguese settlement. The early English and French territories in America presented this same contrast of coast and inland people—the colonists planting themselves on the hem of the continent to preserve maritime connection with the home countries, the aborigines forced back beyond reach of the tide.

Wherever an energetic seafaring people with marked commercial or colonizing bent make a highway of the deep, they give rise to this distinction of coast and inland people on whatever shores they touch. The expanding Angles and Saxons did it in the North Sea and the Channel, where they stretched their *litus Saxonicum* faintly along the coast of the continent to the apex of Brittany, and firmly along the hem of England from Southampton Water to the Firth of Forth;[77] the sea-bred Scandinavians did it farther north in the Teutonic fringe of settlements which they placed on the shores of Celtic Scotland and Ireland.[78]

As a rule it is the new-comers who hold the coast, but occasionally the coast-dwellers represent the older ethnic stock. In the Balkan Peninsula to-day the descendants of the ancient Hellenes are, with few exceptions, confined to the coast. The reason is to be found in the fact that the Slavs and other northern races who have intruded by successive invasions from the plains of southern Russia are primarily inland peoples, and therefore have occupied the core of the peninsula, forcing the original Greek population before them to the edge of the sea.[79] This is the same anthropo-geographical process which makes so many peninsulas the last halting-place of a dislodged earlier race. But the Greeks who line the northern and western shores of Asiatic Turkey are such only in language and religion, because their prevailing broad head-form shows them to be Turks and Armenians in race stock.[80]

Sometimes the distinction of race between coast and interior is obliterated so far as language and civilization are con-

Older ethnic stock in coastlands.

cerned, but survives less conspicuously in head-form and pigmentation. The outermost fringe of the Norwegian coast,
from the extreme south to the latitude of Trondhjem in the
north, is occupied by a broad-headed, round-faced, rather
dark people of only medium height, who show decided affinities with the Alpine race of Central Europe, and who present
a marked contrast to the tall narrow-headed blondes of pure
Teutonic type, constituting the prevailing population from
the inner edge of the coast eastward into Sweden. This
brachycephalic, un-Germanic stock of the Norwegian seaboard seems to represent the last stand made by that once
wide-spread Alpine race, which here has been shoved along
to the rocky capes and islands of the outer edge by a later
Teutonic immigration coming from Sweden.[81] So the largest
continuous area of Negrito stock in the Philippines is found
in the Sierra Madre mountains defining the eastern coast of
northern Luzon.[82] Facing the neighborless wastes of the
Pacific, whence no new settler could come, turned away from
the sources of Malay immigration to the southwest, its location made it a retreat, rather than a gateway to incoming
races. [See map page 147.]

Ethnic amalgamations in coastlands. Where an immigrant population from oversea lands occupies the coastal hem of a country, rarely do they preserve
the purity of their race. Coming at first with marauding or
trading intent, they bring no women with them, but institute
their trading stations or colonies by marriage with the women
of the country. The ethnic character of the resultant population depends upon the proportion of the two constituent
elements, the nearness or remoteness of their previous kinship,
and the degree of innate race antagonism. The ancient
Greek elements which crossed the Aegean from different sections of the peninsula to colonize the Ionian coast of Asia
Minor mingled with the native Carian, Cretan, Lydian,
Pelasgian, and Phœnician populations which they found
there.[83] On all the barbarian shores where the Greeks established themselves, there arose a mixed race—in Celtic Massilia, in Libyan Barca, and in Scythian Crimea—but always
a race Hellenized, born interpreters and mercantile agents.[84]

A maritime people, engrossed chiefly with the idea of trade, moves in small groups and intermittently; hence it modifies the original coastal population less than does a genuine colonizing nation, especially as it prefers the smallest possible territorial base for its operations. The Arab element in the coast population of East Africa is strongly represented, but not so strongly as one might expect after a thousand years of intercourse, because it was scattered in detached seaboard points, only a few of which were really stable. The native population of Zanzibar and Pemba and the fringe of coast tribes on the mainland opposite are clearly tinged with Arab blood. These Swahili, as they are called, are a highly mixed race, as their negro element has been derived not only from the local coast peoples, but also from the slaves who for centuries have been halting here on their seaward journey from the interior of Africa.[85] [See map page 105.]

Coast peoples tend to show something more than the hybridism resulting from the mingling of two stocks. So soon as the art of navigation developed beyond its initial phase of mere coastwise travel, and began to strike out across the deep, all coast peoples bordered upon each other, and the sea became a common waste boundary between. Unlike a land boundary, which is in general accessible from only two sides and tends to show, therefore, only two constituent elements in its border population, a sea boundary is accessible from many directions with almost equal ease; it therefore draws from many lands, and gives its population a variety of ethnic elements and a cosmopolitan stamp. This, however, is most marked in great seaports, but from them it penetrates into the surrounding country. The whole southern and eastern coast population of England, from Cornwall to the Wash, received during Elizabeth's reign valuable accessions of industrious Flemings and Huguenots, refugees from Catholic persecution in the Netherlands and France.[86] Our North Atlantic States, whose population is more than half (50.9 per cent.) made up of aliens and natives born of foreign parents,[87] have drawn these elements from almost the whole circle of Atlantic shores, from Norway to Argentine and from Argentine to Newfoundland. Even the Southern States, so long unattractive to immigrants on account of the low status of

Multiplicity of race elements on coasts.

labor, show a fringe of various foreign elements along the Gulf coast, the deeper tint of which on the census maps fades off rapidly toward the interior. The same phenomenon appears with Asiatic and Australian elements in our Pacific seaboard states.[88] The cosmopolitan population of New York, with its "Chinatown," its "Little Italy," its Russian and Hungarian quarters, has its counterpart in the mixed population of Mascat, peopled by Hindu, Arabs, Persians, Kurds, Afghans, and Baluchis, settled here for purposes of trade; or in the equally mongrel inhabitants of Aden and Zanzibar, of Marseilles, Constantinople, Alexandria, Port Said, and other Mediterranean ports.

Lingua franca of coasts. The cosmopolitanism and the commercial activity that characterize so many seaboards are reflected in the fact that, with rare exceptions, it is the coast regions of the world that give rise to a *lingua franca* or *lingua geral*. The original *lingua franca* arose on the coast of the Levant during the period of Italian commercial supremacy there. It consisted of an Italian stock, on which were grafted Greek, Arabic, and Turkish words, and was the regular language of trade for French, Spanish, and Italians.[89] It is still spoken in many Mediterranean ports, especially in Smyrna, and in the early part of the nineteenth century was in use from Madagascar to the Philippines.[90] From the coastal strip of the Zanzibar Arabs, recently transferred to German East Africa, the speech of the Swahili has become a means of communication over a great part of East Africa, from the coast to the Congo and the sources of the Nile. It is a Bantu dialect permeated with Arabic and Hindu terms, and sparsely sprinkled even with English and German words.[91] "Pidgin English" (business English) performs the function of a *lingua franca* in the ports of China and the Far East. It is a jargon of corrupted English with a slight mixture of Chinese, Malay, and Portuguese words, arranged according to the Chinese idiom. Another mongrel English does service on the coast of New Guinea. The "Nigger English" of the West African trade is a regular dialect among the natives of the Sierra Leone coast. Farther east, along the Upper Guinea littoral, the Eboe family of tribes who extend across the Niger delta from

Lagos to Old Calabar have furnished a language of trade in one of their dialects.[92] The Tupi speech of the Brazilian coast Indians, with whom the explorers first came into contact, became, in the mouth of Portuguese traders and Jesuit missionaries, the *lingua geral* or medium of communication between the whites and the various Indian tribes throughout Brazil.[93] The Chinook Indians, located on our Pacific coast north and south of the Columbia River, have furnished a jargon of Indian, French, and English words which serves as a language of trade throughout a long stretch of the northwest Pacific coast, not only between whites and Indians, but also between Indians of different linguistic stocks.[94]

The coast is the natural habitat of the middleman. One strip of seaboard produces a middleman people, and then sends them out to appropriate other littorals, if geographic conditions are favorable; otherwise it is content with the transit trade of its own locality. It breeds essentially a race of merchants, shunning varied production, nursing monopoly by secrecy and every method to crush competition. The profits of trade attract all the free citizens, and the laboring class is small or slave. Expansion landward has no attraction in comparison with the seaward expansion of commerce. The result is often a relative dearth of local land-grown food stuffs. King Hiram of Tyre, in his letter to King Solomon, promised to send him trees of cedar and cypress, made into rafts and conveyed to the coast of Philistia, and asked in return for grain, "which we stand in need of because we inhabit an island." The pay came in the form of wheat, oil, and wine. But Solomon furnished a considerable part of the laborers—30,000 of them—who were sent, 10,000 at a time, to Mount Lebanon to cut the timber, apparently under the direction of the more skilful Sidonian foresters.[95] A type of true coast traders is found in the Duallas of the German Kamerun, at the inner angle of the Gulf of Guinea. Located along the lower course and delta of the Mungo River where it flows into the Kamerun estuary, they command a good route through a mountainous country into the interior. This they guard jealously, excluding all

Coast-dwellers as middle-men.

competition, monopolizing the trade, and imposing a transit duty on all articles going to and from the interior. They avoid agriculture so far as possible. Their women and slaves produce an inadequate supply of bananas and yams, but crops needing much labor are wholly neglected, so that their coasts have a reputation for dearness of provisions.[96]

Along the 4,500 miles of West African coast between the Senegal and the Kunene rivers the negro's natural talent for trade has developed special tribes, who act as intermediaries between the interior and the European stations on the seaboard. Among these we find the Bihenos and Banda of Portuguese Benguela, who fit out whole caravans for the back country; the Portuguese of Loanda rely on the Ambaquistas and the Mbunda middlemen. The slave trade particularly brought a sinister and abnormal activity to these seaboard tribes,[97] just as it did to the East Coast tribes, and stimulated both in the exploitation of their geographic position as middlemen.[98]

Monopoly of trade with the hinterland. The Alaskan coast shows the same development. The Kinik Indians at the head of Cook's Inlet buy skins of land animals from the inland Athapascans at the sources of the Copper River, and then make a good profit by selling them to the American traders of the coast. These same Athapascans for a long time found a similar body of middlemen in the Ugalentz at the mouth of the Copper River, till the Americans there encouraged the inland hunters to bring their skins to the fur station on the coast.[99] The Chilcats at the head of Lynn Canal long monopolized the fur trade with the Athapascan Indians about Chilkoot Pass; these they would meet on the divide and buy their skins, which they would carry to the Hudson Bay Company agents on the coast. They guarded their monopoly jealously, and for fifty years were able to exclude all traders and miners from the passes leading to the Yukon.[100]

The same policy of monopoly and exclusion has been pursued by the Moro coast dwellers of Mindanao in relation to the pagan tribes of the interior. They buy at low prices the forest and agriculture products of the inland Malays, whom they do not permit to approach either rivers or seaboard, for fear they may come into contact with the Chinese merchants along the coast. So fiercely is their monopoly guarded by this middleman race, that the American Government in the Philippines will be able to break it only by military interference.[101]

Differences of occupation, of food supply, and of climate often further operate to differentiate the coast from the inland people near by, and to emphasize the ethnic difference which is almost invariably present, either inconspicuously from a slight infusion of alien blood, or plainly as in an immigrant race. Sometimes the contrast is in physique. In Finisterre province of western Brittany, the people along the more fertile coastal strip are on the average an inch taller than the inhabitants of the barren, granitic interior. Their more generous food supply, further enriched by the abundant fisheries at their doors, would account for this increased stature; but this must also be attributed in part to intermixture of the local Celts with a tall Teutonic stock which brushed along these shores, but did not penetrate into the unattractive interior.[102] So the negroes of the Guinea Coast, though not immune from fevers, are better nourished on the alluvial lowlands near the abundant fish of the lagoons, and hence are often stronger and better looking than the plateau interior tribes near by. But here, again, an advantageous blending of races can not be excluded as a contributing cause.[103] Sometimes the advantage in physique falls to the inland people, especially in tropical countries when a highland interior is contrasted with a low coast belt. The wild Igorotes, inhabiting the mountainous interior of northern Luzon, enjoy a cooler climate than the lowlands, and this has resulted in developing in them a decidedly better physique and more industrious habits than are found in the civilized people of the coasts encircling them.[104]

Where a coast people is an immigrant stock from some remote oversea point, it brings to its new home a surplus of energy which was perhaps the basis of selection in the exodus from the mother country. Such a people is therefore characterized by greater initiative, enterprise, and endurance than the sedentary population which it left behind or that

Differentiation of coast from inland people.

Early civilization of coasts.

to which it comes; and these qualities are often further stimulated by the transfer to a new environment rich in opportunities. Sea-born in their origin, sea-borne in their migration, they cling to the zone of littoral, because here they find the conditions which they best know how to exploit. Dwelling on the highway of the ocean, living in easy intercourse with distant countries, which would have been far more difficult of access by land-travel over territories inhabited by hostile races, exchanging with these both commodities and ideas, food-stuffs and religions, they become the children of civilization, and their sun-burned seamen the sturdy apostles of progress. Therefore it may be laid down as a general proposition, that the coasts of a country are the first part of it to develop, not an indigenous or local civilization, but a cosmopolitan culture, which later spreads inland from the seaboard.

Retarded coastal peoples.

Exceptions to this rule are found in barren or inaccessible coasts like the Pacific littoral of Peru and Mexico, and on shores like those of California, western Africa and eastern Luzon, which occupy an adverse geographic location facing a neighborless expanse of ocean and remote from the world's earlier foci of civilization. Therefore the descent from the equatorial plateau of Africa down to the Atlantic littoral means a drop in culture also, because the various elements of civilization which for ages have uninterruptedly filtered into Sudan from the Mediterranean and the Red Sea, have rarely penetrated to the western rim of the highland, and hence never reached the coast. Moreover, this steaming lowland, from the Senegal River to the Kamerun Mountains, has been a last asylum for dislodged tribes who have been driven out by expanding peoples of the plateau. They have descended in their flight upon the original coast dwellers, adding to the general condition of political disruption, multiplying the number of small weak tribes, increasing the occasions for intertribal wars, and furthering the prevailing degradation. The seaboard lowlands of Sierra Leone, Liberia and the Ivory Coast have all suffered thus in historic times.[105] All this region was the original home of the low, typical "Guinea Nigger" of the Southern plantation. The coasts of Oregon and California showed a parallel to this in their fragmentary native tribes of retarded development, whose level of culture, low at best, sank rapidly from the interior toward the seaboard. They seem to have been intruders from the central highlands, who further deteriorated in their weakness and isolation after reaching the coast. They bore every mark of degradation in their short stature, linguistic and tribal dismemberment, their low morals and culture, which ranked them little above the brutes. In contrast, all the large and superior Indian groups of North America belonged to the interior of the continent.[106]

The long, indented coast of the Mediterranean has in all ages up to modern times presented the contrast of a littoral more advanced in civilization than the inland districts. The only exception was ancient Egypt before Psammeticus began to exploit his mud-choked seaboard. This contrast was apparent, not only wherever Phœnicians or Greeks had appropriated the remote coast of an alien and retarded people, but even in near-by Thrace the savage habits of the interior tribes were softened only where these dwelt in close proximity to the Ionian colonies along the coast, a fact as noticeable in the time of Tacitus as in that of Herodotus five hundred years before.[107] The ancient philosophers of Greece were awake to the deep-rooted differences between an inland and a maritime city, especially in respect to receptivity of ideas, activity of intellect, and affinity for culture.[108] *Cultural contrast of coast and interior.*

If we turn to the Philippines, we find that 65 per cent. of the Christian or civilized population of the islands live on or near the coast; and of the remaining 35 per cent. dwelling inland, by far the greater part represents simply the landward extension of the area of Christian civilization which had Manila Bay for a nucleus.[109] Otherwise, all the interior districts are occupied by wild or pagan tribes. Mohammedanism, too, a religion of civilization, rims the southernmost islands which face the eastern distributing point of the faith in Java; it is confined to the coasts, except for its one inland area of expansion along the lake and river system of the Rio Grande of Mindanao, which afforded an inland extension of sea navigation for the small Moro boat.

Even the Fiji Islands show different shades of savagery between coasts and interior.[110]

Coasts are areas of out-going and in-coming maritime influences. The nature and amount of these influences depend upon the sea or ocean whose rim the coast in question helps to form, and the relations of that coast to its other tide-washed shores. Our land-made point of view dominates us so completely, that we are prone to consider a coast as margin of its land, and not also as margin of its sea, whence, moreover, it receives the most important contributions to its development. The geographic location of a coast as part of a thalassic or of an oceanic rim is a basic factor in its history; more potent than local conditions of fertility, irregular contour, or accessibility from sea and hinterland. Everything that can be said about the different degrees of historical importance attaching to inland seas and open oceans in successive ages applies equally to the countries and peoples along their shores; and everything that enhances or diminishes the cultural possibilities of a sea—its size, zonal location, its relation to the oceans and continents—finds its expression in the life along its coasts.

The anthropo-geographical evolution which has passed from small to large states and from small to large seas as fields of maritime activity has been attended by a continuous change in the value of coasts, according as these were located on enclosed basins like the Mediterranean, Red, and Baltic; on marginal ones like the China and North seas; or on the open ocean. In the earlier periods of the world's history, a location on a relatively small enclosed sea gave a maritime horizon wide enough to lure, but not so wide as to intimidate; and by its seclusion led to a concentration and intensification of historical development, which in many of its phases left models for subsequent ages to wonder at and imitate. This formative period and formative environment outgrown, historical development was transferred to locations on the open oceans, according to the law of human advance from small to large areas. The historical importance of the Mediterranean and the Baltic shores was transitory, a prelude to the larger importance of the Atlantic littoral of

Europe, just as this in turn was to attain its full significance only when the circumnavigation of Africa and South America linked the Atlantic to the World Ocean. Thus that gradual expansion of the geographic horizon which has accompanied the progress of history has seen a slow evolution in the value of seaboard locations, the transfer of maritime leadership from small to large basins, from thalassic to oceanic ports, from Lubeck to Hamburg, from Venice to Genoa, as earlier from the Piræus to Ostia, and later from England's little *Cinque Ports* to Liverpool and the Clyde.

Though the articulations of a coast determine the ease with which maritime influences are communicated to the land, nevertheless history shows repeated instances where an exceptional location, combined with restricted area, has raised a poorly indented seaboard to maritime and cultural preeminence. Phœnicia's brilliant history rose superior to the limitation of indifferent harbors, owing to a position on the Arabian isthmus between the Mediterranean and the Indian Ocean at the meeting place of Europe, Asia, and Africa. Moreover, the advantages of this particular location have in various times and in various degrees brought into prominence all parts of the Syrian and Egyptian coasts from Antioch to Alexandria. So the whole stretch of coast around the head of the Adriatic, marking the conjunction of a busy sea-route with various land-routes over the encircling mountains from Central Europe, has seen during the ages a long succession of thriving maritime cities, in spite of fast-silting harbors and impeded connection with the hinterland. Here in turn have ruled with maritime sway Spina, Ravenna, Aquileia,[111] Venice, and Trieste. On the other side of the Italian peninsula, the location on the northernmost inlet of the western Mediterranean and at the seaward base of the Ligurian Apennines, just where this range opens two passes of only 1,800 feet elevation to the upper Po Valley, made an active maritime town of Genoa from Strabo's day to the present. In its incipiency it relied upon one mediocre harbor on an otherwise harborless coast, a local supply of timber for its ships, and a road northward across the mountains.[112] The maritime ascendency in the Middle Ages of Genoa, Pisa,

Geographic location of coasts.

Venice, and Barcelona proves that no long indented coast is necessary, but only one tolerable harbor coupled with an advantageous location.

Intermediate location between contrasted coasts.

Owing to the ease and cheapness of water transportation, a seaboard position between two other coasts of contrasted products due to a difference either of zonal location or of economic development or of both combined, insures commercial exchanges and the inevitable activities of the middleman. The position of Carthage near the center of the Mediterranean enabled her to fatten on the trade between the highly developed eastern basin and the retarded western one. Midway between the teeming industrial towns of medieval Flanders, Holland, and western Germany, and the new unexploited districts of retarded Russia, Poland, and Scandinavia, lay the long line of the German Hanseatic towns—Kiel, Lubeck, Wismar, Rostock, Stralsund, Greifswald, Anclam, Stettin, and Colberg, the *civitates maritimæ*. For three centuries or more they made themselves the dominant commercial and maritime power of the Baltic by exchanging Flemish fabrics, German hardware, and Spanish wines for the furs and wax of Russian forests, tallow and hides from Polish pastures, and crude metals from Swedish mines.[113] So Portugal by its geographical location became a staple place where the tropical products from the East Indies were transferred to the vessels of Dutch merchants, and by them distributed to northern Europe. Later New England, by a parallel location, became the middleman in the exchanges of the tropical products of the West Indies, the tobacco of Virginia, and the wheat of Maryland for the manufactured wares of England and the fish of Newfoundland.

Historical decline of certain coasts.

Primitive or early maritime commerce has always been characterized by the short beat, a succession of middlemen coasts, and a close series of staple-places, such as served the early Indian Ocean trade in Oman, Malabar Coast, Ceylon, Coromandel Coast, Malacca, and Java. Therefore, many a littoral admirably situated for middleman trade loses this advantage so soon as commerce matures enough to extend the sweep of its voyages, and to bring into direct contact the two nations for which that coast was intermediary. This is only another aspect of the anthropo-geographic evolution from small to large areas. The decline of the Mediterranean coasts followed close upon the discovery of the sea-route to India; nor was their local importance restored by the Suez Canal. Portugal declined when the Dutch, excluded from the Tagus mouth on the union of Portugal with Spain, found their way to the Spice Isles. Ceylon, though still the chief port of call in the Indian Ocean, has lost its preëminence as chief market for all the lands between Africa and China, which it enjoyed in the sixth century, owing to the "long haul" of modern oceanic commerce.

Not only that far-reaching readjustment of maritime ascendency which in the sixteenth century followed the advance from thalassic to oceanic fields of commerce, but also purely local political events may for a time produce striking changes in the use or importance of coasts. The Piræus, which had been the heart of ancient Athens, almost wholly lost its value in the checkered political history of the country during the Middle Ages, when naval power and merchant marine almost vanished; but with the restoration of Grecian independence in 1832, much of its pristine activity was restored. Up to the beginning of the seventeenth century, Japan had exploited her advantageous location and her richly indented coast to develop a maritime trade which extended from Kamchatka to India; but in 1624 an imperial order withdrew every Japanese vessel from the high seas, and for over two hundred years robbed her busy littoral of all its historical significance. The real life of the Pacific coast of the United States began only with its incorporation into the territory of the Republic, but it failed to attain its full importance until our acquisition of Alaska, Hawaii, and the Philippines. So the coast of the Persian Gulf has had periods of activity alternating with periods of deathlike quiet. Its conquest by the Saracens in the seventh century inaugurated an era of intense maritime enterprise along its drowsy shores. What new awakening may it experience, if it should one day become a Russian littoral!

Sometimes the decline in historical importance is due to

Political factors in this decline.

Physical causes of decline.

physical modifications in the coast itself, especially where the mud transported by a great river to the sea is constantly pushing forward the outer shoreline. The control of the Adriatic passed in turn from Spina to Adria, Ravenna, Aquileia, Venice, and Trieste, owing to a steady silting up of the coast.[114] Strabo records that Spina, originally a port, was in his time 90 stadia, or 10 miles, from the sea.[115] Bruges, once the great *entrepôt* of the Hanseatic League, was originally on an arm of the sea, with which it was later connected by canal, and which has been silted up since 1432, so that its commerce, disturbed too by local wars, was transferred to Antwerp on the Scheldt.[116] Many early English ports on the coast of Kent and on the old solid rim of the Fenland marshes now lie miles inland from the Channel and the Wash.

A people never utilizes all parts of its coast with equal intensity, or any part with equal intensity in all periods of its development; but, according to the law of differentiation, it gradually concentrates its energies in a few favored ports, whose maritime business tends to become specialized. Then every extension of the subsidiary territory and intensification of production with advancing civilization increases the mass of men and wares passing through these ocean gateways. The shores of New York, Delaware, and Chesapeake bays are more important to the country now than they were in early colonial days, when their back country extended only to the watershed of the Appalachian system. Our Gulf coast has gained in activity with the South's economic advance from slave to free labor, and from almost exclusive cotton planting to diversified production combined with industries; and it will come into its own, in a maritime sense, when the opening of the Panama Canal will divert from the Atlantic outlets those products of the Mississippi basin which will be seeking Trans-Pacific markets.

Interplay of geographic factors in coastlands.

A careful analysis of the life of coast peoples in relation to all the factors of their land and sea environment shows that these are multiform, and that none are negligible; it takes into consideration the extent, fertility, and relief of the littoral, its accessibility from the land as well as from the sea, and its location in regard to outlying islands and to opposite shores, whether near or far; it holds in view not only the small articulations that give the littoral ready contact with the sea, but the relation of the seaboard to the larger continental articulations, whether it lies on an out-running spur of a continental mass, like the Malacca, Yemen, or Peloponnesian coast, or upon a retiring inlet that brings it far into the heart of a continent, and provides it with an extensive hinterland; and, finally, it never ignores the nature of the bordering sea, which furnishes the school of seamanship and fixes the scope of maritime enterprise.

All these various elements of coastal environment are further differentiated in their use and their influence accord-ing to the purposes of those who come to tenant such tide-washed rims of the land. Pirates seek intricate channels and hidden inlets for their lairs; a merchant people select populous harbors and navigable river mouths; would-be colonists settle upon fertile valleys opening into quiet bays, till their fields, and use their coasts for placid maritime trade with the mother country; interior peoples, pushed or pushing out to the tidal periphery of their continent, with no mari-time history behind them, build their fishing villages on protected lagoons, and, unless the shadowy form of some outlying island lure them farther, there they tarry, deaf to the siren song of the sea.

NOTES TO CHAPTER VIII

1. Rudolph Reinhard, *Die Wichtigsten Deutschen Seehandelstädte,* pp. 24, 25. Stuttgart, 1901. Joseph Partsch, Central Europe, p. 291. London, 1903.

2. *Ibid.*, p. 301.

3. John Richard Green, The Making of England, Vol. I, pp. 51-54; maps, pp. 36 and 54. London, 1904.

4. *Ibid.*, Vol. I, pp. 12, 63; maps pp. xxii and 54.

5. Ratzel, History of Mankind, Vol. III, pp. 98, 139. London, 1896-1898.

6. Joseph Partsch, Central Europe, pp. 284-288. London, 1903.

7. H. R. Mill, International Geography, p. 251. New York, 1902.

8. Rudolph Reinhard, *Die Wichtigsten Deutschen Seehandelstädte,* pp. 21-22. Stuttgart, 1901.

9. Fitz-Roy and Darwin, Voyage of the Beagle, Vol. II, pp. 140, 178; Vol. III, pp. 231-236. London, 1839.

10. Eleventh Census, Population and Resources of Alaska, pp. 166-171. Washington, 1893.

11. Nordenskiold, The Voyage of the Vega, pp. 327, 334, 335, 365, 366, 412, 416, 459, 467. New York, 1882.

12. G. Frederick Wright, Greenland Icefields, pp. 68-70, 100, 105. New York, 1896. For Eskimo of Hudson Bay and Baffin Land, see F. Boas, The Central Eskimo, pp. 419, 420, 460-462. *Sixth Annual Report of the Bureau of Ethnology.* Washington, 1888.

13. *Bello Gallico*, Book III, chap. 12.

14. Ernst Curtius, History of Greece, Vol. I, p. 15. New York.

15. Strabo's Geography, Book II, chap. V, 4. Book III, chap. I, 4.

16. Grote, History of Greece, Vol. III, pp. 266-267. New York, 1857.

17. Thucydides, Book VI, 2.

18. Grote, History of Greece, Vol. III, p. 273. New York, 1857.

19. Strabo's Geography, Book XVII, chap. III, 13, 14.

20. Thucydides, Book I, 5, 7, 8.

21. Strabo, Book VIII, chap. VI, 2, 4, 13, 14, 22.

22. Grote, History of Greece, Vol. III, pp. 4, 191. New York, 1857.

23. J. Partsch, Central Europe, p. 291. London, 1903.

24. Rudolph Reinhard, *Die Wichtigsten Deutschen Seehandelstädte*, p. 23. Stuttgart, 1901.

25. Grote, History of Greece, Vol. III, p. 273. New York, 1857.

26. Bunbury, History of Ancient Geography, Vol. II, pp. 452-454, 610. London, 1883. Duarte Barbosa, East Africa and Malabar Coasts in the Sixteenth Century, p. 3-16. Hakluyt Society, London, 1866.

27. Ernst Curtius, History of Greece, Vol. I, pp. 433-434. New York.

28. W. B. Weeden, Economic and Social History of New England, Vol. I, p. 93. Boston, 1899.

29. Norway, Official Publication, p. 1. Christiania, 1900.

30. Ratzel, *Deutschland*, pp. 150-151. Leipzig, 1898.

31. J. Partsch, Central Europe, pp. 227-230. London, 1903.

32. Elisée Reclus, The Earth and Its Inhabitants; Europe, Vol. 1, pp. 370-372. New York, 1886.

33. Ernst Curtius, History of Greece, Vol. I, pp. 15-20. New York.

34. Heinrich von Treitschke, *Politik*, Vol. 1, p. 215. Leipzig, 1897.

35. H. J. Mackinder, Britain and the British Seas, pp. 35, 40. London, 1902.

36. William Morris Davis, Physical Geography, pp. 115-122. Boston, 1899.

37. Ratzel, History of Mankind, Vol. III, p. 95. London, 1896-1898.

38. Strabo, Book XVII, chap. I, 18. Diodorus Siculus, Book I, chap. III, p. 36. London, 1814.

39. J. Partsch, Central Europe, pp. 96-98. London, 1903. Ratzel, *Deutschland*, pp. 143-144. Leipzig, 1898.

40. For geomorphology of coasts, see William Morris Davis, Physical Geography, pp. 112-136, 347-383. Boston, 1899.

41. Elisée Reclus, Europe, Vol. II, p. 252. New York, 1886.

42. J. Partsch, Central Europe, p. 231. London, 1903.

43. G. G. Chisholm, Commercial Geography, pp. 44, 446. London, 1904.

44. H. R. Mill, International Geography, p. 1012. New York, 1902. Hereford George, Historical Geography of the British Empire, pp. 278-279. London, 1904.

45. J. E. Thorold Rogers, Six Centuries of Work and Wages, pp. 123-124. New York, 1884.

46. H. R. Mill, International Geography, p. 148. New York, 1902.

47. Diodorus Siculus, Book V, chap. I, p. 304. London, 1814. Strabo, Book V, chap. VI, 6, 7.

48. Helmolt, History of the World, Vol. I, pp. 188-189, 193-195. New York, 1902-1906.

49. Strabo, Book XVI, chap. III, 4, 27. Herodotus, Book I, chap. I; Book VII, chap. 89. J. T. Brent, The Bahrein Islands of the Persian Gulf, Proceedings of the Royal Geographical Society, Vol. XII, pp. 13-16. London, 1890.

50. George Adam Smith, Historical Geography of the Holy Land, pp. 169-170. New York, 1897.

51. Ibid., pp. 179, 185, 286.

52. Ibid., pp. 127-131.

53. Ratzel, History of Mankind, Vol. III, pp. 100-102, 132-145. London, 1896-1898.

54. H. R. Mill, International Geography, p. 985. New York, 1902.

55. D. G. Hogarth, The Nearer East, pp. 84, 166. London, 1902.

56. J. Naken, Die Provinz Kwangtung und ihre Bevölkerung, Petermanns Geographische Mittheilungen, Vol. 24, pp. 409, 420. 1878. Ferdinand von Richthofen, China, Vol. I, pp. 568-569. Berlin, 1877. Cathay and the Way Thither, Vol. I, p. lxxviii. Hakluyt Society, London, 1866.

57. Ratzel, History of Mankind, Vol. I, p. 397. London, 1896-1898. Philippine Census, Vol. I, pp. 438, 481-491. Washington, 1905.

58. Stanford's Australasia, Vol. II, pp. 103, 121, 126-135, 196. London, 1894. Helmolt, History of the World, Vol. II, p. 547. New York, 1902-1906.

59. Ibid., Vol. III, pp. 431, 434. Vol. II, p. 603.

60. Roscher, National-Oekonomik des Handels und Gewerbefleisses, pp. 78-79, 99-100. Stuttgart, 1899. Capt. A. T. Mahan, Influence of Sea Power upon History, pp. 26-28. Boston, 1902.

61. D. G. Hogarth, The Nearer East, pp. 111-112, 152. London, 1902.

62. Ibid., pp. 73-74, 139, 267.

63. Cathay and the Way Thither, Vol. I, p. LXXX. Hakluyt Society. London, 1866. Helmolt, History of the World, Vol. II, p. 548. New York, 1902-1906.

64. The Book of Ser Marco Polo, edited by Sir Henry Yule, Vol. II, Book III, pp. 284, 288, 303. New York, 1903.

65. P. Vidal de la Blache, Géographie de la France, pp. 335-337. Paris, 1903.

66. Elisée Reclus, Europe, Vol. II, p. 252. New York, 1882.

67. Norway, Official Publication, pp. 89-91, map p. 4. Christiania, 1900.

68. D. G. Hogarth, The Nearer East, pp. 114, 140, 163-164, 202, 267. London, 1902.

69. H. F. Tozer, History of Ancient Geography, pp. 276-280. Cambridge, 1897. Strabo, Book XVI, chap. IV, 2, 19.

70. Helmolt, History of the World, Vol. III, p. 433. New York, 1902-1906.

71. James Bryce, Impressions of South Africa, pp. 78-82, 99. New York, 1897.

72. Anatole Leroy-Beaulieu, The Empire of the Tsars, Vol. I, map p. 80. New York, 1893.

73. Census of the Philippine Islands, Vol. I, pp. 412-413, 461, 464, 562. Washington, 1905.

74. *Ibid.*, Vol. I, p. 416.

75. Ratzel, History of Mankind, Vol. III, p. 449. London, 1896-1898.

76. P. Ehrenreich, *Die Eintheilung und Verbreitung der Völkerstämme Brasiliens, Petermanns Mittheilungen*, Vol. 37, pp. 88-89. Gotha, 1891. Helmolt, History of the World, Vol. I, p. 185, map p. 189. New York, 1902-1906.

77. John Richard Green, The Making of England, Vol. I, chap. I. London, 1904.

78. H. J. Mackinder, Britain and the British Seas, p. 189. London, 1904. W. Z. Ripley, Races of Europe, pp. 312-315, map. New York, 1899.

79. D. G. Hogarth, The Nearer East, p. 152. London, 1902. W. Z. Ripley, Races of Europe, pp. 402, 404, map. New York, 1899.

80. *Ibid.*, pp. 117, 404-405, 409-419.

81. *Ibid.*, pp. 206-208, 210-212. Norway, Official Publication, pp. 80-81. Christiania, 1900.

82. Census of the Philippine Islands, Vol. II, p. 52, map p. 50. Washington, 1905.

83. Grote, History of Greece, Vol. III, pp. 175-176, 186-189. New York, 1857.

84. Ernst Curtius, History of Greece, Vol. I, pp. 492-493. New York.

85. Ratzel, History of Mankind, Vol. II, pp. 530-533. London, 1896-1898.

86. H. D. Trail, Social England, Vol. III, pp. 367-368. London and New York, 1895.

87. Twelfth Census, Bulletin No. 103, table 23. Washington, 1902.

88. E. C. Semple, American History and Its Geographic Conditions, pp. 314-328. Boston, 1903.

89. G. G. Chisholm, Commercial Geography, p. 58. London, 1904.

90. Roscher, *National-Oekonomik des Handels und Gewerbefleisses*, p. 85, Note 18. Stuttgart, 1899.

91. Ratzel, History of Mankind, Vol. II, p. 533. London, 1896-1898.

92. *Ibid.*, Vol. III, pp. 139, 145.

93. H. R. Mill, International Geography, p. 869. New York, 1902.

94. D. G. Brinton, The American Race, p. 107. Philadelphia, 1901. H. H. Bancroft, The Native Races, p. 239, footnote p. 274. San Francisco, 1886.

95. Josephus, Antiquities of the Jews, Book VIII, chap. II, 6, 7, 9.

96. J. Scott Keltie, The Partition of Africa, p. 327. London, 1895. Ratzel, History of Mankind, Vol. III, pp. 121-122. London, 1896-1898.

97. *Ibid.*, Vol. III, pp. 121, 132-133.

98. *Ibid.*, Vol. II, p. 239.

99 Eleventh Census, Report on Alaska, p. 70. Washington, 1893.

100. *Ibid.*, p. 156.   E. R. Scidmore, Guidebook to Alaska, p. 94.   New York, 1897.

101. Census of the Philippine Islands, Vol. I, pp. 556-561, 575, 581-583.   Washington, 1905.

102. W. Z. Ripley, Races of Europe, pp. 85-86, 99-101, map pp. 151-152.   New York, 1899.

103. Ratzel, History of Mankind, Vol. III, pp. 97, 106.   New York, 1896-1898.

104. Henry Gannett, The Peoples of the Philippines, in Report of the Eighth International Geographic Congress, p. 673.   Washington, 1904.

105. A. H. Keane, Africa, Stanford's Compendium, pp. 372-376, 385-388.   London, 1895.   Helmolt, History of the World, Vol. III, pp. 402, 456-457, 462.   New York, 1902-1906.

106. H. H. Bancroft, The Native Races, Vol. I, pp. 440-441; Vol. III, pp. 325, 362.   San Francisco, 1886.   McGee and Thomas, Prehistoric North America, pp. 37-38, 78, 88-89, 95-98.   Vol. XIX of History of North America.   Philadelphia, 1905.

107. Grote, History of Greece, Vol. IV, p. 22.   New York, 1857.

108. *Ibid.*, Vol. II, pp. 225, 226.

109. Census of the Philippine Islands, Vol. II, pp. 34, 35.   Washington, 1905.

110. Williams and Calvert, Fiji and the Fijians, pp. 81-82.   New York, 1859.

111. Strabo, Book V, chap. I, 7, 8.

112. Strabo, Book IV, chap. VI, 1, 2; Book V, chap. I, 11.

113. Dietrich Schäfer, *Die Hansestädte und König Waldemar von Dänemark*, pp. 184, 189.   Jena, 1879.

114. W. Deecke, Italy, pp. 89-91.   London, 1904.

115. Strabo, Book III, chap. I, 2.

116. Roscher, *National-Oekonomik des Handels und Gewerbefleisses*, p. 93, Note 1.   Stuttgart, 1899.

CHAPTER IX

OCEANS AND ENCLOSED SEAS

THE water of the earth's surface, viewed from the stand-point of anthropo-geography, is one, whether it appears as atmospheric moisture, spring, river, lake, brackish lagoon, enclosed sea-basin or open ocean. Its universal circulation, from the falling of the dews to the vast sweep of ocean current, causes this inviolable unity. Variations in the geographical forms of water are superficial and constantly changing; they pass into one another by almost impercep-tible gradations, shift their unstable outlines at the bidding of the mobile, restless element. In contrast to the land, which is marked by diversity of geologic structure and geographic form, the world of water is everywhere approximately the same, excepting only the difference in the mineral composi-tion of sea water as opposed to that of spring and stream. Therefore, whenever man has touched it, it has moulded him in much the same way, given the same direction to his activ-ities, dictated the use of the same implements and methods of navigation. As maritime trader or colonist, he has sailed to remote, unknown, yet familiar coasts, and found himself as much at home as on his native shores. He has built up maritime empires, the centre of whose dominion, race and commerce, falls somewhere in the dividing yet uniting sea.

The water a factor in man's mobility.
Man must be grouped with the air and water as part of the mobile envelope of the earth's surface. The mobility which maintains the unity of air and water has caused the unity of the human race. Abundant facilities of dispersal often give animal forms a wide or cosmopolitan distribution. Man, by appropriating the mobile forces in the air and water to increase his own powers of locomotion, has become a cos-mopolitan being, and made the human race reflect the unity of atmosphere and hydrosphere.

Always the eternal unrest of the moving waters has knocked at the door of human inertia to arouse the sleeper within; always the flow of stream and the ebb of tide have sooner or later stirred the curiosity of the land-born barbarian about the unseen destination of these marching waters. Rivers by the mere force of gravity have carried him to the shores of their common ocean, and placed him on this highway of the world. Then from his sea-girt home, whether island or continent, he has timidly or involuntarily followed the track which headland-dotted coast, or ocean current, or monsoon, or trade wind marked out for him across the pathless waters, so that at the gray dawn of history he appears as a cosmopolite, occupying every part of the habitable earth.

These sporadic oversea wanderings, with intervals of centuries or milleniums between, opened to his occupancy strange and remote lands, in whose isolation and new environment he developed fresh variations of mind, body and cultural achievements, to arm him with new weapons in the struggle for existence. The sea which brought him bars him for a few ages from his old home, till the tradition of his coming even is lost. Then with higher nautical development, the sea loses its barrier nature; movements of people and trade recross its surface to unite those who have been long severed and much differentiated in their mutual remoteness. The ensuing friction and mingling weed out the less fit variations of each, and combine in the new race the qualities able to fortify a higher type of man. Not only seas and oceans, but also mountains and deserts serve to isolate the migrant people who once has crossed them; but wastes of water raise up the most effective barriers.

The transformation of the ocean into a highway by the development of navigation is a late occurrence in the history of man and is perhaps the highest phase of his adaptation to environment, because an adaptation which has placed at his disposal that vast water area constituting three-fourths of the earth's surface from which he had previously been excluded. Moreover, it was adaptation to an alien and hostile element, whose violent displays of power recurrently stimulated the human adjustment between attack and defense. Oceans and seas in universal history.

Because adaptation to the sea has been vastly more difficult than to the land, commensurate with the harder struggle it has brought greater intellectual and material rewards. This conquest of the sea is entitled to a peculiarly high place in history, because it has contributed to the union of the various peoples of the world, has formed a significant part of the history of man, whether that history is economic, social, political or intellectual. Hence history has always staged its most dramatic acts upon the margin of seas and oceans; here always the plot thickens and gives promise of striking development. Rome of the seven hills pales before England of the "Seven Seas."

The sea in universal history. Universal history loses half its import, remains an aggregate of parts, fails to yield its significance as a whole, if it does not continually take into account the unifying factor of the seas. Indeed, no history is entitled to the name of universal unless it includes a record of human movements and activities on the ocean, side by side with those on the land. Our school text-books in geography present a deplorable hiatus, because they fail to make a definite study of the oceans over which man explores and colonizes and trades, as well as the land on which he plants and builds and sleeps.

The striking fact about the great World Ocean to-day is the manifold relations which it has established between the dwellers on its various coasts. Marine cables, steamer and sailing routes combine to form a network of paths across the vast commons of the deep. Over these the commercial, political, intellectual, or even purely migrant activities of human life move from continent to continent. The distinctive value of the sea is that it promotes many-sided relations as opposed to the one-sided relation of the land. France on her eastern frontier comes into contact with people of kindred stock, living under similar conditions of climate and soil to her own; on her maritime border she is open to intermittent intercourse with all continents and climes and races of the world. To this sea border must be ascribed the share that France has taken in the history of North and South America, the West Indies, North and Equatorial Africa, India, China and the South Seas. So we find the great maritime peoples of the world, from the Phœnicians to the English, each figuring in the history of the world of its day, and helping weave into a web of universal history the stories of its various parts.

Man's normal contact with the sea is registered in his nautical achievements. The invention of the first primitive means of navigation, suggested by a floating log or bloated body of a dead animal, must have been an early achievement of a great many peoples who lived near the water, or who in the course of their wanderings found their progress obstructed by rivers; it belongs to a large class of similar discoveries which answer urgent and constantly recurring needs. It was, in all probability, often made and as often lost again, until a growing habit of venturing beyond shore or river bank in search of better fishing, or of using the easy open waterways through the thick tangle of a primeval forest to reach fresh hunting grounds, established it as a permanent acquisition.

Origin of navigation.

The first devices were simply floats or rafts, made of light wood, reeds, or the hollow stems of plants woven together and often buoyed up by the inflated skins of animals. Floats of this character still survive among various peoples, especially in poorly timbered lands. The skin rafts which for ages have been the chief means of downstream traffic on the rivers of Mesopotamia, consist of a square frame-work of interwoven reeds and branches, supported by the inflated skins of sheep and goats;[1] they are guided by oars and poles down or across the current. These were the primitive means by which Layard transported his winged bull from the ruins of Nineveh down to the Persian Gulf, and they were the same which he found on the bas-reliefs of the ancient capital, showing the methods of navigation three thousand years ago.[2] Similar skin rafts serve as ferry boats on the Sutlej, Shajok and other head streams of the Indus.[3] They reappear in Africa as the only form of ferry used by the Moors on the River Morbeya in Morocco; on the Nile, where the inflated skins are supplanted by earthen pots;[4] and on the Yo River of semi-arid Sudan, where the platform is made of reeds and is buoyed up by calabashes fastened beneath.[5]

Primitive forms.

Primitive
craft in
arid lands.

In treeless lands, reeds growing on the margins of streams and lakes are utilized for the construction of boats. The Buduma islanders of Lake Chad use clumsy skiffs eighteen feet long, made of hollow reeds tied into bundles and then lashed together in a way to form a slight cavity on top.[6] In the earliest period of Egyptian history this type of boat with slight variations was used in the papyrus marshes of the Nile,[7] and it reappears as the ambatch boat which Schweinfurth observed on the upper White Nile.[8] It is in use far away among the Sayads or Fowlers, who inhabit the reed-grown rim of the Sistan Lake in arid Persia.[9] As the Peruvian balsa, it has been the regular means of water travel on Lake Titicaca since the time of the Incas, and in more primitive form it appears among the Shoshone Indians of the Snake River Valley of Idaho, who used this device in their treeless land to cross the streams, when the water was too cold for swimming.[10] Still cruder rafts of reeds, without approach to boat form, were the sole vehicles of navigation among the backward Indians of San Francisco Bay, and were the prevailing craft among the coast Indians farther south and about the Gulf of Lower California.[11] Trees abounded; but these remnant tribes of low intelligence, probably recent arrivals on the coast from the interior, equipped only with instruments of bone and stone, found the difficulty of working with wood prohibitive.

The second step in the elaboration of water conveyance was made when mere flotation was succeeded by various devices to secure displacement. The evolution is obvious. The primitive raftsman of the Mesopotamian rivers wove his willow boughs and osiers into a large, round basket form, covered it with closely sewn skins to render it water-tight, and in it floated with his merchandise down the swift current from Armenia to Babylon. These were the boats which Herodotus saw on the Euphrates,[12] and which survive to-day.[13] According to Pliny, the ancient Britons used a similar craft, framed of wicker-work and covered with hide, in which they crossed the English and Irish channels to visit their kinsfolk on the opposite shores. This skin boat or coracle or currach still survives on the rivers of Wales and the west coast of Ireland, where it is used by the fishermen and considered the safest craft for stormy weather.[14] It recalls the "bull-skin boat" used in pioneer days on the rivers of our western plains, and the skiffs serving as passenger ferries to-day on the rivers of eastern Tibet.[15] It reappears among the Arikara Indians of the upper Missouri,[16] and the South American tribes of the Gran Chaco.[17] The first wooden boat was made of a tree trunk, hollowed out either by fire or axe. The wide geographical distribution of the dug-out and its survival in isolated regions of highly civilized lands point it out as one of those necessary and obvious inventions that must have been made independently in various parts of the world.

The quieter water of rivers and lakes offered the most favorable conditions for the feeble beginnings of navigation, but the step from inland to marine navigation was not always taken. The Egyptians, who had well-constructed river and marine boats, resigned their maritime commerce to Phœnicians and Greeks, probably, as has been shown, because the silted channels and swamps of the outer Nile delta held them at arm's length from the sea. Similarly the equatorial lakes of Central Africa have proved fair schools of navigation, where the art has passed the initial stages of development. The kingdom of Uganda on Victoria Nyanza, at the time of Stanley's visit, could muster a war fleet of 325 boats, a hundred of them measuring from fifty to seventy feet in length; the largest were manned by a crew of sixty-four paddlers and could carry as many more fighting men.[18] The long plateau course of the mighty Congo has bred a race of river navigators, issuing from their riparian villages to attack the traveler in big flotillas of canoes ranging from fifty to eighty-five feet in length, the largest of them driven through the water by eighty paddlers and steered by eight more paddles in the stern.[19] But the Congo and lake boats are barred from the coast by a series of cataracts, which mark the passage of the drainage streams down the escarpment of the plateau. *Relation of river to marine navigation.*

There are peoples without boats or rafts of any description. Among this class are the Central Australians, Bushmen, Hottentots and Kaffirs of arid South Africa,[20] and with few *Retarded navigation.*

exceptions also the Damaras. Even the coast members of these tribes only wade out into the shallow water on the beach to spear fish. The traveler moving northward from Cape Town through South Africa, across its few scant rivers, goes all the way to Ngami Lake before he sees anything resembling a canoe, and then only a rude dugout. Still greater is the number of people who, though inhabiting well indented coasts, make little use of contact with the sea. Navigation, unknown to many Australian coast tribes, is limited to miserable rafts of mangrove branches on the northwest seaboard, and to imperfect bark canoes with short paddles on the south; only in the north where Malayan influences are apparent does the hollowed tree-stem with outrigger appear.[21] This retardation is not due to fear, because the South Australian native, like the Fuegian, ventures several miles out to sea in his frail canoe; it is due to that deep-seated inertia which characterizes all primitive races, and for which the remote, outlying location of peninsular South America, Southern Africa and Australia, before the arrival of the Europeans, afforded no antidote in the form of stimulating contact with other peoples. But the Irish, who started abreast of the other northern Celts in nautical efficiency, who had advantages of proximity to other shores, and in the early centuries of their history sailed to the far-away Faroes and even to Iceland, peopled southern Scotland by an oversea emigration, made piratical descents upon the English coast, and in turn received colonies of bold Scandinavian mariners, suffered an arrested development in navigation, and failed to become a sea-faring folk.

Regions of advanced navigation. Turning from these regions of merely rudimentary navigation and inquiring where the highest efficiency in the art was attained before the spread of Mediterranean and European civilization, we find that this distinction belongs to the great island world of the Pacific and to the neighboring lands of the Indian Ocean. Sailing vessels and outrigger boats of native design and construction characterize the whole sea-washed area of Indo-Malaysian civilization from Malacca to the outermost isles of the Pacific. The eastern rim of Asia, also, belongs to this wide domain of nautical efficiency, and the coast Indians of southern Alaska and British Columbia may possibly represent an eastern spur of the same,[22] thrown out in very remote times and maintained by the advantageous geographic conditions of that indented, mountainous coast. Adjoining this area on the north is the long-drawn Arctic seaboard of the Eskimo, who unaided have developed in their sealskin kayak and bidarka sea-going craft unsurpassed for the purposes of marine hunting and fishing, and who display a fearlessness and endurance born of long and enforced intimacy with the deep. Driven by the frozen deserts of his home to seek his food chiefly in the water, the Eskimo, nevertheless, finds his access to the sea barred for long months of winter by the jagged ice-pack along the shore.

The highest degree of intimacy is developed in that vast island-strewn stretch of the Pacific constituting Oceanica.[23] Here where a mild climate enables the boatman race to make a companion of the deep, where every landscape is a seascape, where every diplomatic visit or war campaign, every trading journey or search for new coco-palm plantation means a voyage beyond the narrow confines of the home island, there dwells a race whose splendid chest and arm muscles were developed in the gymnasium of the sea; who, living on a paltry 515,000 square miles (1,320,300 square kilometers) of scattered fragments of land, but roaming over an ocean area of twenty-five million square miles, are not more at home in their palm-wreathed islets than on the encompassing deep. Migrations, voluntary and involuntary, make up their history. Their trained sense of locality, enabling them to make voyages several hundred miles from home, has been mentioned by various explorers in Polynesia. The Marshall Islanders set down their geographical knowledge in maps which are fairly correct as to bearings but not as to distances. The Ralick Islanders of this group make charts which include islands, routes and currents.[24] Captain Cook was impressed by the geographical knowledge of the people of the South Seas. A native Tahitian made for him a chart containing seventy-four islands, and gave an account of nearly sixty more.[25] Information and directions supplied

Geographic conditions in Polynesia.

by natives have aided white explorers to many discoveries in these waters. Quiros, visiting the Duff Islands in 1606, learned the location of Ticopia, one of the New Hebrides group, three hundred miles away. Not only the excellent seamanship and the related pelagic fishing of the Polynesians bear the stamp of their predominant water environment; their mythology, their conception of a future state, the germs of their astronomical science, are all born of the sea.

Though the people living on the uttermost boundaries of this island world are 6,000 miles (or 10,000 kilometers) apart, and might be expected to be differentiated by the isolation of their island habitats, nevertheless they all have the same fundamental characteristics of physique, language and culture from Guam to Easter Isle, reflecting in their unity the oneness of the encompassing ocean over which they circulate.[26]

Mediterranean versus Atlantic seamanship.

Midway between these semi-aquatic Polynesians and those Arctic tribes who are forced out upon the deep, to struggle with it rather than associate with it, we find the inhabitants of the Mediterranean islands and peninsulas, who are favored by the mild climate and the tideless, fogless, stormless character of their sea. While such a body of water invites intimacy, it does not breed a hardy or bold race of navigators; it is a nursery, scarcely a training school. Therefore, except for the far-famed Dalmatian sailors, who for centuries have faced the storms sweeping down from the Dinaric Alps over the turbulent surface of the Adriatic, Mediterranean seamanship does not command general confidence on the high seas. Therefore it is the German, English and Dutch steamship lines that are to-day the chief ocean carriers from Italian ports to East Africa, Asia, Australia, North and South America, despite the presence of native lines running from Genoa to Buenos Ayres, Montevideo and New York; just as it was the Atlantic states of Europe, and only these and all of these, except Germany, who, trained to venture out into the fogs and storms and unmarked paths of the *mare tenebrosum*, participated in the early voyages to the Americas. One after the other they came—Norwegians, Spaniards, Portuguese, English, French, Dutch, Swedes and

Danes. The anthropo-geographical principle is not invalidated by the fact that Spain and England were guided in their initial trans-Atlantic voyages by Italian navigators, like Columbus, Cabot and Amerigo Vespucci. The long maritime experience of Italy and its commercial relations with the Orient, reaching back into ancient times, furnished abundant material for the researches and speculations of such practical theorists; but Italy's location fixed the shores of the Mediterranean as her natural horizon, narrowed her vision to its shorter radius. Her obvious interest in the preservation of the old routes to the Orient made her turn a deaf ear to plans aiming to divert European commerce to trans-Atlantic routes. Italy's entrance upon the high seas was, therefore, reluctant and late, retarded by the necessity of outgrowing the old circumscribed outlook of the enclosed basin before adopting the wider vision of the open ocean. Venice and Genoa were crippled not only by the discovery of the sea route to India, but also by their adherence to old thalassic means and methods of navigation inadequate for the high seas.[27] However, these Mediterranean sea folk are being gradually drawn out of their seclusion, as is proved by the increase of Italian oceanic lines and the recent installation of an Hellenic steamship line between Piræus and New York.

The size of a sea or ocean is a definite factor in its power to attract or repel maritime ventures, especially in the earlier stages of nautical development. A broken, indented coast means not only a longer and broader zone of contact between the inhabitants and the sea; it means also the breaking up of the adjacent expanse of water into so many alcoves, in which fisherman, trader and colonist may become at home, and prepare for maritime ventures farther afield. The enclosed or marginal sea tempts earlier because it can be compassed by coastwise navigation; then by the proximity of its opposite shores and its usual generous equipment with islands, the next step to crosswise navigation is encouraged. For the earliest stages of maritime development, only the smaller articulations of the coast and the inshore fringe of sea inlets count. This is shown in the

Three geographic stages of maritime development.

primitive voyages of the Greeks, before they had ventured into the Euxine or west of the forbidding Cape Malia; and in the "inside passage" navigation of the Indians of southern Alaska, British Columbia, and Chile, who have never stretched their nautical ventures beyond the outermost rocks of their skerry-walled coast.

Influence of enclosed seas upon navigation.   A second stage is reached when an enclosed basin is at hand to widen the maritime horizon, and when this larger field is exploited in all its commercial, colonial and industrial possibilities, as was done by the Phœnicians and Greeks in the Mediterranean, the Hanse Towns in the Baltic, the Dutch and English in the North Sea. The third and final stage is reached when the nursery of the inshore estuary or gulf and the elementary school of the enclosed basin are in turn outgrown, and the larger maritime spirit moves on to the open ocean for its field of operation. It is a significant fact that the Norse, bred to the water in their fiords and channels behind their protecting "skerry-wall," then trained in the stormy basins of the North and Irish Seas, were naturally the first people of Europe to cross the Atlantic, because the Atlantic of their shores, narrowing like all oceans and seas toward the north, assumes almost the character of an enclosed basin. The distance from Norway to Greenland is only 1,800 miles, little more than that across the Arabian Sea between Africa and India. We trace, therefore, a certain analogy between the physical subdivisions of the world of water into inlet, marginal sea and ocean, and the anthropo-geographical gradations in maritime development.

The enclosed or marginal sea seems a necessary condition for the advance beyond coastwise navigation and the much later step to the open ocean. Continents without them, like Africa, except for its frontage upon the Mediterranean and the Red Sea, have shown no native initiative in maritime enterprise. Africa was further cursed by the mockery of desert coasts along most of her scant thalassic shores. In the Americas, we find the native races compassing a wide maritime field only in the Arctic, where the fragmentary character of the continent breaks up the ocean into Hudson's Bay, Davis Strait, Baffin Bay, Gulf of Boothia, Melville

Sound and Bering Sea; and in the American Mediterranean of the Caribbean Sea and Gulf of Mexico. The excellent seamanship developed in the archipelagoes of southern Alaska and Chile remained abortive for maritime expansion, despite a paucity of local resources and the spur of hunger, owing to the lack of a marginal sea; but in the Caribbean basin, the Arawaks and later the Caribs spread from the southern mainland as far as Cuba.[28] [See map page 101.]

Enclosed or marginal seas were historically the most important sections of the ocean prior to 1492. Apart from the widening of the maritime horizon which they give to their bordering people, each has the further advantage of constituting an area of close vicinal grouping and constant interchange of cultural achievements, by which the civilization of the whole basin tends to become elevated and unified. This unification frequently extends to race also, owing to the rapidity of maritime expansion and the tendency to ethnic amalgamation characteristic of all coast regions. We recognize an area of Mediterranean civilization from the Isthmus of Suez to the Sacred Promontory of Portugal, and in this area a long-headed, brunette Mediterranean race, clearly unified as to stock, despite local differentiations of culture, languages and nations in the various islands, peninsulas and other segregated coastal regions of this sea.[29] The basin appears therefore as an historical whole; for in it a certain group of peoples concentrated their common efforts, which crossed and criss-crossed from shore to shore. Phœnicia's trade ranged westward to the outer coasts of Spain, and later Barcelona's maritime enterprises reached east to the Levant. Greece's commercial and colonial relations embraced the Crimea and the mouth of the Rhone, and Genoa's extended east to the Crimea again. The Saracens, on reaching the Mediterranean edge of the Arabian peninsula, swept the southern coasts and islands, swung up the western rim of the basin to the foot of the Pyrenees, and taught the sluggish Spaniards the art of irrigation practiced on the garden slopes of Yemen. The ships of the Crusaders from Venice, Genoa and Marseilles anchored in the ports of Mohammedanized Syria, brought the symbol of the cross

(margin note:) Enclosed seas as areas of ethnic and cultural assimilation.

back to its birthplace in Jerusalem, but carried away with them countless suggestions from the finished industries of the East. Here was give and take, expansion and counter-expansion, conquest and expulsion, all together making up a great sum of reciprocal relations embracing the whole basin, the outcome of that close geographical connection which every sharply defined sea establishes between the coasts which it washes.

North Sea and Baltic basins. The same thing has come to pass in the North Sea. Originally Celtic on its western or British side, as opposed to its eastern or Germanic coast, it has been wholly Teutonized on that flank also from the Strait of Dover to the Firth of Tay, and sprinkled with Scandinavian settlers from the Firth of Tay northward to Caithness.[30] The eleventh century saw this ethnic unification achieved, and the end of the Middle Ages witnessed the diffusion of the elements of a common civilization through the agency of commerce from Bruges to Bergen. The Baltic, originally Teutonic only on its northern and western shores, has in historical times become almost wholly Teutonic, including even the seaboard of Finland and much of the coast provinces of Russia.[31] Unification of civilization attended this unification of race. In its period of greatest historical significance from the twelfth to the seventeenth century, the Baltic played the rôle of a northern Mediterranean.[32] The countless shuttles of the Hanse ships wove a web of commercial intercourse between its remotest shores. Novgorod and Abö were in constant communication with Lübeck and Stralsund;[33] and Wisby, on the island of Gotland at the great crossroads of the Baltic,[34] had the focal significance of the Piræus in ancient Aegean trade.

Bering Sea. If we turn to Asia, we find that even the unfavorable Arctic location of Bering Sea has been unable to rob it entirely of historical significance. This is the one spot where a native American race has transplanted itself by its natural expansion to Asiatic shores. The circular rim and island-dotted surface have guided Eskimo emigrants to the coast of the Chukchian Peninsula, where they have become partly assimilated in dress and language to the local Chukches.[35] The same conditions also facilitated the passage of a few

Chukches across Bering Strait to the Alaskan side. At Pak (or Peek) on East Cape and on Diomed Island, situated in the narrowest part of Bering Strait, are the great inter-continental markets of the polar tribes. Here American furs have for many decades been exchanged for the reindeer skins of northern Siberia and Russian goods from far-away Mos-cow.[36] Only the enclosed character of the sea, reported by the Danish explorer Vitus Bering, tempted the land-bred Russians, who reached the northeastern coast of Siberia at the middle of the eighteenth century, to launch their leaky boats of unseasoned timber, push across to the American con-tinent, and make this whole Bering basin a Russian sea;[37] just as a few decades before, when land exploration of Kamchatka had revealed the enclosed character of the Sea of Okhotsk, the Russian pioneers took a straight course across the water to their Pacific outpost of Petropavlovsk near the southern end of the peninsula. But even before the coming of the Slavs to its shores, the Sea of Okhotsk seems to have been an area of native commercial and ethnic intercourse from the Amur River in Siberia in a half circle to the east, through Sakhalin, Yezo, the Kurile Islands and southern Kamchatka,[38] noticeably where the rim of the basin pre-sented the scantiest supply of land and where, therefore, its meager resources had to be eked out by fisheries and trade on the sea.

On the southwest margin of Asia, the Red Sea, despite its desert shores, has maintained the influence of its inter-continental location and linked the neighboring elements of Africa and Asia. Identity of climatic conditions on both sides of this long rift valley has facilitated ethnic exchanges, and made it the center of what Ratzel calls the "Red Sea group of peoples," related in race and culture.[39] The great ethnic solvent here has been Semitic. Under the spur of Islam, the Arabs by 1514 had made the Red Sea an Arabian and Mohammedan sea. They had their towns or trading stations at Zeila on the African side of the Strait of Bab-el-Mandeb, at Dalaqua, the port of Abyssinia, at Massowa, Suakin, and other towns, so that this coast too was called Arabia Felix.[40]

Red Sea basin.

Assimilation
facilitated
by ethnic
kinship.

Vicinal location about an enclosed basin produces more rapidly a unification of race and culture, when some ethnic relationship and affinity already exists among the peoples inhabiting its shores. As in the ancient and medieval Mediterranean, so in the Yellow Sea of Asia, the working of this principle is apparent. The presence along its coasts of divergent but kindred peoples like the Chinese, Koreans and Japanese, allowed these to be easily assimilated to a Yellow Sea race and to absorb quickly any later infusion, like that of the Tatars and Manchus. China, by reason of its larger area, long-drawn coast, massive population, and early civilization, was the dominant factor in this basin; Korea and Japan were its culture colonies—a fact that justifies the phrase calling "China the Rome of the Far East." Historical Japan began on the island of Kiu-sui, facing the Yellow Sea. Like Korea, it derived its writing, its fantastic medical notions, its industrial methods, some features of its government administration, its Buddhism and its religion of Confucius from the people about the lower Hoangho.[41] Three centuries ago Japan had its colony on Korean soil at Fusan, the Calais of the East.[42] For purposes of piracy and smuggling Japanese penetrated far up the rivers of China. Korea has kept in touch with China by an active trade and diplomatic relations through the centuries.

But to-day China is going to school to Japan. Since Japan renounced her policy of seclusion in 1868 along with her antiquated form of government, and since Korea has been forced out of her hermit life, the potency of vicinal location around this enclosed sea has been suddenly restored. The enforced opening of the treaty ports of Japan, Korea and China simply prepared the way for this basin to reassert its power to unite, and to unite now more closely and effectively than ever before, under the law of increasing territorial areas. The stimulus was first communicated to the basin from without, from the trading nations of the Occident and that new-born Orient rising from the sea on the California shores. Japan has responded most promptly and most actively to these over-sea stimuli, just as England has, of all Europe, felt most strongly the

reflex influences from trans-Atlantic lands. The awakening
of this basin has started, therefore, from its seaward rim;
its star has risen in the east. It is in the small countries of
the world that such stars rise. The compressed energies of
Japan, stirred by over-sea contact and an improved government at home, have overleaped the old barriers and are following the lines of slight resistance which this land-bound sea
affords. Helped by the bonds of geographical conditions
and of race, she has begun to convert China and Korea into
her culture colonies. The on-looking world feels that the
ultimate welfare of China and Korea can be best nurtured
by Japan, which will thus pay its old debt to the Middle
Kingdom.

Despite the fact that China's history has always had a Chinese
decidedly inland character, that its political expansion has expansion
been landward, that it has practiced most extensively and seaward.
successively internal colonization, and that its policy of
exclusion has tended to deaden its outlook toward the Pacific,
nevertheless China's direct intercourse with the west and its
westward-directed influence have never, in point of significance, been comparable with that toward the east and
south. Here a succession of marginal seas offered easy
water-paths, dotted with way stations, to their outermost rim
in Japan, the Philippines and remote Australia. About the
South China Sea, the Gulf of Siam, the Sulu, Celebes, and
Java Seas, the coastal regions of the outlying islands have
for centuries received Chinese goods and culture, and a blend
of that obstinately assertive Chinese blood.

The strength of these influences has decreased with every
increase of distance from the indented coasts and teeming,
seafaring population of South China, and with every decrease
in race affinity. They have left only faint traces on the
alien shores of far-away Australia. The divergent ethnic
stock of the widespread Malay world has been little susceptible to these influences, which are therefore weak in the
remoter islands, but clearly discernible on the coasts of the
Philippines,[43] Borneo, the nearer Sunda Islands, and the
peninsula of Malacca, where the Chinese have had trading
colonies for centuries.[44] But in the eastern half of Farther

India, which is grouped with China by land as well as by sea, and whose race stock is largely if not purely Mongolian, these influences are very marked, so that the whole continental rim of the South China Sea, from Formosa to the Isthmus of Malacca, is strongly assimilated in race and culture. Tongking, exposed to those modifying influences which characterize all land frontiers, as well as to coastwise intercourse, is in its people and civilization merely a transcript of China. The coast districts and islands of Annam are occupied by Chinese as far as the hills of Cambodia, and the name of Cochin China points to the origin of its predominant population. One-sixth of the inhabitants of Siam are Chinese, some of whom have filtered through the northern border; Bangkok, the capital, has a large Chinese quarter. The whole economic life and no small part of the intellectual life of the eastern face of Farther India south to Singapore is centered in the activity of the Chinese.[45]

Importance of zonal and continental location. The historical significance of an enclosed sea basin depends upon its zonal location and its position in relation to the surrounding lands. We observe a steady decrease of historical importance from south to north through the connected series of the Yellow, Japan, Okhotsk, Bering Seas and the Arctic basin, miscalled ocean. The far-northern location of the Baltic, with its long winters of ice-bound ports and its glaciated lands, retarded its inclusion in the field of history, curtailed its important historical period, and reduced the intensity of its historical life, despite the brave, eager activity of the Hanseatic League. The Mediterranean had the advantage, not only of a more favorable zonal situation, but of a location at the meeting place of three continents and on the line of maritime traffic across the eastern hemisphere from the Atlantic to the Pacific.

Thalassic character of the Indian Ocean. These advantages it shares in some degree with the Indian Ocean, which, as Ratzel justly argues, is not a true ocean, at best only half an ocean. North of the equator, where it is narrowed and enclosed like an inland sea, it loses the hydrospheric and atmospheric characteristics of a genuine ocean. Currents and winds are disorganized by the close-hugging lands. Here the steady northeast trade wind is replaced by the alternating air currents of the northeast and southwest monsoons, which at a very early date [46] enabled merchant vessels to break away from their previous slow, coastwise path, and to strike a straight course on their voyage between Arabia or the east coast of Africa and India.[47] Moreover, this northern half of the Indian Ocean looks like a larger Mediterranean with its southern coast removed. It has the same east and west series of peninsulas harboring differentiated nationalities, the same northward running recesses, but all on a larger scale. It has linked together the history of Asia and Africa; and by the Red Sea and Persian Gulf, it has drawn Europe and the Mediterranean into its sphere of influence. At the western corner of the Indian Ocean a Semitic people, the Arabs of Oman and Yemen, here first developed brilliant maritime activity, like their Phœnician kinsmen of the Lebanon seaboard. Similar geographic conditions in their home lands and a nearly similar intercontinental location combined to make them the middlemen of three continents. Just as the Phœnicians, by way of the Mediterranean, reached and roused slumberous North Africa into historical activity and became the medium for the distribution of Egypt's culture, so these Semites of the Arabian shores knocked at the long-closed doors of East Africa facing on the Indian basin, and drew this region into the history of southern Asia. Thus the Africa of the enclosed seas was awakened to some measure of historical life, while the Africa of the wide Atlantic slept on.

From the dawn of history the northern Indian Ocean was a thoroughfare. Alexander the Great's rediscovery of the old sea route to the Orient sounds like a modern event in relation to the gray ages behind it. Along this thoroughfare Indian colonists, traders, and priests carried the elements of Indian civilization to the easternmost Sunda Isles; and Oriental wares, sciences and religions moved westward to the margin of Europe and Africa. The Indian Ocean produced a civilization of its own, with which it colored a vast semi-circle of land reaching from Java to Abyssinia, and more faintly, owing to the wider divergence of race, the further stretch from Abyssinia to Mozambique.

The sea route to the Orient.

Thus the northern Indian Ocean, owing to its form, its location in the angle between Asia and Africa and the latitude where, round the whole earth, "the zone of greatest historical density" begins, and especially its location just southeast of the Mediterranean as the eastern extension of that maritime track of ancient and modern times between Europe and China, has been involved in a long series of historical events. From the historical standpoint, prior to 1492 it takes a far higher place than the Atlantic and Pacific, owing to its nature as an enclosed sea.[48] But like all such basins, this northern Indian Ocean attained its zenith of historical importance in early times. In the sixteenth century it suffered a partial eclipse, which passed only with the opening of the Suez Canal. During this interval, however, the Portuguese, Dutch and English had rounded the Cape of Good Hope and entered this basin on its open or oceanic side. By their trading stations, which soon traced the outlines of its coasts from Sofala in South Africa around to Java, they made this ocean an alcove of the Atlantic, and embodied its events in the Atlantic period of history. It is this open or oceanic side which differentiates the Indian Ocean physically, and therefore historically, from a genuine enclosed sea.

Limitation of small area in enclosed seas.   The limitation of every enclosed or marginal sea lies in its small area and in the relatively restricted circle of its bordering lands. Only small peninsulas and islands can break its surface, and short stretches of coast combine to form its shores. It affords, therefore, only limited territories as goals for expansion, restricted resources and populations to furnish the supply and demand of trade. What lands could the Mediterranean present to the colonial outlook of the Greeks comparable to the North America of the expanding English or the Brazil of the Portuguese? Yet the Mediterranean as a colonial field had great advantages in point of size over the Baltic, which is only one-sixth as large (2,509,500 and 431,000 square kilometers respectively), and especially over the Red Sea and Persian Gulf, whose effective areas were greatly reduced by the aridity of their surrounding lands. But the precocious development and early cessa-

tion of growth marking all Mediterranean national life have
given to this basin a variegated history; and in every period
and every geographical region of it, from ancient Phœnicia
to modern Spain and Italy, the early exhaustion of resources
and dwarfing of political ideals which characterize most small
areas become increasingly conspicuous. The history of Sweden, Denmark, and the Hanse Towns in the Baltic tells the
same story, the story of a hothouse plant, forced in germina-
tion and growth, then stifled in the close air.

Growth demands space. Therefore, the progress of his- Successive
tory has been attended by an advance from smaller to larger maritime
marine areas, with a constant increase in those manifold rela- periods in
tions between peoples and lands which the water is able to history.
establish. Every great epoch of history has had its own
sea, and every succeeding epoch has enlarged its maritime
field. The Greek had the Aegean, the Roman the whole
Mediterranean, to which the Middle Ages made an addition
in the North Sea and Baltic. The modern period has had the
Atlantic, and the twentieth century is now entering upon the
final epoch of the World Ocean. The gradual inclusion of
this World Ocean in the widened scope of history has been
due to the expansion of European peoples, who, for the past
twenty centuries, have been the most far-reaching agents in
the making of universal history. Owing to the location and
structure of their continent, they have always found the
larger outlet in a western sea. In the south the field widened
from the Phœnician Sea to the Aegean, then to the Mediterranean, on to the Atlantic, and across it to its western shores;
in the north it moved from the quiet Baltic to the tide-swept
North Sea and across the North Atlantic. Only the South
Atlantic brought European ships to the great world highway of the South Seas, and gave them the choice of an eastern
or western route to the Pacific. Every new voyage in the
age of discovery expanded the historical horizon; and every
improvement in the technique of navigation has helped to
eliminate distance and reduced intercourse on the World
Ocean to the time-scale of the ancient Mediterranean.

It would be a mistake, however, to suppose that the larger
oceanic horizon has meant a corresponding increase in the rel-

ative content and importance of history for the known world
of each period. Such an intense, concentrated national life as
occurred in those little Mediterranean countries in ancient
times is not duplicated now, unless we find a parallel in Japan's recent career in the Yellow Sea basin. There was something as cosmic in the colonial ventures of the Greeks to the
wind-swept shores of the Crimea or barbarous wilds of Massilia, as in the establishment of English settlements on the
brimming rivers of Virginia or the torrid coast of Malacca.
Alexander's conquest of the Asiatic rim of the Mediterranean
and Rome's political unification of the basin had a significance for ancient times comparable with the Russification of
northern Asia and the establishment of the British Empire
for our day.

The ocean has always performed one function in the evolution of history; it has provided the outlet for the exercise
of redundant national powers. The abundance of opportunity which it presents to these disengaged energies depends
upon the size, location and other geographic conditions of
the bordering lands. These opportunities are limited in an
enclosed basin, larger in the oceans, and largest in the northern halves of the oceans, owing to the widening of all land-
masses towards the north and the consequent contraction
of the oceans and seas in the same latitudes.

Contrasted
historical
rôles of
northern
and south-
ern hemi-
spheres.

A result of this grouping is the abundance of land in the
northern hemisphere, and the vast predominance of water
in the southern, by reason of which these two hemispheres
have each assumed a distinct rôle in history. The northern
hemisphere offers the largest advantages for the habitation
of man, and significantly enough, contains a population five
times that of the southern hemisphere. The latter, on the
other hand, with its vast, unbroken water areas, has been
the great oceanic highway for circum-mundane exploration
and trade. This great water girdle of the South Seas had
to be discovered before the spherical form of the earth could
be proven. In the wide territory of the northern hemisphere
civilization has experienced an uninterrupted development,
first in the Old World, because this offered in its large area
north of the equator the fundamental conditions for rapid

evolution; then it was transplanted with greatest success to
North America. The northern hemisphere contains, therefore, "the zone of greatest historical density," from which
the track of the South Seas is inconveniently remote. Hence
we find in recent decades a reversion to the old east-west path
along the southern rim of Eurasia, now perfected by the
Suez Canal, and to be extended in the near future around
the world by the union of the Pacific with the Caribbean
Sea at Panama; so that finally the northern hemisphere will
have its own circum-mundane waterway, along the line of
greatest intercontinental intercourse.

The size of the ocean as a whole is so enormous, and yet **Size of**
its various subdivisions are so uniform in their physical **the oceans.**
aspect, that their differences of size produce less conspicuous historical effects than their diversity of area would lead
one to expect. A voyage across the 177,000 square miles
(453,500 square kilometers) of the Black Sea does not differ
materially from one across the 979,000 square miles (2,-
509,500 square kilometers) of the Mediterranean; or a voyage across the 213,000 square miles (547,600 square kilometers) of the North Sea, from one across the three-hundred-
fold larger area of the Pacific. The ocean does not, like
the land, wear upon its surface the evidences and effects of
its size; it wraps itself in the same garment of blue waves
or sullen swell, wherever it appears; but the outward cloak
of the land varies from zone to zone. The significant
anthropo-geographical influence of the size of the oceans,
as opposed to that of the smaller seas, comes from the larger
circle of lands which the former open to maritime enterprise.
For primitive navigation, when the sailor crept from headland to headland and from island to island, the small enclosed basin with its close-hugging shores did indeed offer
the best conditions. To-day, only the great tonnage of
ocean-going vessels may reflect in some degree the vast areas
they traverse between continent and continent. Coasting
craft and ships designed for local traffic in enclosed seas are
in general smaller, as in the Baltic, though the enormous
commerce of the Great Lakes, which constitute in effect an
inland sea, demands immense vessels.

The vast size of the oceans has been the basis of their neutrality. The neutrality of the seas is a recent idea in political history. The principle arose in connection with the oceans, and from them was extended to the smaller basins, which previously tended to be regarded as private political domains. Their limited area, which enabled them to be compassed, enabled them also to be appropriated, controlled and policed. The Greek excluded the Phœnician from the Aegean and made it an Hellenic sea. Carthage and Tarentum tried to draw the dead line for Roman merchantmen at the Lacinian Cape, the doorway into the Ionian Sea, and thereby involved themselves in the famous Punic Wars. The whole Mediterranean became a Roman sea, the *mare nostrum*. Pompey's fleet was able to police it effectively and to exterminate the pirates in a few months, as Cicero tells us in his oration for the Manilian Law. Venice, by the conquest of the Dalmatian pirates in 991 prepared to make herself *dominatrix Adriatici maris*, as she was later called. By the thirteenth century she had secured full command of the sea, spoke of it as "the Gulf," in her desire to stamp it as a *mare clausum*, maintained in it a powerful patrol fleet under a *Capitan in Golfo*, whose duty it was to police the sea for pirates and to seize all ships laden with contraband goods. She claimed and enforced the right of search of foreign vessels, and compelled them to discharge two-thirds of their cargo at Venice, which thus became the clearing house of the whole Adriatic. She even appealed to the Pope for confirmation of her dominion over the sea.[49] Sweden and Denmark strove for a *dominum maris Baltici;* but the Hanse Towns of northern Germany secured the maritime supremacy in the basin, kept a toll-gate at its entrance, and levied toll or excluded merchant ships at their pleasure, a right which after the fall of the Hanseatic power was assumed by Denmark and maintained till 1857. "The Narrow Seas" over which England claimed sovereignty from 1299 to 1805, and on which she exacted a salute from every foreign vessel, included the North Sea as far as Stadland Cape in Norway, the English Channel, and the Bay of Biscay down to Cape Finisterre in northern Spain.[50]

At the beginning of the sixteenth century the Indian Ocean was a Portuguese sea. Spain was trying to monopolize the Caribbean and even the Pacific Ocean. But the immense areas of these pelagic fields of enterprise, and the rapid intrusion into them of other colonial powers soon rendered obsolete in practice the principle of the *mare clausum*, and introduced that of the *mare liberum*. The political theory of the freedom of the seas seems to have needed vigorous support even toward the end of the seventeenth century. At this time we find writers like Salmasius and Hugo Grotius invoking it to combat Portuguese monopoly of the Indian Ocean as a *mare clausum*. Grotius in a lengthy dissertation upholds the thesis that "*Jure gentium quibusvis ad quosvis liberam esse navigationem*," and supports it by an elaborate argument and quotations from the ancient poets, philosophers, orators and historians.[51] This principle was not finally acknowledged by England as applicable to "The Narrow Seas" till 1805. Now, by international agreement, political domain extends only to one marine league from shore or within cannon range. The rest of the vast water area remains the unobstructed highway of the world.

NOTES TO CHAPTER IX

1. S. M. Zwemer, Arabia the Cradle of Islam, p. 135. New York, 1900.
2. A. H. Layard, Nineveh and Its Remains, Vol. I, p. 277; Vol. II, 79-81. New York, 1849.
3. E. F. Knight, Where Three Empires Meet, pp. 257, 261. London, 1897.
4. Col. Lane Fox, Early Modes of Navigation, *Journal of Anthropological Institute*, Vol. IV, p. 423.
5. Boyd Alexander, From the Niger to the Nile, Vol. I, p. 167. London, 1907.
6. *Ibid.*, Vol. I, p. 324.
7. James H. Breasted, History of Egypt, pp. 89, 91, 97. New York, 1905. Col. Lane Fox, Early Modes of Navigation, *Journal of Anthropological Institute*, Vol. IV, pp. 414-417.
8. G. Schweinfurth, The Heart of Africa, Vol. I, p. 77. London, 1873.
9. E. Huntington, The Depression of Sistan in Eastern Persia, *Bulletin of the American Geographical Society*, Vol. 37, No. 5. 1905.
10. Schoolcraft, The Indian Tribes of the United States, Vol. I, p. 214. Philadelphia, 1853.
11. H. H. Bancroft, The Native Races, Vol. I, pp. 382-383, 408, 564.

San Francisco, 1886. D. G. Brinton, The American Race, pp. 110, 112. Philadelphia, 1901.

12. Herodotus, Book 1, Chap. 194.

13. S. M. Zwemer, Arabia the Cradle of Islam, p. 135. New York, 1900.

14. Cotterill and Little, Ships and Sailors, pp. IX-X, 38. London, 1868.

15. M. Huc, Travels in Tartary, Thibet and China in 1846, Vol. II, p. 251. Chicago, 1898.

16. Elliott Coues, History of the Lewis and Clark Expedition, Vol. I, p. 159. New York, 1893.

17. Col. Lane Fox, Early Modes of Navigation, *Journal of Anthropological Institute*, Vol. IV, pp. 423-425.

18. H. M. Stanley, Through the Dark Continent, Vol. I, pp. 313-314. New York, 1879.

19. *Ibid.*, Vol. II, pp. 184, 219-220, 270-272, 300.

20. Ratzel, History of Mankind, Vol. II, p. 288. London, 1896-1898.

21. *Ibid.*, Vol I, pp. 358-359. Spencer and Gillen, Northern Tribes of Central Australia, pp. 679-680. London, 1904.

22. Ratzel, History of Mankind, Vol. I, pp. 153-154; Vol. II, pp. 91, 100. London, 1896-1898.

23. *Ibid.*, Vol. I, pp. 166-170.

24. Captain Winkler, Sea Charts Formerly Used in the Marshall Islands, Smithsonian Report for 1899, translated from the *Marine Rundschau*. Berlin, 1898.

25. Captain James Cook, Journal of First Voyage Round the World, pp. 70, 105, 119, 221, 230. Edited by W. J. L. Wharton. London, 1893.

26. Ratzel, History of Mankind, Vol. I, pp. 161, 174. London, 1896-1898.

27. The Commercial and Fiscal Policy of the Venetian Republic, *Edinburgh Review*, Vol. 200, pp. 352-353. 1904.

28. H. Helmolt, History of the World, Vol. I, pp. 188-189, 193-195. New York, 1902-1906.

29. G. Sergi, The Mediterranean Race, pp. 29-37. New York, 1901. W. Z. Ripley, Races of Europe, pp. 128-130, 270-273, 387-390, 407, 444, 448. New York, 1899.

30. H. J. Mackinder, Britain and the British Seas, pp. 189-190. London, 1904.

31. Sydow-Wagner *Schul-Atlas, Völker und Sprachenkarten*, No. 13. Gotha, 1905. A. Leroy-Beaulieu, The Empire of the Tsars, map p. 80. New York, 1897.

32. Helmolt, History of the World, Vol. VI, pp. 5-17. New York, 1902-1906.

33. E. C. Semple, The Development of the Hanse Towns in Relation to their Geographical Environment, *Bulletin American Geographical Society*, Vol. XXXI, No. 3, 1899.

34. Helen Zimmern, The Hansa Towns, pp. 24-25, 54-55. New York, 1895.

35. Nordenskiold, The Voyage of the Vega, pp. 565, 588, 591. New York, 1882.

36. *Ibid.*, pp. 375, 403, 405, 487, 563.

37. Agnes Laut, The Vikings of the Pacific, pp. 62-105. New York, 1905.
38. Ratzel, History of Mankind, Vol. III, pp. 446, 449-450. London, 1896-1898.
39. *Ibid.*, Vol. III, pp. 180-195.
40. Duarte Barbosa, The Coasts of East Africa and Malabar, pp. 17-18. Hakluyt Society Publications. London, 1866.
41. Ratzel, History of Mankind, Vol. III, pp. 443-444. London, 1896-1898.
42. Angus Hamilton, Korea, pp. 130-135. New York, 1904.
43. Census of the Philippine Islands, Vol. I, pp. 318-320, 478, 481-495. Washington, 1903.
44. Hans Helmolt, History of the World, Vol. II, pp. 544-545. New York, 1902-1906.
45. Ratzel, History of Mankind, Vol. III, pp. 407-412. London, 1896-1898.
46. Pliny, Natural History, Book VI, chap. 26.
47. Bunbury, History of Ancient Geography, Vol. II, pp. 351, 417-418, 470, 471. London, 1883.
48. For full discussion of Indian Ocean, see Helmolt, History of the World, Vol. II, pp. 580-584, 602-610. New York, 1902-1906. Duarte Barbosa, The Coasts of East Africa and Malabar, pp. 26-28, 41-42, 59-60, 67, 75, 79-80, 83, 166, 170, 174, 179, 184, 191-194, Hakluyt Society. London, 1866.
49. Pompeo Molmenti, Venice in the Middle Ages, Vol. I, pp. 117, 121-123, 130. Chicago, 1906. The Commercial and Fiscal Policy of the Venetian Republic, *Edinburgh Review*, Vol. 200, pp. 341-344, 347. 1904.
50. H. J. Mackinder, Britain and the British Seas, p. 24, note. London, 1904.
51. Hugonis Grotii, *Mare Liberum sive de jure quod Batavis competit ad Indicana commercia dissertatio*, contained in his *De Jure Belli et Pacis. Hagae Comitis*, 1680.

CHAPTER X

MAN'S RELATION TO THE WATER

DESPITE the extensive use which man makes of the water
highways of the world, they remain to him highways, places
for his passing and repassing, not for his abiding. Essentially a terrestrial animal, he makes his sojourn upon the
deep only temporary, even when as a fisherman he is kept
upon the sea for months during the long season of the catch,
or when, as whaler, year-long voyages are necessitated by the
remoteness and expanse of his field of operations. Yet even
this rule has its exceptions. The Moro Bajan are sea gypsies
of the southern Philippines and the Sulu archipelago, of
whom Gannett says "their home is in their boats from the
cradle to the grave, and they know no art but that of
fishing." Subsisting almost exclusively on sea food, they
wander about from shore to shore, one family to a boat, in
little fleets of half a dozen sail; every floating community
has its own headman called the Captain Bajan, who embodies
all their slender political organization. When occasionally
they abandon their rude boats for a time, they do not abandon the sea, but raise their huts on piles above the water
on some shelving beach. Like the ancient lake-dwellers of
Switzerland and Italy, only in death do they acknowledge
their ultimate connection with the solid land. They never
bury their dead at sea, but always on a particular island, to
which the funeral cortege of rude outrigged boats moves to
the music of the paddle's dip.[1]

Protection
of a water
frontier.
    The margin of river, lake and sea has always attracted
the first settlements of man because it offered a ready food
supply in its animal life and an easy highway for communication. Moreover, a water front made a comparatively
safe frontier for the small, isolated communities which constituted primitive societies. The motive of protection, dominant in the savage when selecting sites for his villages, led

him to place them on the pear-shaped peninsula formed by a river loop, or on an island in the stream or off the coast; or to sever his connection with the solid land, whence attack might come, and provide himself with a boundary waste of water by raising his hut on piles above the surface of lake, river or sheltered seacoast, within easy reach of the shore. In this location the occupant of the pile dwelling has found all his needs answered—fishing grounds beneath and about his hut, fields a few hundred feet away on shore, easily reached by his dug-out canoe, and a place of retreat from a land enemy, whether man or wild beast.

Such pile dwellings, answering the primary need of pro- Ancient tection, have had wide distribution, especially in the Tropics, pile vil- and persist into our own times among retarded peoples lages. living in small, isolated groups too weak for effective defence. They were numerous in the lakes of Switzerland[2] and north- ern Italy down to the first century of our era, and existed later in slightly modified form in Ireland, Scotland, England and southern Wales.[3] In ancient Ireland they were con- structed on artificial islands, raised in shallow spots of lakes or morasses by means of fascines weighted down with gravel and clay, and moored to the bottom by stakes driven through the mass. Such groups of dwellings were called *Crannogs;* they existed in Ireland from the earliest historical period and continued in use down to the time of Queen Elizabeth. In the turbulent twelfth century, the warring lords of the soil adopted them as places of refuge and residence.[4] Herodotus describes a pile village of the ancient Thracians in Lake Prasias near the Hellespont, built quite after the Swiss type, with trap doors in the floor for fishing or throwing out refuse. Its inhabitants escaped conquest by the Persians under King Darius, and avoided the fate of their fellow tribesmen on land, who were subdued and removed as colonists to Asia.[5]

Among Europeans such pile villages belong to primitive Present stages of development, chiefly to the Stone, Bronze, and early distribution. Iron Ages. They are widely distributed in modern times among retarded peoples, who in this way seek compensation for their social and economic weakness. In South America, the small timid tribe of the native Warraus till quite recently built their dwellings on platforms over the water in the river network of the Orinoco delta and along the swamp coast as far as the Essequibo. These pile villages, *"fondata sopra l'acqua come Venezia,"* as Vespuccius says, suggested to him the name of Venezuela or little Venice for this coast.[6] A pile village in Jull Lake, a lacustrine expansion in a tributary of the upper Salwin River, is inhabited by the Inthas, apparently an alien colony in Burma. They have added a detail in their floating gardens, rafts covered with soil, on which they raise tomatoes, watermelons and gourds.[7]

In little Lake Mohrya, located near the upper Lualaba River, a southern headstream of the Congo, Cameron found numerous pile dwellings, whose owners moved about in dugout canoes and cultivated fields on land,[8] as did their Swiss confrères .of twenty centuries ago. Livingstone, in descending from Lake Nyassa by the Shire River, found in the lakelet of Pamalombe, into which the stream widened, similar water huts inhabited by a number of Manganja families, who had been driven from their homes by slave raiders. The slender reeds of the papyrus thicket, lining the shore in a broad band, served as piles, number compensating for the lack of strength; the reeds, bent downward and fastened together into a mat, did indeed support their light dwellings, but heaved like thin ice. when the savages moved from hut to hut. The dense forest of papyrus left standing between village and shore effectually screened their retreat, and the abundant fish in the lake provided them with food.[9]

Malayan pile dwellings.   In the vast island world of Indonesia, where constant contact with the sea has bred the amphibian Malay race, we are not surprised to find that the typical Malay house is built on piles above the water; and that when the coast Malay is driven inland by new-comers of his own stock and forced to abandon his favorite occupations of trade, piracy and fishing, he takes to agriculture but still retains his sea-born architecture and raises his hut on poles above the ground, beyond the reach of an enemy's spear-thrust. The Moro Samal Laut of the southern Sulu Archipelago avoid

the large volcanic islands of the group, and place their big
villages over the sea on low coral reefs.   The sandy beaches
of the shore hold their coco-palms, whose nuts by their
milk eke out the scanty supply of drinking water, and whose
fronds shade the tombs of the dead.[10]   The sea-faring Malays
of the Sunda Islands, in thickly populated points of the
coast, often dwell in permanently inhabited rafts moored
near the pile dwellings.   Palembang on the lower swampy
course of the River Musi has a floating suburb of this sort.
It is called the "Venice of Sumatra," just as Banjarmasin,
a vast complex of pile and raft dwellings, is called the
"Venice of Borneo," and Brunei to the north is the "Venice
of the East."[11]   Both these towns are the chief commercial
centers of their respective islands.   The little town of Kil-
waru, situated on a sandbank off the eastern end of Ceram,
seems to float on the sea, so completely has it surrounded
and enveloped with pile-built houses the few acres of dry
land which form its nucleus.   It is a place of busy traffic,
the emporium for commerce between the Malay Archipelago
and New Guinea.[12]

Farther east in Melanesia, whose coast regions are more In Mel-
or less permeated by Malayan stock and influences, pile anesia.
dwellings, both over water and on land form a characteristic
feature of the scenery.   The village of Sowek in Geelvink
Bay, on the northern coast of Dutch New Guinea, consists of
thirty houses raised on piles above the water, connected with
each other by tree trunks but having only boat connection
with the shore.   Similar villages are found hovering over
the lapping waves of Humboldt Bay, all of them recalling
with surprising fidelity the prehistoric lake-dwellings of
Switzerland.[13]   The Papuan part of Port Moresby, on the
southern coast of British New Guinea, covers the whole
water-front of the town with pile dwellings.   In the vicinity
are similar native pile villages, such as Tanobada, Hanua-
bada, Elevara and Hula, the latter consisting of pile dwellings scattered about over the water in a circuit of several
miles and containing about a thousand inhabitants.   Here, too,
the motive is protection against the attacks of inland mountain tribes, with whom the coast people are in constant war.[14]

The Malay fisherman, trader and pirate, with the love of the sea in his blood, by these pile dwellings combines security from his foe and proximity to his familiar field of activity. The same objects are achieved by white traders on the west coast of Africa by setting up their dwellings and warehouses on the old hulks of dismasted vessels, which are anchored for this purpose in the river mouths. They afford some protection against both fever and hostile native, and at the same time occupy the natural focus of local trade seeking foreign exchanges.

River dwellers in populous lands.   When advancing civilization has eliminated the need for this form of protection, water-dwellers may survive or reappear in old and relatively over-populated countries, as we find them universally on the rivers of China and less often in Farther India. Here they present the phenomenon of human life overflowing from the land to the streams of the country; because these, as highways of commerce, afford a means of livelihood, even apart from the food supply in their fish, and offer an unclaimed bit of the earth's surface for a floating home. Canton has 250,000 inhabitants living on boats and rafts moored in the river, and finding occupation in the vast inland navigation of the Empire, or in the trade which it brings to this port of the Si-kiang. Some of the boats accommodate large families, together with modest poultry farms, crowded together under their low bamboo sheds. Others are handsome wooden residences ornamented with plants, and yet others are pleasure resorts with their professional singing girls.[15] In the lakes and swamp-bordered rivers of southern Shantung, a considerable fishing population is found living in boats, while the land shows few inhabitants. This population enjoys freedom from taxation and unrestricted use of the rivers and fisheries. To vary their scant and monotonous diet, they construct floating gardens on rafts of bamboo covered with earth, on which they plant onions and garlic and which they tow behind their boats. They also raise hundreds of ducks, which are trained to go into the water to feed and return at a signal,[16] thus expanding the resources of their river life Bangkok has all its business district afloat on the Menam

River—shops, lumber yards, eating-houses and merchants'
dwellings. Even the street vendor's cart is a small boat,
paddled in and out among the larger junks.[17]

A far more modern type of river-dwellers is found in the
"shanty-boat" people of the western rivers of the United
States. They are the gypsies of our streams, nomads who
float downstream with the current, tying up at intervals
along the bank of some wooded island or city waterfront,
then paying a tug to draw their house-boat upstream. The
river furnishes them with fish for their table and driftwood
for their cooking-stove, and above all is the highway for
the gratification of their nomad instincts. There is no question here of trade and overpopulation.

Pile dwellings and house-boats are a paltry form of
encroachment upon the water in comparison with that extensive reclamation of river swamps and coastal marshes
which in certain parts of the world has so increased the area
available for human habitation. The water which is a
necessity to man may become his enemy unless it is controlled.
The alluvium which a river deposits in its flood-plain, whether
in some flat stretch of its middle course or near the retarding
level of the sea, attracts settlement because of its fertility
and proximity to a natural highway; but it must be protected by dikes against the very element which created it.
Such deposits are most extensive on low coasts at or near the
river's mouth, just where the junction of an inland and
oceanic waterway offers the best conditions for commerce.
Here then is a location destined to attract and support a
large population, for which place can be made only by steady
encroachment upon the water of both river and sea. Diking
is necessitated not only by the demand for more land for the
growing population, but also by the constant silting up of
the drainage outfalls, which increases the danger of inundation while at the same time contributing to the upbuilding of
the land. Conditions here institute an incessant struggle
between man and nature;[18] but the rewards of victory are
too great to count the cost. The construction of sea-walls,
embankment of rivers, reclamation of marshes, the cutting
of canals for drains and passways in a water-soaked land,

Reclama-
tion of
land from
the sea.

the conversion of lakes into meadow, the rectification of tortuous streams for the greater economy of this silt-made soil, all together constitute the greatest geographical transformation that man has brought about on the earth's surface.[19]

The struggle with the water. Though the North Sea lowland of Europe has suffered from the serious encroachment of the sea from the thirteenth to the sixteenth century, when the Zuyder Zee, the Dollart and Jade Bay were formed, nevertheless the counter encroachment of the land upon the water, accomplished through the energy and intelligence of the inhabitants, has more than made good the loss. Between the Elbe and Scheldt more than 2,000 square miles (5,000 square kilometers) have been reclaimed from river and sea in the past three hundred years. Holland's success in draining her large inland waters, like the Haarlem Meer (70 square miles or 180 square kilometers) and the Lake of Ij, has inspired an attempt to recover 800 square miles (2,050 square kilometers) of fertile soil from the borders of the Zuyder Zee and reduce that basin to nearly one-third of its present size.[20] One-fourth of the Netherlands lies below the average of high tides, and in 1844 necessitated 9,000 windmills to pump the waste water into the drainage canals.[21]

The Netherlands, with all its external features of man's war against the water, has its smaller counterpart in the 1,200 square miles of reclaimed soil about the head of the Wash, which constitute the Fenland of England. Here too are successive lines of sea-wall, the earliest of them attributed to the Romans, straightened and embanked rivers, drainage canals, windmills and steam pumps, dikes serving as roads, lines of willows and low moist pastures dotted with grazing cattle. No feature of the Netherlands is omitted. The low southern part of Lincolnshire is even called Holland, and Dutch prisoners from a naval battle of 1652 were employed there on the work of reclamation, which was begun on a large scale about this time.[22] In the medieval period, the increase of population necessitated measures to improve the drainage and extend the acreage; but there was little co-operation among the land owners, and the maintenance of river dikes and sea-walls was neglected, till a succession of disasters from flooding streams and invading tides in the thirteenth and fourteenth centuries led to severe measures against defaulters. One culprit was placed alive in a breach which his own neglect or criminal cutting had caused, and was built in, by way of educating the Fenlanders to a sense of common responsibility.[23]

The fight against the water on the coast begins later than that against rivers and swamps in the interior of the land; it demands greater enterprise and courage, because it combats two enemies instead of one; but its rewards are correspondingly greater. The Netherlands by their struggle have acquired not only territory for an additional half million population, but have secured to themselves a strategic position in the maritime trade of the world.

The abundant fertility of river flood-plains inevitably attracts population and necessitates some kind of artificial protection against inundation. The most primitive form of this protection is obvious and widespread, restricted in neither locality nor race. When the flood season converts the flat plain of the White Nile below Gondokora (7° N. Lat.) into an extensive marsh, countless hills of the white ant emerge over the waters. During the dry season, the ants build up their hills to about ten feet, and then live in safety in the upper section during the flood. They greatly surpass in intelligence and constructive ability the human occupants of the valley, the low and wretched Kytch tribe of the Dinka Negroes, who like the ants are attracted by the natural vegetation of the flood-plain, and who use the ant-hills as refuge stations for themselves and their cattle during the flood.[24] Elsewhere in Africa the natives are more intelligent, for flood-plain villages built on artificial mounds have existed from the earliest times. Diodorus Siculus tells us that those of ancient Egypt, when the Nile was high, looked like the Cyclades Islands.[25] Similar ones are constructed by the Barotse tribe on the upper Zambesi.[26] The Niger River, rising in the Foota Jallon and Kong Mountains which form a region of heavy rainfall from February to July, inundates a plain of several thousand square miles for a distance of 250 miles above Tim-

Mound villages in river flood-plains.

buctoo. Here again the villages of the agricultural Song-
hoi duplicate those of Egypt, built on the same clay mounds,
wreathed in the same feathery palms, and communicating
with one another only by small boats.[27] The same picture
is presented by the Yangtze Kiang plain during the summer
overflow—low artificial hills rising from the expanse of
muddy water and topped with trees and villages, while
sampans moored to their base show the means of communication.[28] In the broad flood-plain of the lower Mississippi
River, the chronicles of the De Soto expedition state that the
Indian villages visited stood "on mounds made by art." The
Yazoo River Indians, at the commencement of the eighteenth
century, had their cabins dispersed over the low deltaic land
on earthen mounds made by their own hands. There is also
strong evidence that some of the works of the Mound-builders
in the "bottoms" of the middle and lower Mississippi served
as protected sites for the dwellings of their chiefs.[29]

Diking of
rivers.

Such meager provisions against inundation suffice for the
sparse population characterizing the lower stages of civilization, but they must be supplemented for the increasing density of higher stages by the embankment of the stream, to
protect also the adjacent fields. Hence the process of confining rivers within dikes goes back into gray antiquity.
Those of the Po and its tributaries were begun before the
political history of the Lombardy plains commenced. Strabo
mentions the canals and dikes of Venetia, whereby a part of
the country was drained and rendered tillable.[30] The main
Po has been embanked for centuries as far up as Cre-
mona, a distance of 600 miles, and the Adige to Verona.[31]
But the most gigantic dike system in the world is that of the
Hoangho, by which a territory the size of England is won
from the water for cultivation.[32] The cost of protecting the
far spread crops against the autumn floods has been a large
annual expenditure and unceasing watchfulness; and this the
Chinese have paid for two thousand years, but have not always
purchased immunity. Year by year the Yellow River mounts
higher and higher on its silted bed above the surrounding
lowlands, increasing the strain on the banks and the area of
destruction, when its fury is uncaged. The flood of 1887

covered an area estimated at 50,000 square miles, wiped out of existence a million people, and left a greater number a prey to famine.[33] So the fertile Chengtu plain of the Min River, supporting four millions of people on its 2,500 square miles of area, owes its prosperity to the embanking and irrigating works of the engineer heroes, Li Ping and his son, who lived before the Christian era. On the temple in their honor in the city of Kuan Hsien is Li Ping's motto, incised in gold: "Dig the bed deep, keep the banks low." For twenty-one centuries these instructions have been carried out. The stone dikes are kept low to permit a judicious amount of flooding for fertilization, and every year five to six feet of silt are removed from the artificial channel of the Min. To this work the whole population of the Chengtu plain contributes.[34] [See map page 8.]

In such organized struggles to reduce the domain of the water and extend that of the dry land, the material gain is not all: more significant by far is the power to co-operate that is developed in a people by a prolonged war against overwhelming sea or river. A common natural danger, constantly and even regularly recurring, necessitates for its resistance a strong and sustained union, that draws men out of the barren individualism of a primitive people, and forces them without halt along the path of civilization. It brings a realizing sense of the superiority of common interests over individual preferences, strengthens the national bond, and encourages voluntary subservience to law. *Social gain by control of the water.*

This is the social or political gain; but this is not all. The danger emanating from natural phenomena has its discoverable laws, and therefore leads to a first empirical study of winds, currents, seasonal rainfall and the whole science of hydraulics. With deep national insight, the Greeks embodied in their mythology the story of Perseus and his destruction of the sea monster who ravaged the coast, and Hercules' killing of the many-headed serpent who issued from the Lernean Marshes to lay waste the country of Argos. Even so early a writer as Strabo states that yet earlier authorities interpreted Hercules' victory over the river god of the Achelous as the embankment of that stream and the draining of its inundated delta tract by the national benefactor.[35]   So the Chinese, whose land abounds in swamps and devastating rivers, have a long list of engineer heroes who embanked and drained for the salvation and benefit of mankind.   It is highly probably that the communal work involved in the construction of dikes and canals for the control of the Hoangho floods cemented the Chinese nationality of that vast lowland plain, and supplied the cohesive force that developed here at a very remote period a regularly organized state and an advancing civilization.

Control of water as factor in early civilizations of arid lands.   The history of Egypt shows a similar effect of the yearly inundation of the Nile Valley.   Here, as in all rainless countries where irrigation must be practiced, the water becomes a potent factor of political union and civilization.   Its scarcity necessitates common effort in the construction and maintenance of irrigation works, and a central control to secure fair distribution of the water to the fields of the inhabitants.   A stimulus to progress is found in the presence of a problem, perennial as the yearly threatenings of the Hoangho, which demands the application of human intelligence and concerted labor for its solution.   Additional arable land for the growing population can be secured only by the wider distribution of the fructifying water; this in turn depends upon corporate effort wisely directed and ably controlled.   Every lapse in governmental efficiency means an encroachment of the desert upon the alluvial fields and finally to the river bank, as to-day in Mesopotamia.

The fact that the earliest civilizations have originated in the sub-tropical rainless districts of the world has been ascribed solely to the regular and abundant returns to tillage under irrigation, as opposed to the uncertain crops under variable meteorological conditions; to the consequent accumulation of wealth, and the emancipation of man for other and higher activities, which follows his escape from the agricultural vicissitudes of an uncertain climate.   When Draper says: "Civilization depends on climate and agriculture," and "the civilization of Egypt depended for its commencement on the sameness and stability of the African climate," and again, "agriculture is certain in Egypt and there man first became civilized,"[36] he seizes upon the conspicuous fact of a stable food supply as the basis of progress, failing to detect those potent underlying social effects of the inundations—social and political union to secure the most effective distribution of the Nile's blessings and to augment by human devices the area accessible to them, the development of an intelligent water economy, which ultimately produced a long series of intellectual achievements.[37]

This unifying and stimulating national task of utilizing and controlling the water was the same task which in various forms promoted the early civilization of the Hoangho and Yangtze basins, India, Mesopotamia, Persia, Peru, Mexico, and that impressive region of prehistoric irrigation canals found in the Salt, Gila River, and upper Rio Grande valleys.[38] Here the arid plateaus of the Cordilleras between the Pueblo district and Central America had no forests in which game might be found; so that the Indian hunter had to turn to agriculture and a sedentary life beside his narrow irrigated fields. Here native civilization reached its highest grade in North America. Here desert agriculture achieved something more than a reliable food supply. It laid the foundation of the first steady integration of wandering Indian hordes into a stable, permanently organized society. Elsewhere throughout the North American continent, we see only shifting groups of hunter and fisher folk, practising here and there a half nomadic agriculture to supplement the chase.

Cultural areas in primitive America.

The primitive American civilization that arose among the Pueblo Indians of New Mexico and Arizona, the only strictly sedentary tribes relying exclusively on agriculture north of the Mexican plateau, was primarily a result of the pressure put upon these people by a restricted water supply.[39] Though chiefly offshoots of the wild Indians of the northern plains, they have been markedly differentiated from their wandering Shoshone and Kiowa kindred by local environment.[40] Scarcity of water in those arid highlands and paucity of arable land forced them to a carefully organized community life, made them invest their labor in irrigation ditches, terraced gardens and walled orchards, whereby they were as firmly rooted in their scant but fertile fields as were their

cotton plants and melon vines;[41] while the towering mesas
protected their homes against marauding Ute, Navajo and
Apache.[42] This thread of a deep underlying connection between civilization and the control of water can be traced
through all prehistoric America, as well as through the
earliest cultural achievements in North Africa and Asia.

Economy
of the
water:
fisheries.

The economy of the water is not confined to its artificial
distribution over arid fields, but includes also the exploitation of the mineral and animal resources of the vast world
of waters, whether the production of salt from the sea, salt
lakes and brine springs, the cultivation of oyster beds, or the
whole range of pelagic fisheries. The animal life of the
water is important to man owing not only to its great abundance, but also to its distribution over the coldest regions of
the globe. It furnishes the chief food supply of polar and
sub-polar peoples, and therefore is accountable for the
far-northern expansion of the habitable world. Even
the reindeer tribes of Arctic Eurasia could hardly subsist without the sea food they get by barter from the
fishermen of the coast. Norway, where civilization has
achieved its utmost in exploiting the limited means of subsistence, shows a steady increase from south to north in the
proportion of the population dependent upon the harvest of
the deep. Thus the fisheries engross 44 per cent. of the
rural population in Nordland province, which is bisected by
the Arctic Circle; over 50 per cent. in Tromso, and about
70 per cent. in Finmarken. If the towns also be included,
the percentages rise, because here fishing interests are especially prominent.[43] Proximity to the generous larder of the
ocean has determined the selection of village sites, as we have
seen among the coast Indians of British Columbia and
southern Alaska, among all the Eskimo, and numerous other
peoples of Arctic lands. [See map page 153.]

Fisheries
as factors
in mari-
time ex-
pansion.

Not only in polar but also in temperate regions, the presence of abundant fishing grounds draws the people of the
nearest coast to their wholesale exploitation, especially if the
land resources are scant. Fisheries then become the starting
point or permanent basis of a subsequent wide maritime
development, by expanding the geographical horizon. It was

the search for the purple-yielding *murex* that first familiarized the Phœnicians with the commercial and colonial possibilities of the eastern Mediterranean coasts.[44]   The royal
dye of this marine product has through all the ages seemed
to color with sumptuous magnificence the sordid dealings of
those Tyrian traders, and constituted them an aristocracy
of merchants.   The shoals of tunny fish, arriving every
spring in the Bosporus, from the north, drew the early
Greeks and Phœnicians after them into the cold and misty
Euxine, and furnished the original impulse to both these
peoples for the establishment of fishing and trading stations
on its uncongenial shores.[45]   To the fisheries of the Baltic
and especially to the summer catch of the migratory herring,
which in vast numbers visited the shores of Pomerania and
southern Sweden to spawn, the Hanse Towns of Germany
owed much of their prosperity.   Salt herring, even in the
twelfth century, was the chief single article of their exchanges
with Catholic Europe, which made a strong demand for the
fish, owing to the numerous fast days.   When, in 1425, by
one of those unexplained vagaries of animal life, the herring
abandoned the Baltic and selected the North Sea for its
summer destination, a new support was given to the wealth
of the Netherlands.[46]   There is a considerable amount of
truth in the saying that Amsterdam was built on herrings.
New England, with an unproductive soil at home, but near
by in the sea a long line of piscine feeding grounds in the
submarine banks stretching from Cape Cod to Cape Race
and beyond, found her fisheries the starting point and base
of her long round of exchanges, a constant factor in her commercial and industrial evolution.[47]

Fisheries have always been the nurseries of seamen, and Fisheries as
hence have been encouraged and protected by governments nurseries of
as providing an important element of national strength.   The seamen.
Newfoundland Banks were the training school which supplied
the merchant marine and later the Revolutionary navy of
colonial New England;[48] ever since the establishment of the
Republic, they have been forced into prominence in our international negotiations with the United Kingdom, with the
object of securing special privileges, because the government

has recognized them as a factor in the American navy. The causal connection between fisheries and naval efficiency was recognized in England in the early years of Elizabeth's reign, by an act aiming to encourage fisheries by the remission of custom duties to native fishermen, by the imposition of a high tariff on the importation of foreign fish in foreign vessels, and finally by a legislative enforcement of fasts to increase the demand for fish, although any belief in the religious efficacy of fasts was frankly disclaimed. Thus an artificial demand for fish was created, with the result that a report on the success of the Fishery Acts stated that a thousand additional men had been attracted to the fishing trade, and were consequently "ready to serve in Her Majesty's ships." [49]

The fishing of the North Sea, especially on the Dogger Bank, is participated in by all the bordering countries, England, the Netherlands, Germany and Belgium; and is valued equally on account of the food supply which it yields and as a school of seamen.[50] The Pomors or "coasters" of Arctic Russia, who dwell along the shores of the White Sea and live wholly by fisheries, have all their taxes remitted and receive free wood from the crown forests for the construction of their ships, on the condition that they serve on call in the imperial navy.[51] The history of Japan affords the most striking illustration of the power of fisheries alone to maintain maritime efficiency; for when by the seclusion act of 1624 all merchant vessels were destroyed, the marine restricted to small fishing and coasting vessels, and intercourse confined to Japan's narrow island world, the fisheries nevertheless kept alive that intimacy with the sea and preserved the nautical efficiency that was destined to be a decisive factor in the development of awakened Japan.

Anthropogeographic importance of navigation. The resources of the sea first tempted man to trust himself to its dangerous surface; but their rewards were slight in comparison with the wealth of experiences and influences to which he fell heir, after he learned to convert the barrier of the untrod waste into a highway for his sailborne keel. It is therefore true, as many anthropologists maintain, that after the discovery of fire the next most important step in the progress of the human race was the invention of the boat.   No other has had such far-reaching results.   Since water covers three-fourths of the earth's surface and permits the land-masses to rise only as islands here and there, it presents to man for his nautical ventures three times the area that he commands for his terrestrial habitat. On every side, the break of the waves and the swell of the tides block his wanderings, unless he has learned to make the water carry him to his distant goal.   Spacially, therefore, the problem and the task of navigation is the most widespread and persistent in the history of mankind.   The numerous coaling-stations which England has scattered over the world are mute witnesses to this spacial supremacy of the water, to the length of ocean voyages, and the power of the ocean to divide and unite.   But had the proportion of land and water been reversed, the world would have been poorer, deprived of all these possibilities of segregation and differentiation, of stimulus to exchange and far-reaching intercourse, and of ingenious inventions which the isolating ocean has caused.   Without this ramifying barrier between the different branches of the human family, these would have resembled each other more closely, but at the cost of development.   The mere multiplicity of races and sub-races has sharpened the struggle for existence and endowed the survivors with higher qualities.   But it was navigation that released primitive man from the seclusion of his own island or continent, stimulated and facilitated the intercourse of peoples, and enabled the human race to establish itself in every habitable part of the world.

NOTES TO CHAPTER X

1. Census of the Philippine Islands, Vol. I, pp. 465, 563-567, 573. Washington, 1905.

2. Sir John Lubbock, Prehistoric Times, pp. 173-223.   New York, 1872.

3. Ferdinand Keller, Lake Dwellings, Vol. I, pp. 2-7, 576.   London, 1876.   English Lake Dwellings, *Westminster Review*, pp. 337-347.   1887.

4. P. W. Joyce, A Social History of Ancient Ireland, Vol. II, pp. 65-66.   London, 1903.

5. Herodotus, V. 16.

6. Alexander von Humboldt, Aspects of Nature, pp. 148-149. Translated by Mrs. Sabine, Philadelphia, 1849. E. F. im Thurn, Among the Indians of Guiana, p. 203. London, 1883.

7. Sir Thomas Holdich, India, p. 184. London, 1905.

8. Verney L. Cameron, Across Africa, pp. 332-334. London, 1885.

9. David and Charles Livingstone, Narrative of Expedition to the Zambezi, p. 414. New York, 1866.

10. Census of the Philippine Islands, Vol. I, pp. 464-466, 565. Washington, 1905.

11. Stanford's Australasia, Vol. II, pp. 256-257. London, 1894.

12. A. R. Wallace, The Malay Archipelago, pp. 368, 381. New York, 1869.

13. Ratzel, History of Mankind, Vol. I, pp. 262-263, 344. London, 1896-1898.

14. Richard Semon, In the Australian Bush, pp. 340-342, 347. London, 1899.

15. John L. Stoddard, Lectures, Vol. III, p. 311. Boston, 1903.

16. John Barrows, Travels in China, pp. 377-379. Philadelphia, 1805.

17. William M. Wood, Fankwei, pp. 169-174. New York, 1859.

18. Edmondo de Amicis, Holland and Its People, pp. 4-13. New York, 1890.

19. G. P. Marsh, The Earth as Modified by Human Action, chap. IV, pp. 330-352. New York, 1871.

20. J. Partsch, Central Europe, pp. 106-108. London, 1903.

21. Roscher, *National-Oekonomik des Ackerbaues*, p. 127, Note 1. Stuttgart, 1888.

22. Elisée Reclus, Europe, Vol. IV, pp. 222-223. New York, 1886. Miller and Skertchley, The Fenland, Past and Present, pp. 7-9. London, 1878.

23. *Ibid.*, pp. 145-147.

24. Sir Samuel W. Baker, The Albert Nyanza, Great Basin of the Nile, pp. 49-50. London and Philadelphia, 1866.

25. Diodorus Siculus, Book I, chap. III, p. 41. Translated by G. Booth. London, 1814.

26. David Livingstone, Missionary Travels in Africa, pp. 234-236, 239, 272. New York, 1858.

27. Felix Dubois, Timbuctoo, pp. 51-55, 145. New York, 1896.

28. Isabella B. Bishop, The Yangtze Valley and Beyond, Vol. I, pp. 8, 10, 97. London and New York, 1900.

29. Cyrus Thomas, Mound Explorations, pp. 626, 650-653. Twelfth Annual Report Bureau of Ethnology, Washington, 1894.

30. Strabo, Book V, chap. I, 4.

31. W. Deecke, Italy, pp. 88-89. London, 1904.

32. John Barrows, Travels in China, p. 349. Philadelphia, 1805.

33. Meredith Townsend, Asia and Europe, pp. 278-284. New York, 1904.

34. Isabella B. Bishop, The Yangtze Valley and Beyond, Vol. II, pp. 72-73, 76-81. New York and London, 1900. For the future of land

reclamation, see N. S. Shaler, Man and the Earth, chap. V. New York, 1906.

35. Strabo, Book X, chap. II, 19.

36. John W. Draper, Intellectual Development of Europe, Vol. I, pp. 84-86. New York, 1876.

37. Winwood Reade, The Martyrdom of Man, pp. 9-17. Eighth Edition, New York.

38. Irrigation, Thirteenth Report of the U. S. Geological Survey, Part III, pp. 133-135. Washington, 1895. J. W. Powell, Twenty-third Annual Report of the Bureau of Ethnology, pp. XII, XIII. Washington, 1904. Cosmos Mindeleff, Aboriginal Remains in the Verde Valley, Arizona, pp. 187, 192-194, 238-245. Thirteenth Annual Report of Bureau of Ethnology. Washington, 1896. V. Mindeleff, Pueblo Architecture, pp. 80, 216-217. Eighth Annual Report of Bureau of Ethnology. Washington, 1891. F. W. Hodge, Prehistoric Irrigation in Arizona, *American Anthropologist*, July, 1893.

39. McGee and Thomas, Prehistoric North America, pp. 105-106, 113, 118, 120-144, 478. Philadelphia, 1905.

40. Eleventh Census, Report on the Indians, pp. 49, 161, 415. Washington, 1894. D. G. Brinton, The American Race, pp. 116-117. Philadelphia, 1901.

41. *Ibid.*, pp. 161, 181, 182, 188, 191, 193, 198, 410, 441-445. M. C. Stevenson, The Zuni Indians, pp. 351-354. Twenty-third Annual Report of Bureau of Ethnology, Washington, 1904.

42. *Ibid.*, pp. 13-14. H. H. Bancroft, The Native Races, Vol. I, pp. 539-547. San Francisco, 1886.

43. Norway, Official Publication, pp. 99-100. Christiania, 1900.

44. Ernst Curtius, History of Greece, Vol. I, pp. 49-50. New York.

45. *Ibid.*, Vol. I, p. 440.

46. Dietrich Schaefer, *Die Hansestädte und König Waldemar von Dänemark*, pp. 255-257. Jena, 1879. Helen Zimmern, Story of the Hansa Towns, pp. 26-27. New York, 1895.

47. W. B. Weeden, Social and Economic History of New England, Vol. I, pp. 17, 18, 90, 91, 128-135, 139. Boston, 1899.

48. *Ibid.*, Vol. I, p. 245.

49. H. D. Traill, Social England, Vol. III, pp. 363-364, 540. London and New York, 1895.

50. J. Partsch, Central Europe, p. 311. London, 1903.

51. Alexander P. Engelhardt, A Russian Province of the North, pp. 54-71. From the Russian. London, 1899.

CHAPTER XI

THE ANTHROPO-GEOGRAPHY OF RIVERS

Rivers as interme-
diaries be-
tween land
and sea.

To a large view, rivers appear in two aspects. They are either part of the general water envelope of the earth, extensions of seas and estuaries back into the up-hill reaches of the land, feeders of the ocean, roots which it spreads out over the surface of the continents, not only to gather its nourishment from ultimate sources in spring and glacier, but also to bring down to the coast the land-born products of the interior to feed a sea-born commerce; or rivers are one of the land forms, merely water filling valley channels, serving to drain the fields and turn the mills of men. In the first aspect their historical importance has been both akin and linked to that of the ocean, despite the freshness and smaller volume of their waters and the unvarying direction of their currents. The ocean draws them and their trade to its vast basin by the force of gravity. It unites with its own the history of every log-stream in Laurentian or Himalayan forest, as it formerly linked the beaver-dammed brooks of wintry Canada with the current of trade following the Gulf Stream to Europe.

Where sea and river meet, Nature draws no sharp dividing line. Here the indeterminate boundary zone is conspicuous. The fresh water stream merges into brackish estuary, estuary into saltier inlet and inlet into briny ocean. Closely confined sea basins like the Black and Baltic, located in cool regions of slight evaporation and fed from a large catchment basin, approach in their reduced salinity the fresh water lakes and coastal lagoons in which rivers stretch out to rest on their way to the ocean. The muddy current of the Yangtze Kiang colors the Yellow Sea, and warns incoming Chinese junks of the proximity of land many hours before the low-lying shores can be discerned.[1] Columbus,

sailing along the Caribbean coast of South America off the
Orinoco mouth, found the ocean waters brackish and surmised the presence of a large river and therefore a large
continent on his left.[2]

The transitional form between stream and pelagic inlet
found in every river mouth is emphasized where strong tidal
currents carry the sea far into these channels of the land.
The tides move up the St. Lawrence River 430 miles (700
kilometers) or half way between Montreal and Quebec, and
up the Amazon 600 miles (1,000 kilometers). Owing to their
resemblance to pelagic channels, the estuaries of the American rivers with their salty tide were repeatedly mistaken, in
the period of discoveries, for the Northwest Passage to the
Pacific. Newport in 1608 explored the broad sluggish course
of the James River in his search for a western ocean. Henry
Hudson ascended the Hudson River almost as far as Albany,
before he discovered that this was no maritime pathway,
like the Bosporus or Dardanelles, leading to an ulterior
sea. The long tidal course of the St. Lawrence westward
into the heart of the continent fed La Salle's dream of finding here a water route to the Pacific, and fixed his village
of "La Chine" above the rapids at Montreal as a signpost
pointing the way to the Indies and Cathay. In the same
way a tidal river at the head of Cook's Inlet on the Alaskan
coast was mistaken for a Northeast Passage, not by Captain
Cook but by his fellow officers, on his Pacific voyage of
1776-1780; and it was followed for several days before its
character as a river was established.[3]

Rivers have always been the great intermediaries between
land and sea, for in the ocean all find their common destination. Until the construction of giant steamers in recent
years, sea navigation has always passed without break into
river navigation. Sailing vessels are carried by the trade
wind 600 miles up the Orinoco to San Fernando. Alexander's discovery of the Indus River led by almost inevitable
sequence to the rediscovery of the Eastern sea route, which
in turn ran from India through the Strait of Oman and
the Persian Gulf up the navigable course of the Euphrates
to the elbow of the river at Thapsacus. Enterprising sea

Sea navigation merges into river navigation.

folk have always used rivers as natural continuations of the marine highway into the land. The Humber estuary and its radiating group of streams led the invading Angles in the sixth century into the heart of Britain.[4] The long navigable courses of the rivers of France exposed that whole country to the depredations of the piratical Northmen in the ninth and tenth centuries. Up every river they came, up the Scheldt into Flanders, the Seine to Paris and the Marne to Meaux; up the Loire to Orleans, the Garonne to Toulouse and the Rhone to Valence.[5] So the Atlantic rivers of North America formed the lines of European exploration and settlement. The St. Lawrence brought the French from the ocean into the Great Lakes basin, whose low, swampy watershed they readily crossed in their light canoes to the tributaries of the Mississippi; and scarcely had they reached the "Father of Waters" before they were planting the flag of France on the Gulf of Mexico at its mouth. The Tupi Indians of South America, a genuine water-race, moved from their original home on the Paraguay headstream of the La Plata down to its mouth, then expanded northward along the coast of Brazil in their small canoes to the estuary of the Amazon, thence up its southern tributary, the Tapajos, and in smaller numbers up the main stream to the foot of the Andes, where detached groups of the race are still found.[6] So the migrations of the Carib river tribes led them from their native seats in eastern Brazil down the Xingu to the Amazon, thence out to sea and along the northern coast of South America, thence inland once more, up the Orinoco to the foot of the Andes, into the lagoon of Maracaibo and up the Magdalena. Meanwhile their settlements at the mouth of the Orinoco threw off spores of pirate colonies to the adjacent islands and finally, in the time of Columbus, to Porto Rico and Haiti.[7] [See map page 101.]

Historical importance of seas and oceans influenced by their debouching streams.

So intimate is this connection between marine and inland waterways, that the historical and economic importance of seas and oceans is noticeably influenced by the size of their drainage basins and the navigability of their debouching rivers. This is especially true of enclosed seas. The only historical importance attached to the Caspian's inland basin

is that inherent in the Volga's mighty stream. The Mediterranean has always suffered from its paucity of long river
highways to open for it a wide hinterland. This lack
checked the spread of its cultural influences and finally
helped to arrest its historical development. If we compare
the record of the Adriatic and the Black seas, the first a
sharply walled *cul de sac*, the second a center of long radiating streams, sending out the Danube to tap the back country
of the Adriatic and the Dnieper to draw on that of the Baltic,
we find that the smaller sea has had a limited range of influence, a concentrated brilliant history, precocious and short-
lived as is that of all limited areas; that the Euxine has exercised more far-reaching influences, despite a slow and still
unfinished development. The Black Sea rivers in ancient
times opened their countries to such elements of Hellenic culture as might penetrate from the Greek trading colonies at
their mouths, especially the Greek forms of Christianity. It
was the Danube that in the fourth century carried Arianism,
born of the philosophic niceties of Greek thought, to the barbarians of southern Germany, and made Unitarians of the
Burgundians and Visigoths of southern Gaul.[8] The Dnieper
carried the religion of the Greek Church to the Russian princes
at Kief, Smolensk, and Moscow. Owing to the southward
course of its great rivers, Russia has found the crux of her
politics in the Black Sea, ever since the tenth century when the
barbarians from Kiev first appeared before Constantinople.
This sea has had for her a higher economic importance than
the Baltic, despite the latter's location near the cultural
center of western Europe.

In other seas, too, rivers play the same part of extending their tributary areas and therefore enhancing their historical significance. The disadvantages of the Baltic's
smaller size and far-northern location, as compared with the
Mediterranean, were largely compensated for by the series
of big streams draining into it from the south, and bringing
out from a vast hinterland the bulky necessaries of life.
Hence the Hanseatic League of the Middle Ages, which had
its origin among the southern coast towns of the Baltic
from Lubeck to Riga, throve on the combined trade of sea

Baltic and
White Sea
rivers.

and river.[9]   The mouths of the Scheldt, Rhine, Weser, Elbe and Thames long concentrated in themselves the economic, cultural and historical development of the North Sea basin. So the White Sea, despite its sub-polar location, is valuable to Russia for two reasons; it affords a politically open port, and it receives the Northern Dwina, which is navigable for river steamers from Archangel south to Vologda, a distance of six hundred miles, and carries the export trade of a large territory.[10]   Similarly in recent years, Bering Sea has gained unwonted commercial activity because the Yukon River serves as a waterway 1,370 miles long to the Klondike gold fields.

Atlantic and Pacific rivers.

If we compare the Atlantic and Pacific oceans in respect to their rivers, we find that the narrow Atlantic has a drainage basin of over 19,000,000 square miles as opposed to the 8,660,000 square miles of drainage area commanded by the vastly larger Pacific.   The Pacific is for the most part rimmed by mountains, discharging into the ocean only mad torrents or rapid-broken streams.   The Atlantic, bordered by gently sloping plains of wide extent, receives rivers that for the most part pursue a long and leisurely course to the sea.   Therefore, the commercial and cultural influences of the Atlantic extend from the Rockies and Andes almost to the heart of Russia, and by the Nile highway they even invade the seclusion of Africa.   Through the long reach of its rivers, therefore, the Atlantic commands a land area twice as great as that of the Pacific; and by reason of this fundamental geographic advantage, it will retain the historical preëminence that it so early secured.   The development of the World Ocean will mean the exploitation of the Pacific trade from the basis of the Atlantic, the domination of the larger ocean by the historic peoples of the smaller, because these peoples have wider and more accessible lands as the base of their maritime operations.

Lack of coast articulations supplied by rivers.

The geographic influence of abundant rivers navigable from the sea is closely akin to that of highly articulated coasts.   The effect of the Hardanger or Sogne Fiord, admitting ocean steamers a hundred miles into the interior of Norway, is similar to that of the Elbe and Weser estuaries, which admit the largest vessels sixty miles upstream to Hamburg and Bremen. Since river inlets can, to a certain extent, supply the place of marine inlets, from the standpoint of anthropo-geographic theory and of human practice, a land dissected by navigable rivers can be grouped with one dissected by arms of the sea. South America and Africa are alike in the unbroken contour of their coasts, but strongly contrasted in the character of their rivers. Hence the two continents present the extremes of accessibility and inaccessibility. South America, most richly endowed of all the continents with navigable streams, receiving ocean vessels three thousand miles up the Amazon as far as Tabatinga in Peru, and smaller steamers up the Orinoco to the spurs of the Andes, was known in its main features to explorers fifty years after its discovery. Africa, historically the oldest of continents, but cursed with a mesa form which converts nearly every river into a plunging torrent on its approach to the sea, kept its vast interior till the last century wrapped in utmost gloom. China, amply supplied with smaller littoral indentations but characterized by a paucity of larger inlets, finds compensation in the long navigable course of the Yangtze Kiang. This river extends the landward reach of the Yellow Sea 630 miles inland to Hanchow, where ocean-going vessels take on cargoes of tea and silk for Europe and America,[11] and pay for them in Mexican dollars, the coin of the coast. Hence it is lined with free ports all the way from Shanghai at its mouth to Ichang, a thousand miles up its course.[12]

Navigable rivers opening passages directly from the sea are obviously nature-made gates and paths into wholly new countries; but the accessibility with which they endow a land becomes later a permanent factor in its cultural and economic development, a factor that remains constantly though less conspicuously operative when railroads have done their utmost to supplant water transportation. The importance of inland waterways for local and foreign trade and intercourse has everywhere been recognized. The peoples who have long maintained preëminence among the commercial and maritime nations of the world have owed this in no

River highways as basis of commercial preeminence.

small part to the command of these natural highways, which have served to give the broad land basis necessary for permanent commercial ascendency.   This has been the history of England, Holland, France and the recent record of Germany.   The medieval League of the Rhine Cities flourished by reason of the Rhone-Rhine highway across western Europe.   The Hanseatic League, from Bruges all the way east to Russian Novgorod, owed their brilliant commercial career, not only to the favorable maritime field in the enclosed sea basins in front of them, but also to the series of long navigable rivers behind them from the Scheldt to the Neva and Volchov.   Wherefore we find the League, originally confined to coast towns, drawing into the federation numerous cities located far up these rivers, such as Ghent, Cologne, Magdeburg, Breslau, Cracow, Pskof and Novgorod.[13]

Importance of rivers in large countries.   In countries of large area, where commerce and intercourse must cover great distances, these natural and therefore cheap highways assume paramount importance, especially in the forest and agricultural stages of development, when the products of the land are bulky in proportion to their value.   Small countries with deeply indented coasts, like Greece, Norway, Scotland, New England, Chile, and Japan, can forego the advantage of big river systems; but in Russia, Siberia, China, India, Canada, the United States, Venezuela, Brazil and Argentine, the history of the country, economic and political, is indissolubly connected with that of its great rivers.   The storm center of the French and English wars in America was located on the upper Hudson, because this stream enabled the English colonies to tap the fur trade of the Great Lakes, and because it commanded the Mohawk Valley, the easiest and most obvious path for expansion into the interior of the continent.   The Spanish, otherwise confining their activities in South America to the Caribbean district and the civilized regions of the Andean highlands, established settlements at the mouth of the La Plata River, because this stream afforded an approach from the Atlantic side toward the Potosi mines on the Bolivian Plateau.   The Yangtze Kiang, that great waterway leading from the sea

across the breadth of China and the one valuable river adjunct of maritime trade in the whole Orient, was early appropriated by the discerning English as the British "sphere of
influence."

No other equally large area of the earth is so generously Rivers as
equipped by nature for the production and distribution of highways
the articles of commerce as southern Canada and that part of expan-
of the United States lying east of the Rocky Mountains. sion.
The simple build of the North American continent, consisting of a broad central trough between distant mountain
ranges, and characterized by gentle slopes to the Atlantic
Ocean and the Gulf of Mexico, has generated great and small
rivers with easy-going currents, that everywhere opened up
the land to explorer, trader and settler.   The rate of expansion from the "Europe-fronting shore" of the continent
was everywhere in direct proportion to the length of the
rivers first appropriated by the colonists.   North of Chesapeake Bay the lure to landward advance was the fur trade.
The Atlantic rivers of the coast pre-empted by the English
were cut short by the Appalachian wall.   They opened up
only restricted fur fields which were soon exhausted, so that
the migrant trapper was here early converted into the agricultural settler, his shifting camp fire into the hearthstone
of the farmhouse.   Expansion was slow but solid.   The
relatively small area rendered accessible by their streams became compactly filled by the swelling tide of immigrants
and the rapid natural increase of population.   In sharp
contrast to this development, the long waterway of the St.
Lawrence and the Great Lakes leading to the still vaster
river system of the Mississippi betrayed the fur-trading
French into excessive expansion, and enabled them to appropriate but not to hold a vast extent of territory.   A hundred years after the arrival of Champlain at Montreal,
they were planting their fur stations on Lake Superior and
the Mississippi, 1,400 miles (2,300 kilometers) back from the
coast, at a time when the English settlements had advanced
little beyond tide-water.   And when after 1770 the westward
movement swept the backwoodsmen of the English colonies
over the Appalachian barrier to the Ohio, Cumberland and

344 ANTHROPO-GEOGRAPHY OF RIVERS

Tennessee, these long westward flowing streams carried them rapidly on to the Mississippi, communicated the mobility and restlessness of their own currents to the eager pioneer, and their capacity to master great distances; so that in forty short years, by 1810, settlements were creeping up the western tributaries of the Mississippi. The abundant water communication in the Mississippi Valley, which even for present large river craft contains 15,410 miles of navigable streams and which had therefore a far greater mileage in the day of canoe and flatboat, afforded outlet for bulky, backwoods produce to the sea at New Orleans. When the English acquired Canada in 1763, they straightway fell under the sway of its harsh climate and long river systems, taking up the life of the fur trader; they followed the now scarcer pelts from the streams of Superior westward by Lake Winnipeg and along the path of the Saskatchewan River straight to the foot of the Rockies.

Siberian rivers and Russian expansion. Rivers have played the same part in expediting Russian expansion across the wide extent of Siberia. Here again a severe climate necessitated reliance on furs, the chief natural product of the country, as the basis of trade. These, as the outcome of savage economy, were gathered in from wide areas which only rivers could open up. Therefore, where the Siberian streams flatten out their upper courses east and west against the northern face of the Asiatic plateau, with low watersheds between, the Russian explorer and sable hunter struck their eastward water trail toward the Pacific. The advance, which under Yermak crossed the Ural Mountains in 1579, reached the Yenisei River in 1610 and planted there the town of Turuchansk as a sort of milestone, almost on the Arctic Circle opposite the mouth of the Lower Tunguska, a long eastern tributary. Up this they passed to the Lena in 1627, thence to Bering Sea by the Kolima and Anadyr rivers, because these arctic fields yielded sable, beaver and fox skins in greatest quantity.[14] The Lena especially, from its source down to its eastern elbow at Yakutsk, that great rendezvous of Siberian fur traders, was a highway for trapper and Cossack tribute-gatherer.[15] From the sources of the Yenisei in Lake Baikal to the navigable course of the Amur was a short step, taken in 1658, though the control of the river, which was claimed by China, was not secured till two hundred years later.[16] [See map page 103.]

As the only highways in new countries, rivers constitute lines of least resistance for colonial peoples encroaching upon the territory of inferior races. They are therefore the geographic basis of those streamers of settlement which we found making a fringe of civilization across the boundary zone of savagery or barbarism on the typical colonial frontier. Ethnic islands of the expanding people cluster along them like iron filings on a magnetized wire. Therefore in all countries where navigable rivers have fixed the lines of expansion, as in the United States, the northern part of the Russian Empire, and the eastern or colonial border of Germany and Austria, there is a strong anthropo-geographic resemblance in the frontiers of successive decades or centuries. But in arid or semi-arid regions like South Africa, the western plains of North America, the steppes of Russian and Chinese Turkestan, the river highway *motif* in expansion is lost in a variety of other geographic and geologic factors, though the water of the streams still attracts trail and settlement.

A river like the Nile, lower Volga, Irtysh or Indus, rising in highlands of abundant rainfall but traversing an arid or desert land, acquires added importance because it furnishes the sole means of water travel and of irrigation. The Nile has for ages constituted the main line of intercourse between the Mediterranean and Equatorial Africa. The Tigris, Euphrates, Indus, and the Niger where it makes its great northern bend into the Sahara near Timbuctoo,[17] attest the value to local fertility and commerce inherent in these rivers of the deserts and steppes. Such rivers are always oasis-makers, whether on their way to the sea they periodically cover a narrow flood-plain like that of the Nile, or one ninety miles wide, like that of the Niger's inland delta above Timbuctoo;[18] or whether they emerge into a silent sea of sand, like the Murghab of Russian Turkestan, which spreads itself out to water the gardens of Merv.

Determinants of routes in arid or semi-arid lands.

Even where such rivers have a volume too scanty to float a raft, they yet point the highway, because they alone supply water for man and beast across the desert tract. The Oxus and Sir Daria have from time immemorial determined the great trade routes through Turkestan to Central Asia. The Platte, Arkansas, Cimarron and Canadian rivers fixed the course of our early western trails across the arid plains to the foot of the Rockies; and beyond this barrier the California Trail followed the long-drawn oasis formed by the Humboldt River across the Nevada Desert, the Gila River guided the first American fur-trapping explorers across the burning deserts of Arizona to the Pacific, and the succession of water-holes in the dry bed of the Mohave River gave direction to the Spanish Trail across the Mohave Desert towards Los Angeles. In the same way, Livingstone's route from the Orange River in South Africa to Lake Ngami, under the direction of native guides, ran along the margin of the Kalahari Desert up the dry bed of the Mokoko River, which still retained an irregular succession of permanent wells.[19]

Wadi routes in arid lands.   In the trade-wind regions of the world, which are characterized by seasons of intense drought, we find rivers carrying a scant and variable amount of water but an abundance of gravel and sand; they are known in different localities as wadis, fiumares and arroyos. Their beds, dry for long periods of the year, become natural roads, paved with the gravel which the stream regularly deposits in the wet season. Local travel in Sicily, Italy [20] and other Mediterranean countries uses such natural roads extensively. Trade routes across the plateau of Judea and Samaria follow the wadis, because these give the best gradient and the best footing for the ascent.[21] Wadis also determine the line of caravan routes across the highlands of the Sahara. In the desert of Southwest Africa, the Khiuseb is the first river north of the Orange to reach the Atlantic through the barrier dunes of the coast. Hence it has drawn to its valley the trade routes from a wide circle of inland points from Ottawe to Windhoek and Rehobeth, and given added importance to the British coast of Walfish Bay, into which it debouches.[22] But just to the north, the broad dry bed of the Swakop offered a natural wagon route into the interior, and has been utilized for the railroad of German Southwest Africa.

The historical importance of a river increases from its source toward its mouth. Its head springs, gushing from the ground, and the ramifying brooks of its highland course yield a widely distributed water supply and thereby exercise a strong influence in locating the dwellings of men; but they play no part in the great movements and larger activities of peoples. Only when minor affluents unite to form the main stream, enlarge it in its lower course by an increasing tribute of water, and extend constantly its tributary area, does a river assume real historical importance. It reaches its fullest significance at its mouth, where it joins the world's highway of the ocean. Here are combined the best geographical advantages—participation in the cosmopolitan civilization characteristic of coastal regions, opportunity for inland and maritime commerce, and a fertile alluvial soil yielding support for dense populations. The predominant importance of the debouchment stretch of a river is indicated by the presence of such cities as London, Rotterdam, Hamburg, Bremen, Bordeaux, Odessa, Alexandria, Calcutta, Rangoon, Bangkok, Hongkong, Canton, Nanking and Shanghai, Montreal and Quebec, New York, Philadelphia, New Orleans, Buenos Ayres and Montevideo. This debouchment stretch gains in practical value and hence in permanent historical importance if it is swept by a scouring tide, which enables the junction of inland and maritime routes to penetrate into the land. Even Strabo recognized this value of tidal reaches.[23] Hence in tideless basins like the Baltic and Caribbean, the great river ports have to advance coastward to meet the sea; and the lower course of even mighty streams like the Volga and Nile achieve a restricted importance.[24]

The control of a river mouth becomes a desideratum or necessity to the upstream people. Otherwise they may be bottled up. Though history shows us countless instances of upstream expansion, nevertheless owing to the ease of down-

[Marginal note: Increasing historical importance from source to mouth.]

stream navigation and this increasing historical importance from source to mouth, the direction of a river's flow has often determined the course of commerce and of political expansion.

The possibility of radial expansion, which we have found to be the chief advantage of a central location, is greatly enhanced if that central location coincides with a hydrographic center of low relief. The tenth century nucleus of the Russian Empire was found about the low nodal watershed formed by the Valdai Hills, whence radiated the rivers later embodied in the Muscovite domain. Here in Novgorod at the head of the Volchov-Ladoga-Neva system, Pskof on the Velikaya, Tver at the head of the navigable Volga, Moscow on the Oka, Smolensk on the Dnieper, and Vitebsk on the Duna, were gathered the Russians destined to displace the primitive Finnish population and appropriate the wide plains of eastern Europe. Everywhere their conquests, colonization, and commercial relations have followed the downstream course of their rivers. The Dnieper carried the Rus of Smolensk and Kief to the Euxine, into contact with the Byzantine world, and brought thence religion, art, and architecture for the untutored empire of the north. The influence of the Volga has been irresistible. Down its current Novgorod traders in the twelfth century sought the commerce of the Caspian and the Orient; and later the Muscovite princes pushed their conquest of the Tartar hordes from Asia. The Northern Dwina, Onega, Mesen and Petchora have carried long narrow bands of Slav settlement northward to the Arctic Ocean. [See map page 225.] Medieval Russian trade from Hanseatic Pskof and Novgorod, and later Russian dominion followed the Narva and Neva to the Baltic. "The Dnieper made Russia Byzantine, the Volga made it Asiatic. It was for the Neva to make it European." [25]

In the same way, when the early French explorers and traders of Canada reached the hydrographic center of the continent about Lakes Superior and Michigan, they quickly crossed the low rim of these basins southward to the Mississippi, and northward to the Rainy Lake and Winnipeg

system draining to Hudson Bay.[26] While it took them from
1608 to 1659 and 1662 to penetrate upstream from Quebec
to this central watershed, only nine years elapsed from
the time (1673) Marquette reached the westward flowing
Wisconsin River to 1682, when La Salle reached the mouth
of the Mississippi.

The effect of mere current upon the course of trade and **Effect of**
political expansion was conspicuous in the early history of **current**
upon trade
the Mississippi Valley, before steam navigation began **and expan-**
to modify the geographic influence of a river's flow. **sion.**
The wide forest-grown barrier of the Appalachian Mountains placed the western pioneers under the geographic
control of the western waters. The bulkiness of their
field and forest products, fitted only for water transportation, and the immense mass of downstream commerce
called loudly for a maritime outlet and the acquisition from
Spain of some port at the Mississippi mouth. For twenty
years the politics of this transmontane country centered
about the "Island of New Orleans," and in 1803 saw its
dream realized by the Louisiana Purchase.

For the western trader, the Mississippi and Ohio were pre-
eminently downstream paths. Gravity did the work. Only
small boats, laden with fine commodities of small bulk and
large value, occasionally made the forty day upstream
voyage from New Orleans to Louisville. Flat boats and
barges that were constructed at Pittsburg for the river
traffic were regularly broken up for lumber at downstream
points like Louisville and New Orleans; for the traders returned overland by the old Chickasaw Trail to the Cumberland and Ohio River settlements, carrying their profits in
the form of gold. The same thing happens today, as it
also happened two thousand years ago, on the Tigris and
Euphrates. The highlander of Armenia or northern Mesopotamia floats down the current in his skin boat or on his
brushwood raft, to sell his goods and the wood forming the
frame-work of his primitive craft in timberless Bagdad and
Busra, as formerly in treeless Babylon. He dries out his
skins, loads them on his shoulders or on a mule brought
down for the purpose, and returns on foot to his highland

village.[27]   The same preponderance of downstream traffic appears to-day in eastern Siberia. Pedlers on the Amur start in the spring from Stretensk, 2025 miles up the river, with their wares in barges, and drift down with the current, selling at the villages *en route*, to the river's mouth at Nikolaievsk. Here they dispose of their remaining stock and also of their barges, the lumber of which is utilized for sidewalks, and they themselves return upstream by steamer. The grain barges of western Siberia, like the coal barges of the Mississippi, even within recent decades, are similarly disposed of at the journey's end.[28]   The tonnage of downstream traffic on the Ohio and Mississippi to-day greatly exceeds that upstream. The fleet of 56 coal boats, carrying about 70,000 tons, which the great towboat Sprague takes in a single trip from Louisville down to New Orleans, all return empty. Of the 15,226,805 net tons of freight shipped in 1906 on the Ohio system, 13,980,368 tons of coal, stone, sand and lumber were carried in unrigged craft, fitted chiefly for downstream traffic.[29]

Importance of mouth to upstream people.   Owing to the strong pull exerted by a river's mouth upon all its basin, current, commerce and people alike tend to reach the ocean. For a nation holding the terrestrial course of a stream, the political fate of its tidal course or mouth must always be a matter of great concern. To the early westerner of the United States, before the acquisition of the Louisiana country, it was of vital importance whether belligerent France or more amenable Spain or the Republic itself should own the mouth of the Mississippi. Germany, which holds 240 miles (400 kilometers) of the navigable Danube,[30] can never be indifferent to the political ownership of its mouth, or to the fact that a great power like Russia has edged forward, by the acquisition of Bessarabia in 1878, to the northern or Kilia debouchment channel.[31]   Such interest shows itself in sustained efforts either to gain political control of the mouth, or to secure the neutrality of the stream by having it declared an international waterway, and thus partially to deprive the state holding its mouth of the advantages of its transit location.

The only satisfactory solution is undivided political ownership.   After France pushed eastward to the Rhine in 1648, she warred for three centuries to acquire its mouth.   Napoleon laid claim to Belgium and Holland on the ground that their soil had been built up by the alluvium of French rivers. Germany's conquest of Schleswig-Holstein in 1864 was significant chiefly because it dislodged Denmark from the right bank of the lower Elbe, and secured undivided control of this important estuary.   The Rhine, which traverses the Empire from north to south and constitutes its greatest single trade route, gives to Germany a more vital interest in Holland than ever France had.   Her most important iron and coal mines and manufacturing industries are located on this waterway or its tributaries, the Ruhr, Mosel, Saar and Main. Hence the Rhine is the great artery of German trade and outlet for her enormous exports, which chiefly reach the sea through the ports of Belgium and Holland.   These two countries therefore fatten on German commerce and reduce German profits.   Hence the Empire, by the construction of the Emden-Dortmund canal, aims to divert its trade from Rotterdam and Antwerp to a German port, and possibly thereby put the screw on Holland to draw her into some kind of a commercial union with Germany.[32]   Heinrich von Treitschke, in his *"Politik,"* deplores the fact that the most valuable part of the great German river has fallen into alien hands, and he declares it to be an imperative task of German policy to recover the mouth of that stream, "either by a commercial or political union."   "We need the entrance of Holland into our customs union as we need our daily bread." [33]

When the middle and upper course of a river system are shared by several nations, their common interest demands that the control of the mouth be divided, as in the case of the La Plata between Argentine and Uruguay; or held by a small state, like Holland, too weak to force the monopoly of the tidal course.   The Treaty of Paris in 1856 extended the territory of Moldavia at the cost of Russia, to keep the Russian frontier away from the Danube.[34]   Her very presence was ominous.   The temptation to giant powers to gobble up these exquisite morsels of territory is irresistible.

Prevention of monopoly of river mouth.

Hence the advisability of neutralizing small states holding such locations, as in the case of Roumania; and making their rivers international waterways, as in the case of the Orinoco,[35] Scheldt, Waal, Rhine and Danube.[36] The Yangtze Kiang mouth, where already the treaty ports cluster thick, will probably be the first part of China to be declared neutral ground, and as such to be placed under the protection of the combined commercial powers,[37] as is even now foreshadowed by the international Conservancy Board of 1910.[38] The United States, by her treaty with Mexico in 1848, secured the right of free navigation on the lower or Mexican course of the Colorado River and the Gulf of California. The Franco-British convention, which in 1898 confirmed the western Sudan to France, also conceded the principle of making the Niger, the sole outlet of this vast and isolated territory, an international waterway, and created two French *enclaves* in British Nigeria to serve as river ports.[39]

Motive for canals in lower course   The mouth of a large river system is the converging point of many lines of inland and maritime navigation. The interests of commerce, especially in its earlier periods of development, demand that the contact here of river and sea be extensive as possible. Nature suggests the way to fulfill this requirement. The sluggish lowland current of a river, on approaching sea level, throws out distributaries that reach the coast at various points and form a network of channels, which can be deepened and rendered permanent by canalization. In such regions the opportunity for the improvement and extension of waterways has been utilized from the earliest times. The ancient Egyptians, Chaldeans, East Indians, and the Gauls of the lower Po for thousands of years canaled the waters of their deltas and coastal lowlands for the combined purpose of irrigation, drainage, and navigation. The great canal system of China, constructed in the seventh century primarily to facilitate inland intercourse between the northern and central sections of the Empire, extends from the sea at Hangchow 700 miles northward through the coastal alluvium of the Yangtze Kiang, Hoangho and Pie-ho to Tientsin, the port of Peking. Only the

canal system of the center, important both for the irrigation of the fertile but porous loess and for the transportation of crops, is still in repair. Here the meshes of the canal
network are little more than half a mile wide; farmers dig
canals to their barns and bring in their produce in barges
instead of hay wagons.[40] Holland, where the ancient Romans constructed channels in the Rhine delta and where the
debouchment courses of the Rhine, Meuse and Scheldt present a labyrinth of waterways, has to-day 1903 miles
(3069 kilometers) of canals, which together with the navigable rivers, have been important geographic factors in the
historical preëminence of Dutch foreign commerce. So on
the lower Mississippi, in the greatest alluvial area of the
United States, the government has expended large sums for
the improvement of the passes and bayous of the river. The
Barataria, Atchafalaya, Terrebonne, Black, Teche and La-
fourche bayous have been rendered navigable, and New Orleans has been given canal outlets to the sea through Lakes
Salvador, Pontchartrain and Borgne.

As the dividing channels of the lower course point to the Watershed
feasibility of amplifying the connection with the ocean canals.
highway, so the spreading branches of a river's source,
which approach other head waters on a low divide, suggest
the extension of inland navigation by the union of two such
drainage systems through canals. Where the rivers of a
country radiate from a relatively low central watershed, as
from the Central Plateau of France and the Valdai Hills of
Russia, nature offers conditions for extensive linking of inland waterways. Hence we find a continuous passway
through Russia from the Caspian Sea to the Baltic by the
canal uniting the Volga and Neva rivers; another from the
Black Sea up the Dnieper, which by canals finds three different outlets to the Baltic through the Vistula, Niemen
and Duna.[41] The Northern Dwina, linked, by canals, with the
Neva through Lakes Onega and Ladoga, unites the White
Sea with the Baltic.[42] Sully, the great minister of Henry IV.
of France, saw that the relief of the country would permit
the linking of the Loire, Seine, Meuse, Saône and Rhine,
and the Mediterranean with the Garonne. All his plans

were carried out by his successors, but he himself, at the end of the sixteenth century, began the construction of the Briare Canal between the Loire near Orleans and the Seine at Fontainebleau [43]   Similarly in the eastern half of the United States, the long, low watershed separating the drainage basin of the St. Lawrence and Great Lakes from that of the Mississippi and the Hudson made feasible the succession of canals completing the "Great Belt" of inland navigation from St. Lawrence and New York bays to the Gulf. Albert Gallatin's famous report of 1808 [44] pointed out the adaptation of the three low divides to canal communication; but long before this, every line of possible canoe travel by river and portage over swamp or lake-dotted watershed had been used by savages, white explorers and French voyageurs, from Lake Champlain to Lake Winnebago, so that the canal engineer had only to select from the numerous portage paths already beaten out by the moccasined feet of Indian or fur-trader.

Rivers and railroads.   The cheapness and ease of river travel have tended to check or delay the construction of highroads and railways, where facilities for inland navigation have been abundant, and later to regulate railway freight charges.   Conversely, riverless lands have everywhere experienced an exaggerated and precocious railroad development, and have suffered from its monopoly of transportation.   Even canals have in most lands had a far earlier date than paved highroads.   This has been true of Spain, France, Holland, and England.[45]   In the Hoang-ho Valley of northern China where waterways are restricted, owing to the rapid current and shallowness of this river, highroads are comparatively common; but they are very rare in central and southern China where navigable rivers and canals abound.[46]   New England, owing to its lack of inland navigation, was the first part of the United States to develop a complete system of turnpikes and late of railroads.   On the other hand, the great river valleys of America have generally slighted the highroad phase of communication, and slowly passed to that of railroads.   The abundance of natural waterways in Russia—51,800 miles including canals—has contributed to the retardation of railroad construction.[47]   The same thing is true in the Netherlands, where 4875 miles (7863 kilometers) of navigable water-ways[48] in an area of only 12,870 square miles (33,000 square kilometers) have kept the railroads down to a paltry 1818 miles (2931 kilometers); but smaller Belgium, commanding only 1375 miles (3314 kilometers) of waterway and stimulated further by a remarkable industrial and commercial development, has constructed 4228 miles (6819 kilometers) of railroad.

If we compare the countries of Central and South America, where railroads are still mere adjuncts of river and coastwise routes, a stage of development prevalent in the United States till 1858, we find an unmistakable relation between navigable waterways and railroad mileage. The countries with ample or considerable river communication, like Brazil, Venezuela, Colombia and Paraguay, are all relatively slow in laying railroads as compared with Mexico and Argentine, even when allowance is made for differences of zonal location, economic development, and degree of European elements in their respective populations. Mexico and Argentine, having each an area only about one-fourth that of Brazil but a railroad mileage nearly one-fourth greater, have been pushed to this development primarily by a common lack of inland navigation. Similarly South Africa, stricken with poverty of water communication south of the Zambesi, has constructed 7500 miles of railroads,[49] in spite of the youth of the country and the sparsity of its white population. Similar geographic conditions have forced the mileage of Australian railways up to twice that of South Africa, in a country which is still in the pastoral and agricultural stage of development, and whose most densely populated province Victoria has only fourteen inhabitants to the square mile. In the almost unpeopled wastes of Trans-Caspia, where two decades ago the camel was the only carrier, the Russian railroad has worked a commercial revolution by stimulating production and affording an outlet for the irrigated districts of the encircling mountains.[50]   In our own Trans-Missouri country, where the scanty volume of the streams eliminated all but the Missouri itself as a dependable

Relation of rivers to railroads in recent colonial lands.

waterway, even for the canoe travel of the early western trappers, railroads have developed unchecked by the competition of river transportation.[51] With no rival nearer than the Straits of Magellan and the Isthmus of Panama for transportation between the Mississippi and the Pacific coast, they have fixed their own charges on a monopoly basis, and have fought the construction of the Isthmian Canal.

Unity of a river system. A river system is a system of communication. It therefore makes a bond of union between the people living among its remoter sources and those settled at its mouth. Every such river system forms geographically an unbroken whole. Only where a wild, torrent-filled gorge, like the Brahmaputra's path through the Himalayas, interrupts communication between the upper and lower course, is human life in the two sections divorced. But such cases are rare. Even the River Jhelam, which springs with mad bounds from the lofty Vale of Kashmir through the outer range of the Himalayas down to its junction with the Indus, carries quantities of small logs to be used as railway sleepers; and though it shatters a large per cent. of them, it makes a link between the lumber men of the Kashmir forests and British railroad engineers in the treeless plains of the Indus.[52]

The effect of common water supply in arid lands. In arid lands, where the scant and variable streams are useless for navigation, but invaluable for irrigation, a rival interest in the limited water supply leads almost inevitably to conflict, and often to the political union of the peoples holding the upper and lower courses, in order to secure adjustment of their respective claims. The ancient Salassi of the upper Doria Baltea Valley in the Alps drew off all the water of the stream for washing gold, and thus deprived the agricultural people lower down the valley of the water necessary for irrigation. The result was frequent wars between the two tribes.[53] The offensive is taken by the downstream people, whose fields and gardens suffer from every extension of tillage or increase of population in the settlements above them. Occasionally a formal agreement is a temporary expedient. The River Firenze and other streams watering southern Trans-Caspia have their sources in the mountains of northern Persia; hence the Russians, in the boundary convention with Persia of 1881, stipulated that no new settlement be established along these streams within Persian territory, no extension of land under cultivation beyond the present amount, and no eduction of the water beyond that necessary to irrigate the existing fields.[54] Russia's designs upon Afghanistan aim not only at access to India, but also at the control of the upper Murghab River, on whose water depends the prosperity of the Pendjeh and Merv oases.[55] In such regions the only logical course is the extension of the political frontier to the watershed, a principle which Russia is applying in western Asia, and which California applied in drawing her eastern boundary to include even Goose Lake.

Rivers unite. Ancient Rome grew up on both banks of the Tiber, and extended her commercial and political supremacy up and down stream. Both sides of the Rhine were originally occupied by the Gallic tribes, whose villages were in some instances bisected by the river. Cæsar found the Menapii, a Belgian people on the lower Rhine, with their fields, farmhouses and villages on both banks.[56] Then the westward advance of the Teutonic tribes gradually transformed the Rhine into a German river, from the island of Batavia at its mouth up to the great elbow at the foot of the Jura Mountains.[57] To the American Indians even the widest rivers were no barriers. Christopher Gist, exploring the Ohio in 1751, found a Shawnee village situated on both sides of the river below the mouth of the Scioto, with about a hundred houses on the north bank and forty on the south.[58] The small and unique nation of the Mandan Indians were found by Lewis and Clark near the northern bend of the Missouri in 1804, in two groups of villages on opposite sides of the river. They had previously in 1772 occupied nine villages lower down the stream, two on the east bank and seven on the west.[59] The Connecticut River settlers of early colonial days laid out all their towns straight across the valley, utilizing the alluvial meadows on both banks for tillage, the terraces for residence sites, and the common river for intercourse.[60]

Every river tends to become a common artery feeding all the life of its basin, and gradually obliterating ethnic and

Union of opposite river banks.

Tendency toward ethnic and cultural unity in a river valley.

cultural differences among the peoples of its valley. The Nile, with its narrow hem of flood-plain on either bank and barrier sands beyond, has so linked race and history in Egypt and Nubia, that the two countries cannot be separated. A common highway from mountains to sea, a common frontier of trackless desert have developed here a blended similarity of race, language and culture from the delta to Kordofan. The Hamitic race seems to have originated in the south and migrated northward down the Nile towards the delta. Later the whole valley, north and south, received the same Semitic or Arab immigration, which spread from Cairo to the old Sudanese capital of Sennar, while a strain of negro blood has filtered in from the equatorial black belt and followed the current down to the sea.[61] The culture of the valley originated in Lower Egypt, and, with that easy transmissibility which characterizes ideas, it moved upstream into Ethiopia, which never evolved a culture of its own. Just as noticeable is the political interplay. The rule of the Pharaohs extended far up the Nile, at times to the Third Cataract at 20° N. L.; and at one period Ethiopian kings extended their sway over Egypt. At another, a large body of mutinous Egyptian soldiers abandoned their country and their wives, and emigrated along the one line of slight resistance open to them into Ethiopia, to found there a new state and new families by marriage with native women, thus contributing to the amalgamation of races in the valley.

Identity of country with river valley.   The most pronounced types of the identity of a country with a river valley are found where strongly marked geographical boundaries, like deserts and mountains, emphasize the inner unity of the basins by accentuating their isolation from without. This is especially the case in high mountain regions; here canton or commune or county coincides with the river valley. Population hugs the margins of the streams where alone is soil fit for cultivation, and fairly level land suitable for dwellings. Above are the unoccupied heights, at once barrier and boundary. In the Alps, Salzburg is approximately identical with the valley of the Salzach, Uri with that of the Reuss, the Valais with the upper Rhone, the Engadine with the upper Inn, Glarus with the Linth, Graubunden or Grisons with the upper Rhine, Valtellina with the Adda. So in the great upheaved area of the Himalayas, the state of Kashmir was originally the valley of the upper Jhelam River, while Assam, in its correct delimitation, is the valley of the Brahmaputra between the Himalayan gorge and the swamps of Bengal.[62]

In mountain regions which are also arid, the identity of a district with a stream basin becomes yet more pronounced, because here population must gather about the common water supply, must organize to secure its fair distribution, and cooperate in the construction of irrigation channels to make the distribution as economical and effective as possible. Thus in Chinese Turkestan, the districts of Yarkand, Kashgar, Aksu and Kut-sha are identical with as many mountain tributaries of the Tarim, whose basin in turn comprises almost the whole of Chinese Turkestan.

In all such desert and mountain-rimmed valleys, the central stream attracts to its narrow hem of alluvial soil the majority of the population, determines the course of the main highroad, and is itself often the only route through the encompassing barriers. Hence the importance attached to the river by the inhabitants, an importance reflected in the fact that the river often gives its name to the whole district. To the most ancient Greeks *Aigiptos* meant the river, whose name was later transferred to the whole land; for the narrow arable strip which constituted Egypt was "the gift of the Nile." The Aryans, descending into India through the mountains on its northwest border, gave the name of *Sindhu*, "the flood" or "the ocean," to the first great river they met. In the mouth of Persians and Greeks the name was corrupted into Indus, and then applied to the whole country; but it still survives in its original form in the local designation of the Sind province, which comprises the valley of the Indus below the confluence of the five rivers, which again formed and named the original Punjab. Significantly enough the western political boundary of the Sind extends into the barren foothills of Baluchistan only so far as the affluents of the Indus render the land arable by irrigation; for the

(margin note: Enclosed river valleys.)

Indus performs for the great province of the Sind, by annual inundation and perennial irrigation, the same service that the Nile does for Egypt. The segregation of such districts, and the concentration of their interests and activities along the central streams have tended to develop in the population an intense but contracted national consciousness, and to lend them a distinctive history. Their rivers become interwoven with their mythology and religion, are gods to be worshipped or appeased, become goals of pilgrimages, or acquire a peculiar sanctity. The Nile, Ganges, Jamna, Jordan, Tiber and Po are such sacred streams, while the Rhine figures in German mythology.

Rivers as boundaries of races and peoples. From the uniting power of rivers it follows that they are poor boundaries. Only mountains and seas divide sharply enough to form scientific frontiers. Rivers may serve as political lines of demarcation and therefore fix political frontiers; but they can never take the place of natural boundaries. A migrating or expanding people tend always to occupy both slopes of a river valley. They run their boundary of race or language across the axis of their river basin, only under exceptional circumstances along the stream itself. The English-French boundary in the St. Lawrence Valley crosses the river in a broad transitional zone of mingled people and speech in and above the city of Montreal. The French-German linguistic frontier in Switzerland crosses the upper Rhone Valley just above Sierre, but the whole canton of Valais above the elbow of the river at Martigny shows fundamental ethnic unity, indicated by identity of head form, stature and coloring.[63] Where the Elbe flows through the low plains of North Germany, its whole broad valley is occupied by a pure Teutonic population—fair, tall, longheaded; a more brunette type occupies its middle course across the uplands of Saxony, and speaks German like the downstream folk; but its upper course, hemmed in by the Erz and Riesen Mountains, shows the short, dark and broad-headed people of the Bohemian basin, speaking the Czech language.[64] On the Danube, too, the same thing is true. The upper stream is German in language and predominantly Alpine in race stock down to the Austro-Hungarian boundary; from this point to the Drave mouth it is Hungarian; and from the Drave to the Iron Gate it is Serbo-Croatian on both banks.[65]   Lines of ethnic demarcation, therefore, cut the Elbe and Danube transversely, not longitudinally. [See map page 223.]

The statements of Cæsar and Pliny that the Seine and Marne formed the boundary between the Gauls and Belgians, and the Garonne that between the Gauls and Aquitanians, must be accepted merely as general and preliminary; for exceptions are noted later in the text.   Parisii, for instance, were represented as holding both banks of the Seine and Marne at their confluence, and the Gallic Bituriges were found on the Aquitanian side of the Garonne estuary.

Only under peculiar conditions do rivers become effective as ethnic, tribal or political boundaries.   Most often it is some physiographic feature which makes the stream an obstacle to communication, and lends it the character of a scientific boundary.   The division of the Alpine foreland of southern Germany first into tribal and later into political provinces by the Iller, Lech, Inn, and Salzach can be ascribed in part to the tumultuous course of these streams from the mountains to the Danube, which renders them useless for communication.[66]   The lower Danube forms a well maintained linguistic boundary between the Bulgarians and Roumanians, except in the northwest corner of Bulgaria, where the hill country between the Timok River and the Danube has enticed a small group of Roumanians across to the southern side.   From this point down the stream, a long stretch of low marshy bank on the northern side, offering village sites only at the few places where the loess terrace of Roumania comes close to the river, exposed to overflows, strewn with swamps and lakes, and generally unfit for settlement, has made the Danube an effective barrier.[67]   Similarly, the broad, sluggish Shannon River, which spreads out to lake breadth at close intervals in its course across the boggy central plain of Ireland, has from the earliest times proved a sufficient barrier to divide the plain into two portions, Connaught and Meath,[68] contrasted in history, in speech and

Scientific river boundaries.

to some extent even in race elements.[69] A different cause gave the Thames its unique rôle among the larger English rivers as a boundary between counties from source to mouth. London's fortified position at the head of the Thames estuary closed this stream as a line of invasion to the early Saxons, and forced them to make detours to the north and south of the river, which therefore became a tribal boundary.[70]

Where navigation is peculiarly backward, a river may present a barrier. An instructive instance is afforded by the River Yo, which flows eastward through northern Bornu into Lake Chad, and serves at once as boundary and protection to the agricultural tribes of the Kanuri against the depredations of the Tibbu robbers living in the Sahara or the northern grassland. But during the dry season from April to August, when the trickling stream is sucked up by the thirsty land and thirstier air, the Tibbu horsemen sweep down on the unprotected Kanuri and retreat with their booty across the vanished barrier. The primitive navigation by reed or brushwood rafts, practiced in this almost streamless district, affords no means of retreat for mounted robbers; so the raiding season opens with the fall of the river.[71]

Rivers as political boundaries. For political boundaries, which are often adopted with little reference to race distribution, rivers serve fairly well. They are convenient lines of demarcation and strategic lines of defense, as is proved by the military history of the Rhine, Danube, Ebro, Po, and countless other streams. On the lower Zambesi Livingstone found the territories of the lesser chiefs defined by the rivulets draining into the main river. The leader of the Makololo formally adopted the Zambesi as his political and military frontier, though his people spread and settled beyond the river.[72] Long established political frontiers may become ethnic boundaries, more or less distinct, because of protracted political exclusion. To the Romans, the Danube and Rhine as a northeastern frontier had the value chiefly of established lines in an imperfectly explored wilderness, and of strategic positions for the defense of an oft assailed border; but the long maintenance of this political frontier resulted in the partial segregation

and hence differentiation of the people dwelling on the opposite banks.

Poor as a scientific boundary, a river is not satisfactory
even as a line of demarcation, because of its tendency to
shift its bed in every level stretch of its course. A political
boundary that follows a river, therefore, is often doomed to
frequent surveys. The plantations on the meanders of the
lower Mississippi are connected now with one, now with the
other of the contiguous states, as the great stream straight-
ens its course after the almost annual overflow.[73] The Rio
Grande has proved a troublesome and expensive boundary
between the United States and Mexico. Almost every rise
sees it cutting a new channel for itself, now through Texas,
now through Mexican territory, occasioning endless contro-
versies as to the ownership of the detached land, and de-
manding fresh surveys. Recent changes in the lower course
of the Helmund between Nasralabad and the Sistan Swamp,
which was adopted in 1872 as the boundary between Afghanistan and Persia, have necessitated a new demarcation of the
frontier; and on this task a commission is at present engaged.[74] In a like manner Strabo tells us that the River
Achelous, forming the boundary between ancient Acarnania
and Aetolia in western Hellas, by overflowing its delta region, constantly obliterated the boundaries agreed upon by
the two neighbors, and thereby gave rise to disputes that
were only settled by force of arms.[75]

Rivers tend always to be centers of population, not out- Fluvial
skirts or perimeters. They offer advantages that have al- settlements
ways attracted settlement—fertile alluvial soil, a nearby and peoples.
water supply, command of a natural highway for intercourse with neighbors and access to markets. Among civilized
peoples fluvial settlements have been the nuclei of broad
states, passing rapidly through an embryonic development
to a maturity in which the old center can still be distinguished by a greater density of population. Only among
savages or among civilized people who have temporarily
reverted to primitive conditions in virgin colonial lands, do
we find genuine riverine folk, whose existence is closely restricted to their bordering streams. The river tribes of the

Congo occupy the banks or the larger islands, while the land only three or four miles back from the stream is held by different tribes with whom the riverine people trade their fish. The latter are expert fishermen and navigators, and good agriculturists, raising a variety of fruits and vegetables. On the river banks at regular intervals are market greens, neutral ground, whither people come from up and down stream and from the interior to trade. Their long riparian villages consist of a single street, thirty feet wide and often two miles long, on which face perhaps three hundred long houses.[76] Fisher and canoe people line the Welle, the great northern tributary of the Congo.[77] The same type appeared in South America in the aboriginal Caribs and Tupis dwelling along the southern tributaries of the Amazon and the affluents of the Paraguay. These were distinctly a water race, having achieved a meager development only in navigation, fishing and the cultivation of their alluvial soil.[78] The ancient mound-builders of America located their villages chiefly, though not exclusively, along the principal watercourses, like the Mississippi, Illinois, Miami, Wabash, Wisconsin, and Fox,[79] on the very streams later dotted by the trading posts of the French voyageurs.

Riparian villages of French Canada. The presence of the great waterways of Canada and the demand of the fur trade for extensive and easy communication made the early French colonists as distinctly a riverine people as the savage Congo tribes. Like these, they stretched out their villages in a single line of cabins and clearings, three or four miles long, facing the river, which was the King's highway. Such a village was called a *côte*. One *côte* ran into the next, for their expansion was always longitudinal, never lateral. These riparian settlements lined the main watercourses of French Canada, especially the St. Lawrence, whose shores from Beaupre, fifteen miles below Quebec, up to Montreal at an early date presented the appearance of a single street. Along the river passed the stately trading ship from France with its cargo of wives and merchandise for the colonists, the pirogue of the *habitant* farmer carrying his onions and grain to the Quebec market, the birchbark canoe of the adventurous voyageur bringing

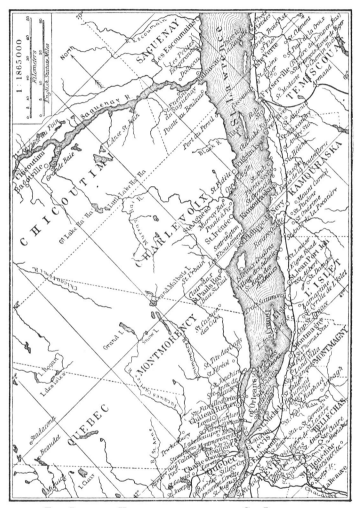

THE RIPARIAN VILLAGES OF THE LOWER ST. LAWRENCE.

down his winter's hunt of furs from the snow-bound forests of the interior, and the fleet of Jesuit priests bound to some remote inland mission.

On this water thoroughfare every dwelling faced. Hence land on the river was at a premium, while that two miles back was to be had for the taking. The original grants measured generally 766 feet in width and 7,660 in depth inland; but when bequeathed from generation to generation, they were divided up along lines running back at right angles to the all important waterway. Hence each *habitant* farm measured its precious river-front by the foot and its depth by the mile, while the cabins were ranged side by side in cosy neighborliness. The *côte* type of village, though eminently convenient for the Indian trade, was ill adapted for government and defense against the savages; but the need for the communication supplied by the river was so fundamental, that it nullified all efforts of the authorities to concentrate the colonists in more compact settlements. Parkman says: "One could have seen almost every house in Canada by paddling a canoe up the St. Lawrence and Richelieu." [80]   The same type of land-holding can be traced today on the Chaudiere River, where the fences run back from the stream like the teeth of a comb. It is reproduced on a larger scale in the long, narrow counties ranged along the lower St. Lawrence, whose shape points to the old fluvial nuclei of settlement. Similarly the early Dutch grants on the Hudson gave to the patroons four miles along the river and an indefinite extension back from the stream. In the early Connecticut River settlements, the same consideration of a share in the river and its alluvial bottoms distributed the town lots among the inhabitants in long narrow strips running back from the banks.[81]

Boatman tribes or castes.

In undeveloped countries, where rivers are the chief highways, we occasionally see the survival of a distinct race of boatmen amid an intruding people of different stock, preserved in their purity by their peculiar occupation, which has given them the aloofness of a caste. In the Kwang-tung province of southern China are 40,000 Tanka boat people, who live in boats and pile-dwellings in the Canton River.

The Chinese, from whom they are quite distinct, regard them as a remnant of the original population, which was dislodged by their invasion and forced to take refuge on the water. They gradually established intercourse with the conquerors of the land, but held themselves aloof. They marry only among themselves, have their own customs, and enjoy a practical monopoly of carrying passengers and messages between the steamers and the shore at Macao, Hongkong and Canton.[82] In the same way, the middle Niger above Gao possesses a distinct aquatic people, the Somnos or Bosos, who earn their living as fishermen and boatmen on the river. They spread their villages along the Niger and its tributaries, and occupy separate quarters in the large towns like Gao and Timbuctoo. They are creatures of the river rather than of the land, and show great skill and endurance in paddling and poling their narrow dugouts on their long Niger voyages.[83]

Reference has been made before to the large river population of China who live on boats and rafts, and forward the trade of the vast inland waterways. These are people, differentiated not in race, but in occupation and mode of life, constantly recruited from the congested population of the land. Allied to them are the trackers or towing crews whose villages form a distinctive feature of the turbulent upper Yangtze, and who are employed, sometimes three hundred at a time, to drag junks up the succession of rapids above Ichang.[84] Similarly the complex of navigable waterways centering about Paris, as far back as the reign of Tiberius Cæsar, gave rise to the *Nautae Parisii* or guild of mariners, from whom the city of Paris derived its present coat of arms—a vessel under full sail. These Lutetian boatmen handled the river traffic in all the territory drained by the Seine, Marne, and Oise. Later, in the reign of Louis the Fat, they were succeeded by the *Mercatores aquae Parisiaci*, and from them sprang the municipal body appointed to regulate the river navigation and commerce.[85]

The location of the ancient tribe of the Parisii is typical of many other weak riverine folk who seek in the islands of a river a protected position to compensate for their

River islands as protected sites.

paucity of number. The Parisii, one of the smallest of the
Gallic tribes, ill-matched against their populous neighbors,
took refuge on ten islands and sandbars of the Seine and
there established themselves.[86]   Stanley found an island in
the Congo near the second cataract of Stanley Falls occupied by five villages of the Baswa, who had taken refuge
there from the attacks of the bloodthirsty Bakuma.[87]   During the Tartar invasions of Russia in the thirteenth and fourteenth centuries, bands of refugees from the surrounding
country gathered for mutual defense on the islands of the
Dnieper River, and became the nucleus of the Dnieper Cossacks.[88]   The Huron tribe of American Indians, reduced to
a mere fragment by repeated Iroquois attacks, fled first to
the islands of St. Joseph and Michilimackinac in Lake Huron, and in 1656 to the Isle of Orleans in the St. Lawrence.
But even this location under the guns of their French allies
in Quebec failed to protect them, for the St. Lawrence was
a highway for the war fleets of their implacable foe.[89]

River and lake is-lands as robber strongholds.   A river island not only confers the negative benefit of
protection, but affords a coign of vantage for raids on
the surrounding country, being to some extent proof against
punitive attacks.   It offers special facilities for depredations on parties crossing the river; here the divided current,
losing something of its force, is less of an obstacle, and the
island serves as a resting place on the passage.   Immunity
from punishment breeds lawlessness.   The Ba Toka who,
fifty years ago, inhabited the islands in the great southern
bend of the Zambesi, utilized their location to lure wandering tribes on to their islands, under the pretext of ferry-
ing them across, and then to rob them, till Sebituane, the
great Makololo chief, cleaned out their fastnesses and opened
the river for trade.[90]   The islands in the wide stretches of
the Lualaba River in the Babemba country were described
to Livingstone as harboring a population of marauders and
robbers, who felt themselves safe from attack.[91]   The same
unenviable reputation attaches to the Budumas of the Lake
Chad islands.   A weak, timid, displaced people, they nevertheless lose no chance of raiding the herds of the Sudanese
tribes inhabiting the shores of the Lake, and carrying off

the stolen cattle on their wretched rafts to their island retreats.[92]

The protection of an island location is almost equalled in the peninsulas formed by the serpentines or meanders of a river. Hence these are choice sites for fortress or settlement in primitive communities, where hostilities are always imminent and rivers the sole means of communication. The defensive works of the mound-builders in great numbers occupied such river peninsulas. The neck of the loop was fortified by a single or double line of ditch and earthen wall, constructed from bank to bank of the encircling stream.[93] This was exactly the location of Vesontio, now Besançon, once the ancient stronghold of the Sequani in eastern Gaul. It was situated in a loop of the Dubis, so nearly a circle that its course seems to have been "described by a compass," Cæsar says, while fortifications across the isthmus made the position of the town almost impregnable.[94] Verona, lying at the exit of the great martial highway of the Brenner Pass, occupies just such a loop of the Adige, as does Capua on the Volturno, and Berne on the Aare. Shrewsbury, in the Middle Ages an important military point for the preservation of order on the marches of Wales, is almost encircled by the River Severn, while a castle on the neck of the peninsula completes the defense on the land side.[95] Graaf Reinett, at one time an exposed frontier settlement of the Dutch in Cape Colony, had a natural moat around it in the Sunday River, which here describes three-fourths of a circle.

The need of protection felt by all colonists in new countries amid savage or barbarous people whom encroachment sooner or later makes hostile, leads them if possible to place their first trading posts and settlements on river islands, especially at the mouth of the streams, where a delta often affords the site required, and where the junction of ocean and river highway offers the best facilities for trade. A river island fixed the location of the English settlement at Jamestown in Virginia, the French at Montreal and New Orleans, the Dutch at Manhattan and Van Renssellær Island in the Hudson, the Swedes at Tinicum Island in the Delaware River a few miles below the mouth

River peninsulas as protected sites.

River islands as sites of trading posts and colonies.

of the Schuylkill.[96] St. Louis, located on a delta island of the Senegal River, is one of the oldest European towns in West Africa; [97] and Bathurst, founded in 1618 on a similar site at the mouth of the Gambia, has for centuries now been the safe outlet for the trade of this stream.[98] Such island settlements at river mouths are a phenomenon of the outer edge of every coastal region; but inland stations for trade or military control also seek the protection of an island site. The Russians in the seventeenth century secured their down-stream conquest of the Amur by a succession of river island forts,[99] which recall Colonel Byrd's early frontier post on an island in the Holston River, and George Rogers Clark's military stockade on Corn Island in the Ohio, which became the nucleus of the later city of Louisville.

Swamps as barriers and boundaries.   More effective than rivers in the protection which they afford are swamps. Neither solid land nor navigable water, their sluggish, passive surface raises an obstacle of pure inertia to the movements of mankind. Hence they form one of those natural boundaries that segregate. In southern England, Romney Marsh, reinforced by the Wealden Forest, fixed the western boundary of the ancient Saxon kingdom of Kent by blocking expansion in that direction, just as the bordering swamps of the Lea and Colne rivers formed the eastern and western boundaries of Middlesex.[100] The Fen-land of the Wash, which extended in Saxon days from the highland about Lincoln south to Cambridge and Newmarket, served to hem in the Angles of Norfolk and Suffolk on the west, so that the occupation of the interior was left to later bands who entered by the estuaries of the Humber and Forth.[101] In northern Germany, the low cross valleys of the Spree, Havel and Netze rivers, bordered by alder swamps, were long a serious obstacle to communication, and therefore became boundaries of districts,[102] just as the Bourtanger Moor drew the dividing line between Holland and Hanover.

Swamps as regions of survival.   Swamp-bordered regions, as areas of natural isolation, guard and keep intact the people which they hold. There-fore they are regions of survival of race and language. The scattered islets of the Fens of England furnished an asylum to the early British Celts from Teutonic attacks,[103] and later protected them against dominant infusion of Teutonic blood. Hence to-day in the Fenland and in the district just to the south we find a darker, shorter people than in the country to the east or west.[104] Similarly the White Russians, occupying the poor, marshy region of uncertain watershed between the sources of the Duna, Dnieper and Volga, have the purest blood of all the eastern Slavs, though this distinction is coupled with poverty and retarded culture,[105] a combination that anthropo-geography often reveals. Wholly distinct from the Russians and segregated from them by a barrier of swampy forests, we find the Letto-Lithuanians in the Baltic province of Courland, speaking the most primitive form of flectional languages classed as Aryan. The isolation which preserved their archaic speech, of all European tongues the nearest to the Sanskrit, made them the last European people to accept Christianity.[106] The great race of the Slavic Wends, who once occupied all northern Germany between the Vistula and Elbe, has left only a small and declining remnant of its language in the swampy forests about the sources of the Spree.[107] [See ethnographical map, p. 223.] The band of marshlands stretching through Holland from the shallow Zuyder Zee east to the German frontier, has given to Friesland and the coast islands of Holland a peculiar isolation, which has favored the development and survival of the peculiar Friesian dialect, that speech so nearly allied to Saxon English, and has preserved here the purest type of the tall, blond Teuton among the otherwise mixed stock of the Netherlands.[108]

Inaccessible to all except those familiar with their treacherous paths and labyrinthine channels, swamps have always afforded a refuge for individuals and peoples; and therefore as places of defense they have played no inconspicuous part in history. What the Dismal Swamp of North Carolina and the cypress swamps of Louisiana were to the runaway slaves, that the Everglades of Florida have been to the defeated Seminoles. In that half-solid, half-fluid area, penetrable only to the native Indian who poles his canoe along its tortuous channels of liquid mud, the Seminoles

Swamps as places of refuge.

have set up their villages on the scattered hummocks of solid land, and there maintained themselves, a tribe of 350 souls, despite all efforts of the United States government to remove them to the Indian Territory. The swamps of the Nile delta have been the asylum of Egyptian independence from the time King Amysis took refuge there for fifty years during an invasion of the Ethiopians,[109] to the retreat thither of Amyrtaeus, a prince of Sais, after his unsuccessful revolt against the Persian conqueror Artaxerxes I.[110] The Isle of Athelney among the marshes of the Parret River afforded a refuge to Alfred the Great and a band of his followers during the Danish invasion of Wessex in 878,[111] while the Isle of Ely in the Fenland was another point of sustained resistance to the invaders. It was the Fenland that two hundred years later was the last stronghold of Saxon resistance to William of Normandy. Here on the Isle of Ely the outlawed leader Hereward maintained Saxon independence, till the Conqueror at last constructed a long causeway across the marshes to the "Camp of Refuge."[112]

The spirit of the marshes. The spirit of the marshlands is the spirit of freedom. Therefore these small and scarcely habitable portions of the land assume an historical dignity and generate stirring historical events out of all proportion to their size and population. Their content is ethical rather than economic. They attract to their fastnesses the vigorous souls protesting against conquest or oppression, and then by their natural protection sustain and nourish the spirit of liberty. It was the water-soaked lowlands of the Rhine that enabled the early Batavians,[113] Ditmarscher and Frieslanders to assert and to maintain their independence, generated the love of independence among the Dutch and helped them defend their liberty against the Spanish[114] and French. So the Fenland of England was the center of resistance to the despotism of King John, who therefore fixed his headquarters for the suppression of the revolt at Lincoln and his military depôt at Lynn. Later in the conflict of the barons with Henry III, Simon de Montfort and other disaffected nobles entrenched themselves in the islands of Ely and Axholm, till the Provisions of Oxford in 1267 secured them some de-

gree of constitutional rights.[115] Four centuries later the
same spirit sent many Fenlanders to the support of Cromwell.

A river that spreads out into the indeterminate earth- Economic
form of a marsh is an effective barrier; but one that gathers and politi-
its waters into a natural basin and forms a lake retains the cal impor-
uniting power of a navigable stream and also, by the exten- lakes.
sion of its area and elimination of its current, approaches
the nature of an enclosed sea. Mountain rivers, characterized
by small volume and turbulent flow, first become navigable
when they check their impetuosity and gather their store of
water in some lake basin. The whole course of the upper
Rhone, from its glacier source on the slope of Mount Furca
to its confluence with the Saone at Lyon, is unfit for navigation, except where it lingers in Lake Geneva. The same
thing is true of the Reuss in Lake Lucerne, the upper Rhine
in Lake Constance, the Aare in Thun and Brienze, and the
Linth in Lake Zurich. Hence such torrent-fed lakes assume
economic and political importance in mountainous regions,
owing to the paucity of navigable waterways. The lakes
of Alpine Switzerland and Italy and of Highland Scotland
form so many centers of intercourse and exchange. Even
such small bodies of water as the Alpine lakes have therefore
become goals of expansion, so that we find the shores of
Geneva, Maggiore, Lugano, and Garda, each shared by two
countries. Switzerland, the Austrian Tyrol, and the three
German states of Baden, Wurtemberg and Bavaria, have all
managed to secure a frontage upon Lake Constance. Lake
Titicaca, lying 12,661 feet (3854 meters) above sea level
but affording a navigable course 136 miles (220 kilometers)
long, is an important waterway for Peru and Bolivia. In
the central Sudan, where aridity reduces the volume of all
streams, even the variable and indeterminate Lake Chad
has been an eagerly sought objective for expanding
boundaries. Twenty years ago it was divided among the
native states of Bornu, Bagirmi and Kanem; today it is
shared by British Nigeria, French Sudan, and German
Kamerun. The erratic northern extension of the German
boundary betrays the effort to reach this goal.

The uniting power of lakes manifests itself in the tendency of such basins to become the nuclei of states. Attractive to settlement in primitive times, because of the protected frontier they afford—a motive finding its most emphatic expression in the pile villages of the early lake-dwellers— later because of the fertility of their bordering soil and the opportunity for friendly intercourse, they gradually unite their shores in a mesh of reciprocal relations, which finds its ultimate expression in political union. It is a significant fact that the Swiss Confederation originated in the four forest cantons of Lucerne, Schwyz, Uri and Unterwalden, which are linked together by the jagged basin of Lake Lucerne or the Lake of the Four Forest Cantons, as the Swiss significantly call it, but are otherwise divided by mountain barriers. So we find that Lake Titicaca was the cradle of the Inca Empire, just as Lake Tezcoco was that of the Toltecs in Mexico and an island in Lake Chalco later that of the Aztec domain.[116]   The most stable of the short-lived native states of Africa have apparently found an element of strength and permanence in a protected lake frontier. Such are the petty kingdoms of Bornu, Bagirmi and Kanem on Lake Chad, and Uganda on Victoria Nyanza.

Large lakes, which include in their area islands, peninsulas, tides, currents, fiords, inlets, deltas, and dunes, and present every geographical feature of an enclosed sea, approach the latter too in historical importance. Some of the largest, however, have long borne the name of seas. The Caspian, which exceeds the Baltic in area, and the Aral, which outranks Lake Michigan, show the closest physical resemblance to thalassic basins, because of their size, salinity and enclosed drainage systems; but their anthropo-geographical significance is slight. The very salinity which groups them with the sea points to an arid climate that forever deprives them of the densely populated coasts characteristic of most enclosed seas, and hence reduces their historical importance. Their tributary streams, robbed of their water by irrigation canals, like "the shorn and parcelled Oxus", renounce their function of highways into the interior. To this rule the Volga is a unique exception. Finally, cut off from union

LAKE OF THE FOUR FOREST CANTONS.
BIRTHPLACE OF THE SWISS CONFEDERATION.

with the ocean, these salt lakes lose the supreme historical advantage which is maintained by freshwater lakes, like Ladoga, Nyassa, Maracaibo and the Great Lakes of North America, all lying near sea level.

Lakes as part of a system of inland waterways may possess commercial importance surpassing that of many seas. This depends upon the productivity, accessibility and extent of their hinterland, and this in turn depends upon the size and shape of the inland basin. The chain of the five Great Lakes, which together present a coastline of four thousand miles and a navigable course as long as the Baltic between the Skager Rack and the head of the Gulf of Bothnia, constitutes a freshwater Mediterranean. It has played the part of an enclosed sea in American history and has enabled the Atlantic trade to penetrate 1400 miles inland to Chicago and Duluth. Its shores have therefore been a coveted object of territorial expansion. The early Dutch trading posts headed up the Hudson and Mohawk toward Lake Ontario, as did the English settlements which succeeded them. The French, from their vantage point at Montreal, threw out a frail casting-net of fur stations and missions, which caught and held all the Lakes for a time. Later the American shores were divided among eight of our states. The northern boundaries of Indiana and Illinois were fixed by Congress for the express purpose of giving these commonwealths access to Lake Michigan. Pennsylvania with great difficulty succeeded in protruding her northwestern frontier to cover a meager strip of Erie coast, while New York's frontage on the same lake became during the period of canal and early railroad construction, a great factor in her development. *Lakes as fresh water seas.*

In 1901, the tonnage of our merchant vessels on the Great Lakes was half that of our Pacific, Atlantic and Gulf coasts combined,[117] constituting a freshwater fleet greater than the merchant marine of either France or sea-bred Norway. A remote but by no means faint echo of this fact is found in the five hundred or more boats, equally available for trade or war, which Henry M. Stanley saw the Uganda prince muster on the shore of Victoria Nyanza Lake.

Ocean, sea, bay, estuary, river, swamp, lake: here is
Nature's great circle returning upon itself, a circle faintly
notched into arcs, but one in itself and one in man's uses.

NOTES TO CHAPTER XI

1. Isabella B. Bishop, The Yangtze Valley and Beyond, Vol. I, pp. 26-
27. New York and London, 1900.

2. Fiske, Discovery of America, Vol. I, p. 492. Boston, 1892.

3. Capt. James Cook, Voyage to the Pacific Ocean, 1776-1780, Vol. 11,
pp. 321-332. New York, 1796.

4. John Richard Green, The Making of England, Vol. I, pp. 63-66, 84-
86, 95, 96. London, 1904.

5. E. Lavisse, *Histoire de France*, Vol. II, Part I, pp. 374-375, 378-379,
381-382, 385-386. Paris, 1903.

6. Helmolt, History of the World, Vol. I, pp. 189-191, map. New
York, 1902-1906.

7. *Ibid.*, Vol. I, pp. 192-194.

8. G. W. Kitchen, History of France, Vol. I, pp. 59-60. Oxford, 1892.

9. Dietrich Schaeffer, *Die Hansestädte und König Waldemar von
Dänemark*, p. 36. Jena, 1879.

10. G. G. Chisholm, Commercial Geography, p. 311. London, 1904.

11. Capt. A. T. Mahan, The Problem of Asia, pp. 41, 60, 120. New
York, 1900.

12. Isabella B. Bishop, The Yangtze Valley and Beyond, Vol. I, pp.
97-98. New York and London, 1900.

13. E. C. Semple, Development of the Hanse Towns in Relation to
their Geographic Environment, Bulletin Amer. Geog. Soc., Vol. 31. No.
3. 1899.

14. Nordenskiold, Voyage of the Vega, pp. 519-530, 552. New York,
1882. Anatole Leroy-Beaulieu, The Empire of the Tsars, Vol. I, Note
pp. 278-281. New York, 1902.

15. Agnes Laut, Voyagers of the Northern Ocean, *Harper's Magazine*,
January, 1906.

16. Alexis Krausse, Russia in Asia, pp. 21-54. New York, 1899.

17 Felix Dubois, Timbuctoo, pp. 198-199, 251-257. New York, 1896.

18. *Ibid.*, p. 38.

19. D. Livingstone, Missionary Travels, pp. 71, 177. New York, 1858.

20. W. Deecke, Italy, p. 87. London, 1904.

21. G. Adam Smith, Historical Geography of the Holy Land, map
facing p. 167; also pp. 287, 327-328. New York, 1897.

22. F. M. Stapff, *Karte des unteren Khiusebthal, Petermanns Mitteilungen*, p. 202. July, 1885.

23. Strabo, Book III, chap. II, 4.

24. For full discussion, see Roscher, *National-Oekonomik des Handels
und Gewerbefleisses*. Stuttgart, 1889.

25. Rambaud, History of Russia, Vol. I, pp. 24-28. Boston, 1886.

26. A. B. Hulbert, Historic Highways of America, Vol. VII, Portage Paths, pp. 182-183, 187-188. Cleveland, 1903.

27. Herodotus, Book I, 194. A H. Layard, Nineveh and Its Remains, Vol. II, pp. 79-81. New York, 1849.

28. Charles W. Hawes, The Uttermost East, p. 60. New York, 1904.

29. Transportation by Water in 1906, Table 30, p. 181. Report of Department of Commerce and Labor, Washington, 1908.

30. G. G. Chisholm, Commercial Geography, p. 277. London, 1904.

31. E. A. Freeman, Historical Geography of Europe, p. 466. London. 1882.

32. J. Ellis Barker, Modern Germany, pp. 68-85. London, 1907.

33. Heinrich von Treitschke, *Politik*, Vol. I, p. 218. Leipzig, 1897.

34. E. A. Freeman, Historical Geography of Europe, p. 466. London, 1882.

35. G. G. Chisholm, Commercial Geography, p. 511. London, 1904.

36. J. Partsch, Central Europe, p. 318. London, 1903.

37. Ratzel, *Politische Geographie*, pp. 739-740. Munich, 1903.

38. Annual Register for 1901, p. 358. New Series, London and New York, 1902.

39. H. R. Mill, International Geography, p. 958. New York, 1902.

40. Ratzel, History of Mankind, Vol. III, p. 473. London, 1896-1898.

41. H. R. Mill, International Geography, p. 406. New York, 1902.

42. G. G. Chisholm, Commercial Geography, map p. 312. London, 1904.

43. Blanqui, History of Political Economy, pp. 273, 277, 296. New York, 1880.

44. Albert Gallatin, American State Papers, Misc. Doc., Vol. I, No. 250. Washington, 1834.

45. Roscher, *National-Oekonomik des Handels und Gewerbefleisses*, pp. 449, 453-454. Stuttgart, 1889.

46. H. R. Mill, International Geography, pp. 530-531. New York, 1902.

47. G. G. Chisholm, Commercial Geography, pp. 310, 312. London, 1904.

48. J. Partsch, Central Europe, p. 314. London, 1903.

49. Statesman's Yearbook for 1907.

50. Henry Norman, All the Russias, pp. 254-255, 285-292. New York, 1902.

51. E. C. Semple, American History and Its Geographic Conditions, pp. 251-255. Boston, 1903.

52. E. F. Knight, Where Three Empires Meet, p. 6. London, 1897.

53. Strabo, Book IV, chap. VI, 7.

54. Alexis Krausse, Russia in Asia, pp. 361-362. New York, 1899.

55. Angus Hamilton, Afghanistan, pp. 137-141. New York and London, 1906. Henry Norman, All the Russias, pp. 276-277. New York, 1902.

56. *Bello Gallico*, Book IV, chap. IV.

57. *Ibid.*, Book I, chap. XXXI; Book II, chap. III; Book IV, chap. I.

58. Journals of Dr. Thomas Walker and Christopher Gist, p. 129. Filson Club Publications, Louisville, 1898.

59. H. R. Schoolcraft, Indian Tribes of the United States, Vol. III, pp. 248-249. Philadelphia, 1853.

60. Martha K. Genthe, The Valley Towns of Connecticut, Bull. of Amer. Geog. Society, Vol. 39, pp. 1-7. New York, 1907.

61. Ratzel, History of Mankind, Vol. III, pp. 181-182, 192. London, 1898.

62. H. R. Mill, International Geography, p. 495. New York, 1902.

63. W. Z. Ripley, Races of Europe, pp. 284-285. New York, 1899.

64. *Ibid.*, Maps pp. 222, 340, 350.

65. *Ibid.*, Maps pp. 402, 429.

66. J. Partsch, Central Europe, pp. 43, 241. London, 1903.

67. *Ibid.*, p. 69. Sydow-Wagner, *Methodischer Schul-Atlas*, compare maps No. 13 and No. 25.

68. Elisée Reclus, Europe, Vol. IV, pp. 380, 389-390. New York, 1882.

69. W. Z. Ripley, Races of Europe, p. 318, map. New York, 1899.

70. H. J. Mackinder, Britain and the British Seas, pp. 202-203. London, 1904.

71. Boyd Alexander, From the Niger to the Nile, Vol. I, pp. 168, 169, 232, 306-307. London, 1907.

72. Livingstone, Missionary Travels, pp. 102, 642. New York, 1858.

73. See Century Atlas, maps of Mississippi, Louisiana and Arkansas for boundary line of 1850.

74. Sir Thomas Holdich, India, p. 57. London, 1905.

75. Strabo, Book X, chap. II, 19.

76. Henry M. Stanley, Through the Dark Continent, Vol. II, pp. 120-124, 155-158, 168, 169, 173, 176, 177, 182, 266-274, 327. New York, 1879.

77. Boyd Alexander, From the Niger to the Nile, Vol. II, pp. 252, 269-270. London, 1907.

78. Helmolt, History of the World, Vol. I, pp. 189, 192-194. New York, 1902-1906.

79. Cyrus Thomas, Mound Explorations, pp. 526-527, 531, 551. Twelfth Annual Report of Bureau of Ethnology, Washington, 1894.

80. Parkman, The Old Regime in Canada, pp. 292-303. Boston, 1904. E. C. Semple, The Influences of Geographic Environment on the Lower St. Lawrence, Bull. of Amer. Geog. Society, Vol. 36, pp. 449-466. 1904.

81. Martha Krug Genthe, Valley Towns of Connecticut, pp. 10-12, figures V. and VI, Bull. of Amer. Geog. Society, Vol. 39, 1907.

82. J. Nacken, *Die Provinz Kwantung und ihre Bevölkerung, Petermanns Mitteilungen*, Vol. 24, p. 421, 1878. W. M. Wood, Fankwei, pp. 276-277. New York, 1859.

83. Felix Dubois, Timbuctoo, pp. 19-22, 38. New York, 1896.

84. Isabella B. Bishop, The Yangtze Valley and Beyond, Vol. I, pp. 164, 174-175, 179, 182, 189, 215. London and New York, 1900.

85. William Walton, Paris, Vol. I, pp. 31-32, 35. Philadelphia, 1899.

86. Cæsar, *Bello Gallico*, Book VIII, chaps, 57, 58.

87. Henry M. Stanley, Through the Dark Continent, Vol. II, pp. 227-228. New York, 1879.

88. Article, Cossack, Encyclopedia Britannica.

89. Parkman, The Jesuits in North America, pp. 292-303, 498-505, 534, 535. Boston, 1904.

90. Livingstone, Missionary Travels, pp. 100, 102. New York, 1858.

91. Livingstone, Last Journals, Vol. I, p. 359. London, 1874.

92. Heinrich Barth, Travels in North and Central Africa, Vol. II, pp. 64, 66, 233. New York, 1857. Boyd Alexander, From the Niger to the Nile, Vol. I, pp. 237, 303-304, 320, 331-336; Vol. II, pp. 54, 56-58, 67-68, 96-99, 104-105. London, 1907.

93. J. P. McLean, The Mound Builders, p. 20. Cincinnati, 1904. Squier and Davis, Ancient Monuments of the Mississippi Valley, pp. 6, 9, 10. New York, 1848.

94. Cæsar, *Bello Gallico*, Book I, chaps. 38, 39.

95. Elisée Reclus, Europe, Vol. IV, pp. 101-102. New York, 1882.

96. John Fiske, Dutch and Quaker Colonies in America, Vol. I, p. 241. Boston.

97. H. R. Mill, International Geography, p. 956. New York, 1902.

98. H. B. George, Historical Geography of the British Empire, pp. 259-260. London, 1904.

99. Alexis Krausse, Russia in Asia, pp. 30-33, 50. New York, 1899.

100. H. J. Mackinder, Britain and the British Seas, pp. 198-199. London, 1904.

101. John Richard Green, The Making of England, Vol. I, pp. 63, 66. London, 1904.

102. J. Partsch, Central Europe, p. 102. London, 1903.

103. Miller and Skertchley, The Fenland Past and Present, pp. 10, 11, 27-30. London, 1878.

104. W. Z. Ripley, Races of Europe, pp. 322-323. Map p. 327. New York, 1899.

105. Anatole Leroy-Beaulieu, The Empire of the Tsars, Vol. I, p. 108. New York, 1893.

106. *Ibid.*, pp. 104-106. W. Z. Ripley, Races of Europe, pp. 340-342, 352, 365. New York, 1899.

107. J. Partsch, Central Europe, p. 135. London, 1903.

108. *Ibid.*, p. 133. W. Z. Ripley, Races of Europe, pp. 294-295. New York, 1899.

109. Herodotus, II, 137, 140.

110. Thucydides, I, 110. Brugsch-Bey, History of Egypt, Vol. II, p. 333. London, 1881.

111. John Richard Green, History of the English People, Vol. I, chap. III, p. 71.

112. Miller and Skertchley, The Fenland Past and Present, pp. 83, 101, 104, 107, 108. London, 1878.

113. Tacitus, History of the Germans, Book VI, chap. VI. Motley, Rise of the Dutch Republic, Vol. I, pp. 2-5, 13. New York, 1885.

114. J. Partsch, Central Europe, p. 299. London, 1903.

115. Miller and Skertchley, The Fenland Past and Present, pp. 113-114. London, 1878.

116. Edward John Payne, History of the New World Called America, Vol. I, pp. 327-328, 502-503. Oxford, 1892. Ratzel, History of Mankind, Vol. II, p. 163. London, 1896-1898.

117. U. S. Report of Commission of Navigation, p. 10. Washington, 1901.

CHAPTER XII

CONTINENTS AND THEIR PENINSULAS

Insularity
of the
land-
masses. THE division of the earth's surface into 28 per cent. land
and 72 per cent. water is an all important fact of physical
geography and anthropo-geography. Owing to this proportion, the land-masses, which alone provide habitats for
man, rise as islands out of the three-fold larger surface of the
uninhabitable ocean. Consequently, the human species, like
the other forms of terrestrial life, bears a deeply ingrained
insular character. Moreover, the water causes different
degrees of separation between the land-masses, according as
it appears as inlet, strait, sea, an island-strewn or islandless
ocean ; it determines the grouping of the habitable areas and
consequently the geographic basis of the various degrees
of ethnic and cultural kinship between the divisions of land.
Finally, since the sea is for man only a highway to some ulterior shore, this geography of the land-masses in relation
to the encompassing waters points the routes and goals of
human wanderings.

Each fragment of habitable land, large or small, continent
or islet, means a corresponding group or detachment of the
vast human family. Its size fixes the area at the service of
the group which occupies it. Its location, however, may
either endow it with a neighborliness like that subsisting
between Africa and Europe and involving an interwoven history ; or remoteness like that of South America from
Australia, so complete that even the close net of intercourse
thrown by modern commerce over the whole world has scarcely
sufficed to bring them into touch. Therefore the highly
irregular distribution of the land areas, here compactly
grouped, there remote, deserves especial attention, since it
produces far-reaching results. Finally, continents and
islands, by their zonal situation, their land forms, rainfall,
river systems, flora and fauna, produce for man varied life

conditions, which in their turn are partially dependent upon the size and grouping of the land-masses.

A comparison of the large and small land-masses of the earth from the standpoint of both physical and anthropological geography yields a classification based upon size and location on the one hand, and historical influences on the other. The following table indicates the relation between the two. *Classification of land-masses according to size and location.*

I. Independent Land-masses.

    A. *Continents.* Independent by reason of size, which enables them to support a large number of people and afford the conditions for civilization.

        (a) Insular continents, whose primitive and modern development are marked by remoteness. Australia.

        (b) Neighboring continents, separated by narrow seas and showing community of historical events. Europe and Africa. Asia and North America around Bering Sea.

    B. *Islands.* Independent by reason of location.

        (a) Oceanic islands, characterized by greatest remoteness from continents and other islands, and also by independent or detached history. St. Helena and Iceland.

        (b) Member of a group of oceanic islands, therefore less independent. Hawaii, Fayal in the Azores, Tongatabu.

        (c) Large islands, approaching by reason of size the independence of continents and thereby finding compensation for a less independent location. New Guinea, Borneo, Madagascar; in a cultural sense, Great Britain and Japan.

II. Dependent Land-masses.

        (a) Inshore or coast islands, whose history is intimately connected with that of the nearby mainland. Euboea, Long Island, Vancouver, Sakhalin, Ceylon.

        (b) Neighboring islands, showing less intimate historical relations. Formosa, the Canaries, Ireland in contrast to Great Britain.

(c) Islands of enclosed or marginal seas, contained in a circle of lands and exposed to constant intercourse from all sides. Jamaica, Java, Crete, Sicily, Zealand, Gotland, St. Lawrence in Bering Sea.

(d) Island groups not to be considered apart from other groups. Samoa, Fiji and Friendly Isles; Philippine, Sulu and Sunda Islands; Greater and Lesser Antilles.

Effect of size of land-masses.

As the homes of man, these land-masses vary greatly owing to difference of size. Only the six continents have been large enough to generate great bodies of people, to produce differentiated branches of the human family, and to maintain them in such numerical force that alien intermixtures were powerless essentially to modify the gradually developing ethnic type. The larger continents are marked by such diversity of climate, relief and contour, that they have afforded the varied environments and the area for the development of several great types or sub-types of mankind. Australia has been just large enough to produce one distinct native race, the result of a very ancient blend of Papuan and Malayan stocks. But prevailing aridity has cast a mantle of monotony over most of the continent, nullifying many local geographic differences in highland and lowland, curtailing the available area of its already restricted surface, and hence checking the differentiation that results either from the competition of large numbers or from a varied environment. We find Australia characterized above all other continents by monotony of culture, mode of life, customs, languages, and a uniform race type from the Murray River to York peninsula.[1] The twin continents of the Americas developed a race singularly uniform in its physical traits,[2] if we leave out of account the markedly divergent Eskimos, but displaying a wide range of political, social and economic developments, from the small, unorganized groups of wandering savages, like the desert Shoshones and coast Fuegians, to the large, stable empire of the Incas, with intensive agriculture, public works, a state religion and an enlightened government.

Even the largest islands of the world, such as **Borneo**,

New Guinea and Madagascar, show no such independent ethnic development. This is the distinguishing characteristic of the largest land-masses. Europe, except on the basis of its size and peninsula form, has no title to the name of continent; certainly not on anthropo-geographical grounds. Its classification as a continent arose in the Mediterranean among the Greeks, as a geographical expression of the antagonism between themselves and their Carian, Phœnician and Persian enemies across the Aegean; the idea had therefore a political origin, and was formed without knowledge of that vast stretch of plains between the Black Sea and the Arctic Ocean, where Asia's climate and races lap over into Europe, and where to-day we find the Muscovite Empire, in point of geographic conditions, its underlying ethnic stock and form of government, as much Asiatic as European. The real or western Europe, which the Roman Empire gradually added to the narrow Europe of the Greeks, and which is strikingly contrasted to Asia in point of size, relief, contour, climate and races, only served to maintain the distinction between the two continents in men's minds. But from a geographical standpoint the distinction is an error. It has confused the interpretation of the history of the Greeks and the development of the Russians. It has brought disorder into the question of the European or Asiatic origin of the Aryan linguistic family, which the anthropo-geographer would assign to the single continent of Eurasia. The independent development that falls to the lot of great world islands like the Americas and Australia is impossible in a peninsular continent like Europe, large as it is.

The independence of a land-mass is based not alone on size: there is also an independence of location. This, owing to the spherical form of the earth, tends to be neutralized by the independence based upon large area. The larger a land-mass is, the nearer it approaches to others. Eurasia, the largest of all the continents, comes into close proximity and therefore close relations with Africa, North America, and even Australia; whereas Australia is at once the smallest and the most isolated of the continents. The remote oceanic islands of the Atlantic Ocean, measuring only a few square

Independence of location versus independence of size.

miles in   area, have a location so independent of other inhabited lands, that before the period of the great discoveries
they had never appeared on the horizon of man.

The case of Asia.

Asia's size and central location to the other continents
were formerly taken as an argument for its correspondingly significant position in the creation and history of man.
Its central location is reflected in the hypothesis of the
Asiatic origin of the Indo-European linguistic group of
peoples; and though the theory has been justly called into
question, these peoples have undoubtedly been subjected to
Asiatic influences. The same thing is true of the native
American race, both as to Asiatic origin and influences; because the approximation of Siberia to Alaska is too close to
exclude human relations between the two continents. The
Malays, too, were probably sprung from the soil of southeastern Asia and spread thence over their close-packed Archipelago. Even the native Australians betray a Malayan and
therefore Asiatic element in their composition,[3] while the
same element can be traced yet more distinctly in the widely
scattered Polynesians and the Hovas of Madagascar. This
radiation of races seems to reflect Asia's location at the core
of the land-masses. Yet the capacity to form such centers
of ethnic distribution is not necessarily limited to the largest
continents; history teaches us that small areas which have
early achieved a relatively dense population are prone to
scatter far their seeds of nations.

Location of hemi- spheres and ethnic kinship.

The continents harbor the most widely different races
where they are farthest apart; where they converge most
nearly, they show the closest ethnic kinships. The same principle becomes apparent in their plants and animals. The
distribution of the land-masses over the earth is conspicuous
for their convergence in the north and divergence in long
peninsular forms toward the south. The contrasted grouping is reflected in both the lower animals and the peoples inhabiting these respectively vicinal and remote lands. Only where
North America and Eurasia stretch out arms to one another
around the polar sea do Eastern and Western Hemisphere
show a community of mammalian forms. These are all strictly
Arctic animals, such as the reindeer, elk, Arctic fox, glutton

and ermine.[4] This is the Boreal sub-region of the Holoarctic zoological realm, characterized by a very homogeneous and very limited fauna.[5] In contrast, the portion of the hemispheres lying south of the Tropic of Cancer is divided into four distinct zoological realms, corresponding to Central and South America, Africa south of Sahara, the two Indian peninsulas with the adjacent islands, and Australia.[6] But when we consider the continental extremities projecting beyond the Tropic of Capricorn, where geographic divergence reaches a climax, we find their faunas and floras utterly dissimilar, despite the fact that climate and physical conditions are very similar.[7] We find also widely divergent races in the southern sections of Africa, Australia or Tasmania and South America, while Arctic Eurasia and America come as near meeting ethnically as they do geographically. Here and here only both Eastern and Western Hemisphere show a strong affinity of race. The Eskimo, long classed as Mongoloid, are now regarded as an aberrant variety of the American race, owing to their narrow headform and linguistic affinity; though in Alaska even their headform closely approximates the Mongoloid Siberian type.[8] But in stature, color, oblique eyes, broad flat face, and high cheek bones, in his temperament and character, artistic productions and some aspects of his culture, he groups with the Asiatic Hyperboreans across the narrow sixty miles of water forming Bering Strait.[9] In the northern part of the earth's land area, the distribution of floras, faunas, and races shows interdependence, intercourse; in the southern, separation, isolation.

What is true where the hemispheres come together is true also where continents converge. The core of the Old World is found in the Mediterranean basin where Europe, Asia and Africa form a close circle of lands and where they are inhabited by the one white Mediterranean race. Contrast their racial unity about this common center with the extremes of ethnic divergence in their remote peripheries, where Teutons, Mongols, Malays and Negroes differ widely from the Mediterranean stock and from each other. Eastern Australia represents the ethnic antipodes of western Asia, in harmony with the great dividing distance between them, but the sides of

Continental convergence and ethnic kinship.

these continents facing each other across the bridge of the Sunda Islands are sparsely strewn with a common Malay element.

Africa's location. Africa's early development was never helped by the fact that the continent lay between Asia and South America. It was subjected to strong and persistent Asiatic influences, but apparently to no native American ones. From that far-off trans-Atlantic shore came no signs of life. Africa appears in history as an appendage of Asia, a cultural peninsula of the larger continent. This was due not only to the Suez Isthmus and the narrowness of the Red Sea rift, but to its one-sided invasion by Asiatic races and trade from the east, while the western side of the continent lay buried in sleep, unstirred by any voice from the silent shores of America. Semitic influences, in successive waves, spread over the Dark Continent as far as Morocco, the Senegal, Niger, Lake Chad, Nyanza, Tanganyika and Nyassa, and gave it such light as it had before the 16th century. Only after the Atlantic gulf was finally crossed did influences from the American side of the ocean begin to impinge upon the West African coast, first in the form of the slave and rum trade, then in the more humane aspect of the Liberian colony. But with the full development of the Atlantic period in history, we see all kinds of Atlantic influences, though chiefly from the Atlantic states of Europe, penetrating eastward into the heart of Africa, and there meeting other commercial and political activities pressing inland from the Indian Ocean.

The Atlantic abyss. The long Atlantic rift between the Eastern and Western Hemispheres, which was such a potent factor in the primitive retardation of Africa is, from the standpoint of anthropogeography, the most important feature in the distribution of the land-masses over the globe. Not till the discovery of America bridged this abyss did the known world become a girdle round the earth. Except the Norse ventures to the American continent by way of Iceland and Greenland between 1000 and 1347, no account of pre-Columbian intercourse between the two shores of the Atlantic has ever been substantiated. Columbus found the opposite land unfamiliar in race as in culture. He described the people as neither whites nor blacks, the two ethnic types which he knew on the eastern side of the Atlantic abyss. He and his successors found in the Americas only a Stone Age culture, a stage already outgrown by Europe and Africa. These continents from Lapland to the Hottentot country were using iron. Prior to the voyage of the great Genoese, Europe gave nothing to America and received nothing from it, except the Gulf Stream's scanty cargo of driftwood stranded on bleak Icelandic shores. The Tertiary land-bridge across the North Atlantic between Norway and Greenland may possibly have guided a pre-Caucasic migration to America and given that continent part of its aboriginal population.[10] However, no trace of any European stock remains.

The collapse of the bridge at the close of the Glacial Epoch left the Atlantic abyss effectually dividing the two hemispheres. Its islands, few and far between, were helpless to maintain intercourse between the opposite shores; this is proven by the fact that all of them from Greenland to Tristan da Cunha, excepting only the Canaries, were uninhabited at the time of their discovery. History records when the first bold voyagers came upon them in that unmarked waste of waters, and gave them their first occupants. The political upheavals of Norway in King Harfagr's time (872) sent to the Faroes and Iceland their first settlers, though these islands were previously known to the Celts of Ireland. The Norse colonists who went to Greenland in the year 1000 seem to have been the first regular settlers on those inhospitable coasts. They found no native inhabitants, but numerous abandoned dwellings, fragments of boats and stone implements,[11] which doubtless recorded the intermittent voyages thither of the Eskimo, preliminary to permanent occupation. The Scandinavians did not encounter natives on the island till the 12th century, when Greenland probably received its first Eskimo immigration.[12]

Atlantic islands uninhabited.

While the Atlantic thus formed a long north-and-south rift across the inhabited world at the period of the great discoveries, the Pacific, strewn with islands and land-rimmed at its northern extremity by the peninsulas of Alaska and eastern Siberia, spread a nebula of population from the dense

Geographical character of the Pacific.

centers of Asia across to the outskirts of America. The general Mongoloid character of the American Indians as a race, the stronger Asiatic stamp of the Western Eskimo, the unmistakeable ethnic and cultural affinities of the Northwest Coast tribes both with southern Polynesians and Asiatics,[13] all point to America as the great eastern wing of the Mongoloid or Asiatic area, and therefore as the true Orient of the world.

Geographic conditions have made this possible or even probable. The winds and currents of the North Pacific set from Japan straight toward the American coast. Junks blown out to sea from China or Japan have been carried by the Kuro Siwo and the prevailing westerlies across the Pacific to our continent. There is record of a hundred instances of this occurence.[14]

Pacific affinities of North-American Indians. The broken bridge across Bering Strait formed by East Cape, Cape Prince of Wales and the Diomede Islands between, and further south the natural causeway of the Commander and Aleutian Islands leading from the peninsula of Kamchatka to that of Unalaska, have facilitated intercourse between Asia and America.[15] Justin Winsor says, "There is hardly a stronger demonstration of such connection between the two continents than the physical resemblances of the peoples now living on opposite sides of the Pacific Ocean in these upper latitudes."[16] This resemblance is by no means confined to the Eskimo and Chukches, who have exchanged colonists across Bering Sea. Recent investigations have revealed a wider kinship. The population of northern Siberia speaks in general Ural-Altaic languages, but it includes a few scattered tribes whose singular speech excludes them from this linguistic group, and who have therefore been placed by ethnologists in a distinct class called "paleasiatics" or "hyperboreans." This class is composed of the Ostyak and Kot on the Yenisei River, the Gilyak and Ainos at the mouth of the Amur and on the Kurile, Sakhalin and Yezo islands, the Kamchadal and Koryak of Kamchatka, and the Chukches and Yukaghir of extreme northeastern Siberia. As far back as 1850, the eminent philologist Robert Latham noted a marked linguistic agreement, both in structure and verbal affinity, between our Northwest Coast tribes and the peoples of the islands and peninsulas fringing northeastern Asia. "Koriak is notably American," he said.[17] The recent Jesup Expedition to the Northwest Coast of America and the nearby coast of Asia investigated the Koryak, to determine whether in the past there had been any connection between the cultures and ethnic types of the Old and New World. These investigations have proved beyond doubt a kinship of culture, attributable either to a remote common origin or to former contact, long and close, between these isolated Siberian tribes and the American aborigines. They show that the Koryak are one of the Asiatic tribes standing nearest to the northwestern American Indian.[18] [See map page 103.]

W. H. Dall finds the inhabitants of the Pacific slope of North America conspicuously allied with Oceanica in cultural achievements, whose origin he therefore assigns to that vast congeries of islands stretching from Asia toward South America in latitude 25° south. These islands, closely clustered as far as the Paumota group, straggle along with widening spaces between, through Easter Isle, which carries the indestructible memorials of a strange civilization, through Sala-y-Gomez, San Felix, and St. Ambrose almost to the threshold of the Peruvian coast. It is to be noted that these islands lie just outside the westward-bearing Equatorial Current and trade-winds, on the margin of the South Pacific anti-cyclonic winds and a southern current which sets towards the Peruvian coast.[19] A more probable avenue for the introduction of these Polynesian or Malayan elements of culture is found in O. T. Mason's theory, that primitive mariners of the southwestern Pacific, led into migration by the eternal food quest, may have skirted the seaboard of East Asia and Northwest America, passing along a great-circle route through the succession of marginal seas and archipelagoes to various ports of entry on the Pacific front of America. Such a route, favored by the prevailing marine currents and winds from the southwest, and used repeatedly during long periods of time, might have introduced trans-Pacific elements of race and culture into the western side of America.[20]

Polynesian affinities.

The real Orient of the world.

Moreover, primitive America resembled Oceanica and

northern Asia in its ignorance of iron, in its Stone Age civilization, and its retarded social and political development. Such affinities as it shows were predominantly Pacific or trans-Pacific.[21] On its Atlantic side, it stood out in striking contrast to the contemporaneous civilizations and races in Europe and Africa; this was its unneighbored shore, lying on the eastern margin of that broad zone of habitation which stretched hence westward on and on around the world, to the outermost capes of Europe and Africa. The Atlantic abyss formed the single gap in this encircling belt of population, to which Columbus at last affixed the clasp. The Atlantic face of the Americas formed therefore the drowsy unstirred Orient of the inhabited world, which westward developed growing activity—dreaming a civilization in Mexico and Peru, roused to artistic and maritime achievement in Oceanica and the Malay Archipelago, to permanent state-making and real cultural development in Asia, and attaining the highest civilization at last in western Europe. There was the sunset margin of the inhabited world, the area of achievement, the adult Occident, facing across the dividing ocean that infant Orient beyond. Here the Old World, the full-grown world, had accumulated in Columbus' time the matured forces of a hemisphere; it was searching for some outlet across the shoreless distances of the Atlantic, waiting for some call from its voiceless beyond.

The Atlantic abyss in historic movements of peoples.   This deep, unbridged chasm of the Atlantic, closed only four hundred years ago, must be taken into account in all investigations of the geographical distribution of races, whether in prehistoric or historic times. The influences of those ages when it formed an impassable gulf are still operative in directing the movements of the peoples to-day inhabiting its shores, because that barrier maintained the continents of America as a vast territorial reserve, sparsely inhabited by a Stone Age people, and affording a fresh field for the superior, accumulated energies of Europe.

Races and continents.   Australia and the double continent of America show each the coincidence of an ethnic realm with an isolated continent. In contrast, when we come to the Old World triad of Europe, Asia and Africa, we find three races, to be sure, but races whose geographical distribution ignores the boundaries of the continents. The White race belongs to all three, and from time immemorial has made the central basin of the Mediterranean the white man's sea. The Mongolian, though primarily at home in Asia, stretches along the coast of the Arctic Ocean to the Atlantic shores of Norway, and in historical times has penetrated up the Danube to the foot of the Alps. Nor was the Negroid stock confined to Africa, though Africa has always been its geographical core. The Indian Peninsula and Malay Archipelago, once peopled by a primitive Negroid race, but now harboring only remnants of them in the Deccan, Malacca, the Philippines and elsewhere, bridge the distance to the other great Negroid center in Melanesia and the derivative or secondary Negroid area of Australia.[22] The Negroid race belongs essentially to the long southern land pendants of the Eastern Hemisphere; and wherever it has bordered on the lighter northern stocks, it has drawn a typical boundary zone of mingled tints which never diverges far from the Equator, from the Atlantic shores of the Sudan to Pacific Fiji.[23] [See map page 105.]

The effort of the old ethnology, as represented by Blumenbach, to make a five-fold division of the races in agreement with the five continents was a mistake. To distinguish between the continents is one thing and to distinguish between the races is another. Neither bio-geography nor anthropo-geography can adopt the continents as geographical provinces, although floras, faunas and races the world over give evidence of partial or temporary restriction to a certain continent, whence they have overflowed to other lands. A ground-plan for the geographical classification of races is to be found, as Tylor says, in the fact that they are not found scattered indiscriminately over the earth's surface, but that certain races belong to certain regions, in whose peculiar environment they have developed their type, and whence they have spread to other lands, undergoing modifications from race intermixture and successive changes of environment on the way.[24]

From this general law of race movements it follows that certain groups of land-masses, favored by location and large

Contrast of the northern and southern continents.

area, play a great imperial rôle, holding other lands as appanages. The Eastern Hemisphere, as we have seen, enjoys this advantage over the Western. Still more the Northern Hemisphere, blessed with an abundance of land and a predominant Temperate Zone location, is able to lord it over the Southern, so insular in its poverty of land. The history of the Northern Hemisphere is marked by far-reaching historical influences and wide control; that of the Southern, by detachment, aloofness and impotence, due to the small area and isolation of its land-masses. A subordinate rôle is its fate. Australia will always follow in the train of Eurasia, whence alone it has derived its incentives and means of progress. Neither the southern half of Africa nor South America has ever in historical times struck out a road to advancement unaided by its northern neighbors. Primitive South America developed the only independent civilization that ever blossomed in the Southern Hemisphere, but the Peruvian achievements in progress were inferior to those of Mexico and Central America.[25]

Isolation of the southern continents.   This subordination of the southern continents is partly due to the fact that they have only one side of contact or neighborhood with any other land, that is, on the north; yet even here the contact is not close. In Australia the medium of communication is a long bridge of islands; in America, a winding island chain and a mountainous isthmus; in Africa, a broad zone of desert dividing the Mediterranean or Eurasian from the tropical and Negroid part of the continent. Intercourse was not easy, and produced clear effects only in the case of Africa. Enlightenment filtering in here was sadly dimmed as it spread. Moreover it was delayed till the introduction from Asia of the horse and camel, which were not native to Africa, and which, as Ratzel points out, alone made possible the long journey across the Sahara. The opposite or peninsular sides, running out as great spurs from the compacter land-masses of the north, look southward into vacant wastes of water, find no neighbors in those Antarctic seas. Owing to this unfavorable location on the edge of things, they were historically dead until four centuries ago, when oceanic navigation opened up the great sea route of the Southern

Hemisphere, and for the first time included them in the world's circle of communication. But even when lifted by the ensuing Europeanizing process, they only emphasize the fundamental dependence of the Southern Hemisphere upon the superior geographical endowments of the Northern.

The build of the land-masses influences fundamentally the movements and hence the development of the races who inhabit them. A simple continental structure gives to those movements a few simple features and a wide monotonous distribution which checks differentiation. A manifold, complex build, varied in relief and ragged in contour, breaks up the moving streams of peoples, turns each branch into a different channel, lends it a distinctive character through isolation, finally brings it up in a *cul de sac* formed by a peninsula or mountain-rimmed basin, where further movement is checked and the process of local individualization begins. Therefore great simplicity of continental build may result in historical poverty, as in the flat quadrangle of European Russia, the level plateau of Africa, and the smooth Atlantic slope of North America, with its neatly trimmed outline. Complexity, abounding in contrasted environments, tends to produce a varied wealth of historical development. Africa lies on the surface of the ocean, a huge torso of a continent, headless, memberless, inert. Here is no diversity of outward form, no contrast of zonal location, no fructifying variety of geographic conditions. Humanity has forgotten to grow in its stationary soil. Only where the Suez Isthmus formed an umbilical cord uniting ancient Egypt to the mother continent of Asia was Africa vitalized by the pulse of another life. European influences penetrated little beyond the northern coast.

Effect of continental structure upon historical development.

Asia, on the other hand, radiating great peninsulas, festooned with islands, supporting the vast corrugations of its highlands and lowlands, its snow-capped mountains and steaming valleys, stretching from the Equator through all the zones to the ice-blocked shores of the Arctic, knowing drought and deluge, tundra waste and teeming jungle, has offered the manifold environment and segregated areas for individualized civilizations, which have produced such far-reaching historical results. The same fact is true of Europe, and that in an intensified degree. Here a complex development of mountains and highlands built on diverse axes, peninsulas which comprise 27 per cent. and islands which comprise nearly 8 per cent. of the total area,[26] vast thalassic inlets cleaving the continent to the core, have provided an abundance of those naturally defined regions which serve as cradles of civilization and, reacting upon the continent as a whole, endow it with lasting historical significance.[27] Even Strabo saw this. He begins his description of the inhabited world with Europe, because, as he says, it has such a "polymorphous formation" and is the region most favorable to the mental and social ennoblement of man.[28]

Structure of North and South America. In North and South America, great simplicity of continental build gave rise to a corresponding simplicity of native ethnic and cultural condition. There is only one marked contrast throughout the length of this double continent, that between its Atlantic and Pacific slopes. On the Atlantic side of the Cordilleras, a vast trough extends through both land-masses from the Arctic Ocean to Patagonia; this has given to migration in each a longitudinal direction and therefore constantly tended to nullify the diversities arising from contrasted zonal conditions. On the Pacific side of North America, there has been an unmistakable migration southward along the accessible coast from Alaska to the Columbia River, and down the great intermontane valleys of the western highlands from the Great Basin to Honduras;[29] while South America shows the same meridional movement for 2,000 miles along the Pacific coast and longitudinal valleys of the Andes system. There was little encouragement to cut across the grain of the continents. The eastern range of the Cordilleras drew in general a dividing line between the eastern and western tribes.[30] Though Athapascans from the east overstepped it at a few points in North America, the Great Divide has served effectually to isolate the two groups from one another and to draw that line of linguistic cleavage which Major Powell has set down in his map of Indian linguistic stocks. Consequently, Americanists recognize a distinct resemblance among the members of the North Atlantic group of Indians, as among those of the South Atlantic group; but they note an equally distinct contrast between each of them and its corresponding Pacific group. Nor is this contrast superficial; it extends to physical traits, temperament and culture,[31] and appears in the use of the vigesimal system of enumeration in primitive Mexico, Central America, among the Tlingits of the Northwest coast and the Eskimo as also among the Chukches and Ainus of Asia, while in the Atlantic section of North America the decimal system, with one doubtful exception, was alone in use.[32]

To the anthropo-geographer, the significant fact is that all the higher phases of native civilization are confined to the Pacific slope group of Indians, which includes the Mexican and Isthmian tribes. From the elongated center of advanced culture stretching from the Bolivian highlands northward to the Anahuac Plateau, the same type shades off by easy transitions through northern Mexico and the Pueblo country, vanishes among the lower intrusive stocks of Oregon and California, only to reappear among the Haidas and Tlingits of British Columbia and Alaska, whose cultural achievements show affinity to those of the Mayas in Yucatan.[33] Dall found certain distinguishing customs or characteristics spread north and south along the western slope of the continent in a natural geographical line of migration. They included labretifery, tattooing the chin of adult women, certain uses of masks, a certain style of conventionalizing natural objects, the use of conventional signs as hieroglyphics, a peculiar facility in carving wood and stone, a similarity of angular designs on their pottery and basketry, and of artistic representations connected with their common religious or mythological ideas. Many singular forms of carvings and the method of superimposing figures of animals one upon another in their totem poles are found from Alaska to Panama, except in California. These distinguishing features of an incipient culture are found nowhere else in North America, even sporadically. Dall therefore concludes that "they have been impressed upon the American aboriginal world from without," and on the ground of affinities, attributes their origin to Oceanica.[34]

Cultural superiority of Pacific slope Indians.

Cyrus Thomas, on the basis of the character and distribution of the archeological remains in North America, concurs in this opinion. He finds that these remains fall into two classes, one east of the Rocky Mountain watershed and the other west. "When those of the Pacific slope as a whole are compared with those of the Atlantic slope, there is a dissimilarity which marks them as the products of different races or as the result of different race influences." He emphasizes the resemblance of the customs, arts and archeological remains of the west coast to those of the opposite shores and islands of the Pacific, and notes the lack of any resemblance to those of the Atlantic; and finally leans to the conclusion that the continent was peopled from two sources, one incoming stream distributing itself over the Atlantic slope, and the other over the Pacific, the two becoming gradually fused into a comparatively homogeneous race by long continental isolation. Yet these two sources may not necessarily include a trans-Atlantic origin for one of the contributing streams; ethnic evidence is against such a supposition, because the characteristics of the American race and of the archeological remains point exclusively to affinity with the people of the Pacific.[35] John Edward Payne also reaches the same conclusion, though on other grounds.[36]

Lack of segregated districts. The one strong segregating feature in primitive America was the Cordilleras, which held east and west apart. In the natural pockets formed by the high intermontane valleys of the Andes and the Anahuac Plateau, and in the constricted isthmian region, the continent afforded a few secluded localities where civilization found favorable conditions of development. But in general, the paucity of large coast articulations, and the adverse polar or subpolar location of most of these, the situation of the large tropical islands along that barren Atlantic abyss, and the lack of a broken or varied relief, have prevented the Americas from developing numerous local centers of civilization, which might eventually have lifted the cultural status of the continents.[37]

Coast articulations of continents. It is necessary to distinguish two general classes of continental articulations; first, marginal dependences, like the fringe of European peninsulas and islands, resulting from a deeply serrated contour; and second, surface subdivisions of the interior, resulting from differences of relief or defined often by enclosing mountains or deserts, like the Tibetan Plateau, the Basin of Bohemia, the Po River trough, or the sand-rimmed valley of the Nile. The first class is by far the more important, because of the intense historical activity which results from the vitalizing contact with the sea. But in considering coast articulations, anthropo-geography is led astray unless it discriminates between these on the basis of size and location. Without stopping to discuss the obvious results of a contrasted zonal location, such as that between Labrador and Yucatan, the Kola Peninsula and Spain, it is necessary to keep in mind always the effect of vicinal location. An outlying coastal dependency like Ireland has had its history impoverished by excessive isolation, in contrast to the richer development of England, Jutland, and Zealand in the same latitude, because these have profited from the closer neighborhood of other peripheral regions. So from ancient times, Greece has had a similar advantage over the Crimea, the Tunisian Peninsula of North Africa over Spain, the Cotentin Peninsula of France over Brittany, and Kent over Cornwall or Caithness in Great Britain.

Articulations on a vast scale, like the southern peninsulas of Asia, produce quite different cultural and historical effects from small physical sub-divisions, like the fiord promontories and "skerries" of Norway and southern Alaska, or the finger peninsulas of the Peloponnesus. The significant difference lies in the degree of isolation which the two types yield. Large continental dependencies of the Asiatic class resemble small continents in their power to segregate; while overgrown capes like ancient Attica and Argolis or the more bulky Peloponnesus have their exclusiveness tempered by the mediating power of the small marine inlets between them. Small articulations, by making a coast accessible, tend to counteract the excessive isolation of a large articulation. They themselves develop in their people only minor or inner differentiations, which serve to enrich the life of the island or peninsula as a whole, but do not invade its essential unity. The contrast in the history of Hellas and the Peloponnesus

Importance of size in continental articulations.

was due largely to their separation from one another; yet neither was able to make of its people anything but Greeks. Wales and Cornwall show in English history the same contrast and the same underlying unity.

Historical contrast of large and small peninsulas.
In discussing continental articulations, therefore, it makes a great difference whether we draw our deductions from small projections of the coast, like Wales, the Peloponnesus, Brittany and the Crimea, whose areas range from 7442 to 10,023 square miles (19,082 to 25,700 square kilometers); or the four Mediterranean peninsulas, which range in size from the 58,110 square miles (149,000 square kilometers) of the Apennine Peninsula to the 197,600 square miles (506,-600 square kilometers) of Asia Minor and the 227,700 square miles (584,000 square kilometers) of the Iberian; or the vast continental alcoves of southern Asia, like Farther India with its 650,000 square miles (1,667,000 square kilometers), Hither India with 814,320 square miles (2,088,000 square kilometers) and Arabia with 1,064,700 square miles (2,730,-000 square kilometers).[38] The fact that the large compound peninsula of western Europe which comprises Spain, Portugal, France, Jutland, Belgium, Holland, Switzerland, Italy and western Germany, and has its base in the stricture between the Adriatic and the Baltic, is about the size of peninsular India, suggests how profound may be the difference in geographic effects between large and small peripheral divisions. The three huge extremities which Asia thrusts forward into the Indian Ocean are geographical entities, which in point of size and individualization rank just below the continents; and in relation to the solid mass of Central Asia, they have exhibited in many respects an aloofness and self-sufficiency, that have resulted in an historical divergence approximating that of the several continents. India, which has more productive territory than Australia and a population not much smaller than that of Europe, becomes to the administrators of its government "the Continent of India," as it is regularly termed in the Statistical Atlas published at Calcutta. Farther India has in the long-drawn pendant of Malacca a sub-peninsula half as large again as Italy. The Deccan has in Ceylon an insular dependency the size of Tas-

mania. The whole scale is continental. It appears again somewhat diminished, in the largest articulations of Europe,
in Scandinavia, the British Isles, the Iberian and Balkan peninsulas. This continental scale stamps also the anthropo-
geography of such large individualized fields. They are big
enough for each to comprise one or even several nations, and
isolated enough to keep their historical processes for long
periods at a time to a certain extent detached from those of
their respective continents.

The most favorable conditions for historical development
obtain where the two classes of marginal articulation are
combined, and where they occur in groups, as we find them in
the Mediterranean and the North Sea-Baltic basin. Here the
smaller indentations multiply contact with the sea, and provide the harbors, bays and breakwaters of capes and promontories which make the coast accessible. The larger
articulations, by their close grouping, break up the sea into
the minor thalassic basins which encourage navigation, and
thus insure the exchange of their respective cultural achievements. In other words, such conditions present the pre-
eminent advantages of vicinal location around an enclosed
sea.

*Peninsular
conditions
most favor-
able to his-
torical de-
velopment.*

The enormous articulations of southern Asia suffer from
their paucity of small indentations, all the more because of
their vast size and sub-tropical location. The Grecian type
of peninsula, with its broken shoreline, finds here its large-
scale homologue only in Farther India, to which the Sunda
Islands have played in history the part of a gigantic
Cyclades. The European type of articulation is found only
about the Yellow-Japan Sea, where the island of Hondo and
the peninsulas of Shangtung and Korea reproduce approximately the proportions of Great Britain, Jutland and Italy
respectively. Arabia and India, like the angular shoulder
of Africa which protrudes into the Indian Ocean, measure
an imposing length of coastline, but this length shrinks in
comparison with the vast area of the peninsulas. The contour of a peninsula is like the surface of the brain: in both
it is convolutions that count. Southern Asia has had
lobes enough but too few convolutions. For this reason, the

northern Indian Ocean, despite its exceptional location as the eastward extension of the Mediterranean route to the Orient, found its development constantly arrested till the advent of European navigators.

Length of coastline. Although the peripheral articulations of a continent differ anthropo-geographically according to their size, their zonal and vicinal location, yet large and small, arctic and tropical, are grouped indiscriminately together in the figures that state the length of coastlines. For this reason, statistics of continental coastlines have little value. For instance, the fact that Eurasia has 67,000 miles (108,000 kilometers) and North America 46,500 miles (75,000 kilometers) of contact with the ocean is not illuminating; these figures do not reveal the fact that the former has its greatest coastal length on its tropical and sub-tropical side, while the latter continent has wasted inlets and islands innumerable in the long, bleak stretch from Newfoundland poleward around to Bering Sea.

The continental base of peninsulas. Peninsulas are accessible from the sea according to the configuration of their coasts, but from their hinterland, according to the length and nature of their connection with the same. This determines the degree of their isolation from the land-mass. If they hang from the continent by a frayed string, as does the Peloponnesus, Crimea, Malacca, Indian Gutjerat, and Nova Scotia, they are segregated from the life of the mainland almost as completely as if they were islands. The same effects follow where the base of a peninsula is defined by a high mountain barrier, as in all the Mediterranean peninsulas, in the two Indias, and in Korea; or by a desert like that which scantily links Arabia to Egypt, Syria and Mesopotamia; or by a blur of swamps and lakes such as half detaches Scandinavia, Courland, Estland and Finland from Russia.

Held to their continents by bonds that often fail to bind, subjected by their outward-facing peripheral location to every centrifugal force, feeling only slightly the pull of the great central mass behind, peninsulas are often further detached economically and historically by their own contrasted local conditions. A sharp transition in geological formation and therefore in soil, a difference of climate, rainfall, drainage system, of flora or fauna, serve greatly to emphasize the lack of community of interests with the continental interior, and therefore produce an inevitable diversity of historical development.[39] Hence, many peninsulas insulate their people as completely as islands. It is hard to say whether the Pyrenean peninsula or Sicily, Scandinavia or Great Britain, has held itself more aloof from the political history of remaining Europe; whether Korea is not more entitled to its name of the Hermit Kingdom than island Japan could ever be; whether the Peloponnesus or Euboea was more intimately associated with the radiant life of ancient Hellas. These questions lead to another, namely, whether a high mountain wall like the Pyrenees, or a narrow strait like that of Messina is the more effective geographical boundary.

Peninsulas not infrequently gain in breadth as they approach the continent; here they tend to abate their distinctive character as lobes of the mainland, together with the ethnic and historical marks of isolation. Here they form a doubtful boundary zone of mingled continental and peninsular development. Such peninsulas fall naturally, therefore, into a continental and a peninsular section, and reveal this segmentation in the differentiated history of the two portions. That great military geographer Napoleon distinguished the Italy of the Po basin as *Italie continentale*, and the Apennine section as *Presqu'ile*. Not only is the former broader, but, expanding like a tree trunk near the ground, it sends its roots well back into the massive interior of the continent; it is dominated more by the Alps than by the Apennines; it contains a lowland and a river of continental proportions, for which there is no space on the long, narrow spur of southern Italy. If its geographical character approximates that of the mainland, so does its ethnic and historical. The Po basin is a well defined area of race characterization, in which influences have made for intermixture. South of the crest of the Apennines the Italian language in its purity begins, in contrast to the Gallo-Italian of the north. This mountain ridge has also held apart the dark, short dolichocephalic stock of the Mediterranean race from the fairer, taller, broad-headed Celts, who have moved down into the

Continental base a zone of transition.

Po basin from the Alps, and the Germans and Illyrians who have entered it from the northeast.[40] Northern Italy is therefore allied ethnically, as it has often been united politically, to the neighboring countries abutting upon the Alps, so that it has experienced only in a partial degree that detachment which has stamped the history of the Apennine section.

Historical contrast between base and extremity. The Balkan Peninsula tells much the same story of contrasted geographic conditions and development in its continental and peninsular sections. Greece proper, in ancient as in modern times, reached its northern confines where the peninsula suddenly widens its base through Macedonia and Thrace. In this narrow southern section to-day, especially in isolated Peloponnesus, Attica, and the high-walled garden of Thessaly, are found people of the pure, long-headed, Hellenic type, and here the Greek language prevails.[41] But that broad and alien north, long excluded from the Amphictyonic Council and a stranger to Aegean culture in classical times, is occupied to-day by a congeries of Slavs, who form a southwestern spur of the Slav stock covering eastern Europe. Its political history shows how often it has been made a Danubian or continental state,—by Alexander of Macedon, by the Romans, Bulgarians, and Ottoman Turks,[42] as it may be some day by Russia; and also how often its large and compact form has enabled it to dominate the tapering peninsular section to the south.

In the same way, the vast Ganges and Indus basins, which constitute the continental portion of India, have received various Tibetan, Scythian, Aryan, Pathan, and Mongol-Tartar ingredients from Central Asia; and by reason of the dense populations supported by these fruitful river plains, it has been able to dominate politically, religiously and culturally the protruding triangle of the Deccan. [See maps pages 8 and 102.] The continental side of Arabia, the Mesopotamian valley which ties the peninsula to the highlands of Persia and Armenia, has received into its Semitic stock constant infiltrations of Turanian and Aryan peoples from the core of Asia. This process has been going on from the ancient Elamite and Persian conquests of Mesopotamia down to the Ottoman invasion and the present periodic visits of Kurdish shepherds to the pastures of the upper Tigris.[43] Here we have the same contrast of geographic conditions as in Italy and India, a wide, populous alluvial plain occupying the continental section of the peninsula, and a less attractive highland or mountainous region in the outlying spur of land.

These continental sections of peninsulas become there-fore strongly marked as areas of ethnic characterization and differentiated historical development. Their threshold loca-tion, by reason of which they first catch any outward migra-tion from the core of the continent, and their fertility, which serves as a perennial lure to new comers, whether peaceful or warlike, combine to give them intense historical activity. They catch the come and go between their wide hinterland and the projection of land beyond, the stimulus of new arrivals and fresh blood. But tragedy too is theirs. The Po Valley has been called "the cockpit of Europe." Even the little Eider, which marks the base of Jutland, has been the scene of war between Danes and Germans since the tenth century.[44] The Indus Valley has again and again felt the shock of conflict with invading hordes from the central high-lands, and witnessed the establishment of a succession of empires. Peace at the gates of the Balkan Peninsula has never been of long duration, and the postern door of Korea has been stormed often enough. *Continental base a scene of invasion and war.*

In contrast to these continental sections which stand in contact with the solid land-mass behind, the extremities of the peninsulas are areas of isolation and therefore generally of ethnic unity. They often represent the last stand of displaced people pressed outward into these narrow quarters by expanding races in their rear. The vast triangle of the Deccan, which forms the essentially peninsular part of India, is occupied, except in the more exposed northwest corner, by the Dravidian race which once occupied all India, and afterward was pushed southward by the influx of more energetic peoples.[45] Here they have preserved their speech and nationality unmixed and live in almost primitive sim-plicity.[46] In the peninsular parts of Great Britain, in northern Scotland, Wales and Cornwall, we find people of *Peninsular extremities as areas of isolation.*

Celtic speech brought to bay on these remote spurs of the land, affiliating little with the varied folk which occupied the continental side of the island, and resisting conquest to the last.[47] The mountainous peninsula of western Connaught in Ireland has been the rocky nucleus of the largest Celtic-speaking community in the island.[48] Brittany, with a similar location, became the last refuge of Celtic speech on the mainland of Europe,[49] the seat of resistance to Norman and later to English conquest, finally the stronghold of conservatism in the French Revolution.

Ethnic unity of peninsulas.

The northern wall of the Apennines and the outpost barrier of the Alps have combined to protect peninsular Italy from extensive ethnic infusions from the direction of the continent. This portion of the country shows therefore, as the anthropological maps attest, a striking uniformity of race. It has been a melting-pot in which foreign elements, filtering through the breaches of the Apennines or along the southern coast, have been fused into the general population under the isolating and cohesive influences of a peninsular environment.[50] The population of the Iberian Peninsula is even more unified, probably the most homogeneous in Europe. Here the long-headed Mediterranean race is found in the same purity as in island Corsica and Sardinia.[51] Spain's short line of contact with France and its sharp separation by the unbroken wall of the Pyrenees robs the peninsula of any distinctly continental section, and consequently of any transitional area of race and culture; hence the unity of Spain as opposed to that twofold balanced diversity which we find in Italy and India. The Balkan Peninsula, on the other hand, owing to the great predominance of its continental section and the confused relief of the country, has not protected its distinctively peninsular or Greek section from the southward migrations of Slavs, Albanians, Wallachians, and other continental peoples.[52] It has been like a big funnel with a small mouth; the pressure from above has been very great. Hellas and even the Peloponnesus have had their peninsularity impaired and their race mixed, owing to the predominant continental section to the north.

Peninsulas as intermediaries.

Peninsulas, so far as they project from their continents,

are areas of isolation; but so far as they extend also toward some land beyond, they become intermediaries. The isolating and intermediary aspects can be traced in the anthropo-geographical effects of every peninsula, even those which, like Brittany and Cornwall, project into the long uncharted waste of the Atlantic. In the order of historical development, a peninsula first isolates, until in its secluded environment it has molded a mature, independent people; then, as that people outgrows its narrow territory, the peninsula becomes a favorable base for maritime expansion to distant lands, or becomes a natural avenue for numerous reciprocal relations with neighboring lands beyond. Korea was the bridge for Mongolian migration from continental Asia to the Japan islands, and for the passage thither of Chinese culture, whether intellectual, esthetic, industrial or religious.[53] It has been the one country conspicuous in the foreign history of Japan. Conquered by the island empire in 1592, it paid tribute for nearly three centuries and yielded to its foreign master the southeastern port of Fusan, the Calais of Korea.[54] Since the treaty of Portsmouth in 1905 made it subject to Japan, it has become the avenue of Japanese expansion to the mainland and the unwilling recipient of the modern civilization thrust upon it by these English of the East. In like manner the Pyrenean peninsula has always been the intermediary between Europe and northwest Africa. Its population, as well as its flora and fauna, group with those of the southern continent. It has served as transit land between north and south for the Carthaginians, Vandals and Saracens; and in modern times it has maintained its character as a link by the Portuguese occupation of the Tangiers peninsula in the fifteenth cen-, tury,[55] and the Spanish possession of Ceuta and various other points along the Moroccan coast from the year 709 A. D. to the present.[56]

This rôle of intermediary is inevitably thrust upon all peninsulas which, like Spain, Italy, Greece, Asia Minor, Arabia, Farther India, Malacca, Chukchian Siberia, and Alaska, occupy an intercontinental location. Arabia especially in its climate, flora, races and history shows the haul and

Peninsulas of intercontinental location.

pull now of Asia, now of Africa. From it Asiatic influences have spread over Africa to Morocco and the Niger River on the west, and to Zanzibar on the south, permeated Abyssinia, and penetrated to the great Equatorial Lakes, whether in the form of that Mecca-born worship of Allah, or the creeping caravans and slave-gangs of Arab trader. Of all such inter-continental peninsulas, Florida alone seems to have had no rôle as an intermediary. Its native ethnic affinities were wholly with its own continent. It has given nothing to South America and received nothing thence. The northward expansion of Arawak and Carib tribes from Venezuela in historic times ceased at Cuba and Hayti. The Straits drew a dividing line. Local conditions in Florida itself probably furnish the explanation of this anomaly. Extensive swamps made the central and southern portion of the peninsula inhospitable to colonization from either direction, transformed it from a link into a barrier.

Atlantic peninsulas of Europe. Peninsulas which conspicuously lack an intercontinental location must long await their intermediary phase of development, but do not escape it. The Cornish, Breton and Iberian peninsulas were all prominent in the trans-Atlantic enterprises of Europe from the end of the fifteenth century. The first French sailors to reach the new world were Breton and Norman fishermen. Plymouth, as the chief port of the Cornish peninsula, figures prominently in the history of English exploration and settlement in America. It seems scarcely accidental that most of Queen Elizabeth's great sea captains were natives of this district—Sir Francis Drake, Sir John Hawkins, Sir Humphrey Gilbert, and Sir Walter Raleigh, the latter holding the office of vice-admiral of Cornwall and Devon. It was the peninsula-like projection of South America about Cape St. Roque, twenty degrees farther east than Labrador, that welcomed the ships of Cabral and Americus Vespucius, and secured to Portugal a foothold in the Western Hemisphere.

NOTES TO CHAPTER XII

1. Ratzel, History of Mankind, Vol. I, p. 336. London, 1896-1898.
2. D. G. Brinton, The American Race, p. 41. Philadelphia, 1901.

3. D. G. Brinton, Races and Peoples, pp. 239-240. Philadelphia, 1901. Ratzel, History of Mankind, Vol. I, p. 336. London, 1896-1898.

4. A. R. Wallace, Island Life, p. 14. New York, 1892.

5. A. Heilprin, Geographical Distribution of Animals, p. 69, map. 1887.

6. *Ibid.*, pp. 78, 82, 90, 100.

7. Darwin, Origin of Species, Chap. XII. New York, 1895. A. R. Wallace, Island Life, p. 6. New York, 1892.

8. W. Z. Ripley, Races of Europe, Map on p. 43. New York, 1899.

9. *Ibid.*, pp. 39, 50, 80. Ratzel, History of Mankind, Vol. II, pp. 100-110. London, 1896-1898.

10. A. H. Keane, Ethnology, pp. 231-232, 362. Cambridge, 1896.

11. McGee and Thomas, Prehistoric North America, p. 56, Vol. XIX of History of North America. Philadelphia, 1905.

12. Fiske, Discovery of America, Vol. I, p. 224. Boston, 1893.

13. For various Asiatic and Oceanic elements, see Franz Boas, The Indians of British Columbia, *Bull. of the Amer. Geog. Society*, Vol. 28, p. 229. The Northwest Coast Tribes, Science, Vol. XII, pp. 194-196. Niblack, The Indians of the Northwest Coast, p. 385, Washington. H. H. Bancroft, The Native Races, Vol. I, pp. 177, 178, footnote; pp. 210, 225. San Francisco, 1886. W. Z. Ripley, Races of Europe, map p. 42. New York, 1899.

14. T. W. Higginson and William Macdonald, History of the United States, p. 21. New York and London, 1905.

15. Edward John Payne, History of the New World Called America, Vol. II, pp. 64-68, 74-77, 305, 388-389. Oxford, 1899.

16. Justin Winsor, Narrative and Critical History, Vol. I, p. 60. Boston, 1889.

17. Cited by E. J. Payne, History of the New World Called America, Vol. II, p. 292, footnote p. 294. Oxford, 1899.

18. Waldemar Jochelson, The Mythology of the Koryak, *The American Anthropologist*, Vol. VI, pp. 415-416, 421-425. 1904.

19. W. D. Dall, Masks, Labrets, and Certain Aboriginal Customs, Third Annual Report of Bureau of Ethnology, pp. 46-147. Washington, 1884.

20. O. T. Mason, Migration and the Food Quest, pp. 275-292. Washington, 1894.

21. McGee and Thomas, Prehistoric North America, pp. 51, 58-82. Philadelphia, 1905. Ratzel, History of Mankind, Vol. I, pp. 5-7, 145-147, 153-154. London, 1896-1898.

22. Ripley, Races of Europe, map p. 42, pp. 43-44. New York, 1899.

23. Ratzel, History of Mankind, Vol. I, p. 7. London, 1896-1898.

24. Tylor, Anthropology, pp. 86-87. New York, 1881.

25. E. J. Payne, History of the New World Called America, Vol. II, pp. 554-555. Oxford, 1899.

26. Justus Perthes, *Taschen Atlas*, p. 17. Gotha, 1905.

27. Carl Ritter, Comparative Geography, pp. 188-212. Translated by W. L. Gage, Philadelphia, 1865. N. S. Shaler, Nature and Man in America, pp. 11-18, 151-165. New York, 1896.

28. Strabo, Book II, chap. V. 26.

29. McGee and Thomas, Prehistoric North America, p. 3, map. Philadelphia, 1905.

30. D. G. Brinton, Races and Peoples, pp. 248-249. Philadelphia, 1901.

31. D. G. Brinton, The American Race, pp. 58, 103-104. Philadelphia, 1901. McGee and Thomas, Prehistoric North America, p. 86. Philadelphia, 1905 Ratzel, History of Mankind, Vol. I, pp. 5-7, 145-147, 153-

32. *Ibid.*, p. 293. E. J. Payne, History of the New World Called America, Vol. II, p. 315. Oxford, 1899.

33. *Ibid.*, Vol. II, pp. 412-417. McGee and Thomas, Prehistoric North America, pp. 72-75. Philadelphia, 1905.

34. W. H. Dall, Masks, Labrets, and Certain Aboriginal Customs, Third Annual Report of Bureau of Ethnology, pp. 146-147. Washington, 1884.

35. Cyrus Thomas, Report of Mound Explorations, pp. 522-523, 722-728. Twelfth Annual Report of the Bureau of Ethnology, Washington, 1894.

36. E. J. Payne, History of the New World Called America, Vol. II, pp. 382-383. Oxford, 1899.

37. N. S. Shaler, Nature and Man in America, pp. 151, 168-173. New York, 1891.

38. Justus Perthes, *Taschen Atlas*, p. 9. Gotha, 1905.

39. Carl Ritter, Comparative Geography, pp. 191-192. Translated by W. L. Gage, Philadelphia, 1865.

40. W. Z. Ripley, Races of Europe, pp. 247-258. New York, 1899.

41. *Ibid.*, pp. 403-409.

42. E. A. Freeman, Historical Geography of Europe, Atlas, Maps, 34, 49. London, 1882.

43. For race elements in Mesopotamia, see D. G. Hogarth, The Nearer East, Maps, pp. 173 and 176. London, 1903.

44. E. A. Freeman, Historical Geography of Europe, pp. 201-202, 506-508, 535-536, 541. London, 1882.

45. Imperial Gazetteer of India, Vol. I, pp. 293-297. Oxford, 1907.

46. Sir Thomas Holdich, India, Ethnographical map, p. 201, pp. 202, 213-216. London, 1905. B. H. Baden-Powell, The Indian Village Community, pp. 111, 116, 119, 161. London, 1896.

47. W. Z. Ripley, Races of Europe, pp. 312-321. New York, 1899. E. Reclus, Europe, Vol. IV, pp. 73, 83-84. New York, 1882.

48. H. J. Mackinder, Britain and the British Seas, Ethnographic map, p. 184, and p. 306. London, 1904.

49. W. Z. Ripley, Races of Europe, pp. 22, 23, 150-151. New York, 1899.

50. *Ibid.*, pp. 248, 258, 272.

51. *Ibid.*, pp. 247, 273.

52. *Ibid.*, pp. 401-409, and map.

53. F. Brinkley, Japan, Vol. I, pp. 38-42, 70, 75-80, 83-84, 126. Boston and Tokyo, 1901. W. E. Griffis, The Mikado's Empire, Vol. I, pp. 73, 83. New York, 1903.

54. Henry Dyer, Dai Nippon, pp. 59, 69. New York, 1904.

55. E. A. Freeman, Historical Geography of Europe, p. 558. London, 1882.

56. *Ibid.*, pp. 559, 561. Gibbon, Decline and Fall of the Roman Empire, Vol. V, p. 248. New York, 1858.

CHAPTER XIII

ISLAND PEOPLES

THE characteristics which mark peninsulas, namely, ample contact with the sea, small area as compared with that of the continents, peripheral location, more or less complete isolation, combined, however, with the function of bridge or passway to yet remoter lands, are all accentuated in islands. A list of the chief peninsulas of the world, as compared with the greatest islands, shows a far larger scale of areas for the former, even if the latter be made to include the vast ice-capped land-mass of Greenland (2,170,000 square kilometers or 846,000 square miles). New Guinea, the largest habitable island, has only one-fourth the area of Arabia, the largest of the peninsulas.[1] Therefore, both the advantages and disadvantages incident to a restricted area may be expected to appear in an intensified degree in islands.

Peninsulas are morphologically transition forms between mainland and islands; by slight geological changes one is converted into the other. Great Britain was a peninsula at the end of the Tertiary period, before subsidence and the erosion of Dover Channel combined to sever it from the continent. It bears to-day in its flora and fauna the evidence of its former broad connection with the mainland.[2] In Pliocene times, Sicily and Sardinia were united by a land bridge with the Tunisian projection of North Africa; and they too, in their animal and plant life, reveal the old connection with the southern continent.[3] Sometimes man himself for his own purposes converts a peninsula into an island. Often he constructs a canal, like that at Kiel or Corinth, to remove an isthmian obstruction to navigation; but occasionally he transforms his peninsula into an island for the sake of greater protection. William of Rubruquis tells us that in 1253 he found the neck of the Crimea cut through by a ditch from sea to sea by the native Comanians, who had

Physical relationship between islands and peninsulas.

taken refuge in the peninsula from the Tartar invaders, and in this way had sought to make their asylum more secure.[4]

The reverse process in nature is quite as common. The Shangtung Peninsula rises like a mountainous island from the sea-like level of alluvial plains about it, suggesting that remote time when the plains were not yet deposited and an arm of the Yellow Sea covered the space between Shangtung and the highlands of Shansi.[5] The deposition of silt, aided often by slight local elevation of the coast, is constantly tying continental islands to the mainland. The Echinades Archipelago off the southwest coast of ancient Acarnania, opposite the mouth of the Achelous River, Strabo tells us, was formerly farther from shore than in his time, and was gradually being cemented to the mainland by Achelous silt. Some islets had already been absorbed in the advancing shoreline, and the same fate awaited others.[6] Farther up this western coast of Greece, the island of Leukas has been converted into a peninsula by a sickle-shaped sandbar extending across the narrow channel.[7] Nature is working in its leisurely way to attach Sakhalin to the Siberian coast. The strong marine current which sets southward from the Okhotsk Sea through the Strait of Tartary carries silt from the mouth of the heavy laden Amur River, and deposits it in the "narrows" of the strait between Capes Luzarev and Pogobi, building up sandbars that come dangerously near the surface in mid channel.[8] Here the water is so shallow that occasionally after long prevailing winds, the ground is left exposed and the island natives can walk over to Asia.[9] The close proximity of Sakhalin to the mainland and the ice bridge covering the strait in winter rob the island of much of its insular character and caused it to pass as a peninsula until 1852. Yet that five-mile wide stretch of sea on its western coast determined its selection as the great penal station of the Russian Empire. The fact that peninsular India accords in so many points of flora, fauna and even primitive ethnic stock with Madagascar and South Africa, indicates its former island nature, which has been geographically cloaked by its union with the continent of Asia.

Character of insular flora and fauna.

Islands, because of their relatively limited area and their

clearly defined boundaries, are excellent fields for the study of floral, faunal, and ethnic distribution. Small area and isolation cause in them poverty of animal and plant forms and fewer species than are found in an equal continental area. This is the curse of restricted space which we have met before. The large island group of New Zealand, with its highly diversified relief and long zonal stretch, has only a moderate list of flowering plants, in comparison with the numerous species that adorn equal areas in South Africa and southwestern Australia.[10] Ascension possessed originally less than six flowering plants. The four islands of the Greater Antilles form together a considerable area and have all possible advantages of climate and soil; but there are probably no continental areas equally big and equally favored by nature which are so poor in all the more highly organized groups of animals.[11] Islands tend to lop off the best branches. Darwin found not a single indubitable case of terrestrial mammals native to islands situated more than three hundred miles from the mainland.[12] The impoverishment extends therefore to quality as well as quantity, to man as well as to brute. In the island continent of Australia, the native mammalia, excepting some bats, a few rodents, and a wild dog, all belong to the primitive marsupial subclass; its human life, at the time of the discovery, was restricted to one retarded negroid race, showing in every part of the island a monotonous, early Stone Age development. The sparsely scattered oceanic islands of the Atlantic, owing to excessive isolation, were all, except the near-lying Canaries, uninhabited at the time of their discovery; and the Canary Islanders showed great retardation as compared with their parent stock of northern Africa. [See map page 105.]

Despite this general poverty of species, island life is distinguished by a great proportion of peculiar or endemic forms, and a tendency toward divergence, which is the effect of isolation and which becomes marked in proportion to the duration and effectiveness of isolation. Isolation, by reducing or preventing the intercrossing which holds the individual true to the normal type of the species, tends to produce divergences.[13] Hence island life is more or less differentiated

Endemic forms.

from that of the nearest mainland, according to the degree of isolation. Continental islands, lying near the coast, possess generally a flora and fauna to a large extent identical with that of the mainland, and show few endemic species and genera; whereas remote oceanic islands, which isolation has claimed for its own, are marked by intense specialization and a high percentage of species and even genera found nowhere else.[14] Even a narrow belt of dividing sea suffices to loosen the bonds of kinship. Recent as are the British Isles and near the Continent, they show some biological diversity from the mainland and from each other.[15]

Paradoxical influences of island habitats upon man. The influence of an island habitat upon its human occupants resembles that upon its flora and fauna, but is less marked. The reason for this is twofold. The plant and animal life are always the older and therefore have longer felt the effects of isolation; hence they bear its stamp in an intensified degree. Man, as a later comer, shows closer affinity to his kin in the great cosmopolitan areas of the continents. More than this, by reason of his inventiveness and his increasing skill in navigation, he finds his sea boundary less strictly drawn, and therefore evades the full influence of his detached environment, though never able wholly to counteract it. For man in lowest stages of civilization, as for plants and animals, the isolating influence is supreme; but with higher development and advancing nautical efficiency, islands assume great accessibility because of their location on the common highway of the ocean. They become points of departure and destination of maritime navigation, at once center of dispersal and goal, the breeding place of expansive national forces seeking an outlet, and a place of hospitality for wanderers passing those shores. Yet all the while, that other tendency of islands to segregate their people, and in this aloofness to give them a peculiar and indelible national stamp, much as it differentiates its plant and animal forms, is persistently operative.

Conservative and radical tendencies. These two antagonistic influences of an island environment may be seen working simultaneously in the same people, now one, now the other being dominant; or a period of undisturbed seclusion or exclusion may suddenly be followed by one of extensive intercourse, receptivity or expansion. Recall the contrast in the early and later history of the Canaries, Azores, Malta, England, Mauritius and Hawaii, now a lonely, half-inhabited waste, now a busy mart or teeming way-station. Consider the pronounced insular mind of the globe-trotting Englishman, the deep-seated local conservatism characterizing that world-colonizing nation, at once the most provincial and cosmopolitan on earth. Emerson says with truth, "Every one of these islanders is an island himself, safe, tranquil, incommunicable."[16] Hating innovation, glorifying their habitudes, always searching for a precedent to justify and countenance each forward step, they have nevertheless led the world's march of progress. Scattered by their colonial and commercial enterprises over every zone, in every clime, subjected to the widest range of modifying environments, they show in their ideals the dominant influence of the home country. The trail of the Oxford education can be followed over the Empire, east to New Zealand and west to Vancouver. Highschool students of Jamaica take Oxford examinations in botany which are based upon English plant life and ignore the Caribbean flora! School children in Ceylon are compelled to study a long and unfamiliar list of errors in English speech current only in the London streets, in order to identify and correct them on the Oxford papers, distributed with Olympian impartiality to all parts of the Empire. Such insularity of mind seems to justify Bernard Shaw's description of Britain as an island whose natives regard its manners and customs as laws of nature. Yet these are the people who in the Nile Valley have become masters of irrigation, unsurpassed even by the ancient Egyptians; who, in the snow-wrapped forests of Hudson Bay, are trappers and hunters unequalled by the Indians; who, in the arid grasslands of Australia, pasture their herds like nomad shepherd or American cowboy, and in the Tropics loll like the natives, but somehow manage to do a white man's stint of work.

In Japan, isolation has excluded or reduced to controllable measure every foreign force that might break the continuity of the national development or invade the integrity of the

The case of Japan.

national ideal. Japan has always borrowed freely from neighboring Asiatic countries and recently from the whole world; yet everything in Japan bears the stamp of the indigenous. The introduction of foreign culture into the Empire has been a process of selection and profound modification to accord with the national ideals and needs.[17] Buddhism, coming from the continent, was Japanized by being grafted on to the local stock of religious ideas, so that Japanese Buddhism is strongly differentiated from the continental forms of that religion.[18] The seventeenth century Catholicism of the Jesuits, before it was hospitably received, had to be adapted to Japanese standards of duty and ritual. Modern Japanese converts to Christianity wish themselves to conduct the local missions and teach a national version of the new faith.[19] But all the while, Japanese religion has experienced no real change of heart. The core of the national faith is the indigenous Shinto cult, which no later interloper has been permitted to dislodge or seriously to transform; and this has survived, wrapped in the national consciousness, wedded to the national patriotism, lifted above competition. Here is insular conservatism.

Japan's sudden and complete abandonment of a policy of seclusion which had been rigidly maintained for two hundred and fifty years, and her entrance upon a career of widespread intercourse synchronously with one of territorial expansion and extensive emigration, form one of those apparently irreconcilable contradictions constantly springing from the isolation and world-wide accessibility of an island environment; yet underlying Japan's present receptivity of new ideas and her outwardly indiscriminate adoption of western civilization is to be detected the deep primal stamp of the Japanese character, and an instinctive determination to preserve the core of that character intact.

Islands as nurseries and disseminators of distinctive civilizations.

It is this marked national individuality, developed by isolation and accompanied often by a precocious civilization, in combination with the opposite fact of the imminent possibility of an expansive unfolding, a brilliant efflorescence followed by a wide dispersal of its seeds of culture and of empire, which has assigned to islands in all times a great historical rôle. Rarely do these wholly originate the elements of civilization. For that their area is too small. But whatever seed ripen in the wide fields of the continents the islands transplant to their own forcing houses; there they transform and perfect the flower. Japan borrowed freely from China and Korea, as England did from continental Europe; but these two island realms have brought Asiatic and European civilization to their highest stage of development. Now the borrowers are making return with generous hand. The islands are reacting upon the continents. Japanese ideals are leavening the whole Orient from Manchuria to Ceylon. English civilization is the standard of Europe. "The Russian in his snows is aiming to be English," says Emerson. "England has inoculated all nations with her civilization, intelligence and tastes."[20]

The recent discoveries in Crete show beyond doubt that the school of Aegean civilization was in that island. Ancient Phœnicia, Argos, even Mycenæ and Tiryns put off their mask of age and appear as rosy boys learning none too aptly of their great and elderly master. Borrowing the seeds of culture from Asia and Egypt,[21] Crete nursed and tended them through the Neolithic and Bronze Age, transformed them completely, much as scientific tillage has converted the cotton tree into a low shrub. The precocity of this civilization is clear. At early as 3000 B. C. it included an impressive style of architecture and a decorative art naturalistic and beautiful in treatment as that of modern Japan.[22] From this date till the zenith of its development in 1450 B. C., Crete became a great artistic manufacturing and distributing center for stone carving, frescoes, pottery, delicate porcelain, metal work, and gems.[23] By 1800 B. C., seven centuries before Phœnician writing is heard of, the island had matured a linear script out of an earlier pictographic form.[24] This script, partly indigenous, partly borrowed from Libya and Egypt, gives Crete the distinction of having invented the first system of writing ever practised in Europe.[25]

Yet all this wealth of achievement bore the stamp of the indigenous; nearly every trace of its remote Asiatic or Egyptian origin was obliterated. Here the isolation of an

Ancient Cretan civilization.

island environment did thoroughly its work of differentiation, even on this thalassic isle which maintained constant intercourse with Egypt, the Cyclades, the Troad and the Greek peninsula.[26]   Minoan art has a freshness, vivacity, and modernity that distinguishes it fundamentally from the formal products of its neighbors. "Many of the favorite subjects, like the crocus and wild goat, are native to the islands . . . Even where a motive was borrowed from Egyptian life, it was treated in a distinctive way," made tender, dramatic, vital. "In religion, as in art generally, Crete translated its loans into indigenous terms, and contributed as much as it received."[27] The curator of Egyptian antiquities in the New York Metropolitan Art Museum examined five hundred illustrations of second and third millenium antiquities from Gournia and Vasiliki in Crete, made by Mrs. Harriet Boyd Hawes during her superintendence of the excavations there, and pronounced them distinctly un-Egyptian, except one vase, probably an importation.[28] All this was achieved by a small insular segment of the Mediterranean race, in their Neolithic and Bronze Age, before the advent of those northern conquerors who brought in an Aryan speech and the gift of iron. It was in Crete, therefore, that Aegean civilization arose. On this island it had a long and brilliant pre-Hellenic career, and thence it spread to the Greek mainland and other Aegean shores.[29]

Limitation of small area in insular history.

A small cup soon overflows. Islands may not keep; they are forced to give, live by giving. Here lies their historical significance. They dispense their gifts of culture in levying upon the resources of other lands. But finally more often than not, the limitation of too small a home area steps in to arrest the national development, which then fades and decays. To this rule Great Britain and Japan are notable exceptions, owing partly to the unusual size of their insulaɪ territory, partly to a highly advantageous location. Minoan Crete, in that gray antiquity when Homeric history was still unborn, gave out of its abundance in art, government, laws and maritime knowledge to the eastern Mediterranean world, till the springs of inspiration in its own small land were exhausted, and its small population was unable to resist the flood of northern invasion. Then the dispenser of gifts had to become an alms-taker from the younger, larger, more resourceful Hellenic world.

The same story of early but short lived preëminence comes from other Aegean islands. Before the rise of Athens, Samos under the great despot Polykrates became "the first of all cities, Hellenic or barbaric," a center of Ionian manners, luxury, art, science and culture, the seat of the first great thalassocracy or sea-power after that of Cretan Minos, a distributing point for commerce and colonies.[30] Much the same history and distinction attached to the island of Rhodes long before the first Olympiad,[31] and to the little island of Aegina.[32] If we turn to the native races of America, we find that the Haida Indians of the Queen Charlotte Archipelago are markedly superior to their Tlingit and Tsimshean kinsmen of the nearby Alaskan and British Columbian coast. In their many and varied arts they have freely borrowed from their neighbors; but they have developed these loans with such marvelous skill and independence that they greatly surpass their early masters, and are accredited with possessing the creative genius of all this coast.[33] Far away, on the remote southeastern outskirts of the island world of the Pacific, a parallel is presented by little Easter Isle. Once it was densely populated and completely tilled by a people who had achieved singular progress in agriculture, religion, masonry, sculpture in stone and wood carving, even with obsidian tools, and who alone of all the Polynesians had devised a form of hieroglyphical writing.[34] Easter Isle to-day shows only abandoned fields, the silent monuments of its huge stone idols, and the shrunken remnant of a deteriorated people.[35]

Isolation and accessibility are recorded in the ethnic stock of every island. Like its flora and fauna, its aboriginal population shows an affinity to that of the nearest mainland, and this generally in proportion to geographical proximity. The long line of deposit islands, built of the off-scourings of the land, and fringing the German and Netherland coast from Texel to Wangeroog, is inhabited by the same Frisian folk which occupies the nearby shore. The

Sources of ethnic stock of islands.

people of the Channel Isles, though long subject to England, belong to the Franco-Gallic stock and the *langue d'oïl* linguistic family of northern France. The native Canary Islanders, though giving no evidence of previous communication with any continental land at the time of their discovery, could be traced, through their physical features, speech, customs and utensils, to a remote origin in Egypt and the Berber regions of North Africa prior to the Mohammedan conquest.[36] Sakhalin harbors to-day, besides the immigrant Russians, five different peoples—Ainos, Gilyaks, Orochons, Tunguse, and Yakuts, all of them offshoots of tribes now or formerly found on the Siberian mainland a few miles away.[37]

Ethnic divergence with increased isolation.   Where the isolation of the island is more pronounced, owing either to a broader and more dangerous channel, as in the case of Madagascar and Formosa, or to the nautical incapacity of the neighboring coast peoples, as in the case of Tasmania and the Canary Islands, the ethnic influence of the mainland is weak, and the ethnic divergence of the insular population therefore more marked, even to the point of total difference in race. But this is generally a case of survival of a primitive stock in the protection of an unattractive island offering to a superior people few allurements to conquest, as illustrated by the ethnic history of the Andaman and Kurile Isles.

Differentiation of peoples and civilization on islands.   The sea forms the sharpest and broadest boundary; it makes in the island which it surrounds the conditions for differentiation. Thus while an insular population is allied in race and civilization to that of the nearest continent, it nevertheless differs from the same more than the several sub-groups of its continental kindred differ from each other. In other words, isolation makes ethnic and cultural divergence more marked on islands than on continents. The English people, despite their close kinship and constant communication with the Teutonic peoples of the European mainland, deviate from them more than any of these Germanic nations deviate from each other. The Celts of Great Britain and Ireland are sharply distinguished from the whole body of continental Celts in physical features, temperament, and cultural development. In Ireland the primitive Catholic

Church underwent a distinctive development. It was closely bound up in the tribal organization of the Irish people, lacked the system, order and magnificence of the Latinized Church, had its peculiar tonsure for monks, and its own date for celebrating Easter for nearly three hundred years after the coming of St. Patrick.[38] The Japanese, in their physical and mental characteristics, as in their whole national spirit, are more strikingly differentiated from the Chinese than the agricultural Chinese from the nomadic Buriat shepherds living east of Lake Baikal, though Chinese and Japanese are located much nearer together and are in the same stage of civilization. The Eskimo, who form one of the most homogeneous stocks, and display the greatest uniformity in language and cultural achievements of all the native American groups, have only one differentiated offshoot, the Aleutian Islanders. These, under the protection and isolation of their insular habitat from a very remote period, have developed to a greater extent than their Eskimo brethren of the mainland. The difference is evident in their language, religious ceremonies, and in details of their handiwork, such as embroidery and grass-fiber weaving.[39] The Haidas of the Queen Charlotte Archipelago show such a divergence in physique and culture from the related tribes of the mainland, that they have been accredited with a distinct origin from the other coast Indians.[40]

The differentiating influence is conspicuous in the speech of island people, which tends to form a distinct language or dialect or, in an archipelago, a group of dialects. The Channel Isles, along with their distinctive breeds of cattle, has each its own variant of the *langue d'oïl*.[41] According to Boccaccio's narrative of a Portuguese voyage to the Canaries in 1341, the natives of one island could not understand those from another, so different were their languages. The statement was repeated by a later authority in 1455 in regard to the inhabitants of Lancerote, Fuerteventura, Gomera and Ferro, who had then been Christianized. A partial explanation is supplied by the earlier visitors, who found the Canary Guanches with no means of communication between the several islands except by swimming.[42] In the Visayan group

Differentiation of language in islands.

of the Philippines, inhabited exclusively by the civilized Visayan tribes except for the Negritos in the mountainous interior, the people of Cebu can not understand their brethren in the adjacent islands; in Cuyos and Calmanianes, dialects of the Visayan are spoken.[43] [See map page 147.]

The differentiation of language from the nearby continental speech may be due to a higher development, especially on large islands affording very advantageous conditions, such as Great Britain and Japan. Japanese speech has some affinity with the great Altaic linguistic family, but no close resemblance to any sub-group.[44] It presents marked contrasts to the Chinese because it has passed beyond the agglutinative stage of development, just as English has sloughed off more of its inflectional forms than the continental Teutonic languages.

Archaic forms of speech in islands. More often the difference is due to the survival of archaic forms of speech. This is especially the case on very small or remote islands, whose limited area or extreme isolation or both factors in conjunction present conditions for retardation. The speech of the Sardinians has a strong resemblance to the ancient Latin, retains many inflectional forms now obsolete in the continental Romance languages; but it has also been enlivened by an infusion of Catalan words, which came in by the bridge of the Balearic Islands during the centuries of Spanish rule in Sardinia.[45] Again, it is in Minorca and Majorca that this Catalan speech is found in its greatest purity to-day. On its native soil in eastern Spain, especially in Barcelona, it is gradually succumbing to the official Castilian, and probably in a few centuries will be found surviving only in the protected environment of the Balearic Isles. Icelandic and the kindred dialects of the Shetland and Faroe Islands had their origin in the classic Norse of the ninth century, and are divergent forms of the speech of the Viking explorers.[46] The old Frisian tongue of Holland, sister speech to Anglo-Saxon, survives to-day only in West Friesland beyond the great marshlands, and in the long-drawn belt of coastal islands from Terschelling through Helgoland to Sylt, as also on the neighboring shores of Schleswig-Holstein.[47] This region of linguistic survival, insulated partially by the marshes or completely by the shallow "Wattenmeer" of this lowland coast, reminds us of the protracted life of the archaic Lithuanian speech within a circle of sea and swamp in Baltic Russia, and the survival of the Celtic tongue in peninsular Brittany, Cornwall, Wales, in Ireland, and the Highlands and islands of Scotland.

Islanders are always coast dwellers with a limited hinter- Unification land. Hence their stock may be differentiated from the of race in mainland race in part for the same reason that all coastal islands. folk in regions of maritime development are differentiated from the people of the back country, namely, because contact with the sea allows an intermittent influx of various foreign strains, which are gradually assimilated. This occasional ethnic intercrossing can be proved in greater or less degree of all island people. Here is accessibility operating against the underlying isolation of an island habitat. The English to-day represent a mixture of Celts with various distinct Teutonic elements, which had already diverged from one another in their separate habitats—Jutes, Angles, Saxons, Danes, Norse and Norman French. The subsequent detachment of these immigrant stocks by the English Channel and North Sea from their home people, and their arrival in necessarily small bands enabled them to be readily assimilated, a process which was stimulated further by the rapid increase of population, the intimate interactive life and unification of culture which characterizes all restricted areas. Hence islands, like peninsulas, despite ethnic admixtures, tend to show a surprising unification of race; they hold their people aloof from others and hold them in a close embrace, shut them off and shut them in, tend to force the amalgamation of race, culture and speech. Moreover, their relatively small area precludes effective segregation within their own borders, except where a mountainous or jungle district affords a temporary refuge for a displaced and antagonized tribe. Hence there arises a preponderance of the geographic over the ethnic and linguistic factors in the historical equation.

The uniformity in cranial type prevailing all over the British Isles is amazing; it is greater than in either Spain or Scandinavia. The cephalic indices range chiefly between

77 and 79, a restricted variation as compared with the ten points which represents the usual range for Central Europe, and the thirteen between the extremes of 75 and 88 found in France and Italy.[48] Japan stands in much the same ethnic relation to Asia as Britain to Europe. She has absorbed Aino, Mongolian, Malay and perhaps Polynesian elements, but by reason of her isolation has been left free to digest these at her leisure, so that her population is fairly well assimilated, though evidences of the old mixture can be discerned.[49] In Corsica and Sardinia a particularly low cephalic index, dropping in some communes to 73, and a particularly short stature point to a rare purity of the Mediterranean race,[50] and indicate the maintenance here of one ethnic type, despite the intermittent intrusion of various less pure stocks from the Italian mainland, Africa, Phœnicia, Arabia, and Spain. The location of the islands off the main routes of the basin, their remoteness from shore, and the strong spirit of exclusiveness native to the people,[51] bred doubtless from their isolation, have combined to reduce the amount of foreign intermixture.

Remoter sources of island populations. Islands do not necessarily derive their population from the land that lies nearest to them. A comparatively narrow strait may effectively isolate, if the opposite shore is inhabited by a nautically inefficient race; whereas a wide stretch of ocean may fail to bar the immigration of a seafaring people. Here we find a parallel to the imperfect isolation of oceanic islands for life forms endowed with superior means of dispersal, such as marine birds, bats and insects.[52] Iceland, though relatively near Greenland, was nevertheless peopled by far away Scandinavians. These bold sailors planted their settlements even in Greenland nearly two centuries before the Eskimo. England received the numerically dominant element of its population from across the wide expanse of the North Sea, from the bare but seaman-breeding coasts of Germany, Denmark and Norway, rather than from the nearer shores of Gaul. So the Madeira and Cape Verde Isles had to wait for the coming of the nautical Portuguese to supply them with a population; and only later, owing to the demand for slave labor, did they draw upon the human stock of nearby Africa, but even then by means of Portuguese ships.

Owing to the power of navigation to bridge the intervening spaces of water and hence to emphasize the accessibility rather than the isolation of these outlying fragments of land, we often find islands facing two or three ways, as it were, tenanted on different sides by different races, and this regardless of the width of the intervening seas, where the remote neighbors excel in nautical skill. Formosa is divided between its wild Malay aborigines, found on the eastern, mountainous side of the island, and Chinese settlers who cultivate the wide alluvial plain on the western side.[53] Fukien Strait, though only eighty miles wide, sufficed to bar Formosa to the land-loving northern Chinese till 1644, when the island became an asylum for refugees from the Manchu invaders; but long before, the wider stretches of sea to the south and north were mere passways for the sea-faring Malays, who were the first to people the island, and the Japanese who planted considerable colonies on its northern coasts at the beginning of the fifteenth century. [See map page 103.]

In a similar way Madagascar is divided between the Malayan Hovas, who occupy the eastern and central part of the island, and the African Sakalavas who border the western coast. [See map page 105.] This distribution of the ethnic elements corresponds to that of the insect life, which is more African on the western side and more Indo-Malayan on the eastern.[54] Though the population shows every physical type between Negro and Malayan, and ethnic diversity still predominates over ethnic unity in this vast island, nevertheless the close intercourse of an island habitat has even in Madagascar produced unification of language   Malayan speech of an ancient form prevails everywhere, and though diversified into dialects, is everywhere so much alike that all Malagasies can manage to understand one another.[55] The first inhabitants were probably African; but the wide Mozambique Current (230 miles), with its strong southward flow, was a serious barrier to fresh accessions from the mainland, especially as the nautical development of the African tribes was always low. Meanwhile, however, successive relays of sea-bred Malay-

Double sources.

Polynesians crossed the broad stretch of the Indian Ocean, occupied the island, and finally predominated over the original Negro stock.[56] Then in historic times came Arabs, Swahilis, and East Indians to infuse an Asiatic element into the population of the coasts, while Portuguese, English, Dutch and French set up short-lived colonies on its shores. But despite this intermittent foreign immigration, the fundamental isolation of Madagascar, combined with its large area, enabled it to go its own slow historical gait, with a minimum of interference from outside, till France in 1895 began to assume control of the island.

Mixed population of small thalassic isles. Small thalassic islands, at an early date in their history, lose their ethnic unity and present a highly mixed population. The reasons for this are two. The early maritime development characterizing enclosed seas covers them with a network of marine routes, on which such islands serve as way stations and mid-sea markets for the surrounding shores. Sailors and traders, colonists and conquerors flock to them from every side. Such a nodal location on commercial routes insures to islands a cosmopolitanism of race, as opposed to the ethnic differentiation and unity which follows an outlying or oceanic situation. Here the factor of many-sided accessibility predominates over isolation.

The prevailing small area of such thalassic islands, moreover, involves a population so small that it is highly susceptible to the effects of intercrossing. Too restricted to absorb the constant influx of foreign elements, the inhabitants tend to become a highly mixed, polyglot breed. This they continue to be by the constant addition of foreign strains, so long as the islands remain foci of trade or strategic points for the control of the marine highways. Diomede Island in Bering Strait is the great market place of the polar tribes. Here Siberian Chukches and Alaskan Eskimos make their exchanges. The Eskimo of St. Lawrence Island in Bering Sea, from long intercourse, have adopted certain articles of dress, the boats and part of the vocabulary of the Chukches.[57] Kilwauru, located on a sand-bank at the eastern end of Ceram, on the border between Malayan and Papuan island districts, is the metropolis of native traders in the Far East. Here gather the *praus* of the sea-faring Bugis bringing manufactured goods from Singapore, and boats laden with the natural products of New Guinea.[58] The smaller these island marts and the wider their circle of trade, the more mixed is their population. Thursday Isle, an English coaling-station in Torres Strait, is a port of call for all steamers bound from Europe or China for east Australian ports, besides being a center of a big local trade in pearl shell and tripang. Hence its population of 526 souls comprises 270 Europeans of various nationalities, including British, Germans, Scandinavians, Danes, Spanish, Portuguese, French and Australians of European origin, besides 256 South Sea Islanders, Papuans, Africans, Philippinos, Chinese and other Asiatics.[59]

Antiquity shows the same thing on a smaller scale, which **Mixed** grew, however, with the expansion of the circle of commerce. **population** Ancient Aegina in the Saronic Gulf received inhabitants **of island** from Crete, Argos, Epidaurus in eastern Argolis and Athens; **markets.** it became a central maritime market and its people sea-traders, whose goods of a certain small kind became known as "Aegina wares."[60] Delos at the crossroads of the Aegean was the center of longer radii. It became the inn for travelers and merchants sailing from Asia and Egypt to Italy and Greece, and hence drew to itself the trade and people of the whole Mediterranean basin.[61] The northwestern Indian Ocean had a similar emporium in the ancient Dioscoridis, (Sokotra) which focused on itself the trade between Arabia and eastern Africa.[62]

Ceylon's location made it in ancient and medieval times the common meeting place for Arab traders from the west and Chinese merchants from the east; it thus became the Sicily of the semi-enclosed North Indian Ocean. To-day its capital Colombo is "the Clapham Junction of the Eastern Seas," where passengers change steamers for China, India and Australia; a port of call for vessels passing from the Straits of Malacca to the Persian Gulf or Mediterranean. Hence Ceylon's solid nucleus of Singhalese and Tamil population, protected against absorption by the large area of the island (25,365 square miles) is interspersed in the coastal

districts with Arabs, Portuguese, Eurasians dating from the
old Portuguese occupation, and some ten thousand Europeans.[63] The island of Gotland, located at the crossroads of
the Baltic, was early adopted by the Hanseatic merchants
as their maritime base for the exploitation of Swedish, Finnish, and Russian trade. Here were "peoples of divers
tongues," so the old chronicles say, while the archeological
finds of Byzantine, Cufic, Roman, Anglo-Saxon and German
coins testify to the wide circle of trade whose radii focused
at this nodal point of the Baltic.[64]

Significant
location of
island way
stations. The great importance of such islands has been due solely
to their location. Their size and resources are negligible
quantities, but their natural position as way stations lent
them preëminence so long as navigation held to short "laps,"
and was restricted to enclosed seas. In the wide expanse of
the open ocean, similar sparsely scattered isles, like Ascension,
St. Helena, the Canaries and Hawaii, assumed importance
in proportion to their scarcity. Though never the centers
of rife intercourse like Delos and Gotland, those lying conspicuously in the track of commerce have succeeded in drawing to themselves the typical polyglot nodal population.
Mauritius, located at the southwestern entrance of the Indian
Ocean about equally distant from Aden, Ceylon, Bombay,
Singapore and West Australia, and possessing the best
harbor within many hundred miles, has been held successively
by Dutch, French and English, and to-day has a dense population of French, English and Hindus.[65] A situation at the
northeast entrance to the Caribbean Sea, keystone of the
vast arch formed by the Greater and Lesser Antilles, made
the island of St. Thomas a natural distributing point for this
whole basin. Facing that much traveled Virgin Passage,
and forming the first objective of vessels bound from Europe
to Panama, it became a great ship rendezvous, and assumed
strategic and commercial importance from early times. We
find the same political owners here as in Mauritius and in the
same order—Dutch, French and English, though in 1671
the island was occupied by the Danes, then from 1807 to
1815 by the English again, and finally secured by the
Danes.[66] The history of the Falkland Islands is a significant

reflection of their location on the south oceanic trade route, where they command the entrance to the Magellan Straits and the passage round the Horn. Here on the outskirts of the world, where they form the only break in the wide blank surface of the South Atlantic, they have been coveted and held in turn by the chief European powers having colonies in the Orient,—by France, Spain, England, Spain again, England again, by Argentine in 1820, and finally by England since 1833. Their possession was of especial advantage to Great Britain, which had no other base in this part of the world intermediate between England and New Zealand.

Islands located in enclosed seas display the transitional character of border districts. They are outposts of the surrounding shores, and become therefore the first objective of every expanding movement, whether commercial or political, setting out from the adjacent coasts. Such islands are swept by successive waves of conquest or colonization, and they carry in their people and language evidences of the wrack left behind on their shores. This has been the history of Aegina, Cyprus, Rhodes, Crete, Malta, Corfu, Sicily and Sardinia. That of Cyprus is typical. It was the first island base for the ancient Tyrian fleets, and had its Phœnician settlements in 1045 B. C. From that time it was one of the many prizes in the Mediterranean grab-bag for the surrounding nations. After the decline of Tyre, it was occupied by Greeks, then passed in turn to Assyrians, Egyptians, Persians, Romans, Saracens, Byzantines, and in 1191 was seized by the Crusaders. Later it fell to Egypt again; but in 1373 was taken by Genoa, in 1463 by Venice, in 1571 by the Turks, and finally in 1878 was consigned to England.[67] All these successive occupants have left their mark upon its people, speech, culture and architecture. In the same way Sicily, located at the waist of the Mediterranean, has received the imprint of Greeks, Carthagenians, Romans, Saracens, Normans, Spaniards and Italians.[68] Its architectural remains bear the stamp of these successive occupants in every degree of purity and blending. The Sicilians of to-day are a mixture of all these intrusive stocks and speak a form of Italian corrupted by the infusion of Arabic words.[69] In 1071 when

Thalassic islands as goals of expansion.

the Normans laid siege to Palermo, five languages were spoken on the island,—Greek, Latin, Hebrew, Arabic and vulgar Sicilian, evidence enough that it was the meeting ground of the nations of Europe, Asia and North Africa.[70] Polyglot Malta to-day tells the same story of successive conquests, the same shuttlecock history.[71] Almost every language of Europe is spoken here; but the native Maltese speech is a corrupt form of Arabic mixed with modern Italian and ancient Phœnician words.[72] The whole island is ethnographically a border hybrid of Europe and North Africa. The Channel Isles are to-day the only spot in Europe where French and English survive side by side as official and commercial languages. French and Italian meet on equal terms in Corsica. Chinese, Japanese and Malays have traded and warred and treated on the debatable land of Formosa. The Aru, Ke, and other small archipelagoes of the Banda Sea link together the pure Malay and the pure Papuan districts, between which they lie.

From the border character of many islands there follow often far-reaching historical effects. Like all border regions they are natural battlegrounds. Their historical episodes are small, often slow and insidious in their movement, but large in their final content; for they are prone to end in a sudden dramatic *denouement* that draws the startled gaze of all the neighboring world. It was the destiny of Sicily to make and unmake the fortunes of ancient Carthage. Ceylon, from the dawn of history, lured traders who enriched and conquerors who oppressed peninsular India. The advance of Spain to the Canary Isles was the drowsy prologue to the brilliant drama of American discovery. The island of Tsushima in the Korean Strait was seized by the forces of Kublai Khan in 1280 as the base of their attack upon Japan;[73] and when in 1857 the Russian bear tried to plant a foot on this island, Japan saw danger in the movement and ordered him off.[74] Now we find Japan newly established in Sakhalin, the Elliot Islands and Formosa, by means of which and her own archipelago she blankets the coast of Asia for twenty-two hundred miles. This geographical situation may be productive of history.

Islands are detached areas physically and readily detached

Political detachability of islands.

politically. Though insularity gives them some measure of protection, their relatively small size and consequently small populations make them easy victims for a conquering sea power, and easy to hold in subjection. The security of an island habitat against aggression therefore, increases with its size, its efficiency in naval warfare, and its degree of isolation, the last of which factors depends in turn upon its location as thalassic or oceanic. Islands of enclosed seas, necessarily small and never far from the close encircling lands, are engulfed by every tide of conquest emanating from the nearby shores. Oesel and Dago have been held in succession by every Baltic power, by the Teutonic Orders, Denmark, Sweden and Russia. Gotland has acknowledged allegiance to the Hanseatic League, to Denmark and Sweden. Sardinia, occupying the center of the western Mediterranean, has figured in a varied series of political combinations,—with ancient Carthage, Rome, the Saracens of North Africa, with Sicily, Pisa, Aragon, Piedmont, and finally now with united Italy.[75] To the land-bred Teutonic hordes which swept over western Europe in the early centuries of our era, a narrow strip of sea was some protection for Sicily, Corsica, Sardinia, Malta and the Balearic Isles. Hence we find these islands slow in succumbing to their non-maritime conquerors, and readily regained by the energetic Justinian. Later they fell victim to the sea-wise Saracens, but again gravitated back to their closer and more natural European connections.

More often the small area of an island facilitates its re- Insular tention in bondage, when the large and less isolated conti- weakness nental districts have thrown off an unwelcome yoke. Athens, due to small area. with her strong navy, found it an easy task to whip back into the ranks of the Delian Confederacy her recalcitrant island subjects like Naxos, Samos and Thasos; but her mutinous cities in peninsular Chalcidice and isthmian Megara, incited to revolt and aided by their neighbors,[76] were less at her mercy. This principle was recognized by Thucydides,[77] and taken advantage of by the Lacedæmonians during the great war for Spartan supremacy. England has been able to hold Ireland in a vise. Of all her former French territory, she retains only the Channel Isles. Cuba and Porto Rico remained in the crushing grasp of Spain sixty-four years after the continental Greeks had made good their claim to South America, by mutual help and encouragement, had secured independence. The islands found that the isolation which confers protection from outside aggression meant for them detachment from friendly sources of succor on the mainland. The desultory help of filibuster expeditions, easily checked at the port of departure or landing, availed little to supplement the inadequate forces of rebellion pent up on their relatively small areas. By contrast, Mexico's larger area and population, continually stirred by American example and encouragement, reinforced by American volunteers and even by United States army officers, found revolt from 1812 to 1824 a comparatively easy task.

Cuba suffered from its geographic aloofness. So did little Crete, which submitted to Turkish oppression sixty years after the continental Greeks had made good their claim to freedom. Nor was this the first time that Cretan liberty had suffered from the detachment of an island environment. Aristotle recognized the principle when he wrote: "The people of Crete have hitherto submitted to the rule of the leading families as *Cosmi*, because the insular situation of Crete cuts off the interference of strangers or foreigners which might stir up rebellion against the unjust or partial government." And then he adds that this insular exclusion of outside incitement long rendered the fidelity of the *Perioeci* or serf-like peasants of Crete a striking contrast to the uneasy spirit of the Spartan Helots, who were constantly stirred to revolt by the free farmers of Argos, Messinia and Arcadia.[78] Thus ancient like modern Crete missed those beneficient stimuli which penetrate a land frontier, but are cut off by the absolute boundary of the sea.

Island remains of broken empires. Island fragments of broken empires are found everywhere. They figure conspicuously in that scattered location indicative of declining power. Little St. Pierre and Miquelon are the last geographical evidences of France's former dominion in Canada. The English Bermudas and Bahamas point back to the time when Great Britain held the long-drawn opposite coast. The British, French, Dutch, Danish, as once even Swedish, holdings in the Lesser Antilles are island monuments to lost continental domains, as recently were Cuba and Porto Rico to Spain's once vast American empire. Of Portugal's widespread dominion in the Orient there remain to her only the island fragments of Timor, Kambing, Macao and Diu, besides two coastal points on the western face of peninsular India. All the former continental holdings of the Sultan of Zanzibar have been absorbed into the neighboring German and British territories, and only the islands of Zanzibar and Pemba remain to him by the temporary indulgence of his strong neighbors. The Sheik of the Bahrein Islands originally held also the large kingdom of El Hasa on the nearby Persian Gulf littoral of Arabia; but he lost this to the Turks in 1840, and now retains the Bahrein Islands as the residuum of his former territories.[79]

The insular remnants of empires are tolerated, because Security their small size, when unsupported by important location, of such usually renders them innocuous; and their geographic isola- remnants tion removes them from international entanglements, unless passive. some far-reaching anthropo-geographic readjustment lends them a new strategic or commercial importance. The construction of the Suez Canal gave England a motive for the acquisition of Cyprus in 1878, as a nearer base than Malta for the protection of Port Said, just as the present Panama Canal project led the United States to re-open negotiations for the purchase of the Danish Isles. One cannot get away from the impression that the law of political detachability will operate again to make some new distribution of the particolored political holdings in the Lesser Antilles. The small size of these islands, and their thalassic location commanding approaches to a large region of only partially developed resources and to the interoceanic passway across it, will pitch them into the dice-box on the occasion of every naval war between their sovereign powers.

The shifting fate of political detachability becomes moderated in islands of the open ocean, because of their remoteness from the colonizing or conquering movements emanating from the continents. In contrast to the changing political connections of thalassic isles, consider the calm or

monotonous political history of outlying islands like the
Shetland, Faroes, Iceland, Canaries, Madeira, Cape Verde,
Azores, St. Helena, Ascension and Hawaii. The Norse colony
of Iceland, as a republic, maintained loose connections with
its mother country from 874 to 1264; then for nearly six
centuries it followed the political fate of Norway till 1814,
when an oversight left it in the hands of Denmark on the
dissolution of the union of Denmark and Norway. The
Azores have known no history except that which came to
them from Portugal; even their discovery goes back to a
Saracen navigator who, in 1147, sailed from the mouth of
the Tagus a thousand miles straight into the sunset.[80] For
two hundred years thereafter extreme isolation kept them
outside the pale of history till their rediscovery by Prince
Henry, the Navigator.

Political autonomy of islands based upon area and location. Land-masses, as we have found, are independent by location or independent by size. Large islands, especially where
they occupy an outskirt locaton, may long succeed in maintaining an independent national existence; but to render this
permanent, they must supplement their area by the acquisition of continental lands, according to the law of increasing
territorial aggregates. Great Britain and Japan, though
ethnically and culturally appendages of the nearby mainland, were large enough, aided by the dividing sea, to
maintain political autonomy. They absorbed all the insular
fragments lying about them to extend their areas, and then
each in turn entered upon a career of continental expansion.
To Japan this movement as a determined policy came late,
only when she faced the alternative of absorbing territory
or being absorbed by all-devouring Russia. The isolation
of Madagascar resulted in only slight community of race
with Africa, and combined with large area, has kept
the island to a great extent distinct from the political history
of Africa. The impulses which swept the eastern coast of
the continent reached the outlying island with abated force.
Arab, Portuguese, Dutch and English only scratched its
rim. The character of its western coasts, of its vigorous
Malayan population, and of the intervening Mozambique
Current rendered conquest difficult from the African shore.

Its large size, with the promise of abundant resources, offered a bait to conquest, yet put a barrier in its way. Hence we find that not till 1895, when the partition of continental Africa was almost accomplished, did the French conquest of Madagascar occur.

By contrast, the closely grouped East Indies, long coveted for their tropical products, suffered a contagion of conquest. The large size of these islands, so far from granting them immunity, only enabled the epidemic of Portuguese and Dutch dominion to pass from one to the other more readily, and that even when the spice and pepper trade languished from a plethora of products. But even here the size of the islands, plus the sub-equatorial climate which bars genuine white colonization, has restricted the effective political dominion of Europeans to the coasts, and thus favored the survival of the natives undisturbed in the interior, with all their primitive institutions. The largest islands, like Borneo and Sumatra, have vast inland tracts still unexplored and devoted to savagery, thus illustrating the contrast between center and periphery. When Australia, the largest of all the Pacific island group, became an object of European expansion, its temperate and sub-tropical location adapted it for white colonization, and the easy task of conquering its weak and retarded native tribes encouraged its appropriation; but the natural autonomy which belongs to large area and detached location asserted itself in the history of British Australia. The island continent is now erected into a confederation of states, enjoying virtual independence. In New Zealand, we find the recent colonists taking advantage of their isolation to work out undisturbed certain unique social theories. Here, against a background of arrested aboriginal development, another race evinces a radical spirit of progress; and to these contrasted results equally the detached island environment has contributed its share.

The historical development of island peoples bears always in greater or less degree the stamp of isolation; but this isolation may lead to opposite cultural results. It may mean in one case retardation, in another accelerated development. Its geographical advantages are distinctly

Historical effects of island isolation: primitive retardation.

relative, increasing rapidly with a rising scale of civilization. Therefore in an island habitat the race factor may operate with or against the geographic factor in producing a desirable historical result. If the isolation is almost complete, the cultural status of the inhabitants low, and therefore their need of stimulation from without very great, the lack of it will sink them deeper in barbarism than their kinsmen on the mainland. The negroes of Africa, taken as a whole, occupy a higher economic and cultural rank than the black races of Australia and Melanesia; and for this difference one cause at least is to be found in the difference of their habitats. The knowledge of iron, stock-raising, and many branches of agriculture were continental achievements, which belonged to the great eastern land-mass and spread from Egypt over Africa even to the Hottentot country; the lack of them among the Australians must be attributed to their insularity, which barred them from this knowledge, just as the ignorance of iron and other metals among the native Canary Islanders[81] can only be ascribed to a sea barrier fifty-two miles wide. The scant acquaintance of the Balearic Islanders with iron in Roman days[82] points to insular detachment. The lack of native domesticable animals in the Pacific archipelagoes illustrates another limitation incident to the restricted fauna of islands, though this particular lack also retarded the cultural development of primitive North America.

Later stimulation of development.   On the other hand, people who have already secured the fundamental elements of civilization find the partial seclusion of an island environment favorable to their further progress, because it permits their powers to unfold unhindered, protects them from the friction of border quarrels, from the disturbance and desolation of invading armies, to which continental peoples are constantly exposed. But even here the advantage lies in insulation but not in isolation,[83] in a location like that of England or Japan, near enough to a continent to draw thence culture, commerce and occasional new strains of blood, but detached by sea-girt boundaries broad enough to ward off overwhelming aggressions. Such a location insures enough segregation for protection, but also opportunity for universal contact over the vast commons of the sea.

Excessive isolation may mean impoverishment in purse Excessive and progress even for an advanced race. Ireland has long isolation. suffered from its outskirt location. It lies too much in the shadow of England, and has been barred by the larger island from many warming rays of immigration, culture and commerce that would have vitalized its national existence. The "round barrow" men of the Bronze Age, the Romans, and the Normans never carried thither their respective contributions to civilization. The Scandinavians infused into its population only inconsiderable strains of their vigorous northern blood.[84] In consequence the Irish are to-day substantially the same race as in Cæsar's time, except for the small, unassimilated group of antagonistic English and Lowland Scotch, both Teutonic, in Ulster.[85] Barred by Great Britain from direct contact with the Continent and all its stimulating influences, suffering from unfavorable conditions of climate and topography, Ireland's political evolution progressed at a snail's pace. It tarried in the tribal stage till after the English conquest, presenting a primitive social organization such as existed nowhere in continental Europe. Property was communal till the time of the Tudors, and all law was customary.[86] Over-protected by excessive isolation, it failed to learn the salutary lesson of political co-operation and centralization for defense, such as Scotland learned from England's aggressions, and England from her close continental neighbors. Great Britain, meanwhile, intercepted the best that the Continent had to give, both blows and blessings, and found an advantage in each. The steady prosecution of her continental wars demanded the gradual erection of a standing army, which weakened the power of feudalism; and the voting of funds for the conduct of these same wars put a whip into the hand of Parliament.

The history of Iceland illustrates the advantage and sub- The case sequently the drawback of isolation. The energetic spirits of Iceland. who, at the end of the ninth century, resented the centralization of political power in Norway and escaped from the turmoil and oppression of the home country to the remote asylum offered by Iceland, maintained there till 1262 the only absolutely free republic in the world.[87] They had brought with them various seeds of culture and progress, which grew and flowered richly in this peaceful soil. Iceland became the center of brilliant maritime and colonial achievements, the home of a native literature which surpassed that of all its contemporaries except Dante's Italy.[88] But after the decay of the Greenland colonies converted Iceland from a focal into a remote terminal point, and after the progress of the world became based upon complex and far-reaching commercial relations, the blight of extreme isolation settled upon the island; peace became stagnation.

Protection of an island environment. The concomitant of isolation is protection. Though this protection, if the result of extreme isolation, may mean an early cessation of development, history shows that in the lower stages of civilization, when the social organism is small and weak, and its germs of progress easily blighted, islands offer the sheltered environment in which imported flowers of culture not only survive but improve; in less protected fields they deteriorate or disappear. When learning and Christianity had been almost wiped out on the continent of Europe by the ravages of barbarian invasion between 450 and 800 A. D., in Ireland they grew and flourished. In the seventh and eighth centuries, the high scholarship of the Irish monks and their enthusiastic love of learning for its own sake drew to their schools students of the noblest rank from both England and France.[89] It was from Irish teachers that the Picts of Scotland and the Angles of northern England received their first lessons in Christianity. These fixed their mission stations again on islands, on Iona off southwestern Scotland and on Lindisfarne or Holy Isle near the east coast of Northumbria.[90] It was in the protected environment of the medieval Iceland that Scandinavian literature reached its highest development.

Insular protection was undoubtedly a factor in the brilliant cultural development of Crete. The progress of the early civilization from the late Stone Age through the Bronze Age was continuous; it bears no trace of any strong outside influence or sudden transition, no evidence of disturbance like an invasion or conquest by an alien people till 1200 B. C. when the latest stage of Minoan art was crushed by barbarian incursion from the north.[91]

The early history of the Singhalese monarchy in Ceylon from 250 B. C. to 416 A. D., when even the narrow moat of Palk Strait discouraged Tamil invasions from the mainland, shows the brilliant development possible under even a slight degree of protection.[92] However, in the case of these Ceylon Aryans, as in that of the Icelandic Norse, we must keep in mind the fact that the bearers of this culture were picked men, as are early maritime colonists the world over. The sea selects and then protects its island folk. But the seclusion of Ceylon was more favorable to progress than the mainland of India, with its incessant political and religious upheavals. Japan, in contrast to China's long list of invasions, shows the peace of an insular location. She never suffered any overwhelming influx of alien races or any foreign conquest. The armada sent by Kublai Khan in 1281 to subdue the islands paralleled the experience of the famous Spanish fleet three centuries later in English waters. This is the only attempt to invade Japan that recorded history shows.[93] In the original peopling of the island by Mongolian stock at the cost of the Aino aborigines, there is evidence of two distinct and perhaps widely separated immigrations from the mainland, one from Korea and another from more northern Asia. Thus Japan's population contained two continental elements, which seem to have held themselves in the relation of governing and governed class, much as Norman and Saxon did in England, while the Ainos lingered in the geographical background of mountain fastness and outlying islands, as the primitive Celts did in the British Isles. In the case both of England and Japan, the island location made the occupation by continental races a fitful, piecemeal process, not an inundation, because only small parties could land from time to time. The result was gradual or partial amalgamation of the various stocks, but nowhere annihilation.

But island location was not the sole factor in the equation. Similarity of race and relative parity of civilization between the successive immigrants and the original population, as

Factor of protection in Ceylon and Japan.

Character of the invaders as factor.

well as the small numbers of the invaders, made the struggle for the ownership of the island not wholly one-sided, and was later favorable to amalgamation in England as in Japan; whereas very small bands of far-coming Spaniards in the Canaries, Cuba, and Porto Rico resulted in the extinction of the original inhabitants, by the process operating now in New Zealand and Australia. Prior to the arrival of the Europeans in the Antilles, the conquest of these islands by South American Caribs had resulted in race intermixture. These sea-marauders brought no women with them in their small boats from the distant mainland, so they killed off the men and married the Arawak women of the islands. Here again insular location plus similarity of race and culture produced amalgamation, as opposed to extermination of the vanquished by over-sea invaders.

While the insular security of a primitive folk like the Tasmanians, Hawaiians and Malagasies is only passive, that of a civilized people like the English and modern Japanese is active, consciously utilized and reinforced. It is therefore more effective, and productive of more varied political and cultural results. Such people can allow themselves extensive contact with other nations, because they know it is in their power to control or check such contact at will. Japan took refuge in its medieval period in a policy of seclusion suggested by its island habitat,[95] relying on the passive protection of isolation. England, on the other hand, from the time of King Alfred, built up a navy to resist invasion. The effect, after the political unification of Great Britain, was a guarantee of protection against foreign attack, the concentration of the national defenses in a navy,[96] the elimination of the standing army which despotic monarchs might have used to crush the people, the consequent release of a large working force from military service, and the application of these to the development of English industry.[97]

Islands as places of refuge.

Islands, as naturally protected districts, are often sought as places of refuge by the weak or vanquished, and thus are drawn into the field of historical movement. We find this principle operating also in the animal world. The fur seals of the North Pacific have fled from the American coasts and found an asylum on the Pribiloff Islands of Bering Sea, where their concentration and isolation have enabled them to become wards of the United States government, though this result they did not foresee. The last Rhytina or Arctic sea-cow was found on an island in Bering Strait.[98]   So the Veneti of Northern Italy in the fifth century sought an asylum from the desolating Huns and, a century later, from the Lombards, in the deposit islands at the head of the Adriatic, and there found the geographic conditions for a brilliant commercial and cultural development.   Formosa got its first contingent of Chinese settlers in the thirteenth century in refugees seeking a place of safety from Kublai Khan's armies ; and its second in 1644 in a Chinese chief and his followers who had refused to submit to the victorious Manchus.   In 1637 Formosa was an asylum also for Japanese Christians, who escaped thither from the persecutions attending the discovery of Jesuit conspiracies against the government.[99]   The Azores, soon after their rediscovery in 1431, were colonized largely by Flemish refugees,[100] just as Iceland was peopled by rebellious Norwegians.   To such voluntary exiles the dividing sea gives a peculiar sense of security, this by a psychological law.   Hence England owing to its insular location, and also to its free government, has always been an asylum for the oppressed.   The large body of Huguenot refugees who sought her shores after the revocation of the Edict of Nantes added a valuable element to her population.

Islands find their populations enriched by the immigration of this select class who refuse to acquiesce in oppression and injustice.   But the geographic conditions which make islands natural asylums make them also obvious places of detention for undesirable members of society; these conditions render segregation complete, escape difficult or impossible, and control easy.   Hence we find that almost all the nations of the world owning islands have utilized them as penal stations. From the gray dawn of history the Isles of the Blessed have been balanced by the isles of the cursed.   The radiant Garden of Hesperides has found its antithesis in the black hell of Norfolk Isle, peopled by the "doubly condemned" criminals whom not even the depraved convict citizens of

Convict islands.

Botany Bay could tolerate.[101]   There is scarcely an island
of the Mediterranean without this sinister vein in its history.
The archipelagoes of the ancient Aegean were constantly
receiving political exiles from continental Greece. Augustus
Cæsar confined his degenerate daughter Julia, the wife of
Tiberius, on the island of Pandateria, one of the Ponza
group; and banished her paramour, Sempronius Gracchus,
to Cercina in the Syrtis Minor off the African coast.[102]
Other Roman matrons of high degree but low morals and
corrupt officials were exiled to Corsica, Sardinia, Seriphos,
Amorgos and other of the Cyclades.[103]   To-day Italy has
prisons or penal stations in Ischia, the Ponza group, Procida,
Nisida, Elba, Pantellaria, Lampedusa, Ustica, and especially
in the Lipari Isles, where the convicts are employed in mining
sulphur, alum and pumice from the volcanic cones.[104]

Penal colonies on unin-habited islands.

In modern times many remote oceanic islands have gotten
their first or only white settlers from this criminal class.
Such are the citizens whom Chile has sent to Easter Isle
twenty-five hundred miles away out in the Pacific.[105]   The
inhabitants of Fernando Noronha, 125 miles off the eastern
point of South America, are convicts from Brazil, together
with the warders and troops who guard them.[106]   In 1832
Ecuador began to use the uninhabited Gallapagos Islands,
lying 730 miles west of its coast, as a penal settlement.[107]
The history of St. Helena is typical. Its first inhabitants
were some Portuguese deserters who in punishment were
marooned here from a Portuguese ship with a supply of seed
and cattle. They proved industrious and had cultivated a
good deal of the land when four years later they were removed
to Portugal. The next inhabitants were a few slaves of both
sexes who escaped from a slave ship that had stopped here
for wood and water. These multiplied, worked and restored
the overgrown plantations of their predecessors, till a Portuguese vessel about twenty years later was sent to exterminate
them. A few escaped to the woods, however, and were found
there in prosperity in 1588.[108]   From 1815 till 1821 St.
Helena was the prison of Napoleon.

Many of these penal islands seem chosen with a view to
their severe or unhealthy climate, which would forever repel

free immigration and therefore render them useless for any other purpose. This is true of the French Isles du Salut off the Guiana coast, of Spanish Fernando Po in the Gulf of Guinea, of the Andaman and Nicobar Islands, notoriously unhealthy, which receive the criminals of British India,[109] and of numerous others. A bleak climate and unproductive soil have added to the horror of exile life in Sakhalin, as they overshadowed existence in the Falkland Islands, when these were a penal colony of Spain and later of Argentine.[110]

In the case of political offenders and incorrigibles, the island prison is as remote and inaccessible as possible. The classic example is Napoleon's consignment to Elba and subsequently to St. Helena, whence escape was impossible. Spain has sent its rebellious subjects, even university professors of independent views, to Fernando Po in the Gulf of Guinea and Teneriffe in the Canaries.[111] Russian political offenders of the most dangerous class are confined first in the Schlüsselberg prison, situated on a small island in Lake Ladoga near the effluence of the Neva. There they languish in solitary confinement or are transferred to far-off Sakhalin, whose very name is taboo in St. Petersburg.[112] During our Civil War, one of the Dry Tortugas, lying a hundred miles west of the southern point of Florida and at that time the most isolated island belonging to the American government, was used as a prison for dangerous Confederates; and here later three conspirators in the assassination of President Lincoln were incarcerated.[113] Far away to the southeast, off the coast of South America, are the Isles du Salut, a French penal station for criminals of the worst class. The Isle du Diable, ominous of name, lies farthest out to sea. This was for five years the prison of Dreyfus. Its other inhabitants are lepers. Isles of the cursed indeed! *Island prisons for political offenders.*

What islands have they tend to hold, to segregate, secrete from meddling hands, preserve untouched and unaltered. Owing to this power to protect, islands show a large percentage of rare archaic forms of animal and plant life. The insular fauna of Australia, Tasmania, New Guinea and Madagascar display a succession of strange, ancestral forms going back to the biological infancy of the world. The *Islands as places of survival.*

Canaries in the Atlantic and Celebes in the Pacific are museums of living antiquities, some of them dating probably from Miocene times.[114] Such survivals are found elsewhere only in high mountains, whose inaccessible slopes also offer protection against excessive competition. Hence some of the antiquated species of insular Celebes, Formosa, Japan and Hainon occur again on the Asiatic mainland only in the Himalayas.[115]

For man, too, islands and their sister areas of isolation, mountains, are areas of survivals. The shrinking remnants of that half-dwarf Negrito stock which may have formed the aboriginal population of southern Asia are found to-day only in the mountains of peninsular India and in island groups like the Andaman and the Philippines. But even in the Philippines, they are confined either to the mountainous interiors of the larger islands, or to little coastal islets like Polillo, Alabat, Jomalig, and others.[116] [See map page 147.] Yezo, Sakhalin and the Kurile Isles harbor the last feeble remnants of the Ainos, a primitive people who formerly occupied a long stretch of the Asiatic coast south of the Amur mouth. The protected environment of these islands has postponed the doom of extinction toward which the Ainos are hastening.[117] With insular conservatism they dress, live and seek their food on the sea to-day, just as depicted in Japanese art and literature at the dawn of history.[118] [See map page 103.]

Insular survivals of manners and customs It is chiefly on islands of harsh climatic conditions, like Sakhalin, or of peculiarly restricted resources and area, like the Andaman, or of remote, side-tracked location, like Iceland, Sardinia and Cape Breton, that the stamp of the primitive or antiquated is strongest. Even when not apparent in race stock, owing to the ubiquitous colonization of maritime peoples, it marks the language and customs of even these late-coming occupants, because an island environment asserts always some power to isolate. This is due not only to the encircling moat of sea, but also to the restricted insular area, too small to attract to itself the great currents of human activity which infuse cosmopolitan ideas and innovations, and too poor to buy the material improvements which progress offers. If the tourist in Sicily finds the women of

Taormina or Girgenti spinning with a hand spindle, and the express trains moving only twelve miles an hour, he can take these two facts as the product of a small, detached area, although this island lies at the crossroads of the Mediterranean. Corsica and Sardinia, lying off the main routes of travel in this basin, are two of the most primitive and isolated spots of Europe. Here the old wooden plow of Roman days is still in common use as it is in Crete, and feudal institutions of the Middle Ages still prevail to some extent,[119] —a fact which recalls the long survival of feudalism in Japan. The little Isle of Man, almost in sight of the English coast, has retained an old Norse form of government. Here survives the primitive custom of orally proclaiming every new law from the Tynwald Hill before it can take effect,[120] and the other ancient usage of holding the court of justice on the same hill under the open sky. The Faroe Islands and Iceland are museums of Norse antiquities. The stamp of isolation and therefore conservatism is most marked in the remoter, northern islands. Surnames are rare in Iceland, and such as exist are mostly of foreign origin. In their place, Christian names followed by the patronymic prevail; but in the Faroes, these patronymics have in a great many cases become recognized as surnames. So again, while the Faroese women still use a rude spinning-wheel introduced from Scotland in 1671, in Iceland this spinning-wheel was still an innovation in 1800, and even to-day competes with spindles. Hand-querns for grinding wheat, stone hammers for pounding fish and roots, the wooden weighing-beam of the ancient Northmen, and quaint marriage customs give the final touch of aloofness and antiquity to life on these remote islands.[121]

As all island life bears more or less the mark of isolation, so it betrays the narrow area that has served at its base. Though islands show a wide variation in size from the 301,-000 square miles (771,900 square kilometers) of New Guinea or the 291,000 square miles (745,950 square kilometers) of Borneo to the private estates like the Scilly Isles, Gardiner and Shelter islands off Long Island, or those small, sea-fenced pastures for sheep and goats near the New England coast

Effects of small area in islands.

and in the Aegean, yet small islands predominate; the large ones are very few. Islands comprise a scant seven per cent. of the total land area of the earth, and their number is very great,—nine hundred, for instance, in the Philippine group alone. Therefore small area is a conspicuous feature of islands generally. It produces in island people all those effects which are characteristic of small, naturally defined areas, especially early or precocious social, political and cultural development. The value of islands in this respect belongs to the youth of the world, as seen in the ancient Mediterranean, or in the adolescence of modern primitive races; it declines as the limitations rather than the advantages of restricted territory preponderate in later historical development.

Political dominion of small islands. This early maturity, combined with the power to expend the concentrated national or tribal forces in any given direction, often results in the domination of a very small island over a large group. In the Society Islands, Cook found little Balabola ruling over Ulietea (Raitea) and Otaha, the former of these alone being over twice the size of Bolabola, whose name commanded respect as far as Tahiti.[122] The Fiji Archipelago was ruled in pre-Christian days by the little islet of Mbau, scarcely a mile long, which lies like a pebble beside massive Viti Levu. It was the chief center of political power and its supremacy was owned by nearly all the group. The next important political center was Rewa, no larger than Mbau, which had for its subject big Mbengga.[123] In the same way, the Solomon group was ruled by Mongusaie and Simbo, just as tiny New Lauenberg lorded it over the larger islands of the Bismarck Archipelago.[124] When the Dutch in 1613 undertook the conquest of the coveted Spice Isles, they found there two rival sultans seated in the two minute islets of Ternate and Tidore off the west coast of Gilolo. Their collective possessions, which the Dutch took, comprised all the Moluccas, the Ke and Banda groups, the whole of northwestern New Guinea, and Mindanao of the Philippines.[125]

It was no unusual thing for classic Aegean isles to control and exploit goodly stretches of the nearest coast, or to exercise dominion over other islands. Aristotle tells us that

Crete's location across the southern end of the Aegean Sea confirmed to it by nature the early naval empire of the Hellenic world. Minos conquered some of the islands, colonized others,[126] and, according to the story of Theseus and the Minotaur, laid Athens under tribute; but his suppression of piracy in these waters and his conspicuous leadership in the art of navigation point to a yet more significant supremacy. So insular Venice ruled and exploited large dependencies. The island of Zealand, strategically located at the entrance to the Baltic, has been the heart and head and strong right arm of the Danish dominion, through all its long history of fluctuating boundaries. England's insularity has been the strongest single factor in the growth of her vast colonial empire and in the maintenance of its loyal allegiance and solidarity. The widely strewn plantation of her colonies is the result of that teeming island seed-bed at home; while the very smallness of the mother country is the guarantee of its supremacy over its dependencies, because it is too small either to oppress them or to get along without them. Now an Asiatic variant of English history is promised us by growing Japan.

Though political supremacy is possible even to an island of insignificant size, both the advantages and the grave disadvantages of small area are constantly asserting themselves. Some developments peculiar to large territory are here eliminated at the start. For instance, robbery and brigandage, which were so long a scourge in peninsular Greece, were unheard of on the small Aegean islands. Sheep-raising was at an early date safer in England than on the Continent, because wolves were earlier exterminated there. Bio-geography shows an increasing impoverishment in the flora and fauna of small islands with distance from the mainland. In the Pacific Ocean, this progressive impoverishment from west to east has had great influence upon human life in the islands. In Polynesia, therefore, all influences of the chase and of pastoral life are wanting, while in Melanesia, with its larger islands and larger number of land animals, hunting still plays an important part, and is the chief source of subsistence for many New Guinea villages.[127] Therefore a corresponding decay of projectile weapons is to be traced west to east,

Economic limitations of their small area.

and is conspicuous in those crumbs of land constituting Polynesia and Micronesia. The limit of the bow and arrow includes the northeastern portion of the Philippine group, cuts through the Malay Archipelago so as to include the Moluccas and Flores, includes Melanesia as far as Tonga or the Friendly Isles, but excludes Micronesia, Polynesia and Australia. Even in Melanesia, however, bows and arrows are not universal; they are lacking in peripheral islands like New Caledonia and New Ireland.[128]

The restriction of trees, also, with the exception of the coco-palm and pandanus, has had its effect upon boat making. This general impoverishment is unmistakably reflected in the whole civilization of the smaller islands of Polynesia and Micronesia, especially in the Paumota and Pelew groups. In the countless coralline islands which strew the Pacific, another restricting factor is found in their monotonous geological formation. Owing to the lack of hard stone, especially of flint, native utensils and weapons have to be fashioned out of wood, bones, shells, and sharks' teeth.[129]

Poverty of alluvial lowlands in islands. Nor does the geographical limitation end here. Islands have proportionately a scanter allowance of fertile alluvial lowlands than have continents. This follows from their geological history, except in the case of those low deposit islands built up from the waste of the land. Most islands are summits of submerged mountain ranges, like Corsica and Sardinia, the Aegean archipelagoes, the Greater Antilles, Vancouver, and the countless fiord groups; or they are single or composite volcanic cones, like the Canaries, Azores, Lipari, Kurile, Fiji, Ascension, St. Helena and the Lesser Antilles; or they are a combination of highland subsidence and volcanic out-thrust, like Japan, the Philippines, the long Sunda chain and Iceland. Both geologic histories involve high reliefs, steep slopes, a deep surrounding sea, and hence rarely a shallow continental shelf for the accumulation of broad alluvial lowlands. Among the Aegean Isles only Naxos has a flood plain; all the rest have steep coasts, with few sand or gravel beaches, and only small deposit plains at the head of deep and precipitous embayments. Japan's area of arable soil is to-day only 15.7 per cent. of its total surface, even after the gentler slopes of its mountains have been terraced up two thousand feet. Some authorities put the figure lower, at 10 and 12 per cent.

Yet in spite of limited area and this paucity of local re- **Dense** sources, islands constantly surprise us by their relatively **populations** dense populations. More often than not they show a density **of islands.** exceeding that of the nearest mainland having the same zonal location, often the same geologic structure and soil. Along with other small, naturally defined areas, they tend to a closer packing of the population. Yet side by side with this relative over-population, we find other islands uninhabited or tenanted only by sheep, goats and cattle.

In the wide Pacific world comprising Australia and Ocean- ica, islands take up fifteen per cent. of the total land area, but they contain forty-four per cent. of the population.[130] The insular empire of Japan, despite the paucity of its arable soil, has a density of population nearly twice that of China, nearly three times that of Korea, and exceeding that of any political subdivision of continental Asia; but Japan, in turn, is surpassed in congestion only by Java, with a density of 587 to the square mile,[131] which almost equals that of Belgium (643) and England (600). Great Britain has a density of population (453 to the square mile) only exceeded in continental Europe by that of Belgium, but surpassed near- ly threefold by that of the little Channel Isles, which amounts to 1254 to the square mile.[132] If the average density of the United Kingdom is greatly diminished in Ireland, just as Italy's is in Sardinia and France's in Corsica, this fact is due primarily to a side-tracked or overshadowed location and adverse topography, combined with misgovernment.

If we compare countries which are partly insular, partly continental, the same truth emerges. The kingdom of Greece has fifteen per cent. of its territory in islands. Here again population reaches its greatest compactness in Corfu and Zante, which are nearly thrice as thickly inhabited as the rest of Greece.[133] Similarly the islands which constitute so large a part of Denmark have an average density of 269 to the square mile as opposed to the 112 of Jutland. The figures rise to 215 to the square mile in the Danish West

Indies, but drop low in the bleak, subarctic insular dependencies of Greenland, Iceland and the Faroes. Portugal's density is tripled in the Madeiras[134] and doubled in the Azores,[135] but drops in the badly placed Cape Verde Island, exposed to tropical heat and the desiccating tradewinds blowing off the Sahara. Spain's average rises twenty-five per cent. in the Canary Islands, which she has colonized, and France's nearly doubles in the French West Indies. The British West Indies, also, with the exception of the broken coral bank constituting the Bahamas, show a similar surprising density of population, which in Bermuda and Barbadoes surpasses that of England, and approximates the teeming human life of the Channel Isles.

Density of population in Polynesia.

This general tendency toward a close packing of the population in the smaller areas of land comes out just as distinctly in islands inhabited by natural peoples in the lower stages of development. Despite the retarded economic methods peculiar to savagery and barbarism, the Polynesian islands, for instance, often show a density of population equal to that of Spain and Greece (100 to the square mile) and exceeding that of European Turkey and Russia. "Over the whole extent of the South Sea," says Robert Louis Stevenson, "from one tropic to another, we find traces of a bygone state of over-population, when the resources of even a tropical soil were taxed, and even the improvident Polynesian trembled for the future."[136] He calls the Gilbert atolls "warrens of men."[137] One of them, Drummond's Island, with an area of about twenty square miles, contained a population of 10,000 in 1840, and all the atolls were densely populated.[138] To-day they count 35,000 inhabitants in less than 200 square miles. The neighboring Marshall group has 15,000 on its 158 square miles of area. The Caroline and Pelew archipelagoes show a density of 69 to the square mile, the Tonga or Friendly group harbor about 60 and the French holdings of Futuma and Wallis (or Uea) the same.[139] So the Bismarck Archipelago, Solomon, Hawaiian, Samoan and Marianne islands have to-day populations by no means sparse, despite the blight that everywhere follows the contact of superior with primitive peoples.

In all these cases, if economic status be taken into account,
we have a density bordering on congestion; but the situation
assumes a new aspect if we realize that the crowded inhabitants of small islands often have the run of the coco
plantations and fishing grounds of an entire archipelago.
The smaller, less desirable islands are retained as fish and
coco-palm preserves to be visited only periodically. Of a
low, cramped, monotonous coral group, often only the largest
and most productive is inhabited,[140] but that contains a
population surprising in view of the small base, restricted
resources and low cultural status of its inhabitants. The
population of the wide-strewn Paumota atolls was estimated
as about 10,000 in 1840. Of these fully one-half lived on
Anaa or Chain Island, and one-fourth on Gambier, but they
levied on the resources of the other islands for supplies.[141]
The Tonga Islands at the same time were estimated to have
20,000 inhabitants, about half of whom were concentrated on
Tongatabu, while Hapai and Varao held about 4,000
each.[142]

This is one of the sharp contrasts in island life,—here
density akin to congestion, there a few miles away a deserted
reef or cone rising from the sea, tenanted only by sheep or
goats or marine birds, its solitude broken only by the occasional crunching of a boat's keel upon its beach, as some
visitant from a neighboring isle comes to shear wool, gather
coco-nuts, catch birds or collect their eggs. All the 500 inhabitants of the Westman Isles off the southern coast of Iceland live in one village on Heimey, and support themselves
almost entirely by fishing and fowling birds on the wild crags
of the archipelago.[143] An oceanic climate, free contact with
the Gulf Stream, and remoteness from the widespread ice
fields of Iceland give them an advantage over the vast island
to the north. Only twenty-seven of the ninety islands com-
posing the Orkney group are inhabited, and about forty
smaller ones afford natural meadows for sheep on their old
red sandstone soil;[144] but Pomona, the largest Orkney has
17,000 inhabitants on its 207 square miles of territory or
85 to the square mile. The Shetlands tell the same story—29
out of 100 islands inhabited, some of the *holms* or smaller islets

serving as pastures for the sturdy ponies and diminutive cattle, and Mainland, the largest of the group, showing 53 inhabitants to the square mile. This is a density far greater than is reached in the nearby regions of Scotland, where the county of Sutherland can boast only 13 to the square mile, and Invernesshire 20. Here again insularity and contracted area do their work of compressing population.

The causes of this insular density of population are not far to seek. Islands can always rely on the double larder of land and sea. They are moreover prone to focus in themselves the fishing industry of a large continental area, owing to their ample contact with the sea. Shetland is now the chief seat of the Scotch herring fishery, a fact which contributes to its comparatively dense population. The concentration of the French export trade of Newfoundland fish in little St. Pierre and Miquelon accounts for the relatively teeming population (70 to the square mile) and the wealth of those scraps of islands. So the Lofoden Islands of Norway, like Iceland, Newfoundland and Sakhalin, balance a generous sea against an ungenerous soil, and thus support a population otherwise impossible.

Oceanic climate as factor.

For these far northern islands, the moderating effect of an oceanic climate has been a factor in making them relatively populous, just as it is on tropical isles by mitigating heat and drought. The prosperity and populousness of the Bermuda Islands are to be explained largely by the mild, equable climate which permits the raising of early vegetables and flowers for English and American markets. Like climatic conditions and a like industry account for the 2,000 souls living on the inhabited islands of the Scilly group. Here intensive horticulture supports a large force of workmen and yields a profit to the lord proprietor. Syros in the Cyclades fattens on its early spring vegetable trade with Athens and Constantinople.[145]

In the Mediterranean lands, where drought and excessive heat during the growing season offer adverse conditions for agriculture, the small islands, especially those of fertile volcanic soil, show the greatest productivity and hence marked density of population. Though the rainfall may be slight, except where a volcanic peak rises to condense moisture, heavy dews and the thick mists of spring quicken vegetation. This is the case in Malta, which boasts a population of 2,000 to the square mile, exclusive of the English garrison.[146] Little Limosa and Pantellaria, the merest fragments of land out in the mid-channel of the Mediterranean, have a population of 200 to the square mile.[147] The Lipari group north of Sicily average nearly 400 on every square mile of their fertile soil;[148] but this average rises in Salina to 500, and in Lipari itself, as also in Ponza of the Pontine group, to nearly 1300. Here fertile volcanic slopes of highly cultivated land lift vineyards, orchards of figs, and plantations of currants to the sunny air. But nearby Alicuri, almost uncultivated, has a sparse population of some five hundred shepherds and fishermen. Panaria and Filicuri are in about the same plight. Here again we find those sharp island contrasts.

The insular region of the Indian Ocean, which is inhabited by peoples quite different in race and cultural status from those of the Mediterranean, yet again demonstrates the power of islands to attract, preserve, multiply and concentrate population. This is especially true of the smaller islands, which in every case show a density of population many times that of the neighboring mainland of Africa. Only vast Madagascar, continental in size, repeats the sparsity of the continent. An oceanic climate increases the humidity of the islands as compared with the mainland lying in the same desiccating tradewind belt. Moreover their small area has enabled them to be permeated by incoming Arab, English, and French influences, which have raised their status of civilization and therewith the average density of population. This culminates in English Mauritius, which shows 540 inhabitants to the square mile, occupied in the production of sugar, molasses, rum, vanilla, aloes, and copra. In Zanzibar this density is 220 to the square mile; in Reunion 230; in Mayotte, the Comores and Seychelles, the average varies from 100 to 145 to the square mile, though Mahe in the Seychelles group has one town of 20,000 inhabitants.[149]

In the Malay Archipelago, an oceanic climate and tropical location have combined to stimulate fertility to the

Relation of density to area.

greatest extent; but this local wealth has been exploited in the highest degree in the smaller islands having relatively the longest coastline and amplest contact with the sea. The great continent-like areas of Borneo, New Guinea and Sumatra show a correspondingly sparse population; Java, smaller than the smallest of these and coated with mud from its fertilizing volcanoes, supports 587 inhabitants to the square mile; but this exceptional average is due to rare local productivity. Java's little neighbors to the east, Bali and Lombok, each with an area of only about 2100 square miles, have a density respectively of 333 and 195 to the square mile. This density rises suddenly in small Amboina (area 264 square miles), the isle of the famous clove monopoly, to 1000,[150] drops in the other Moluccas, where Papuan influences are strong, even to 20, but rises again in the pure Malayan Philippines to 69. In the Philippines a distinct connection is to be traced between the density of population and smallness of area. The explanation lies in the attraction of the coast for the sea-faring Malay race, and the mathematical law of increase of shoreline with decrease of insular area. Since 65 per cent. of the whole Philippine population inhabits coastal municipalities, it is not surprising that the 73 islands from ten to a hundred square miles in area count 127 inhabitants to the square mile, and those of less than ten square miles, of which there are nearly a thousand, have a density of 238.[151]

This same insular density, supported by fertility, fisheries and trade, appears again in the West Indies, and also the contrast in density between large and small islands down to a certain limit of diminutiveness. The Greater Antilles increase in density from Cuba through smaller Haiti and Jamaica down to little Porto Rico, which boasts 264 inhabitants to the square mile. In the smaller area of the Danish Indies and Guadeloupe about this same density (215 and 274) reappears; but it mounts to 470 in Martinique and to 1160 in Barbadoes.[152]

Island resorts.   Climate advantages often encourage density of population on islands, by attracting to them visitors who make a local demand for the fruits of the soil and thereby swell the income of the islands. For instance, about the densely populated region of the Gulf of Naples, Procida has 14,000 inhabitants on its one and a half square miles of area, while fertile Ischia and Capri have 1400 to the square mile. Here a rich volcanic soil, peaks which attract rain by their altitude and visitors by their beauty, and a mild oceanic climate delightful in winter as in summer, all contribute to density of population. Sicily, Malta and Corfu also gain in the same way in winter. The Isle of Man owes some of its recent increase of population, now 238 to the square mile, to the fact that it has become the summer playground for the numerous factory workers of Lancashire in England.

Sometimes climatic advantages are reinforced by a favorable focal point, which brings the profits of trade to supplement those of agriculture. This factor of distributing and exporting center has undoubtedly contributed to the prosperity and population of Reunion, Mahe, Mauritius and Zanzibar, as it did formerly to that of ancient Rhodes and modern St. Thomas at the angle of the Antilles. Barbadoes, by reason of its outpost location to the east of the Windward Isles, is the first to catch incoming vessels from England, and is therefore a focus of steamship lines and a distributing point for the southern archipelago, so that we find here the greatest density of any island in the West Indies.[153] The 9405 inhabitants of Charlotte Amalie on St. Thomas and the 15,000 of Willemsted on Curaçao give these also a characteristic insular density. Samos, blessed with good soil, an excellent position on Aegean maritime routes, and virtual autonomy, supports a population of 300 to the square mile.[154]

Focal location alone can often achieve this density. Syros, one of the smallest and by nature the most barren of the Cyclades, though well tilled is the great commercial and shipping center of the Aegean, and has in Hermupolis with its 17,700 population by far the largest town of the archipelago.[155] This development has come since Greece achieved its independence. It reminds us of the distinction and doubtless also population that belonged to Delos in ancient days. Advantageous commercial location and density of population characterize Kilwauru and Singapore at the east and west extremi-

Density of population affected by focal location for trade.

ties of the Malay Archipelago. The Bahrein Islands, which England has acquired in the Persian Gulf, serve as an emporium of trade with eastern Arabia and have a local wealth in their pearl fisheries. These facts account for the 68,000 inhabitants dwelling on their 240 square miles (600 square kilometers) of sterile surface.[156]

Overflow of island population to the mainland.
The concentration of population in these favored spots of land with inelastic boundaries, and the tendency of that population to increase under the stimulating, interactive life make the restriction of area soon felt. For this reason, so many colonies which are started on inshore islets from motives of protection have to be transferred to the mainland to insure a food supply. A settlement of Huguenots, made in 1555 on an island in the harbor of Rio Janeiro, found its base too small for cultivation, but feared the attack of the hostile Indians and Portuguese on the mainland. After three years of a struggling existence, it fell a prey to the Portuguese.[157] De Monts' short-lived colony on an island in the mouth of the St. Croix River in 1604 had an excellent site for defence, but was cut off by the drifting ice in winter from mainland supplies of wood, water and game, while no cultivation was possible in the sandy soil.[158]

Such sites suffice for mere trading posts, but are inadequate for the larger social group of a real colony. The early Greek colonists, with their predilection for insular locations, recognized this limitation and offset it by the occupation of a strip of the nearest mainland, cultivated and defended by fortified posts, as an adjunct to the support of the islands. Such a subsidiary coastal hem was called a *Paraea.* The ancient Greek colonies on the islands of Thasos and Samothrace each possessed such a Paraea.[159] The Aeolian inhabitants of Tenedos held a strip of the opposite Troad coast north of Cape Lekton, while those of Lesbos appropriated the south coast of the Troad.[160] In the same way Tarentum and Syracuse, begun on inshore islands, soon overflowed on to the mainland. Sometimes the island site is abandoned altogether and the colony transferred to the mainland. The ancient Greek colony of Cyrene had an initial existence on the island of Platea just off the Libyan coast, but, not flourishing there, was moved after an interval of several years to the African mainland, where "the sky was perforated" by the mountains of Barca.[161] De Monts' colony was removed from its island to Port Royal in Nova Scotia.

Where an island offers in its climate and soil conditions favorable to agriculture, tillage begins early to assume an intensive, scientific character, to supply the increasing demand for food. The land, fixed in the amount of area, must be made elastic in its productivity by the application of intelligence and industry. Hence in island habitats, an early development of agriculture, accompanied by a parallel skill in exploiting the food resources of the sea, is a prevailing feature. In Oceanica, agriculture is everywhere indigenous, but shows greatest progress in islands like Tonga and Fiji, where climate and soil are neither lavish nor niggardly in their gifts, but yield a due return for the labor of tillage. The Society[162] and Samoan Islands, where nature has been more prodigal, rank lower in agriculture, though George Forster found in Tahiti a relatively high degree of cultivation.[163] The small, rocky, coralline Paumotas rank lower still, but even here plantains, sugar-cane, sweet potatoes, yams, taro and solanum are raised. The crowded atolls of the Gilbert group show pains-taking tillage. Here we find coco-palms with their roots fertilized with powdered pumice, and taro cultivated in trenches excavated for the purpose and located near the lagoons, so that the water may percolate through the coral sand to the thirsty roots.[164] To lonely Easter Isle nature has applied a relentless lash. At the time of Cook's visit it was woodless and boatless except for one rickety canoe, and therefore was almost excluded from the food supplies of the sea. Hence its destitute natives, by means of careful and often ingenious tillage, made its parched and rocky slopes support excellent plantations of bananas and sugar-cane.[165]

The islands of Melanesia show generally fenced fields, terrace farming on mountain sides, irrigation canals, fertilized soils, well trimmed shade trees and beautiful flower gardens,[166] proof that the cultivation of the ground has advanced to the aesthetic stage, as it has in insular Japan.

Precocious development of island agriculture.

In Tonga the coco-palm plantations are weeded and manured. Here, after a devastating war, the victorious chief devotes his attention to the cultivation of the land, which soon assumes a beautiful and flourishing appearance.[167] In Tongatabu, which is described by the early visitors as one big garden, Cook found officials appointed to inspect all produce of the island and to enforce the cultivation of a certain quota of land by each householder.[168] Here agriculture is a national concern.

Melanesian agriculture. In the minute land fragments which constitute Micronesia, fishing is the chief source of subsistence; agriculture, especially for the all important taro, is limited to the larger islands like the Pelews. In the vast islands of western Melanesia, agriculture is on the whole less advanced. New Guinea, where the chase yields support to many villages, has large sections still a wilderness, though some parts are cultivated like a garden. In the smaller Melanesian islands, such as New Hebrides, New Britain and the Solomon group, we find extensive plantations laid out on irrigated terraces. In New Hebrides and the Banks Islands every single village has its flowers and aromatic herbs.[169] But it is in Fiji that native island agriculture seems to culminate. Here a race of dark, frizzly haired savages, addicted to cannibalism, have in the art of tillage taken a spurt forward in civilization, till in this respect they stand abreast of the average European. The German asparagus bed is not cultivated more carefully than the yam plants of Fiji; these also are grown in mounds made of soil which has been previously pulverized by hand. The variety and excellence of their vegetable products are amazing, and find their reflection in an elaborate national cuisine, strangely at variance with the otherwise savage life.[170]

West of Melanesia, the Malay Archipelago shows a high average of tillage. The inhabitants of Java, Madura, Bali, Lombok and Sumbawa are skilled agriculturists and employ an elaborate system of irrigation,[171] but the natives of Timor, on the other hand, have made little progress. In the Philippines a rich and varied agriculture has been the chief source of wealth since the Spanish conquest early in the sixteenth century, proving a native aptitude which began to develop long before.[172]

The dense population of the Mediterranean islands is the concomitant of an advanced agriculture. The connection between elaborate tillage and scant insular area is indicated in the earliest history of classic Aegina. The inhabitants of this island were called Myrmidons, Strabo tells us, because by digging like ants they covered the rocks with earth to cultivate all the ground; and in order to economize the soil for this purpose, lived in excavations under ground and abstained from the use of bricks.[173] To-day, terraced slopes, irrigation, hand-made soils, hoe and spade tillage, rotation of crops, and a rich variety of field and garden products characterize the economic history of most Mediterranean islands, whether Elba, the Lipari, Ponza, Procida, Capri, Ischia, Pantellaria, Lampedusa,[174] or the Aegean groups. The sterile rock of Malta has been converted for two-thirds of its area into fertile gardens, fields and orchards. The upper stratum of rock has been pulverized and enriched by manure; the surface has been terraced and walled to protect it against high winds. In consequence, the Maltese gardens are famous throughout the Mediterranean.[175] In the Cyclades every patch of tillable ground is cultivated by the industrious inhabitants. Terraced slopes are green with orchards of various southern fruits, and between the trees are planted melons and vegetables. Fallow land and uncultivated hillsides, as well as the limestone islands fit only for pastures, are used for flocks of sheep and goats.[176]

Intensive tillage.

It is in Japan that agriculture has attained a national and aesthetic importance reached nowhere else. Of the 150,-000 square miles constituting Japan proper, two-thirds are mountains; large tracts of lowlands are useless rock wastes, owing to the detritus carried down by inundating mountain torrents.[177] Hence to-day arable land forms only 15.7 per cent. of the whole area. During the two hundred and fifty years of exclusion when emigration and foreign trade were forbidden, a large and growing population had to be supplied from a small insular area, further restricted by reason of the configuration of the surface. Here the geographical effects

Japanese agriculture.

of a small, naturally defined area worked out to their logical conclusion. Consequently agriculture progressed rapidly and gave the farmer a rank in the social scale such as he attained nowhere else.[178] His methods of tillage are much the same as in overcrowded China, but his national importance and hence his ranking in society is much higher. In Japan to-day farming absorbs 60 per cent. of the population. The system of tillage, in many respects primitive, is yet very thorough, and by means of skilful manuring makes one plot of ground yield two or three crops per annum.[179] Every inch of arable land is cultivated in grain, vegetables and fruits. Mountains and hills are terraced and tilled far up their slopes. Meadows are conspicuously absent, as are also fallow fields. Land is too valuable to lie idle. Labor is chiefly manual and is shared by the women and children; mattock and hoe are more common than the plow.[180] Such elaborate cultivation and such pressure of population eventuate in small holdings. In Japan one hectar (2 1-2 acres) is the average farm per family.

The case of England. While Japan's agriculture reflected the small area of an island environment, and under its influence reached a high development, England's from the beginning of the fifteenth century declined before the competition of English commerce, which gained ascendency owing to the easy accessibility of Great Britain to the markets of Europe. The ravages of the Black Death in the latter half of the fourteenth century produced a scarcity of agricultural laborers and hence a prohibitive increase of wages. To economize labor, the great proprietors resorted to sheep farming and the raising of wool, which, either in the raw state or manufactured into cloth, became the basis of English foreign trade. A distinct deterioration in agriculture followed this reversion to a pastoral basis of economic life, supplemented by a growing commerce which absorbed all the enterprise of the country. The steady contraction of the area under tillage threw out of employment the great mass of agricultural laborers, made them paupers and vagrants.[181] Hence England entered the period of maritime discoveries with a redundant population. This furnished the raw material for her colonies, and made her territorial expansion assume a solid, permanent character, unknown to the flimsy trading stations which mark the mere extension of a field of commerce.

Even when agriculture, fisheries and commerce have done their utmost, in the various stages of civilization, to increase the food supply, yet insular populations tend to outgrow the means of subsistence procurable from their narrow base. Hence islanders, like peninsula peoples, are prone to emigrate and colonize. This tendency is encouraged by their mobility, born of their nautical skill and maritime location. King Minos of Crete, according to Thucydides and Aristotle, colonized the Cyclades.[182] Greece, from its redundant population, peopled various Aegean and Ionian islands, which in turn threw off spores of settlements to other isles and shores. Corcyra, which was colonized from the Peloponnesus, sent out a daughter colony to Epidamnos on the Illyrian coast. Andros, one of the Cyclades, as early as 654 B. C., colonized Acanthus and Stagirus in Chalcidice.[183] Paros, settled first by Cretans and then by Ionians, at a very early date sent colonies to Thasos and to Parium on the Propontis, while Samos was a perennial fountain emitting streams of settlement to Thrace, Cilicia, Crete, Italy and Sicily. [Map page 251.]

Emigration and colonization from islands.

This moving picture of Greek emigration is duplicated in the Malay Archipelago, especially in the smaller eastern islands. Almost every Malay tribe has traditions based upon migrations. The southern Philippines derived the considerable Mohammedan element of their populations from the Samal Laut, who came from Sumatra and the islands of the Strait of Malacca.[184] A Malayan strain can be traced through Polynesia to far-off Easter Isle. Sometimes the emigration is a voluntary exile from home for a short period and a definite purpose. The inhabitants of Bouton, Binungku, and the neighboring islets, all of them located southeast of Celebes, have for the past twenty-five years come in great numbers to the larger islands of Ceram, Buru, Amboina and Banda, where they have laid out and carefully cultivated plantations of maize, tobacco, bananas and coco-palms. Generally only the men come, work two years, save their profits and then return home. These ambitious tillers look like savages, are shy as wild things of the woods, and work naked to the waist.[185]

Polynesia, Melanesia and Micronesia, where every condition of land and sea tends to develop the migratory spirit, form a region of extensive colonization.[186] Settlements of one race are scattered among the island groups of another, making the ethnic boundaries wide penumbras. In some smaller islands of Melanesia the Polynesian colonists have exterminated or expelled the original inhabitants, and are found there now with all their distinctive race characteristics; but in the larger islands, they have been merged in the resident population, and their presence is only to be surmised from the existence of Polynesian customs, such as father-right in New Hebrides and Solomon Island side by side with the prevailing Melanesian mother-right.[187] In small islands, like Tongatabu, Samoa and Fiji, emigration becomes habitual, a gradual spilling over of the redundant population and hence not a formidable inundation. In all this insular region of the Pacific, the impulse to emigration is so persistent, that the resulting inter-insular colonization obliterates sharp distinctions of race; it annuls the segregation of an island environment, and makes everywhere for amalgamation and unification, rather than differentiation.[188]

Modern emigration from islands.

Among highly civilized peoples, where better economic methods bring greater density of population and set at the same time a higher standard of living, emigration from islands is especially marked. Japan has seen a formidable exodus since an end was put to its long period of compression. This has taken the form of widespread emigration to various foreign lands, notably the Hawaiian Islands and the United States, and also of internal colonization in its recently acquired territory in Formosa and Korea.[189] The Maltese have spread from their congested island, and are found to-day as gardeners, sailors and traders along all the Mediterranean coasts.[190] Majorca and the more barren Cyclades[191] tell the same story. The men of Capri go in considerable numbers to South America, but generally return home again. The Icelanders often pull themselves out of the stagnation of their lonely, ungenerous island to become thrifty citizens of western Canada.

Emigration from islands readily throws itself into the Maritime enterprise as outlet. channel of navigation and foreign trade. The northern Sporades, especially Skiathos and Skopelos, are the home of sailors who can be found over all the world.[192] In this appetency for a nautical career, small inshore islets are often distinguished from the nearby mainland. Nearly all the masculine population of the Frisian Islands were seamen prior to 1807. In the eighteenth century a third of the Hamburg vessels were commanded by captains from the little island of Sylte, and a third of the Greenland fleet of the Netherlands by natives of Föhr.[193]

In England the exodus took the form of trading expeditions and the foundation of commercial colonies long before the food resources of the island had been even considerably developed. The accessible sea offered lines of least resistance, while the monopoly of the land by a privileged aristocracy and the fiercely defended corn laws made the limitations of a small area more oppressive. In Ireland, a landless peasantry in a grainless land, dulled by deprivation of opportunity, found in emigration an escape from insupportable evils.

While emigration draws off the surplus population, there Artificial checks to population. tend to develop in islands, as also in barren highlands where population early reaches the point of saturation, various devices to restrict natural increase. The evils of congestion are foreseen and guarded against. Abbé Raynal, writing of islanders in general, remarked as far back as 1795, "It is among these people that we trace 'the origin of that multitude of singular institutions which retards the progress of population. Anthropophagy, the castration of males, the infibulation of females, late marriages, the consecration of virginity, the approbation of celibacy, the punishments exercised against girls who become mothers at too early an age," he enumerates as such checks. Malthus, in his Essay on Population, commenting on this statement, notes that the bounds to the number of inhabitants on islands, especially small ones, are so narrow and so obvious that no one can ignore them.[194]

The checks to population practiced on islands are either

preventive or positive. The extreme measure to restrict marriage is found among the wretched Budumas who inhabit the small, marshy islands of Lake Chad. Tribal custom allows only the chiefs and headmen to have wives. A brass crescent inserted in the ear of a boy indicates the favored one among a chief's sons destined to carry on his race. For his brothers this is made physically impossible; they become big, dull, timid creatures contributing by their fishing to the support of the thinly populated villages. The natives of the Shari River delta on the southern shore of Lake Chad use Buduma as a term of contempt for a man.[195]

Polyandry. In islands, as in unproductive highlands where hunger stalks abroad, marriage readily takes the form of polyandry. On the Canary Islands, at the time of their conquest in 1402, polyandry existed in Lancerote and possibly in Fuerteventura, often assigning one woman to three husbands; but in the other islands of the group monogamy was strictly maintained.[196] In Oceanica polygamy, monogamy or polyandry prevails according to a man's means, the poverty of the islands, and the supply of women. A plurality of wives is always the privilege of the chiefs and the wealthy, but all three forms of marriage may be found on the same island. Scarcity of women gives rise to polyandry in Tahiti,[197] and consigns one woman to four or five men. In old Hawaii, where there were four or five men to one woman a kind of incipient polyandry arose by the addition of a countenanced paramour to the married couple's establishment.[198] Robert Louis Stevenson found the same complaisant arrangement a common one in the Marquesas, where the husband's deputy was designated by the term of *pikio* in the native vocabulary.[199] Polyandry existed in Easter Isle, among whose stunted and destitute population the men far exceeded the women, and children were few, according to reports of the early visitors.[200] Numerous other instances make this connection between island habitat, deficiency of women, need of checking increase, and polyandrous marriages an obvious one.[201]

Infanticide. This disproportion of the sexes in Oceanica is due to the murder of female infants, too early child-bearing, overwork, privation, licentiousness, and the violence of the men.[202] The imminence of famine dictates certain positive checks to population, among which infanticide and abortion are widespread in Oceanica. In some parts of the New Hebrides and the Solomon groups it is so habitual, that in some families all children are killed, and substitutes purchased at will.[203] In the well-tilled Fiji Islands, a pregnant girl is strangled and her seducer slain. The women make a practice of drinking medicated waters to produce sterility. Failing in this, the majority kill their children either before or after birth. In the island of Vanua Levu infanticide reaches from one-half to two-thirds of all children conceived; here it is reduced to a system and gives employment to professional murderers of babies, who hover like vultures over every child-bed. All destroyed after birth are females.[204] And yet here, as on many other islands of Melanesia and Polynesia, such offspring as are spared are treated with foolish fondness and indulgence.[205] The two facts are not incompatible.

Geographic conditions made infanticide a state measure in these crowded communities. On the small coral atolls, where the food supply was scantest, it was enforced by law. On Vaitupu, in the Ellice group, only two children were allowed to a couple; on Nukufelau, only one. Any violation of this unique sumptuary law was punished by a fine.[206] On the congested Gilbert atolls, a woman rarely had more than two children, never more than three. Abortion, produced by a regular midwife, disposed of any subsequent offspring. Affection for children was very strong here, and infanticide of the living was unknown.[207] In Samoa, also, Turner found the practice restricted to the period before birth; but in Tahiti and elsewhere it was enforced by the tribal village authorities on the born and unborn.[208] In pre-Christian Hawaii, two-thirds of all children, and especially girls, were killed by their parents either before or after birth. The result was a decay of the maternal instinct and the custom of farming out children to strangers. This contributed to the excess of infant mortality, the degeneration of morals and the instability of the family.[209] So in Japan the pressure of population led to infanticide and the

Approved by the state.

sale of daughters to a life of ignominy, which took them out of the child-bearing class.[210] Nor was either custom under the ban.

The result is a deterioration of morals, an invasion of the family bond, and a decay of the finer sentiments therewith connected. Captain Cook in 1770 found in Tahiti *Eareeoie* or *Arreoys* societies, which were free-love associations including in their number "over half of the better sort of the inhabitants." The children begotten of these promiscuous unions were smothered at birth. Obscene conversations, indecent dances and frank unchastity on the part of girls and women were the attendant evils of these loose morals.[211] Cook was sure that "these societies greatly prevent the increase of the superior classes of people of which they are composed." Malthus reports a similar association in the Marianne Islands, distinguished by a similar name, devoted to race suicide.[212] Everywhere in Oceanica marriage is unstable, and with few exceptions unchastity prevails. Stevenson thinks it chiefly accountable for the decline of population in the islands.[213] However, in the detailed *taboos* laid upon women in Fiji, Marquesas, and other Polynesian islands we have the survival of an early measure to increase reserve between the sexes, long after regard for chastity has vanished.[214]

Low valuation of human life. The constant pressure of population upon the limits of subsistence throughout Oceanica has occasioned a low valuation of human life. Among natural peoples the helpless suffer first. The native Hawaiians, though a good-natured folk, were relentless towards the aged, weak, sick, and insane. These were frequently stoned to death or allowed to perish of hunger.[215] In Fiji, the aged are treated with such contempt, that when decrepitude or illness threatens them, they beg their children to strangle them, unless the children anticipate the request.[216] In Vate (or Efate) of the New Hebrides, old people are buried alive, and their passage to another world duly celebrated by a feast.[217] However, in the Tonga Islands and in New Zealand, great respect and consideration are shown the aged as embodying experience.[218] The harsher custom recalls an ancient law of Aegean Ceos, which ordained that all persons over sixty years of age should be compelled to drink hemlock, in order that there might be sufficient food for the rest.[219]

Many customs of Oceanica can be understood only in the Cannibal-light of the small value attached to human life in this island ism in world. The overpopulation which lies back of their coloniza- islands. tion explains the human sacrifices in their religious orgies and funeral rites, as also the widespread practice of cannibalism. This can be traced in vestigial forms, or as an occasional or habitual custom from one end of the Pacific to the other, from the Marquesas to New Guinea and from New Zealand to Hawaii. All Melanesia is tainted with it, and Micronesia is not above suspicion. The cause of this extensive practice, Stevenson attributes to the imminence of famine and the craving for flesh as food in these small islands, which are destitute of animals except fowls, dogs and hogs. In times of scarcity cannibalism threatens all; it strikes from within or without the clan.[220] Ratzel leans to the same opinion.[221] Captain Cook thought the motive of a good full meal of human flesh was often back of the constant warfare in New Zealand, and was sometimes the only alternative of death by hunger. Cannibalism was not habitual in the Tonga Islands, but became conspicuous during periods of famine.[222] In far-away Tierra del Fuego, where a peculiarly harsh climate and the low cultural status of the natives combine to produce a frightful infant mortality and therefore to re-press population, cannibalism within the clan is indulged in only at the imperious dictate of mid-winter hunger. The same thing is true in the nearby Chonos Archipelago.[223]

These are the darker effects of an island habitat, the vices of its virtues. That same excessive pressure of population which gives rise to infanticide also stimulates agriculture, industry and trade; it develops ingenuity in making the most of local resources, and finally leads to that widespread emigration and colonization which has made islanders the great distributors of culture, from Easter Isle to Java and from ancient Crete to modern England.

NOTES TO CHAPTER XIII

1. Table of areas of peninsulas and islands, Justus Perthes, *Taschen Atlas*, p. 9. Gotha, 1905.
2. H. J. Mackinder, Britain and the British Seas, pp. 105-108. London, 1904.
3. W. Deecke, Italy, p. 45. London, 1904.
4. Journey of William de Rubruquis, pp. 187, 204. Hakluyt Society Publication, London, 1903.
5. Archibald Little, The Far East, pp. 35, 45. Oxford, 1905.
6. Strabo, Book X, chap. II, 19.
7. Ratzel, *Die Erde und das Leben*, Vol. I. pp. 312-313. Leipzig, 1901.
8. Charles H. Hawes, In the Uttermost East, p. 103. New York, 1904.
9. W. E. Griffis, The Mikado's Empire, Vol. I, pp. 26-27. New York, 1904.
10. Darwin, Origin of Species, Vol. II, chap. XIII, p. 178. New York, 1895.
11. A. R. Wallace, Geographical Distribution of Animals, Vol. II, p. 61. London, 1876.
12. Darwin, Origin of Species, Vol. II, chap. XIII, p. 183. New York, 1895.
13. *Ibid.*, Vol. II, chap. XIII, pp. 178-180.
14. A. R. Wallace, Island Life, pp. 331-332, 338-389, 393, 402, 409-410, 449, 456-463. New York, 1893.
15. *Ibid.*, 342, 370-371.
16. Emerson, English Traits, chap. VI.
17. Capt. F. Brinkley, Japan, Vol. I, p. 50. Boston and Tokyo, 1901.
18. W. E. Griffis, The Mikado's Empire, Vol. I, p. 198. New York, 1904.
19. Arthur M. Knapp, Feudal and Modern Japan, Vol. I, pp. 211, 220, 221. New York, 1900.
20. Emerson, English Traits, chap. III.
21. Ronald M. Burrows, The Discoveries in Crete, pp. 134-136, 141, 162, 177. New York, 1907.
22. *Ibid.*, chapters IV and V.
23. *Ibid.*, p. 179. Angelo Mosso, The Palaces of Crete, pp. 46, 54-55, 61-62, 81. London, 1907.
24. Ronald M. Burrows, The Discoveries in Crete, pp. 64-65, 82, 84, 147-150. New York, 1907. James Baikie, The Sea Kings of Crete, pp. 235-237. London, 1910.
25. J. B. Bury, History of Greece, pp. 8-10. New York, 1909.
26. R. M. Burrows, The Discoveries in Crete, pp. 36, 44-46, 50-51, 85, 149-150, 179. New York, 1907.
27. *Ibid.*, 136-137.
28. Private communication from Mrs. Harriet Boyd Hawes.
29. Recent Discoveries in Crete, *The Chautauquan*, Vol. 43, p. 220. 1906. R. M. Burrows, The Discoveries in Crete, pp. 103, 162. New York, 1907.
30. Grote, History of Greece, Vol. IV, pp. 244-245. New York, 1857.

31. Strabo, Book XIV, chap. II, 7-13.

32. Strabo, Book VII, chap. VI, 16.

33. A. P. Niblack, Coast Indians of Southern Alaska and Northern British Columbia, pp. 382-384. House Misc. Doc. 142. Washington. Dr. George Dawson, The Haidas, *Harper's Monthly*, August, 1882.

34. Ratzel, History of Mankind, Vol. I, p. 180. London, 1896-1898.

35. Article, The National Academy of Sciences, *Nation*, Vol. LXXX, p. 328. 1905. Capt. James Cook, A Voyage Towards the South Pole, 1772-1775, Vol. I, p. 284, 288-296. London. 1777. George Forster, Voyage Round the World, Vol. I, pp. 566-567, 580-581, 586-591. London, 1777.

36. G. Sergi, The Mediterranean Race, chap. VII. London and New York, 1901. Helmolt, History of the World, Vol. IV, pp. 222-223. New York, 1902-1906.

37. Charles W. Hawes, The Uttermost East, pp. 113-116. New York, 1904.

38. William Bright, Early English Church History, pp. 224-234. Oxford. 1897. P. W. Joyce, Social History of Ireland, Vol. I, pp. 320, 389, 390. London, 1903.

39. W. H. Dall, Masks and Labrets, p. 137. Third Annual Report of Bureau of Ethnology, Washington, 1884.

40. A. P. Niblack, Coast Indians of Southern Alaska and Northern British Columbia, pp. 236-382. Washington.

41. H. R. Mill, International Geography, p. 187. New York, 1902.

42. A. B. Ellis, The West African Islands, p. 202. London, 1885. History of the Conquest of the Canaries, Introduction, pp. XIII, XVII, XXXIII, XXXIV. Hakluyt Society, London, 1872.

43. Henry Gannett, People of the Philippines, Report of the Eighth International Geographical Congress, Washington, 1904.

44. H. R. Mill, International Geography, p. 549. New York, 1903.

45. W. Deecke, Italy, p. 451. London, 1904.

46. Nelson Annandale, The Faroes and Iceland, p. 14. Oxford, 1905.

47. J. Partsch, Central Europe, Map, p. 131, and p. 133. London, 1903.

48. W. Z. Ripley, Races of Europe, pp. 272, 304, 305, 317. New York, 1899.

49. *Ibid.*, p. 303.

50. *Ibid.*, Map, p. 251, and p. 253.

51. W. Deecke, Italy, p. 451. London, 1904.

52. Darwin, Origin of Species, Vol. II, chap. XIII, pp. 179, 180, 184. New York, 1895. A. R. Wallace, Island Life, pp. 284-285, 290-291. London and New York, 1892.

53. H. R. Mill, International Geography, p. 554. New York, 1902.

54. Ratzel, *Die Erde und das Leben*, Vol. I, p. 364. Leipsig, 1901.

55. Ratzel, History of Mankind, Vol. I, pp. 454-456. London, 1896-1898. H. R. Mill, International Geography, p. 1018. New York, 1902.

56. Ratzel, History of Mankind, Vol. I, p. 456. London, 1896-1898.

57. Nordenskiold, Voyage of the Vega, pp. 563, 588, 591. New York, 1882.

58. A. R. Wallace, Malay Archipelago, pp. 368, 380, 381. New York, 1869.

59. Richard Semon, In the Australian Bush, pp. 277-278. London, 1899.

60. Strabo, Book VIII, chap. VI, 16.

61. Pliny, *Naturalis Historia*, Book IV, 12.

62. *Ibid.*, Book VI, chap. 32.

63. Hereford George, Historical Geography of the British Empire, pp. 130-133. London, 1904.

64. Dietrich Schaefer, *Die Hansestädte und König Waldemar von Dänemark*, pp. 37-44. Jena, 1879.

65. Hereford George, Historical Geography of the British Empire, pp. 127-128. London, 1904.

66. The Danish West Indies, pp. 2767, 2769. Summary of Commerce and Finance for January, 1902. Washington.

67. E. A. Freeman, Historical Geography of Europe, pp. 22, 29, 37, 65, 77, 384, 412-415, 419, 426, 465. London, 1882.

68. *Ibid.*, 35, 48, 49, 54-55, 80, 379, 382-385, 409, 411, 556, 557. E. A. Freeman, Sicily, chaps. I, II. New York and London, 1894.

69. W. Deecke, Italy, pp. 132, 445. London, 1904. W. Z. Ripley, Races of Europe, p. 271. New York, 1899.

70. Elisée Reclus, Europe, Vol. I, p. 320. New York, 1886.

71. W. Deecke, Italy, pp. 448, 453. London, 1904.

72. H. R. Mill, International Geography, p. 367. New York, 1902.

73. David Murray, Story of Japan, p. 156. New York, 1894.

74. Henry Dyer, Dai Nippon, p. 61. New York, 1904.

75. E. A. Freeman, Historical Geography of Europe, pp. 55, 245, 252, 257, 258, 264, 556. London, 1882.

76. Thucydides I, 114; IV, 57-59, 62.

77. *Ibid.*, IV, 120-122.

78. Aristotle, Politics, Book XI, chaps. 7, 8.

79. J. T. Bent, The Bahrein Islands in the Persian Gulf, *Proceedings of the Roy. Geog. Soc.*, Vol. XII, p. 1. London, 1890.

80. W. F. Walker, The Azores, p. 22. London, 1886.

81. A. B. Ellis, West African Islands, p. 203. London, 1885.

82. Strabo, Book III, chap. V, 1.

83. H. J. Mackinder, Britain and the British Seas, pp. 10-12. London, 1904.

84. W. Z. Ripley, Races of Europe, pp. 301, 311. New York, 1899.

85. H. B. George, Historical Geography of the British Empire, pp. 10Q, 103, 104. London, 1904.

.86. J. R. Green, The Making of England, Vol. II, pp. 30, 31, 35. London, 1904.

87. James Bryce, Holy Roman Empire, p. 185. London, 1890. George Webbe Dasent, The Story of Burnt Njal, or Life in Iceland at the End of the Tenth Century, Vol. I, pp. LII-LXVIII. Edinburgh, 1861.

88. Dahlmann, *Geschichte von Dänemark*, Vol. II, pp. 265-268. Hamburg, 1857. James Bryce, Introduction to Helmolt, History of the World, Vol. I, p. XXII. New York, 1902.

89. George T. Stokes, Ireland and the Celtic Church, pp. 206-230. London, 1886.

90. J. R. Green, History of the English People, Vol. I, pp. 48-49.

91. Recent Discoveries in Crete, *The Chautauquan*, Vol. XLIII, p. 220. 1906. Angelo Mosso, The Palaces of Crete, p. 325. London, 1907.

92. Helmolt, History of the World, Vol. II, pp. 496-504. New York, 1902-6.

93. David Murray, Story of Japan, p. 156. New York, 1894. W. E. York, 1902-6.
Griffis, The Mikado's Empire, Vol. I, pp. 176-181. New York, 1903.
94. J. R. Green, History of the English People, Vol. I, pp. 30-33. New York.
95. Capt. F. Brinkley, Japan, Vol. I, p. 8. Boston and Tokyo, 1901.
96. Capt. A. T. Mahan, Influence of Sea Power upon History, p. 29. New York, 1902.
97. H. J. Mackinder, Britain and the British Seas, pp. 341, 343. London, 1904.
98. Ratzel, *Die Erde und das Leben*, Vol. I, p. 362. Leipzig, 1901.
99. W. E. Griffis, The Mikado's Empire, Vol. I, p. 258. New York, 1903.
100. W. F. Walker, The Azores, p. 2. London, 1886.
101. F. W. Wines, Punishment and Reformation, pp. 166-167, 184-188. New York, 1895.
102. Tacitus, Annals, Book I, chap. XIII.
103. *Ibid.*, Book IV, chaps. III, XV. Book II, chap. XIX.
104. W. Deecke, Italy, pp. 270, 410, 413, 448, 450. London, 1904.
105. Longmans Gazetteer of the World, Article Easter Isle.
106. Darwin and Fitzroy, Voyage of the Beagle, Vol. II, p. 59. London, 1839.
107. *Ibid.*, Vol. II, pp. 490-492.
108. A. B. Ellis, West African Islands, pp. 1-3. London, 1885.
109. Longmans Gazetteer of the World, Andaman and Nicobar.
110. Darwin and Fitzroy, Voyage of the Beagle, Vol. III, p. 245. London, 1839.
111. A. B. Ellis, West African Islands, pp. 72, 73, 241. London, 1885.
112. Charles H. Hawes, The Uttermost East, p. 345. New York, 1904.
113. The Dry Tortugas, *Harper's Monthly*, Vol. 37, p. 260. 1868.
114. A. R. Wallace, Island Life, pp. 332, 371, 410, 457, 460-461, 464. London, 1892.
115. *Ibid.*, pp. 407, 408, 410, 462.
116. Census of the Philippine Islands of 1903, Vol. I, p. 456. Washington, 1905.
117. Ratzel, History of Mankind, Vol. III, pp. 446, 449, 451. London, 1896-1898.
118. W. E. Griffis, The Mikado's Empire, Vol. I, pp. 30-31. New York, 1903.
119. W. Z. Ripley, Races of Europe, p. 271. New York, 1899.
120. Hereford George, Historical Geography of the British Empire, pp. 106-107. London, 1904.
121. Nelson Annandale, The Faroes and Iceland, pp. 19, 20, 33, 37, 64-65, 148, 193-194, 198, 206, 208. Oxford, 1905.
122. Capt. James Cook, Voyage to the Pacific Ocean, 1776-1780, Vol. II, pp. 69-70, 75-78. New York, 1796.
123. Williams and Calvert, Fiji and the Fijians, pp. 5-7, 14, 15. New York, 1859. Basil Thomson, The Fijians, pp. 23-32. London, 1908.
124. Mahler, *Siedelungsgebiete und Siedelungslage in Ozeanien.* Melching *Staatenbildung in Melanesien*, Leipzig, Dissertations, 1897.
125. H. R. Mill, International Geography, p. 570. New York, 1902.

126. Aristotle, Politics, Book II, chap. 8.

127. Ratzel, History of Mankind, Vol. I, 297-299. London, 1896-1898.

128. *Ibid.*, Vol. I, Map, p. 145, pp. 234, 251.

129. *Ibid.*, Vol. I, pp. 204-214.

130. Justus Perthes, *Taschen Atlas*, p. 67. Gotha, 1910.

131. *Ibid.*, p. 60.

132. *Ibid.*, p. 37.

133. *Ibid.*, p. 51.

134. *Ibid.*, pp. 37, 67.

135. Lippincott's New Gazetteer of the World, Madeira and Azores.

136. R. L. Stevenson, The South Seas, p. 37. New York, 1903.

137. *Ibid.*, p. 222.

138. J. S. Jenkins, United States Exploring Squadron under Capt. Wilkes, 1838-1842, pp. 401-403. New York, 1855.

139. Justus Perthes, *Taschen Atlas*, p. 70. Gotha, 1905.

140. Ratzel, History of Mankind, Vol. I, pp. 158, 179. London, 1896-1898.

141. J. S. Jenkins, United States Exploring Squadron under Capt. Wilkes, 1838-1842, p. 462. New York, 1855.

142. *Ibid.*, p. 314.

143. Nelson Annandale, The Faroes and Iceland, pp. 93-129. Oxford, 1905.

144. Elisée Reclus, Europe, Vol. IV, p. 344. New York, 1886.

145. John Murray, Handbook to Greece and the Ionian Isles, p. 329. London, 1872.

146. Hereford George, Historical Geography of the British Empire, p. 119. London, 1904.

147. W. Deecke, Italy, pp. 449-450. London, 1904.

148. *Ibid.*, pp. 447-448, 410-411.

149. Statistics from Justus Perthes, *Taschen Atlas*, p. 65. Gotha, 1910.

150. Longmans Gazetteer of the World, Amboina.

151. Census of the Philippine Islands of 1903. Vol. II, p. 30. Washington, 1905.

152. Justus Perthes, *Taschen Atlas*, pp. 75, 77. Gotha, 1910.

153. Hereford George, Historical Geography of the British Empire, pp. 238-240. London, 1904.

154. D. G. Hogarth, The Nearer East, pp. 243-244. London, 1902.

155. Dr. A. Philippson, The Greek Islands of the Aegean, *Scottish Geographical Magazine*, Vol. XIII, p. 489. 1897.

156. J. T. Brent, The Bahrein Islands in the Persian Gulf, *Proceedings of the Roy. Geog. Society*, Vol. XII, pp. 1-19, 1890; and Justus Perthes, *Taschen Atlas*, p. 55. Gotha, 1910.

157. Parkman, Pioneers of France in the New World, pp. 26-32. Boston, 1900.

158. *Ibid.*, pp. 253-262.

159. Thucydides, I, 100, 101. Herodotus, VII, 108, 109.

160. Grote, History of Greece, Vol. III, pp. 195, 197. New York, 1857.

161. *Ibid.*, Vol. IV, pp. 30-33.

162. Capt. James Cook, Voyage to the Pacific Ocean, 1776-1780, Vol. II, pp. 85-86, 88. New York. 1796.

163. George Forster, Voyage Round the World, Vol. I, p. 274, 280, 281, 285. London, 1777.

164. J. S. Jenkins, United States Exploring Squadron under Capt. Wilkes, 1838-1842, p. 402. New York, 1855.

165. George Forster, Voyage Round the World, Vol. I, pp. 571, 578, 587, 595. London, 1777.

166. R. H. Codrington, The Melanesians, pp. 303-304. Oxford, 1891.

167. William Mariner, Natives of the Tonga Islands, Vol. II, p. 30. Edinburgh, 1827.

168. Capt. James Cook, Voyage to the Pacific Ocean, 1776-1780, Vol. I, p. 302. New York, 1796.

169. Ratzel, History of Mankind, Vol. I, pp. 254-256. London, 1896-1898.

170. Williams and Calvert, Fiji and the Fijians, pp. 8, 46-49. New York, 1859. Basil Thomson, The Fijians, p. 339. London, 1908.

171. H. R. Mill, International Geography, pp. 562, 564, 572. New York, 1902.

172. Census of the Philippine Islands of 1903, Vol. IV, pp. 1-2. Washington, 1905.

173. Strabo, Book VIII, chap. VI, 16.

174. W. Deecke, Italy, pp. 380, 448-450. London, 1904.

175. Ibid., p. 452.

176. Dr. A. Philippson, The Greek Islands of the Aegean, Sottish Geographical Magazine, Vol. XIII, pp. 489-490. 1897. John Murray, Handbook to Greece and the Ionian Isles. London, 1872.

177. W. E. Griffis, The Mikado's Empire, Vol. I, pp. 17-20. New York, 1904.

178. Henry Dyer, Dai Nippon, pp. 238-244. New York, 1903. Arthur M. Knapp, Feudal and Modern Japan, Vol. I, pp. 78, 79, 116, 117. New York, 1900.

179. Alfred Stead, Japan by the Japanese, p. 413. London, 1904.

180. Sir Rutherford Alcock, Three Years in Japan, Vol. I, pp. 83, 84, 283-286. New York, 1868.

181. H. D. Traill, Social England, Vol. II, pp. 243-246, 547-554; Vol. III, pp. 114-121, 239-241, 253-255, 351-359. London, 1905.

182. Thucydides, Book 1, 4. Aristotle, Politics, Book II, chap. 7, 2. Herodotus, Book VII, 170.

183. Thucydides, Book IV, chaps. 84, 88.

184. Census of the Philippine Islands in 1903, Vol. I, pp. 412-414. Washington, 1905.

185. Richard Semon, In the Australian Bush, p. 517. London, 1899.

186. Ratzel, History of Mankind, Vol. I, pp. 174-177. London, 1896-98.

187. Ibid., Vol. I, pp. 178-179.

188. Ibid., Vol. I, pp. 157-161, 165.

189. Henry Dyer, Dai Nippon, pp. 250-257, 266. New York, 1904.

190. Elisée Reclus, Europe, Vol. I, p. 337. New York, 1886. Hereford George, Historical Geography of the British Empire, pp. 118-119. London, 1904.

191. D. G. Hogarth, The Nearer East, p. 244. London, 1902.

192. Dr. A. Philippson, The Greek Islands of the Aegean, Scottish Geographical Magazine, Vol. XIII, p. 488. 1897.

193. Jensen, *Die Nordfrieschen Inseln*, p. 133. 1891.

194. Malthus, Essay on Population, Book I, chap. V, p. 67. London, 1826. This whole chapter on "Checks to Population in the Islands of the South Seas" is valuable.

195. Boyd Alexander, From the Niger to the Nile, Vol. II, pp. 108-110. London, 1907.

196. History of the Conquest of the Canaries, p. xxxix. Hakluyt Society, London, 1872.

197. Ratzel, History of Mankind, Vol. I, pp. 273, 299-300. London, 1896-98.

198. *Ibid.*, Vol. I, pp. 270, 274-275. Adolf Marcuse, *Die Hawaiischen Inseln*, p. 108. Berlin, 1894.

199. R. L. Stevenson, The South Seas, pp. 138-139. New York, 1903.

200. George Forster, Voyage Round the World, Vol. I, p. 564, 569, 572, 577, 584, 586, 596. London, 1777.

201. Westermarck, History of Human Marriage, pp. 116, 441, 462-463, 450-452, 454, 457. London, 1891.

202. Ratzel, History of Mankind, Vol. I, p. 270. London, 1896-1898.

203. R. H. Codrington, The Melanesians, p. 229. Oxford, 1891.

204. Basil Thomson, The Fijians, pp. 221-227. London, 1908. Williams and Calvert, Fiji and the Fijians, pp. 132, 142. New York, 1859.

205. *Ibid.*, p. 130. R. L. Stevenson, The South Seas, pp. 38, 40. New York, 1903.

206. *Ibid.*, p. 38.

207. J. S. Jenkins, United States Exploring Squadron under Capt. Wilkes, 1838-1842, pp. 404-405. New York, 1855.

208. Ratzel, History of Mankind, Vol. I, pp. 270, 299. London, 1896-98.

209. Adolf Marcuse, *Die Hawaiischen Inseln*, p. 109. Berlin, 1894.

210. G. W. Knox, Japanese Life in Town and Country, p. 188. New York, 1905.

211. Capt. Cook's Journal, First Voyage Round the World in the Endeavor, 1768-1771, pp. 95, 96. Edited by W. J. L. Wharton. London, 1893.

212. Malthus, Essay on Population, Book I, chap. V.

213. R. L. Stevenson, The South Seas, p. 39. New York, 1903.

214. *Ibid.*, p. 52.

215. Adolf Marcuse, *Die Hawaiischen Inseln*, p. 109. Berlin, 1894.

216. Williams and Calvert, Fiji and the Fijians, pp. 144-146. New York, 1859.

217. Ratzel, History of Mankind, Vol. I, p. 330. London, 1896-1898.

218. William Mariner, Natives of the Tonga Islands, Vol. II, pp. 95, 134-135. Edinburgh, 1827. Capt. Cook's Journal, First Voyage Round the World in the Endeavor, 1768-1771, pp. 220-221. Edited by W. J. L. Wharton. London, 1893.

219. Strabo, Book X, chap. V, 6.

220. R. L. Stevenson, The South Seas, pp. 98-104. New York, 1903.

221. Ratzel, History of Mankind, Vol. I, pp. 297-299. London, 1896-1898.

222. William Mariner, Natives of the Tonga Islands, Vol. II, pp. 108-109. Edinburgh, 1827.

223. Darwin and Fitzroy, Voyage of the Beagle, Vol. II, pp. 183, 189-190. London, 1839.

CHAPTER XIV

PLAINS, STEPPES AND DESERTS

Relief of the sea floor. ANTHROPO-GEOGRAPHY has to do primarily with the forms and relief of the land. The relief of the sea floor influences man only indirectly. It does this by affecting the forms of the coast, by contributing to the action of tides in scouring out river estuaries, as on the flat beaches of Holland and England, by determining conditions for the abundant littoral life of the sea, the fisheries of the continental shelf which are factors in the food quest and the distribution of settlements. Moreover, the ocean floor enters into the problem of laying telegraph cables, and thereby assumes a certain commercial and political importance. The name of the Telegraph Plateau of the North Atlantic, crossed by three cables, points to the relation between these and submarine relief. So also does the erratic path of the cable from southwestern Australia to South Africa via Keeling Island and Mauritius.

Submarine reliefs have yet greater significance in their relation to the distribution of the human race over the whole earth; for what is now a shallow sea may in geologically recent times have been dry land, on which primitive man crossed from continent to continent. It is vital to the theory of the Asiatic origin of the American Indian that in Miocene times a land bridge spanned the present shallows of Bering Sea. Hence the slight depth of this basin has the same biogeographical significance as that of the British seas, the waters of the Malay Archipelago, and the Melanesian submarine platform. The impressive fact about "Wallace's Line" is the depth of the narrow channel which it follows through Lombok and Macassar Straits and which, in recent geological times, defined the southeastern shore of Asia. In all these questions of former land connection, anthropogeography follows the lead of bio-geography, whose deductions, based upon the dispersal of countless plant and animal forms, point to the paths of human distribution.

Mean elevations of the continents.   The mean elevation of the continents above sea level indicates the average life conditions of their populations as dependent upon relief. The 1010 meters (3313 feet) of Asia indicate its predominant highland character. The 330 meters (1080 feet) representing the average height of Europe, and the 310 meters (1016 feet) of Australia indicate the preponderance of lowlands. Nevertheless, anthropo-geography rarely lends itself to a mathematical statement of physical conditions. Such a statement only obscures the facts. The 660 meters (2164 feet) mean elevation of Africa indicates a relief higher than Europe, but gives no hint of the plateau character of the Dark Continent, in which lowlands and mountains are practically negligible features; while the almost identical figure (650 meters or 2132 feet) for both North and South America is the average derived from extensive lowlands in close juxtaposition to high plateaus capped by lofty mountain ranges. Such mathematical generalizations indicate the general mass of the continental upheaval, but not the way this mass is divided into low and high reliefs.[1]

The method of anthropo-geography is essentially analytical, and therefore finds little use for general orometric statements, which may be valuable to the science of geo-morphology with its radically different standpoint. For instance, geo-morphology may calculate from all the dips and gaps in the crest of a mountain range the average height of its passes. Anthropo-geography, on the other hand, distinguishes between the various passes according as they open lines of greater or less resistance to the historical movement across the mountain barriers. It finds that one deep breach in the mountain wall, like the Mohawk Depression[2] and Cumberland Gap in the Appalachian system,[3] Truckee Pass in the Sierra Nevada[4] and the Brenner in the Alps,[5] has more far-reaching and persistent historical consequences than a dozen high-laid passes that only notch the crest. Pack-trail, road and railroad seek the former, avoid the latter; one draws from a wide radius, while the other serves a restricted local need. Therefore anthropo-geography, instead of clumping the

passes, sorts them out, and notes different relations in each.
In continents and countries the anthropo-geographer looks Distribu-
to see not what reliefs are present, but how they are dis- tion of re-
tributed; whether highlands and lowlands appear in un- liefs.
broken masses as in Asia, or alternate in close succession as
in western Europe; whether the transition from one to the
other is abrupt as in western South America, or gradual as
in the United States. A simple and massive land structure
lends the same trait of the simple and massive to every kind
of historical movement, because it collects the people into
large groups and starts them moving in broad streams, as it
were. This fact explains the historical preponderance of
lowland peoples and especially of steppe nomads over the
small, scattered groups inhabiting isolated mountain valleys.
The island of Great Britain illustrates the same principle on
a small scale in the turbid, dismembered history of independent Scotland, with its Highlanders and Lowlanders, its tribes
and clans separated by mountains, gorges, straits, and
fiords,[6] in contrast to the smoother, unified course of history
in the more uniform England. Carl Ritter compares the dull
uniformity of historical development and relief in Africa with
the variegated assemblage of highlands and lowlands, nations
and peoples, primitive societies and civilized states in the
more stimulating environment of Asia.[7]

The chief features of mountain relief reappear on a Homolo-
large scale in the continents, which are simply big areas of gous relief
upheaval lifted above sea level. The continents show there- and homol-
fore homologous regions of lowlands, uplands, plateaus and ogous his-
mountains, each district sustaining definite relations to the tories.
natural terrace above or below it, and displaying a history
corresponding to that of its counterpart in some distant part
of the world, due to a similarity of relations. This appears
first in a specialization of products in each tier and hence
in more or less economic interdependence, especially where civilization is advanced. The tendency of conquest to unite such
obviously complementary districts is persistent. Hence the
Central Highland of Asia is fringed with low peripheral
lands like Manchuria, China, India and Mesopotamia, into
whose history it has repeatedly entered as a disturbing force.

All the narrow Pacific districts of the Americas from Alaska to Patagonia are separated by the Cordilleras from the lowlands on the Atlantic face of the continents; all reveal in their history the common handicap arising from an overwhelming preponderance of plateau and mountain and a paucity of lowlands. Colombia, Ecuador and Peru have in the past century been stretching out their hands eastward to grasp sections of the bordering Amazon lowlands, where to-day is the world's great field of conflicting boundary claims. Chile would follow its geographical destiny if it should supplement its high, serrated surface by the plateaus and lowlands of Bolivia, as Cyrus the Persian married the Plateau of Iran to the plains of the Tigris and Euphrates, and Romulus joined the Alban hills to the alluvial fields of the Tiber.

Anthropo-geography of low-lands.

Well-watered lowlands invite expansion, ethnic, commercial and political. In them the whole range of historical movements meet few obstacles beyond the waters gathering in their runnels and the forests nourished in their rich soils. Limited to 200 meters (660 feet) elevation, lowlands develop no surface features beyond low hills and undulating swells of land. Uniformity of life conditions, monotony of climate as of relief, except where grades of latitude intervene to chill or heat, an absence of natural boundaries, and constant encouragement to intercourse, are the anthropo-geographic traits of lowlands, as opposed to the arresting, detaining grasp of mountains and highland valleys. Small, isolated lowlands, like the mountain-rimmed plains of Greece and the Aegean coast of Asia Minor, the Nile flood-plain, Portugal, and Andalusia in Spain, may achieve precocious and short-lived historical importance, owing to the fertility of their alluvial soils, their character as naturally defined districts, and their advantageous maritime location; but while in these restricted lowlands the telling feature has been their barrier boundaries of desert, mountains and sea, the vast level plains of the earth have found their distinctive and lasting historical importance in the fact of their large and unbounded surface.

Such plains have been both source and recipient of every form of historical movement. Owing to their prevailing fitness for agriculture, trade and intercourse, they are favored regions for the final massing of a sedentary population. The areas of greatest density of population in the world, harboring 150 or more to the square kilometer (385 to the square mile), are found in the lowlands of China, the alluvial plains of India, and similar level stretches in the Neapolitan plain and Po Valley, the lowlands of France, Germany, Holland, Belgium, England and Scotland. Such a density is found in upland districts (660 to 2000 feet, or 200 to 600 meters) bordering agricultural lowlands, only where industries based upon mineral wealth cause a concentration of population. [See maps pages 8, 9, 559.]

The level or undulating surface of extensive lowlands is not favorable to the early development of civilization. Not only do their wide extent and absence of barriers postpone the transition from nomadism to sedentary life, but their lack of contrasting environments and contrasted developments, which supplement and stimulate, puts chains upon progress. A flat, monotonous relief produces a monotonous existence, necessarily one-sided, needing a complement in upland or mountain. To the pioneer settlers in the lowlands of Missouri the Ozark Plateau was a boon, because its streams furnished water-power for much needed saw and flour mills. Treeless Egypt even before 2500 B. C. depended upon the cedars of the Lebanon Mountains for the construction of its ships; so that the conquest of Lebanon, begun by Thutmose I. and completed by Thutmose III. in about 1470 B. C., had a sound geographical basis.[8] Similarly the exploitation of the copper, malachite, turquoise and lapis-lazuli of Mount Sinai, minerals not found in the Nile plain, led the ancient Egyptians into extensive mining operations there before 3000 B. C., and resulted in the establishment of Egyptian political supremacy in 2900 B. C., as a measure to protect the mines against the depredations of the neighboring Bedouin tribes.[9] Lowlands lack the distinctive advantages of highlands found in diversity of climate, water-power, generally in more abundant forests and minerals. The latter are earlier discovered and worked in the tilted strata of mountains and uplands.

Extensive plains unfavorable to early development.

Plain countries suffer particularly from a paucity of varied geographic conditions and of resulting contrasts in their population. Their national characters tend to be less richly endowed; their possibilities for development are blighted or retarded, because even racial differences are rapidly obliterated in the uniform geographic environment. A small diversified country like Crete, Great Britain, Italy, Portugal, Saxony, or Japan, is a geographical *multum in parvo*. The western half of Europe bears the same stamp, endowing each country and nation with marked individuality born of partial isolation and a varied combination of environment. The larger eastern half of the continent embraced in the plains of Poland and Russia shows monotony in every aspect of human life. This comes out anthropologically in the striking similarity of head-form found everywhere north and east of the Carpathian Mountains, except in the secluded districts of Lithuania and Crimea, which shelter remnants of distinct races. Over all this vast territory the range of cephalic variation is only five units or one-third that in the restricted but diversified territory of western Europe. Italy, only one-eighteenth the size of European Russia, has a range of fifteen units, reflecting in the variety of its human types the diversity of its environment.[10]

Conditions for fusion in plains. In the plains geography makes for fusion. Russia shows this marked homogeneity, despite a motley collection of race ingredients which have entered into the make-up of the Russian people. Without boundary or barrier, the country has stood wide open to invasion; but the intruders found no secluded corners where they could entrench themselves and preserve their national individuality.[11] They dropped into a vast melting-pot, which has succeeded in amalgamating the most diverse elements. The long-drawn Baltic-North Sea plain of Europe shows the same power to fuse. Here is found a prevailing blond, long-headed stock from the Gulf of Finland to the Somme River in France.[12] Yet this natural boulevard has been a passway for races. Prehistoric evidences show that the dark, broad-headed Celtic folk once overspread this plain east to the Weser;[13] it still tends to trickle down from the southern uplands into the Baltic lowland, and modify the Teutonic type along its southern margin throughout Germany.[14]   The Slavs in historic times reached as far west as the Weser, while the expansion of the Teutons has embraced the whole maritime plain from Brittany to the Finnish Gulf. Here it is difficult to draw an ethnic boundary on the basis of physical differences.   The eastern Prussians are Slavonized Teutons, and the adjacent Poles seem to be Teutonized Slavs, while the purest type of Letto-Lithuanian at the eastern corner of the Baltic coast approximates closely to the Anglo-Saxon type which sprang from the western corner.[15]   A similar amalgamation of races and peoples has taken place in the lowlands of England and Scotland, while diversity still lingers in the highlands.   In the Lowlands of Scotland, Picts in small numbers, Britons, Scots from Ireland, Angles, Frisians, Northmen and Danes have all been blended and assimilated in habits, customs and speech.[16]

This uniformity is advantageous to early development in a small plain, because of the juxtaposition of contrasted environments, but is stultifying to national life in an immense expanse of monotony like that of Russia.   Here sameness leaves its stamp on everything.   Language is differentiated with only two dialects, that of the Great Russians of the north and the Little Russians of the southern steppes, who were so long exposed to Tartar influences.   Most other languages of Europe, though confined to much smaller areas, show far greater diversity.[17]   While the Russian of Kazan or Archangel can converse readily with the citizen of Riga or St. Petersburg, Germans from highland Bavaria and Swabia are scarcely intelligible to Prussian and Mecklenberger.   And whereas Germany a few decades ago could count over a hundred different kinds of national dress or *Tracht*, Great Russia alone, with six times the area, had only a single type with perhaps a dozen slight variations.   Leroy-Beaulieu comments upon this eternal sameness.   "The cities are all alike; so are the peasants, in looks, habits, in mode of life.   In no country do people resemble one another more; no other country is so free from political complexity, those oppositions in type and character, which even yet we encounter in Italy and Spain, in France and Germany.   The nation is

Retardation due to monotonous environment.

made in the likeness of the country; it shows the same unity, we might say the same monotony, as the plains on which it dwells."

Influence of soils in low plains.

The more flat and featureless a lowland is, the more important become even the slightest surface irregularities which can draw faint dividing lines among the population. Here a gentle land-swell, river, lake, forest, or water-soaked moor serves as boundary. Especially apparent is the differentiating influence of difference of soils. Gravel and alluvium, sand and clay, chalk and more recent marine sediments, emphasize small geographical differences throughout the North German lowland and its extension through Belgium and Holland; here various soils differentiate the distribution of population. In the Netherlands we find the Frisian element of the Dutch people inhabiting chiefly the clay soils and low fens of the west and northwest, the Saxon in the diluvial tracts of the east, and the Frankish in the river clays and diluvium of the south. All the types have maintained their differences of dialect, styles of houses, racial character, dress and custom.[18] The only distinctive region in the great western lowland of France, which comprises over half of the country, is Brittany, individualized in its people and history by its peninsula form, its remote western location, and its infertile soil of primary rocks. Within the sedimentary trough of the Paris Basin, a slight Cretacean platform like the meadow land of Perche[19] (200 to 300 meters elevation) introduces an area of thin population devoted to horse and cattle raising in close proximity to the teeming urban life of Paris. The eastern lowland of England also can be differentiated economically and historically chiefly according to differences of underlying rocks, Carboniferous, Triassic, Jurassic, chalk, boulder clays, and alluvium, which also coincide often with slight variations of relief.[20] In Russia the contrast between the glaciated surface of the north and the Black Mould belt of the south makes the only natural divisions of that vast country, unless we distinguish also the arid southeastern steppes on the basis of a purely climatic difference. [See map page 484.]

The broad coastal plain of our South Atlantic States contains only low reliefs, but it is diversified by several soil belts, which exert a definite control over the industries of the inhabitants, and thereby over the distribution of the negro population. In Georgia, for instance, the rich alluvial soil of the swampy coast is devoted to the culture of rice and sea-island cotton, and contains over 60 per cent. of negroes in its population. This belt, which is only 25 miles wide, is succeeded inland by a broader zone of sandy pine barrens, where the proportion of negroes drops to only 20 or 30 per cent. of the total. Yet further inland is another fertile belt, devoted chiefly to the cultivation of upland cotton and harboring from 35 to over 60 per cent. of negroes in its population.[21] Alabama shows a similar stratification of soils and population from north to south over its level surface. Along the northern border of the state the cereal belt coincides with the deep calcareous soil of the Tennessee River Valley, where negroes constitute from 35 to 60 per cent. of the inhabitants. Next comes the mineral belt, covering the low foot-hills of the Appalachian Mountains. It contains the densest population of the state, less than 17 per cent. of which is negro. South of this is the broad cotton belt of various rich soils, chiefly deep black loam of the river bottoms, which stretches east and west across the state and includes over 60 per cent. of negroes in its population. This is succeeded by the low, coastal timber belt, marked by a decline in the quality of the soil and the proportion of negro inhabitants.[22]

In the dead level of extensive plains even slight elevations are seized upon for special uses, or acquire peculiar signifi- *Value of slight elevations.* cance. The Kurgans or burial mounds of the prehistoric inhabitants of Russia, often twenty to fifty feet high, serve to-day as watch-towers for herdsmen tending their flocks.[23] Similarly the Bou-bous, inhabiting the flat grasslands of the French Congo between the Shari and Ubangui Rivers, use the low knolls dotted over their country, probably old ant-hills, as lookout points against raiders.[24] The sand hills and ridges which border the southern edges of the North German lowland form districts sharply contrasted to the swampy, wooded depressions of the old deserted river valleys just to the north. Early occupied by a German stock, they furnished the first German colonists to displace the primitive Slav

population surviving in those unattractive, inaccessible
regions, as seen in the Spreewald near Kottbus to-day.

Plains and political expansion.   The boundless horizon which is unfavorable to a nascent
people endows them in their belated maturity with the power
of mastering large areas.   Political expansion is the dominant characteristic of the peoples of the plains.   Haxthausen observed that handicapped and retarded Russia
commands every geographic condition and national trait
necessary for virile and expansive political power.[25]   Muscovite expansion eastward across the lowlands of Europe
and Asia is paralleled by the rapid spread of American
settlement and dominion across the plains and prairies of the
Mississippi Valley, and Hungarian domination of the wide
Danubian levels from the foot-hills of the Austrian Alps to
the far Carpathian watershed.   It was the closely linked
lowlands of the Seine and Loire which formed the core of
political expansion and centralization in France.   Nearly the
whole northern lowland of Germany has been gradually absorbed by the kingdom of Prussia, which now comprises in
its territory almost two-thirds of the total area of the Empire.   Prussian statesmen formulated the policy of German
unification and colonial expansion, and to Prussia fell the
hereditary headship of the Empire.

Lowland states tend to stretch out and out to boundaries
which depend more upon the reach of the central authority
than upon physical features.   We have seen American settlement and dominion overleap one natural boundary after another between the Mississippi River and the Pacific, from 1804
to 1848.   Russia in an equally short period has pushed forward
its Asiatic frontier at a dozen points, despite all barriers of
desert and mountain.   Argentina, blessed with extensive plains,
fertile soil and temperate climate, which have served to augment its population both by natural increase and steady immigration (one-fourth of its population is foreign), has expanded
across the Rio Negro over the grasslands of the Patagonian
plain, and thereby enlarged its area by 259,620 square miles
since 1881.   The statesman of the plains is a nature-made im-
perialist; he nurses wide territorial policies and draws his
frontiers for the future.   To him a "far-flung battle line" is

significant only as a means to secure a far-flung boundary line. From these low, accessible plains of adequate rainfall, **Arid** which at first encourage primitive nomadism but finally make **plains.** it yield to sedentary life and to dense populations spreading their farms and cities farther and farther over the unresisting surface of the land, we turn to those boundless arid steppes and deserts which Nature has made forever the homes of restless, rootless peoples. Here quiescence is impossible, the *Völkerwanderung* is habitual, migration is permanent. The only change is this eternal restlessness. While the people move, progress stands still. Everywhere the sun-scorched grasslands and waterless waste have drawn the dead-line to the advance of indigenous civilization. They permit no accumulation of productive wealth beyond increasing flocks and herds, and limit even their growth by the food supply of scanty, scattered pasturage. The meager rainfall elimi-nates forests and therewith a barrier to migrations; it also restricts vegetation to grasses, sedges and those forms which can survive a prolonged summer drought and require a short period of growth.

The union of arid plains and steppe vegetation is based **Distribution** upon climate, and is therefore a widely distributed phenom- **and extent** enon. These plains, whether high or low, are found in their **of arid** greatest extent in the dry trade-wind belts, as in the deserts **plains.** and steppes of Arabia, Persia, Sudan, the Sahara, South Africa and Central Australia; and in vast continental in-teriors, where the winds arrive robbed of their moisture in passing intervening highlands, as in the grasslands of our western plains, the llanos and pampas of South America, and the steppes of Central Asia. But wherever they occur, whether in Argentina or Russian Turkestan or the higher plains of Mongolia and Tibet, they present the same general characteristics of land surface, climate, flora and fauna, and the same nomadic populations of pastoral or hunting tribes. In them the movement of peoples reaches its culminat-ing point, permanent settlement its nil point. Here the hunting savage makes the widest sweep in pursuit of buffalo or antelope, and pauses least to till a field; here the pastoral nomad follows his systematic wandering in search of pas-

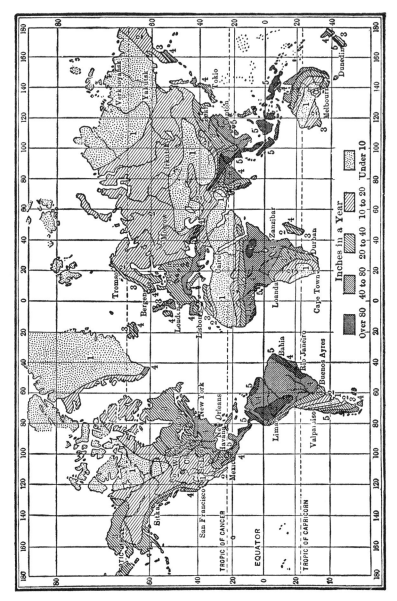

'ANNUAL RAINFALL OF THE WORLD.

turage and his hardly less systematic campaigns of conquest. It is the vast area and wide distribution of these arid plains, combined with the mobility which they impose on native human life, that has lent them historical importance, and reproduced in all sections of the world that significant homologous relation of arid and well-watered districts.

The grasslands of the old world developed historical **Pastoral** importance only after the domestication of cattle, sheep, **life.** goats, asses, horses, camels and yaks. This step in progress resulted in the evolution of peoples who renounced the precarious subsistence of the chase and escaped the drudgery of agriculture, to devote themselves to pastoral life. It was possible only where domesticable animals were present, and where the intelligence of the native or the peculiar pressure exerted by environment suggested the change from a natural to an artificial basis of subsistence. Australia lacked the type of animal. Though North America had the reindeer and buffalo, and South America the guanaco, llama and alpaca, only the last two were domesticated in the Andean highlands; but as these were restricted to altitudes from 10,000 to 14,000 feet, where pasturage was limited, stock raising in primitive South America was merely an adjunct to the sedentary agriculture of the high intermontane valleys, and never became the basis for pastoral nomadism on the grassy plains. However, when the Spaniards introduced horses and cattle into South America, the Indians and half-breeds of the llanos and pampas became regular pastoral nomads, known as llaneros and gauchos. They are a race of horsemen, wielding javelin and lasso and bola, living on meat, often on horse-flesh like the ancient Huns, dwelling in leather tents made on a cane framework, like those of the modern Kirghis and medieval Tartars, dressed in cloaks of horsehide sewn together, and raiding the Argentinian frontier of white settlement for horses, sheep and cattle, with the true marauding instinct of all nomads.[26]

Aridity is not the only climatic condition condemning a **Pastoral** people to nomadic life. Excessive cold, producing the tundra **nomads of** wastes of the far north, has the same effect. Therefore, **Arctic** throughout Arctic Eurasia, from the Lapp district of Nor- **plains.**

way to the inland Chukches of eastern Siberia, we have a succession of Hyperborean peoples pasturing their herds of reindeer over the moss and lichen tundra, and supplementing their food supply with hunting and fishing. The reindeer Chukches once confined themselves to their peninsula, so long as the grazing grounds were unexhausted; but they now range as far west as Yakutsk on the Lena River. The Orochones of the Kolima River district in eastern Siberia, who live chiefly by their reindeer, have small herds. A well-to-do person will have 40 to 100 animals, and the wealthiest only 700, while the Chukches with herds of 10,000 often seek the pasture of the Kolima tundra.[27] Farther west, the Samoyedes of northern Siberia and Russia and the Zirians of the Petchora River range with their large herds northward to the Yalmal Peninsula and Vaygats Isle in summer, and southward in winter. [See map pages 103, 225.] Here a herd of fifty head, which just suffices for the support of one family of four souls, requires 10 square versts, or 4.44 square miles of tundra pasturage.[28] Hence population must forever remain too sparse ever to attain historical significance. [See map page 8.] The Russian Lapps, too, lead a semi-nomadic life. Each group has a particular summer and winter settlement. The winter village is located usually inland in the Kola Peninsula, where the forests lend shelter to the herds, and the summer one near the tundra of the coast, where fishing is accessible. In winter, like the nomads of the deserts, they add to their slender income by the transport of goods by their reindeer and by service at the post stations.[29]

Historical importance of steppe nomads.   These nomads of the frozen north, scattered sparsely over the remote periphery of the habitable world, have lacked the historical importance which in all times has attached to the steppe nomads, owing to their central location. The broad belt of deserts and grasslands which crosses the old world diagonally between 10° and 60° North Latitude from the Atlantic in Africa to the Pacific in Asia, either borders or encompasses the old domains of culture found in river oases, alluvial lowlands or coastal plains of the Torrid and Temperate Zones. The restless, mobile, unbound shepherds of the arid lands have never long been contained by the

country which bred them.   They have constantly encroached
upon the territory of their better placed neighbors, invading,
conquering, appropriating their fields and cities, disturbing
but at the same time acquiring their culture, lording it over
the passive agriculturists, and at the same time putting iron
into their weaker blood.   It is the geographical contact between arid steppes and moist river valley, between land of
poverty and land of plenty, that has made the history of the Mobility
two inseparable.[30]   of pastoral
Every aspect of human life in the steppes bears the stamp nomads.

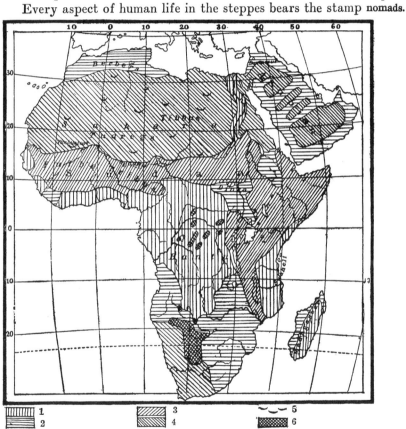

CULTURAL REGIONS OF AFRICA AND ARABIA.

1. Agricultural tribes.   2. Combined agricultural and grazing.
3. Agricultural tribes under dominion of pastoral nomads.   4. Deserts.   5. Oases, combining tillage and grazing.   6. Hunting tribes.

of mobility. The nomad tolerates no clog upon his movements. His dwelling is the tent of skin or felt as among Kalmucks and Kirghis, or the tent wagon of the modern Boer[31] and the ancient Scythian as described by Herodotus.[32] "This device has been contrived by them as the country is fit for it," he says,—level, grassy, treeless. The temporary settlement of shepherd tribes is the group of tents, or the ancient *carrago* camp of the nomadic Visigoths,[33] or the *laager* of the pastoral Boers, both a circular barricade or corral of wagons.

Tendency to trek.

Constant movement reduces the impedimenta to a minimum. The Orochones, a Tunguse nomadic tribe of eastern Siberia, have no furniture in their tents, and keep their meager supply of clothing and utensils neatly packed on sledges, as if to start at a moment's notice.[34] The only desirable form of capital is that which transports itself, namely, flocks and herds. Beyond that, wealth is limited to strictly portable forms, preferably silver, gold and jewels. It was in terms of these, besides their herds, that the riches of Abraham and Lot were rated in the Bible. That the Israelites when traveling through the wilderness should have had the gold to make the golden calf accords strictly with the verisimilitude of pastoral life.[35] Moreover, that these enslaved descendants of the Sheik Abraham, with their traditions of pastoral life, should have simply trekked—ruptured the frail ties of recently acquired habit which bound them to the Nile soil, is also in keeping with their inborn nomadic spirit. Similar instances occur among modern peoples. The Great Trek of the South African Boers in 1836, by which they renounced not only their unwelcome allegiance to England, but also their land,[36] was another exodus in accordance with the instinct of a pastoral people. They adopted no strange or difficult course, but traveled with their families as they were wont in their every day life of cattle-tenders, took all their chattels with them, and headed for the thin pastures of the far-reaching veldt. The Russian government has had to contend with a like fluidity in her Cossack tribes of the steppes, who have been up and off when imperial authority became oppressive. In the summer of 1878 West Siberia lost about 9000 Kirghis, who left the province Semipalatinsk to seek Mongolia.

Environment determines the nomadic habits of the dweller of desert and steppe. The distribution of pasture and water fixes the scope and the rate of his wandering; these in turn depend upon geographic conditions and vary with the season. The Papago Indians of southern Arizona range with their cattle over a territory 100 by 150 miles in extent, and wander across the border into Mexico. When their main water supply, derived from wells or artificial reservoirs near their summer villages, is exhausted, they migrate to the water-holes, springs or streams in the cañons. There the cattle graze out on the plains and return to the cañons to drink.[37] Every Mongol tribe and clan has its seasonal migration. In winter the heavier precipitation and fuller streams enable them to collect in considerable groups in protected valleys; but the dry summer disperses them over the widest area possible, in order to utilize every water-hole and grass spot. The hotter regions of the plains are abandoned in summer for highlands, where the short period of warmth yields temporary pastures and where alone water can be found. The Kirghis of Russian Turkestan resort in summer to the slopes and high valleys of the Altai Mountains, where their auls or tent villages may be seen surrounded by big flocks of sheep, goats, camels, horses and cattle.[38] The Pamir in the warm months is the gathering place for the nomads of Central Asia. The naked desert of Arabia yields a rare herbage during the rainy season, when the Bedouin tribes resort to it for pasturage;[39] but during the succeeding drought they scatter to the hills of Yemen, Syria and Palestine,[40] or migrate to the valley of the Nile and Euphrates.[41] The Arabs of the northern Sahara, followed by small flocks of sheep and goats, vibrate between the summer pastures on the slopes of the Atlas Mountains and the scant, wiry grass tufts found in winter on the borders of the desert.[42] When the equatorial rains begin in June, the Arabs of the Atbara River follow them north-westward into the Nubian desert, and let their camel herds graze on the delicate grass which the moisture has conjured up from the sandy soil. The

Seasonal migrations.

country about Cassala, which is flooded during the monsoon rains by the rivers from the Abyssinian Mountains, is reserved for the dry season.[43] In the same way the Tartar tribes of the Dnieper, Don, Volga and Ural Rivers in the thirteenth century moved down these rivers in winter to the sea coast, and in summer up-stream to the hills and mountains.[44] So for the past hundred years the Boers of the South African grasslands have migrated in their tent wagons from the higher to the lower pastures, according to the season of the year, invading even the Karroo Desert after the short summer rains.[45]

Marauding expeditions.   This systematic movement of nomads within their accepted boundaries leads, on slight provocation, to excursions beyond their own frontiers into neighboring territories. The growing herd alone necessitates the absorption of more land, more water-holes, because the grazed pastures renew their grass slowly under the prevailing conditions of drought. An area sufficient for the support of the tribe is inadequate for the sustenance of the herd, whose increase is a perennial expansive force. Soon the pastures become filled with the feeding flocks, and then herdsmen and herds spill over into other fields. Often a season of unusual drought, reducing the existing herbage which is scarcely adequate at best, gives rise to those irregular, temporary expansions which enlarge the geographical horizon of the horde, and eventuate in widespread conquest. Such incursions, like the seasonal movements of nomads, result from the helpless dependence of shepherd tribes upon variations of rainfall.

The nomad's basis of life is at best precarious. He and want are familiar friends. A pest among his herds, diminished pasturage, failing wells, all bring him face to face with famine, and drive him to robbery and pillage.[46] Marauding tendencies are ingrained in all dwellers of the deserts and steppes.[47] Since the days of Job, the Bedouins of Arabia have been a race of marauders; they have reduced robbery to a system. Predatory excursions figure conspicuously in the history of all the tribes. Robber is a title of honor.[48] Pliny said that the Arabs were equally addicted to theft and trade. They pillaged caravans and held them for ransom, or gave them safe conduct across the desert for a price. Formerly the Turkoman tribes of the Trans-Caspian steppes levied on the bordering districts, notably the northern part of Khorasan, which belonged more to the Turkomans, Yomut and Goklan tribes of the adjoining steppe than to the resident Persians. The border districts of Herat, Khiva, Merv and Bukhara used to suffer in the same way from the raids of the Tekkes, till the Russians checked the evil.[49] The Tekkes had depopulated whole districts, invaded Persian towns of considerable size, and carried off countless families into slavery. Both Turkomans and Kirghis tribes prior to 1873 raided caravans and carried off the travelers to the slave markets of Bukhara and Samarkand.[50] [See map page 103.]

Among these tribes no young man commanded respect in his community till he had participated in a *baranta* or cattle-raising.[51] For centuries the nomadic hordes of the Russian steppes systematically pillaged the peaceful agricultural Slavs, who were threatening to encroach upon their pasture lands. The sudden, swift descent and swift retreat of the mounted marauders with the booty into the pathless grass-lands, whither pursuit was dangerous, their tendency to rob and conquer but never to colonize, involved Russia in a long struggle, which ceased only with the extension of Muscovite dominion over the steppes.[52]

All the Saharan tribes are marauders, whether Arabs, Berber Tuaregs, or Negroid Tibbus. The desert has made them so. The Tuaregs are chronic freebooters; they keep the Sahara and especially the caravan routes in constant insecurity. They stretch a cordon across these routes from Ghadames and Ghat in the east to the great oases of Insalah and Twat in the west; and from the oases and hills forming their headquarters they spread for pasturage and blackmail over the desert.[53] They exact toll over and over again from a caravan, provide it with a military escort of their own tribesmen, and then pillage it on the way.[54] This has been the experience of Barth[55] and other explorers. Caravans have not been their only prey. The agricultural peoples in the Niger flood-plain, the commerce on the river, and the markets of Timbuctoo long suffered from the raids of the

Depreda-tion and conquests of African nomads.

Tuaregs of the Sahara. They collected tribute in the form of grain, salt, garments, horses and gold, typical needs of a desert people, imposed tolls on caravans and on merchant fleets passing down the Niger to Timbuctoo. In 1770 they began to move from the desert and appropriate the fertile plains in the northern part of the Niger Valley, and in 1800 they conquered Timbuctoo; but soon they had to yield to another tribe of pastoral nomads, the Fulbes from the Senegal, who in 1813 established a short-lived but well organized empire on the ruins of the Tuareg dominion.[56] [See map page 105.] The other agricultural states of the Sudan have had the same experience. The Tibbus, predatory nomads of the French Sahara just north of Lake Chad and the River Yo, mounted on camels and ponies, cross the shrunken river in the dry season and raid Bornu for cattle, carry off women and children to sell as slaves, pillage the weekly markets on the Yo, and plunder caravans of pilgrims moving eastward to Mecca.[57] Nowhere can desert nomads and the civilized peoples of agricultural plains dwell side by side in peace. Raids, encroachments, reprisals, finally conquest from one side or the other is the formula for their history. [See map page 487.]

Forms of defense against nomad depredations. The raided territory, if a modern civilized state, organizes its border communities into a native mounted police, as the English have done in Bornu, Sokoto and the Egyptian Sudan, and as the Russians did with their Cossack riders along the successive frontiers of Muscovite advance into the steppes; or it takes into its employ, as we have seen, the nearest nomad tribes to repress or punish every hostile movement beyond. Among the ancient states the method was generally different. Since the nomad invaders came with their flocks and herds, a barrier often sufficed to block their progress. For this purpose Sesostris built the long wall of 1500 stadia from Pelusium to Heliopolis as a barricade against the Arabians.[58] Ancient Carthage constructed a ditch to check the depredations of the nomads of Numidia.[59] The early kings of Assyria built a barrier across the plains of the Euphrates above Babylon to secure their dominion from the incursions of the desert Medes.[60] In the fifth century of our era, the "Red Wall" was constructed near the northern frontier of Persia as a bulwark against the Huns. It stretched for a hundred and fifty miles from the Caspian Sea at the ancient port of Aboskun eastward to the mountains, and thus enclosed the populous valley of the Gurgen River.[61] In remote ages the neck of the Crimean Peninsula was fortified by a wall against the irruptions of the Tauro-Scythians.[62] The Russians early in their national history used the same means of defense against Tartar incursions. One wall was built from Pensa on the Sura River to Simbirsk on the Volga, just south of Kazan; another, further strengthened by a foss and palisades, extended from the fortress of Tsaritzin at the southern elbow of the Volga across the fifty-mile interval to the Don, and was still defended in 1794 by the Cossacks of the Don against the neighboring Kirghis hordes.[63] The classic example of such fortifications against pastoral nomads, however, is the Great Wall of China.

The nomad is economically a herdsman, politically a conqueror, and chronically a fighter. Strife over pasturage and wells meets us in the typical history of Abraham, Lot and Isaac;[64] it exists within and without the clan. The necessity of guarding the pastures, which are only intermittently occupied, involves a persistent military organization. The nation is a quiescent army, the army a mobilized nation.[65] It carries with it a self-transporting commissariat in its flocks and herds. Constant practice in riding, scouting and the use of arms, physical endurance tested by centuries of exertion and hardship, make every nomad a soldier. Cavalry and camel corps add to the swiftness and vigor of their on-slaught, make their military strategy that of sudden attack and swifter retreat, to be met only by wariness and extreme mobility. The ancient Scythians of the lower Danubian steppes were all horse archers, like the Parthians. "If the Scythians were united, there is no nation which could compare with them or would be capable of resisting them; I do not say in Europe, but even in Asia," said Thucydides.[66] In this opinion Herodotus concurred.[67] The nomad's whole existence breeds courage. The independent, hazardous life of the desert makes the Arab the bravest of mankind, but

Pastoral life as a training for soldiers.

the settled, agricultural Arab of Egypt and Mohammedan Spain lost most of his fighting qualities.[68]

Military organization of nomads.   The daily life of a nomad horde is a training school for military organization. In the evening the flocks and herds are distributed with system around the camp to prevent confusion. The difficult art of a well ordered march, of making and breaking camp, and of foraging is practiced almost daily in their constant migrations.[69] The usual order of the Bedouin march could scarcely be surpassed by an army. In advance of the caravan moves a body of armed horsemen, five or seven kilometers ahead; then follows the main body of the tribesmen mounted on horses and camels, then the female camels, and after these the beasts of burden with the women and children. The encampment of tents with the places for men, arms and herds is also carefully regulated. More than this, the horde is organized into companies with their superior and subordinate leaders.[70] John de Carpini describes Genghis Khan's military organization of his vast Tartar horde by tens, hundreds and thousands, his absolute dominion over his conquered subjects, and prompt absorption of them into his fighting force, by the compulsory enlistment of soldiers out of every freshly subjugated nation.[71] In the same way the Hebrew tribes, when preparing for the conquest of Canaan, adopted from the desert Midianites the organization of the horde into tens, hundreds and thousands under judges, who were also military leaders in time of war.

Capacity for conquest and political consolidation.   Thus certain geographic conditions produce directly the habitual and systematic migration of the nomads, and through this indirectly that military and political organization which has given the shepherd races of the earth their great historical mission of political consolidation. Agriculture, though underlying all permanent advance in civilization, is handicapped by the lack of courage, mobility, enterprise and large political outlook characterizing early tillers of the soil. All these qualities the nomad possesses. Hence the union of these two elements, imperious pastor superimposed upon peaceful tiller, has made the only stable governments among savage and semi-civilized races.[72] The politically invertebrate peoples of dark Africa have secured the backbone to erect states only from nomad conquerors. The history of the Sudan cannot be understood apart from a knowledge of the Sahara and its peoples. All the Sudanese states were formed by invaders from the northern desert, Hamitic or Semitic. [See map page 487.] The Galla or Wahuma herdsmen of East Africa founded and maintained the relatively stable states of Uganda, Kittara, Karague, and Uzinza in the equatorial district; the conquerors remained herders while they lorded it over the agricultural aborigines.[73] In prehistoric times when the various peoples of the Aryan linguistic family were spreading over Europe and southern Asia, the superiority of the shepherd races must have been especially marked, because in that era only the unobstructed surface of the steppes permitted the concentration of men on a vast scale for migration and conquest. Everywhere else regions of broken relief and dense forests harbored small, isolated peoples, to whom both the idea and the technique of combined movement were foreign.

The rapidity and wide scope of such conquests is explained largely by the fact that nomads try to displace only the ruling classes in the subjugated territory, leaving the mass of the population practically undisturbed. Thus they spread themselves thin over a wide area. How lasting are the results of such conquests depends upon the degree of social evolution attained by the herdsmen. Genghis Khan and Tamerlane, after the manner of overlords, organized their conquered nations, but left them under the control of local princes,[74] while their tribute gatherers annually swept the country like typical nomad marauders. The Turks are still only encamped in Europe. They too make taxation despoliation. And though their dominion has produced no assimilation between victor and vanquished, it has given political consolidation to a large area occupied by varied peoples. The Hyksos conquest of Egypt found the Nile Valley divided into several petty principalities under a nominal king. The nomad conquerors possessed political capacity and gave to Egypt a strong, centralized government, which laid the basis for the power and glory of the Eighteenth Dynasty. The Tartars in 1279 A. D. and the Manchus in 1664 con-

Scope of nomad conquests.

quered China, extended its boundaries, governed the country as a ruling class, and left the established order of things undisturbed. The Saracen conquest of North Africa and Spain showed for a time organization and a permanence due to the advanced cultural status of the sedentary Arabs drawn into the movement by religious enthusiasm. The environment of Spain tended to conserve the knowledge of agriculture, industry, architecture, and science which they brought in and which might have cemented Spaniard and Moor, had it not been for the intense religious antagonism existing between the two races.

The history of nomad conquerors shows that they become weakened by the enervating climate and the effeminating luxury of the moist and fertile lowlands. They lose eventually their warlike spirit, like the Fellatah or Fulbe founders of the Sudanese states,[75] and are either displaced from their insecure thrones by other conquerors sprung from the same nomad-breeding steppe, as the Aryan princes of India by the Mongol Emperor, and the Saracen invaders of Mesopotamia by the victorious Turkomans; or they are expelled in time by their conquered subjects, as the Tartars were from Russia, the Moors from Spain, and the Turks from the Danube Valley.

Centralization versus decentralization in nomadism. Nomad hordes unite for concerted action to resist encroachment upon their pastures, or for marauding expeditions, or for widespread conquest; but such unions are from their nature temporary, though a career of conquest may be sustained for decades. The geographically determined mobility which facilitates such concentration favors also dispersal, decentralization. This is the paradox in nomadism. Geographic conditions in arid lands necessitate sparse distribution of population and of herds. Pastoral life requires large spaces and small social groups. When Abraham and Lot went to Canaan from Egypt, "the land was not able to bear them that they might dwell together, for their substance was great." Strife for the pasturage ensued between their respective herdsmen, so the two sheiks separated, Lot taking the plains of Jordan and Abraham the hill pastures of Hebron. Jacob and Esau separated for the same reason. The encampment of the Kirghis shepherds rarely averages over five or six tents, except on the best grazing grounds at the best season of the year. The flow of spring, well or stream also helps to regulate their size. The groups of Mongol yurts or felt tents along the piedmont margin of the Gobi vary from four tents to a large encampment, according to water and grass.[76] Prevalsky mentions a population of 70 families or 300 souls in the Lob Nor district distributed in 11 villages, or less than 28 in each group.[77] Barth noticed the smallness of all the oasis towns of the Sahara, even those occupying favorable locations for trade on the caravan routes.[78]

The nature-made necessity of scattering in small groups to seek pasturage induces in the nomad a spirit of independence. The Bedouin is personally free. The power of the sheik is only nominal,[79] and depends much upon his personal qualities. The gift of eloquence among the ancient Arabs has been attributed to the necessity of persuading a people to whom restraint was irksome.[80] Political organization is conspicuously lacking among the Tibbus of the Sahara[81] and the Turkoman tribes of the Trans-Caspian steppes. "We are a people without a head," they say. The title of sheik is an empty one. Custom and usage are their rulers.[82] Though the temporary union of nomadic tribes forms an effective army, the union is short-lived. Groups form, dissolve and re-form, with little inner cohesion. The Boers in South African grasslands showed the same development. The government of the Dutch East India Company in Cape Colony found it difficult to control the wandering cattlemen of the interior plateau. They loved independence and isolation; their dissociative instincts, bred by the lonely life of the thin-pastured veldt, were overcome only by the necessity of defense against the Bushmen. Then they organized themselves into commandos and sallied out on punitive expeditions, like the Cossack tribes of the Don against marauding Tartars. Scattered over wide tracts of pasture land, they were exempt from the control of either Dutch or English authority; but when an energetic administration pursued them into their widespread ranches, they eluded

Spirit of independence among nomads.

control by trekking.[83]   Here was the independent spirit of the steppe, reinforced by the spirit of the frontier.

Resistance to conquest.

Though the desert and steppe have bred conquerors, they are the last parts of the earth's surface to yield to conquest from without. The untameable spirit of freedom in the shepherd tribes finds an ally against aggression in the trackless sands, meager water and food supply of their wilderness. Pursuit of the retreating tribesmen is dangerous and often futile. They need only to burn off the pasture and fill up or pollute the water-holes to cripple the transportation and commissariat of the invading army. This is the way the Damaras have fought the German subjugation of Southwest Africa.[84]   Moreover, the paucity of economic and political possibilities in deserts and grasslands discourages conquest. Conquest pays only where it is a police measure to check depredations on the bordering agricultural lands, or where such barren areas are transit lands to a desirable territory beyond. It is chiefly the "Gates of Herat" and the lure of India which have drawn Russian dominion across the scorched plains of Turkestan. France has assumed the big task of controlling the Sahara to secure a safe passway between French Tunisia and the rich Niger basin of the French Sudan. The recent British-Egyptian expansion southward across the Nubian steppes had for its objective the better watered districts of the upper Nile above Khartum. This desert advance is essentially a latter day phenomenon, the outcome of modern territorial standards; it is attended or secured by the railroad. To this fact the projected Trans-Saharan line is the strongest witness.

Nature everywhere postpones, obstructs, jeopardizes the political conquest of arid lands. The unstable, fanatical tribesmen of the Egyptian Sudan, temporarily but effectively united under the Mahdi, made it necessary for Kitchener to do again in 1898 the work of subjugation which Gordon had done thirty years before. The body of the Arabian people is still free. The Turkish sovereignty over them to-day is nominal, rather an alliance with a people whom it is dangerous to provoke and difficult to attack. Only the coast provinces of Hejaz, Yemen and Hasa are subject to Turkey, while the tribes of the interior and of the southeastern sea-board are wholly independent.[85]   The Turkoman tribes of Trans-Caspia have been subordinated to Russia largely by a process of extermination.[86]   China is satisfied with a nominal dominion over the roaming populations of Mongolia and Chinese Turkestan.   The French pacification and control of Northwest Africa meets a peculiar problem, due to the ex-treme restlessness and restiveness of the dominant Arab race. The whole population is unstable as water; a disturbance or movement in one tribe is soon communicated to the whole mass.[87]

The steppe or desert policy for the curtailment of nomad-ism, and the reclamation of both land and people is to encourage or enforce sedentary life.   The French, to settle the wandering tribes on the Atlas border of the Sahara, have opened a vast number of artesian wells through the agency of skillful engineers, and thus created oases in which the fecund sands support abundant date-palm groves.[88]   The method pursued energetically by the Russians is to compress the tribes into ever narrowing limits of territory, taking away their area of plunder and then so restricting their pasture lands, that they are forced to the drudgery of irrigation and tillage.   In this way the Yomuts and Goklans occupying the Caspian border of Trans-Caspia have been compelled to abandon their old marauding, nomadic life and become to some extent agriculturists.[89]   The method of the Chinese is to push forward the frontier of agricultural settlement into the grasslands, dislodging the shepherd tribes into poorer pas-tures.   They have thus reclaimed for grain and poppy fields considerable parts of the Ordos country in the great northern bend of the Hoangho, which used to be a nursery for nomadic invaders.   A similar substitution of agriculture for pastoral nomadism of another type has in recent decades taken place in the semi-arid plains of the American West.   Sheep-grazing on open range was with difficulty dislodged from the San Joaquin Valley of California by expanding farms in the six-ties.   More recently "dry farming" and scientific agriculture adapted to semi-arid conditions have "pushed the desert off the map" in Kansas, and advanced the frontier of tillage

Curtail-ment of nomadism.

across the previous domain of natural pastures to the western border of the state.

Pastoral nomadism has been gradually dislodged from Europe, except in the salt steppes of the Caspian depression, where a vast tract, 300,000 square miles in area and wholly unfit for agriculture, still harbors a sparse population of Asiatic Kalmuck and Kirghis hordes, leading the life of the Asiatic steppes.[90] In Asia, too, the regions of pastoral nomadism have been curtailed, but in Africa they still maintain for the most part the growing, expanding geographical forms which they once showed in Europe, when nomadism prevailed as far as the Alps and the Rhine. In Africa shepherd tribes cover not only the natural grasslands, but lap over into many districts destined by nature for agriculture. Hence it is safe to predict that a conspicuous part of the future economic and cultural history of the Dark Continent will consist in the release of agricultural regions from nomad occupancy and dominion.

Supplementary agriculture of pastoral nomads.

Though agriculture is regarded with contempt and aversion by pastoral nomads and is resorted to for a livelihood only when they lose their herds by a pest or robbery, or find their pasture lands seriously curtailed, nevertheless nomadism yields such a precarious and monotonous subsistence that it is not infrequently combined with a primitive, shifting tillage. The Kalmucks of the Russian steppes employ men to harvest hay for the winter feeding. The Nogai Tartars practice a little haphazard tillage on the alluvial hem of the steppe streams.[91] Certain Arab tribes living east of the Atbara and Gash Rivers resort with their herds during the dry season to the fruitful region of Cassala, which is inundated by the drainage streams from Abyssinia, and there they cultivate dourra and other grains.[92] The Bechuana tribes inhabiting the rich, streamless grassland of the so-called Kalahari Desert rear small herds of goats and cultivate melons and pumpkins; among the other Bechuana tribes on the eastern margin of the desert, the men hunt, herd the cattle and milk the cows, while the women raise dourra, maize, pumpkins, melons, cucumbers and beans.[93] [Compare maps pages 105, 487.]

Such supplementary agriculture usually shifts with the

nomad group. But where high mountains border rainless tracts, their piedmont districts regularly develop permanent cultivation. Here periodic rains or melting snows on the ranges fill the drainage streams, whose inundation often converts their alluvial banks into ready-made fields. The reliability of the water supply anchors here the winter villages of the nomads, which become centers of a limited agriculture, while the pasture lands beyond the irrigated strips support his flocks and herds. Where the piedmont of the Kuen Lun Mountains draws a zone of vegetation around the southern rim of the Takla Makan Desert, Mongol shepherds raise some wheat, maize and melons as an adjunct to their cattle and sheep; but their tillage is often rendered intermittent by the salinity of the irrigating streams.[94] Along the base of the Tian Shan Mountains, the felt yurt of the Gobi nomad gives place to Turki houses with wheat and rice fields, and orchards of various fruits; so that the whole piedmont highway from Hami to Yarkand presents an alternation of desert and oasis settlement.[95] Even the heart of arid Arabia shows fertile oases under cultivation where the lofty Nejd Plateau, with its rain-gathering peaks over five thousand feet high, varies its wide pastures with well tilled valleys abounding in grain fields and date-palm groves.[96] Along the whole Saharan slope of the Atlas piedmont a series of parallel wadis and, farther out in the desert, a zone of artesian wells, sunk to the underground bed of hidden drainage streams from the same range, form oases which are the seat of permanent agriculture and more or less settled populations. The Saharan highlands of Tibesti, whose mountains rise to 8,300 feet, condense a little rain and permit the Tibbus to raise some grain and dates in the narrow valleys.[97]

The few and limited spots where the desert or steppe affords water for cultivation require artificial irrigation, the importation of plants, and careful tillage, to make the limited area support even a small social group. Hence they could have been utilized by man only after he had made considerable progress in civilization.[98] Oasis agriculture is predominantly intensive. Gardens and orchards tend to prevail over field tillage. The restricted soil and water must be forced to yield

Irrigation and horticulture.

their utmost. While on the rainy or northern slope of the Atlas in Algiers and Tunis farms abound, on the Saharan piedmont are chiefly plantations of vegetables, orchards and palm groves.[99] In Fezzan at the oasis of Ghat, Barth found kitchen gardens of considerable extent, large palm groves, but limited fields of grain, all raised by irrigation; and in the flat hollow basin forming the oasis of Murzuk, he found also fig and peach trees, vegetables, besides fields of wheat and barley cultivated with much labor.[100] In northern Fezzan, where the mountains back of Tripoli provide a supply of water, saffron and olive trees are the staple articles of tillage. The slopes are terraced and irrigated, laid out in orchards of figs, pomegranates, almonds and grapes, while fields of wheat and barley border the lower courses of the wadis.[101] In the "cup oases" or depressions of the Sahara, the village is always built on the slope, because the alluvial soil in the basin is too precious to be used for house sites.[102]

Effect of diminishing water supply. The water supply in deserts and steppes, on which permanent agriculture depends, is so scant that even a slight diminution causes the area of tillage to shrink. Here a fluctuation of snowfall or rainfall that in a moist region would be negligible, has conspicuous or even tragic results. English engineers who examined the utilization of the Afghan streams for irrigation reported that the natives had exploited their water supply to the last drop; that irrigation converted the Kabul River and the Heri-rud at certain seasons of the year into dry channels.[103] In the Turkoman steppes it has been observed that expanding tillage, by the multiplication of irrigation canals, increased the loss of water by evaporation, and hence diminished the supply. Facts like these reveal the narrow margin between food and famine, which makes the uncertain basis of life for the steppe agriculturist. Even slight desiccation contracts the volume and shortens the course of interior drainage streams; therefore it narrows the piedmont zone of vegetation and the hem of tillage along the river banks. The previous frontier of field and garden is marked by abandoned hamlets and sand-buried cities, like those which border the dry beds of the shrunken Khotan rivers of the Tarim basin.[104] The steppe regions in the New World

as well as the Old show great numbers of these ruins.
Barth found them in the northern Sahara, dating from
Roman days.[105]   They occur in such numbers in the
Syrian Desert, in the Sistan of Persia, in Baluchistan, the
Gobi, Takla Makan Desert, Turfan and the Lop Nor basin,
that they indicate a marked but irregular desiccation of
central and western Asia during the historical period.[106]

If a scant water supply places sedentary agriculture in Scant diet
arid lands upon an insecure basis, it makes the nomad's of nomads.
sources of subsistence even more precarious.   It keeps him
persistently on low rations, while the drought that burns
his pastures and dries up well and wadi brings him face to
face with famine.   The daily food of the Bedouin is meal
cooked in sour camel's milk, to which bread and meat are
added only when guests arrive.   His moderation in eating
is so great that one meal of a European would suffice for six
Arabs.[107]   The daily food of the shepherd agriculturists on
the Kuen Lun margin of the Takla Makan Desert is bread
and milk; meat is indulged in only three or four times a
month.[108]   The Tartars, even in their days of widest conquest,
showed the same habitual frugality.   "Their victuals are all
things that may be eaten, for we saw some of them eat lice."
The flesh of all animals dying a natural death is used as
food; in summer it is sun-dried for winter use, because at
that time the Tartars live exclusively on mare's milk which
is then abundant.   A cup or two of milk in the morning suffices till evening, when each man has a little meat.   One
ram serves as a meal for fifty or a hundred men.   Bones are
gnawed till they are burnished, "so that no whit of their food
may come to naught."   Genghis Khan enacted that neither
blood nor entrails nor any other part of a beast which might
be eaten should be thrown away.[109]   Scarcity of food among
the Tibetan and Mongolian nomads is reflected in their habit
of removing every particle of meat from the bone when eating.[110]   A thin decoction of hot tea, butter and flour is their
staple food.   Many Turkoman nomads, despite outward appearance of wealth, eat only dried fish, and get bread only
once a month, while for the poor wheat is prohibited on account of its cost.[111]   The Saharan Tibbus, usually on a

starvation diet, eat the skin and powdered bones of their dead animals.[112]

The privations and hardships of life in the deserts and steppes discourage obesity. The Koko-Nor Mongols of the high Tibetan plateau are of slight build, never fat.[113] The Bedouin's physical ideal of a man is spare, sinewy, energetic and vigorous, "lean-sided and thin," as the Arab poet expresses it.[114] The nomadic tribesmen throughout the Sahara, whether of Hamitic, Semitic or Negro race, show this type, and retain it even after several generations of settlement in the river valleys of the Sudan. The Bushmen, who inhabit the Kalahari Desert, have thin wiry forms and are capable of great exertion and privations.[115]

Checks to population. Though the conquering propensities of nomadic tribes make large families desirable, in order to increase the military strength of the horde, and though shepherd folk acquiring new and rich pastures develop patriarchal families, as did the Jews after the conquest of Canaan, nevertheless the limited water and food supply of desert and grassland, as well as the relatively low-grade economy of pastoral life, impose an iron-bound restriction upon population, so that as a matter of fact patriarchal families are rare. When natural increase finds no vent in emigration and dispersal, marriage among nomads becomes less fruitful.[116] Artificial limitation of population occurs frequently among desert-dwellers. In the Libyan oasis of Farafeah, the inhabitants never exceed eighty males, a limit fixed by a certain Sheik Murzuk.[11] Poverty of food supply explains the small number of children in the typical Turkoman family. Among the Koko-Nor Tibetans, monogamy is the rule, polygamy the exception and confined to the few rich, while families never include more than two or three children.[118] According to Burckhardt, three children constitute a large family among the Bedouins, much to the regret of the Bedouins themselves. Mohammedans though they are, few practice polygamy, while polyandry and female infanticide existed in heathen times.[119] Desert peoples seem to be naturally monogamous.[120]

Trade of nomads. The prevailing poverty, monotony and unreliability of subsistence in desert and steppe, as well as the low industrial status, necessitate trade with bordering agricultural lands. The Bedouins of Arabia buy flour, barley for horse feed, coffee and clothing, paying for them largely with butter and male colts. The northern tribes resort every year to the confines of Syria, when they are visited by pedlers from Damascus and Aleppo.[121] The tribes from Hasa and the Nejd pasture land bring horses, cattle and sheep to the city of Koweit at the head of the Persian Gulf to barter for dates, clothing and firearms; and large encampments of them are always to be seen near this town.[122] Arabia and the Desert of Kedar sold lambs, rams and goats to the markets of ancient Tyre.[123] The pastoral tribes of ancient Judea in times of scarcity went to Egypt for grain, which they purchased either with money or cattle. The picture of Jacob's sons returning from Egypt to Canaan with their long lines of asses laden with sacks of corn is typical for pastoral nomads; so is their ultimate settlement, owing to protracted famine, in the delta land of Goshen. The Kirghis of the Russian and Asiatic steppes barter horses and sheep for cereals, fine articles of clothing, and coarse wooden utensils in the cities of Bukhara and the border districts of Russia. Occasionally the land of the nomad yields other products than those of the flocks and herds, which enter therefore into their trade. Such is the salt of the Sahara, secured at Taudeni and Bilma, the gums of the Indus desert, and balm of Gilead from the dry plateau east of Jordan.

The systematic migrations of nomads, their numerous beasts of burden, and the paucity of desert and steppe products determine pastoral tribes for the office of middlemen;[124] and as such they appear in all parts of the world. The contrast of products in arid regions and in the bordering agricultural land, as also in the districts on opposite sides of these vast barriers, stimulates exchanges. This contrast may rest on a difference of geographic conditions, or of economic development, or both. The reindeer Chukches of Arctic Siberia take Russian manufactured wares from the fur stations on the Lena River to trade at the coast markets on Bering Sea for Alaskan pelts. The sons of Jacob, pasturing their flocks on the Judean plateau, saw "a company of

Pastoral nomads as middlemen.

Ishmaelites come from Gilead with their camels bearing spicery and balm and myrrh, going to carry it down to Egypt."¹²⁵ This caravan of Arabian merchants purchased Joseph as a slave, a characteristic commodity in desert commerce from ancient times to the present. The predatory expeditions of nomads provide them with abundant captives, only few of which can be utilized as slaves in their pastoral economy. In the same way the Kirghis manage the caravan trade between Russia and Bukhara, sometimes adding captured travelers to their other wares. In ancient times Nubian shepherd folk acted as migrant middlemen between Egypt and Meroe near the junction of the Atbara River and the Nile, as did also the desert tribe of the Nasamones between Carthage and interior Africa.¹²⁶ From remote ages an active caravan trade was carried on between the productive districts of Arabia Felix and the cities of Mesopotamia, Syria and Egypt. Mohammed himself was a caravan leader; in the faith which he established religious pilgrimages and commercial ventures were inextricably united, while to the mercantile spirit it gave a fresh and vigorous impetus.¹²⁷ The caravan trade of the Sahara was first organized by Moorish and Arab tribes who dwelt on the northern margin of the desert, rearing herds of camels. These they hired to merchants for the journey between Morocco and Timbuctoo, in return for cereals and clothing. Hence Morocco has been the chief customer of the great desert town near the Niger, and sends thither numerous caravans from Tendouf (Taredant) Morocco, Fez and Tafilet. Algiers dominates the less important route via the oasis of Twat, and Tripolis that through Ghadames to the busy towns in the Lake Chad basin.¹²⁸

Desert markets. If the camel is "the ship of the desert," the market towns on the margin of the sandy wastes are the ports of the desert. Their bazaars hold everything that the nomad needs. Their suburbs are a shifting series of shepherd encampments or extensive caravanseries for merchant and pack animal, like the *abaradion* of Timbuctoo, which receives annually from fifty to sixty thousand camels.¹²⁹ Their industries develop partly in response to the demand of the desert or trans-desert population. The fine blades of Damascus reflected the Bedouin's need of the best weapon. Each city has its sphere of desert influence. The province of Nejd in Central Arabia is commercially subservient to Bagdad, Busrah, Koweit and Bahrein.[130] The bazaars of Samarkand and Tashkent exist largely for the scattered nomads of Turkestan. Ancient Gaza[131] and Askelon fattened on the Egyptian trade across the Desert of Shur, as Petra, Bostra and Damascus on the thin but steady streams of nomad products flowing in from the Syrian Desert.

The abundant leisure of nomadic life encourages the begin- Nomad in-
ning of industry, but rarely advances it beyond the house- dustries.
hold stage, owing to the thin, family-wise dispersion of popu-
lation which precludes division of labor. Such industry as exists consists chiefly in working up the raw materials yielded by the herds. Among the Bedouins, blacksmiths and sad-dlers are the only professional artisans; these are regarded with contempt and are never of Bedouin stock.[132] In the ancient world, industry reached its zero point in Arabia, and in modern times shows meager development there. On the other hand the Saharan Arabs developed an hereditary guild of expert well-makers, which seems to date back to remote times, and is held in universal honor.[133]

It is to the tent-dwellers of the world, however, that we ap- Oriental
parently owe the oriental rug. This triumph of the weaver's art rugs.
seems to have originated among pastoral nomads, who devel-oped it in working up the wool and hair of their sheep, goats and camels; but it early became localized as a specialized in-dustry in the towns and villages of irrigated districts on the borders of the grazing lands, where the nomads had advanced to sedentary life. Therefore in the period of the Caliphate, from 632 to 1258, we find these brilliant flowers of the loom, blooming like the Persian gardens, in Persian Farsistan, Khusistan, Kirman and Khorasan. We find them spreading the mediaeval fame of Shiraz, Tun, Meshed, Amul, Bukhara and Merv. The secret of this preeminence lay partly in the weaver's inherited aptitude and artistic sense for this textile work, derived from countless generations of shepherd ances-tors; partly in their proximity to the finest raw materials,

whose quality was equalled nowhere else, because it depended upon the character of the pasturage, probably also upon the climatic conditions affecting directly the flocks and herds.[134]

A map showing the geographical distribution of Eastern rug-making reveals the relation of the industry to semi-arid or saline pastures, and makes the mind revert at once to the blankets of artistic design and color, woven by the Navajo Indians of our own rainless Southwest. Rug weaving in the Old World reached its finest development in countries like Persia, Turkestan, western Afghanistan, Baluchistan, western India and the plateau portions of Asia Minor, countries where the rainfall varies from 10 to 20 inches or even less, [See map page 484.] where nomadism claims a considerable part of the population, and where the ancestry of all traces back to some of the great shepherd races, like Turkomans and Tartars. These peoples are hereditary specialists in the care, classification, and preparation of wools.[135] Weavers of rugs form an industrial class in the cities of Persia and Asia Minor, where they obey largely the taste of the outside world in regard to design and color;[136] whereas the nomads, weaving for their own use, adhere strictly to native colors and designs. Their patterns are tribal property, each differing from that of the other; and though less artistic than those of the urban workers, are nevertheless interesting and consistent, while the nomad's intuitive sense of color is fine.[137]

Architecture of nomad conquerors. The principles of design and color which these tent-dwellers had developed in their weaving, they applied, after their conquest of agricultural lands, to stone and produced the mosaic, to architecture and produced the Alhambra and the Taj Mahal.[138] Whether Saracens of Spain or Turkoman conquerors of India, they were ornamentists whose contribution to architecture was decoration. Working in marble, stone, metals or wood, they wrought always in the spirit of color and textile design, rather than in the spirit of form. The walls of their mosques, palaces and tombs reproduce the beauty of the rugs once screening the doors of their felt tents. The gift of color they passed on to the West, first through the Moors of Sicily and Spain, later through Venetian commerce. Their influence can be seen in the exquisite mosaic decoration in the cloister of Mont Reale of once Saracenic Palermo, and in the Ducal Palace and St. Mark's Cathedral of beauty-loving Venice.[139] This has been almost their sole contribution to the art of the world.

Pastoral nomads can give political union to civilized peoples; they can assimilate and spread ready-made elements of civilization, but to originate or develop them they are powerless. Between the art, philosophy and literature of China on the one side, and of the settled districts of Persia on the other, lies the cultural sterility of the Central Asia plateau. Its outpouring hordes have only in part acquired the civilization of the superior agricultural peoples whom they have conquered; from Kazan and Constantinople to Delhi, from Delhi to Peking they have added almost nothing to the local culture.

Deserts and steppes lay an arresting hand on progress. Their tribes do not develop; neither do they grow old. They are the eternal children of the world. Genuine nomadic peoples show no alteration in their manners, customs or mode of life from millennium to millennium. The interior of the Arabian desert reveals the same social and economic status,[140] whether we take the descriptions of Moses or Mohammed or Burckhardt or more recent travelers. The Bedouins of the Nubian steppes adhere strictly to all their ancient customs, and reproduce to-day the pastoral nomadism of Abraham and Jacob.[141] Genealogies were not more important to the biblical house of David and stem of Jesse than they are for the modern Kirghis tribesman, who as a little child learns to recite the list of his ancestors back to the seventh generation. The account which Herodotus gives of the nomads of the Russian steppes agrees in minute details with that of Strabo written five centuries later,[142] with that of William de Rubruquis in 1253, and with modern descriptions of Kalmuck and Kirghis life. The Gauchos or Indian pastoral halfbreeds of the Argentine plains were found by Wappäus in 1870 to accord accurately with Avara's description of them at the end of the eighteenth century.[143] The restless tenants of the grasslands come and go, but their type never materially changes. Their culture is stationary amid persistent movement. Only when here or there in some small and favored spot they are forced to make

Arid lands as areas of arrested development.

the transition to agriculture, or when they learn by long and close association with sedentary nations the lesson of drudgery and progress, do the laws of social and economic development begin to operate in them. As a rule, they must first escape partly or wholly the environment of their pasture lands, either by emigration or by the intrusion into their midst of alien tillers of the soil.

But while the migrant shepherd originates nothing, he plays an historical rôle as a transmitter of civilization. Asiatic nomads have sparsely disseminated the culture of China, Persia, Egypt and Yemen over large areas of the world. The Semite shepherds of the Red Sea deserts, through their merchants and conquerors, long gave to the dark Sudan the only light of civilization which it received. Mohammed, a Bedouin of the Ishmaelite tribe, caravan leader on the desert highways between Mecca and Syria, borrowed from Jerusalem the simple tenets of a monotheistic religion, and spread them through his militant followers over a large part of Africa and Asia.

Mental and moral qualities of nomads. The deserts and grasslands breed in their sons certain qualities and characteristics—courage, hardihood, the stiff-necked pride of the freeman, vigilance, wariness, sense of locality,[144] keen powers of observation stimulated by the monotonous, featureless environment, and the consequent capacity to grasp every detail.[145] Though robbery abroad is honorable and marauder a term with which to crown a hero, theft at home is summarily dealt with among most nomads. The property of the unlocked tent and the far-ranging herd must be safeguarded.[146] The Tartars maintained a high standard of honesty among themselves and punished theft with death.[147] Wide dispersal in small groups is reflected in the diversity of dialects among desert peoples;[148] in the practice of hospitality, whether among Bedouins of the Nejd, Kirghis of the Central Asia plateau,[149] or semi-nomadic Boers of South Africa;[150] in the persistence of feuds and of the duty of blood revenge, which is sanctioned by the Koran.

Isolation tends to breed among nomads pride of race and a repugnance to intermixture. The ideal of the pastoral

Israelites was a pure ethnic stock, protected by stern inhibition of intermarriage with other tribes. Therefore, Moses
enjoined upon them the duty of exterminating the peoples
of Canaan whom they dispossessed.[151]   While the urban
Arabs show a medley of breeds, dashed with a strain of negro
blood, among the nomad Bedouins, mixture is exceptional
and is regarded as a disgrace.[152]   The same thing is true
among the nomad Arabs of Algeria, and there it has placed
a stumbling block in the way of the French colonial administration, by preventing the appearance of half-breeds who
might bridge the gap between the colonials and natives.
Where pastoral Semites have settled in agricultural lands,
inermixture on a wide scale has followed, as in the Sudan
from Niger to Nile; but even here, when a tribe or clan has
retained a strictly pastoral life in the grassland, and has held
itself aloof from the agricultural districts of the Negro villages, relatively pure survivals are to be found, as among
the Cow or Bush Fulani of Bornu.[153]   On the other hand, the
Hausa, a migrant trading folk of mingled Arab and Negro
blood, spread northward along the trans-Saharan caravan
route to the oasis of Air before the fourteenth century, and
there have infused into the local Berber stock a strong Negro
strain.[154] ,Among the nomads of Central Asia, one wave of
race movement has so often followed and overtaken another,
that it has produced a confused blending of breeds. The
mixtures are so numerous that pure types are exceptional,[155]
and the exclusiveness of the desert Semites disappears.

    Though all these desert-born characteristics and customs **Religion**
have a certain interest for the sociologist, they possess only **of pas-**
minor importance in comparison with the religious spirit of **toral**
pastoral nomads, which is always fraught with far-reaching **nomads.**
historical results. The evidence of history shows us that there
is such a thing as a desert-born genius for religion. Huc
and Gabin testify to the deeper religious feeling of the Buddhist nomads of the Central Asia plateaus, as compared with
the lowland Chinese. The three great monotheistic religions
of the world are closely connected in their origin and development with the deserts of Syria and Arabia. The area of
Mohammedism embraces the steppe zone of the Old World[156]

from Senegambia and Zanzibar in Africa to the Indus, Tarim and the upper Obi, together with some well watered lands on its margins. It comprises in this territory a variety of races —Negroes, Hamites, Semites, Iranians, Indo-Aryans, and a long list of Mongoloid tribes. Here is a psychological effect of environment. The dry, pure air stimulates the faculties of the desert-dweller, but the featureless, monotonous surroundings furnish them with little to work upon. The mind, finding scant material for sustained logical deduction, falls back upon contemplation. Intellectual activity is therefore restricted, narrow, unproductive; while the imagination is unfettered but also unfed. First and last, these shepherd folk receive from the immense monotony of their environment the impression of unity.[157] Therefore all of them, upon outgrowing their primitive fetish and nature worship, gravitate inevitably into monotheism. Their religion is in accord with their whole mental make-up; it is a growth, a natural efflorescence. Therefore it is strong. Its tenets form the warp of all their intellectual fabrics, permeate their meager science and philosophy, animate their more glorious poetry. It has moreover the fanaticism and intolerance characterizing men of few ideas and restricted outlook upon life. Therewith is bound up a spirit of propaganda. The victories of the Jews in Palestine, Syria and Philistia were the victories of Jehovah; the conquests of Saladin were the conquests of Allah; and the domain of the Caliphate was the dominion of Islam.

Fanaticism as a force in nomad expansion.

The desert everywhere, sooner or later, drives out its brood, ejects its people and their ideas, like those exploding seed-pods which at a touch cast their seed abroad. The religious fanaticism of the shepherd tribes gives that touch; herein lies its historical importance. Mohammedism, fierce and militant, conduced to those upheavals of migration and conquest which since the seventh century have so often transformed the political geography of the Old World. The vast empire of the Caliphate, from its starting point in Arabia, spread in eighty years from the Oxus River to the Atlantic Ocean.[158] The rapid rise and spread between 1745 and 1803 of the Wahaby clan and sect, the Puritans of Islam, which resulted for a time in their political and religious domination

Distribution of Religions in the Old World

of much of Arabia from their home in the Nejd, recalls the stormy conquests of Mohammed's followers. Islam is to-day a persistent source of ferment in Algeria, the Sahara, and the Sudan. On the other hand, Buddhism serves to cement together the diverse nomadic tribes of the Central Asia plateaus, and keep them in spiritual subjection to the Grand Lama of Lhassa. The Chinese government makes political use of this fact by dominating the Lama and employing him as a tool to secure quiet on its long frontier of contact with its restless Mongol neighbors. Moreover the religion of Buddha has restrained the warlike spirit of the nomads, and by its institution of celibacy has helped keep down population below the boiling-point. [Compare maps pages 484 and 513.]

The faith of the desert. The faith of the desert tends to be stern, simple and austere. The indulgence which Mohammed promised his followers in Paradise was only a reflex of the deprivation under which they habitually suffered in the scant pastures of Arabia. The lavish beauty of the Heavenly City epitomized the ideals and dreams of the desert-stamped Jew. The active, simple, uncramped life of the grasslands seems essential to the preservation of the best virtues of the desert-bred. These disappear largely in sedentary life. The Bedouin rots when he takes root. City life contaminates, degrades him. His virile qualities and his religion both lose their best when he leaves the desert. Contact with the cities of Philistia and the fertile plains of the Canaanites, with their sensual agricultural gods, demoralized the Israelites.[159] The prophets were always calling them back to the sterner code of morals and the purer faith of their days of wandering. Jeremiah in despair holds up to them as a standard of life the national injunction of the pastoral Rechabites, "Neither shall ye build house nor sow corn nor plant vineyard, but all your days ye shall dwell in tents."[160] The ascent in civilization made havoc with Hebrew morals and religion, because ethics and religion are the finest and latest flower of each cultural stage. Transition shows the breaking down of one code before the establishment of another.

Judaism has always suffered from its narrow local base. Even when transplanted to various parts of the earth, it has remained a distinctly tribal religion. Intense conservatism in doctrine and ceremonial it still bears as the heritage of its desert birth. Islam too shows the limitations of its original environment. It embodies a powerful appeal to the peoples of arid lands, and among these it has spread and survives as an active principle. But it belongs to an arrested economic and social development, lacks the germs of moral evolution which Christianity, born in the old stronghold of Hebraic monotheism, but impregnated by all the cosmopolitan influences of the Mediterranean basin and the *Imperium Romanum*, amply possesses.

NOTES TO CHAPTER XIV

1. Figures taken from Albrecht Penck, *Morphologie der Erdoberfläche*, Vol. I, p. 151. Stuttgart, 1894.
2. A. P. Brigham, Geographic Influences in American History, Chap. IV. Boston, 1903.
3. E. C. Semple, American History and Its Geographic Conditions, pp. 65-69, 230, 288, 385. Boston, 1903.
4. *Ibid.*, pp. 218, 221, 393.
5. H. R. Mill, International Geography, p. 127. New York, 1902.
6. Henry Buckle, History of Civilization in England, Vol. II, pp. 126-136. New York, 1871.
7. Carl Ritter, Comparative Geography, pp. 191-192, 201. Philadelphia, 1865.
8. J. H. Breasted, History of Egypt, pp. 142, 144, 261-265, 293-302, 513-517. New York, 1905.
9. *Ibid.*, 6, 48, 93, 114, 119, 127, 134, 136, 163, 164, 182, 190, 191, 507.
10. W. Z. Ripley, Races of Europe, pp. 340-343, map. New York, 1899.
11. Anatole Leroy-Beaulieu, The Empire of the Tsars, Vol. I, pp. 57-60. New York, 1893.
12. W. Z. Ripley, Races of Europe, Maps, pp. 53 and 66. New York, 1899.
13. Hans Helmolt, History of the World, Vol. VI, p. 130, map of ancient distribution of Germans and Celts. New York, 1907.
14. W. Z. Ripley, Races of Europe, pp. 216-218. New York, 1899.
15. *Ibid.*, 344-347, 356, 365.
16. Elisée Reclus, Europe, Vol. IV, pp. 309-310. New York, 1882.
17. Anatole Leroy-Beaulieu, Empire of the Tsars, Vol. I, p. 107. New York, 1893.
18. H. R. Mill, International Geography, pp. 220-222. New York, 1902.
19. Vidal-Lablache, *Atlas Général*, Maps pp. 63, 64, 93. Paris, 1909.
20. H. R. Mill, International Geography, 174, 177-182. New York, 1902.
21. Twelfth Census, Bulletin of Agriculture No. 181, p. 2, compared with Eleventh Census, Statistics of Population, map of negro distribution, p.XCVII. Washington, 1895.

22. Twelfth Census, Bulletin of Agriculture, No. 155, p. 2. Washington, 1902.
23. W. Z. Ripley, Races of Europe, p. 353. New York, 1899.
24. Boyd Alexander, From the Niger to the Nile, Vol. II, p. 238. London, 1907.
25. Haxthausen, *Studien*, Vol. I, p. 309. *Die ländliche Verfassung Russlands*, pp. 3, 7. Leipzig, 1866.
26. Ratzel, History of Mankind, Vol. II, pp. 79-83. London, 1896-1898. J. Wappäus, *Handbuch der Geographie und Statistik des ehemaligen spanischen Mittel- und Sud-Amerika*, pp. 978-980, 1019. Leipzig, 1863-1870.
27. Ratzel, History of Mankind, Vol. II, pp. 206-208. London, 1896-1898.
28. Nordenskiold, Voyage of the Vega, pp. 60, 156, 452. New York, 1882. Alexander P. Engelhardt, A Russian Province of the North, pp. 291-295. London, 1899.
29. *Ibid.*, pp. 83, 88-91.
30. Ratzel, History of Mankind, Vol. III, pp. 166-167. London, 1896-1898.
31. James Bryce, Impressions of South Africa, p. 107. New York, 1897.
32. Herodotus, Melpomene, 19, 46.
33. Thomas Hodgkin, Italy and Her Invaders, Vol. I, p. 262. Oxford, 1892.
34 Ratzel, History of Mankind, Vol. II, p. 220. London, 1896-1898.
35. Genesis, XIII, 2, 5.
36. James Bryce, Impressions of South Africa, p. 474. New York, 1897.
37. Eleventh Census, Indian Report, pp. 143-144. Washington, 1894.
38. Sven Hedin, Central Asia and Tibet, Vol. I, pp. 18-20. London and New York, 1903.
39. J. L. Burckhardt, Notes on the Bedouins and Wahabys, Vol. I, pp. 32-33. London, 1831.
40. George Adam Smith, Historical Geography of the Holy Land, pp. 8-10. New York, 1897.
41. Gibbon, Decline and Fall of the Roman Empire, Vol. V, pp. 78-79. New York, 1858.
42. L. March Phillipps, In the Desert, p. 95. London, 1905.
43. Sir Samuel W. Baker, The Nile Tributaries of Abyssinia, pp. 88, 128, 129, 135. Hartford, 1868.
44. Journey of John de Carpini and William de Rubruquis in 1253, pp. 8, 217. Hakluyt Society, London, 1903.
45. James Bryce, Impressions of South Africa, pp. 107, 421. New York, 1897.
46. Wilhelm Roscher, *National-Oekonomik des Ackerbaues*, p. 44. Stuttgart, 1888.
47. A full discussion in Malthus, Principles of Population, Book I, chap. 7.
48. J. L. Burckhardt, Notes on the Bedouins and Wahabys, Vol. I, pp. 133-144, 157-160. London, 1831. S. M. Zwemer, Arabia, The Cradle of Islam, 155-157. New York, 1900.
49. Vambery, *Reise in Mittelasien*, pp. 285, 289-297. Leipzig, 1873.
50. Alexis Krausse, Russia in Asia, pp. 127-129. New York, 1899.

51. Ratzel, History of Mankind, Vol. III, pp. 174-175. London, 1896-1898.

52. Wallace, Russia, pp. 340-342. New York, 1904.

53. L. March Phillipps, In the Desert, pp. 17, 63-66. London, 1905.

54. Felix Dubois, Timbuctoo, pp. 256, 324-325. Translated from the French, New York, 1896.

55. Heinrich Barth, Travels in North and Central Africa, Vol. I, pp. 287-288, 293, 305. New York, 1857.

56. Felix Dubois, Timbuctoo, pp. 133-134, 203, 206-207, 229, 232, 239-245. New York, 1896.

57. Boyd Alexander, From the Niger to the Nile, Vol. II, pp. 1-2, 6, 16-18, 80. London, 1907.

58. Gibbon, Decline and Fall of the Roman Empire, Vol. V, p. 87. New York, 1858.

59. Pliny, *Historia Naturalis*, V, 3.

60. Gibbon, Decline and Fall of the Roman Empire, Vol. II, p. 495. New York, 1858.

61. Ellsworth Huntington, The Pulse of Asia, p. 340. Boston, 1907.

62. Pallas, Travels in the Southern Provinces of Russia in 1793-1794, Vol. II, p. 4. London, 1812.

63. *Ibid.*, Vol. I, pp. 94, 256.

64. Genesis, XIII, 7-8; XXI, 25-30; XXVI, 15-22.

65. Herbert Spencer, Principles of Sociology, Vol. I, p. 545. New York, 1887.

66. Thucydides, Book II, 96.

67. Herodotus, IV, 46.

68. Meredith Townsend, Asia and Europe, Chapter on Arab Courage. New York, 1904.

69. Wilhelm Roscher, *National-Oekonomik des Ackerbaues*, p. 44. Stuttgart, 1888.

70. J. L. Burckhardt, Notes on the Bedouins and Wahabys, Vol. I, pp. 35-36. London, 1831.

71. John de Plano Carpini, Journey to the Northeast, pp. 114-117, 120-125. Hakluyt Society, London, 1904.

72. Ratzel, History of Mankind, Vol. I, p. 28. London, 1896-1898.

73. J. H. Speke, Discovery of the Source of the Nile, pp. 241-244. New York, 1868.

74. Journey of William de Rubruquis, pp. 18-27. Hakluyt Society, London, 1900.

75. Jerome Dowd, The Negro Races, Vol. I, pp. 225-232. New York, 1907.

76. Sir Francis Younghusband, The Heart of a Continent, pp. 85-98. London, 1904.

77. Ratzel, History of Mankind, Vol. I, p. 170. London, 1896-1898.

78. Heinrich Barth, Travels in North and Central Africa, Vol. I, pp. 148, 152, 204, 210, 303. New York, 1857.

79. J. L. Burckhardt, Notes on the Bedouins and Wahabys, Vol. I, pp. 115-119, 284-286, 296-300. London, 1831.

80. Gibbon, Decline and Fall of the Roman Empire, Vol. V, pp. 85-87. New York, 1857.

81. Jerome Dowd, The Negro Races, Vol. I, pp. 234-235. New York, 1907.

82. Vambery, *Reise in Mittel Asien*, pp. 288-290. Leipzig, 1873.

83. James Bryce, Impressions of South Africa, pp. 108, 128, 129, 155, 199, 452-453. New York, 1897.

84. For vivid description of desert defensive warfare, see Gustav Frensen, Peter Moore's Journey to Southwest Africa. Translated from the German, 1908. Based upon interviews with hundreds of returning German soldiers from the Damara campaign.

85. H. R. Mill, International Geography, p. 454. New York, 1902.

86. Henry Norman, All the Russias, p. 273. New York, 1902.

87. L. March Phillipps, In the Desert, pp. 54-56. London, 1905.

88. *Ibid.*, pp. 161-164.

89. Ratzel, History of Mankind, Vol. III, p. 177. London, 1896-1898.

90. Anatole Leroy-Beaulieu, The Empire of the Tsars, Vol. I, pp. 29-30. New York, 1893.

91. Pallas, Travels through the Southern Provinces of Russia, Vol. I, pp. 532-533. London, 1812.

92. Sir S. W. Baker, Nile Tributaries of Abyssinia, p. 88. Hartford, 1868.

93. David Livingstone, Mssionary Travels, pp. 53-56, 169. New York, 1858.

94. Sven Hedin, Central Asia and Tibet, Vol. I, pp. 96, 136, 359. New York and London, 1903. Ellsworth Huntington, The Pulse of Asia, pp. 193, 202, 212, 213. Boston, 1907.

95. Sir Francis Younghusband, The Heart of a Continent, pp. 103, 104, 107, 112-116, 120, 125-128, 137, 138, 143. London, 1904.

96. S. W. Zwemer, Arabia the Cradle of Islam, pp. 147, 151. New York, 1900. D. G. Hogarth, The Nearer East, pp. 185, 195, 265. London, 1902.

97. Nachtigal, *Sahara und Sudan*, Vol. I, pp. 214-218, 267-269. Berlin, 1879.

98. Ratzel, History of Mankind, Vol. III, p. 168. London, 1896-1898.

99. H. R. Mill, International Geography, pp. 906, 914. New York, 1902.

100. H. Barth, Travels in North and Central Africa, Vol. I, pp. 152, 207, 210, 211. New York, 1857.

101. *Ibid.*, 41-44, 52, 61-64, 67, 76, 93, 95, 99, 103, 105.

102. L. March Phillipps, In the Desert, p. 174. London, 1905.

103. Sir Thomas Holdich, India, pp. 91-93. London, 1905.

104. M. A. Stein, The Sand-Buried Ruins of Khotan, pp. 275-324, 354-408. London, 1903.

105. H. Barth, Travels in North and Central Africa, Vol. I, chap. III. New York, 1857.

106. Ellsworth Huntington, The Pulse of Asia, pp. 160-190, 209, 304, 309-310, 315, 367. Boston, 1907.

107. J. L. Burckhardt, Notes on the Bedouins and Wahabys, Vol. I, pp. 57-64, 238-242. London, 1831.

108. E. Huntington, The Pulse of Asia, pp. 137-138. Boston, 1907.

109. John de Plano Carpini, Journey to the Northeast, pp. 109-111, 120. Hakluyt Society, London, 1904. Journey of William de Rubruquis, pp. 191-193, 203, 224. Hakluyt Society, London, 1903.

110. W. W. Rockhill, The Land of the Lamas, p. 80. New York, 1891.

111. Vambery, *Reise in Mittel Asien*, p. 295. Leipzig, 1873.

112. Nachtigal, *Sahara und Sudan*, Vol. I, pp. 257, 268. Berlin, 1879.
113. E. Huntington, The Pulse of Asia, p. 74. Boston, 1907.
114. L. March Phillipps, In the Desert, pp. 198-201. London, 1905.
115. D. Livingstone, Travels and Researches in South Africa, p. 55.
New York, 1859.
116. W. Roscher, *Grundlagen der Nationalökonomik*, Book VI, chap. II,
p. 244. Stuttgart, 1886.
117. Ratzel, History of Mankind, Vol. III, p. 170. London, 1896-98.
118. W. W. Rockhill, Land of the Lamas, p. 80. New York, 1891.
119. J. L. Burckhardt, Notes on the Bedouins and Wahabys, Vol. I, pp.
106, 187. London, 1831. S. M. Zwemer, Arabia the Cradle of Islam, pp.
162, 268. New York, 1900.
120. Westermarck, History of Human Marriage, p. 429, notes 2 and 5,
p. 440, note 2, p. 507. London, 1891.
121. J. L. Burckhardt, Notes on the Bedouins and Wahabys, Vol. I,
pp. 47, 48, 70, 71, 191-192, 239. London, 1831.
122. S. M. Zwemer, Arabia the Cradle of Islam, p. 128. New York,
1900.
123. Ezekiel, Chap. XXVII, 21.
124. For economic principle, see W. Roscher, *Handel und Gewerbefleiss*,
pp. 141-147. Stuttgart, 1899.
125. Genesis, Chap. XXXVII, 25-28, 36.
126. W. Roscher, *National-Oekonomik des Ackerbaues*, p. 39, Note 11.
Stuttgart, 1888.
127. S. P. Scott, History of the Moorish Empire in Europe, Vol. III, p.
616. Philadelphia, 1904.
128. Felix Dubois, Timbuctoo, pp. 251-252. New York, 1896.
129. *Ibid.*, pp. 257-264.
130. S. M. Zwemer, Arabia the Cradle of Islam, p. 151. New York,
1900.
131. George Adam Smith, Historical Geography of the Holy Land, pp.
182-184. New York, 1897.
132. J. L. Burckhardt, Notes on the Bedouins and Wahabys, Vol. I, p.
65. London, 1831.
133. L. March Phillipps, In the Desert, pp. 130-134. London, 1903.
134. F. R. Martin, A History of Oriental Carpets before 1800, pp. 9,
29, 69 et seq., 101, 121. Vienna, 1908. G. LeStrange, Land of the
Eastern Caliphates, pp. 37, 293-294, 353, 363, 471. Cambridge, 1905.
135. J. K. Mumford, Oriental Rugs, pp. 23-40, 100-111. New York,
1895.
136. D. G. Hogarth, The Nearer East, pp. 197-198. London, 1902.
137. J. K. Mumford, Oriental Rugs, p. 61. New York, 1895.
138. J. Ferguson, History of Architecture, Vol. II, pp. 277-278, 499,
500. New York. J. Ferguson, History of Indian and Eastern Architecture, Vol. 11, pp. 210-214. New York, 1891.
139. Wilhelm Bode, *Vorderasiatische Knüpfteppiche*, pp. 3-4. Leipzig.
140. Gibbon, Decline and Fall of the Roman Empire, Vol. V, p. 78.
New York, 1858.
141. Sir S. W. Baker, Exploration of the Nile Tributaries of Abyssinia,
pp. 148-152. Hartford, 1868.
142. Strabo, Book VII, chap. III, 7, 17; chap. IV, 6. Book XI, chap.
II, 1, 2, 3.

143. J. Wappäus, *Handbuch der Geographie und Statistik des ehemaligen spanischen Mittel- und Sud-Amerika*, p. 1019. Leipzig, 1863-1870.
144. Sir F. Younghusband, The Heart of a Continent, pp. 72, 74. London, 1904. Alfred Kirchoff, Man and Earth, pp. 58-71. London.
145. J. L. Burckhardt, Notes on the Bedouins and Wahabys, Vol. I, pp. 374-377. London, 1831. L. March Phillipps, In the Desert, pp. 98-100. London, 1905.
146. Exodus, Chap. XXII, 1-4, 23.
147. John de Plano Carpini, Journey to the Northeast in 1246, pp. 110, 111, 113. Hakluyt Society, London, 1904.
148. Gibbon, Decline and Fall of the Roman Empire, Vol. V, p. 89. New York, 1858. H. Barth, Travels in North and Central Africa, Vol. I, p. 144. New York, 1857.
149. E. Huntington, The Pulse of Asia, pp. 121-123. Boston, 1907.
150. James Bryce, Impressions of South Africa, p. 422. New York, 1897.
151. Deuteronomy, VII, 1-3.
152. Ratzel, History of Mankind, Vol. III, p. 184. London, 1896-1898.
153. Boyd Alexander, From the Niger to the Nile, Vol. I, pp. 190-197. London, 1907.
154. H. Barth, Travels in North and Central Africa, Vol. I, pp. 202, 277-281. New York, 1857.
155. Ratzel, History of Mankind, Vol. III, p. 173. London, 1896-1898.
156. *Ibid.*, Vol. III, Chapter on Islam, pp. 195-204.
157. George Adam Smith, Historical Geography of the Holy Land, pp. 28-30. New York, 1897. L. March Phillipps, In the Desert, pp. 101-105. London, 1905.
158. E. A. Freeman, Historical Geography of Europe, pp. 114-116. London, 1882.
159. George Adam Smith, Historical Geography of the Holy Land, pp. 88-90. New York, 1897.
160. Jeremiah, Chap. XXXV, 6-14.

CHAPTER XV

MOUNTAIN BARRIERS AND THEIR PASSES

THE important characteristic of plains is their power
to facilitate every phase of historical movement; that of
mountains is their power to retard, arrest, or deflect it.
Man, as part of the mobile envelope of the earth, like air and
water feels always the pull of gravity. From this he can
never fully emancipate himself. By an output of energy he
may climb the steepest slope, but with every upward step the
ascent becomes more difficult, owing to the diminution of
warmth and air and the increasing tax upon the heart.[1]
Maintenance of life in high altitudes is always a struggle.
The decrease of food resources from lower to higher levels
makes the passage of a mountain system an ordeal for every
migrating people or marching army that has to live off the
country which it traverses. Mountains therefore repel population by their inaccessibility and also by their harsh conditions of life, while the lowlands attract it, both in migration
and settlement. Historical movement, when forced into the
upheaved areas of the earth, avoids the ridges and peaks,
seeks the valleys and passes, where communication with the
lowlands is easiest.

Man as part of the mobile envelope of the earth.

High massive mountain systems present the most effective
barriers which man meets on the land surface of the earth.
To the spread of population they offer a resistance which
long serves to exclude settlers. The difficulty of making
roads up steep, rocky slopes and through the forests usually
covering their rain-drenched sides, is deterrent enough; but
in addition to this, general infertility, paucity of arable land,
harsh climatic conditions, and the practical lack of communication with the outside world offer scant basis for subsistence.
Hence, as a rule, only when pressure of population in the lowlands becomes too great under prevailing economic methods,
do clearings and cabins begin to creep up the slopes. Moun-

Inaccessi-
bility of
mountains.

tains are always regions of late occupation. Even in the Stone Age, we find the long-headed race of Mediterranean stock, who originally populated Europe, distributed over the continent close up to the foot of the high Alps, but not in the mountains themselves, and only scantily represented in the Auvergne Plateau of France. The inhospitable highlands of Switzerland, the German Alps, and the Auvergne received their first population later when the Alpine race began to occupy western Europe.[2] The *Mittelgebirge* of Germany were not settled till the Middle Ages. In the United States, the flood of population had spread westward by 1840 to the ninety-fifth meridian and the north-south course of the Missouri River; but out of this sea of settlement the Adirondack Mountains, a few scattered spots in the Appalachians, and the Ozark Highlands rose as so many islands of uninhabited wilderness, and they remain to-day areas of sparser population. In 1800, the "bare spots" in the eastern mountains were more pronounced. [See map page 156.] Great stretches of the Rocky Mountains, of the Laurentian Highlands of Canada, like smaller patches in the Scandinavian and Swiss Alps, are practically uninhabited.

Mountains as transit regions. Mountain regions, like deserts and seas, become mere transit districts, which man traverses as quickly as possible. Hence they often lie as great inert areas in the midst of active historical lands, and first appear upon the historical stage in minor rôles, when they are wanted by the plains people as a passway to desirable regions beyond. Then, as a rule, only their transit routes are secured, while the less accessible regions are ignored. Cæsar makes no mention of the Alps, except to state that he has crossed them, until some of the mountain tribes try to block the passage of Roman merchants or armies; then they become important enough to be conquered. It was not till after the Cimbri in 102 B. C. invaded Italy by the Brenner route, that the Romans realized the value of Rhaetia (Tyrol) as a thoroughfare from Italy to Germany, and began its conquest in 36 B. C. This was the same value which the Tyrol so long had for the old German Empire and later for Austria,—merely to secure connection with the Po Valley. The need of land communication with the

Rhone Valley led the Romans to attack the Salyes, who inhabited the Maritime Alps, and after eighty years of war to force from them the concession of a narrow transit strip, twelve stadia or one and a half miles wide, for the purpose of making a road to Massilia.[3] The necessity of controlling such transit lands has drawn British India into the occupation of mountain Baluchistan, Kashmir and Sikkim, just as it has caused the highlands of Afghanistan to figure actively in the expansion policy of both India and Russia. The conquest of such transit lands has always been attended by road building, from the construction of the Roman highway through the Brenner Pass to the modern Russian military road through the Pass of Dariel across the Caucasus, and the yet more recent Indian railroad to Darjeeling, with the highway extension beyond to the Tibetan frontier through Himalayan Sikkim.

Such mountain regions attain independent historical importance when their population increases enough to form the nucleus of a state, and to acquire additional territory about the highland base either by conquest or voluntary union, while they utilize their naturally protected location and their power to grant safe transit to their allies, as means to secure their political autonomy. Therefore to mountain regions so often falls the rôle of buffer states. Such were medieval Burgundy and modern Savoy, which occupied part of the same territory, Navarre which in the late Middle Ages controlled the important passway around the western end of the Pyrenees, and Switzerland which commands the passes of the central Alps. The position of such mountain states is, however, always fraught with danger, owing to the weakness inherent in their small area and yet smaller allowance of productive soil, to their diverse ethnic elements, and the forces working against political consolidation in their deeply dissected surface. Political solidarity has a hard, slow birth in the mountains.

Transition forms of relief between highlands and lowlands

In view of the barrier character of mountains, a fact of immense importance to the distribution of man and his activities is the rarity of abrupt, ungraded forms of relief on the earth's surface. The physiographic cause lies in the elasticity of the earth's crust and the leveling effect of weathering and denudation. Everywhere mountains are worn down and rounded off, while valleys broaden and fill up to shallow trough outlines. Transition forms of relief abound. Human intercourse meets therefore few absolute barriers on the land; but these few reveal the obstacles to historical movement in perpendicular reliefs. The mile-high walls of the Grand Cañon of the Colorado are an insuperable obstacle to intercourse for a stretch of three hundred miles. The glacier-crowned ridge of the Bernese Alps is crossed by no wagon road between the Grimsel Pass and the upper Rhone highway around their western end, a distance of 100 kilometers (62 miles). The Pennine Alps have no pass between the Great St. Bernard and the Simplon, a distance of 90 kilometers (54 miles).

Importance of transition slopes.   Gentle transition slopes or terrace lands facilitate almost everywhere access to the lowest, most habitable and therefore, from the human standpoint, most important section of mountains. They combine the ease of intercourse characteristic of plains with many advantages of the mountains, and especially in warm climates they unite in a narrow zone both tropical and temperate vegetation. The human value of these transition slopes holds equally of single hills, massive mountain systems, and continental reliefs. The earth as a whole owes much of its habitability to these gently graded slopes. Continents and countries in which they are meagerly developed suffer from difficulty of intercourse, retarded development and poverty of the choicest habitable areas. This is one disadvantage of South Africa, emphasized farther by a poor coastline. The Pacific face of Australia would gain vastly in historical importance, if the drop from the highlands to the ocean were stretched out into a broad slope, like that which links our Atlantic coastal plain with the Appalachian highlands. There each river valley shows three characteristic anthropo-geographical sub-divisions—the active seaports and tide-water tillage of its lower course, the contrasted agriculture of its hilly course, the upland farms, waterpower industries and mines of its headstream valleys, each landscape giving its population distinctive characteristics.

The same natural features, with the same effect upon human activities and population, appear in the long seaward slopes of France, Germany and northern Italy.

At the base of the mountains themselves, where the bold relief begins, is always a piedmont zone of hilly surface but gentler grade, at whose inner or upland edge every phase of the historical movement receives a marked check. Here is a typical geographical boundary, physical and human. It shifts slightly in different periods, according to the growing density of population in the plains below and improved technique in industry and road-making. It is often both an ethnic and cultural boundary, because at the rim of the mountains the geologic and economic character of the country changes.[4] The expanding peoples of the plains spread over the piedmont so far as it offers familiar and comparatively favorable geographic conditions, scatter their settlements along the base of the mountains, and here fix their political frontier for a time, though later they may advance it to the crest of the ridge, in order to secure a more scientific boundary. The civilized population of the broad Indus Valley spread westward up the western highlands, only so far as the shelving slopes of the clay and conglomerate foothills, which constitute the piedmont of the Suleiman and Kirthar Mountains, afforded conditions for their crops. Thus from the Arabian Sea for 600 miles north to the Gomal River, the political frontier of India was defined by the line of relief dividing the limestone mountains from the alluvial plain, the marauding Baluch and Afghan hill tribes from the patient farmers of the Sind.[5] This line remained the border of India from pre-British days till the recent annexation of Baluchistan.

Piedmont belts as boundary zones.

These piedmont boundaries are most clearly defined in point of race and civilization, where superior peoples from the lowlands are found expanding at the cost of retarded mountain folk. Romans and Rhaetians once met along a line skirting the foot of the eastern Alps, as Russians to-day along the base of the Caucasus adjoin the territories of the heterogeneous tribes occupying that mountain area.[6] [See map page 225.] The plains-loving Magyars of Hungary have pushed up to the rim of mountainous Siebenburgen or Transylvania from Arad on the Maros River to Sziget on the upper Theiss, while the highland region has a predominant Roumanian population. A clearly defined linguistic and cultural boundary of Indo-Aryan speech and religion, both Hindu and Mohammedan, follows the piedmont edges of the Brahmaputra Valley, and separates the lowland inhabitants from the pagans of Tibeto-Burman speech occupying the Himalayan slope to the north and the Khasia Mountains to the south. The highland race is Mongoloid, while the Bengali of an Aryan, Dravidian and Mongoloid blend fill the river plain.[7] Such piedmont boundary lines tend to blur into bands or zones of ethnic intermixture and cultural assimilation. The western Himalayan foothills show the blend of Mongoloid and Aryan stocks, where the vigorous Rajputs of the plains have encroached upon the mountaineer's land.[8] Of almost every mountain folk it can be assumed that they once occupied their highlands to the outermost rim of the piedmont, and retired to the inner rim of this intermediary slope only under compulsion from without.

Density of population in piedmont belts. The piedmont boundary also divides two areas of contrasted density of population. Mountain regions are, as a rule, more sparsely settled than plains. The piedmont is normally a transition region in this respect; but where high mountains rise as climatic islands of adequate water supply out of desert and steppes, they concentrate on their lower slopes all the sedentary population, making their piedmonts zones of greatest density. Low mountains in arid regions become centers of population; here their barrier nature vanishes. In the Sudanese state of Darfur, the Marra Mountains are the district best watered and most thickly populated. Nowhere higher than 6000 feet (1850 meters), they afford running water at 4000 feet elevation and water pools in the sandy beds of their wadis at 3200 feet. Below this, water disappears from the surface, and can be found only in wells whose depth and scarcity increase with distance from the central mountains.[9] The neighboring kingdom of Wadai shows similar conditions and effects.[10] In the heart of Australia, where utter desert reigns, the Macdonnell Ranges form the nucleus of the northern area occupied by the Arunta tribe of natives; farther north the Murchison Range, usually abounding in water-holes, is the center and stronghold of the Warramunga tribe.[11]

Mineral wealth or waterpower in the mountains serves to collect an urban and industrial population along their rim, as we see it about the base of the Erz Mountains in Saxony, the Riesen range in Silesia, the coal-bearing Pennine Mountains of northwestern England, and the highlands of southern Wales, all which piedmont zones show a density of over 150 to the square kilometer (385 to the square mile). Hence the original Swiss Confederation, which included only the mountain cantons of Schwyz, Uri and Unterwalden, was greatly ˙trengthened by the accession of the piedmont cantons of Lucerne, Zurich, Zug and Bern in the early fourteenth century, as later by St. Gall, Aargau and Geneva. These marginal cantons to-day show a density of population exceeding 385 to the square mile, and rising to 1356 in the canton of Geneva.

Piedmont belts tend strongly towards urban development, **Piedmont** even where rural settlement is sparse. Sparsity of popula- **towns and** tion and paucity of towns within the mountains cause main **roads.** lines of traffic to keep outside the highlands, but close enough to their base to tap their trade at every valley outlet. On the alluvial fans or plains of these valley outlets, where mountain and piedmont road intersect, towns grow up. Some of them develop into cities, when they command transverse routes of communication quite across the highlands. The ancient *Via Aemilia* traced the northern base of the Apennines from Ariminum on the Adriatic to Dertona at the foot of the Ligurian range back of Genoa, and connected a long line of Roman colonies. The modern railroad follows almost exactly the course of the old Roman road,[12] while a transverse line southward across the Apennines, following an ancient highway over the Poretta Pass to the Arno Valley, has maintained the old preëminence of Bologna. A line of towns, connected by highways or railroads, according to the economic development of the section, defines the bases of the Pyrenees, Alps, Jura, Apennines, Harz, Vosges, Elburz and numerous other ranges. Along the Elburz piedmont runs the imperial road of Persia from Tabriz through Teheran to Meshed. In arid regions these piedmont roads are an unfailing feature, but their towns shrink to rural settlements, except at the junction of transmontane routes.

Piedmont termini of transmontane routes.

Piedmont cities draw their support from plain, mountain and transmontane region, relying chiefly on the fertile soil of the level country to feed their large populations. Sometimes they hug the foot of the mountains, as Bologna, Verona, Bergamo, Zurich, Denver and Pittsburg do; sometimes, like Milan, Turin, and Munich, they drop down into the plain, but keep the mountains in sight. They flourish in proportion to their local resources, in which mineral wealth is particularly important, and to the number and practicability of their transmontane connections. Hence they often receive their stamp from the mountains behind them as well as from the bordering plain. The St. Gotthard route is flanked by Lucerne on the north and Milan on the south. The Brenner has its urban outlets at Munich and Verona. Narbonne and Barcelona form the termini of the route over the eastern Pyrenees; Toulouse commands the less used central passes, and Bayonne the western. Tiflis is situated in the great mountain trough connecting the Black Sea and the Caspian; but over the Caucasus by the Pass of Dariel come the influences which make it a Russian town. Peshawar, situated in the mountain angle of the Punjab, depends more upon the Khaibar Pass and its connections thereby with Central Asia than upon the plains of the Indus; its population, in appearance and composition nearly as much Central Asiatic as Indian, is engaged in traffic between the Punjab and the whole trans-Hindu Kush country.[13]

Where a mountain system describes a semi-circular course, its transit routes tend to converge on the inner side, and at their foci fix the sites of busy commercial centers. Turin draws on a long series of Alpine and Apennine routes from the Pass of Giovi (1548 feet or 472 meters) leading up from Genoa on the south, to the Great St. Bernard on the north. Milan gets immense support from the St. Gotthard and Simplon railroads over the Alps, besides wagon routes over several minor passes. Kulm, Balkh and Kunduz in the piedmont of northern Afghanistan are fed by twenty or more passes over the Hindu Kush and Pamir. Bukhara is the remoter focus of all these routes, and also of the valley highways of the western Tian Shan. It therefore occupies a location which would make it one of the great emporiums of the world, were it not for the expanse of desert to the west and the scantiness of its local water supply, which is tapped farther upstream for the irrigation of Samarkand. In its bazaars are found drugs, dyes and teas from India; wool, skins and dried fruit from Afghanistan; woven goods, arms, and books from Persia; and Russian wares imported by rail and caravan. English goods, which formerly came in by the Kabul route from India, have been excluded since Russia established a protectorate over the province of Bukhara. Across the highlands to the east, the cities of Kashgar and Yarkand, situated in that piedmont zone of vegetation where mountain and desert meet, are enclosed by a vast amphitheater formed by the Tian Shan, the Pamir Highlands, and the Karakorum range. Stieler's atlas marks no less than six trade routes over the passes of these mountains from Kashgar to the headstreams of the Sir-daria and Oxus, and six from Yarkand to the Oxus and Indus. Kashgar is a meeting ground of many nationalities. To its bazaars come traders from China, India, Afghanistan, Bukhara, and Russian Turkestan.[14] The Russian railway up the Sir-daria to Andizhan brings European goods within relatively easy reach of the Terek Davan Pass, and makes serious competition for English wares entering by the more difficult Karakorum Pass from India.[15]

Where mountains drop off into a desert, as these Central Asiatic ranges do, their piedmont cities are confined to a narrow zone between mountains and arid waste. Bordering two transit regions of scant population and through travel, they become natural outfitting points, centers of exchange rather than production. Where mountains drop off into the sea and the piedmont therefore becomes a coastal belt, again it borders two transit regions; but here the ports of the desert are replaced by maritime ports, which command the world

Cities of coastal piedmonts.

thoroughfare of the ocean. They therefore tend to concentrate population and commerce wherever a good harbor coincides with the outlet of a transmontane route, as in Genoa and Bombay.

Piedmonts as colonial or backwoods frontiers. Since mountains are inhospitable to every phase of the historical movement, they long remain regions of retardation. Hence to their bordering plains they sustain the relation of young undeveloped lands, so that life in their piedmont belts tends to show for a long time all the characteristics of a new colonial frontier. The rim of the Southern Appalachians abundantly illustrates this principle even to-day. During the westward expansion of the American people from 1830 to 1850, the eastern rim of the Rocky Mountains was dotted with trading posts like that of the Missouri Fur Company at the forks of the Missouri River, Forts Laramie and Platte on the North Fork of the Platte, Vrain's Fort and Fort Lancaster on the South Fork, Bent's Fort at the mountain exit of the Arkansas River, and Barclay's in the high Mora Valley of the upper Canadian. These posts gathered in the rich pelts which formed the one product of this highland area susceptible of bearing the cost of transportation to the far away Missouri River. Though they developed into way-stations on the overland trails, when the movement of population to California and Oregon in the forties and fifties made the Rocky Mountains a typical highland transit region, yet they long remained frontier posts.[16] Later the abundant water supply of this piedmont district, as compared with the arid plains below, and the mineral wealth of the mountains concentrated here an agricultural and industrial population.

In Sze Chuan province of western China, the piedmont of a vast highland hinterland shows a similar development. Here the towns of Matang, Sungpan, Kuan Hsien, and even the capital Chengtu, situated in the high Min Valley at the foot of the mountains walling them in on the west, are emporiums for trade with the Tibetans, who bring hither furs, hides and wool from their plateau pastures, and musk from the musk deer on the Koko Nor plains.[17] Just to the north, Sian (Singan), capital of the highland province of Shensi, concentrates the fur trade of a large mountain wilderness to the west. Several blocks on the main street form a great fur market for the sale of mink and other skins used to line the official robes of mandarins.[18]

Like seas, deserts, and other geographical transit regions, mountains too under primitive conditions develop their professional carriers. These collect in the piedmont, where highway and mule train cease, and where the steep track admits only human beasts of burden, trained by their environment to be climbers and packers. These mountain carriers are found on the Pacific face of the coast ranges of North and South America from the peninsula of Alaska to the Straits of Magellan. They are able to pack from 100 to 160 pounds up a steep grade. The Chilkoot Indians, men, women and children, did invaluable service on the White Horse and Chilkoot passes during the early days of the Klondike rush. They had devised a well-arranged harness, which enabled them better to carry their loads. Farther south in British Columbia the piedmont tribes had once a like importance; there they operated especially from the town of Hope on the lower Frazer River as a distributing center. The Mexican carrier is so efficient and so cheap that he enters into serious competition with modern schemes to improve transportation, especially as the rugged relief of this country makes those schemes expensive.[19] The Indians of the eastern slope of the Andes pack India rubber, in loads of 150 pounds each, from the upper Purus and Madeira rivers up to the Andean plateau at a height of 15,000 feet, and there transfer their burdens to mules for transport down to the Peruvian port of Mollendo.[20]

The retarded mountain peoples on the borders of the Central Asia plateau employ the same primitive means of transportation. The roads leading from the Sze Chuan province of western China over the mountain ranges to Tibet are traversed by long lines of porters, men, women and children, laden with bales of brick tea,[21] the strongest of them shouldering 350 pounds. The Bhutia coolies of Sikkim act as carriers on military and commercial expeditions on the track across the Himalayas between Darjeeling and Shigatze. Colonel Younghusband found that these Bhutias, who were

Mountain carriers.

paid by the job, would carry a pack of 250 to 300 pounds, or three times the usual burden of a Central Asia carrier. Landon cites the case of a Bhutia lady who was said to have carried a piano on her head from the plains up to Darjeeling (7150 feet).[22] In Nepal, women and girls, less often men, have long been accustomed to carry travellers and merchandise over the Himalayan ranges.[23] In the marginal valleys of the Himalayas, like Kashmir and Baltistan, the natives are regularly impressed for *begar* or carrier service on the English military roads to strategic points on the high mountain frontier of the Indian Empire.[24] So the Igorots of the Luzon province of Benguet pack all goods and supplies from Naguilian in the lowlands up 4000 feet in a distance of 25 miles to their little capital of Baguio; for this service they are now paid one peso (46 cents in 1901) a day with food, or ten times as much as under the Spanish rule.[25]

Power of mountain barriers to block or deflect.
If the historical movement slackens its pace at the piedmont slope, higher up the mountain it comes to a halt. Only when human invention has greatly improved communication across the barrier are its obstacles in part overcome. The great highland wall stretching across southern Europe from the Bay of Biscay to the Black Sea long cut off the solid mass of the continent from the culture of the Mediterranean lands. Owing to these mountains Central Europe came late into the foreground of history, not till the Middle Ages. Even the penetrating civilization of Greece reached it only by long detours around the ends of the mountain barrier; by Massilia and the Rhone, by Istria and the Danube, Greek commerce trickled through to the interior of the continent.

Where mountains fail to check, they deflect the historical movement. The wall of the Carpathians, bulwark of Central Europe, split the westward moving Slav hordes in the 6th century, diverting one southward up the Danube Valley to the Eastern Alps, and turning one northward along the German lowlands.[26] The northward expansion of the Romans, rebuffed by the high double wall of the Central Alps, was bent to the westward over the Maritime, Cottine and Savoy Alps, where the barrier offered the shortest and easiest transmontane routes.   Hence Germany received the elements of Mediterranean culture indirectly through Gaul, second-hand and late.   The ancient Helvetians, moving southward from northern Switzerland into Gaul, took a route skirting the western base of the Alps by the gap at Geneva, and thus threatened Roman Provincia.   Cæsar's campaigns into northern Gaul were given direction by the massive Central Plateau of France.[27]   The rugged and infertile area of the Catskills long retarded the westward movement in colonial New York and deflected it northward through the Mohawk depression, which therefore had its long thin line of settlements when the neighboring Catskills were still a "bare spot."

In their valleys, mountains lose something of their barrier nature, and approximate the level of the plains.   Here they harbor oases of denser population and easier intercourse. Valleys favor human settlement through the milder climate of their lower elevation, the accumulation of soil on their floors, their sheltered environment, and their command of such routes of communication as the highlands afford.   They are the avenues into and within a mountain system, and therefore radically influence its history by their direction and location.   The Central Plateau of France, through the valleys of the Alliers and upper Loire, is most accessible from the north; therefore in that direction it has maintained its most important historical connections,[28] from the days of Cæsar and Vercingetorix.   The massive highland region of Transylvania, which opens long accessible valleys westward toward the plains of the Theiss and Danube, has since the eleventh century received thence Hungarian immigration and political dominion.[29] Its dominant Roumanian population, however, seems to have fled thither from the Tartar-swept plains to the southeast.

The anthropo-geography of mountain valleys depends upon the structure of the highlands themselves, whether they are fold mountains, whose ranges wall in longitudinal valleys, or dissected plateaus, whose valleys are mostly transverse river channels leading from the hydrographic center out to the rim of the highlands.   Longitudinal valleys are not only long, but also broad as a rule and often show a nearly level

Signifi-cance of mountain valleys.

floor.[30]   They therefore form districts of considerable size, fertility, and individuality, and play distinct historical rôles in the history of their respective highlands. Such are the upper Rhone Valley with its long line of flourishing towns and villages, the Hither Rhine, the Inn of the Tyrol and the Engadine, the fertile trough of the meandering Isère above Grenoble,[31] the broad Orontes-Leontes valley between the Lebanon and Anti-Lebanon where Kadesh and Baalbec were once the glory of northern Syria. Such is the central trough of the Appalachian Mountains, known as the Great Appalachian Valley, seventy-five miles wide, subdivided into constituent valleys of similar character by parallel, even-crested ridges following the trend of the mountains. These are drained by broad, leisurely rivers, bordered by fertile farms and substantial towns. Transverse valleys, on the other hand, are generally narrow, with steep slopes rising almost from the river's edge and supporting only small villages and farms. A comparison of the spacious, smooth-floored valley of Andermatt with the wild Reuss gorge, of the fertile and populous Shenandoah Valley in the Southern Appalachians with the cañon of the Kanawha in the Cumberland Plateau, makes the contrast striking enough.

Longitudinal valleys.   Longitudinal valleys, by reason of their length and their branching lateral valleys, are the natural avenues of communication within the mountains themselves. They therefore give a dominant direction to such phases of the historical movement as succeed in passing the outer barrier. The series of parallel ranges which strike off from the eastern end of the Tibetan plateau southward into Farther India have directed along their valleys the main streams of Mongolian migration and expansion, heading them toward the river basins of Burma and Indo China, and away from India itself.[32] While Tibetan elements have during the ages slowly welled over the high Himalayan brim and trickled down toward the Gangetic plain, Burma has been deluged by floods of Mongolians pouring down the runnels of the land. A carriage road follows the axis of the Central Alps from Lake Geneva to Lake Constance by means of the upper Rhone, Andermatt, and upper Rhine valleys, linked by the Furca and

Oberalp passes. The Roman and Medieval routes north-ward across the Central Alps struck the upper Rhine Valley above Coire, (the ancient Curia Rhaetorum); this natural groove gave them a northeastward direction, and made them emerge from the mountains directly south of Ulm, which thereby gained great importance. The trade routes from Damascus and Palmyra which once entered the Orontes-Leontes trough in the Lebanon system found their Mediterranean termini south near Tyre or north near Antioch, and thus contributed to the greatness of those ancient emporiums. The Great Appalachian Valley used to be a highway for the Iroquois Indians, when they took the warpath against the Cherokee tribes of Tennessee. Later it gave a distinct southwestward trend to pioneer movements of population within the mountains, blending in its common channel the Quakers, Germans and Scotch-Irish from Pennsylvania, with the English and Huguenot French of the more southern colonies. In the Civil War its fertile fields were swept by marching armies, all the way from Chattanooga to Gettysburg.

The barrier nature of mountains depends upon their **Passes in** height and structure, whether they are massive, unbroken **mountain** walls like the Scandinavian Alps and the Great Smoky range; **barriers.** or, like the Welsh Highlands and the Blue Ridge, are studded with low passes. The Pyrenees, Caucasus and Andes, owing to the scarcity and great height of their passes, have always been serious barriers. The Pyrenees divide Spain from France more sharply than the Alps divide Italy from France; owing to their rampart character, they form the best and most definite natural boundary in Europe.[33] Epirus and Aetolia, fenced in by the solid Pindus range, took little part in the common life of ancient Greece; but the intermittent chains of Thessaly offered a passway between Macedon and Hellas. The Alps have an astonishing number of excellent passes, evenly distributed for the most part. These, in conjunction with the great longitudinal valleys of the system, offer transit routes from side to side in any direction. The Appalachian system is some three hundred miles broad and thirteen hundred miles long, but it has many easy gaps among its parallel ranges, so that it offered natural though circuitous highways to the early winners of the West. The long line (400 miles) of the Hindu Kush range, high as it is, forms no strong natural boundary to India, because it is riddled with passes at altitudes from 12,500 to 19,000 feet.[34] The easternmost group of these passes lead down to Kashmir, and therefore lend this state peculiar importance as guardian of these northern entrances to India.[35] The Suleiman Mountains along the Indo-Afghan frontier are an imperfect defence for the same reason. They are indented by 289 passes capable of being traversed by camels. The mountain border of Baluchistan contains 75 more, the most important of which focus their roads upon Kandahar. Hence the importance to British India of Kandahar and Afghanistan. Across this broken northwest barrier have come almost all the floods of invasion and immigration that have contributed their varied elements to the mixed population of India. Tradition, epic and history tell of Asiatic highlanders ever sweeping down into the warm valley of the Indus through these passes; Scythians, Aryans, Greeks, Assyrians, Medes, Persians, Turks, Tartars, and Mongols have all traveled these rocky roads, to rest in the enervating valleys of the peninsula.[36]

Breadth of mountain barriers.   Mountains folded into a succession of parallel ranges are greater obstructions than a single range like the Erz, Black Forest, and Vosges, or a narrow, compact system like the Western Alps, which can be crossed by a single pass. Owing to this simple structure the Western Alps were traversed by four established routes in the days of the Roman Empire. These were: 1. The *Via Aurelia* between the Maritime Alps and the sea, where now runs the Cornice Road. II. The *Mons Matrona* (Mont Genevre Pass, 6080 feet or 1854 kilometers) between the headstream of the Dora Riparia and that of the Durance, which was the best highway for armies. III. The Little St. Bernard (7075 feet or 2157 meters), from Aosta on the Dora Baltea over to the Isère and down to Lugdunum (Lyons). IV. The Great St. Bernard (8109 feet or 2472 meters) route, which led northward from Aosta over the Pennine Alps to Octodurus at the elbow of the upper Rhone, where Martigny now stands. Across the broad double rampart of the Central Alps the Roman used chiefly the Brenner route, which by a low saddle unites the deep reëntrant valleys of the Adige and Inn rivers, and thus surmounts the barrier by a single pass. However, a short cut northward over the Chalk Alps by the Fern Pass made closer connection with Augusta Vindelicorum (Augsburg). The Romans seem to have been ignorant of the St. Gotthard, which, though high, is the summit of an unbroken ascent from Lake Maggiore up the valley of the Ticino on one side, and from Lake Lucerne up the Reuss on the other.

Mountains which spread out on a broad base in a series of parallel chains, and through which no long transverse valleys offer ready transit, form serious barriers to every phase of intercourse. The lofty boundary wall of the Pyrenees, a folded mountain system of sharp ranges and difficult passes, has successfully separated Spain from continental Europe; it has given the Iberian Peninsula, in the course of a long history, closer relations with Morocco than with its land neighbor France. It thus justifies the French saying that "Africa begins at the Pyrenees." The Andalusian fold mountains stretching across southern Spain in a double wall from Trafalgar to Cape Nao, accessible only by narrow and easily defended passes, enabled the Moors of Granada to hold their own for centuries against the Spaniard Christians. The high thin ridges of the folded Jura system, poor in soil and sparsely populated, broken by occasional "cluses" or narrow water-gaps admitting the rivers from one elevated longitudinal valley to another, have always been a serious hindrance to traffic.[37]

Such mountains can be crossed only by circuitous routes from pass to pass, ascending and descending each range of the system. The Central Alps, grooved by the longitudinal valleys of the upper Rhone, Rhine and Inn, make transit travel a series of ups and downs. The northern range must be crossed by some minor pass like the Gemmi, (7553 feet) or Panixer (7907 feet) to the longitudinal valleys, and the southern range again by the Simplon (6595 feet), San Bernadino (6768 feet), Splügen (6946 feet) or Septimer (7582 feet) to the Po basin. Across the corrugated

Circuitous routes through folded mountains.

highland of the Hindu Kush, lying between the plains of the Indus and the Oxus, the caravans of western Asia seek the market of the Punjab by a circuitous route through the Hajikhak Pass (12,188 feet) or famous Gates of Bamian over the main range of the Hindu Kush, by the Unai Pass over the Paghman Mountains to Kabul at 5740 feet, and then by gorges of the Kabul River and the Khaibar Pass (6825 feet) down to Peshawar. This road presents so many difficulties that caravans from Turkestan to India prefer another route from Merv up the valley of the Heri-Rud through the western hills of the Hindu Kush to Herat, thence diagonally southeast across Afghanistan to Kandahar, and thence by the Bolan Pass down to the Sind. The broad, low series of forested mountains consisting of the Vindhyan and Kaimur Hills, reinforced by the Satpura, Kalabet, Gawilgarh ranges, Mahadeo Hills, Maikal Range and Chutia Nagpur Plateau as a secondary ridge to the south, forms a double barrier across the base of peninsular India. It divides the Deccan from Hindustan so effectually that it has sufficed to set limits to any Aryan advance *en masse* southward. It kept southern India isolated, and admitted only later Aryan influences which filtered through the barrier. To people accustomed to treeless plains, these wide belts of wooded hills were barrier enough. Even a few years ago their passes were dreaded by cartmen; most of the carriage of the country was effected by pack-bullocks. Even when roads were cleared through the forests, they were likely to be rendered impassable by torrential rains.[38]

Dominant transmontane routes. Where a broad, complex mountain system contracts to narrow compass, or is cut by deep reëntrant valleys leading up to a single pass, the transmontane route here made by nature assumes great historical importance. The double chain of the mighty Caucasus, from 120 to 150 miles wide and 750 miles long, stretches an almost insuperable barrier between the Black Sea and the Caspian. But nearly midway between these two seas it is constricted to only 60 miles by a geographical and geological gulf, which penetrates from the steppes of Russia almost to the heart of the system.[39] This gulf forms the high valley of the Terek River, beyond whose headstream lies the Dariel defile (7503 feet or 2379 meters), which continues the natural depression across to the short southern slope. All the other passes of the Caucasus are 3000 meters or more high, lie above snow line and are therefore open only in summer. The Dariel Pass alone is open all the year around.[40] Here runs the great military road from Vladicaucas to Tiflis, which the Russians have built to control their turbulent mountaineer subjects; and here are located the Ossetes, the only people among the variegated tribes of the whole Caucasus who occupy both slopes. All the other tribes and languages are confined to one side or the other.[41] Moreover, the Ossetes, occupying an exposed location in their highway habitat, lack the courage of the other mountaineers, and yielded without resistance to the Russians. In this respect they resemble the craven-spirited Kashmiri, whose mountain-walled vale forms a passway from Central Asia down to the Punjab.

The Pass of Dariel, owing to its situation in a retarded corner of Asia, has never attained the historical importance which attaches to the deep saddle of the Brenner Pass (4470 feet) in the Central Alps. Uniting the reëntrant valleys of the Inn and Adige rivers only 2760 feet above the Inn's exit from the mountains upon the Bavarian plateau, it forms a low, continuous line of communication across the Central Alps. The Brenner was the route of the Cimbri invading the Po Valley, and later of the Roman forces destined for frontier posts of the Empire on the upper Danube. In the Middle Ages it was the route for the armies of the German Emperors who came to make good their claim to Italy. By this road came the artists and artisans of the whole north country to learn the arts and crafts of beauty-loving Venice. From the Roman road-makers to the modern railroad engineer, with the concomitant civilization of each, the Brenner has seen the march of human progress. *Brenner route.*

Farther to the west, the wall of highlands stretching across southern Europe is interrupted by a deep groove formed by the mountain-flanked Rhone Valley and the Pass of Belfort, or Burgundian Gate, which lies between the Vosges and Jura system, and connects the Rhone road with the long *Pass of Belfort.*

rift valley of the middle Rhine. This pass, broad and low (350 meters or 1148 feet) marks the insignificant summit in the great historic route of travel between the Mediterranean and the North Sea, from the days of ancient Etruscan merchants to the present. This was the route of the invading Teuton hordes which the Roman Marius defeated at Aquae Sextiae, and later, of the Germans under Ariovistus, whom Cæsar defeated near the present Mühlhausen. Four centuries afterward came the Alamannians, Burgundians and other Teutonic stocks, who infused a tall blond element into the population of the Rhone Valley.[42] The Pass of Belfort is the strategic key to Central Europe. Here Napoleon repeatedly fixed his military base for the invasion of Austria, and hither was directed one division of the German army in 1870 for the invasion of France. The gap is traversed to-day by a canal connecting the Doubs and the Rhine and by a railroad, just as formerly by the tracks of migrating barbarians.

Mohawk route.   The natural depression of the Mohawk Valley, only 445 feet (136 meters) above sea level, is the only decided break across the entire width of the long Appalachian system. This fact, together with its ready accessibility from the Hudson on the east and Lake Ontario on the west, lent it importance in the early history of the colonies, as well as in the later history of New York. It was an easy line of communication with the Great Lakes, and gave the colonists access to the fur trade of the Northwest, then in the hands of the French. So when French and English fought for supremacy in the New World, the Mohawk and Hudson valleys were their chief battleground; elsewhere the broad Appalachian barrier held them apart. Again in the Revolution, control of the Mohawk-Hudson route was the objective of the British armies mobilized on the Canadian frontier, because it alone would enable them to co-operate with the British fleet blockading the coast cities of the colonies. In the War of 1812, it was along this natural transmontane highway that supplies were forwarded to the remote frontier, to support Perry's fight for control of the Great Lakes. The war demonstrated the strategic necessity of a protected, wholly American line of water communication between the Hudson and our western frontier, while the commercial and political advantage was obvious. Hence a decade after the conclusion of the war, this depression was traced by the Erie Canal, through which passed long lines of boats to build up the commercial greatness of New York City.

Other structural features being the same, mountains are barriers also in proportion to their height; for, with few exceptions, the various anthropo-geographic effects of up-heaved areas are intensified with increase of elevation. Old, worn-down mountains, like the Appalachians and the Ural, broad as they are, have been less effective obstacles than the towering crests of the Alps and Caucasus. The form of the elevation also counts. Easy slopes and flat or rounded summits make readier transit regions than high, thin ridges with escarpment-like flanks. Mountains of plateau form, though reaching a great altitude, may be relatively hospitable to the historical movement and even have a regular nomadic population in summer. The central and western Tian Shan system is in reality a broad, high plateau, divided into a series of smoothly floored basins and gently rolling ridges lying at an elevation of 10,000 to 12,000 feet above the sea. Its pamirs or plains of thick grass, nourished by the relatively heavy precipitation of this high altitude, and forming in summer an island of verdure in the surrounding sea of sun-scorched waste, attract the pastoral nomads from all the bordering steppes and deserts.[43] Thus it is a meeting place for a seasonal population, sparse and evanescent, but its uplifted mass holds asunder the few sedentary peoples fringing its piedmont. The corrugated dome of the Pamir highland, whose valley floors lie at an elevation of 11,000 to 13,000 feet, draws to its summer pastures Kirghis shepherds from north, east and west; and their flocks in turn attract the raids of the marauding mountaineers occupying the Hunza Valley to the south. The Pamir, high but accessible, was a passway in the tenth century for Chinese caravans bound from "Serica" or the "Land of Silk" to the Oxus River and the Caspian. Here Marco Polo and many travelers after him found fodder for their pack animals and food for themselves, because they

[margin note: Height in mountain barriers.]

could always purchase meat from the visiting shepherds. The possibilities of the Pamir as a transit region are apparent to Russia, who in 1886 annexed most of it to the government of Bukhara.

Contrasted accessibility of opposite slopes. Mountains are seldom equally accessible from all sides. Rarely does the crest of a system divide it symmetrically. This means a steep, difficult approach to the summit from one direction, and a longer, more gradual, and hence easier ascent from the other. It means also in general a wide zone of habitation and food supply on the gentler slope, a better commissary and transport base whence to make the final ascent, whether in conquest, trade or ethnic growth. Mountain boundaries are therefore rarely by nature impartial. They do not umpire the great game of expansion fairly. They lower the bars to the advancing people on one side, and hold them relentlessly in place to the other. To the favored slope they give the strategic advantage of a swift and sudden descent beyond the summit down the opposite side. The political boundary of France along the watershed of the Vosges Mountains is backed by a long, gradual ascent from the Seine lowland and faces a sharp drop to the rift valley of the middle Rhine. Its boundary along the crest of the Alps from Mont Blanc to the Mediterranean brings over two-thirds of the upheaved area within the domain of France, and gives to that country great advantages of approach to the Alpine passes at the expense of Italy. With the exception of the ill-matched conflict between the civilized Romans and the barbarian Gauls, it is a matter of history that from the days of Hannibal to Napoleon III, the campaigns over the Alps from the north have succeeded, while those from the steep-rimmed Po Valley have miscarried. The Brenner route favored alike the Cimbri hordes in 102 B. C. and later the medieval German Emperors invading Italy from the upper Danube. The drop from the Brenner Pass to Munich is 2800 feet; to Rovereto, an equally distant point on the Italian side, the road descends 3770 feet.

Its ethnic effects. The inequality of slope has ethnic as well as political effects, especially where a latitudinal direction also makes a sharp contrast of climate on the two sides of the mountain system. Except in the Roman period, the southern face of the Alps has been an enclosing wall to the Italians. The southern cultivator penetrated its high but sunny valleys only when forced by poverty, while the harsh climate on the long northern slope effectively repelled him. On the other hand, Switzerland has overstepped the Alpine crest in the province of Ticino and thrust its political boundary in a long wedge down to the lowland of the Po near Como; and the Alpine race, spilling everywhere over the mountain rim into the inviting Po basin, has given to this lowland population a relatively broad skull, blond coloring and tall figure, sharply contrasted with the pure Mediterranean race beyond the crest of the Apennines.[44]

The long northward slope of the Alps in Switzerland and Tyrol, and the easy western grade toward France, have enabled Germanic and Gallic influences of various kinds to permeate the mountains. A strong element of blond, long-headed Germans mingles in the population of the Aar and Rhine valleys up to the ice-capped ridge of the Glarner and Bernese Alps,[45] while the virile German speech has pushed yet farther south to the insuperable barrier of the Monte Rosa group. The abrupt southward slope of the Himalayas has repelled ethnic expansion from the river lowlands of northern India, except in the mountain valleys of the Punjab streams and Nepal, where the highland offered asylum to the Rajput race when dislodged by a later Aryan invasion, or when trying their energies in expansion and conquest.[46] The Tibetan people, whose high plateaus rise almost flush with the Himalayan passes, have everywhere trickled through and given a Mongoloid mountain border to Aryan India,[47] even though their speech has succumbed to the pervasive Aryan language of the piedmont, and thus confused the real ethnic boundary. [See map page 102.] The retarded and laborious approach of British "influence" up this steep ascent to Lhassa, as opposed to the long established suzerainty of the Chinese Emperor in Tibet, can be attributed in part to the contrasted accessibility from north and south.

Mountains influence the life of their inhabitants and their

Persistence of barrier nature.

neighbors fundamentally and variously, but always reveal their barrier nature. For the occupants of one slope they provide an abundant rainfall, hold up the clouds, and rob them of their moisture; to the leeward side they admit dry winds, and only from the melting snow or the precipitation on their summits do they yield a scanty supply of water. The Himalayas are flanked by the teeming population of India and the scattered nomadic tribes of Tibet. Mountains often draw equally clear cut lines of cleavage in temperature. The Scandinavian range concentrates upon Norway the warm, soft air of the Atlantic westerlies, while just below the watershed on the eastern side Sweden feels all the rigor of a sub-Arctic climate. In history, too, mountains play the same part as barriers. They are always a challenge to the energies of man. Their beauty, the charm of the unknown beyond tempts the enterprising spirit; the hardships and dangers of their roads daunt or baffle the mediocre, but by the great ones whose strength is able to dwarf these obstacles is found beyond a prize of victory. Such were Hannibal, Napoleon, Suvaroff, Genghis Khan, and those lesser heroes of the modern work-a-day world who toiled across the Rockies and Sierras in the feverish days of '49, or who faced the snows of Chilkoot Pass for the frozen gold-fields of the Yukon.

Importance of mountain passes.

For migrating, warring and trading humanity therefore, the interest of the mountains is centered in the passes. These are only dents or depressions in the great up-lifted crest, or gaps carved out by streams, or deeper breaches in the mountain wall; but they point the easiest pathway to the ultramontane country, and for this reason focus upon themselves the travel that would cut across the grain of the earth's wrinkled crust. Their influence reaches far. The Brenner, by its medieval trade, made the commercial greatness of Augsburg, Ratisbon, Nuremberg, and Leipzig to the north, and promoted the growth of Venice to the south. The Khaibar Pass and the Gates of Herat in Afghanistan have for long periods dominated the Asiatic policy of Russia and British India. The Mohawk depression and Cumberland Gap for decades gave direction to the streams of population moving westward into the Mississippi basin in the early history of the Republic. Where Truckee Pass (7017 feet) makes a gash in the high ridge of the Sierra Nevada, the California Trail in 1844 sought the line of least resistance across the barrier mass, and deposited its desert-worn immigrants about the Sacramento Valley and San Francisco Bay. There they made a nucleus of American population in Mexican California, and in 1846 became the center of American revolt.

Though modern engineering skill, especially when backed by a political policy, may cause certain passes to gain in historical importance at the cost of others, the rule holds that passes are never quite insignificant. Their influence is persistent through the ages. They are nature-made thoroughfares, traversed now by undisciplined hordes of migrating barbarians, now by organized armies, now by the woolly flocks and guardian dogs of the nomad shepherd, now by the sumpter mule of the itinerant merchant, now by the wagon-trains of over-mountain settlers, now by the steam engine panting up the steep grade. Nowhere does history repeat itself so monotonously, yet so interestingly as in these mountain gates. In the Pass of Roncesvalles, notching the western Pyrenees between Pamplona in Spain and St. Etienne in France, fell the army of Charlemagne surprised and beset by the mountain tribes in 778;[48] through this breach the Black Prince in 1367 led his troops to the victory of Navarette; in the Peninsular War a division of Wellington's army in 1813 moved northward up this valley, driving the French before them; and by this route Soult advanced southward across the frontier for the relief of the French forces shut up in Pamplona. The history of Palestine may be read in epitome in the annals of the Vale of Jezreel, where the highlands of Palestine sink to a natural trough before rising again to the hill country of Galilee and the mountain range of high Lebanon. This was the avenue for war and trade between the Nile and Euphrates, between Africa and Asia. Here the Canaanites expanded eastward from the coast, cutting off northern Israel in Galilee from Samaria and Judea. Here Gideon turned back the incursions of the Midianites or western Arabs. Here was the open road for Assyrians, Egyptians, for Greek armies under Antiochus, and Roman

Persistent influence of passes.

armies under Pompey, Mark Antony, Vespasian and Titus. Hither came the Saracens from the east in 634 A. D. to rout the Greek army, and later the Crusaders from the west, to secure with castle and fortress this key to the Holy Land. Finally, hither came Napoleon from Egypt in 1799 on his way to the Euphrates.[40]

Geographic factors in the historical importance of passes.   The historical importance of passes tends to increase with the depth of the depression, since the lowest gap in a range relegates the others to only occasional or local use; and with their rarity, in consequence of which intercourse between opposite slopes is concentrated upon one or two defiles. The low dips of the Central American Cordilleras to 262 feet (80 meters) at Panama, 151 feet (46 meters) in the Nicaraguan isthmus, and 689 feet (210 meters) at Tehuantepec, present a striking contrast both orographically and historically to the South American Andes, where from the equator to the Uspallata or Bermejo Pass (12,562 feet or 3842 meters) back of Valparaiso, a stretch measuring 33 degrees of latitude, the passes all reach or exceed 10,000 feet or 3000 meters. The southern or Pennine range of the Alps, stretching as a snow-wrapped barrier from Mont Blanc 90 miles to the central Alpine dome of the St. Gotthard, is notched only by the Great St. Bernard and Simplon passes, which have therefore figured conspicuously in war and trade, since very early times. The Pass of Thermopylæ, as the only route southward along the flank of the Pindus system, figures in every land invasion of Greece from Xerxes to the Greek war of independence. All movements back and forth across the Caucasus wall have been confined to the Pass of Dariel and the far lower Pass of Derbent, or *Pylæ Albaniæ* of the ancients, which lies between the Caspian and the last low spurs of the mountains as they drop down to the sea. The latter, as the easier of the two passes, has had a longer and richer history. It alone enabled the ancient Persians temporarily to force a wedge of conquest to the northern foot of the Caucasus, and it has been in all ages a highway for peoples entering Persia and Georgia from the north. It has so far been the only practicable route for a railway from the Russian steppes to the southern base of the Caucasus. While Vladicaucas and Tiflis have direct connection by the military highway over the Pass of Dariel, the railroad between these two points makes a detour of 300 miles to the east.

Intermarine mountains as a rule offer the easiest passways **Inter-** where they sink to meet the flanking seas. The Pyrenees **marine** are crossed by only two railroads, the Bayonne-Burgos line, **mountains.** along the shore of the Bay of Biscay, and the Narbonne-Barcelona line, overlooking the Mediterranean. Between these extremities the passes are very high and only two are practicable for carriages, the Col de la Perche (5280 feet or 1610 meters) between the valleys of the Tet and the upper Segre, and the Port de Canfranc (7502 feet or 2288 meters) on the old Roman road from Saragossa to Oloron. The coastal road around the eastern end of the Cheviot Hills has been the great intermediary between England and Scotland. It was the avenue for early Teutonic expansion into the Scotch Lowlands, the thoroughfare for all those armies which for centuries made Berwick a chronic battleground.

For purposes of trade these intermarine mountains are less serious barriers, because they can be avoided by an easier and cheaper sea route. Hence on each side of such ranges grow up active ports, like Narbonne and Barcelona, Bayonne and Bilbao with San Sebastian, on the piedmont seaboard of the Pyrenees; Petrovsk and Baku on the Caspian rim of the Caucasus, balancing the Crimean ports and Poti with Trebizond on the Black Sea. Analogous is the position of Genoa and Marseilles in relation to the Maritime Alps. Such ports are inevitably the object of attack in time of hostilities. In the Peninsular War almost the first act of the French was to seize Barcelona, San Sebastian and Bilbao; and throughout the seven years of the conflict these points were centers of battle, blockade and siege. If Russia ever tries to wrench the upper Euphrates Valley from Turkey, Trebizond will repeat the history of Barcelona in the Peninsular War.

As the world's roads are used primarily for commerce, **Pass roads** pass routes rank in importance according to the amount of **between** trade which they forward; and this in turn is decided by **regions of** the contrast in the lands which they unite. The passes of **contrasted** the Alps and the Pass of Belfort have been busy thorough- **production.**

fares from the early Middle Ages, because they facilitate exchanges between the tropical Mediterranean and the temperate regions of Central Europe. Or the contrast may be one of economic and social development. The Mohawk depression forwards the grain of the agricultural Northwest in return for the manufactured wares of the Atlantic seaboard. The passes of the Asiatic ranges connect the industrial and agricultural lowlands of India and China with the highland pastures of Mongolia, Tibet, Afghanistan and Russian Turkestan. Hence they forward the wool, skins, felts, cloth and carpets of the wandering shepherds in exchange for the food stuffs and industrial products of the fertile, crowded lowlands. Where passes open a highway for inland countries to the sea, their sphere of influence is greatly increased. San Francisco, New York, Marseilles, Genoa, Venice, Beirut and Bombay are seaports which owe their importance in no small degree to dominant pass routes into their hinterland.

Passes determine transmontane roads. In plains and lowlands highways may run in any direction expediency suggests, but in mountain regions the pass points the road. In very high ranges there is no appeal from this law; but in lower systems and especially in old mountains which have been rounded and worn down by ages of denudation, economic and social considerations occasionally transcend orographical conditions in fixing the path of highways. Scarcely less important than pass or gap is the avenue of approach to the same. This is furnished by lateral or transverse valleys of erosion. The deeper their reëntrant angles cut back into the heart of the highlands, the more they facilitate intercourse and lend historical importance to the pass route. The Alpine passes which are approached by a single valley from each side are those crossed by railroads to-day,—Mont Cenis, Simplon, St. Gotthard and the Brenner. The Alpine chain is trenched on its inner or southern side by a series of transverse erosion valleys, such as the Dora Baltea, Sesia, Tosa, Ticino, Adda, Adige, and Tagliamento, which carry roads up to the chief Alpine passes. The coincidence of the Roman and medieval roads over the Alps with the modern railroads is striking, except in the single point of elevation. Railroads tend to follow lower levels. Modern engineering skill enables them to tunnel the crest, to cut galleries in the perpendicular walls of gorges, and to embank mountain torrents against the spring inundation of the roadbed, where it drops to the valley floor.

Where gaps are low and the approaching waters are Navigable navigable, at least for the small craft of early days, they river ap- combine to enhance the historical importance of their routes. proaches The Mohawk River, navigable for the canoe of Indian and to passes. fur trader, greatly increased travel and traffic through the Mohawk depression. The Pass of Belfort is the greatest historic gateway of western Europe, chiefly because it unites the channels of the Rhone, Saône and Rhine. Lake Lucerne brings the modern tourist by boat to the foot of the railroad ascent to the St. Gotthard Pass, as the long gorge of Lake Maggiore receives him at the southern end. Lake Maggiore is the water outlet also of the Simplon Pass from the upper Rhone, the Lukmanier (6288 feet or 1917 meters) from the Hither Rhine, and the San Bernadino (6766 feet or 2063 meters) from the Hinter Rhine.[50] This geographical fact explains the motive of Swiss expansion in the fifteenth century in embracing the Italian province of Ticino and the upper end of Lake Maggiore. A significance like that of the Swiss and Italian lakes for the Alpine passes appears emphasized in the Sogne Fiord of Norway. This carries a marine highway a hundred miles into the land; from its head, roads ascend to the only two dents in the mountain wall south of the wide snowfield of the Jotun Fjeld, and they lead thence by the valleys of Hallingdal and Valders down to the plains of Christiania.

Genuine mountain passes have only emergency inhabitants Types of —the monks and dogs of the hospice, the road-keepers in settlements their refuge huts or *cantonière*, or the garrison of a fort in the valley ap- guarding these important thoroughfares. The flanking val- proaches. leys of approach draw to themselves the human life of the mountains. Their upper settlements show a certain common physiognomy, born of their relation to the barren transit region above, except in those few mountain districts of advanced civilization where railroads have introduced through traffic over the barrier. At the foot of the final ascent to the pass, where often the carriage road ends and where mule-path or foot-trail begins, is located a settlement that lives largely by the transmontane travel. It is a place of inns, hostelries, of blacksmith shops, where in the busy season the sound of hammer and anvil is heard all night; of stables and corrals crowded with pack and draft animals; of storehouses where the traveler can provide himself with food for the journey across the barren, uninhabited heights. It is the typical outfitting point such as springs up on the margin of any pure transit region, whether mountain or desert. Such places are Andermatt and Airolo, lying at an altitude of 4000 feet or more on the St. Gotthard road, St. Moritz below the Maloja Pass, Jaca near the Pass de Canfranc over the Pyrenees, Kugiar and Shahidula[51] at an elevation of 10,775 feet or 3285 meters on the road up to the Karakorum Pass (18,548 feet or 5655 meters), which crosses the highest range of the Himalayas between Leh in the upper Indus Valley and Yarkand in Chinese Turkestan.

Lower settlements. Farther down the transverse valley the type of settlement changes where side valleys, leading down from other passes, converge and help build up a distributing center for a considerable highland area. Such a point is Chiavenna in northern Italy, located above the head of Lake Como at the junction of the Mera and Liro valleys, which lead respectively to the Splügen and Maloja passes. It lies at an altitude of 1090 feet (332 meters) and has a population of 4000. Such a point is Aosta (1913 feet or 583 meters elevation) in the Dora Baltea Valley, commanding the Italian approaches to the Great St. Bernard Pass, and the less important Col de Fenêtre leading to the upper Rhone, the Little St. Bernard highway to the valley of the Isère, and Col de la Seigne path around the Mont Blanc range to the valley of the Arve. Aosta was an important place in the Roman period and has to-day a population of about 8000. Kokan, in the upper Sir-Daria Valley in Russian Turkestan, commands the approach to the passes of the western Tian Shan and the northern Pamir. Its well-stocked bazaars, containing goods from Russia, Persia and India, testify to its commercial location.

When the highland area is very broad and therefore neces- Pass cities
sitates long transit journeys, genuine pass cities develop and their
at high altitudes, and become the termini of the transmontane markets.
trade. Such is the Leh (11,280 feet or 3439 meters) on the
caravan route from Central Asia over the Karakorum Pass
down to Kashmir, and such is Srinagar (5252 feet or 1603
meters) in Kashmir. To their markets come caravans from
Chinese Turkestan, laden with carpets and brick tea, and
Tibetan merchants from Lhassa, bringing wool from their
highland pastures to exchange for the rice and sugar of lowland India.[52] Leh is conveniently situated about half way
between the markets of India and Central Asia. Therefore
it is the terminus for caravans arriving from both regions, and
exchange place for products from north and south. Seldom
do caravans from either direction go farther than this point.
Here the merchants rest for a month or two and barter their
goods. Tents of every kind, camels, yaks, mules and horses,
coolie transports of various races, men of many languages
and many religions, give to this high-laid town a truly cosmopolitan stamp in the summer time when the passes are open.[53]
Kabul, which lies at an altitude of nearly 6000 feet near the
head of the Kabul River, is the focus of numerous routes
over the Hindu Kush, and dominates all routes converging
on the northwest frontier of the Punjab.[54] It is therefore
the military and commercial key to India. Its narrow
winding streets are obstructed by the picturesque *kafilas* of
Oriental merchants, stocked with both Russian goods from the
Oxus districts and British goods from India in evidence of
its intermediary location.[55]

Occasionally a very high market develops for purely local
use. The Indian Himalayan province of Kumaon contains
the market town of Garbyang, at an elevation of 10,300 feet
or about 3000 meters, on the Kali River road leading by
the Lipu Lekh Pass (16,780 feet or 5115 meters) over to
Tibet. It has grown up as a trade center for the Dokpa
Tibetans, who will not descend below 10,000 feet because their
yak and sheep die at a lower altitude.[56] Farther east in the
Sikkim border, Darjeeling (7150 feet or 2180 meters elevation) is center of the British wool trade with Tibet.

Often the exchange point moves nearer the summit of the pass, dividing the journey more equally between the two areas of production. Here develops the temporary summer market. High up on the route between Leh and Yarkand is Sasar, a place of unroofed enclosures for the deposit of cotton, silk and other goods left there by the caravans plying back and forth between Leh and Sasar, or Sasar and Yarkand.[57] Nearly midway on the much frequented trade route between Leh and Lhassa, at a point 15,100 feet (nearly 500 meters) above sea level, just below the Schako Pass, lies Gartok in western Tibet, in summer a busy market surrounded by a city of tents, and the summer residence of the two Chinese viceroys, who occupy the only two substantial dwellings in the place. Here at the end of August is held a great annual fair, which is attended by traders from India, Kashmir, Mongolia, Chinese Turkestan, China proper, and Lhassa; but by November the place is deserted. The traders disperse, and the few residents of Gartok, together with the viceroys, retire down the Indus Valley to the more sheltered village of Gargunza (14,140 feet or 4311 meters elevation), which represents the limits of permanent settlement in these altitudes.[58] The Sutlej Valley route from the Punjab to Lhassa is capped near its summit at an altitude of about 5000 meters by the summer market of Gyanema, whose numerous types of tents indicate the various homes of the traders from Lhassa to India.[59]

Pass peoples.

Natural thoroughfares, whether river highways or mountain pass routes, draw to themselves migration, travel, trade and war. They therefore early assume historical importance. Hence we find that peoples controlling transmontane routes have always been able to exert an historical influence out of proportion to their size and strength; and that in consequence they early become an object of conquest to the people of the lowlands, as soon as these desire to control such transit routes. The power of these pass tribes is often due to the trade which they command and which compensates them for the unproductive character of their country. In the eastern Himalayas the Tomos of the Chumbi Valley are intermediaries of trade between Darjeeling and Tibet. In the western

Himalayas, the Kumaon borderland of northern India, which commands some of the best passes, has made its native folk or Bhutias bold merchants who jealously monopolize the trade over the passes to the Tibetan markets. They stretch for a zone of thirty miles south of the boundary from Nepal to Garhwal along the approach to every pass, each sub-group having its particular trade route.[60]

It is always possible for such pass tribes to levy a toll or **Transit** transit duty on merchandise, or in lieu of this to rob. Cæsar **duties.** made war upon the Veragri and Seduni, who commanded the northern end of the Great St. Bernard Pass, in order to open up the road over the Alps, which was traversed by Roman merchants *magno cum periculo magnisque cum portoriis.*[61] The Salassi, who inhabited the upper Dora Baltea Valley and hence controlled the Little St. Bernard wagon road leading over to Lugdunum or Lyons, regularly plundered or taxed all who attempted to cross their mountains. On one occasion they levied a toll of a drachm per man on a Roman army, and on another plundered the treasure of Cæsar himself. After a protracted struggle they were crushed by Augustus, who founded Aosta and garrisoned it with a body of Praetorian cohorts to police the highway.[62] The Iapodes in the Julian Alps controlled the Mount Ocra or Peartree Pass, which carried the Roman wagon road from Aquileia over the mountains down to the valley of the Laibach and the Save. This strategic position they exploited to the utmost, till Augustus brought them to subjection as a preliminary to Roman expansion on the Danube.[63]

Turning to another part of the world, we find that the Afghan tribes commanding the passes of the Suleiman Mountains have long been accustomed to impose transit duties upon caravans plying between Turkestan and India. The merchants have regularly organized themselves into bands of hundreds or even thousands to resist attack or exorbitant exactions. The Afghans have always enforced their right to collect tolls in the Khaibar and Kohat passes, and have thus blackmailed every Indian dynasty for centuries. In 1881 the British government came to terms with them by paying them an annual sum to keep these roads open.[64] Just to the south the Gomal Pass, which carries the main traffic road over the border mountains between the Punjab and the Afghan city of Ghazni, is held by the brigand tribe of Waziris, and is a dangerous gauntlet to be run by every armed caravan passing to and from India.[65] The Ossetes of the Caucasus, who occupy the Pass of Dariel and the approaching valleys, regularly preyed upon the traffic moving between Russia and Georgia, till the Muscovite government seized and policed the road.[66]

Strategic power of pass states.   The strategic importance of pass peoples tends early to assume a political aspect. The mountain state learns to exploit this one advantage of its ill-favored geographical location. The cradle of the old Savoyard power in the late Middle Ages lay in the Alpine lands between Lake Geneva and the western tributaries of the Po River. This location controlling several great mountain routes between France and Italy gave the Savoyard princes their first importance.[67] The autonomy of Switzerland can be traced not less to the citadel character of the country and the native independence of its people, than to their political exploitation of their strategic position. They profited, moreover, by the wish of their neighbors that such an important transit region between semi-tropical and temperate Europe should be held by a power too weak to obstruct its routes. The Amir of Kabul, backed by the rapacious Afridi tribes of the Suleiman Mountains, has been able to play off British India against Russia, and thereby to secure from both powers a degree of consideration not usually shown to inferior nations. Similarly in colonial America, the Iroquois of the Mohawk depression, who commanded the passway from the Hudson to the fur fields of the Northwest and also the avenue of attack upon the New York settlements for the French in Canada, were early conciliated by the English and used by them as allies, first in the French wars and afterward in the Revolution.

NOTES TO CHAPTER XV

1. For physical effects, see Angelo Mosso, Life of Man on the High Alps. Translated from the Italian. London, 1898.

2. W. Z. Ripley, Races of Europe, pp. 463-465. New York, 1899.

3. Strabo, Book IV, chap. VI, 3.

4. W. Z. Ripley, Races of Europe, pp. 31-32. New York, 1899.

5. Sir Thomas Holdich, India, pp. 32-33. London, 1905.

6. W. Z. Ripley, The Races of Europe, Map p. 439. New York, 1899.

7. Imperial Gazetteer of India, Vol. I, pp. 294-295. Oxford, 1907. Sir Thomas Holdich, India, relief map on p. 171 compared with linguistic map p. 201. London, 1905.

8. Census of India for 1901, Risley and Gait, Vol. I, Part I, p. 2. Calcutta, 1903. B. H. Baden-Powell, The Indian Village Community, pp. 40, 130, 131. London, 1896.

9. Count Gleichen, The Egyptian Sudan, Vol. I, pp. 184, 185, 190. London, 1905.

10. Gustav Nachtigal, *Sahara und Sudan*, Vol. III, pp. 178, 188-192. Leipzig, 1889.

11. Spencer and Gillen, The Northern Tribes of Central Australia, pp. 6, 13. London, 1904.

12. W. Deecke, Italy, p. 365. London, 1904.

13. Sir Thomas Holdich, India, pp. 295-296. London, 1905. G. W. Steevens, In India, pp. 202-204. New York, 1899.

14. Francis Younghusband, The Heart of a Continent, pp. 138, 140, 145, 272-273. London, 1904.

15. E. Huntington, The Pulse of Asia, p. 87. Boston, 1907.

16. E. C. Semple, American History and Its Geographic Conditions, pp. 184-185. Boston, 1903.

17. Isabella Bird Bishop, The Yangtze Valley and Beyond, Vol. II, pp. 70-72, 88, 91. London, 1900.

18. Francis H. Nichols, Through Hidden Shensi, pp. 170-171. New York, 1902.

19. Otis T. Mason, Primitive Travel and Transportation, pp. 450-454, 474-475. Smithsonian Report, Washington, 1896.

20. Col. George E. Church, The Acre Territory and the Caoutchouc Regions of Southwestern Amazonia, *Geog. Jour.* May, 1904. London.

21. M. Huc, Journey through the Chinese Empire, pp. 39-40. New York, 1871.

22. Perceval Landon, The Opening of Tibet, pp. 54-55. New York, 1905.

23. Jean Baptiste Tavernier, Travels in India. Vol. II, p. 264. Translated from the French of 1676. London, 1889.

24. E. F. Knight, Where Three Empires Meet, pp. 231, 274, 276, 286-289. London, 1897.

25. Census of the Philippine Islands, Vol. I, p. 544. Washington, 1905.

26. Joseph Partsch, Central Europe, p. 134. London, 1903.

27. M. S. W. Jefferson, Cæsar and the Central Plateau of France, *Journal of Geog.*, Vol. VI, p. 113. New York, 1897.

28. P. Vidal de la Blache, *Tableau de la Géographie de la France*, p. 276. Paris, 1903.

29. E. A. Freeman, Historical Geography of Europe, Vol. I, p. 450-453. London, 1882.

30. William Morris Davis, Physical Geography, p. 183. Boston, 1899.

31. P. Vidal de la Blache, *Tableau de la Géographie de la France*, p. 260, map p. 261. Paris, 1903.

556 MOUNTAIN BARRIERS AND PASSES

32. Indian Census for 1901, Risley and Gait, Vol. I, Part I, pp. 1, 2. Calcutta, 1903.
33. Hans Helmolt, History of the World, Vol. IV, p. 479. New York, 1902.
34. Sir Thomas Holdich, India, p. 67, cartogram of Hindu Kush orography. London, 1905.
35. *Ibid.*, pp. 102-104.
36. *Ibid.*, p. 26.
37. J. Partsch, Central Europe, p. 27. London, 1903.
38. B. H. Baden-Powell, The Indian Village Community, pp. 40-45, 111, 116. London, 1896.
39. H. R. Mill, International Geography, pp. 394-395. New York, 1902.
40. Gottfried Merzbacher, *Aus den Hochregionen des Kaukasus*, pp. 73-78. Leipzig, 1901.
41. W. Z. Ripley, The Races of Europe, p. 438. New York, 1899.
42. *Ibid.*, Maps pp. 143, 147, text p. 148.
43. E. Huntington, The Pulse of Asia, pp. 106-109. Boston, 1907.
44. W. Z. Ripley, The Races of Europe, pp. 249-253. New York, 1899.
45. *Ibid.*, p. 282 and cartogram, p. 284.
46. Sir Thomas Holdich, India, p. 201. London, 1905. Imperial Gazetteer of India, Vol. I, p. 295. Oxford, 1907.
47. Census of India, 1901, Ethnographic Appendices, Vol. I, p. 60, by H. H. Risley, Calcutta, 1903. C. A. Sherring, Western Tibet and the British Borderland, pp. 341-353. London, 1906.
48. E. Lavisse, *Histoire de France*, Vol. II, Part 1, p. 294. Paris, 1903.
49. George Adam Smith, Historical Geography of the Holy Land, pp. 383, 384, 391-400, 407, 409. New York, 1897.
50. Wilhelm Deecke, Italy, pp. 20, 21. London, 1904.
51. Francis Younghusband, The Heart of a Continent, pp. 150, 194, 199. London, 1904.
52. E. F. Knight, Where Three Empires Meet, pp. 12, 88, 157-159, 231. London, 1897.
53. *Ibid.*, pp. 173, 177.
54. Sir Thomas Holdich, India, map p. 85, pp. 86, 89. London, 1905.
55. Vambery, *Reise in Mittelasien*, pp. 371-375. Leipzig, 1973.
56. C. A. Sherring, Western Tibet and the British Borderland, p. 136. London, 1906.
57. O. P. Crosby, Tibet and Turkestan, pp. 112-116. New York, 1903.
58. Elisée Reclus, Asia, Vol. II, pp. 50-51. C. A Sherring, Western Tibet and the British Borderland, pp. 146-148, 152, 157, 300-303. London, 1906.
59. *Ibid.*, pp. 326-327.
60. *Ibid.*, pp. 4, 61-64, 310-311.
61. *Bello Gallico*, Book III, chap. I.
62. Strabo, Book IV, chap. VI, 7, 11.
63. Strabo, Book IV, chap. VI, 10.
64. Sir Thomas Holdich, The Indian Borderland, p. 48. London, 1909.
65. H. R. Mill, International Geography, p. 467. New York, 1902.
66. Pallas, Travels Through the Southern Provinces of Russia, Vol. I, p. 431. London, 1812.
67. E. A. Freeman, Historical Geography of Europe, Vol. I, pp. 286-287. London, 1882.

CHAPTER XVI

INFLUENCES OF A MOUNTAIN ENVIRONMENT

THERE are zones of latitude and zones of altitude. To Zones of altitude. every mountain region both these pertain, resulting in a nice interplay of geographic factors. Every mountain slope from summit to piedmont is, from the anthropo-geographical standpoint, a complex phenomenon. When high enough, it may show a graded series of contrasted complementary locations, closely interdependent grouping of populations and employments, every degree of density from congestion to vacancy, every range of cultural development from industrialism to nomadism. The southern slope of the Monte Rosa Alps, from the glacier cap at 4500 meters to the banks of the Po River, yields within certain limits a zonal epitome of European life from Lapland to the Mediterranean. The long incline from the summit of Mount Everest (8840 meters) in the eastern Himalayas, through Darjeeling down to sea level at Calcutta, comprises in a few miles the climatic and cultural range of Asia from Arctic to Tropic.

For the state, a territory of varied relief is highly benefi- Politico-economic value of varied relief. cial, because it combines manifold forms of economic activity, a wide range of crops, areas of specialized production mutually interdependent. It induces a certain balance of urban and rural life, which contributes greatly to the health of the state.[1] The steep slopes of Dai Nippon, fertile only under spade tillage, will forever insure Japan the persistence of a numerous peasantry. For geological and geographical reasons, as from national motives, therefore, Japan will probably never sacrifice its farmer to its industrial class, as England has done. On the other hand, contrasted reliefs on a great territorial scale tend to invade political solidarity. Tidewater and mountain Virginia were poor running-mates for a century before the Civil War, and then the mountain region broke out of harness. Geographical contrasts made the unification of Germany difficult, and yet they have added to the economic and national strength of the Empire. The history of Switzerland shows the high Alpine cantons always maintaining a political tug of war with the cantons of the marginal plain, and always suffering a defeat which was their salvation.

Relief and climate.

The chief effect of a varied relief is a varied climate. This changes with altitude in much the same way as with latitude. Heat and absolute humidity diminish, generally speaking, as height increases, while rainfall becomes greater up to a certain level. The effect of ascending and descending currents of air is to diminish the range of temperature on mountain slopes and produce rather an oceanic type of climate. The larger and more uniform a climatic district, the more conspicuously do even slight elevations form climatic islands, like the Harz Mountains in the North German lowlands. A land of monotonous relief has a uniform climate, while a region rich in vertical articulations is rich also in local varieties of climate.[2] A highland of considerable elevation forms a cold district in the Temperate Zone, a temperate one in the Tropics, and a moist one in a desert or steppe. Especially in arid and torrid belts does the value of elevation for human life increase.

Altitude zones of economic and cultural development.

The highlands of Mexico, South America and the Himalayan rim of India show stratified zones of tropical, temperate, and arctic climate, to which plant, animal and human life conform. The response is conspicuous in the varying density of population in the successive altitude zones. Central Asia shows a threefold cultural stratification of its population, each attended by the appropriate density, according to location in steppe, piedmont and mountain. The steppes have their scattered pastoral nomads; the piedmonts, with their irrigation streams, support sedentary agricultural peoples, concentrated at focal points in commercial and industrial towns; the higher reaches of the mountains are occupied by sparse groups of peasants and shepherds, wringing from upland pasture and scant field a miserable subsistence. The same stratification appears in the Atlas Mountains, intensified on the southern slope by the contrast between the closely populated belt of the piedmont and the wandering Tuareg tribes of the Sahara on the one hand, and the sparse Berber settlements of the Atlas highlands on the other. The long slope of Mount Kilimanjaro in German East Africa descends to a coastal belt of steppe and desert, inhabited by Swahili cattle-breeders. Its piedmont, from 1000 feet above the plain up to 2400 feet, constitutes a zone of rich irrigated plantations and gardens, densely populated by peaceful folk of mingled Bantu and Hamitic blood. At 6000 feet, where forests cease, are found the kraals, cattle, sheep and goats of the semi-nomadic Masai of doubtful Hamitic stock, who raid the coastal lowlands for cattle, and purchase all their vegetable food from the tillage belt.[3] [See maps page 105 and 487.]

This stratification assumes marked variations in the different geographical zones. In Greenland life is restricted

DENSITY OF POPULATION IN ITALY.

to the piedmont coastal belt; above this rises the desert waste of the ice fields. Norway shows a tide-washed piedmont, containing a large majority of the population; above this, a steep slope sparsely inhabited; and higher still, a wild plateau summit occupied in summer only by grazing herds or migrant reindeer Lapps. Farther south the Alps show successive tiers of rural economy, again with their appropriate density of settlement. On their lower slope is found the vineyard belt, a region of highly intensive tillage, large returns upon labor, and hence of closely distributed settlement. Above that is the zone of field agriculture, less productive and less thickly peopled. Higher still is the wide zone of hay farming and stock-raising, supporting a sparse, semi-nomadic population and characterized by villages which diminish with the altitude and cease beyond 2000 meters. On Aetna, located in the tropical Mediterranean, three girdles of altitude have long been recognized,—the girdle of agriculture, the forest belt, and the desert summit. But the tourist who ascends Aetna, passes from the coast through a zone of orange and lemon groves, which are protected by temporary matting roofs against occasional frosts; then through vineyards and olive orchards which rise to 800 meters; then through a belt of summer crops rising to 1550 meters, and varied between 1400 and 1850 meters elevation by stretches of chestnut groves, whose green expanse is broken here and there by the huts of the forest guards, the highest tenants of the mountain. From these lonely dwellings down to the sea, density of population increases regularly to a maximum of over 385 to the square mile (150 to the square kilometer) near the coast.

Altitude and density belts in tropical highlands. In the tropical highlands of Mexico, Central and South America, on the other hand, concentration of population and its concomitant cultural development begin to appear above the 2000 meter line. Here are the chief seats of population. Mexico has three recognized altitude zones, the cold, the temperate and the hot, corresponding to plateau, high slopes and coastal piedmont up to 1000 meters or 3300 feet; but the first two contain nine-tenths of the people. While the plateau has in some sections a population dense as that of France, the lowlands are sparsely peopled by wild Indians and lumbermen. Ecuador has three-fourths of its population crowded into the plateau basins (mean elevation 8000 feet or 2500 meters) enclosed by the ranges of the Andes. Peru presents a similar distribution, with a comparatively dense population on a plateau reaching to 11,000 feet (3500 meters) or more, though its coastal belt, being healthful, dry, and fairly well supplied with irrigation streams from the Andes, is better developed than any other similar district in tropical America.[4] In Bolivia, 72 per cent. of the total population live at an altitude of 6000 to 14,000 feet, while five out of the nine most densely peopled provinces lie at elevations over 11,000 feet.[5] [See map page 9.]

From Mexico to central Chile, the heavy rains from the trade-winds clothe the slopes with dense forests, except on the lee side of the high Andean wall of Peru and Chile, and reduce much of the piedmont to malarial swamp and jungle. The discouragement to primitive tillage found in the unequal fight with a tropical forest, the dryer, more bracing and healthful climate of the high intermontane basins, their favorable conditions for agriculture by irrigation, and their naturally defined location stimulating to early cultural development, all combined to concentrate the population of prehistoric America upon the high valleys and plateaus. In historic times these centers have persisted, because the civilized or semi-civilized districts could be best exploited by the Spanish conquerors and especially because they yielded rich mineral wealth. Furthermore, the white population which has subsequently invaded tropical America has to a predominant degree reinforced the native plateau populations, while the imported negroes and mulattoes have sought the more congenial climatic conditions found in the hot lowlands.

The relativity of geographical advantages in different historical periods warns us against assuming in all times a sparsity of population in mountains, even when the adjoining lowlands offer many attractions of climate and soil. In ages of incessant warfare, when the motive of safety has strongly influenced distribution of population, protected mountain sites have attracted settlement from the exposed plains, and thus increased the relative density of population on the steep

Increasing density with motive of protection.

slopes. The corrugated plateau of Armenia and Kurdistan, located on the uneasy political frontier of Russia, Persia and Asiatic Turkey, exposed for centuries to nomadic invasion from the east, shows a sparser population on its broad intermontane plains than on the surrounding ranges. Security makes the latter the choicer places of residence. Hence they are held by the overbearing and marauding Kurds, late-comers into the land, while the older and numerically weaker Armenians cower down on the lower levels.[6] Here is an inversion of the usual order. The militantly stronger intruders, with no taste for agriculture, have seized the safer and commanding position on the hills, descending in winter with their cattle and horses to pasture and prey upon field and granary of the valley folk, whose better soil is a questionable advantage.

Motive of protection in primitive peoples. Instances of this sort, rare in modern times, because of general economic and social progress, multiply when we go into the history of primitive or ancient peoples. The Cherokee Indians of the Southern Appalachians, surrounded by powerful neighbors in the Chickasaws, Creeks and the encroaching whites of the seaboard colonies, attacked by war parties of Shawnees and Iroquois from the north, located the bulk of their nation in the mountains. The Overhill and Middle towns, numbering together thirty-three and situated wholly in the mountains, comprised four-fifths of their fighting force in 1775, while the nine towns distributed in the flat lands of Georgia and South Carolina were small and unimportant. The Indians themselves distinguished these two divisions of their country, the one as *Otarre* or mountainous, and the others as *Ayrate* or low.[7] Similarly in ancient Gaul the three strongest tribes, the Sequani, Aedui, and Arverni, all had a large mountain nucleus. The Sequani held the Jura range with part of the Saône Valley; the Aedui held the northeast corner of the Central Plateau and some lands on the Saône, while the Arverni inhabited the western and central portion of the same highland. In a period of constant tribal migrations and war, the occupants of these high, protected locations were better able to defend themselves, and they maintained an adequate food supply by holding some of the adjoining lowland. Archaeologists generally agree that in central and southern Italy settlement first took place in the mountains, gradually extending thence down into the plains. The superiority of the upland climate, the more abundant rainfall, the greater security against attack offered by mountain sites, and the excellent soil for agriculture resulting from the geological make-up of the Apennines, all combined to draw thither primitive and later settlement.[8] [See map page 559.] Similarly in Britain of the Bronze Age, before the peoples of Aryan speech began to swarm over the island, the primitive inhabitants, involved in constant clan or tribal warfare, placed their villages on the hills, and left in the indestructible terraces on their slopes the evidences of a vanished race and an outgrown social order.[9]

The advance of civilization, which brought the ancient pirate-ridden city from the inner edge of the coastal zone down to the wave-washed strand, also drew the hill town down to the plain, and the mountain population from their inaccessible strongholds to the more accessible and productive valleys. These facts contain a hint. The future investigation of archaeological remains in high mountain districts may reveal at considerable elevations the oldest and hence lowest strata of prehistoric development, strata which, in the more attractive valleys, have been obliterated or overlaid by later invasions of peoples and cultures. Ignoring this temporary attraction of population to protected mountain locations in ages of persistent warfare, we find that a comparison of many countries reveals a decreasing food supply and decreasing density of population, with every increase of height above a certain altitude, except in favored mining regions and in some tropical lands, where better climatic conditions and freedom from malaria distribute settlements far above the steaming and forest-choked lowlands. The density of population in mountains is influenced also by the composition of the soil, which affects its fertility; by the grade and exposure of the slopes, which determine the ease and success of tillage; by the proximity of the highlands to teeming centers of lowland population, and by the general economic development of the people.

Geographic conditions affecting density of mountain population.

In Great Britain, the sparsest population is found in the sterile highland moors of Scotland, where the county of

Sutherland has only 11 inhabitants to the square mile, Inverness only 20.[10] These figures reveal also the remoteness of a far northern location. In the southern half of the island the sparsest populations are found in the Welsh county of Radnor, with 49 to the square mile, and in English Westmoreland with 85, both of them mountain regions, but reflecting in their larger figures their close proximity to the teeming industrial centers of South Wales and Lancashire respectively. In France the most thinly settled *départements* are Basses-Alpes with 43 to the square mile and Hautes-Alpes with 50, which again owe even these figures in part to their situation on the margin of the densely populated valley of the middle Rhone. [See map page 559.] Norway, almost wholly a mountain country, averages only 18 souls to the square mile. Less than a thousand square miles of its territory are under cultivation, and these are distributed in small deltas at the heads of the fiords, in low strips here and there along its western coasts, or in the openings of its mountain valleys to the southeast. Here too is massed the larger part of its inhabitants. A barren granitic soil, unfavorable zonal location, excessive rainfall, paucity of level land, leaving the "upright farm" predominant, and remoteness from any thickly settled areas, together with the resulting enormous emigration, have combined to keep down Norway's population.

Sparsity of population in the Alps. If we turn to Switzerland, a country poor in the resources of its land but rich in the resourcefulness of its people, we find a high average density, 218 to the square mile; but this is due to the surprising industrial development of the marginal plains, which show in the Canton of Geneva 1356 to the square mile, and in Canton Zurich 705, while the rugged upland of Graubünden (Grisons) shows only 38 to the square mile, Uri only 48, and Wallis (Valais) only 59. How limited is the food supply of the country is evident from the fact that only 2400 square miles, or fifteen per cent. of its area, can be ranked as arable land, fit for garden, orchard or grain field, while a larger proportion, or twenty-eight per cent, is made wholly useless by watercourses, glaciers, rock and detritus. One half of the entire country lies above the region where agriculture is possible. In the Cantons of Uri and Valais, more than half the area is absolutely unproductive, scarcely less in the Grisons, and a third even in sunny Ticino.[11] The three strictly Alpine provinces of Austria, Tyrol, Salzburg and Carinthia, reproduce approximately these geographic conditions. Nearly half of their area is uninhabited, and only one-seventh consists of arable land. In consequence they support only 75 inhabitants to the square mile, while just outside the mountains, in the piedmont or Alpine fore-land, this density is doubled.[12] Many tracts of the Carpa-thians, especially about the sources of the Theiss and Pruth and the wooded mountain borders of Transylvania, are among the most sparsely inhabited parts of Europe.[13] Japan, ridged by steep volcanic ranges, drenched by mountain-born rains, strewn with detritus from plunging torrents, can cultivate only 15.7 per cent. of its area, and is forced to leave 59 per cent. in forest reserves.[14]

These figures tell of the hard conditions of life character- Terrace
istic of most mountain regions. Population under normal agriculture.
circumstances settles in the narrow valleys between the ranges and along the borders of their drainage stream. Soon, however, the food supply becomes inadequate for the growing numbers, so that artificial means have to be employed to ex-pand the area of arable land. The soil on the mountain slopes is so thin that it yields only a scanty return to the labor of tillage. Moreover, under the operations of plough-ing and harrowing, it is exposed to the danger of washing; so that after a few croppings the underlying rock of the mountain side may be laid bare, and all that was valuable in the quondam field deposited in the valley as silt or swept away to enrich the distant delta of the nearest trunk river.

To obviate this difficulty and to secure the desired increase of arable land, mountain peoples the world over have resorted to terrace agriculture. This means hand-made fields. Par-allel walls, one above the other, are constructed on horizontal lines across the face of the steep slopes, and the intervals between are filled with earth, carried thither in baskets on the peasants' backs. The soil must be constantly renewed and enriched by manure in the same way, and the masonry of the retaining walls kept in repair. Whenever possible these costly terraced fields are located by preference on southward facing slopes, where the tilt of the land makes the fields catch the rays of the sun almost at right angles and thus counteracts the chill of the higher altitude, while the mountain behind protects the growing crops from cold northern winds. Good arable land, being limited in amount, commands a high price; and especially do choice terraced fields in vine-growing countries, since they make the best vineyards. Such fields in Switzerland will bring from $300 to $2,000 an acre, and are estimated to produce annually two bottles of wine for every square foot.[15]

Geographical distribution.   Terrace agriculture, rare in new countries, in the more densely populated Old World is widely distributed in mountainous areas. In Germany, where it is nearly identical with the culture of the vine, it is found along the steep slopes overlooking the valley of the Moselle and the Rhine; also in the Vosges Mountains, the Black Forest and the Swabian Jura, to the limited altitude in which the vine will flourish in these northern regions. In the Alps it is widespread, and not confined to the culture of the vine. The traveler passing along the upper Rhone through the sunny Canton of Valais follows these terraced fields almost as far as Fiesch (altitude 3458 feet), beyond which agriculture proper becomes more and more restricted on account of the elevation, and passes rapidly into the mere hay-making of a pastoral community. Between Leuk and Sierre, not only the mountain sides, but also the steep gravel hills constituting the old terminal moraine deposited by the receding Rhone glacier across the valley floor, are terraced to their very tops.

Terrace cultivation prevails in the mountains of Italy; it is utilized not only for the vine, but for olives, maize, oats, hemp, rye and flax. On the gentler declivities of the Apennines, the terraced walls are wider apart and lower than on the steep slopes of the Ligurian Apennines and along the Riviera of the Maritime Alps, where the mountains rise abruptly from the margin of the sea.[16] Careful and laborious terrace cultivation has produced in Italy a class of superior gardeners. The Genoese are famous for their skill in this sort of culture. The men from the Apennine plateau of the

Abruzzi readily find positions in the lowlands as expert gardeners.[17]

The Saracens of Spain in the tenth century converted Terrace every mountain slope into a succession of green terraces. culture They built walls of heavy masonry, and brought water, loam, of the and fertilizing materials from great distances. The slopes of Saracens. Granada back of Malaga and Almeria were covered with vineyards. Every foot of land susceptible of cultivation was turned to account, every drop of water from the ill-timed winter rains was conserved for the growing season. The application of intelligence and labor to tillage enabled the Hispano-Arab provinces to support a dense population.[18] These Saracen cultivators had come from the severest training school in all Eurasia. Where the arid tableland of Arabia is buttressed on the southwestern front by high coast ranges (6000 to 10,500 feet or 2000 to 3200 meters) is Yemen, rich in its soil of disintegrated trap rock, adequately watered by the dash of the southwest monsoons against its towering ridges; but practically the whole country is atilt. Consequently the mountains have been terraced from the base often up to 6000 feet. The country presents the aspect of vast agricultural amphitheaters, in which the narrow paths of ancient paving zigzag up and up through successive zones of production. Here is a wide range of fruits—oranges, lemons, figs, dates, bananas and coffee; then apricots, apples, plums, grapes, quinces, peaches, together with grains of various zonal distribution, such as millet, maize, wheat and barley. The terrace walls are from five to eight feet high, but toward the top of the mountains they often increase to fifteen feet. Though laid without mortar, they are kept in perfect repair. Reservoirs filled with water from the two rainy seasons, supply the irrigation channels.[19] In the narrow valleys of the Nejd plateau in central Arabia and on the mountain slopes of Oman are found the same irrigated gardens and terraced plantations. This laborious tillage underlay the prosperity of the ancient Sabaean monarchy of Yemen, as it explains the population of 35,000 souls who occupy the modern capital of Sanaa, located at an altitude of 7600 feet (2317 meters).[20] In the

Turning eastward, we find terrace agriculture widely dis- Himalayas.

tributed in Himalayan lands. The steep mountain sides of the Vale of Kashmir are cultivated thus to a considerable height. The terraces are irrigated by contour channels constructed along the hillsides, which bring the water for miles from distant snow-fed streams. Their shelf-like fields are green with fruit orchards and almond groves, with vineyards and grain fields.[21] The terraced slopes about the Himalayan hill-station of Simla (elevation 7100 to 8000 feet) feed the summer population of English, who there take refuge from the deadly heat of the plains. The mountain sections of the native states of Nepal and Bhutan present the view of slopes cut into gigantic stairs, each step a field of waving rice kept saturated by irrigating streams from abundant mountain springs. Farther north, where Himalayas and Hindu Kush meet, terrace agriculture is combined with irrigation in the high Gilgit valleys, and farther still along that mere gash running down from the Pamir dome, called the Hunza Valley. Here live the once lawless robber tribes of the Hunzas and Nagaris, whose conquest cost the British a dangerous and expensive campaign in 1892, but whose extensive terraces of irrigated fields and evidences of skillful tillage gave the whole country an appearance of civilization strangely at variance with the barbarous character of its inhabitants.[22]

In Tibet and China. North of the outer Himalayan range, near the sources of the Indus and Sutlej rivers in Ladak or Western Tibet, this same form of cultivation has been resorted to by the retarded and isolated Mongolian inhabitants. Here at an altitude of 11,000 feet or more (3354 meters), along mountain ranges of primitive rock yielding only a scant and sterile soil, terraces are laboriously constructed; their surfaces are manured with burnt remains of animal excrements, which must first serve as fuel in this timberless land before they are applied to the ground. In this stronghold of Buddhism almost every lamasery has its terraced fields yielding good crops of grain and fruit.[23] In the densely populated Sze Chuan province of western China, cultivation has climbed from the fertile basins of the Min and upper Yangtze rivers far up the surrounding mountains, where it is carried on terraces to the foot of vertical ,cliffs.[24] Farther north where the mountain province of Shensi occupies the rise of land from the Chinese lowlands to the central highlands of Asia, terraces planted with wheat or other grains cover the mountain slopes.[25]

Terrace tillage is rare in new countries of extensive plains, In ancient like the United States and Canada, where the level lands still Peru. suffice for the agricultural needs of the people; but in the confined mountain basins and valleys which made up the Inca's territory in ancient Peru, every available natural field was utilized for cultivation, and terraces brought the obstinate mountain sides under the dominion of the Andean peasant. They were constructed, a hundred or more in number, rising 1000 or 1500 feet above the floor of the highland valley, contracting in width as they rose, till the uppermost one was a narrow shelf only two feet broad. These were extended by communal labor year after year, with increase of population, just as to-day in Java and the neighboring islands, and became the property of the Inca. Streams from the higher slopes were conducted in canals and distributed from terrace to terrace, to irrigate and fertilize. These terraces therefore yielded the best crops of potatoes, maize and pulse. The cultivable area was further extended by floating gardens, consisting of rafts covered with earth, which floated on the surface of lakes.[26] They existed in ancient Mexico also,[27] and are used to-day in the lakes and streams of Tibet and Kashmir[28] and the rivers of overcrowded China.

Mountainous islands, born of volcanic forces or the partial Terrace submergence of coastal ranges, have steep surfaces and scant agriculture lowlands. Their inhabitants command limited area at best. in moun- tainous Driven to agriculture by their isolation, drawn to it by the islands. favorable oceanic climate, such islands develop terrace tillage in its most pronounced form. On the precipitous pitch of Teneriffe, every particle of alluvial soil is collected to make gardens. Long lines of camels, laden with boxes of earth, may be seen coming almost daily into the town of Santa Cruz, bringing soil for the terraces.[29] This is desperate agriculture. Irrigated terraces scar the steep slopes of many Polynesian islands.[30] They are highly developed among the Malay Battaks of Sumatra, especially for rice culture.[31] In Java, Bali and Lombok they reach a perfection hardly equalled elsewhere in the world. In Java they begin at an altitude of 1000 feet, cutting main and branch valleys into amphitheaters, and covering hundreds of square miles.[32] On the volcanic slopes of Lombok the terrace plots vary from many acres to a few square yards, according to the grade, while a complete system of irrigation uses every brook to water the terraces. Here as in Java the work began at a very early period, when it was probably introduced among the native Malays by Brahmans from India.[33] Japan, two-thirds of whose area is mountainous, has terraced its steep valley walls often up to 2000 feet or more, and utilized every patch of ground susceptible of tillage.[34]

Among mountain savages. A mountain environment often occasions a forced development in the form of agriculture among peoples who otherwise still linger in a low stage of barbarism or savagery. The wild, head-hunting Igorots, inhabiting the Cordilleras of north central Luzon, have levelled the face of their mountains into a series of platforms, held by retaining walls from twenty to thirty feet high. On these they cultivate upland rice at an altitude of 5000 feet. The Igorot province of Bontoc contains valleys in which every available foot of land is terraced for rice, and which present artificial landscapes vividly recalling Japan. Labor is the heritage of each inhabitant. Every man, woman and child down to ten years of age shares in the work of providing food.[35] Africa shows parallel cases. The Angoss people, a savage negro tribe who occupy part of the Murchison Range in northern Nigeria, have mapped out all their sloping land into little terraces, sometimes only a foot or two wide. One of their peaks, 4135 feet high, has its plateau top covered with populous villages, owing to the protection of the site, and every inch of its slope cut into terraces planted with millet and guinea corn.[36] A more primitive form of this tillage is found in the country of the Marunga negroes, who occupy the steep western face of the rift valley filled by Lake Tanganyika. Here Cameron found the surface not regularly terraced, but retaining walls of loose stones disposed at intervals, which served to hold the soil in place, without greatly altering the natural slope. The scene recalled the terraced heights of Switzerland, and the people working there looked like flies on a wall.[37] In the semi-arid country of Sudanese Darfur, where only the mountain districts are well watered and thickly populated, small terraces for grain and melons cover all the slopes.[38]

Mountain agriculture is necessarily laborious. The paucity of arable land precludes the possibility of letting fields lie fallow. These, to prevent exhaustion, must be constantly and abundantly fertilized, all the more as conditions of excessive subaërial denudation found in the steep slope and usual heavy rainfall of mountains, as well as possible glacial scouring of the land in the past, have greatly attenuated the layer of soil called upon to support plant life. The Swiss or Tyrolese farmer cherishes his manure pile as at once source and badge of his wealth. After harvest it is carted or carried in baskets not only to the terraces, but also to the wide alluvial fan that grows his oats and rye, to his meadows and hay fields. Both in Mexico and Peru the soil received a dressing of poudrette. Manuring was most extensive where population was densest, as in the isolated mountain valleys opening out upon the desert coast of Peru. Every kind of organic refuse was utilized, and fish was buried with the kernels of maize as a fertilizer. The deposits of guano found on the headlands and off-shore islands were used from the remotest times. Different guano beds were assigned to the several provinces, and the breeding places of the birds were protected by law.[39] Ashes and decayed wood were employed for the same purpose, or plants were dug into the soil, while human manure was in Mexico a marketable commodity as in China.[40]

Fertilizing.

In all mountain regions where population has begun to press upon the meager limits of subsistence, level land and soil are at a premium. In ancient Peru space was begrudged for the dead.[41] Cities covered considerable space on the roomy intermontane plateaus; but in the narrow lateral valleys, houses and temples were built on rocks, in order to reserve every fertile spot for agriculture.[42] The traveler notices the same thing throughout the Alps. Compact villages cling to the mountain sides, leaving the alluvial hem of

Economy of level land for houses and villages.

the stream or level glacial terrace free for the much needed fields. Only in broad longitudinal valleys, like that of Ander-matt, do the settlements complacently spread out their skirts, or on wide alluvial fans where transverse valleys debouch upon the plains. The mountaineers of the Crimea construct their houses against the precipices, excavating into their face and building up the front with stones, and thus reserve the gentler slopes for vineyards and gardens.[43] In the Kangra, Kumaon, and Garhwal districts of the British Hima-layas, the large Indian villages of the plains give place to small hamlets or detached homesteads, scattered here and there wherever occasional patches of soil on a hillside or in a narrow valley offer hope of sustenance. These hamlets or dwellings are located on the sides of the mountains, because level spots which can be irrigated must be reserved for rice fields.[44] The high site is also freer from malaria.

Perpen-dicular villages. In the high Himalayan province of Ladak or Western Tibet, this principle of land economy reaches a climax. All settlement is on the perpendicular. The abrupt mountain sides are honey-combed with tombs, villages and Buddhist lamaseries in the detached localities where population occurs. A pleasure walk through one of these Tibetan towns means a climb by steep flights of steps hewn out of the rock, varied by a saunter up ladders, where the sheer face of a cliff must be surmounted to reach the houses on a ledge above.[45] Pictures of these recall forcibly the cliff-dwellings of the Pueblo Indians. Even the important market city of Leh covers the lower slope of the mountain at an altitude of 11,500 feet, and from its height overlooks the cultivated fields in the sandy valley bed below, made fertile by irrigating streams from debouching cañons.[46] The Ladak villages always shun the plains. The desire to economize level arable land does not alone dictate this choice of sites, however; the motive of pro-tection against inundation, when the snows melt and the streams swell, and also, to some degree, against hostile attack, is an additional factor. In the mountainous parts of over-crowded China, again, the food problem is the dominant motive. In the rugged highland province of Shensi, a village of several hundred people covers only a few acres, and rises in closely packed tiers of houses against the mountain side.[47] In the wilder, half-conquered parts of Sze Chuan the villages crown the lower peaks, cling to the base of the mountains, or are perched on ledges of rock overlooking the gorges. Among the steep cliffs bordering the upper Yangtze, occupied chiefly by the timid, displaced Mantze aborigines, at an altitude of 10,000 feet, small platforms resting on beams projecting from the sheer mountain face support minute houses, whose backs burrow into the cliff behind. The small children are tied to the door post, to keep them from falling into the millet field below. The house is accessible only by bolts driven into the cliff. Above and below is the farm—small patches of tilled soil, often not larger than a bath towel, to which the cultivator lowers himself by a rope.[48] Here life hovers on the brink of death and despair.

Paucity of arable land in mountain regions leads to the utilization of the untillable slopes for stock grazing. This industry is always a valuable ally to mountain agriculture on account of the manure which it yields; but in high altitudes, where the steepness or rockiness of the soil, cold and the brevity of the growing season restrict or eliminate cereal crops, it becomes the dominant occupation of the inhabitants, while agriculture takes a subordinate place, limited to the production of hay and fodder for the winter feeding of the stock. Above the line of tree growth flourish the natural summer pastures up to the border of perpetual snow; and just below lies a zone which, if cleared of its forests, supports a thick carpet of grass and herbage, though too cold to ripen grain.

Mountain pastures and stock-raising.

The high pastures are particularly nourishing. Cows feeding here in the Alps give better milk than the "home" or valley cows, though a smaller quantity. Sheep and goats do equally well, but swine are profitable only as a by-product, to utilize the refuse of the cheese and butter industry. The area of these pastures far exceeds that of arable land in mountain regions. In Switzerland they comprise about 27 per cent. of the total productive area; hay meadows 24 per cent., but fields and gardens only 20 per cent.[49] In the Austrian province of Salzburg, pastures make up 13.3 per cent., hay meadows 34.5 per cent., and tilled fields only 11.7

per cent. of the total productive area. In the Tyrol the figures are much the same.[50] Since Norway has over 67 per cent. of its total area in bare mountains, snow fields, bogs and lakes, it is not surprising to find only 7.6 per cent. in pastures, 2.2 per cent. in meadows, and 0.7 per cent. in grain fields; but here the pastures are ten times the arable area.[51] The season of the summer feeding on the grass lands is short. In the so-called High Alps it frequently lasts only six or seven weeks, in the Grisons at most thirteen weeks,[52] and in Norway from two to three months.[53]

High mountain regions, practically restricted to this *Graswirthschaft*, soon reach their maximum of prosperity and population. The amount of hay secured for the winter feeding limits the number of cattle, and the number of the cattle, through their manure, fixes the valley hay supply. Alpine pastures cannot be enlarged, and they may be reduced by accidents of nature, such as landslides, devastating torrents, or advance of ice fields or glaciers. They cannot be improved by capital and labor, and they may deteriorate chemically by exhaustion. The constant export of butter and cheese from Alpine pastures in recent times, without substitution by any fertilizer beyond the local manure, has caused the diminution of phosphoric acid in the soil and hence impoverishment. Canton Glarus has shown a steady decline since 1630 in the number of cows which its mountain pastures can support.[54] Many other Alpine districts show the same deterioration.

Mountain herdsmen and shepherds.

The remoteness of these highland pastures from the permanent villages necessitates *Sennenwirthschaft*, or the maintenance of out-farms and shepherds on the mountains during the grazing season. This involves a semi-nomadic existence for such inhabitants as serve as herdmen. In June, as soon as the high pastures begin to grow green, cattle, sheep and goats ascend step by step in the wake of summer, as she climbs the slope, and they return in autumn to the valleys. There they feed on the stubble of hay and grain fields, till the increasing cold confines them to their low stables. The hut of the *Senner* or *Saeter*, as the herdsman is variously called in Switzerland and Norway, consists of a living room and a smaller apartment for making butter and cheese, while against the steep slope is a rude stone shelter for the cattle and goats. The predominance of summer pastures has made cattle-raising a conspicuous part of agriculture in the Alps and in Norway. In many parts of Switzerland, cattle are called "wares" and the word cheese is used as a synonym for food, as we use bread. A Swiss peasant who has a reputation for cheese making is popular with the girls.[55] Here even Cupid turns dairy expert.

Since it is scarcely practicable to divide these highland pastures, they have generally remained communal property, whether in Norway,[56] Switzerland, the Bavarian Alps, the British Himalayan districts,[57] Nepal and Bhutan,[58] or Kashmir.[59] In Europe their use is generally regulated. As a rule, a Swiss villager may keep on the *Allmende* during the summer as many head of cattle as he is able to stall-feed during the winter. Any in excess of this number must be paid for at a fixed rate to the village or commune treasury.[60] Hay-sheds and herdsmen's huts mark these districts of temporary occupation near the altitude limits of human life throughout Europe. In Asia, likewise, are to be found small villages, inhabited only in summer by herdsmen tending their flocks. Such is the hamlet of Minemerg, located at an altitude of about 8000 feet at the southern entrance to the Borzil Pass over the Western Himalayas, and Sonamerg (altitude 8650 feet or 2640 meters) just below the Zogi La Pass, both of them surrounded by rich meadows on the northern rim of the Vale of Kashmir.[61]

Communal ownership of mountain pastures.

The utilization of mountain pastures for stock raising is almost universal. In the arid highlands of Central Asia, it is the essential supplement to the pastoral nomadism of the steppes and deserts, and to the limited sedentary agriculture found along the irrigated piedmont slopes. Here and elsewhere the animal raised varies widely—the llama and vicuna in Peru, which thrive best at 10,000 to 13,000 feet elevation, and multiply rapidly on the *ichu* or coarse grass which clothes the slopes of the higher Andes up to snow line; sheep, goats, yaks and herds of dzo, a useful hybrid between yak and cow, in the highland districts of Sze Chuan. Here the Mantze mountaineers lock their houses and leave their villages deserted, while they camp with their herds on the high pastures at 10,000 feet or more.[62] Only economical, ingenious Japan has failed to develop stock raising, though mountains comprise two-thirds of its area. The explanation has often been sought in Buddhism, which inhibits the use of animal food; but this religious rule probably found ready acceptance in Japan, just because the paucity of animal food made its observance easy, for the fish industry of the Empire never suffered from the inhibition. The reason is probably to be sought elsewhere. The native grass of Japan, which relentlessly crowds out all imported grazing crops, is a bamboo grass with sharp, hard, serrated edges, and is said to cut the entrails of horses and sheep.[63]

Haymaking in high mountains. While the high pastures are ample for the summer feeding, the chief problem of mountain stock-farmers is to secure feed for the winter support of their animals. This taxes their industry and ingenuity to the utmost. While the herdsmen are away tending their charges on the heights, the rest of the population are kept busy at home, getting fodder for the six or seven months of stall-feeding. This includes the cultivation of hardy crops like oats, rye and barley, which will mature at a great altitude, hay-making and collecting twigs and even leaves for the less fastidious goats. In Switzerland as in Norway the art of mowing has reached its highest pitch. Grass only three inches high is cut thrice yearly. The Norwegian peasant gathers a small hay harvest from the roofs of his house and barns, and from the edges of the highways. In Switzerland not a spear of grass escapes. In places inaccessible to cattle and goats, the peasant gathers hay by the handful with crampons on his feet, generally from the ledges of cliffs. He stacks it in one spot, and brings it down to the valley by sledge in winter. He is the *Wildheuer* or wild hay gatherer. His life is so dangerous, that the law permits only one *Wildheuer* to a family.[64] In high Alpine cantons this office is the privilege of the poor.[65] The traveler in Norway frequently sees huge bundles of hay sliding down to the valley on wires stretched from some high point on the precipitous fiord wall. This represents the harvest from isolated spots or from the field of the summer shepherd. In the vicinity of every *saeter* hut, a plot of ground is fenced in, enriched with the manure gathered during the summer, and utilized to grow fine nourishing grass, which is mown and transported down to the valley farm.[66] Here economy of vegetative resources reaches its climax.

In mountain regions of heavy rainfall, thick dew and numerous cloudy days, it becomes a problem to get the hay dried and stored before a drenching shower comes. In many parts of Switzerland, therefore, the peasant on a clear morning cuts a limited amount of grass. This, with the help of his wife and children, he diligently turns and tosses at short intervals all day long, thus subjecting it to a rapid curing process by the action of the wind and the sun, whose rays are doubly effective in the rarefied air of the heights. In the evening the hay is made up into bundles and carried on his back to the barn. In other parts of Switzerland the green hay is hung on horizontal poles arranged against the sunny side of the chalet and under its projecting roof, thus exposed to the heat and protected from the rain till cured. In Norway the same purpose is achieved by setting up in the fields racks supporting long horizontal bars, over which the newly cut grass is hung. There it is exposed to the gentle fanning of the wind and penetrated by the warmth of the sun, in the short intervals when the sky is not overcast; and during a shower it sheds the water immediately, so that a minimum of harm is done. In the mountains of Germany, the hay is stacked on cone-shaped racks made of poles, with lateral projections which support the grass; thus the air can circulate freely inside the hollow cone, which is lifted well above the ground. Elsewhere sharpened stakes provided with cross bars are simply driven into the ground, and on these the hay is draped till cured.

Mountain hay-making leaves nothing to chance; too much depends upon the crop. In fact, at high altitudes it becomes the only crop. Cereal culture drops off with every increase of elevation. Norway has few fields above 1600 feet;[67] even barley fails to ripen above 2600 feet. In the mountains of Würtenberg we find pure *Graswirthschaft* at 3000 feet elevation, with only a small garden patch near the dwell-

Methods of curing hay in mountains.

ing.[68] It is interesting to take a tramp up one of the longitudinal or lateral valleys of the Alps, and observe the economic basis of life gradually change from agriculture to hay-making, till in some high-laid Alpine cirque, like Bad Leuk or Barmaz at the head of the Val d'Ilez, one sees only meadows and an occasional potato patch, which impresses the lowlander as a last despairing effort in the struggle for existence.

Winter industries of mountain peoples.

Where climate and soil do so little for the support of life, man must do much. Work must in some way be made to compensate for an ungenerous Nature. The closely housed existence necessitated by the long severe winters of high altitudes stimulates industries in the home. The winter feeding of the stock involves little labor, so the abundant leisure would otherwise be wasted. Hence it is no accident that we find almost everywhere native mountain industries in a high state of development, and often characterized by an artistic beauty which seems to be the one flower of this barren environment. They are naturally based upon the local raw materials of the mountains, such as wood, metals, clays, and especially the wool of sheep and goats. Moreover, their products are articles of small bulk and large value, adapted to costly mountain transportation. Those of Kashmir are typical—carved wood, artistic metal work in silver and copper, puttoo cloth, carpets and the famous Kashmir shawls.[69] The stark life of Tibet shows in its industries an unexpected richness and beauty. The men spin and weave wool into puttoo cloth of all grades; some of it is extraordinarily fine in texture and color, and is exported by caravan in considerable quantity to northern China and Mongolia. Pastil sticks, made of aromatic wood and impregnated with musk and gold-dust, are a conspicuous commodity in the trade with Peking. Tibet is rich in metals, especially silver and gold. Even the nomad shepherds of the tablelands know how to purify gold-dust over a fire of argols; hence it is not surprising that the settlements in the irrigated mountain valleys should develop real artists in metallurgy.[70] The province of Dérgé, which excels in metal work, produces swords, guns, teapots, bells and seals of extremely artistic design and perfect finish.[71] The jewelry of Tibet suggests Byzantine work. It includes ear-rings and charm boxes of gold and carved turquoise, and is marked by the same delicate finish. But whether the Tibetan is working in wood, gold, brass, or wool, he uses native designs of real merit, and shows the expert craftsman's hand.[72] His activities recall the metal work of the Caucasus and the famous rugs of Daghestan.

Turning to Europe we find watch and clock making in the Black Forest and the Jura, wood-carving in the Swiss and Norwegian mountains, bobbin lace in the Erz range and in Alpine Appenzell, and the far more beautiful Italian product of the rugged Abruzzi and the Frioulian Alps. The Slovaks of highland Hungary are expert in wire-drawing,[73] and the peasant of the central Apennines makes from the gut of his goats the finest violin strings in the world, the so-called Roman strings.[74] The low Thuringian and Franconian Forests, which harbor denser populations, have by a minute subdivision of labor turned their local resources to the making of dolls, which they supply to the markets of the world. Here too the manufacture of glass articles, porcelains, majolica and terra-cotta flourishes.[75] Most of these mountain industries merely supplement the scant agricultural resources; they represent the efforts of industrious but hard pressed people to eke out their meager subsistence.

The application of steam to industry has converted Overpopu- mountain regions of abundant mineral wealth into centers of lation and production for the markets of the world. But this is the his- emigration. tory of only the last century, and of only favored mountain regions. The utilization of waterpower for electricity in factories is transforming the piedmont belts of the Alps and Apennines; but life in the interior of these ranges remains unaltered by the denser population at their base, except for the increased demand for the butter, milk and cheese of the highland pastures. For the world at large, therefore, the obvious and persistent fact of mountain economy is a scanty food supply secured by even the most intelligent and untiring labor, and a fixed tendency to overpopulation. The simplest remedy for this evil is emigration, a fact which Malthus observed.[76] Hence emigration is an almost universal phenomenon in highland regions. Sometimes it is only seasonal. It takes place in the fall after the field work is over, and is due to the paucity of industries possible in the mountains during the winter. It seems to be a recurrence of that nomadic note in the *motif* of mountain life—that migration in summer upward to the borders of the snow, in winter downward to the sun-warmed plains. In autumn the Swiss descend from the Jura and Alps in great numbers to cities, seeking positions as servants or pastry-cooks. The Auvergnats leave their home by the thousand in the fall, when snow covers the mountains, to work in the cities as hewers of stone and drawers of water, then return in summer to resume their tasks in field and pasture, bringing back sums of money which noticeably enrich the home districts.[77]

Forms of temporary emigration. This seasonal emigration often assumes the form of peddling, in order to dispose of small home-made wares. From the Basilicata and Modena Apennines the young men follow the pedler's trade, but the Basilicata village of Viggiano furnishes Italy with many wandering musicians.[78] The Kabyles of the Atlas Mountains go out in parties of two or three in the fall, and hawk every kind of goods, bringing back from their journey quantities of wool for home weaving.[79] The emigration may last for several years, but finally the love of home generally calls the mountaineer back to his rugged hills. The Galicians of the Cantabrian Mountains of northern Spain leave their poor country for a time for the richer provinces of Portugal and Spain, where they become porters, water-carriers and scavengers, and are known as boorish, but industrious and honest. The women from the neighboring mountain province of Asturias are the professional wet-nurses of Spain. They are to be seen in every aristocratic household of Madrid, but return to the mountains with their savings when their period of service ends.[80] In mountainous Basutoland, the Kaffir Switzerland of South Africa, arable land and pastures are utilized as completely as local methods of husbandry permit; and yet the native Kaffirs go in large numbers—28,000 out of a total population of 220,000 in 1895—to work in the mines of Kimberley and the Witwatersrand. They also return in time with their savings.[81] Similarly the Battaks of the rugged mountain-rimmed plateau of western Sumatra emigrate in increasing numbers to the lowlands, and hire them-

selves out for a term of years on the Dutch plantations.[82]
Another interesting and once rather widespread phase of
this temporary emigration appears in the mercenary troops
formerly drawn from mountain regions. After the Burgundian wars of the fifteenth century, the Swiss became the
mercenaries of Europe, and in 1503 were first employed as
papal life-guards. They served the kings of France from
Louis XI. till the tragedy of the Tuileries in 1792; and in
that country and elsewhere they made the name "Switzer"
a synonym for guard or attendant,[83] till in 1848 the mercenary system was abolished. The pressure of population at home
and the military spirit of the Scotch Highlanders once led the
young Gaels to seek their fortunes in military service abroad,
as in the army of Gustavus Adolphus of Sweden.[84] Gurkhas
from Himalayan Nepal, an independent state, are employed in
considerable numbers in the Indian army to-day, and constitute one of the most reliable divisions of the native troops. In
January, 1901, there were 12,797 Gurkhas drawing pay from
the Indian government as soldiers, besides 6000 more employed
as military police, porters, and in other capacities.[85] Similarly ancient Arcadia, the mountain core of Peloponnesus, was
a constant hive of mercenaries.

Often, however, permanent emigration is the result, robbing **Permanent**
the mountain population of its most enterprising element. **emigration.**
Piedmontese, Bergamese, and Frioulians from the Italian Alps
leave their country in large numbers. Many of them find
work in Marseilles and other towns of southern France, infusing an Italian strain into the population there and making serious competition for the local French. A proverb says there is
no country in the world without sparrows and Bergamese.[86]
Geneva, once the citadel of Calvinism, is to-day a Catholic
town, owing to the influx of Catholic laborers from Alpine
Savoy. The overflow of the redundant population of this
mountain province has given the Swiss canton a character
diametrically opposed to its traditions.[87] The Chinese provinces of Chili and Manchuria have been largely populated by
immigrants from the barren mountain peninsula of Shantung;
Manchuria has thereby been converted from an alien into
a native district.[88]

Emigration on so large a scale exercises far-reaching economic and historical influences. Norse colonization contributed interesting chapters to the history of Europe in the ninth and tenth centuries. Norwegians who have flocked to America have made a deep impress upon our Northwestern States. Switzerland in 1902 and 1903 gave us 9500 of its subjects, a valuable contribution. Scotchmen of Highland birth are scattered over the whole world, carrying with them everywhere their sturdy qualities of character. Even the stay-at-home French lose emigrants from their mountain districts. The people of the Basses-Alps go to Mexico, and the Basques from the French Pyrenees seek Argentine.[89] The honesty, industry, and frugality of these mountain emigrants make them desirable elements in any colonial population, and insure their success when they seek their fortunes in the uncrowded western world.

Preventive checks to increase of population. The alternative to overpopulation and its remedy emigration is found in preventive checks to increase. These sometimes take the form of restricted or late marriages, as Malthus found to be the case in Norway and Switzerland in 1799,[90] before the introduction of steam or electric motive power had stimulated the industries of these countries or facilitated emigration thence. The same end is achieved by the widespread religious celibacy which sometimes characterizes mountain communities. In the barren Auvergne Plateau of France, the number of younger sons who become priests is extraordinary. Many daughters become nuns. Celibacy, seconded by extensive emigration, clears the field for the eldest son and the system of primogeniture which the poverty of this rugged highland has established as a fixed institution in the Auvergne.[91] A careful statistical investigation of the geographical origins of the Catholic priesthood in Europe might throw interesting light on the influences of environment. The harsh conditions of mountain life make the monastery a line of least resistance, while geographical isolation nourishes the religious nature and benumbs the intellectual activities.

It is in the corrugated highland of Tibet, chilled to barrenness by an elevation of 12,000 feet or more (4000 meters), sterile and treeless from aridity, carved by cañon-cutting streams into deep gorges offering a modicum of arable soil for irrigation, that monasticism has developed into an effective system to keep down population. Buddhism, with its convents and lamaseries, naturally recommended itself to a country where asceticism was obviously expedient. The world shows nowhere else so large a celibate class. In Tibet, monks are estimated at 175,000 to 500,000 in a total population of three millions. Archibald Little estimates their number at one-third of the total male population.[92] Derge, which is the most productive district both agriculturally and industrially of eastern Tibet and is also most densely inhabited, counts at least 10,000 lamas in a total population of about 42,000.[93] Not less than one-sixth of the inhabitants of Ladak are in religious houses as monks and nuns.[94] Families in Tibet are small, yet each devotes one or more children to convent or monastic life.[95] In western Tibet, especially about Taklakot in the Himalayan border, one boy in every family is invariably devoted to the priesthood, and one or more daughters must become nuns. But the nun generally resides with her family or lives in some monastery—with unspeakable results.[96]

The Tibetans seem to be enthusiastic Malthusians, with Polyandry. all the courage of their convictions. Religious celibacy among them is only an adjunct to another equally effective social device for restricting population. This is the institution of polyandry, which crops out in widely distributed mountain regions of limited resources, just as it appears not infrequently in primitive island societies. Its sporadic occurrence in extensive lowlands, as among the Warraus of Guiana and certain tribes of the Orinoco, is' extremely rare, as also its occasional appearance among pastoral steppe-dwellers, like the Hottentots and Damaras.[97] It is often associated with polygamy where wealth exists, and is never the exclusive form of marriage, yet its frequency among mountain peoples is striking. Strabo describes fraternal polyandry as it existed in mountainous Yemen. There among a Semitic people, as to-day in Mongolian Tibet and among the aboriginal Todas of the Nilgiri Hills in peninsular India, the staff of one husband left at the door of the house excluded the others.[98] In modern times the institution is found throughout Tibet, and in the Himalayan and sub-Himalayan districts adjoining it, as in Ladak, Kunawar, Kumaon, Garhwal, Spiti, Sirmur, among the Miris, Daphlas, Abors and Bhutias occupying the southern slope of the Himalayans eastward from Sikkim, and the Murmese tribes of the Khasia Hills just to the south. The same practice occurs among the Coorgs of the Western Ghats, among the Nairs at the coastal piedmont of this range, among the Todas of the mountain stronghold known as the Nilgiri Hills (peaks 8000 feet or 2630 meters), and it crops out sporadically among certain mountain Bantu tribes of South Africa.[99]

Female infanticide. There seems little doubt that polyandry, as Herbert Spencer maintains, has been adopted as an obvious and easy check upon increase of population in rugged countries.[100] It is generally coupled with other preventive checks. In the Nilgiri Hills, as we found also to be the case on many Polynesian islands, it is closely associated with female infanticide.[101] The Todas in 1867 showed a proportion of two men to one woman, but later, with the decline of infanticide under British rule, a proportion of 100 men to 75 women, and a resulting modification of the institution of polyandry.[102] It may well be that the paucity of women suggested this form of marriage, whose expediency as an ally to infanticide in checking population later became apparent. The Todas are a very primitive folk of herdsmen, living on the produce of their buffaloes, averse to agriculture, though not inhibited from it by the nature of their country, therefore prone to seek any escape from that uncongenial employment,[103] and relying on the protected isolation of their habitat to compensate for the weakness inherent in the small number of the tribe.

Throughout Tibet and Ladak polyandry works hand in hand with the lamaseries in limiting population. The conspicuous fact in Tibetan polyandry is its restriction to the agricultural portion of the population. The pastoral nomads of the country, depending on their yaks, sheep and goats, wandering at will over a very wide, if desolate territory, practice monogamy and polygamy.[104] The sedentary population, on the other hand, is restricted to tillable lands so small that each farm produces only enough for one family. Subdivision under a divided inheritance would be disastrous to these dwarf estates, especially owing to possible complications growing out of irrigating rights.[105] Polyandry leaves the estate and the family undivided, and by permitting only one wife to several fraternal husbands restricts the number of children. It does this also in another way by diminishing the fertility of the mothers; for all travelers comment upon the paucity of children in polyandrous families.

Westermarck lays stress upon the fact that polyandry prevails chiefly in sterile countries. He regards it less as a conscious device to check increase of population than a result of the disproportion of males to females in polyandrous communities. The preponderance of male births he attributes to the excessive endogamy bordering on inbreeding which tends to prevail in all isolated mountain valleys; and also, as a possibility, to the undernourished condition of the parents caused by scanty food supplies, which Dusing found to be productive of a high percentage of male births in proportion to female.[106] The motive of restricting population seems entitled to more weight than Westermarck concedes to it; for he slurs over the fact that in Tibet polyandry gives rise to a large number of superfluous women who fill the nunneries,[107] while in the Nilgiri Hills redundant females were eliminated by infanticide. The fact seems to be that in the institution of polyandry we have a social and psychological effect of environment, reinforced by a physiological effect.

A comparison of social conditions in the adjoining provinces of Baltistan and Ladak, which together comprise the Himalayan valley of the Indus, reveals the character of polyandry as a response to geographic environment. Both provinces are inhabited by a Mongolian stock, but the Ladaki living on the uppermost stretch of the basin near Tibet are Buddhists and polyandrists, while the Baltis farther down the valley are Mussulmen and polygamists. The Baltis, with their plurality of wives and numerous children, are wretchedly poor and live in squalor on the verge of starvation; but as the elevation of their valley ranges only from 4000 to 8500 feet, they are inured to heat, and therefore emigrate in large numbers to the neighboring Mohammedan province of the Punjab,

Effects of polyandry and polygamy.

where they work as coolies and navvies. The Ladakis, on the other hand, living 9000 to 13,000 feet above the sea, die of bilious fever when they reach the lowlands. Cut off from emigration, they curtail population by means of polyandry and lamaseries. Consequently they show signs of prosperity, are well fed, well clothed and comfortably housed.[108] Baltistan's social condition illustrates in a striking way the power of an idea like an alien creed, assimilated as the result of close vicinal location, to counteract for a time the influences of local geographic conditions.

Marauding tendencies in mountaineers. The less civilized mountain peoples, whose tastes or low economic status unfit them for emigration, solve the problem of a deficient food supply by raiding the fields and stores of their richer neighbors. Predatory expeditions fill the history of primitive mountain peoples, and of the ancient occupants of highland regions which are now devoted to honest industry. The ancient Alpine tribes were one and all, from the Mediterranean to the Danube, "poor and addicted to robbery," as Strabo says. He analyzes their condition with nice discrimination. "The greater part [of the Alps], especially the summits of the mountains inhabited by robbers, are barren and unfruitful, both on account of the frost and the ruggedness of the land. Because of the want of food and other necessaries, the mountaineers have sometimes been obliged to spare the inhabitants of the plains, that they might have some people to supply them."[109] The freebooters usually descended into the lowlands of Italy, Gaul and Helvetia, but the pass peoples lay in wait for their prey on the mountain roads. Strabo described the same marauding habits arising from the same cause among the mountaineers of northern Spain,[110] the Balkan range,[111] and the highlands encircling the Mesopotamian plains.[112]

Hunger is usually the spur. The tribesmen who inhabit the Hunza gorge were notorious robbers till their recent conquest by the British. Despite the most careful terrace tillage, their country was much overpopulated. The supply of grain was so inadequate, that during the summer the people subsisted wholly on fruit, reserving the grain for winter use. Therefore, when early summer opened the passes of the Karakoram and Himalayan ranges, and caravans began to move over the trade route between Kashmir and Yarkand, when the Kirghis nomads from the plains sought the pastures of the Pamir, the Hunza tribesmen found raiding caravans and herds, and pillaging the Gilgit Valley of Baltistan the easiest means of supplementing their slender resources. Hardy mountaineers as they were, and born fighters, they always conducted their forays successfully, and returned to the shelter of their fastnesses, laden with plunder and driving their captive flocks before them. The perpetual menace of these Hunza raids caused large districts in the Gilgit Valley to be abandoned by their inhabitants, and cultivated land to lapse into wilderness,[113] while the Chilas to the south pillaged the Astor Valley of Baltistan, carrying away crops and cattle, enslaving women and children.[114]

Marauding propensities are marked among all retarded **Cattle-** mountain peoples of modern times. The cattle-lifting clans **lifting.** of the Scotch Highlands, who preyed upon the Lowlands, have their counterpart in the Pathans of the Suleiman and Baluch mountain border who, till curbed by the British power in India, systematically pillaged the plains of the Sind.[115] The forest Bhils of the Vindhyan and Satpura ranges are scarcely yet married to agriculture; so when in time of drought their crops fail and the game abandons the hill forests to seek water in the lowland jungles, the Bhils cheerfully revert to their ancestral habit of cattle-lifting.[116]

The Caucasus was long a breeding place for robber tribes who made their forays into the pastures and fields of southern Russia. Robbery was part of the education of every Circassian prince, while one group of the Abassines conferred their chieftainship upon the most successful robber or the man of largest family.[117] The Kurdish hillmen of the Armenian ranges descend with their herds of horses in winter to the warmer plains, where they exhaust the pastures and subject the Armenian villages to a regular system of blackmail.[118] The wide grassy plains about Koukou Nor Lake, near the Chinese border of Tibet, attract numerous Mongol nomads with their herds; but these rich pastures are exposed to the depredation of Si Fan brigand tribes, who have their haunts in the deep, impenetrable gorges of the neighboring mountains, and carefully guard all the approaches to the same. They are Buddhists, but worship a special Divinity of Brigandage, to whom their lamas offer prayers for the success of every foray.[119] Hence, among mountain as among desert peoples, robbery tends to become a virtue; environment dictates their ethical code.

Historical results of mountain raiding.

These depredations reflect to a great degree the complementary relation of highlands and lowlands. The plains possess what the mountains lack. This is a fundamental fact of economic geography, and inevitably leads to historical results. The marauding expeditions of mountain peoples first acquire historical importance, either when the raids after long continuance end in the conquest of the lowlands, and thus augment the resources and population of the highland state; or, as is often the case, the raiders call down upon themselves the vengeance of the plainsmen, are subdued, and embodied in the lowland state. The conquest of ancient Assyria and the destruction of Nineveh by the mountain Medes seems to have been a process of this kind. Long before their descent upon Mesopotamia, they were known as the "dangerous Medes," were constantly threatening the Assyrian frontiers and occupying isolated tracts.[120] The predatory incursions of the Samnites of the Apennines into the fertile fields of Campania eventuated in the conquest of ancient Capua and other cities, and greatly strengthened the Samnite Confederacy. But this encroachment of the mountain tribes upon the plains aroused the cupidity and alarm of the Romans, who in turn bent their energies toward the final subjugation of the Samnites.[121] Himalayan Nepal, after the unification of its petty Rajah states by the Gurkha conquest between 1768 and 1790, began encroachments and ravages upon the Indian Terai or fertile alluvial lowland at the foot of the mountains; and finally by 1858 had acquired title to a considerable strip of it, which by its rice fields and forests greatly strengthened the geographic and economic base of the highland state.[122] The Malay Hovas, inhabiting the central plateau of Madagascar, braced to effort by its temperate climate and not over-generous soil, have almost everywhere subdued the better fed but sluggish lowlanders of the coast.[123] There can be little doubt that the beneficent effects of an invigorating mountain climate, especially in tropical and subtropical latitudes, have helped the hardy, active hill people to make easy conquest of the enervated plainsmen.

It is more often the case, however, that the scant resources, small number, and divided political condition of the mountain tribes make such conquest impossible. Their depredations provoke reprisals from the stronger states of the plain, who bring the mountain region under subjection, merely to police their frontier. Strabo makes it clear that the Romans, having secured certain passes over the Alps, neglected the conquest of the ranges, till the increase of Roman colonies along the piedmont rim excited the cupidity of the mountaineers. Muscovite dominion was extended over the Caucasus, both in order to check the persistent raids of its tribes into the Russian plains, and to secure control of its passes. The state of Kashmir, guided by a purely local policy, for years tried to conquer the robber tribes on its northwestern frontier, merely to protect its own border provinces. Then the British authorities of the Indian Empire began the same process, but from a radically different motive. They saw the Gilgit and Hunza valleys, like the Chitral to the west, as highways through a mountain transit land, whose opposite approaches were held by the Russians.[124]

Such conquests, whatever be their motive, profit the vanquished in the end more than the victor. They result in the systematic and intelligent development of the mountain resources, and the maintenance of ampler social and economic relations between highland and lowland through the construction of roads, which must always represent the reach of the governing authority. The conquest of mountain peoples means always expensive and protracted campaigns. The invader has always two enemies to fight, Nature and the armed foe. There is a saying in India that "In Gilgit a small army is annihilated and a large army starves to death." Hunger is king in high altitudes, and comes always to the defense of mountain independence. Moreover, the inaccessibility of such districts, the difficulty of maintaining lines of communication,

Conquest of mountain regions.

ignorance of by-paths and trails which forever offer strategic opportunities to the natives or escape at a crisis, all serve to protract the war. The independent spirit of the mountaineer, his endurance of hardships, his mastery of mountain tactics, and his obstinate resistance after repeated defeat, give always a touch of heroism to highland warfare. Consequently, history abounds in examples of unconquered mountain peoples, or of long sustained resistance, like that which for sixty years under the heroic leadership of Kadi Mulah and Shamyl used up the treasure and troops of Russia in the impregnable defiles of the Caucasus. In the end, however, the highland tribes succumb to numbers and the road-making engineer.

Political dismemberment of mountain peoples. Political dismemberment, lack of cohesion due to the presence of physical barriers impeding intercourse, is the inherent weakness of mountain peoples. Political consolidation is never voluntary. It is always forced upon them from without, either by foreign conquest or by the constant menace of such conquest, which compels the mountain clans to combine for common defense of their freedom. The combination thus made is reluctant, loose, easily broken, generally short-lived. It becomes close and permanent only under a constant pressure from without, and then assumes a form allowing to the constituent parts the greatest possible measure of independence. The Swiss canton and commune are the result of a segregating environment; the Swiss Republic is the result of threatened encroachments by the surrounding states. It owed its first genuine federal constitution to Napoleon.

A report on the situation in the Caucasus, addressed to Czar Nicholas in 1829, contains an epitome of the history of mountain peoples. It runs as follows: "The Circassians bar out Russia from the south, and may at their pleasure open or close the passage to the nations of Asia. At present their intestine dissensions, fostered by Russia, hinder them from uniting under one leader; but it must not be forgotten that, according to traditions religiously preserved among them, the sway of their ancestors extended as far as to the Black Sea. * * * The imagination is appalled at the consequence which their union under one leader might have for Russia, which has no other bulwark against their ravages than a military line, too extensive to be very strong."[125] Here we have the whole story—a mountain people pillaging the lowlands, exercising a dangerous and embarrassing control over the passes, and thereby calling down upon themselves conquest from without; weakened by a contracting territory within the highlands and a shrinking area of plunder without, doomed to eventual defeat by the yet more ominous weakness of political dismemberment.

Mountain tribes are always like a pack of hounds on the leash, each straining in a different direction. Wall-like barriers, holding them apart for centuries, make them almost incapable of concerted action, and restive under any authority but their own. Clan and tribal societies, feudal and republican rule, always on a small scale, characterize mountain sociology. All these are attended by an exaggerated individualism and its inevitable concomitant, the blood feud. Mountain policy tends to diminish the power of the central authority to the vanishing point, giving individualism full scope. Social and economic retardation, caused by extreme isolation and encouraged by protected location, tend to keep the social body small and loosely organized. Every aspect of environment makes against social integration. *Individualism and independence.*

The broken relief of ancient Greece produced the small city state; but in the rugged mountains of Arcadia the principle of physical and political subdivision went farther. Here, for four centuries after the first Olympiad, the population, poorest and rudest of all Greece, was split up into petty hill villages, each independent of the other.[126] The need of resisting Spartan aggression led for the first time, in 371 B. C., to the formation of a *commune Arcadum,* a coalescence of all the fractional groups constituting the Arcadian folk;[127] but even this union, effected only by the masterly manipulation of the Theban Epaminondas, proved short-lived and incomplete. What was true of the Arcadian villages was true of the city states of Greece. The geography of the land instilled into them the principle of political aloofness, except when menaced by foreign conquest. Coöperation is efficient only when it springs from a habit of mind. Greek union against the Persians was very imperfect; and against the Roman, the feeble leagues were wholly ineffective. The influence of this dismembering environment still persists. As ancient Greece was a complex of city states, modern Greece is a complex of separate districts, each of which holds chief place in the minds of its citizens, and unconsciously but steadily operates against the growth of a national spirit in the modern sense.[128]

Types of mountain states. A mountain environment encourages political disunion in several forms. Sometimes it favors the survival of a turbulent feudal nobility, based upon clan organization, as among the medieval Scotch, who were not less rebellious toward their own kings than toward the English conquerors.[129] Feudal rule seems congenial to the mountaineer, whose conservative nature, born of isolation, clings to hereditary chiefs and a long established order. Feudal communities and dwarf republics exist side by side in the northern Caucasus,[130] attended by that primitive assertion of individual right, the blood feud.[131] Often the two forms of government are combined, but the feudal element is generally only a dwindling survival from a remote past. The little Republic of Andorra, which for a thousand years has preserved its existence in the protection of a high Pyrenean valley, is a self-governing community, organized strictly along the lines of a Tyrolese or Swiss commune; but the two *viguiers* or agents, who in some matters outrank the president, are official appointments tracing back to feudal days, when Andorra was a seigneurie of the Comté of Urgel.[132] Tyrol offers a striking parallel to this. In its local affairs it has in effect a republican form of government, enjoying as high degree of autonomy as any Swiss canton; but the great Brenner route, which could confer both power and wealth on its possessor, made the Tyrol an object of conquest to the feudal nobles of the early Middle Ages. Their hereditary dominion is now vested in the archdukes of Austria, to whom the Tyrolese have shown unfailing fidelity, but from whom they have exacted complete recognition of their rights.[133]

Tyrol's neighbor Switzerland illustrates the pure form of commune, canton and republic, which is the logical result of a rugged mountain relief. Here commune and canton are the real units of government. In the federal power at Bern the

Swiss peasant takes little interest, often not even knowing the name of the national president. In the highest ranges a canton coincides with a mountain-rimmed valley—Valais with the basin of the upper Rhone, Glarus with the upper Linth, Uri with the Reuss, Graubünden with the upper Rhine, to which is joined by many pass routes the sparsely peopled Engadine, Ticino with the drainage basin of upper Lake Maggiore, Unterwalden with the southern drainage valleys of Lake Lucerne. Where the mountains are lower, or where passes connect valleys of high levels, cantonal boundaries may overstep geographical barriers. A commune generally consists of the villages strung along a narrow lateral valley, isolated and sufficient unto itself politically. A close parallel to the Alpine commune is found among the Kabyles of the Atlas Mountains. Their political structure is based upon the *Jemaa* or commune, a small sovereign republic whose independence is fiercely defended. It enjoys complete local autonomy, is governed by an assembly of all the adult male inhabitants, and grants this body the usual functions except the administration of justice, which, characteristically, is replaced by blood feuds as the inalienable right of the individual. Romans, Arabs, Turks and French have in turn exercised over these mountain Berbers only nominal control, except when their internal dissensions made them vulnerable.[134]

The mountains, by the segregating power of their ridges and ranges, first produce these little independent communities, and then, throwing around them strong protecting arms, enfold them in an embrace which long provides security to them in their weakness. These minute mountain states, therefore, tend to reflect in their size the isolation of their environment, and indirectly the weakness of the surrounding nations. The original Swiss *Eidgenossensschaft* of the four forest cantons, embedded in the high Alps, braced against a mountain wall, held its own against the feeble feudal states of ,Austria and ˙Germany. The rugged relief of Graubünden and the spirit of freedom cradled there enabled its peasants in the Middle Ages to overthrow the feudal lords, and to establish a federal republic. This typical mountain state was a league composed of three other leagues. Each

Significance of their small size.

component league consisted of a group of districts, having the power of sovereign states, and consisting in turn of a group of communes, which were quite independent in local affairs. This triune league formed in time an alliance with the Swiss Confederation, but did not become a member of it till the Vienna adjustment of 1815. Similar is the story of the mountain shepherds of Appenzell, who formed a little peasant republic, despite their bishop overlord of St. Gall; and who later during the Reformation, on the ground of religious differences, divided into two yet smaller states.[135] The relation between size and inaccessibility is most strikingly illustrated in the high Himalayan ranges west of Kashmir and north of the Punjab. Here is the Shinaka district, which includes the Chilas, Darel, Tanger and other valleys branching off from the Indus, and which is inhabited by Dards of Indo-European stock. Each Shinaka valley is a small cantonal republic, and each village of each republic is a commune managing its own affairs by an assembly. One settlement of only twelve houses enjoys complete autonomy. Besides the village assemblies there is a state parliament handling questions of general policy, to which each village sends representatives. One dissentient vote can defeat a measure. The majority cannot control the minority; for if one village of a state disagrees with the others, it is free to carry out its own policy, even in the matter of foreign alliances.[136] Here is home rule run to seed.

Slight power of mountain chiefs. Small size is sometimes coupled with monarchical rule, degenerating occasionally into despotism among aggressive robber tribes. The inaccessible Hunza Valley is occupied on opposite sides of its deep gorge by two rival states, the Hunzas and the Nagaris, whose combined population amounts to scarcely 25,000 souls. Hostile to each other, they unite only to resist an invading force. While the Hunza Thum is a tyrant, the Nagari ruler has little voice in the government. The Tibeto-Burman hill folk of the eastern Himalayas are divided into clans, and concede a mild authority to a chief who rules a group of clan villages, but only rarely is able to secure power over a larger district. The Khasia Hills of Assam are broken up into twenty-three petty states, each under its own Rajah or chief, who has, however, little authority beyond the administration of justice.[137]

Everywhere in mountain regions appears this repugnance to centralized authority. Protection by environment obviates the necessity of protection through combination. The spirit of clan exclusiveness, the absence of a common national sentiment, characterize equally the tribesmen of mountainous Albania, of Persian Luristan,[138] and highland Kurdistan. Along the rugged upheaved area which forms the western boundary of India from the Khaibar Pass to the sea, British officials have had to negotiate with the native Pathan and Baluch "jirgahs," assemblies of the chief men of the countless clans into which the tribes are divided, as the only visible form of authority tolerated.[139] Combination must be voluntary and of a type to exact a modicum of submission. These requirements are best answered by the confederation, which may gradually assume a stable and elaborate form among an advanced people like the Swiss; or it may constitute a loose yet effective union, as in the famous Samnite confederacy of the central Apennines; or a temporary league like that of the ancient Arcadians, or the group of confederated sheiks of Bellad el Kobail, the "Country of the Highlanders" in mountainous Yemen, who in 1790 established a republican form of union for defense against their more powerful neighbors.[140]

The power of mountains to protect makes them asylums of refuge for displaced peoples. This fact explains the confused ethnology which often characterizes these isolated regions, especially when they lie near or across natural highways of human migration. As a tide of humanity sweeps around or across the mountains, a branch stream turns into a side valley, where it is caught and held. There it remains unaltered, crystallizing in its seclusion, subjected for ages to few modifying influences from without. Its people keep their own language and customs, little affected by a totally different race stock similarly placed in a neighboring alcove of the mountains. Lack of communication engenders an endless multiplication of dialects, as we find them in the Alps, the Caucasus, in Kafirstan of the Hindu Kush and in Nepal.

Mountain isolation and differentiation.

Diversity of speech, itself a product of isolation, reacts upon that political and social aloofness of mountain folk, to emphasize and fix it.

Survival of primitive races in mountains. From this principle it follows that the same highland region shows strong differentiation and marked social individuality from one district to another, and from one valley to the next, despite a prevailing similarity of local geographic conditions. In fact, the very similarity of those conditions, strong in their power to isolate, present the conditions for inevitable variation. A mountain region gets its population from diverse sources, or, which is quite as important, at different times from the same source. For instance, Nepal received contingents of Rajput conquerors, dislodged from the Punjab, in the seventh century, the eleventh, and finally the dominant Gurkhas at the end of the eighteenth. To-day these represent different degrees of amalgamation with the local Tibetan stock of Nepal. They are distinguished from each other by a diversity of languages, and a multiplicity of dialects, while the whole piedmont of the country shows a yet different blend with the Aryan Hindus of the Ganges valley, who have seeped into the Terai and been drawn up, as if by capillary attraction, into the hill valleys of the outer range. The Vindhyan Range and its associated highlands, long before the dawn of Indian history, caught and held in their careful embrace some of the fragile aboriginal tribes like the Kolarian Ho, Santals and Korkus. Centuries later the Dravidian Bhils and Gonds sought refuge here before the advancing Indo-Aryans, and found asylums in the secluded valleys.[141] Finally those same northern plains whence the Dravidians had come, after the Mohammedan conquest of central India in the sixteenth century, sent flying to the refuge of the hills a large contingent of Hindus of mingled Dravidian and Aryan stocks, but stamped with the culture of the Ganges basin. These occupied the richer valleys and the more accessible plateaus of the highlands, driving the primitive Gonds and Bhils back into the remoter recesses of the mountains.[142] Dravidians and aboriginal Kolarians survive in their purity in the wilder and more inaccessible regions, but in the lower valleys their upper classes show signs of mixtures with the Rajput invaders, while the lower classes betray little Aryan blood.[143]

Afghanistan, of disordered relief, set as a transit region between the plains of Mesopotamia, the Oxus and the Indus, has a confused ethnology in keeping with the tangle of dissected plateaus and mountain systems which constitute its surface. Here we find three distinct branches of the Indo-European race, divided up into various peoples of diverse tongues and subdivided further into countless tribes; and two branches of Mongol-Tartars scattered, as if out of a pepper box, from the Helmund to the Oxus, tossed in among diverse peoples of Iranic and Galcha origin in hopeless confusion. The various Afghan tribes, separated from each other by natural barriers and intervening alien stocks, though similar in physical type, speech, religion and culture, have no sense of unity, no common political aims, while the appalling list of tribes constituting the population of the country[144] offers little hope of Afghanistan ever developing national cohesion. Kafiristan alone, which lies in the Hindu Kush range for the most part at an altitude of 12,000 feet or more, harbors in its recesses many remnants of primitive peoples, speaking various languages and dialects, strangers alike to any native affinity or political union. It is a mere agglomeration of ethnic fragments, in which the people of one village are often unable to converse with those of the next.[145] Relief has fashioned the ethnology of the Caucasus in the same way. No other equally small area in the world contains such a variety of peoples and tongues, differing from one another in race, language, and customs so fundamentally as the Caucasus. From the heterogeneous survivals of extremely old ethnic stocks, lodged in the high valleys, to the intrusive Russians of the lower piedmont, the Caucasus might be called an ethnographical sample card.[146]

The rugged configuration of the Alps, from the Rhone to the Danube, has preserved the broad-headed Alpine race, which was perhaps the primitive stock of Central Europe. The great river valleys leading into this massive highland, like the Rhine, Aar, Inn and Adige, show the intrusion of a long-headed race from both north and south; but lofty and

Diversity of peoples and dialects.

remote valleys off the main routes of travel, like the Hither Rhine about Dissentis, the little Stanzerthal of the upper Inn, and the Passierthal of the upper Adige above Meran, show the race preserved in its purity by the isolating environment.[147] Here each segregated lateral valley becomes an area of marked linguistic and social differentiation; only where it opens into the wider longitudinal valleys are its peculiarities of speech and custom diluted by the intrusive current of another race. Switzerland has received three different streams of language, and broken them up into numerous rivulets of dialect. On its small area of 16,125 square miles (41,346 square kilometers) thirty-five dialects of German are spoken, sixteen of French, eight of Italian and five of Romansch, a primitive and degenerate Latin tongue, surviving from the ancestral days of Roman occupation.[148] The yet smaller territory of the Tyrol has all these languages except French, whose place is taken by various forms of Slavonic speech which have entered by the western tributaries of the Danube.[149]

Constriction of mountain areas of ethnic survivals. Rarely is a polyglot mountain population able to work out its own political salvation, as the Swiss have done. More often political union must be forced upon them from without. Oftener still, when the highlanders are primitive survivals, ill-matched against the superior invaders from the plain, they are doomed to a process of constriction of territory and deterioration of numbers, which proceeds slowly or rapidly according to the inaccessibility of their environment and the energy of the intruders. Deliberate, unenterprising nations, like the Chinese, Turks and Indo-Aryans long tolerate the presence of alien mountain tribes, who remain like enemies brought to bay in their isolated fortresses. The conquerors throw around them at their leisure a cordon of settlement, which, slowly ascending the piedmont, draws closer and closer about the mountaineers. The situation of many mountain tribes reminds one of a besieged stronghold. Russian wars against the Caucasus have rightly been described as protracted sieges. The heroic history of Switzerland in relation to its neighbors has been that of a skillfully conducted defense, both military and diplomatic. The territory of China is dotted over with detached groups of aborigines, who have survived wherever a friendly mountain has offered them an asylum. Variously known as Lolos, Mantze or Miaotse, they have preserved everywhere a semi-independence in pathless mountains, whither Chinese troops do not dare to follow them;[150] but the more numerous and patient Chinese agriculturalists are in many sections slowly encroaching upon their territories, driving them farther and farther into the recesses of their highlands. The same process goes on in Formosa, where the Chinese have gradually forced the native Malays into mountain fastnesses among the peaks which rise to 14,000 feet (4500 meters). There, split up by internecine feuds into numberless clans and tribes, ignorant of one another's languages, raiding each other's territories and the coastal plains tilled by Chinese colonists, they await their doom, while the piedmont zone between has already given birth to a typical border race of halfbreeds, more Chinese than Malay.[151]

"To have and to hold" is the motto of the mountains. Like remote islands, they are often museums of social antiquities. Antiquated races and languages abound. The mountaineers of the Southern Appalachians speak to-day an eighteenth century English. Their literature is the ballad poetry of old England and Scotland, handed down from parent to child. Clan feuds settle questions of justice, as in the Caucasus and the Apennines. Religion is orthodox to the last degree, sectarianism is rigid, and Joshua's power over the sun remains in some lonely valleys undiscounted.[152] These are all the marks of isolation and retardation which appear in similar environments elsewhere. Especially religious dogmas tend to show in mountains a tenacity of life impossible in the plains. The Kafirs, inhabiting the high Hindu Kush Mountains of Badakshan, and apparently of Pelasgic, early Greek, or Persian origin, have a religion blended of paganism, Zoroastrianism and Brahmanism.[153] One intruding faith has been unable to dislodge the previous incumbent, so the three have combined. The great historical destiny of the small, barren, isolated Judean plateau was to hold aloof the chaste religion of the desert-bred Jews from the sensuous agricultural gods of the Canaanites; to conserve and fix it; if need be, to narrow it to a provincial tribal faith, to stamp it with ex-

Isolation and retardation of mountain regions.

clusiveness, conservatism, and formalism, as its adherents with bigotry,[154] for this is always the effect of geographical seclusion. But when all these limitations of Judaism are acknowledged, the fact remains that that segregated mountain environment performed the inestimable service for the world of keeping pure and undefiled the first and last great gift of the desert, a monotheistic faith.

Buddhism, once the official religion of Korea but disestablished three centuries ago, has taken refuge in the Diamond Mountains, far from the main roads; there a dull, moribund form of the faith dozes on in the monasteries and monastic shrines of these secluded highlands.[155] Driven out of India, Buddhism survives only in the Himalayan border of the country among the local Tibeto-Burman peoples, and in Ceylon, whose mountain city of Kandy is its stronghold. The persecuted Waldenses, a heretic sect who fled in 1178 from the cities of France to the Alps, took refuge in the remote valleys of the Pellice, Chisone, and Augrogne some thirty miles southwest of Turin. There, protected equally against attack and modification, the Waldenses have maintained the old tenets and organization of their religion.[156]

Conservatism of mountain peoples.

The mountain-dweller is essentially conservative. There is little in his environment to stimulate him to change, and little reaches him from the outside world. The "spirit of the times" is generally the spirit of a past time, when it has penetrated to his remote upland. He is strangely indifferent to what goes on in the great outstretched plains below him. What filters in to him from the outside has little suggestion for him, because it does not accord with the established order which he has always known. Hence innovation is distasteful to him. This repugnance to change reaches its clearest expression, perhaps, in the development and preservation of national costumes. *Tracht*, which is crystallized style in dress, appears nowhere so widespread and so abundantly differentiated as in mountain districts. In Switzerland, every canton has its distinctive costume which has come down from a remote past. The peasants of Norway, of the German and Austrian Alps, of the Basque settlements in the Pyrenees, of mountain-bound Alsace and Bohemia, give local color to the

INFLUENCES MOUNTAIN ENVIRONMENT 601

landscape by the picturesqueness of their national dress. With this conservatism of the mountaineer is generally coupled suspicion toward strangers, extreme sensitiveness to criticism, superstition, strong religious feeling, and an intense love of home and family. The bitter struggle for existence makes him industrious, frugal, provident; and, when the marauding stage has been outgrown, he is peculiarly honest as a rule. Statistics of crime in mountain regions show few crimes against property though many against person. When the mountain-bred man comes down into the plains, he brings with him therefore certain qualities which make him a formidable competitor in the struggle for existence,—the strong muscles, unjaded nerves, iron purpose, and indifference to luxury bred in him by the hard conditions of his native environment.

Mental and moral qualities.

NOTES TO CHAPTER XVI

1. Heinrich von Treitschke, *Politik*, Vol. I, p. 218. Leipzig, 1897.
2. For full discussion, see H. R. Mill, International Geography, pp. 79-81. New York, 1902.
3. J. Thomson, Through Masai Land, pp. 78-82, 113-115, 122, 140-141, 163-167, 406-407. London, 1885.
4. J. Russell Smith, Plateaus in Tropical America, in Report of Eighth International Geographical Congress, pp. 829-831. Washington, 1905.
5. Isaiah Bowman, The Distribution of Population in Bolivia, *Bulletin American Geographical Society*, pp. 74-78, Vol. VII. 1909.
6. D. G. Hogarth, The Nearer East, p. 157. London, 1902.
7. Roosevelt, Winning of the West, Vol. I, pp. 52-56. New York, 1895. C. C. Royce, The Cherokee Nation of Indians, Fifth Annual Report of Bureau of Ethnology, pp. 140-143. Washington, 1887.
8. W. Z. Ripley, The Races of Europe, pp. 253-254. New York, 1899.
9. G. L. Gomme, The Village Community, pp. 72, 75-95. New York, 1890.
10. H. R. Mill, International Geography, pp. 148, 154, 155. New York, 1902.
11. J. Partsch, Central Europe, pp. 204, 207. London, 1903.
12. H. R. Mill, International Geography, p. 304. New York, 1902.
13. J. Partsch, Central Europe, p. 221. London, 1903.
14. Alfred Stead, Japan by the Japanese, p. 425. London, 1904. Henry Dyer, Dai Nippon, p. 241. New York, 1904.
15. Boyd Winchester, The Swiss Republic, pp. 307-308. Phila., 1891.
16. Wilhelm Deecke, Italy, pp. 190, 358-361. London, 1904.
17. Elisée Reclus, Europe, Vol. I, p. 284. New York, 1882.
18. S. P. Scott, History of the Moorish Empire in Spain, Vol. III, pp. 610-613. Philadelphia, 1904.

602 INFLUENCES MOUNTAIN ENVIRONMENT

19. M. Niebuhr, Travels Through Arabia, Vol. I, pp. 290-291, 300. Edinburgh, 1792. S. M. Zwemer, Arabia the Cradle of Islam, pp. 57, 68, 69, 415. New York, 1900.

20. D. G. Hogarth, The Nearer East, pp. 75, 140, 267. London, 1902.

21. E. F. Knight, Where Three Empires Meet, p. 10. London, 1897.

22. *Ibid.*, pp. 312, 460, 463, 468, 475.

23. *Ibid.*, 118, 119, 160, 200.

24. Isabella Bird Bishop, The Yangtze Valley and Beyond, Vol. I, pp. 176, 183, 294; Vol. II, p. 107. New York and London, 1900.

25. F. H. Nichols, Through Hidden Shensi, pp. 51, 54. New York, 1902.

26. E. J. Payne, History of the New World, Vol. I, pp. 375-378. Oxford, 1892.

27. Ratzel, History of Mankind, Vol. II, p. 162. London, 1896-1898.

28. E. F. Knight, Where Three Empires Meet, pp. 86-87. London, 1897.

29. A. B. Ellis, West African Islands, p. 248. London, 1885.

30. Ratzel, History of Mankind, Vol. I, p. 254. London, 1896-1898.

31. *Ibid.*, Vol. I, pp. 426-428.

32. A. R. Wallace, The Malay Archipelago, p. 122. New York, 1869.

33. *Ibid.*, 174.

34. W. E. Griffis, The Mikado's Empire, Vol. I, p. 90. New York, 1903.

35. Census of the Philippine Islands, Vol. I, pp. 458, 541, 543; and Vol. IV, pp. 88-89. Washington, 1905. Gazetteer of the Philippine Islands, photographs, pp. 352-353. Washington, 1902.

36. Boyd Alexander, From the Niger to the Nile, Vol. I, pp. 96-97. London, 1907.

37. V. L. Cameron, Across Africa, p. 221. London, 1885.

38. Count Gleichen, The Egyptian Sudan, Vol. I, p. 190. London, 1905.

39. Prescott, Conquest of Peru, Vol. I, pp. 134-136. New York, 1848.

40. Ratzel, History of Mankind, Vol. II, p. 176. London, 1896-1898.

41. *Ibid.*, Vol. II, p. 176.

42. E. J. Payne, History of the New World, Vol. I, p. 377. Oxford, 1892.

43. Pallas, Travels Through the Southern Provinces of Russia, Vol. II, p. 346. London, 1812.

44. B. H. Baden-Powell, The Indian Village Community, pp. 57, 58, 61. London, 1896.

45. E. F. Knight, Where Three Empires Meet, pp. 148, 151, 154, 163, 203, 238 *et passim*. London, 1897.

46. *Ibid.*, 70-73.

47. F. H. Nichols, Through Hidden Shensi, p. 52. New York, 1902.

48. Isabella Bird Bishop, The Yangtze Valley and Beyond, Vol. I, pp. 163, 176; Vol. II, pp. 126, 147. New York and London, 1900.

49. Boyd Winchester, The Swiss Republic, p. 307. Philadelphia, 1891.

50. Wilhelm Roscher, *National-oekonomik des Ackerbaues*, p. 656, Note 1. Stuttgart, 1888.

51. Norway, Official Publication, p. 307. Christiania, 1900.

52. Roscher, *National-oekonomik des Ackerbaues*, p. 656, Note 4. Stuttgart, 1888.

53. Norway, Official Publication, p. 325. Christiania, 1900.

54. Roscher, *National-oekonomik des Ackerbaues*, p. 657, Note 7. Stuttgart, 1888.

55. *Ibid.*, p. 655, Note 1.

56. Norway, Official Publication, p. 310. Christiania, 1900.

57. B. H. Baden-Powell, The Indian Village Community, pp. 58-59. London, 1896.

58. McCullough, Geographical Dictionary, Article Nepal. J. C. White, Journeys in Bhutan, *Geographical Journal*, Vol. 35, p. 33. London, 1910.

59. E. F. Knight, Where Three Empires Meet, p. 10. London, 1897.

60. Boyd Winchester, The Swiss Republic, p. 310. Philadelphia, 1891. A. von Miaskowski, *Die schweizerische Allmend*, pp. 88-89, 175, 178, 179, 198. *Staats- und socialwissenschaftliche Forschungen*, Vol. II, No. 4, Leipzig, 1879.

61. E. F. Knight, Where Three Empires Meet, pp. 98, 248, 329. London, 1897.

62. Isabella Bird Bishop, The Yangtze Valley and Beyond, Vol. II, pp. 181, 187, 224. London and New York, 1900.

63. Carter Harrison, A Race with the Sun, p. 63. New York, 1889.

64. Boyd Winchester, The Swiss Republic, pp. 325-327. Phila. 1891.

65. A von Miaskowski, *Die schweizerische Allmend*, pp. 164-166. *Staats- und socialwissenschaftliche Forschungen*, Vol. II, No. 4. Leipzig, 1879.

66. Norway, Official Publication, p. 325. Christiania, 1900.

67. *Ibid.*, p. 59.

68. Roscher, *National-oekonomik des Ackerbaues*, p. 655, Note 1. Stuttgart, 1888.

69. E. F. Knight, Where Three Empires Meet, pp. 40, 41, 77. London, 1897.

70. M. Huc, Travels in Tartary, Thibet and China in 1846, Vol. II, pp. 151-156. Chicago, 1898.

71. W. W. Rockhill, The Land of the Lamas, p. 228. New York, 1891.

72. Perceval Landon, The Opening of Tibet, pp. 110, 111, 205-206. New York, 1905.

73. J. Partsch, Central Europe, pp. 197, 248. London, 1903.

74. Wilhelm Deecke, Italy, p. 220. London, 1904.

75. J. Partsch, Central Europe, pp. 269-270. London, 1903.

76. Malthus, Essay on Population, Book II, chap. V.

77. Cliffe Leslie, Auvergne, *Fortnightly Review*, p. 741, Vol. XVI. 1874.

78. Wilhelm Deecke, Italy, pp. 243, 409. London, 1904.

79. Ratzel, History of Mankind, Vol. III, p. 252. London, 1896-1898.

80. L. Higgin, Spanish Life in Town and Country, pp. 27, 29, 292-293. New York, 1902.

81. James Bryce, Impressions of South Africa, p. 350. New York, 1897.

82. Von Bremer, Land of the Battaks, *Geographical Journal*, Vol. VII, pp. 76-80. London, 1896.

83. B. Winchester, The Swiss Republic, pp. 229-232. Phila., 1891.

84. James Logan, The Scottish Gael or Celtic Manners, p. 78. Hartford, 1849.

85. Indian Census for 1901, Vol. I, Part I, p. 93, by Risley and Gait. Calcutta, 1903.

86. Elisée Reclus, Europe, Vol. I, p. 219. New York, 1882.

87. Heinrich von Treitschke, *Politik*, Vol. I, p. 228. Leipzig, 1897.

88. Archibald Little, The Far East, pp. 47, 167. Oxford, 1905.

89. H. R. Mill, International Geography, p. 243. New York, 1902.

90. Malthus, Essay on Population, Book II, chap. I.

91. Cliffe Leslie, Auvergne, *Fortnightly Review*, Vol. XVI, pp. 741-742. 1874.

92. Oscar P. Crosby, Tibet and Turkestan, pp. 153, 156. London and New York, 1905. A. Little, The Far East, p. 217. Oxford, 1905.

93. W. W. Rockhill, The Land of the Lamas, p. 227. New York, 1891.

94. E. F. Knight, Where Three Empires Meet, p. 218. London, 1897.

95. W. W. Rockhill, The Land of the Lamas, p. 212. New York, 1891.

96. C. A. Sherring, Western Tibet and the British Borderland, p. 188. London, 1906.

97. Westermarck, History of Human Marriage, pp. 451, 452. London, 1891.

98. Strabo, Book XVI, chap. IV, 25.

99. For authorities, see Westermarck, History of Human Marriage, pp. 452-455. London, 1891. McLennan, Primitive Marriage, pp. 178-179, 184-189. Edinburgh, 1865. C. A. Sherring, Western Tibet and the British Borderland, pp. 14, 15, 88-89, 177, 305. London, 1906.

100. Spencer, Principles of Sociology, Vol. I, pp. 646-649. New York, 1887.

101. W. H. R. Rivers, The Todas, incorporated in W. I. Thomas' Source Book for Social Origins, pp. 485-486. Chicago, 1909.

102. Westermarck, History of Human Marriage, p. 463. London, 1891.

103. Sir Thomas Holdich, India, pp. 216, 217. London, 1905.

104. W. W. Rockhill, The Land of the Lamas, pp. 211-212. New York, 1891.

105. Oscar P. Crosby, Tibet and Turkestan, pp. 148-151. New York and London, 1905.

106. Westermarck, History of Human Marriage, pp. 470-483, 547-548. London, 1891.

107. Perceval Landon, The Opening of Tibet, p. 193. New York, 1905.

108. E. F. Knight, Where Three Empires Meet, pp. 137-141. London, 1897.

109. Strabo, Book IV, chap. VI, 6, 7, 8, 10.

110. *Ibid.*, Book III, chap. III, 5, 7, 8.

111. *Ibid.*, Book VII, chap. VI, 1.

112. *Ibid.*, Book XI, chap. XII, 4; chap. XIII, 3, 6.

113. E. F. Knight, Where Three Empires Meet, pp. 346-349, 460-464. London, 1897.

114. *Ibid.*, 280-282.

115. Sir Thomas Holdich, India, p. 33. London, 1905.

116. *Ibid.*, 219-221.

117. Pallas, Travels Through the Southern Provinces of Russia, Vol. I, pp. 386-390, 406-407. London, 1812.

118. D. G. Hogarth, The Nearer East, p. 246-249. London, 1902.

119. M. Huc, Travels in Tartary, Thibet, and China in 1846, Vol. II, pp. 90-93, 100-101, 129-132. Chicago, 1898.

120. Hans Helmolt, History of the World, Vol. III, pp. 131, 133-135. New York and London, 1902-1906.

121. Strabo, Book V, chap. IV, II.

122. Article Nepal, Encyclopædia Britannica.
123. C. Keller, Madagascar, pp. 24-26, 72, 85. London, 1901.
124. E. F. Knight, Where Three Empires Meet, pp. 280, 288-289. London, 1897.
125. Walter K. Kelly, History of Russia, Vol. II, p. 392. London, 1881.
126. Grote, History of Greece, Vol. II, p. 441. New York, 1859.
127. *Ibid.*, Vol. X, pp. 208, 215, 224-225.
128. D. G. Hogarth, The Nearer East, p. 235. London, 1902.
129. Henry Buckle, History of Civilization in England, Vol. II, pp. 125, 136-137. New York, 1871.
130. W. K. Kelly, History of Russia, Vol. II, p. 394. London, 1881.
131. Pallas, Travels Through the Southern Provinces of Russia, Vol. I, pp. 391, 404-405. London, 1812.
132. H. Spencer, A Visit to Andorra, *Fortnightly Review*, Vol. 67, pp. 53-60. 1897.
133. Article Tyrol, Encyclopædia Britannica.
134. Ratzel, History of Mankind, Vol. III, pp. 253-254. London, 1896-1898.
135. H. J. Mackinder, The Rhine, pp. 27-31, 47-49, 56, 57. London, 1908.
136. E. F. Knight, Where Three Empires Meet, pp. 305-306. London, 1897.
137. B. H. Baden-Powell, The Indian Village Community, pp. 136, 143-146. London, 1896.
138. D. G. Hogarth, The Nearer East, pp. 229-231, 248, 252-253. London, 1902.
139. Sir Thomas Holdich, India, pp. 243-244. London, 1905.
140. Niebuhr, Travels Through Arabia, Vol. II, pp. 50-51. Edinburgh, 1792.
141. B. H. Baden-Powell, The Indian Village Community, pp. 40, 47, 110, 121, 151-154, 159. London, 1896.
142. Captain J. Forsythe, The Highlands of Central India, pp. 10-15, 23-24, 123-125. London, 1889.
143. *Ibid.*, 6, 7, 10-12, 141-147.
144. Angus Hamilton, Afghanistan, pp. 262-268. New York, 1906.
145. Sir Thomas Holdich, India, pp. 98-99. London, 1905.
146. Merzbacher, *Aus den Hochregionen des Kaukasus*, Vol. I, pp. 55-56, 156. Leipzig, 1901.
147. W. Z. Ripley, The Races of Europe, pp. 281-283, 289-290, map p. 285. New York, 1899.
148. *Ibid.*, 282.
149. Article Tyrol, Encyclopædia Britannica.
150. Archibald Little, The Far East, 131-132. Oxford, 1905. Isabella Bird Bishop, The Yangtze Valley and Beyond, Vol. II, 132-133, 146-147, 166, 174, 207-210. New York and London, 1900. S. Wells Williams, The Middle Kingdom, Vol. I, p. 43, New York, 1904. J. Naken, *Die Provinz Kwangtung und ihre Bevölkerung, Petermanns Geographische Mittheilungen*, Vol. 24, p. 421. 1878.
151. Archibald Little, The Far East, pp. 307-308. Oxford, 1905.
152. E. C. Semple, The Anglo-Saxons of the Kentucky Mountains, *Geographical Journal*, Vol. XVII, pp. 588-623. London, 1901.

153. Sir Thomas Holdich, The Origin of the Kafir of the Hindu Kush, *Geographical Journal*, Vol. VII, p. 42. London, 1896.

154. George Adam Smith, Historical Geography of the Holy Land, pp. 259-261. New York, 1897.

155. Isabella Bird Bishop, Korea and Her Neighbors, pp. 21, 134-135, 140, 142. New York, 1897.

156. Article Waldenses, Encyclopædia Britannica.

CHAPTER XVII

THE INFLUENCE OF CLIMATE

CLIMATE enters fundamentally into all consideration of geographic influences, either by implication or explicitly. It is a factor in most physiological and psychological effects of environment. It underlies the whole significance of zonal location, continental and insular. Large territorial areas are favorable to improved variation in men and animals partly because they comprise a diversity of natural conditions, of which a wide range of climates forms one. This is also one advantage of a varied relief, especially in the Tropics, where all the zones may be compressed into a small area on the slopes of high mountains like the Andes and Kilimanjaro. Climate fixes the boundaries of human habitation in Arctic latitudes and high altitudes by drawing the dead-line to all organic life. It dominates life in steppes and torrid deserts as in sub-polar wastes. It encourages intimacy with the sea in tropical Malays and Polynesians, and like a slave-driver, scourges on the fur-clad Eskimo to reap the harvest of the deep. It is always present in that intricate balance of geographic factors which produces a given historical result, throwing its weight now into one side of the scales, now into the other. It underlies the production, distribution and exchange of commodities derived from the vegetable and animal kingdoms, influences methods of agriculture, and the efficiency of human labor in various industries.[1] Hence it is a potent factor in the beginning and in the evolution of civilization, so far as this goes hand in hand with economic development. *Importance of climatic influences.*

The foregoing chapters have therefore been indirectly concerned with climate to no small degree, but they have endeavored to treat the subject analytically, showing climate as working with or against or in some combination with other geographic factors. This course was necessary, because climatic influences are so conspicuous and so important that by *Climate in the interplay of geographic factors.*

the older geographers like Montesquieu[2] and others, they have been erected into a blanket theory, and made to explain a wide range of social and historical phenomena which were properly the effect of other geographic factors.

Direct and indirect effects of climate.

For a clear understanding of climatic influences, it is necessary to adhere to the chief characteristics of the atmosphere, such as heat and cold, moisture and aridity, and to consider the effect of zonal location, winds and relief in the production and distribution of these; also to distinguish between direct and indirect results of climate, temporary and permanent, physiological and psychological ones, because the confusion of these various effects breeds far-fetched conclusions. The direct modification of man by climate is partly an *a priori* assumption, because the incontestable evidences of such modification are not very numerous, however strong the probability may be. The effect of climate upon plant and animal life is obvious, and immediately raises the assumption that man has been similarly influenced. But there is this difference: in contrast to the helpless dependence upon environment of stationary plants and animals, whose range of movement is strictly determined by conditions of food and temperature, the great mobility of man, combined with his inventiveness, enables him to flee or seek almost any climatic condition, and to emancipate himself from the full tyranny of climatic control by substituting an indirect economic effect for a direct physical effect.

The direct results of climate are various, though some are open to the charge of imperfect proof. Even the relation of nigrescence to tropical heat, which seems to be established by the geographical distribution of negroid races in the Old World, fails to find support from the facts of pigmentation among the American Indians from Alaska to Tierra del Fuego. Nevertheless climate undoubtedly modifies many physiological processes in individuals and peoples,[3] affects their immunity from certain classes of diseases and their susceptibility to others, influences their temperament, their energy, their capacity for sustained or for merely intermittent effort, and therefore helps determine their efficiency as economic and political agents.

While producing these direct effects, climate also influences man indirectly by controlling the wide range of his life conditions dependent upon the plant and animal life about him. It dictates what crops he may raise, and has it in its power to affect radically the size of his harvest. It decides which flocks and herds are best suited to his environment, and therefore directs his pastoral activities, whether he keeps reindeer, camels, llamas, horses or horned cattle. By interdicting both agriculture and stock-raising, as in Greenland whose ice cap leaves little surface free even for reindeer moss, it condemns the inhabitants forever to the uncertain subsistence of the hunter. Where it encourages the growth of large forests which harbor abundant game and yield abundant fruits, as in the hot, moist equatorial belt and on rainy mountain slopes, it prolongs the hunter stage of development, retards the advance to agriculture. Climate thus helps to influence the rate and the limit of cultural development. It determines in part the local supply of raw material with which man has to work, and hence the majority of his secondary activities, except where these are expended on mineral resources. It decides the character of his food, clothing, and dwelling, and ultimately of his civilization.

The very ground under man's feet, moreover, feels the molding hand of climate. In one region a former age of excessive cold has glaciated the surface and scoured off the fertile loam down to the underlying rock, or left the land coated with barren glacial drift or more productive clays. In another, the cold still persists and caps the land with ice and snow, or, as in the tundra, underlays it with a stratum of frozen earth, which keeps the surface wet and chilled even in the height of summer. In yet other regions, abundant moisture combined with heat covers the ground with a pad of fertile humus, while some hundred miles away drying trade winds parch and crack the steppe vegetation, convert most of its organic substance into gases, and leave only a small residue to enrich the soil. Rain itself modifies the relief of the land, and therefore often decides in a slow, cosmic way what shall be the ultimate destination of its precious store of water. A heavy precipitation on the windward side of a

Effect of climate upon relief.

mountain range, by increasing the mechanical force of its drainage streams, makes them bite their way back into the heart of the system and decapitate the rivers on the leeward side, thus diminishing the volume of water left to irrigate the rainless slope. Thus the hydra-headed Amazon has been spreading and multiplying its sources among the Andean valleys, to the detriment of agriculture on the dry Pacific slope; thus the torrents of the Western Ghats, gorged by the monsoon rains from the Indian Ocean, are slowly nipping off the streams of the ill-watered Deccan. [See map page 484.] All these direct and indirect effects of climate may combine to produce ultimate politico-geographical results which manifest themselves in the expansion, power and permanence of states.

Climate limits the habitable area.   Climatic conditions limit the habitable area of the earth. This is their most important anthropo-geographic effect. At either pole lurks an invincible foe, with whom expanding humanity must always reckon, and who brooks little encroachment upon his territory. His weapon is the restriction of organic life, without which man cannot exist. The geographical boundaries of organic life, however, are wider than those of human life. The consequence of this climatic control, therefore, is not only a narrowed distribution of the human race, but a concentration which intensifies the struggle for existence, forces the utilization of all the available area, and thereby in every locality stimulates adaptation to environment.

Adaptability of man to climatic extremes.   Man ranks among the most adaptable organic beings on the earth. No climate is absolutely intolerable to him. Only the absence of food supply or of all marketable commodities will exclude him from the most inhospitable region. His dwellings are found from sea level up to an altitude of 5000 meters or more, where the air pressure is little over one half that on the coast.[4] Seventeen per cent. of the towns and cities of Bolivia are located at an elevation above 13,000 feet (4000 meters), while Aullagas occupies a site 15,700 feet or nearly 5000 meters above the sea.[5] Mineral wealth explains these high Bolivian settlements, just as it draws the Mexican sulphur miners to temporary residence in the crater of Popocatepetl at an altitude of 17,787 feet (5420 meters), from their permanent dwellings a thousand meters below.[6] The laborers employed in the construction of the Oroya railroad in Peru became rapidly accustomed to work in the rarefied air at an elevation of 4000 to 4800 meters. The trade routes over the Andes and Himalayan ranges often cross passes at similar altitudes; the Karakorum road mounts to 18,548 feet (5,650 meters). Yet these great elevations do not prevent men going their way and doing the day's work, although the unacclimated tenderfoot is liable to attacks of mountain sickness in consequence of the rarefied air.[7]

Man makes himself at home in any zone. The cold pole of the earth, so far as recorded temperatures show, is the town of Verkhoyansk in northeastern Siberia, whose mean January temperature is 54 F. below zero (—48 Centigrade). Massawa, one of the hottest spots in the furnace of Africa is the capital of the Italian colony of Eritrea. However, extremes both of heat and cold reduce the density of population, the scale and efficiency of economic enterprises. The greatest events of universal history and especially the greatest historical developments belong to the North Temperate Zone. The decisive voyages of discovery emanated thence, though the needs of trade and the steady winds of low latitudes combined to carry them to the Tropics. The coldest lands of the earth are either uninhabited, like Spitzenbergen, or sparsely populated, like northern Siberia. The hottest regions, also, are far from being so densely populated as many temperate countries.[8] [See maps pages 8, 9, and 612.] The fact that they are for the most part dependencies or former colonial possessions of European powers indicates their retarded economic and political development. The contrast between the Mongol Tunguse, who lead the life of hunters and herders in Arctic Siberia, and the related Manchus, who conquered and rule the temperate lands of China, shows how climates help differentiate various branches of the same ethnic stock; and this contrast only parallels that between the Eskimo and Aztec offshoots of the American Indians, the Norwegian and Italian divisions of the white race.

Temperature as modified by oceans and winds.

The zonal location of a country indicates roughly the degree of heat which it receives from the sun. It would do this

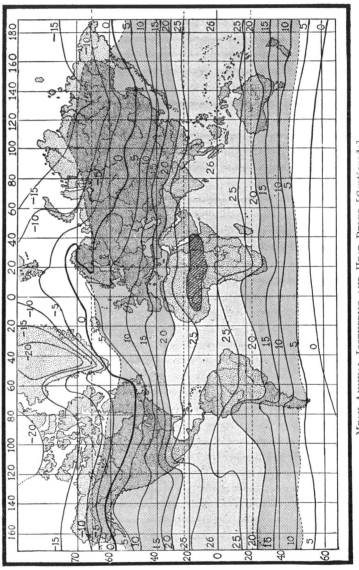

MEAN ANNUAL ISOTHERMS AND HEAT BELTS [Centigrade]
0°C.=32°F.   20°C.=68°F.   30°C.=86°F.

accurately if variations of relief, prevailing winds and proximity of the oceans did not enter as disturbing factors. Since
water heats and cools more slowly than the land, the ocean is
a great reservoir of warmth in winter and of cold in summer,
and exercises therefore an equalizing effect upon the temperature of the adjacent continents, far as these effects can be
carried by the wind. The ocean is also the great source of
moisture, and this, too, it distributes over the land through
the agency of the wind. Where warm ocean currents, like the
Gulf Stream and Kuro Siwa, penetrate into temperate or
sub-polar latitudes, or where cool ones, like the Peruvian and
Benguela Currents wash the coasts of tropical regions, they
enhance the power of the ocean and wind to mitigate the
extremes of temperature on land. The warm currents, moreover, loading the air above them with vapor, provide a store
of rain to the nearest wind-swept land. Hence both the rainfall and temperature of a given country depend largely upon
its neighboring water and air currents, and its accessibility to
the rain-bearing winds. If it occupies a marked central position in temperate latitudes, like eastern Russia or the Great
Plains of our semi-arid West, it receives limited moisture and
suffers the extreme temperatures of a typical continental
climate. The same result follows if it holds a distinctly
peripheral location, and yet lies in the rain-shadow of a
mountain barrier, like western Peru, Patagonia and Sweden
north of the sixtieth parallel. [See map page 484.]

Owing to the prevalence of westerly winds in the Temperate
Zones and particularly in the North Temperate Zone, the
mean annual temperature is high on the western face of the
northern continents, but drops rapidly toward the east.[9]
This is especially true of winter temperatures, which even
near the eastern coast show the severity of a continental climate. Sitka and New York, Trondhjem and Peking have the
same mean January temperatures, though Peking lies in about
the latitude of Madrid, over twenty-three degrees farther
south.

Europe's location in the path of the North Atlantic westerlies, swept by winds from a small and narrow ocean which
has been super-heated by the powerful Gulf Stream, secures

Effect of the westerlies.

for that continent a more equable climate and milder winters than corresponding latitudes on the western coasts of North America, whose winds from the wide Pacific are not so warm.[10] Moreover, a coastal rampart of mountains from Alaska to Mexico restricts the beneficial influences of the Pacific climate to a narrow seaboard, excludes them from the vast interior, which by reason of cold or aridity or both must forever renounce great economic or historical significance, unless its mineral resources developed unsuspected importance. In Europe, the absence of mountain barriers across the course of these westerly winds from Norway to central Spain, and the unobstructed avenue offered to them by the Mediterranean Sea during fall and winter, enable all the Atlantic's mitigating influences of warmth and moisture to penetrate inland, and temper the climate of Europe as far east as St. Petersburg and Constantinople. Thus several factors have combined to give the western half of Europe an extraordinarily favorable climate. They have therefore greatly broadened its zone of historical intensity toward the north, pushed it up to the sixtieth parallel, while the corresponding zone in eastern Asia finds its northern limit at the fortieth degree.

Rainfall.   Moisture and warmth are essential to all that life upon which human existence depends. Hence temperature and rainfall are together the most important natural assets of a country, because of their influence upon its productivity. The grazing capacity and wheat yield of southern Australia increase almost regularly with every added inch of rainfall.[11] The map of population for the Empire of India clearly shows that a high degree of density accompanies a high and certain rainfall. Exceptions occur only where hilly or mountainous tracts offer scant arable areas, or where plains and valleys are sparsely populated owing to political troubles or unhealthiness. Nearly three-tenths of the population are found crowded together on the one-tenth of India's level territory which is blessed with a rainfall above the average for the country.[12] Deserts which yield nothing are purely climatic phenomena. Steppes which facilitate the historical movement, and forests which block it, are products of scant or ample precipitation. The zonal distribution of rainfall, with its maxima in the Tropics and the Temperate Zones, and its minima in the trade-wind belts and polar regions, reinforces and emphasizes the influence of temperature in determining certain great cultural and economic zones.

In equatorial regions, which have an abundant rainfall throughout the year, agriculture is directed toward fruits and roots; only in certain districts can it include cereals, and then only rice and maize. The temperate grains demand some dry summer weeks for their maturity. Excessive moisture in Ireland has practically excluded wheat-growing, which in England and Scotland also is restricted chiefly to the drier eastern counties.[13] It thrives, on the other hand, in Manitoba and the Red River region even with a short season of scant rainfall, because this comes in the spring when moisture is most needed.[14] Most important to man, therefore, is the question how and when the rainfall is distributed, and with what regularity it comes. Monsoon and trade-wind districts labor under the disadvantage of a wet and dry season, and a variability which brings tragic results, since it easily reduces a barely adequate rainfall to disastrous drought. These are the lands where wind and weather lord it over man. If the rains hold off too long, or stop too soon, or withhold even a small portion of their accustomed gift, famine stalks abroad.

Temperature, the other important element of climate, depends primarily upon zonal location, which has far different historical results from central and peripheral location, continental and insular. It determines the amount of heat received from the⸳sun, though air and ocean currents may redistribute that heat within certain limits, and humidity or aridity modify its effects. Still zonal distinctions remain. The great climatic regions of the earth, like the hot, wet equatorial belt or the warm, dry trade-wind belts or the cool, well-watered temperate zones, constitute, through the medium of their economic products and their climatically imposed methods of production, so many socio-political areas, regardless of ethnic and political boundaries. The Berber nomads of the northern Sahara live much as the Semitic Bedouins of the Syrian desert or the Turkoman stock of arid Turkestan. *Temperature and zonal location.*

They have the same tribal government, the same scattered distribution in small groups, the same economic basis of subsistence, though of different races and dominated respectively by France, Turkey and Russia. The history of the tropical Antilles has in both its economic and political features paralleled that of the East Indies since the early 16th century. Temperate South America promises to follow in the historical footsteps of temperate North America, South Africa in those of Europe and temperate Australia.

Reactions of contrasted zones. While people of the same latitude live approximately under the same temperature conditions, those of contrasted zones are subjected to markedly different influences. They develop different degrees of civilization, wealth, economic efficiency, and density of population; hence they give rise to great historical movements in the form of migration, conquest, colonization, and commerce, which, like convection currents, seek to equalize the differences and reach an equilibrium. Nature has fixed the mutual destiny of tropical and temperate zones, for instance, as complementary trade regions. The hot belt produces numerous things that can never grow in colder countries, while a much shorter list of products, coupled, however, with greater industrial efficiency, is restricted to the Temperate Zone. This explains the enormous importance of the East Indian trade for Europe in ancient and medieval times, the value of tropical possessions for commercial countries like England and Holland. It throws light upon the persistence of the tropical plantation system in the Dutch East Indies and republican Mexico, as formerly in the sugar and cotton fields of the Southern States, with its relentless grip upon the throat of national life in hot lands.

Temperate products from tropical highlands. Tropical regions, however, may profit by the fact that their mountains and plateaus permit the cultivation of temperate crops. India during the last century has introduced tea culture extensively on the Assam and Nilgiri Hills, and in the Himalayan valleys up to an altitude of 7000 feet.[15] Besides this temperate product, it has put large areas into cotton, chiefly in the peninsular plateau of the Deccan, and by means of these two crops has caused a considerable readjustment in world commerce.[16] Nevertheless, here the infringe-

ment of the principle of tropical production in the torrid zone
is after all slight. In tropical America, on the other hand,
the case is quite different; this region presents an interesting
paradox in relation to its foreign commerce. Here the highlands are the chief seats of population. They contain,
moreover, the most industrious and intelligent native stock,
due to geographical and historical causes running back into
the ancient civilizations, as well as the largest proportions of
immigrant Europeans. This is true not only of the
Cordilleran states from northern Mexico to the borders of
Chile, but also of Brazil, whose center of population falls on
the plateau behind Rio de Janeiro and Santos. The isolation
of these high plateaus excludes them to a serious extent from
foreign trade, while their great altitude permits only temperate products, with the exception of sub-tropical coffee,
which is their only crop meeting a great demand. The
world wants, on the other hand, the long list of lowland
tropical exports which torrid America furnishes as yet in
inadequate amounts, owing to the lack of an industrious and
abundant lowland population. Commerce will eventually experience a readjustment in these localities to the natural
basis of tropical production; but how soon or how effectively
this change will take place depends upon the question of immigration of foreign tropical peoples, or the more difficult
problem of white acclimatization.[17]

Despite some purely climatological objections, anthropo- Isothermal
geography finds the division of climatic zones according to lines in
certain isothermal lines of mean annual temperature the most anthropo-
expedient one for its purpose. The hot zone may be taken as geography.
the belt north and south of the equator enclosed between the
annual isotherms of 20° C. (68° F.) These hold a course
generally far outside the two tropics, and in the northern
continents frequently reach the thirty-fifth parallel. The
temperate climatic zones extend from the annual isotherm of
20° C. to that of 0° C. (32° F.), which bears little relation
to the polar circles forming the limits of the solar Temperate Zone. The north temperate climatic zone has been
further sub-divided along the annual isotherm of 5° C. (41°
F.), distinguishing thus the warmer southern belt, which

forms preëminently the zc ie of greatest historical intensity. The areas beyond the annual isotherms of 0° C. belong to the barren cold zones. [See map page 612.]

Historical effect of compressed isotherms.

This isothermal division of the climatic zones is abundantly justified, because the duration of a given degree of heat or cold in any region is a dominant factor in its human, animal, and plant life. A map of the mean annual isotherms of the earth is therefore eloquent of the relation between historical development and this one phase of climate. Where the lines run far apart, they enclose extensive areas of similar temperature; and where they approach, they group together regions of contrasted temperatures. The compression of climatic differences into a small area enlivens and accentuates the process of historical development. It produces the same sort of effect as the proximity of contrasted reliefs. Nowhere else in the world do the tropical and frigid climatic areas, as defined on the north and south by the annual isothermal lines of 20° C. and 0° C. respectively, lie so near together as in Labrador and northern Florida. Separated here by only twenty degrees of latitude, on the opposite side of the Atlantic they diverge so sharply as to include the whole western face of Europe, from Hammerfest and the North Cape down to the Canary Islands and the crest of the Atlas Mountains in Africa, a stretch of forty-two degrees of latitude. This approximation of contrasted climatic districts in North America was an immense force in stimulating the early economic development of the Thirteen Colonies, and in maturing them to the point of political autonomy. It gave New England commerce command of a nearby tropical trade in the West Indies, of sub-tropical products in the southern colonies, in close proximity to all the contrasted products of a cold climate—dense northern forests for naval stores and lumber, and an inexhaustible supply of fish from polar currents, which met a strong demand in Europe and the Antilles. The sudden southward drop of the 0° C. annual isothermal line toward the St. Lawrence and the Great Lakes brought the northwestern fur trade to the back gate of New York, where it opened on the Mohawk and upper Hudson, and brought prosperity to the young colony. Even to-day the center of

collection for the Canadian fur fields is Quebec, located at
47° north latitude, while the corresponding point of concentration in Europe for the furs of Russia and Siberia is
Nizhni-Novgorod, which lies ten degrees farther north.[18]

This compression of the isotherms emphasizes the differ- Effect of
ences of national characters produced in part by dissimilar slight cli-
climatic conditions. Contrasts in temperament, manner of matic dif-
life, and point of view, like that between the New Englander ferences.
and Virginian, Chilean and Bolivian in the Americas, Breton
and Provençal in France, Castilian and Andalusian in Spain,
Gurkha and Bengali in India, seem to bleach out when they
are located far apart, owing to many grades of transition
between; but they become striking, stimulating, productive
of important economic and political results, when close juxtaposition enables them to react sharply one upon the other.
In effecting these nice differentiations of local types, climate
is nearly always one of the factors at work, emphasizing
perhaps an existing ethnic difference. Even the slight variations of temperature to be found in the same zone or the
same climatic region produce distinct results, especially
where they are harnessed, as is usually the case, with some
other geographic condition of relief, area or soil, pulling in
the same direction. Mexico, Peru, Italy, Switzerland, Greece
and Asia Minor, with its high plateau interior and its contrasted Euxine and Aegean coasts, represent each a complex
of climatic differences, which, reinforced by other geographic
factors, have made in these regions a polychrome picture of
national life.

Climatic contrasts aid differentiation also by influencing Effect of
both natural and artificial selection in the distribution of climate
peoples. This effect is conspicuous in the distribution of upon dis-
immigrants in all colonial lands like Africa, South America tribution
and in every part of the United States.[19] The warm, moist of immi-
air of the Gulf and South Atlantic States is attracting back gration.
to the congenial habitat of the "black belt" the negroes of
the North, where, moreover, their numbers are being further
depleted by a harsh climate, which finds in them a large
proportion of the unfit. The presence of a big negro laboring
class in the South, itself primarily a result of climate, has long

served to exclude foreign immigration, which sought therefore the unoccupied lands and the congenial climate of the more bracing North. Hence it is both a direct and indirect effect of climate that the North shows a large proportion of aliens, and the white population of the South an almost unadulterated English stock.

Climate and race temperament. The influence of climate upon race temperament, both as a direct and indirect effect, can not be doubted, despite an occasional exception, like the cheery, genial Eskimos, who seem to carry in their sunny natures an antidote to the cold and poverty of their environment. In general a close correspondence obtains between climate and temperament. The northern peoples of Europe are energetic, provident, serious, thoughtful rather than emotional, cautious rather than impulsive. The southerners of the sub-tropical Mediterranean basin are easy-going, improvident except under pressing necessity, gay, emotional, imaginative, all qualities which among the negroes of the equatorial belt degenerate into grave racial faults. If, as many ethnologists maintain, the blond Teutons of the north are a bleached out branch of the brunette Mediterranean race, this contrast in temperament is due to climate. A comparison of northern and southern peoples of the same race and within the same Temperate Zone reveals numerous small differences of nature and character, which can be traced back directly or indirectly to climatic differences, and which mount up to a considerable sum total. The man of the colder habitat is more domestic, stays more in his home. Though he is not necessarily more moderate or continent than the southerner, he has to pay more for his indulgences, so he is economical in expenditures. With the southerner it is "easy come, easy go." He therefore suffers more frequently in a crisis. The low cost of living keeps down his wages, so that as a laborer he is poorly paid. This fact, together with his improvidence, tends to swell the proletariat in warm countries of the Temperate Zone; and though here it does not produce the distressing impression of a proletariat in Dublin or Liverpool or Boston, it is always degrading. It levels society and economic status downward, while in the cooler countries of the Temperate Zone, the process is upward.

The laborer of the north, owing to his providence and larger profits, which render small economies possible, is constantly recruited into the class of the capitalist.

Everywhere a cold climate puts a steadying hand on the human heart and brain. It gives an autumn tinge to life. Among the folk of warmer lands eternal spring holds sway. National life and temperament have the buoyancy and thoughtlessness of childhood, its charm and its weakness. These distinctions and contrasts meet us everywhere. The southern Chinese, and especially the Cantonese, is more irresponsible and hot-blooded than the Celestial of the north, though the bitter struggle for existence in the over-crowded Kwangtung province has made him quite as industrious; but on his holidays he takes his pleasure in singing, gambling, and various forms of dissipation. The southern Russian is described as more light-hearted than his kinsman of the bleaker north, though both are touched with the melancholy of the Slav. In this case, however, the question immediately arises, how far the dweller of the southern wheat lands owes his happy disposition to the easy conditions of life in the fertile Ukraine, as opposed to the fiercer struggle for subsistence in the glaciated lake and forest belt of the north. Similar distinctions of climate and national temperament exist in the two sections of Germany. The contrast between the energetic, enterprising, self-contained Saxon of the Baltic lowland and the genial, spontaneous Bavarian or Swabian is conspicuous, though the only geographical advantage possessed by the latter is a warmer temperature attended by a sunnier sky. He contains in his blood a considerable infusion of the Alpine stock and is therefore racially differentiated from the northern Teuton,[20] but this hardly accounts for the difference of temperament, because the same Alpine stock is plodding, earnest and rather stolid on the northern slope of the Alps, but in the warm air and sunshine of the southern slope, it abates these qualities and conforms more nearly to the Italian type of character. The North Italian, however, presents a striking contrast to the indolent, irresponsible, improvident citizens of Naples, Calabria and Sicily, who belong to the contrasted Mediterranean race, and have been

Contrasted temperaments in the same nation.

longer subjected to the relaxing effects of sub-tropical heat.

Complexity of the geographic problem. Where the climatic difference is small, it is nevertheless often conspicuous enough to eclipse other concomitant factors which are at work, and hence to encourage the formation of some easy blanket theory of climatic influences. But just because the difference is slight, all attending geographic and ethnic circumstances ought to be scrutinized, to insure a correct statement of the geographical equation. The contrast between the light-hearted, gracious peasants of warm, sunny Andalusia and the reserved, almost morose inhabitants of cool and cloudy Asturias is the effect not only of climate but of the easy life in a fertile river plain, opposed to the bitter struggle for existence in the rough Cantabrian Mountains. Moreover, a strong infusion of Alpine blood has given this group of Spanish mountaineers the patience and seriousness which characterizes the race in other parts of continental Europe.[21] The conditions which have differentiated Scotch from English have been climate, relief, location, geologic composition of the soil, and ethnic composition of the two peoples. The divergent development of Northerners and Southerners in America arose from contrasts in climate, soil and area. It was not only the enervating heat and moisture of the Southern States, but also the large extent of their fertile area which necessitated slave labor, introduced the plantation system, and resulted in the whole aristocratic organization of society in the South.[22]

Monotonous climatic conditions. When one type of climate extends monotonously over a vast area, as in Russia, Siberia, Central Asia or immense tracts of Africa, the differences of temperature which prick and stimulate national endeavor in small climatic districts here lose much of their force. Their effects flatten out into insignificance, overwhelmed by the encounter with too large a territory. All the southern continents are handicapped by the monotony of their zonal location. The map of annual isotherms shows Africa quite enclosed between the two torrid lines of 20° Centigrade, except for a narrow sub-tropical belt along the Barbary coast in the north, and in the south an equally narrow littoral extending east and north from the Cape of Good Hope. At first glance, the large area of South Africa lying on the temperate side of the Tropic of Capricorn raises hopes for a rich economic, social and cultural development here; but these are dashed by an examination of the isotherms. Excessive heat lays its retarding touch upon everything, while a prevailing aridity (rainfall less than 10 inches or 25 centimeters), except on the narrow windward slope of the eastern mountains, gives the last touch of climatic monotony. The coastal belt of Cape Colony and Natal raise tropical and sub-tropical products[23] like all the rest of the continent, while the semi-arid interior is committed with little variations to pastoral life. [See maps pages 484 and 487.] Climatic monotony, operating alone, would have condemned South Africa to poverty of development, and will unquestionably always avail to impoverish its national life. South African history has been made by its mines and by its location on the original water route to India; the first have dominated its economic development, and the latter has largely determined its ethnic elements—English, Dutch, and French Huguenots, while the magnet of the mines has drawn other nationalities and especially a large Jewish contingent into the urban centers of the Rand.[24] In the background is the native Kaffir and Hottentot stocks, whose blood filters into the lower classes of the white population. The diversity of these ethnic elements may compensate in part for the monotony of climatic conditions, which promise to check differentiation. However, climatic control is here peculiarly despotic. We see how it has converted the urban merchants of Holland and the skillful Huguenot artisan of France into the crude pastoral Boer of the Transvaal.

In contrast to South Africa, temperate South America has an immense advantage in its large area lying outside the 20°C. isotherm, and in the wide range of mean temperatures (from 20°C. to 5°C.) found between the Tropic of Capricorn and Tierra del Fuego. Climate and relief have combined to make the mouth of the La Plata River the site of the largest city of the southern hemisphere. Buenos Ayres, with a population of over a million, reflects its large temperate hinterland. The effects

Frigid zones and the Tropics alike suffer from monotony, of Arctic the one of cold and the other of heat. The Arctic climatic cold.

belt, extending from the isotherm of 0°C. (32°F.) to the pole, includes inhabited districts where the mean annual temperature is less than --15°C. (or 5°F.), as at the Greenland village of Etah on Smith's Sound and the Siberian town of Verkhoyansk. Here the ground is covered with ice or snow most of the year, and permanently frozen below the surface. Animal and plant life are reduced to a minimum on the land, so that man, with every poleward advance of his thin-strung settlements, is forced more and more to rely on the sea for his food. Hence he places his villages on narrow strips of coast, as do the Norse of Finmarken, the Eskimo and the Tunguse inhabiting the Arctic rim of Asia. Products of marine animals make the basis of his domestic economy. Farther inland, which means farther south, all tribes live by hunting and fishing. The Eurasian Hyperboreans find additional subsistence in their reindeer herds, which they pasture on the starchy lichen (Cladonia rangiferina) of the tundra. [See maps pages 103, 153.]

Similarity of cultural development.   Though these Arctic folk are sprung from diverse race stocks, close vicinal location around an enclosed sea has produced some degree of blood relationship. But whatever their origins, the harsh conditions of their life have imposed upon them all a similar civilization. All population is sparse and more or less nomadic, since agriculture alone roots settlement. They have the same food, the same clothing, the same types of summer and winter dwellings, whether it is the earth hut of the Eskimo or of the coast Lapp, the Siberian Yukagirs of the Kolima River, or the Samoyedes of northeastern Russia.[25] The spur of necessity has aroused their ingenuity to a degree found nowhere in the drowsy Tropics of Africa. Dread of cold led the Yakuts of the Lena Valley to glaze the windows of their huts with slabs of ice, which are better nonconductors of heat and cold, and can be made more perfectly air-tight than glass. Hence these windows have been adopted by Russian colonists. The Eskimo devised the oil lamp, an invention found nowhere else in primitive America, and fishing tackle so perfect that white men coming to fish in Arctic waters found it superior to their own.

Owing to the inexorable restriction of their natural resources, contact with European commerce has impoverished

the Hyperborean natives. It has caused the rapid and ruthless exploitation of their meager resources, which means
eventual starvation. So long as the Ostyaks, before the coming
of the Russians, were sole masters of the vast forests of the
Obi Valley, they commanded a supply of fish and fur animals
which sufficed for their sparse population. But the greed of
the Russian fish dealers and fur traders, and the devastating
work of the lumbermen have made double war upon Ostyak
sources of subsistence.[26] The appearance of the white man
in Alaskan waters was the signal for the indiscriminate killing
of seal and other marine animals, till the Eskimo's supply of
food and furs has been seriously invaded, from Greenland to
the outermost Aleutian Islands. In all this wide territory,
climatic conditions forbid any substitute for the original
products, except the domesticated reindeer on the tundra of
the mainland; but this would necessitate the transformation
of the Eskimo from a hunting to a pastoral people. This
task the government at Washington has undertaken, but with
scant success.

In contrast to the numerous indirect effects of a frigid Cold
climate, no direct physiological effect can be positively as- and
cribed to intense cold. It lays no bodily handicap on health health.
and energy, as does the excessive heat of the Tropics. The
coldest regions where tillage is possible are tolerable places of
residence, because their winters are intensely dry. That of
central Siberia, which is drier than the driest desert, makes
tent life comfortable in the coldest season, provided the tenter
be clad in furs. The low temperatures of the Canadian
Northwest for the same reason have not repelled settlers even
from the Southern States. Negroes, however, meet a climatic
barrier in America at the isotherm of 5° Centigrade (41° F.).
They are found in New England and Nova Scotia, generally
with a large admixture of white blood; but there and farther
north where the climate is moist as well as cold, they show
a fatal tendency to pulmonary diseases.

The acclimatization of tropical people in temperate regions The small
will never be a question of widespread importance. The amount of
negroes were involuntary immigrants to America, under con- tropical
ditions that can never recur. Their concentration in the emigration.

"black belt," where they find the heat and moisture in which they thrive, and their climatically conditioned exclusion from the more northern states are matters of local significance. Economic and social retardation have kept the hot belt relatively underpopulated. The density map shows much the largest part of it with a population less than 25 to the square mile. Only the small portion contained in India, southernmost China, and Java shows a density over 125 to the square mile (or 50 to the square kilometer). This density has to rise to 500 or more to the square mile before emigration begins. The would-be exiles then have a wide choice of new homes in other tropical lands, where they find congenial climate and phases of economic development into which they will fit. East Indian coolies are found in Cape Colony, Natal, Zanzibar, Trinidad, and British Guiana, where they constitute 38 per cent. of the population.

Effects of tropical climate. The redundant population of crowded western and southern Europe also seek these sparsely inhabited Tropics, but they come heavily handicapped by the necessity of acclimatization. They leave their homes from Trondhjem and Stockholm in the north to the Mediterranean in the south, where the mean annual temperatures vary from 5° to 17° C. (41° to 63° F.), to seek the Torrid Zone which averages 25° C. or 77° F. over most of its territory. The effects of a tropical climate are due to intense heat, to its long duration without the respite conferred by a bracing winter season, and its combination with the high degree of humidity prevailing over most of the Torrid Zone. These are conditions advantageous to plant life, but hardly favorable to human development. They produce certain derangements in the physiological functions of heart, liver, kidneys and organs of reproduction. Bodily temperature rises, while susceptibility to disease and rate of mortality show an increase ominous for white colonization. The general effect is intense enervation; this starts a craving for stimulants and induces habits of alcoholism which are accountable for many bodily ills usually attributed to direct climatic influences. Transfer to the Tropics tends to relax the mental and moral fiber, induces indolence, self-indulgences and various excesses which lower the physical tone.[27] The social control of public opinion in the new environment is weak, while temptation, due to both climatic and social causes, is peculiarly strong. The presence of an inferior, more or less servile native population, relaxes both conscience and physical energy just when both need a tonic. The result is general enervation, deterioration both as economic and political agents.

This is the effect of climate which has had the most far-reaching and persistent historical consequences. Our study of the historical movements of peoples in the northern hemisphere revealed a steady influx from colder into tropical and sub-tropical lands, followed always by enervation and loss of national efficiency, due partly to the debilitating heat of the new habitat, partly to its easier conditions of living, whether the intruders came as conquerors and appropriated the fat of the land, or as immigrant colonists who dropped into slack methods of agriculture, because rain and sun and soil made their reluctant labor scarcely necessary. Everywhere in the Tropics the enervating effects of heat, moisture, and abundance make not only the natives averse to steady work, but start the energetic European immigrant down the same easy descent to Avernus. Passing over the deterioration of the Aryans in India, the Persians in Mesopotamia, and the Vandals in Africa, we find that modern instances show the transformation to be very rapid. The French who since 1715 have occupied the islands of Réunion and Mauritius have lost much of their thrift and energy, though their new homes lie just within the southern tropic, and are blessed with an oceanic climate. Yet the volunteer troops sent by Réunion to aid in the recent subjugation of the Hovas in Madagascar proved to be utterly useless.[28] The Spaniards who come to-day to Mexico have great energy, born of their former hard conditions of life in Spain. But their children are reared in a country whose mean annual temperature, even on the plateau, exceeds that of Spain by 10°C. (or 18°F.), a difference equal to that between Mobile and New York, or Madrid and Christiania. Hence they are less energetic and vigorous, while the third generation are typical Mexicans in their easy-going way of life.[29] The Germans who recently have colonized southern Brazil in great numbers show a similar

Historical signifi-cance of deteriora-tion.

deterioration under similar increase of mean annual temperature, combined with somewhat greater humidity, which intensifies the debilitating effects of the heat. An investigation
made in 1900 by the International Harvester Company of
America revealed the fact that the German farmer in the
State of Santa Catharina rarely cultivated over one acre of
grain.[30] Much of the iron in the blood and conscience of the
New England missionary stock which went to Hawaii two
generations ago has been dissolved out by the warm rain
and balmy air of the islands.

The problem of acclimatization.

In all these instances the white race has been successfully
transplanted. It has domiciled itself on the borders of the
Tropics and has propagated its kind, though it has abated some
of the vigorous qualities which characterized it in its temperate fatherland. In the real Tropics like India, Cochin China,
the Malay Archipelago, and Central Africa, the whole per-
plexing and urgent problem of European colonization turns
on the difficulty or impossibility of acclimatization; and this
in turn affects the whole economic, ethnic and political destiny
of present colonial holdings. If acclimatization is impossible,
the alternative is an imported ruling class, constantly inva-
lided and as constantly renewed, aided by a similar commercial
body acting as superintendents of labor; the whole machine of
government and economic exploitation is supported by a
permanent servile native population, doing the preëminently
tropical work of agriculture, which is so fatal to the white
man in a torrid climate. This means that the conquering white
race of the Temperate Zone is to be excluded by adverse climatic
conditions from the productive but undeveloped Tropics, unless
it consents to hybridization, like the Spaniards and Portuguese of tropical America. In that national struggle for
existence which is a struggle for space, it means an added
advantage for the Mediterranean peoples, that they are more
tolerant of a torrid climate than the blond Teutons, whose
disability in this regard is pronounced; it means that the

Historical importance of the temperate zones.

aptitude of the Chinese for a wide range of climatic accom-
modation, from the Arctic circle to the equator, lends color
to "the yellow peril."

In contrast to the monotonous extremes of climate in the

hot and cold zones, temperate lands are characterized by the intermediate degrees of annual temperature and marked seasonal diversity which are so favorable to human development. In Arctic lands labor is paralyzed by cold as it is by heat in the enervating and overproductive Tropics. In one, the growing season is too short and ill-favored; in the other, too long to stimulate man to sustained industry. Hence the Temperate Zones, whose climate avoids both these extremes and abounds in contrasts, whose summers are productive enough to supply food for the winter, and whose winters give both motive and energy for the summer's work, are richer in cultural possibilities and hence in historical importance.

The advantage of the Temperate Zone is not only its moderate and adequate allowance of heat, but its contrast of seasons. Beyond the range of a vertical sun, grades of temperature change rapidly from latitude to latitude and from summer to winter. The seasons bring variety of activities, which sharply react upon one another. Manufactures were in their origin chiefly winter industries, as they still are in small isolated communities. The modern factory system flourishes best in cooler parts of the Temperate Zone, where the agricultural demands of the summer, spreading over a shorter period, leave a longer time for winter work, and where that once long winter of the Glacial Period, by the scouring action of the ice cap, has reduced the fertile area of the northern fields. The factory system is also favored, as Heinrich von Treitschke maintains, by the predominance of cool or cold weather, which facilitates the concentration of numerous workmen in large buildings, and renders possible long labor hours the year round,[31]—conditions unthinkable in a warm climate. The iron and steel industries which have grown up about Birmingham, Alabama, find that the long hot summers and mild winters reduce the efficiency of their skilled labor imported from the North. *Effects of contrasted seasons.*

The length of the seasons is of conspicuous importance. It determines, for instance, whether a given climate permits continuous field work with summer and winter crops, whether field work is possible at all, and how long it is interrupted by excessive cold. Buckle maintains that climate not only *Effects of length of seasons.*

enervates or invigorates man, but affects also the constancy of his work and his capacity for sustained labor throughout the year. He considers "that no people living in a very northern latitude have ever possessed that steady and unflinching industry for which the inhabitants of temperate regions are remarkable," and assigns as a reason "that the severity of the weather, and, at some seasons, the deficiency of light, render it impossible for the people to continue their usual out-of-door employments." The result of this he finds to be desultory habits of work, which help to make the national character fitful and capricious. He cites in illustration of his principle the people of the Scandinavian and Iberian peninsulas, whom he finds marked "by a certain instability and fickleness of character," owing to the fact that in Norway and Sweden agricultural labor experiences long interruptions, due to the severity of the winter and the shortness of the days; in Spain and Portugal owing to the heat and drought of summer.[32] The extreme continental climate of northern Russia with its violent contrast of the seasons, its severe and protracted winters, enables Leroy-Beaulieu to make a safer application of this principle to the empire of the Czars, which, unlike Scandinavia, feels no ameliorating effect from the mild Atlantic winds and commands no alternative industries like dairy farming, fisheries, and maritime trade.[33] Hence Leroy-Beaulieu attributes the unsystematic, desultory habits of work prevailing among the northern peasants to the long intermission of labor in winter, and to the alternation of a short period of intense activity with a long period of enforced idleness. He finds them resembling southern peoples in their capacity for sudden spurts of energy rather than sustained effort, thinks them benumbed by the sloth of the far north, which is not unlike the sloth of the south.[34]

Effect of long winters.

The dominant continental and central location of Russia enables its climatic extremes to operate with little check. The peripheral location of Scandinavia in the path of the Atlantic winds modifies its climate to a mild oceanic type, and its dominant maritime situation gives its people the manifold resources of a typical coast land. Hence Buckle's estimate of national character in the Scandinavian Peninsula has little basis as to fact or cause. Irregularity of agricultural labor does not mean here cessation of all labor, and hence does not produce the far-reaching effect ascribed to it. Only about one-third of the Norwegian population is engaged in agriculture. The restriction of its arable and meadow land to 3 per cent. of the whole territory, and the fact that a large proportion of the people are employed in shipping and the fisheries,[35] are due to several geographic factors besides climate. The same thing is true of Sweden in a modified degree.

Caution should be exercised in drawing conclusions from climate alone or from only one phase of its influence. The duration and intensity of the seasons affects not only the manner of work, but the whole mode of life of a people. On the Yukon, in Iceland, and the high mountain valleys of the Alps, winter puts a check not only upon out-of-door labor, but upon all public or community life. Intercourse stops or is greatly restricted. The outside world drops away. In Iceland, the law courts are in session only in summer when the roads by sea and land are open. In the Kentucky mountains the district schools close before Christmas, when the roads become impassable from rain and snow; the summer is the gala time for funeral services, for only then can the preacher or "circuit-rider" reach the graves made in the winter. Therefore the funerals in one community accumulate, so to speak, and finally, when leisure comes after the August harvest, they make the occasion for important social gatherings. Much of the influence of winter lies in its power to isolate.

Complexity of climatic effects.

It is the economic effects of such periods of enforced idleness which are most obvious, both in their power to restrict national wealth and keep down density of population. When long, they limit subsistence to the products of a short growing season, except where local mining adds considerable sources of revenue. In the Russian government of Yaroslaf, located on the northernmost bend of the Volga within the agricultural belt, and containing the chief inland wheat market of the Empire, the field labor of four months must support the population for the remaining eight months of the year. The half of Russia included in the cold forest zone of the north maintains meagerly a sparse population, and

can hope for an increase of the same only by the encouragement of industrial pursuits.   Here the long winter leisure has
created the handicrafts on which so many villages rely, and
which in turn have given rise to peddling,[36] as we have
seen it do in high mountain regions where altitude intensifies
and prolongs the winter season.   Agricultural and industrial
life are still undivorced, just as in primitive communities.   The
resulting population has also the primitive mark of great
sparsity, so that modern industry, which depends upon a
concentrated labor force, is here inhibited.   Hence Russian
manufactures, which are so active in the governments of Vla-
dimir, Moscow, and St. Petersburg, cease beyond the sixtieth
parallel, which defines the northern limit of the agricultural
belt and the beginning of the forest and the fur zone.[37]   [See
maps pages 8 and 612.]

Social
effects
of long
winters.

The rigorous climate of Russia was undoubtedly one
cause for the attachment of the peasants to the soil in 1593.
This measure was resorted to at a time when the Muscovite
dominion from its center in Great Russia had recently been
extended at the expense of the Tartars, and had thus embraced
fertile southern lands, which tempted the northern peasant
away from his unfruitful fields.[38]   This attraction, coupled with
the free and hopeful life of the frontier, met the migrant
instinct bred in the peasant by the wide plains and far horizon
of Russia, so that the north threatened to be left without
cultivators.   Later, the harsh climatic conditions of the north
were advanced as an argument against the abolition of serf-
dom, on the ground that this system alone secured to the
landed proprietor a steady labor supply, and guaranteed to
the peasant his maintenance during the long, idle winter.

The duration and severity of the cold season has put a
drag upon the wheel of enterprise in Canada, as opposed
to the warmer United States.   The prairies of the Canadian
Northwest, whose fertile soil should early have attracted
settlement, were a closed land till railroads could pour into
it every summer from the warmer south and east a seasonal
tide of laborers.   These follow the harvest as it advances from
point to point, and then withdraw in autumn either to the
lumber camps of eastern Canada, Minnesota and Wisconsin,

or to seek other forms of out-door labor in the more southern states, thus lifting from the Canadian farmer the burden of their winter support.

In the lower latitudes of the Temperate Zones, where the growing season is long and the dormant period correspondingly short and mild, we find agriculture based upon clearly distinguished winter and summer crops, as in the northern Punjab (30° to 34° N. L.) ;[39] or producing a quick succession of valuable crops, where the fertility of the soil can be maintained by manures or irrigating streams, as in many of the warmer Southern States and in Spain[40] respectively. In Argentine, where tillage is extensive, land abundant, and population sparse, where, in fact, "skimp farming" is the rule, the shrewd cultivator takes advantage of the long growing season to stretch out his period of sowing and reaping, and thus tills a larger area. The International Harvester Company of America, investigating the reason for the small number of reaping machines employed in Argentine in proportion to the area under cultivation, found that the simple climatic condition of a long growing season enabled one reaper to serve about twice the acreage usual in the United States, because it could work twice as long.[41]

Over and beyond slight local variations of climate and season within the same zone, which contribute their quota to economic and historical results, it is the fundamental differences between the hot, cold and temperate climatic zones that produce the most conspicuous and abiding effects. These broad belts, each with its characteristic climatic conditions and appropriate civilization, form so many girdles of culture around the earth. They have their dominant features of heat and cold, variously combined with moisture and aridity, which give a certain zonal stamp to human temperature and development. *Zones of culture.*

The two cold belts have little claim to the name of cultural zones, since their inability to support more than an insignificant population has made them almost a negligible factor in history. [Compare maps pages 8, 9, and 612.] The discoveries and settlements of the Northmen in Greenland remained a barren historical event, though the vikings' ships reached a new hemisphere. Iceland is the only land in this sub-arctic region which ever figured upon the stage of history; and its rôle was essentially passive. Such prominence as it acquired was due to its island nature and its situation in a swirl of the Gulf Stream, which ameliorates the worst climatic effects of its far northern location, and brings it just within the upper limit of the temperate belt. The wide sub-arctic lowlands of Russia and Siberia, which, from the Ural Mountains to the lower Amur River, stretch the cold zone well below the sixtieth parallel, have at times in the last three centuries and especially in the past decade thrown their great mass into the scale of eastern Asiatic history. This has been possible because the hot summer characteristic of continental climates forces the July isotherm of 20° C. northward over the vast heated surface of Asia nearly to the sixtieth parallel, well within the borders of Siberia. It gives that belt the short but warm growing season with protracted hours of sunshine which is so favorable to cereals, lending to Omsk, Tomsk, Vitimsk and all the stretch of Russian settlements in Siberia, an admirable summer climate like that of the Canadian Northwest.[42]

The cradle of civilization. The North Temperate Zone is preëminently the culture zone of the earth. It is the seat of the most important, most steadily progressive civilizations, and the source of all the cultural stimuli which have given an upward start to civilization in other zones during the past three centuries. It contains the Mediterranean basin, which was the pulsing heart of ancient history, and all the modern historically important regions of Europe, Asia, Africa, and America. The temperate belt of the southern hemisphere also is following its lead, since European civilization has been transplanted to other parts of the world. This is the zone which least suffers from the drawbacks of climatic monotony or extremes, and best combines, especially in the northern hemisphere, the wide range of annual and seasonal variety so favorable to economic and cultural development, with the incalculable advantage of large land area.

Man grew in the temperate zone, was born in the Tropics. There, in his primitive, pre-civilized state, he lived in a moist, warm, uniform climate which supplied abundantly his simple wants, put no strain upon his feeble intellect and will. That first crude human product of Nature's Pliocene workshop turned out in the steaming lowland of Java, and now known to us as the *Pithecanthropus erectus*, found about him the climatic conditions generally conceded to have been necessary for man in his helpless, futile infancy. Where man has remained in the Tropics, with few exceptions he has suffered arrested development. His nursery has kept him a child. Though his initial progress depended upon the gifts which Nature put into his hands, his later evolution depended far more upon the powers which she developed within him. These have no limit, so far as our experience shows; but their growth is painful, reluctant. Therefore they develop only where Nature subjects man to compulsion, forces him to earn his daily bread, and thereby something more than bread. This compulsion is found in less luxurious but more salutary geographic conditions than the Tropics afford, in an environment that exacts a tribute of labor and invention in return for the boon of life, but offers a reward certain and generous enough to insure the accumulation of wealth which marks the beginning of civilization.[43]

Most of the ancient civilizations originated just within the mild but drier margin of the Temperate Zone, where the cooler air of a short winter acted like a tonic upon the energies relaxed by the lethargic atmosphere of the hot and humid Tropics; where congenial warmth encouraged vegetation, but where the irrigation necessary to secure abundant and regular crops called forth inventiveness, coöperation, and social organization, and gave to the people their first baptism of redemption from savagery to barbarism. Native civilizations of limited development have arisen in the Tropics, but only where, as in Yemen, Mexico and Peru, a high, cool, semi-arid plateau, a restricted area of fertile soil, and a protected location alternately coddled and spurred the nascent people.

As the Tropics have been the cradle of humanity, the Temperate Zone has been the cradle and school of civilization. Here Nature has given much by withholding much. Here man found his birthright, the privilege of the struggle.

NOTES TO CHAPTER XVII

1. G. G. Chisholm, Commercial Geography, p. 15. London, 1904.
2. Montesquieu, The Spirit of Laws, Vol. I, Book XIV. London, 1906.
3. W. Z. Ripley, Races of Europe, pp. 574-578. New York, 1899.
4. Julius Hann, Handbook of Climatology, Part I, pp. 223-224. New York, 1903.
5. Isaiah Bowman, Distribution of Population in Bolivia, *Bulletin of Geographical Society of Philadelphia*, Vol. VII, pp. 40, 41.
6. Ratzel, *Aus Mexico*, p. 415, Note 14. Breslau, 1878.
7. Julius Hann, Handbook of Climatology, Part I, pp. 224-227. New York, 1903.
8. G. G. Chisholm, Commercial Geography, p. 23. London, 1904.
9. Julius Hann, Handbook of Climatology, Part I, pp. 171-173. New York, 1903.
10. *Ibid.*, pp. 188-189.
11. *Ibid.*, pp. 57-58.
12. Risley and Gait, Census of India for 1901, Vol. I, Part 1, pp. 14-21, map p. 4. Calcutta, 1903.
13. H. J. Mackinder, Britain and the British Seas, pp. 173-174. London, 1904.
14. G. G. Chisholm, Commercial Geography, pp. 65-66. London, 1904.
15. *Ibid.*, 126-128. Holdich, India, p. 259. London, 1905.
16. G. G. Chisholm, Commercial Geography, pp. 114, 382. London, 1904.
17. J. Russell Smith, The Economic Importance of the Tropical Plateaus in America, House Doc. 460, 58-3—53, pp. 829-835. Washington, 1904.
18. G. G. Chisholm, Commercial Geography, p. 160. London, 1904.
19. E. C. Semple, American History and Its Geographic Conditions, Chap. XV. Boston, 1903.
20. W. Z. Ripley, Races of Europe, pp. 215-238. New York, 1899.
21. *Ibid.*, p. 276, Map p. 274.
22. E. C. Semple, American History and Its Geographic Conditions, p. 280-283. Boston, 1903.
23. G. G Chisholm, Commercial Geography, pp. 434, 436. London, 1904.
24. H. R. Mill, International Geography, p. 1009. New York, 1902.
25. Ratzel, History of Mankind, Vol. II, pp. 218-225. London, 1896-1898.
26. *Ibid.*, Vol. II, p. 217.
27. W. Z. Ripley, Races of Europe, Chap. XXI. New York, 1899.
28. Dr. C. Keller, Madagascar, Mauritius, and Other East African Islands, pp. 172-175. London, 1901.
29. Matthias Romero, Mexico and the United States, Vol. I, p. 79. New York, 1898.
30. From a personal interview with the supervising agent for South America.
31. Heinrich von Treitschke, *Politik*, Vol. I, p. 212 et seq. Leipzig, 1897.
32. Henry Buckle, History of Civilization in England, Vol. I, p. 32. New York, 1884.

33. G. G. Chisholm, Commercial Geography, pp. 320-324. London, 1904.
34. Anatole Leroy-Beaulieu, Empire of the Tsars, Vol. I, pp. 6, 139-144. New York, 1893.
35. Norway, Official Publication, p. 308. Christiania, 1900.
36. A. Leroy-Beaulieu, Empire of the Tsırs, Vol. I, pp. 19, 142, 327. New York, 1893.
37. G. G. Chisholm, Commercial Geography, pp. 214, 315. London, 1904.
38. A. Leroy-Beaulieu, Empire of the Tsars, Vol. I, pp. 412-413. New York, 1893.
39. Holdich, India, pp. 255-257. London, 1905.
40. G. G. Chisholm, Commercial Geography, p. 329. London, 1904.
41. From an interview with the supervising agent for South America.
42. G. G. Chisholm, Commercial Geography, p. 356. London, 1904.
43. Henry Buckle, History of Civilization in England, Vol. I, pp. 31-33. New York, 1884.

INDEX

INDEX

INDEX

INDEX

INDEX

INDEX

INDEX

INDEX

Erz Mts., 224, 360, 527, 536, 579
Eskimos, coast settlements of, 152, 154, 248, 249, 299, 304, 330, 624; distribution of, 88, 107, 304, 387, 422, 424; influence of climate upon civilization of, 10, 41, 58, 63, 611, 624-625; race of, 76, 123, 173, 382, 385, 387, 388, 395, 419
Esk River, 236
Essartage, 182
Essequibo River, 320
Essex, 74
Estland, 272, 400
Etah, 207, 624
Ethiopia, 99, 358, 372
Ethnology, and geography, 121-122
Etruscans, 97, 180, 264
Euboea, 381, 401
Euphrates River, as highway, 296, 337, 345, 349; plains, 152, 230, 476; nomad invasion of, 7, 489, 492. See also Mesopotamia
Eurasia, area of, 169-170, 172, 179, 383; Arctic, 172, 485-486; coastline, 400; location of, 383-385
Europe, Asiatic side of, 129, 148, 254, 348; Atlantic front of, 30, 82, 99, 149, 282-283, 301, 398; climate of, 109, 613-614, 618, 620-621; location of, 149, 150, 380-381, 383; peripheral articulations of, 131, 144, 254, 255, 258, 264, 394, 399, 405; races of, 74, 76, 104, 110, 112, 121, 477; varied structure and relief of, 117, 174, 199-200, 311, 339, 383, 389, 390, 394, 474-475, 478, 539
Europeans, expansion, 82, 106-107, 145, 151, 174, 311; trade with the Orient, 82, 270, 309-310, 616
Everglades, 371
Evolution, of geographic influences, 24-25, 282-283, 285, 433-434, 436, 444, 561-562; of geographic relations, 12-14, 67-69, 76, 78, 149-150, 282-283, 301-302, 311-313
Expansion, commercial and political, 65-68; commercial and ethnic, 196-197; ethnic and political, 183-187, 190-192; excessive, 134, 212-213, 343-344; geographic conditions for, 139, 343-345, 482; geographic marks of, 83, 139, 161-163, 165, 208-212; in new and old countries, 189-190, 198-200

Falkland Islands, 35, 44, 426-427
Faroe Islands, 88, 137, 264, 298, 387, 420, 432, 443, 448
Farralone Islands, 29
Farsistan, 507
Farther India, Asiatic peninsula, 131, 398-400; Chinese in, 307-308; intercontinental location of, 405; river valleys of, 259, 534; river-boat people, 322-323
Fayal, 381
Fenland of England, 245; reclamation of, 107-108, 286, 324-325; refuges and strongholds in, 370-372
Fernando Noronha Isle, 153, 440
Fernando Po Island, 441
Fern Pass, 537
Ferro, 419
Feuds, in mountains and deserts, 113, 237, 570, 591-592
Fez, 506
Fezzan, 502
Fiesch, 566
Fiji Islands, 282, 382, 446; effects of small, insular area, 455-456, 460, 463-464; government of, 6, 56, 444; races in, 77, 165, 391
Finisterre Province, 279
Finland, 400; maritime development of, 15, 71, 144, 262; Russian occupation of, 119, 177, 181, 189; Swedes in coasts of, 225, 272, 304
Finmarken Province, 152-153, 330, 624
Finns, in Russia, 77, 119, 159, 165, 224-226, 348; in Scandinavia, 119, 218
Fiord coasts, 261-262
Firenze River, 356-357
Firth of Forth, 273, 370
Tay, 304
Fisheries, and maritime expansion, 187, 330-331, 406, 618; and seamanship, 295, 299, 331-332; in Arctic economy and settlement, 152, 207, 248-249, 299, 330, 486, 624-625; in small or sterile lands, 15, 261, 264, 269, 305, 449-450, 455, 456; river, 108, 322
Fisher tribes, 56-57
Fiume, 14, 140, 258
Flanders, 284, 338

INDEX

INDEX

INDEX

INDEX

INDEX

INDEX

Manchuria, 415, 475, 611; Chinese expansion into, 189, 581; Russian expansion into, 143, 188, 211, 213, 229, 271
Manchus, 184, 306, 423, 495-496
Mandan Indian villages, 98, 357
Manganja tribe, 320
Mangyan tribe, 272
Manhattan Island, 369
Manila Bay, 281
Manitoba, 615
Mantze tribes, 234, 573
Maoris, 103, 177-178, 438
Marches, see Boundaries
Marcomanni War, 85, 86
Marco Polo, 269, 541
Mare clausum, 314-315
Marianne Islands, 448, 464
Maritime development, see Coasts and Navigation; periods of history, 311-312. See also Aegean, Atlantic and Mediterranean periods
Marius, Caius, 540
Markets, border, 207-208, 227, 364; coast, 267, 305, 505; desert, 505-507; island, 108, 285, 305, 321, 413, 424-426, 505; mountain, 100, 551-553; piedmont, 527-531
Marne River, 338, 361, 367
Maros River, 526
Marquesas Islands, 462, 464-465
Marquette, Jacques, 98, 349
Marra Mts., 526
Marseilles, 276, 303, 547, 581
Marshall Islands, 299, 448
Martigny, 360, 536
Martinique, 452
Marunga negroes, 570
Maryland, tidewater country of, 16, 61, 261; wheat of, 47, 284
Masai tribes, 559
Mascat, 145, 268, 269, 276
Mason, Otis, 78, 389
Massachusetts, 11
Massilia, 274, 312, 523, 532
Massowa, 305, 611
Matto Grosso, 38
Mauritius Island, 473, 627; density of population in, 451, 453; oceanic market, 108, 269, 413, 426, 453
Mayas, civilization of, 157, 395
Mayotte Island, 451
Mbau, 444
Mbengga, 444
Meath, 361

Meaux, 338
Mecca, 99, 111, 129, 153, 185, 492, 510, 512
Mecklenburg, 479
Medes, 492, 588
Media, 91
Mediterranean race, 97, 132, 222, 303-304, 306, 385, 391, 401, 404, 416, 422, 522, 543, 620, 621, 628; in England, 75; relation of Teutonic race to, 121
Mediterranean Sea, as an enclosed basin, 191-192, 254, 282-283, 284, 300-301, 310-311; climate of, 109, 136, 557; contrasted eastern and western basins of, 13, 96, 145, 152, 249, 266, 284, 429; early civilization of, 84, 122, 130, 131, 136, 262, 280, 281, 303-304, 306, 515, 634; European front of, 148-250, 258, 339, 532; intercontinental location of, 308, 385; islands of, 427, 450-451, 457; maritime development in, 107, 131, 187, 252, 284, 300-301; period of history, 82, 311; political union of, under Romans, 136, 191, 192, 194, 311-312; trade with the North Sea, 82, 540; trade with the Orient, 16, 18, 28, 131, 270, 276, 283, 425
Megara, 250, 429
Mekong River, 259
Melanesia, agriculture in, 56, 455-456; area and fauna of, 445-446, 465; artificial checks to population in, 463, 465; negroid race of, 38, 100, 124, 165, 272, 391, 434; Polynesian and Malay immigrants in, 77, 272, 460
Melville Sound, 312
Menam River, 259, 322-323
Menapii, Rhine villages of, 357
Mera Valley, 550
Mercenaries, 581
Meroe, 506
Mersey River, 149
Merv, 163, 345, 357, 491, 507, 538
Mesas, pueblos in, 329
Mesen River, 348
Meshed, 507, 528
Mesopotamia, civilization and irrigation in, 329, 352; desert border of, 400, 506; mountain border of, 402-403, 475, 476, 586, 588; nomads in, 47, 109; river

INDEX

INDEX

INDEX

INDEX

INDEX

INDEX